Contents

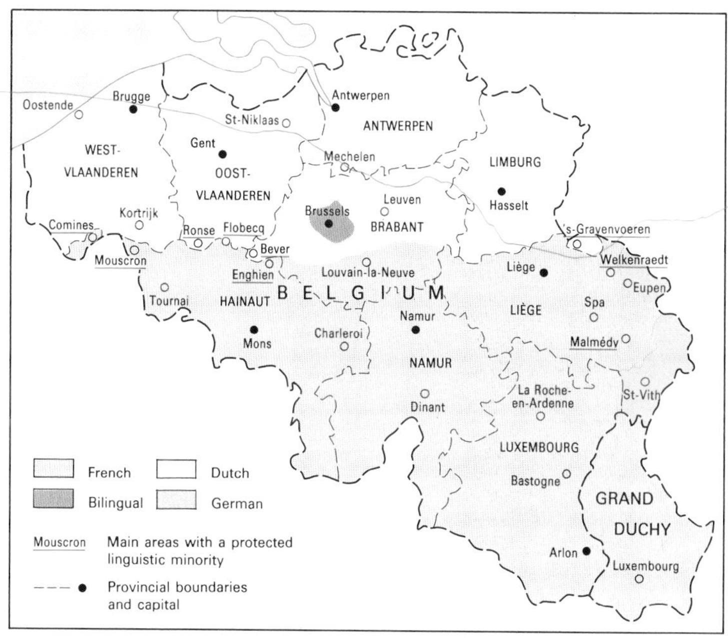

Oostende
Brugge
Antwerpen
St-Niklaas
ANTWERPEN
Gent
WEST-VLAANDEREN
OOST-VLAANDEREN
Mechelen
LIMBURG
Hasselt
Leuven
Brussels
BRABANT
Kortrijk
Comines
Ronse
Flobecq
Bever
's-Gravenvoeren
Mouscron
Enghien
Louvain-la-Neuve
Liège
Welkenraedt
Eupen
Tournai
HAINAUT
BELGIUM
Namur
LIÈGE
Spa
Mons
Charleroi
Malmédy
NAMUR
Dinant
La Roche-en-Ardenne
St-Vith
LUXEMBOURG
Bastogne
GRAND DUCHY
Arlon
Luxembourg
French
Dutch
Bilingual
German
Mouscron
Main areas with a protected linguistic minority
Provincial boundaries and capital

PRINCIPAL SIGHTS

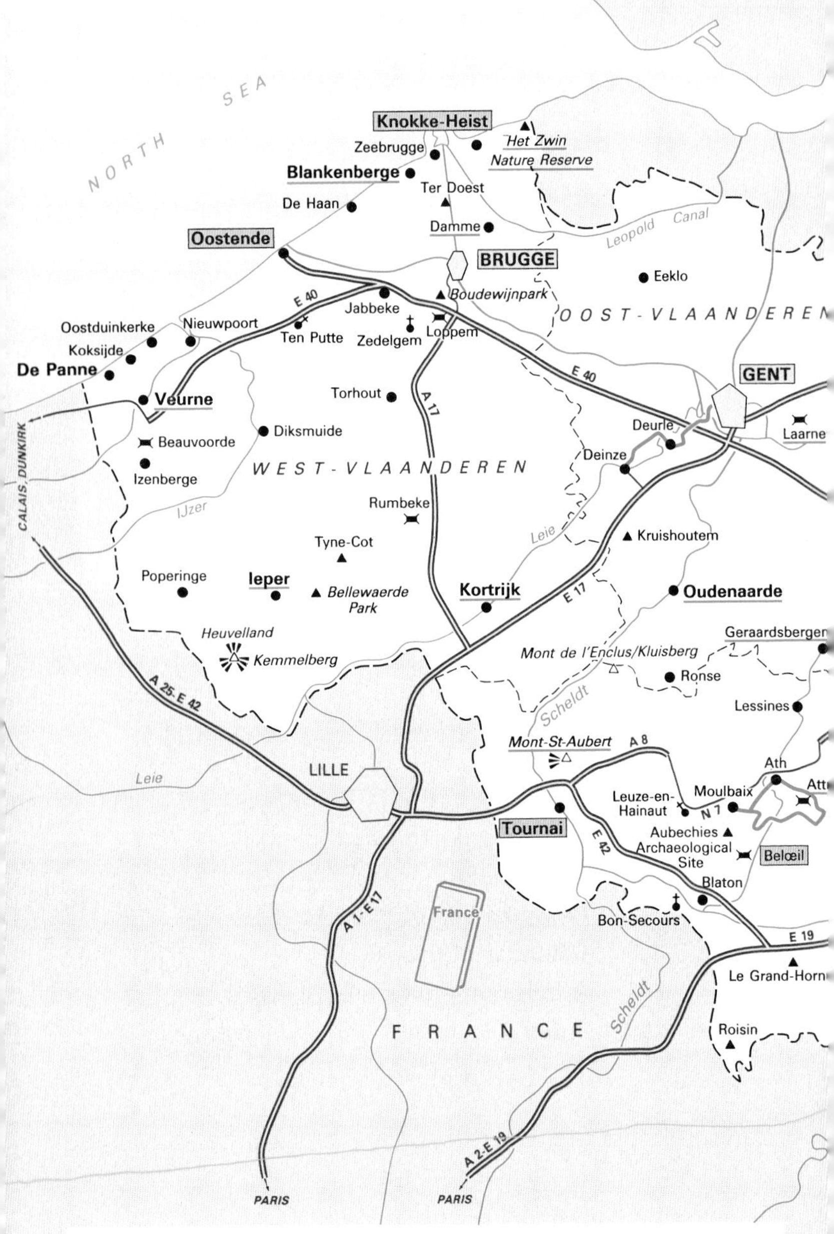

BILINGUAL LIST OF PLACE NAMES

Place names given on this map are those in official use. The list below gives French translations of Dutch names; official names are in bold type; English names are given in brackets where they differ from the official one.

Aalst	Alost	Luik	**Liège**
Antwerpen (Antwerp)	Anvers	**Mechelen**	Malines
Baarle-Hertog	Baerle-Duc	**Nieuwpoort**	Nieuport
Bergen	**Mons**	**Oostende** (Ostend)	Ostende
Brugge (Bruges)	Bruges	**Oost-Vlaanderen**	(East Flanders)
Brussel (Brussels)	**Bruxelles**	**Oudenaarde**	Audenarde
Dendermonde	Termonde	**De Panne**	La Panne
Diksmuide	Dixmude	**Ronse**	Renaix
Doornik	**Tournai**	**Scherpenheuvel**	Montaigu
Gent (Ghent)	Gand	**Sint-Niklaas**	St-Nicolas
Geraardsbergen	Grammont	**Sint-Truiden**	St-Trond
De Haan	Le Coq	**Tienen**	Tirlemont
Halle	Hal	**Tongeren**	Tongres
Ieper (Ypres)	Ypres	**Veurne**	Furnes
Koksijde	Coxyde	**Vilvoorde**	Vilvorde
Kortrijk	Courtrai	**West-Vlaanderen**	(West Flanders)
Leuven	Louvain	**Zoutleeuw**	Léau
Lier	Lierre		

A more comprehensive list of place names will be found in the Practical Information section at the end of the guide. Michelin map 409 also has a bilingual list of place names.

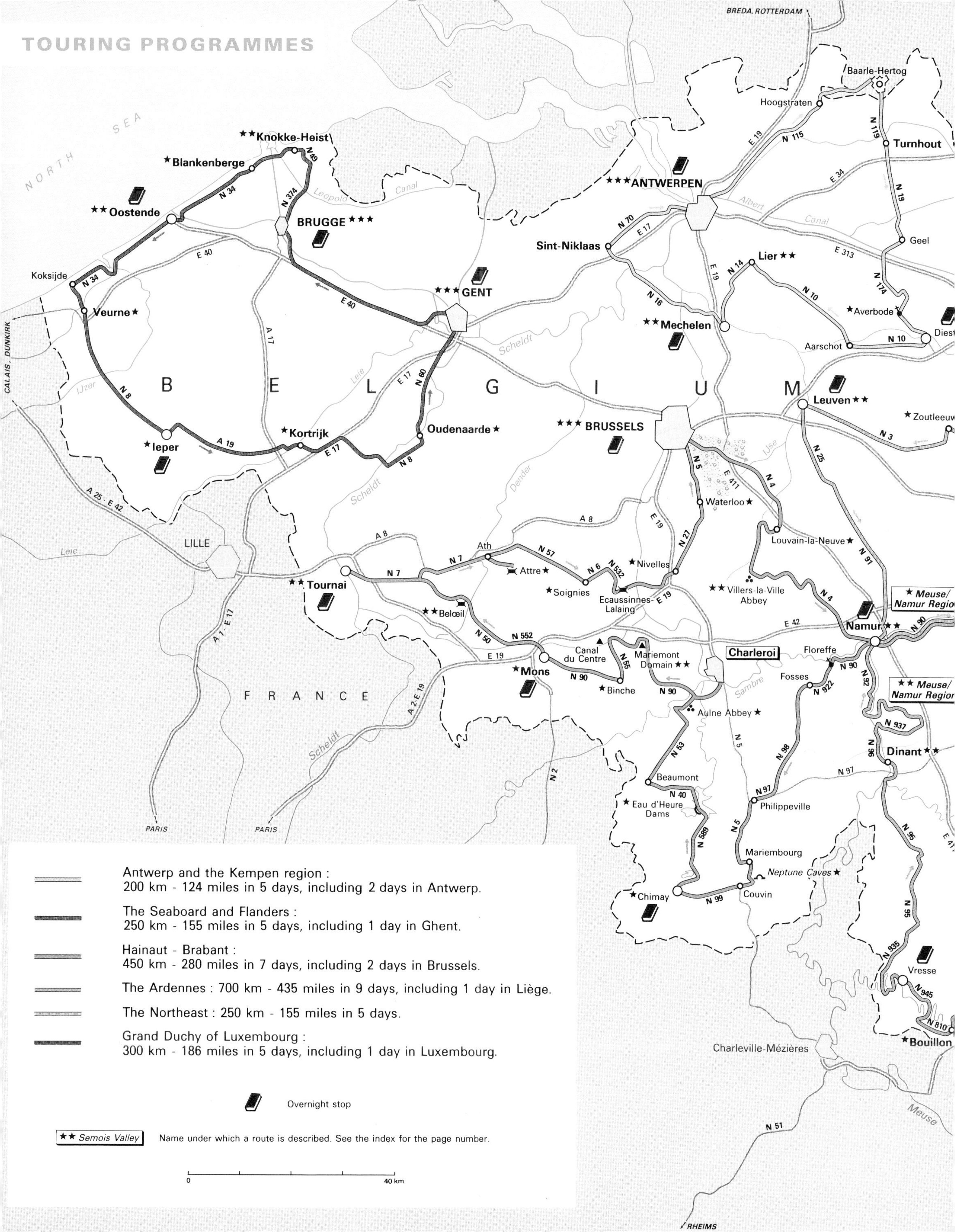

TOURING PROGRAMMES
BREDA, ROTTERDAM
NORTH SEA
Baarle-Hertog
Hoogstraten
Turnhout
★★Knokke-Heist
★Blankenberge
★★Oostende
BRUGGE★★★
★★★ANTWERPEN
Leopold Canal
Albert Canal
Sint-Niklaas
Lier★★
Geel
Koksijde
Veurne★
★★★GENT
★★Mechelen
★Averbode
Diest
Aarschot
CALAIS, DUNKIRK
B E L G I U M
Leuven★★
★Zoutleeuw
★Ieper
★Kortrijk
Oudenaarde★
★★★BRUSSELS
Waterloo★
Louvain-la-Neuve★
LILLE
Ath
Attre★
★Nivelles
★★Tournai
★Soignies
Ecaussinnes-Lalaing
★★Villers-la-Ville Abbey
★Meuse/Namur Region
Namur★★
★★Belœil
Canal du Centre
Mariemont Domain★★
Charleroi
Floreffe
★Mons
★Binche
Fosses
★★Meuse/Namur Region
Aulne Abbey★
F R A N C E
Dinant★★
Beaumont
★Eau d'Heure Dams
Philippeville
Mariembourg
Neptune Caves★
★Chimay
Couvin
Vresse
★Bouillon
Charleville-Mézières
Meuse
PARIS
PARIS
RHEIMS
Scheldt
Leie
IJzer
Dender
Sambre
Antwerp and the Kempen region :
200 km - 124 miles in 5 days, including 2 days in Antwerp.
The Seaboard and Flanders :
250 km - 155 miles in 5 days, including 1 day in Ghent.
Hainaut - Brabant :
450 km - 280 miles in 7 days, including 2 days in Brussels.
The Ardennes : 700 km - 435 miles in 9 days, including 1 day in Liège.
The Northeast : 250 km - 155 miles in 5 days.
Grand Duchy of Luxembourg :
300 km - 186 miles in 5 days, including 1 day in Luxembourg.
Overnight stop
★★ Semois Valley
Name under which a route is described. See the index for the page number.
0
40 km

Worth a journey ★★★
Worth a detour ★★
Interesting ★
The names of sights described in the guide appear in black on the map. See the index for the page number.
0
20 km
BREDA, ROTTERDAM
AMSTERDAM
Netherlands
EINDHOVEN
NETHERLANDS
DUISBURG
GERMANY
Germany
BELGIUM
ANTWERPEN
LIMBURG
BRABANT
LIÈGE
HAINAUT
NAMUR
LUXEMBOURG
GRAND DUCHY
Baarle-Hertog
De Kalmthoutse Heide Nature Reserve
Hoogstraten
Turnhout
Brasschaat
Postel
Kasterlee
Vrieselhof
Zilvermeer
Lommel
Kattenbos
Herentals
Mol
Geel
Albert Canal
Lier
Tongerlo
Fonteintje
Molenheide
Maaseik
Meuse
Old Scheldt
Fort Breendonk
St-Amands
Tessenderlo
Averbode
Kelchterhoef
Zwartberg
De Mechelse Heide Nature Reserve
Mechelen
Dendermonde
Tremelo
Aarschot
Diest
Heusden-Zolder
Bokrijk
Genk
De Maten
Plankendael
Scherpenheuvel
Hasselt
Bouchout Domain
Grimbergen
Vilvoorde
Horst
Maastricht
Leuven
Zoutleeuw
Alden Biesen
BRUSSELS
Tervuren
Tienen
Hakendover
Sint-Truiden
Colen
Tongeren
AACHEN
Gaasbeek
Soignes Forest
Beersel
Ijse Valley
Voerstreek (Les Fourons)
Visé
Triple Milestone
Halle
Jodoigne
Val-Dieu
Henri-Chapelle
Blégny Trembleur
Waterloo
Wavre
Rixensart
Eupen
Rebecq
Bois Seigneur-Isaac
Louvain-la-Neuve
LIÈGE
Verviers
Limbourg
Vesdre Dam
Ronquières Inclined Plane
Aigremont
Chaudfontaine
Gileppe Dam
Villiers-la-Ville Abbey
Tilff
Vesdre
Nivelles
Gembloux
Jehay
Amay
Neuville-en-Condroz
Tancrémont
Hautes Fagnes
Ecaussinnes-Lalaing
Franc-Waret
Sougné-Remouchamps
Theux
Corroy-le-Château
Meuse
Huy
St-Séverin
Spa
Reinhardstein
Comblain-au-Pont
Namur
Andenne
Mons
Canal du Centre
Mariemont Domain
Charleroi
Samson Valley
Modave
Ourthe
Amblève Valley
Malmédy
Bütgenbach
Stavelot
Coo
Cuesmes
Binche
Fosses-la-Ville
Gesves
Bois-et-Borsu
Bomal
Sambre
Amblève
Trois-Ponts
Bonne-Espérance
Lobbes
Aulne Abbey
Profondeville
Meuse/Namur Region
Durbuy
Aisne Valley
Lienne
Annevoie-Rouillon
Thuin
Anhée
Spontin
Erezée
Our
Furnaux
Jannée
Hotton Caves
Molignée Valley
Dinant
Valéry Cousin
Valley
Reuland
Beaumont
Walcourt
Freÿr
Celles
Marche-en-Famenne
Hastière-Lavaux
Vêves
Chevetogne
Waha
Six Ourthes Viewpoint
Anseremme
La Roche en-Ardenne
Eau d'Heure Dams
Philippeville
Lesse Valley
Rochefort
Troisvierges
Houffalize
Rance
Lavaux-Ste-Anne
Han Cave
Hachiville
Mariembourg
Beauraing
Fourneau-St-Michel
Clervaux
Dasburg
Virelles Lake
Neptune Caves
Our Valley
Couvin
St-Hubert
Bastogne
Redu-Transinne
Chimay
Euro Space Center
Wiltz
Bivels
Brûly-de-Pesche
Lesse
Grenglay
Vianden
Esch-s-Sûre
Petit Fays Gorges
Diekirch
Sûre Valley
Vresse
Ettelbruck
Chau de Beaufort
Berdorf
Hochfels
Rindschleiden
Rochehaut
Semois Valley
Bohan
Botassart
Larochette
Echternach
Luxembourg's « Petite Suisse »
Herbeumont
Mersch
Bouillon
Wasserbillig
Charleville-Mézières
Eisch Valley
Chiny
Semois
Arlon
Grevenmacher
Koerich
Alzette
Florenville
Luxembourg Moselle Valley
Orval Abbey
Montauban
Victory Memorial Museum
LUXEMBOURG
Virton
Bascharage
Rodange
Bettembourg
Mondorf-les-Bains
Schwebsange
Montquintin
Esch-s-A.
Rumelange
Torgny
Schengen
METZ
RHEIMS
COLOGNE
E 19
E 34
E 313
E 17
E 314
E 40
A 2
N 3
N 275
A 8
E 411
E 42
N 90
N 92
N 942
N 59
N 5
N 97
N 633
N 629
N 672
N 676
N 632
N 86
E 25
N 89
N 62
N 4
N 7
N 10
N 973
N 43
A 203
N 884
N 83
N 51
N 153
N 165
N 287

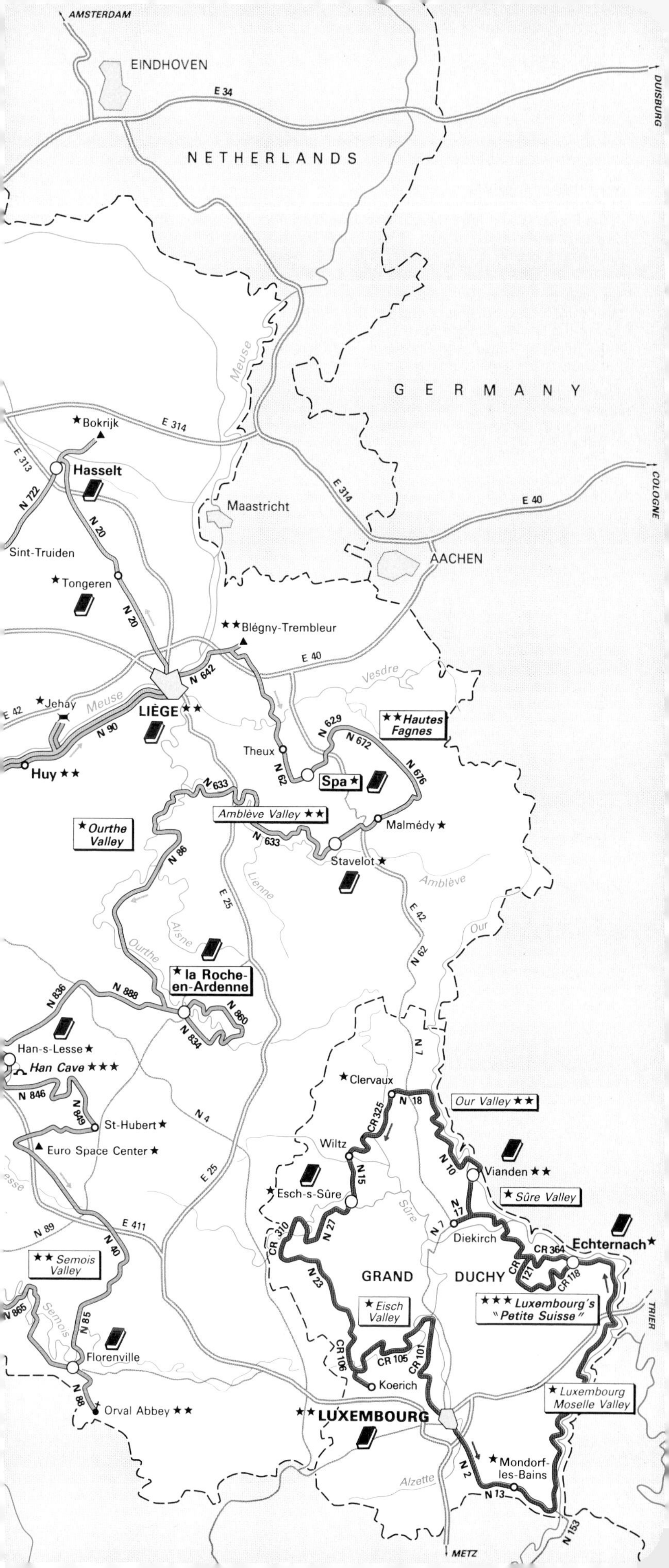
AMSTERDAM
EINDHOVEN
E 34
DUISBURG
NETHERLANDS
Meuse
GERMANY
Bokrijk
E 314
E 313
Hasselt
N 722
N 20
Maastricht
E 314
E 40
COLOGNE
Sint-Truiden
AACHEN
Tongeren
Blégny-Trembleur
E 40
N 642
Vesdre
Jehay
Meuse
E 42
LIÈGE
N 90
Huy
Hautes Fagnes
Theux
N 629
N 672
N 62
Spa
N 676
N 633
Amblève Valley
Ourthe Valley
N 633
Malmédy
Stavelot
N 86
Lienne
Amblève
E 25
E 42
Aisne
Ourthe
Our
N 62
la Roche-en-Ardenne
N 836
N 888
N 860
N 834
N 7
Han-s-Lesse
Han Cave
Clervaux
N 846
N 18
Our Valley
N 849
St-Hubert
N 4
CR 325
Euro Space Center
Wiltz
N 10
Vianden
N 15
E 25
Esch-s-Sûre
Sûre Valley
Sûre
N 17
N 89
E 411
N 27
N 7
Diekirch
CR 310
Echternach
N 40
CR 364
Semois Valley
CR 121
CR 118
GRAND
DUCHY
N 23
Luxembourg's "Petite Suisse"
TRIER
Eisch Valley
N 865
N 85
Semois
CR 106
CR 105
CR 101
Florenville
Koerich
Luxembourg Moselle Valley
N 88
Orval Abbey
LUXEMBOURG
Mondorf-les-Bains
N 2
Alzette
N 13
N 153
METZ

LANGUAGES, POLITICS AND GOVERNMENT

BELGIUM

Belgium's multilingualism has important consequences for the political and administrative structure of the country.

A trilingual country – Three languages are spoken in Belgium: Dutch in Flanders (60% of the Belgian population), French in Wallonia (39%) and German or a Germanic dialect in the Eupen region (slightly less than 1%). The linguistic borders correspond roughly to those of the provinces, except in Brabant *(see map p 3)*. Brussels is a sort of enclave within the Flemish region, being bilingual with a French-speaking majority. Dutch is one of the western branches of the Germanic language and resembles both German and English.

The dialects – There are as many of these in Flanders as in Wallonia. They have left their mark on place names and are the origin of a great number of local idiosyncracies in the spoken language. There are three large areas of Walloon dialects situated around Liège, Namur and Charleroi. The Picardian dialect in the Tournai region and the Gaume Lorraine dialect around Virton constitute two special cases.

The linguistic quarrel – The linguistic border dates back as far as the 5C, when Rome abandoned the north of the country to the Germanic tribes. The Gallo-Roman language in the south resisted Germanic influence despite Salian Frank occupation. "Walha" (the origin of the word "Walloon") meant "foreigner" to the Franks.
Dutch literature developed in Flanders from the 12C, but disappeared entirely after the break from the Netherlands at the end of the 16C. It was not until the reign of William I from 1814 to 1830 that a certain rebirth of Dutch took place; in reaction to this the members of the 1831 Constituent Assembly imposed French as the only official language. Since then the sometimes violent antagonism between Flemish and French speakers has dominated Belgium's domestic history. There have been successive measures to "reinstate" the Dutch language:

- 1898: the Coremans-De Vriendt decrees that all laws should be passed in Dutch and French; the king has to take his oath in both languages.
- 1930: the University of Ghent adopts Flemish.
- 1932: regional monolingualism replaces bilingualism, except in Brussels.
- 1963: three laws formalise this separation as well as the linguistic status of the 19 communities constituting the Brussels conurbation; dissatisfied Flemish autonomists call for a completely independent statute for the Flemish-speaking regions; this federalist goal has also been adopted by some Walloon citizens in the hope of preserving particularism and of preventing Flemish from becoming more frequently used in Brussels. Belgium is divided culturally into the Flemish-, French- and German-speaking communities.
- 1968: scission of the University of Leuven.
- 1970: four linguistic regions are constitutionally established: Flanders, Wallonia, the German language cantons and Brussels. The case of the Brussels conurbation remains the subject of heated debate, as many French speakers work in the capital and live nearby in Flemish-speaking communities.
- 1993: The St Michael's Agreement makes Belgium a federal state. The councils of the communities and regions are elected by direct franchise.

Political and administrative organisation – Belgium is a parliamentary, representative, constitutional monarchy. Its constitution dates from 1831 and has had several revisions, the last one in 1993. The king chooses the prime minister, who then forms his own government. The legislation is represented by two Chambers: the Senate (183 senators) and the Chamber of Representatives (212). The composition of the two Chambers has been fundamentally altered by the St Michael's Agreement. The power of the Senate has been reduced. Every royal act must be co-signed by a minister. The legislative elections are held by direct, universal franchise.

Political and administrative organisations linked to the linguistic communities – On one hand, there is a division into three **Communities** – Flemish, French and German-speaking – responsible for cultural affairs, health, social affairs and education (which is conducted in each language). On the other, the country is also divided into three **Regions** – Brussels, Flanders and Wallonia – responsible for everything on a regional level: housing, employment, the environment, economic development. Since 1980 Flanders and Wallonia have had actual legislative assemblies elected by universal franchise, and their own executive agents chosen from within each region.
By the law of 12 January 1989 Brussels Capital has become a political region in its own right, with a Council, an Executive and extensive powers. On 18 June 1989 there was an institutional first performance: Council elections for the region of Brussels Capital. For the first time in Belgium the inhabitants themselves elected those who would be their representatives in the regional Council.

Administrative divisions – Belgium is currently divided into nine Provinces, although the State Reform means that Belgium will soon have a tenth province. Each province has a capital where the provincial government is located.

LUXEMBOURG

Languages – Three languages are spoken in the Grand Duchy of Luxembourg. The Luxembourg dialect, a Moselle patois, is used everyday. German is used for culture in general. French is the official language, and that used for literature. It is taught in all schools and at all educational levels; at secondary school most classes are held in French.

Political organisation – The constitution dates from 17 October 1868 and has been revised several times. The Grand Duke holds executive power and chooses his own government. Legislative power belongs to the Chamber of Deputies; the members are elected every five years by direct universal franchise.

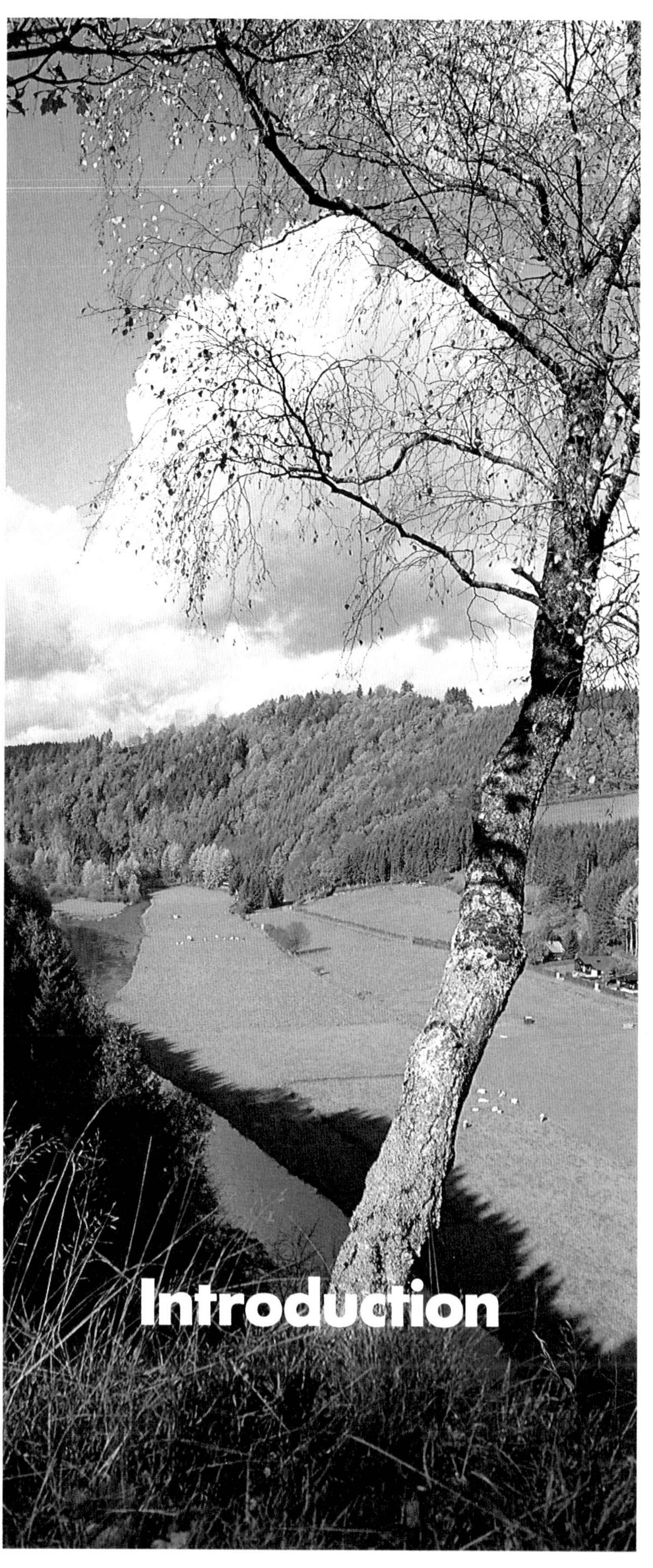

Introduction

REGIONS AND LANDSCAPES

Although Belgium covers a rather small geographical area – 30 513 km² (11 781 sq miles) – it has a population of 9 875 716 (January 1989). This is one of the highest population densities in Europe: 324 inhabitants per km² (Great Britain: 228). The Grand Duchy of Luxembourg has a population of 378 400 in a geographical area of 2 586km² (998 sq miles), and a population density of 146 inhabitants per km². People and merchandise in the two States circulate freely, thanks to a remarkable communications infrastructure (numerous waterways – both rivers and canals – and a very comprehensive road network); in Belgium this infrastructure is such that it permits daily population displacements of a size unparalleled anywhere else in the world. Almost half of the Belgian and Luxembourg workforce is employed in industry alone, with the most important sectors being metallurgy, textiles and the chemical industry in Belgium, and iron and steel works in Luxembourg.

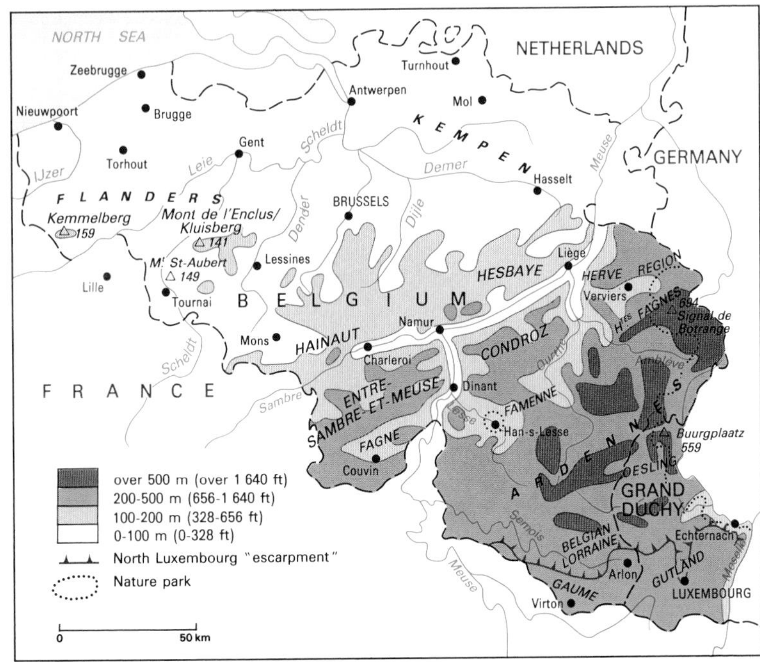

BELGIUM

At its widest point, southeast to northwest, Belgium measures 329km – 204 miles across. It has relatively diverse scenery, and the Belgian territory itself is divided into three groups *(see map above)*.

Lower Belgium (up to 100m - 328ft in altitude)

Antwerpen
Principal cities: **Antwerp**, Mechelen
Area: 2 867km² - 1 782 sq miles
Population: 1 597 000

Limburg
Principal city: **Hasselt**
Area: 2 422km² – 1 505 sq miles
Population: 745 000

West-Vlaanderen
Principal cities: **Bruges**, Ostend, Kortrijk
Area: 3 134km² - 1 0947 sq miles
Population: 1 102 500

Oost-Vlaanderen
Principal city: **Ghent**
Area: 2 982km² - 1 853 sq miles
Population: 1 331 600

The coast – The 70km - 43.5 miles of straight coastline is the only part of Belgium which borders the sea. The beautiful beaches of fine white sand have made this coast into a much-frequented holiday resort. The other side of the coin is that they have not made it easy to build ports, for which costly special arrangements (access canals, outer ports) have been necessary to compensate for their distance from the coast. The seafront has only one sheltered place, the indentation at Nieuwpoort where the River IJzer (Yser) spills into the ocean. Zeebrugge is an artificial fishing port. Antwerp *(qv)*, Belgian's great commercial port, is at the far end of a very long estuary which crosses the Dutch province of Zeeland.
The coast has developed out of all recognition since the Middle Ages and is now edged with esplanades for strolling and cycling alternating with wide strips of **dunes** covered with seagrass. In the past, it was marshy land crisscrossed by an infinite number of waterways. As time passed these gradually became choked with mud, as in the case of the silting up of the Zwin tributary, which ruined Bruges as a centre of commerce. Man himself completed the work of Nature by creating a polder zone beyond the dunes.

The polders – Although they are not the size of the Dutch ones, the polders have been created in the same way. They were once swamps, which have been drained and dried out, and which are now protected against the tides by locks. In 1914 it only took the opening of Nieuwpoort's sluice gates to flood the entire countryside behind them *(see Nieuwpoort)*. The soil of the polders is very fertile.

Kempen – What was once known as Taxandria extends over several provinces and into the Netherlands. The sands and pebbles borne by the rivers Scheldt, Meuse and Demer have accumulated in this vast plain between these rivers. Lakes and marshland are scattered over the Kempen region, with only heather and Norwegian pines growing on its poor soil.

Although there are now few inhabitants in Kempen, it was once a favourite place for the monks to build their monasteries (Postel, Westmalle and Tongerlo). Some of the land was reclaimed and cultivated in the 19C, while other areas were used for military manoeuvres (Leopoldsburg, founded in 1850). More recently the region has become home to a Centre of Nuclear Studies at Mol (1952) as well as to some industrial concerns, attracted by the presence of the Albert Canal built in 1939. The only valuable natural resource is coal; this was discovered at the end of the 19C near Genk, but the coal seams have been gradually abandoned because it is no longer cost-effective to mine them.

Another sandy region – This region, with its occasional valleys, extends throughout Flanders between the coast and the polders and the rivers Leie and Scheldt. Several peaks are all that remain of the more resistant terrain: **Kemmelberg, Mont de l'Enclus (Kluisberg)** and **Mont St Aubert**.

The ground is cultivated much more intensively here than in Kempen, and it is much more densely populated. The cultivated fields have borders of green walls of poplars. Low farmhouses are dotted around the countryside. The textile industry has established itself near the Scheldt and in the regions surrounding Kortrijk, Tournai and Ghent in particular.

Some regions are thickly wooded, such as **Houtland**, near Torhout.

The ancient ground is easily broken up, making it possible to create many quarries (porphyry in Lessines and Tournai). The towns are numerous, since urbanisation of this region dates back as far as the great drapers' era during the Middle Ages. The great cities of Ghent, Antwerp and Brussels developed in these regions so accessible to transport.

Central Belgium (100-200m - 328-656ft in altitude)

Brabant
Principal city: **Brussels**
Area: 3 358km² - 1 296 sq miles
Population: 2 243 000

Hainaut
Principal cities: Tournai, **Mons**, Charleroi
Area: 3 785km² - 1 461 sq miles
Population: 1 278 000

A cretaceous plain extends over the centre of the countryside, surrounding the Sambre and Meuse Valleys, rising gradually from a moderate altitude towards the Ardennes massif to the south, finally reaching an altitude of about 200m - 656ft. The soil is a mixture of clay and silt in the plain and loess on the slopes; this relatively fertile land is used for both agriculture and pastureland. The forest of the charcoal burner, which covered a good part of the country during the Roman period, has virtually disappeared; **Soignes Forest** *(qv)* is all that now remains.The **Hesbaye** plateau to the east and the **Hainaut** to the west are covered with a layer of very fertile loess. This is agricultural country, where villages tuck themselves away in valleys, and farms are large and isolated. The limestone, sandstone or brick buildings (the latter often whitewashed) usually surround a vast central courtyard, which is reached through a single, sometimes monumental, gateway. The **coal-mining basin** is to the south of Central Belgium, at the point where it meets the Ardennes mountains, where a fault brought the carboniferous layers to the surface; it lies in a long hollowed out tract of land which is crossed by the rivers Sambre and Meuse from Charleroi to Liège and extended by the coal-mining area around Mons, the Borinage. The highest concentration of metallurgical industry is found on this "Sambre-Meuse furrow" (the Liège, Charleroi and Louvière regions).

Ardennes

Namur
Principal cities: **Namur**, Dinant
Area: 3 666km² - 1 415 sq miles
Population: 421 000

Luxembourg
Principal cities: La Roche-en-Ardenne, **Arlon**
Area: 4 439km² - 1 713 sq miles
Population: 230 800

Liège
Principal cities: **Liège**, Spa
Area: 3 862km² – 1 490 sq miles
Population: 998 200

The **Signal de Botrange** (beacon), at an altitude of 694m - 2 276ft, is the highest point in Belgium; it is actually the remains of a worn mountain massif from the Primary era which extends the German Eifel range. The parallel mountain folds roll from east to west, making it difficult to establish communication routes outside the valleys running from south to north.

This region, well-known for the forests dating from the Roman period (the name "Ardennes" comes from the name of a goddess, Arduinna), can be divided into the Lower and Upper Ardennes.

Lower Ardennes – This series of plateaux, at an average altitude of 200-500m - 656-1 640ft, is located south of the Meuse. The **Condroz** (named after the Germanic tribe, the Condrusi) is quite a fertile region, composed of limestone and schist; the capital is Ciney. **Entre-Sambre-et-Meuse** is south of Charleroi; the great hollows of **Famenne** (capital: Marche-en-Famenne) and **Fagne** are typically swampy, wooded regions of sandstone and schist. Deep, narrow valleys run between these plateaux – the rivers Lesse, Ourthe and Meuse – in which caves open off all along the valley sides *(see below)*.

The humid **Herve region**, used mostly for pastureland, and the Verviers region are part of Lower Ardennes. The French border region south of Couvin *(qv)*, known as the **Pays des Rièzes et des Sarts**, is at over 300m - 984ft in altitude. This is one point where the Ardennes shelf emerges.

Upper Ardennes – These plateaux, over 500m - 1 640ft in altitude, are essentially convex. The most rugged crests make up the inhospitable area of Hautes Fagnes, which includes the highest point in Belgium. Peat bogs have developed on the very water-logged, poorly drained ground here.

Part of this region has been planted with coniferous trees, spruces for the most part. The winding river valleys, such as that of the Amblève, are more welcoming.

The typical Ardennes farmhouse is a great forbidding barracks of a place; a cube of rough-rendered walls, with the living areas and the barn under the same ridged roof. One of the sides is sometimes half-timbered.

The region of the Upper Ardennes, lacking in natural resources and ill-favoured by the harsh climate and difficulty of access, did not develop at the same pace as the rest of the country for many years; it has now opened up to tourism.

The **Belgian Lorraine** (Arlon) and the **Gaume** (Virton) regions belong geologically to the southern part of Luxembourg. As in France, the Lorraine village consists of rows of closely built farms on either side of very wide streets. In southern Gaume the houses have Romanesque tiling, which is not at all usual in Belgium.

Hautes Fagnes

THE GRAND DUCHY OF LUXEMBOURG

Capital: **Luxembourg**
Area: 2 586km² - 1 606 sq miles
Population: 378 400

Luxembourg consists of two very different geographical regions.

Oesling, in the north, is a plateau which joins the Ardennes and Eifel ranges; at its highest point it reaches 559m - 1 833ft (Buurgplaatz). The harsh climate is comparable to that of the Ardennes. Oesling is a region of forests, which occupy about one third of the territory of the Grand Duchy of Luxembourg.

Gutland to the south has a milder climate as it is at a lower altitude, sloping gently down towards the French Lorraine. It is formed of superposed strata of sandstone and limestone, alternating with clay and marl. The Luxembourg vineyards *(see Luxembourg Moselle Valley)* are southeast of the Gutland, on the hills overlooking the Moselle region.

Erosion has created **"escarpments"** where the hard rock of the ancient mountain massif meets softer rock. These long, sheer rock faces, running in an irregular line from east to west, are covered with beech forests. The northern one, of Luxembourg sandstone, crosses the Arlon region at Echternach and runs along the north of Luxembourg's "Petite Suisse". The southern one extends along the border and carries on into Belgium to just south of Virton.

CAVES

A complete circle of rivers – the Meuse, the Ourthe and the Lesse – encloses the region of Condroz, on the central Ardennes plateau. The rivers flow on the perimeter of the plateau, cutting through schist and limestone to form deep river beds.

Water infiltration – The effect of water is particularly noticeable in the calcareous areas, where it erodes the plateau surface to form chasms such as the **Fondry des Chiens** in Nismes, or the various types of abysses known as "chantoirs" (the Chantoirs Valley at Sougné-Remouchamps), "aiguigeois" or "adugeoirs", which can be found here and there throughout the region.

Cave formation – Water flowing into these chasms dissolves the limestone stratum in some places. In this way it forms subterranean rivers, which are often no more than the underground stretch of a river at ground level. The Lesse is such an example, disappearing near Han to reappear 10km - 6.25 miles further on. It runs through the **Han Cave**, the most famous in Belgium, renowned for its great chamber. The great chamber at **Rochefort Cave**, Sabbath Hall, is equally impressive.
In most cases the subterranean river has a tendency to cut deeper and deeper; for this reason the old river bed higher up fills up only during floods, and otherwise dries up completely. It is sometimes possible to take a boat through the lower gallery; at **Remouchamps**, the boat trip lasts for about 1km - 0.5 mile.
Some of the caves formed in this way were inhabited during the prehistoric period (Goyet, Furfooz, Han, etc.).

Concretions – Underground, the water deposits the limestone it has accumulated from filtering through the soil, thus forming the fantastic shapes of concretions. **Stalactites**, projections downwards from the roof, are the best known, along with **stalagmites**, columns rising up from the floor. Juxtaposed stalactites form draperies, and a stalactite meeting a stalagmite creates a pillar.
Gravity-defying eccentrics are the delicate concretions produced by crystallisation, which often "grow" diagonally. Although they are generally white and formed of calcite, they are sometimes tinted with minerals: for example, iron oxide produces a reddish colour, and manganese gives a brownish one.

Resurgence – Water running through subterranean galleries eventually comes up against the side of a slope, through which it re-emerges at ground level once more. At Han-sur-Lesse the resurgent river is visible near the visitors' exit.

Remouchamps Cave

FLORA AND FAUNA

Reserves and nature parks are particularly carefully managed, as much in the most densely populated areas as in the Ardennes, to protect flora and fauna.

Nature reserves – These areas are strictly protected by the various regions themselves or by private associations such as the RNOB (Réserves Naturelles et Ornithologiques de Belgique). Some of these nature reserves are open to the public, at least in part; others may only be visited with a guide. Particularly good reserves in Flanders include **De Kalmthoutse Heide**, **De Mechelse Heide**, where heather is the predominant vegetation, and **Het Zwin**, which is more ornithologically orientated. In the Ardennes there is the **Hautes Fagnes**, famous for its peat bogs, in the province of Namur the **Lesse and Lomme nature reserve** and the **Furfooz** nature reserve (these two reserves are known locally as "parcs naturels"), and in the province of Hainaut the **Virelles** lake at Chimay.

Nature parks – These parks include valleys, forests, villages, etc. which are to be protected. A distinction is made between national nature parks, designated by the State, and regional nature parks, designated by some other public authority. Belgium has a large national nature park, the **Hautes Fagnes-Eifel** *(qv)*, which extends into Germany.
Like Belgium, Luxembourg shares a large nature reserve with Germany, the **Germano-Luxembourg nature park**. Indicated by signs marked with a sprig of holly, it extends across particularly wild or picturesque areas; Luxembourg's "Petite Suisse" region, the lower Sûre Valley, the Our Valley, as well as including the major tourist centres of Echternach, Vianden and Clervaux.

Leisure parks – In these parks the natural setting is maintained for the maximum benefit of visitors, sports enthusiasts and ramblers alike. The estate belongs either to the province or to the State and is called a "domain". Some parks contain an ornithological nature reserve or a game park, others a stretch of water making it possible to engage in various water sports. The leisure parks are quite numerous in the Kempen region, where they can usually be found in the midst of extensive pine forests.

HISTORICAL TABLE AND NOTES

CELTS AND ROMANS

BC The Belgians, of Celtic origin, fight vainly against Julius Caesar, who finally suppresses them in 57. Three years later the Eburones revolt, led by Ambiorix, is crushed.

AD **Pax Romana** – modern Belgium is divided into three Roman provinces: Belgica Prima (capital: Trier), Belgica Secunda (capital: Rheims) and Germania Secunda (capital: Cologne). Tongeren and Tournai are important cities.

4C-5C Barbarian invasions – the Franks settle in Taxandria (Kempen) and Luxembourg. The first conversions to Christianity take place.

MEROVINGIANS TO FEUDAL SYSTEM

5C Tournai comes under the rule of the Salian Franks. Childeric, father of Clovis, founds the Merovingian dynasty. Clovis makes Tournai an episcopal seat following his conversion.

7C Second wave of conversions to Christianity. Blossoming of the great abbeys.

843 **Treaty of Verdun** – the Carolingian Empire is divided between France (to the west of the Scheldt) and Germania, leaving a narrow band of territory between the two, running from the North Sea to the Mediterranean, which is given to Lothair I. Upon his death this territory is divided into three parts: Italy, Burgundy and **Lotharingia**; the frontiers of the latter correspond approximately to modern Belgium, minus Flanders (which depends on the French crown).

862 Baldwin of the Iron Arm becomes first Count of **Flanders** *(see Kortrijk: Excursion)*.

962 Lotharingia is annexed to the Germanic Holy Roman Empire.

963 Count Sigefroi of the Moselle founds the county of Luxembourg *(see Luxembourg)*.

980 **Notger**, prince-bishop of **Liège** *(qv)*, gains temporal power over his territory.

Early 11C Flanders expands at the expense of Imperial territories; this is the rise of Imperial Flanders. The Count of Flanders is vassal to both the King of France and the Germanic Emperor.

12C-13C **Emancipation of the Flemish cities** – the period from the 12C to the 14C is marked by growth in trade, particularly in the weaving of wool. The new wealth of the cities gives them communal autonomy. This is the golden age for Bruges *(qv)*. Although a vassal of the king of France, Flanders' economic activities link it loosely to England and the Germanic Empire; this causes a rift between the people with an eye to their economic interests and the nobility supported by the French. The king of France, **Philippe Auguste**, makes heavy claims on the northern States and a coalition forms against him. The Flemish are supported by King John (Lackland) of England and Emperor Otto IV of Germany. Nevertheless, in 1214 Philippe Auguste wins victory at the **Battle of Bouvines**, where the Count of Flanders, Ferrand, suffers the greatest losses.

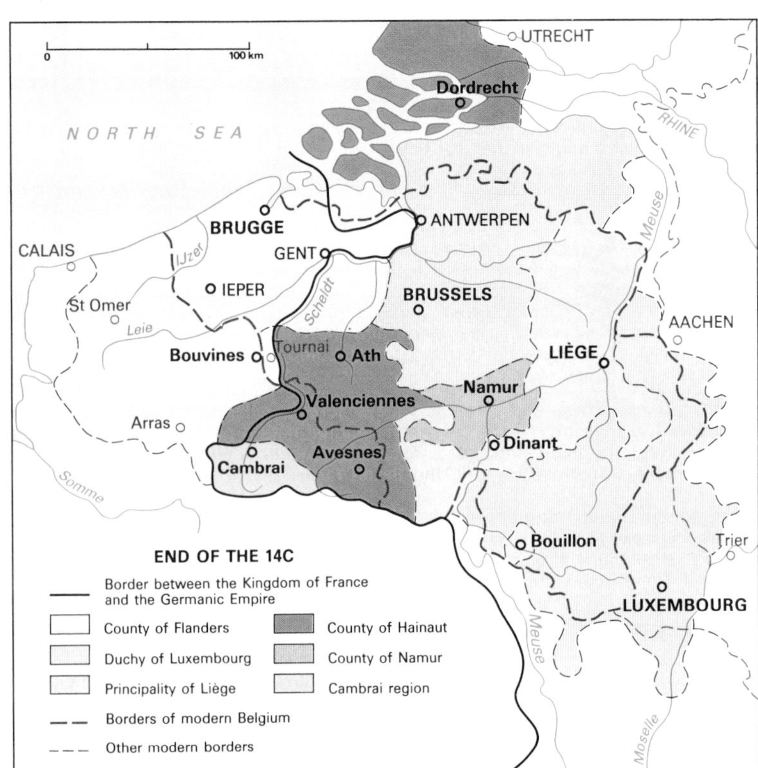

1300 Philip the Fair annexes Flanders, but the population revolts, and on 11 July 1302 the **Battle of the Golden Spurs** *(qv)* ends in victory for the Flemings over Philip the Fair's French knights.

1308 Henri VII of Luxembourg becomes Germanic Emperor under the name of Henry IV *(see Luxembourg)*.

1337 Beginning of the **Hundred Years War** between the English and the French, in dispute over the French crown. Revolt against the Count of Flanders in Ghent *(qv)*.

1354 The county of Luxembourg is raised to the status of duchy.

1369 The Duke of Burgundy, **Philip the Bold**, marries Margaret of Male, daughter of the Count of Flanders, Louis of Male.

FOREIGN AEGIS

The Dukes of Burgundy

1384 On the death of Louis of Male, Philip the Bold inherits his territories; thus Flanders becomes part of the Duchy of Burgundy.

1429-1477 Reigns of the Dukes of Burgundy **Philip the Good** and **Charles the Bold**. A great period of prosperity. Philip the Good founds the **Order of the Golden Fleece** at the time of his marriage with Isabella of Portugal. With the acquisition of Luxembourg in 1441, he completes the unification of the countries this side of the border (as opposed to those the other side, in Burgundy). The Dukes of Burgundy are surrounded by a sumptuous court, an incomparable centre of art with artists such as Jan Van Eyck, Petrus Christus, Memling.
In 1468, Charles the Bold sacks the town of Liège, which is in revolt, and annexes the principality. On his death in 1477 his daughter **Mary of Burgundy** inherits his territories and marries Maximilian of Austria. The two-headed eagle replaces the Burgundian coat of arms.

The Habsburgs

1482-1519 On the death of Mary of Burgundy, Maximilian becomes regent of the Low Countries (thus named to differentiate them from the High Countries, or Upper Germany, his country). In 1494 Maximilian gives the Low Countries to his son **Philip the Handsome**. In 1496 Philip marries Joanna, daughter of the Catholic King of Spain. Their son Charles is born in 1500 in Ghent; he is the future **Emperor Charles V**. He is brought up in Flanders, partly by his aunt, Margaret of Austria, daughter of Maximilian *(see also Mechelen)*, who becomes governor after the death of Philip the Handsome in 1506.

1519-1555 **Reign of Emperor Charles V** – Charles I, King of Spain, becomes Emperor Charles V on the death of Maximilian. His empire, "where the sun never sets", includes the Burgundian lands, the Austrian Empire and Spain, together with all the American and Asian colonies. He extends the territory of the Low Countries both to the north and to the south. In 1548 Emperor Charles V establishes Franche-Comté and the seventeen provinces of the Low Countries in the "Burgundy circle", with Brussels as capital.

The Spanish Netherlands

1555-1598 **Reign of Philip II of Spain** – in 1555 Emperor Charles V hands over the rule of the Low Countries to his son, Philip II. While Emperor Charles V had been strongly attached to the country of his birth and had protected it fiercely, his son is just as passionately a Spaniard above all else. A fervent Catholic, he fights against the Protestants ("iconoclasts"), who ransack the churches of his religion. During his reign, the nationalistic spirit of the Low Countries boils over, and the struggle for political liberties keeps pace with the battle of the Calvinists for religious tolerance. In 1567 Philip II appoints the **Duke of Alva** governor of the Low Countries and charges him with quashing the Calvinistic "heresy" and with combatting the Dutch revolt, led by guerilla-style groups of "Geuzen" (rebel-nobility). This is when the execution of the Counts of Egmont and Hornes takes place in Brussels *(qv)*. In 1576 the "Spanish Fury" is unleashed in Antwerp, then in Ghent. In the wake of this Philip II is forced to concede the **Pacification of Ghent** which liberates the seventeen provinces of the Low Countries from Spanish troops. In 1579, after the **Confederation of Arras** brings together the Catholic provinces which have chosen to stay under Spanish rule, the Protestant provinces form the **Union of Utrecht** (the provinces of the present Netherlands), followed by the republic of the United Provinces.

1598-1621 Reign of Archdukes Albert and Isabella, daughter of Philip II.

1648 With the **Treaty of Münster** Philip IV of Spain recognises the independence of the United Provinces and yields to them northern Brabant, northern Limburg and Flemish Zeeland. Belgium's future territory begins to take shape.

1659-1678 The **Treaty of the Pyrénées** between France and Spain places Artois under French rule and decides the marriage of Louis XIV with Maria Theresa of Spain. According to a Brabant custom favouring children of a first marriage, she stands to inherit this entire region through her mother. In 1663 Louis XIV declares the **War of Devolution** against the Spanish Netherlands to take possession of his wife's inheritance. He thus annexes southern Flanders (Lille). The Triple Alliance ends this war with the **Treaty of Aachen**. However, Louis XIV declares the **War of the Netherlands** in 1678, which concludes with the **Treaty of Nijmegen** in 1678; Flanders and Hainaut are excised.

The Austrian Netherlands

1701-1713 **War of the Spanish Succession** – Charles II of Spain dies with no direct descendants, leaving as heir Philip of Anjou, the grandson of his sister Maria Theresa and Louis XIV. However, England, Holland, Denmark and the German princes back the Archduke of Austria against France in the claim to succession.

1740-1748 War of the Austrian Succession. Louis XV invades Belgium, which is returned to Austria under the terms of the Treaty of Aachen.

1780-1789 **Emperor Joseph II**, an enlightened despot, nonetheless fails to take local idiosyncracies into account, thus sparking the peoples' revolt: Belgian nationalism becomes a reality. In 1789 the Brabant Revolution drives out the Austrians and assembles the States General in Brussels. The Austrians are temporarily expelled.

French Rule

1795 After the victories at Jemappes (1792) and Fleurus (1794), Republican France annexes the Austrian Netherlands and the principality of Liège. It establishes nine *départements* which are eventually to become the nine present provinces.

The Kingdom of the Netherlands

1814 **Napoleon's Defeat** – Belgium and Holland form the Kingdom of the Netherlands, with William I of Orange as sovereign; he also becomes Grand Duke of Luxembourg.

1815 The **Battle of Waterloo**, followed by the **Congress of Vienna** – Eupen and Malmédy are thus annexed to Prussia.

1830 Belgium finally wins independence from Holland, which has held dominion over the Belgians since the Congress of Vienna following the Brussels Revolution *(see Brussels)*. Belgium renounces its claims on Flemish Zeeland, northern Brabant and part of Limburg. The German-speaking part of Luxembourg remains under the rule of William I.

FROM INDEPENDENCE TO THE PRESENT DAY

1831 The London Conference acknowledges Belgian independence. The Constitution is drawn up and the crown given to Leopold of Saxe-Coburg-Gotha, who becomes first King of the Belgians under the name of **Leopold I** (1831-1865). War breaks out between the Belgians and the Dutch.

1839 William I acknowledges Belgian independence.
Belgium overcomes severe economic difficulties (famine in Flanders, 1845-1848) and involves itself in the Industrial Revolution. Luxembourg, tied economically to Germany from 1842, experiences substantial industrial growth.

1865-1909 Reign of **Leopold II**.

1890 **Independence of Luxembourg** - **Adolphe of Nassau** is Grand Duke from 1890 to 1905. **William IV** succeeds him (1905-1912).

1894 Universal suffrage is established in Belgium.

1908 The Congo, which has been Leopold II's personal property since 1855, becomes a Belgian colony.

1909 **Albert I** becomes King of the Belgians.

1912 **Marie-Adelaide** becomes Grand Duchess of Luxembourg.

1914-1918 **First World War** – Germany occupies Luxembourg and virtually all of Belgium, where Albert I, the "Soldier King", heads the resistance. Liège is captured, then Namur, Brussels and Antwerp. The Belgian army falls back to the coast; the Battle of the IJzer (Yser) takes place, brought to a close by the flooding of the polders. The front settles on the Ypres salient, then the hills of Flanders.

1919 Treaty of Versailles: Belgium regains Eupen, Malmédy, Moresnet and St-Vith.
Grand Duchess Charlotte of Luxembourg succeeds her sister Marie-Adelaide, who is forced to abdicate.

1922 Economic union concluded between Belgium and Luxembourg.

1934 Accidental death of Albert I *(qv)*. **Leopold III** succeeds him (1934-1944). His Queen Astrid meets an accidental death the following year (1935).

1940-1944 **Second World War** – Germany occupies Belgium and Luxembourg. Battle of the Bulge *(see Bastogne)*.

1944-1951 Charles of Belgium is Regent.

1948 The economic union of Benelux is concluded: **Be**lgium-**Ne**therlands-**Lux**embourg.

1951 Leopold III abdicates in favour of his son, who becomes King of the Belgians under the name of **Baudouin I**.

1957 Belgium and Luxembourg become members of the EEC (European Economic Community). Brussels is the capital of the EEC.

1960 The economic union of Benelux, instituted in 1958, gathers momentum. The Eyskens government grants independence to the Belgian Congo, which becomes the Congo-Kinshasa, then Zaïre.
Marriage of King Baudouin with Doña Fabiola de Mora y Aragón.

1964 **Jean of Nassau**, Grand Duke of Luxembourg, succeeds Grand Duchess Charlotte.

1977 Agreement drawn up establishing three federal regions: Brussels, Flanders, Wallonia.

1980 Referendum on regionalisation; new institutions in Flanders and Wallonia.

1993 Baudouin I dies and is succeeded by **Albert II**.

ART AND ARCHITECTURE

Over the centuries various peoples have flocked into Belgium and Luxembourg, bearing great artistic movements with them: the Romans, the French, the Germans, the Burgundians, the Austrians, the Spanish, the Dutch. Each left its trace.
Nevertheless two very distinct and original styles, both of which gave rise to real masterpieces, were born and developed in Belgian cities: the Mosan school of art in the principality of Liège; and the Flemish school of art, which flourished especially under the Dukes of Burgundy.

From Prehistory to the Carolingian Empire

There are a few megaliths (Wéris) which are still standing from the prehistoric era. Excavations carried out in the towns once occupied by the Romans have brought to light a multitude of objects bearing witness to the skill of the craftsmen: pottery, glass, bronze statuettes, terracotta, jewellery. The **Treviri Region** (Arlon and Luxembourg) has produced innumerable statues, votive stelae, including the famous stones of four divinities, funerary monuments on which the bas-reliefs, now in museums, evoke scenes of everyday life *(illustration p 53)*. Funerary artefacts from the 5C to the 9C, in the regions under the Salian Franks (Tournai) and the Ripuarian Franks (Arlon and Luxembourg), included damascene (inlaid) iron weapons, jewellery and brooches in bronze or gold, set with glass beads.
Charlemagne set up court at Aachen and introduced Christianity throughout his empire. He was at the root of a cultural renewal which manifested itself above all in the art of illumination. The churches of Lobbes and Theux are characteristic of the Carolingian style with their avant-corps, their wooden ceilings, their square pillars and the tribune located west of the nave.

Romanesque art (11C, 12C)

Towns and abbeys developed during this period. Belgium was divided into two parts: west of the Scheldt, Flanders belonged to France; regions to the east, through which the River Meuse flowed, belonged to the Germanic Empire. Romanesque art spread in particular along the trade routes lying in these two valleys.
Two distinct movements formed: Scaldian art (from Scaldis, or the Scheldt) and Mosan art (named after the Meuse). Both were full of originality, even though churches in both regions share many common characteristics, such as basilical layout, transept, chancel with radiating chapels and flat wooden ceiling.

Scaldian Romanesque art

In the Scaldian regions, devastated by the passage of hordes of marauding Vikings, Romanesque architecture is now evident only in isolated buildings such as the collegiate church of **Soignies**. The building of **Tournai Cathedral** led to the construction in the 12C of several churches based on the same architectural style. The outside of these buildings is characterised by a tower at the transept crossing and turrets on the west front; inside, the Norman influence in the tribunes and galleries is also typical.
Some civic buildings are also examples of Scaldian art (Tournai, Ghent, Aalst). Above the ground floor with round-arched openings, the windows, divided into two by a colonnette, are aligned between two stone string courses. In Gravensteen castle in Ghent, the Romanesque arches of the windows divided by colonnettes bring to mind those of private houses.
Sculpture in the region from the 12C onwards, favoured by the availability of local Tournai stone *(see Tournai)*, is quite remarkable: doorways and capitals (Tournai Cathedral) and fonts (Zedelgem, Dendermonde).

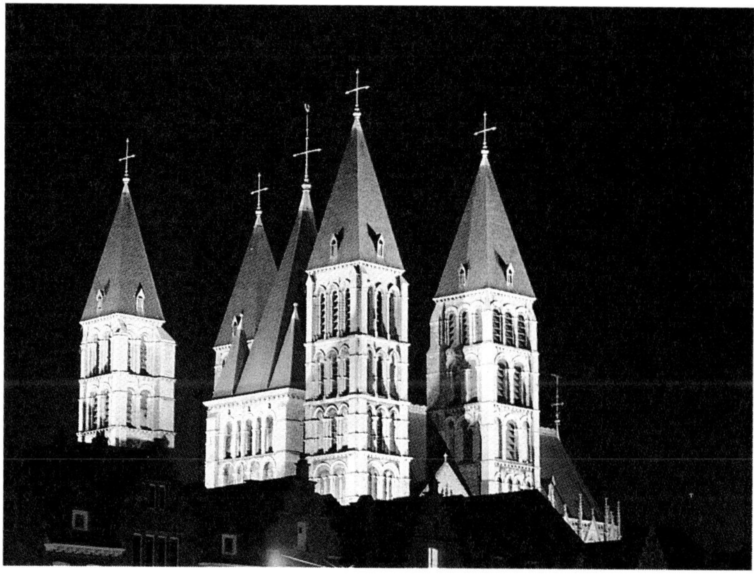

Cathedral, Tournai

Mosan Romanesque art

The art which developed in the diocese of Liège (that is to say, the Meuse valley and the surrounding countryside), in particular during the 11C and 12C, is known as Mosan Romanesque art. The **principality of Liège**, which included Aachen, was already an important artistic centre during the Gallo-Roman period and came very much under Carolingian influence. Later, owing to particularly close relations with the archbishopric of Cologne (on which the diocese of Liège depended) and the Rhine, the Rhenish Romanesque style began to exercise an influence as well.
In the 13C, French style predominated. This put an end to Mosan influence on architecture.

Architecture – Mosan regional Romanesque architecture retained a number of elements from Carolingian art, of which it is in some ways the continuation. First of all Ottonian architecture, which spread in the 10C and at the beginning of the 11C under Otto I, left its mark on part of the **Nivelles collegiate church**, which was consecrated in 1046. Nivelles belonged at that time to the bishopric of Liège, part of the Holy Empire.
The avant-corps of the churches became more imposing in the 12C, being flanked with staircase turrets (churches of St Denis and St John in Liège) or, more rarely, two square towers (St Bartholomew's in Liège). The outside of the church was decorated with Lombard arches. The apse was occasionally doubled by an exterior gallery (St Peter's in Sint-Truiden). There was often a crypt in the church, and sometimes a beautiful cloister (Nivelles, Tongeren).
Several of these characteristics can be seen in the later section of the Nivelles collegiate church, as well as in many rural churches (Hastières-par-delà, Celles, Xhignesse).

Copper-, Gold- and Silversmithing – The art of melting and beating copper or brass, practised in the Meuse Valley first in Huy, then in Dinant, is probably at the root of the great liturgical goldsmithing tradition which was to spread throughout the Mosan region, resulting in the production of immensely ornate shrines, reliquaries, crucifixes and book bindings.
From 1107 to 1118 **Renier de Huy** executed the famous brass font of St Bartholomew's in Liège; it is of a classic perfection quite exceptional for the period.
From this time on each work becomes more complex, more elaborate in subject matter and more varied in materials used. **Godefroy de Huy** used champlevé enamel for most of his work, in particular for the main reliquary of the pope St Alexander; this piece was made for the Abbey of Stavelot and is now exhibited in the Cinquantenaire Museum in Brussels.

Font by Renier de Huy,
St. Bartholomew's Church, Liège

Nicolas de Verdun, who marked the transition from Romanesque to Gothic, created the shrine of Our Lady for Tournai cathedral in 1205.
The monk **Hugo d'Oignies** chiselled his delicate, sophisticated works at the beginning of the 13C. They are now on display in Namur, in Oignies Convent. There are also many anonymous works, such as the 12C Visé shrine, or the 13C Stavelot one *(illustration p 188)* which fall within the limits of Mosan art.

Sculpture – Mosan art produced superb sculptures in wood: the Tongeren Christ, the famous Virgins in Majesty known as the **Sedes Sapientiae**, or Seat of Wisdom. Further examples include the Walcourt pieces in the Museum of Religious and Mosan Art as well as in St John's Church in Liège.
The sculptures in stone are equally interesting, especially the capitals (Tongeren) and the bas-reliefs (*Dom Rupert Madonna*, in the Curtius Museum in Liège). Many Mosan church fonts have basins carved with heads on each of the four corners (Waha) and the lip decorated with ornamental foliage and animals (St-Séverin).

Gothic Art (13C to 15C)

Religious architecture – Rhenish art in ecclesiastical buildings gradually gave way to the French Gothic style, which was brought by the monastic communities from France, or which was spread through Tournai as intermediary.
Nevertheless, Gothic art appears later in Belgium than in France. The first example was the **Tournai cathedral chancel** (1243), which took Soissons cathedral (Aisne, France) as its inspiration. The style spread slowly. Certain variations distinct to Belgium or to particular regions can be distinguished. The Gothic church is wider in Belgium than in France and is often not as high. On the other hand, the bell tower reaches quite an imposing height (123m - 403ft in Antwerp), even when it has been left unfinished, as in Mechelen.

Scaldian Gothic – This style retains some Romanesque features, but its main particularity is the development of triple lancet windows, or **triplets** (O.L.-Vrouwekerk van Pamele in Oudenaarde, St Nicholas's in Ghent).

Brabant Gothic – It was not until the 14C that Gothic art appeared in Brabant. The architects took their inspiration from the great French cathedrals (St Michael's in Brussels). However, their modifications created a distinct style which spread outside the province (Antwerp cathedral). Otherwise, this art remained rather sobre and never developed the excesses of Flamboyant Gothic.

The Brabant church is a large building with three naves and an ambulatory with radiating chapels. It is distinguished by the massive tower forming the west porch (the most beautiful is in Mechelen), and side aisle chapels surmounted by triangular gables recalling those of the houses. There is often no transept (Halle basilica), and the rose windows have commonly been replaced with larger windows.
The interior has a very distinctive style. The nave is supported by solid cylindrical pillars, whose capitals were originally decorated with a double row of curly cabbage leaves; large statues of the Apostles were later added to the other side of these pillars. The vaulting is of a fairly early Gothic style. The side aisle chapels communicate from one to the other, creating in this way new naves. Finally, the triforium has sometimes been replaced by a very intricately decorated balustrade, without a gallery.
The most representative of churches of this type is the basilica at Halle.

Civic architecture – From the end of the 13C, architectural originality manifested itself predominantly in **civic buildings**, especially in Flanders: belfries, covered markets or town halls.
The draper's trade brought about the creation and growth of the towns. The inhabitants defended their prosperity by obtaining certain privileges, town charters providing guarantees for their industry. For their meetings and their commercial activities they constructed imposing monuments which bore witness to jealously defended local autonomy and active community life. These buildings were arranged around the central market square (Grand-Place/Grote Markt).

Belfries – The belfry towers over the market square, symbolising the power of the community. It stands alone (Tournai, Ghent) or as part of a public building, such as a covered market (Bruges, Ieper) or the town hall (Brussels).
It is designed as a keep with watch turrets and battlements. The prison is below ground level, with two rooms, one on top of the other, above it, with a cantilevered oriel window or balcony from which proclamations were made. The bell room containing the chimes *(see Townscapes below)* is at the top, along with the lodge for the watchmen and heralds. Crowning everything is a weathervane symbolising the city: a dragon, the Flemish lion, a warrior, a saint (Brussels), a local character (Oudenaarde).

Covered Markets – The community developed hand in hand with the draper's trade. In the 15C there were 4 000 weavers in Ghent out of 50 000 inhabitants. Certain covered markets even had the privilege of offering official sanctuary normally provided only by churches and cemeteries.
The covered market consisted of a rectangular building divided into spaces for stalls inside. The area devoted to meetings and storage was upstairs.
The most beautiful of these markets are in Bruges, dating from the end of the 13C, and in Ieper, dating from the same period and rebuilt after the First World War.
In both Bruges and Ieper the covered market contains the belfry because up to the end of the 14C it generally served as a community building.

Town Halls – The most beautiful town halls (Bruges, Leuven, Brussels, Oudenaarde) were built from the late 14C onwards, when the wool trade was declining.
The Bruges town hall constructed in 1376 set a good precedent; the architecture still resembles that of a chapel. Brussels town hall followed; those in Leuven and Ghent were built during the Renaissance; that in Oudenaarde is the synthesis of its predecessors.
Outside, the façade is decorated with recesses, which contain representations of Flemish counts and countesses and the patron saints of the community.
On the first floor the great aldermen's hall is richly decorated (frescoes, tapestries or paintings, and always with a massive fireplace); it serves as a meeting room presided over by the burgomaster, as well as a hall for local festivities.
The ground floor of the town hall in Damme is used as a covered market.
The Gothic style is also evident in Flemish private houses; this is especially true of Bruges where the 16C saw the development of a very distinctive style tending toward Flamboyant architecture. Windows were surmounted by a moderately ornate tympanum; later, the windows and tympanum were both set beneath ogee arches.

Town Hall, Brussels

Sculpture – A school of sculpture developed in Brabant (Brussels, Leuven) and in Antwerp and Mechelen during the second half of the 15C and the beginning of the 16C. It produced innumerable wooden altarpieces of a remarkably fine craftsmanship, marked by a picturesque realism with traces of Gothic techniques.
An outstanding example of these **Brabant altarpieces**, besides that by Hakendover in 1430, one of the oldest and also one of the most elegantly executed, is the magnificent 1493 altarpiece of St George exhibited in the Cinquantenaire Museum in Brussels.
The same picturesque quality marks the sculpture on **church stalls**. The armrests and misericords (seat supports) in Brabant churches are decorated with satirical figures full of imagination, unforgiving illustrations of the human vices. Those in Diest are among the most remarkable examples.

Decorative arts – The Belgian Gothic style exhibits great originality particularly in the decoration of the interiors of ecclesiastical or civic buildings. Work in wood (altarpieces, statues, stalls, beams) is as remarkable as that in stone, as illustrated by the Flamboyant **rood-screens** in Lier, Walcourt and Tessenderlo. Mosan gold- and silversmithing did not survive beyond the 13C; coppersmithing, however, spread throughout the country, giving rise to magnificent chandeliers, fonts, or lecterns in the shape of eagles, pelicans or griffins.
Exceptional works were also produced in painting and tapestry *(see below).*

The Renaissance (16C)

The Italian Renaissance had little impact on Belgium, and then not until 1530.

Architecture – While ecclesiastical buildings retained the Gothic style, civic architecture gradually adopted that of the Italian Renaissance.
Oudenaarde Town Hall (1526-1530) is faithful in part at least to the Gothic style, whereas that in Antwerp (1564) is not. Constructed in 1564 by **Cornelis Floris de Vriendt** (1514-1575), it reflects a change in tastes, as do the courtyard of the Prince-Bishops' palace in Liège (1526) and the guild halls on Antwerp Market Square (end of the 16C).
This is particularly evident on the façades: engaged columns, pilasters and statues (Antwerp Town Hall), friezes (the Old Court Records Office in Bruges), gables trimmed with spiral scrolls and crowned with statues (Veurne Town Hall). The windows often have moulded tympana above them, a regional characteristic inherited from the Gothic style.
Indeed, the extent and exuberance of this decoration has earned Flemish Renaissance style the name **"pre-baroque"**.
During the second half of the 16C, during the period of Spanish rule, a style known as **hispano-flemish** developed in castle architecture. It is typified by onion domes such as those at Ooidonk, turrets as at Rumbeke, or crowstepped gables like those at Beersel *(illustration p 92)*. These decorative elements give the buildings a picturesque and characteristic appearance, as do the onion domes which feature on top of church bell towers.

Sculpture – Renaissance sculpture in Belgium is best manifested in the somewhat intellectual works by the Mons artist **Jacques Du Broeucq** (*c*1500-1584), most of which are kept in Mons' collegiate church of St Waudru (*qv* – statues of the Virtues). He also designed the plans for the castles in Binche and Mariemont, which have since disappeared.
Cornelis Floris de Vriendt, architect of Antwerp Town Hall, also created the magnificent tabernacle in Zoutleeuw.
The works of **Jerome Duquesnoy the Elder** (*c*1570-1641), renowned for his *Manneken Pis (illustration p 93)*, recall those of Cornelis Floris, especially the Aalst tabernacle.
Jean Mone (died 1548), sculptor to Emperor Charles V, born in Metz, France, created funerary monuments (Enghien, Hoogstraten) and altarpieces (Halle) in the purest Italian tradition.

Baroque art (17C)

The early 17C was a period of relative peace after the wars of religion and independence. Spain was represented by Archdukes Albert and Isabella, whose sumptuous court was in Brussels. These catholic sovereigns had many ecclesiastical buildings constructed.
Until the middle of the century, however, the great artistic centre was still Antwerp *(qv)*, where Rubens died in 1640.

Religious architecture – **Coebergher** *(qv)* completed the dome-topped Scherpenheuvel basilica at the beginning of the century, at the request of the archdukes; it is this building which marks the birth of the baroque style in Belgium.
Numerous ecclesiastical buildings were constructed for the Society of Jesus (Jesuits), such as St Charles Borromeo's in Antwerp, St Loup's in Namur, St Michael's in Leuven; they drew their inspiration from the Gesù church built in Rome in the previous century.
By the end of the century several Premonstratensian abbey churches had adopted the baroque style: Grimbergen, Averbode, Ninove. These are grandiose structures, their floor plan resembling a trefoil cross with the particularly long chancel reserved for the monks. Sometimes the churches are topped with a cupola, as is the case in Grimbergen.

Famous Belgian belfries include: Antwerp, Bruges, Florenville, Ghent, Leuven, Mechelen, Mons, Nieuwpoort.

Civic architecture – Noteworthy buildings from this period include the Mons belfry.
The most beautiful urban construction in the baroque style is to be found on the **Grand-Place, Brussels**. Rebuilt after the 1695 bombardment, it bears witness to a decorative verve run wild, but nonetheless faithful to a certain Renaissance spirit, evident in the Doric, Ionic and Corinthian orders, which lend rhythm to the façades, as well as in the balustrades of some pediments.
In the Mosan region, 17C private houses are characteristically bereft of any flights of fancy; the brick walls are cut by seams of stone, between which there are tall mullion windows, as at the Curtius Museum in Liège.

Belfry, Mons

Sculpture – Many churches of the period were decorated inside with sculptures by the Antwerp artist **Artus Quellin the Elder** (1609-1668); he was very much influenced by Rubens, or his cousin **Artus Quellin the Younger** (1625-1697).
Lucas Faydherbe (1617-1697), the artist from Mechelen who was also a student of Rubens, created enormous statues resting against columns in the nave and on altarpieces.
François Duquesnoy (1597-1643), son of Jerome *(see above)* worked mainly in Rome. He was known for his baby angels, or "putti", which were amiable figurines in marble, terracotta or ivory. He is also credited, together with his brother **Jerome Duquesnoy the Younger** (1602-1654), with producing numerous ivory crucifixes which resemble each other in the delicacy and elegance of their execution (Spontin castle).
Jean Delcour (1627-1707) in Liège *(qv)* collaborated with Bernini in Rome and sculpted elegant effigies of Madonnas and saints.
Antwerp artist **Hendrik Frans Verbruggen** (1655-1724) won renown for his work in wood: the Grimbergen confessionals, decorated with life-size figures, show a remarkable vigour and sense of movement. They were frequently imitated.
For St Michael's in Brussels, Verbruggen produced a forerunner of the pulpits known in Belgium as **truth pulpits**, on which sculptures and immense figures depict the truths of the Gospels.
The church stalls in Averbode, Floreffe and Vilvoorde, decorated with figures, are also remarkable examples of Belgian baroque sculpture.

The 18C

Baroque style persisted in ecclesiastical buildings, but at the end of the century, under the rule of Charles of Lorraine (1744-1780), the neo-classical style began to spread. The **Place Royale in Brussels** was constructed in this style by the Frenchmen Guimard and Barré.
Laurent Dewez (1731-1812), architect to this governor, built Orval abbey church in 1760 (since destroyed) in the same style, then the church at Gembloux (1762-1779) and finally that of Bonne-Espérance (1770-1776).
Baroque sculpture was still prolific in churches. Pulpits tended more towards rococo, for example the elegant construction in oak and marble in St Bavo's, Ghent. This was created by **Laurent Delvaux** (1696-1778), who thereafter adopted the neo-classical style.
Theodoor Verhaegen (1700-1759), in addition to several pulpits, executed a splendid confessional with majestic figures carved in wood in Ninove.
Michiel Vervoort the Elder (1667-1737) produced pulpits and confessionals decorated with statues, such as those in St Charles' church in Antwerp.
The decorative arts came into their own in the 18C; tapestry and lace *(see below)*, Tournai ceramics *(see Tournai)*, as well as cabinet-making in Liège *(see Liège)*. These pieces of furniture, drawing inspiration from the French style, adorned sumptuous interiors hung with painted leather or tapestries (Ansembourg Museum in Liège). In Liège, the richness of the castles' interior decoration contrasts with the austerity of local architecture (Aigremont).

The 19C and 20C

Architecture – At the beginning of the 19C, neo-classicism triumphed in Brussels (St Hubert Arcades, Congress Column, Théâtre de la Monnaie) and in Ghent (Grote Schouwburg and Law Courts). The end of the century saw a taste for architecture imitating the buildings of Classical Antiquity; the most beautiful example is the Graeco-Roman Law Courts in Brussels, designed by **Poelaert** (1817-1879).
However, from 1890 onwards certain architects revolted against this plagiarism of the past and sought new forms and materials. Belgium was one of the first countries to subscribe to the Art Nouveau movement, with architects such as **Paul Hankar** (1859-1901), **Henry Van de Velde** (1863-1957) and above all **Victor Horta** (1861-1947). Traditional materials (stone, glass, wood) or new ones (steel, concrete) were used for rationally studied compositions where the structure was linked harmoniously to the décor until it became in itself a decorative element. The interior of the house by Horta (Horta Museum in St-Gilles), of the Palais des Beaux-Arts, of the Waucquez shops containing Brussel's Comic Strip Centre and of the Tournai Fine Art Museum all demonstrate the attention to detail, form and originality which characterise this highly productive innovator.

After Horta, several architects plunged into modernism and attempted to resolve the problem of collective residences. This gave birth to the garden-cities of the 1920s, created by architects **Eggerickx** and **Van der Zwaelmen** ("Floréal" urban park at Boitsfort, *qv*), Victor Bourgeois, **Huib Hoste** and **Adolphe Puissant.**
More modern works include those of **André Jacqmain** in Louvain-la-Neuve, **Claude Strebelle** in Sart Tilman, and **Roger Bastin** in Brussels (Museum of Modern Art).

Sculpture – **Willem Geefs** (1805-1883), representing neo-classicism, created the statue of Leopold I at the top of Congress Column in Brussels.
From 1830, the influence of romanticism and the taste for quattrocento are evident in the sculptures of **Charles Fraikin** (1817-1893) and **Julien Dillens** (1849-1904) who participated with the exiled Rodin in decorating the Bourse in Brussels. **Thomas Vinçotte** (1850-1925) created the group of charging horses on the Cinquantenaire Triumphal Arch. **Jef Lambeaux** (1852-1908) casts his spell over viewers with the surging passion emanating from his works, reminiscent of Jordaens (Brabo Fountain in Antwerp).
Constantin Meunier (1831-1905) was a painter before turning to sculpture in 1885; he felt at one with the new industrial era and committed himself to representing the working man, the miner at his job.
The Impressionist period is represented, above all, by **Rik Wouters** (1882-1916), whose spontaneity bursts out of boldly executed works such as the *Crazy Girl.*
Georges Minne (1866-1941) pioneered Expressionism, whose principal representatives were to be **Oscar Jespers** (1887-1970) and **Joseph Cantré**. A return to fundamental themes can be seen in the works of **Georges Grard** (1901-1984) which celebrates the fertile image of the female form. By the 1920s, non-representational art had already appeared in the works of **Servranckx**, who was also a painter.
Notable post-war pioneers include **Maurice Carlier** and **Félix Roulin** (born in 1931), the latter of whom hammered out a highly personal world in copper in which traces of the human body (hands, mouths, arms, etc.) are scattered over various reliefs. **Jacques Moeschal** (born in 1913), architect and sculptor, marks out distinct motorways and urban spaces in his works of steel and concrete. **Pol Bury** (born in 1922) inherited the Surrealist tradition in addition to being close to the Cobra group *(see Painting below)*. Since the 1950s he has devoted himself to designing "Kinetic" sculptures (continuously moving sculptures with motors or balls, hydraulic sculptures, etc.)

PAINTING

It is in painting most particularly that the people of Belgium, fond of colour and receptive to the world around them, have found their most characteristic mode of expression.

The Primitives – The 15C is the golden age of Flemish painting. A naturalist movement had already appeared by the end of the 14C, with Hennequin (or Jan) de Bruges, who drew the tapestry cartoons for *The Apocalypse* in Angers, and Melchior Broederlam, painter of the altarpieces for the Champmol charterhouse in Burgundy.
Their art remained nonetheless closely related to the art of **illumination** in which the Flemings excelled under the patronage of the Dukes of Burgundy. In the early 15C the Pol friars, Jan and Herman Van Limburg, **miniaturists** of the *Book of Very Rich Hours of the Duke of Berry* (*Les Très Riches Heures du Duc de Berry*, in Chantilly Château, France) displayed an astonishingly detailed and vivid realism in their art of illumination.
The greatest painter was **Jan Van Eyck** (*d*1441). The *Mystic Lamb* altarpiece *(qv)* remains one of the great wonders of painting of all time, by dint of his use of perspective, realistic detail and bright colours softened by light. Van Eyck is also credited by many with the invention of oil painting.
Robert Campin, thought by some scholars to be the Master of Flémalle, worked in Tournai during the same period. One of his students was **Rogier Van der Weyden** (Rogier de la Pasture) *(qv)*, who influenced among others **Dirk Bouts** *(qv)*.
Van Eyck was succeeded by the Bruges School *(see Bruges)*, which included **Petrus Christus**, the great portraitist, and **Hans Memling**, who offers a charming synthesis of the pictorial themes of his period in his work, as much in his calm sophisticated religious compositions as in his exceptional, masterfully executed portraits. **Gérard David** continued in his vein.
In Ghent, **Hugo Van der Goes** *(qv)* painted panels demonstrating an original sense of composition.

Virgin with Child by Hugo van der Goes, Museum of Ancient (15C-19C) Art, Brussels

The Renaissance – 16C. **Quentin Metsys** (1466-1530) was the first painter to reveal Renaissance inspirations in his tasteful, sophisticated works. **Joachim Patinir** *(qv)* and **Herri met de Bles** *(qv)* devoted themselves to landscapes. **Pieter Brueghel the Elder** (c1525-1569), influenced by Hieronymous Bosch, produced lively, picturesque works revealing his gift for observation. His son Pieter Brueghel, known as **Hell Brueghel**, imitated him with not inconsiderable talent.

17C – Like the 15C this was a golden age for painting.
Pieter Paul Rubens *(qv)* was a universal artist who was sensitive to all the promptings of flesh and spirit; it was he who struck a balance between Flemish realism and Italian harmony.
Anthony Van Dyck (1599-1641), who lived in England from 1632 onwards, was a student of Rubens. He was an extraordinary draughtsman who painted often dark and melancholy works; he was the creator of religious scenes and elegant society portraits.
Jacob Jordaens (1593-1678) was among Rubens' colleagues. He painted colourful works with a vigourous relief, often depicting earthy, realistic scenes. The animal painter **Frans Snyders** (1579-1657) taught **Paul De Vos** among his students, whose brother **Cornelis De Vos** specialised in portraits. Jan Brueghel, known as **Velvet Brueghel**, is famous for his paintings of flowers and landscapes. His son-in-law **David Teniers the Younger** (1610-1690) created a fashion in Belgium for scenes of peasant life, or genre painting. Developments slowed down somewhat in the 17C with the religious paintings of **Pieter Jozef Verhaghen** (1728-1811) *(qv)*, who continued in Rubens' style.

19C-20C – The style of the excellent portraitist François Joseph **Navez** (1787-1869), a student of David, was essentially neo-classical. Antoine **Wiertz** (1806-1865) was more Romantic.
In 1868 the Société Libre des Beaux-Arts of Brussels brought together the Realist painters **Félicien Rops** (1833-1898) *(qv)*, **Charles De Groux** (1867-1930), **Alfred-Émile Stevens** (1823-1906) and **Constantin Meunier**.
Except for **Théo van Rysselberghe** (1862-1926), who adopted Seurat's pointillist style, the painters of the late 19C paid no attention to new movements, in particular Impressionism. **Emile Claus** (1848-1924) depicted tranquil country life. **Henri Evenepoel** (1872-1899) studied daily life, whereas **Henri De Braekeleer** (1840-1888) lent a luminous poetry to scenes of bourgeois life. Jakob Smits *(qv)* was the painter of the Kempen region.
The **Symbolist movement** attracted William Degouves de Nuncques (1867-1935), Xavier Mellery (1845-1921) and Fernand Khnopff (1858-1921), who painted strange, sphinx-like women.
James Ensor *(qv)* set himself apart from artistic movements, demonstrating an unrivalled originality and talent.
Belgian painting made good progress with the work of the **Sint Martens-Latem group** *(qv)*. **Valerius de Saedeleer** painted landscapes in the style of Brueghel, while **Gustave van de Woestijne** painted everyday people. The second wave of the Latem group's work was Expressionist, with **Albert Servaes**, who tended towards mysticism in his work, **Gust** (Gustave) **De Smet** and **Frits van den Berghe**, who was more Surrealist. **Constant Permeke** *(qv)* led this group. His landscapes and figures have a calm vigour about them and, like his sculptures, are endowed with a fairly primitive lyricism. Fauvism was as important a movement in Brabant as Expressionism was in Flanders. The leading proponent was **Rik Wouters** (1882-1916), whose paintings showed a tendency towards constructivism (influenced by Cézanne). In the same school, **Jean Brusselmans** (1884-1953) drew his inspiration from his surroundings: working class women, labourers, landscapes, backstreet interiors. Surrealism made its mark with **René Magritte** (1898-1967) and his fantastic worlds in which his precise technique was put to the service of his imagination. **Paul Delvaux** *(qv)* painted characters roaming around against theatrical backdrops.
Joseph Peeters (1895-1960) and **Victor Servranckx** (1897-1965) were both precursors and theoreticians of abstract art in Belgium; Servranckx's geometric abstract works bring to mind Fernard Léger.
La Jeune Peinture Belge was founded just after the Second World War, in July 1945, bringing together Gaston Bertrand, Louis Van Lint, **Anne Bonnet**, Antoine Mortier and **Marc Mendelson**. This was the second wave of abstract art.
In 1948 the **Cobra** group (**Co**penhagen, **Br**ussels, **A**msterdam) was founded by the Belgian writer Christian Dotremont and the Experimental Group of painters from Amsterdam: principal exponents were the Dane Asger Jorn, the Dutchman Karel Appel and the Belgians **Pierre Alechinsky** and Corneille (Cornelis van Beverloo). Cobra aimed to be a way of life, art freed from the intellect to express all types of experience, in particular the unconscious.
Since 1960 Belgian painters have followed the great international movements.

TAPESTRY

Tapestry, designed to ornament the walls of castles and churches, first appeared in Europe at the end of the 8C. The art of tapestry-making developed in particular from the 14C onwards and assumed considerable importance in Belgium.
Brussels had over 1 500 tapestry-makers at the beginning of the 16C. Tapestries woven in Belgium were ordered by the greatest princes in Europe, by the kings of Spain and by the Pope.
Tapestry is woven on a loom on which a parallel series of coloured threads (the warp) has another parallel series of threads (the weft) interwoven with it at right angles to form patterns following a painted design or "cartoon". If the warp threads are laid horizontally, the loom is said to be "low-warp". If they are vertical, the loom is "high-warp". The latter is the most common type in Belgium. The weft consists of threads of wool, often mixed with threads of silk, gold or silver.
The first tapestries were most usually religious compositions. Historic scenes appeared later, as did hunting scenes, allegorical and mythological scenes. Several tapestries illustrating the same theme are known as a set, or up to the 19C as a "room" (the latter generally included tapestry upholstery for furniture etc. as well as wall hangings). Compositions were set against a background of flower-filled meadows.

Tournai – The main centre of production was initially Arras, under the rule of the Dukes of Burgundy. Its decline began in 1477, when the town was captured by Louis XI. Tournai, which was already the main rival of Arras, ended up by eclipsing it all together. Tournai compositions have no border; the story is depicted in several episodes in close juxtaposition. There are no empty spaces; the areas between the sumptuously robed figures are filled in with plant-like decoration. The compositions are highly stylised, even when the subject is taken from a painting such as **The Judgement of Trajan and Herkenbald** (Bernese Historical Museum, Berne, Switzerland), which was inspired by works by Van der Weyden which have since been destroyed.
The more famous Tournai tapestries include in particular: *Sheep-shearing; The Story of Gideon* (disappeared) (1449-1453); *The Story of Alexander* (1459), which was woven for Philip the Good; and *The Battle of Roncevaux* (second half of the 15C).

Legend of Notre-Dame-du-Sablon,
Royal Museums of Art and History, Brussels

Brussels – Tapestry had a place of honour in Brussels from the 14C onwards; nevertheless, the oldest known works from Brussels only date back to the second half of the 15C. In 1466, the Dukes of Burgundy commissioned their first tapestries. Highly sophisticated in technique, the compositions were still essentially Gothic in style, as illustrated by the early 16C **David and Bathsheba**.
Brussels tapestry making reached its peak not long after this. A new style evolved under the impetus of **Van Orley** (*c*1488-1541). The composition became monumental, and the scenes from then on very elaborate, dealing with a single, strongly emphasised subject. The figures are dressed in sumptuous costumes, the landscapes enriched with Renaissance buildings, plants are painstakingly reproduced, and the borders are filled with flowers, fruit and grotesques involving either animal or arabesque motifs. From 1525 it is possible to discern the initials BB (Brussels Brabant) in the border framing the composition. Van Orley designed the series entitled **Honours**, commissioned by Emperor Charles V (*c*1520), **The Legend of Notre-Dame du Sablon** (1515-1518) and the **Hunts of Maximilian**, which was executed by Willem de Pannemaker, a member of a highly talented family of tapestry-makers. Nature is depicted in a remarkable way in the latter series. Raphael painted the cartoons for the **Acts of the Apostles** (1515-1519), commissioned by Pope Leo X.
The painter **Pieter Coecke** produced the cartoons for *Capital Sins* and *The Story of St Paul. The Legend of Herkenbald* (1513) and the series **Virtues and Vices** are equally admirable works.
At the beginning of the 17C Brussels fell from supremacy, although commissions continued to pour in. Many tapestries, such as *The Triumphs of the Holy Sacrament*, were made following cartoons by **Rubens**. They are distinguished by their sense of drama, their perspective effects and the importance of the border as a feature. Jordaens himself created several cartoons, including *Proverbs* and *Country Life*.
Antwerp, Bruges, Enghien and Geraardsbergen also wove tapestries during this period. At the end of the 17C and 18C Rubens' cartoons were still used, but rustic subjects were more the vogue, and so paintings by **David Teniers the Younger** were frequently reproduced.

Oudenaarde – In Oudenaarde, where tapestry had been a great art since the 16C, the subjects were of a more modest type than in Brussels. The 18C witnessed the rise to triumph of the landscapes called **verdures** *(see Oudenaarde)*, which other centres of tapestry production had been making since the 16C, such as Enghien and Geraardsbergen. Oudenaarde, like Brussels, imitated the rustic paintings of David Teniers the Younger.

Contemporary Tapestry – The art of tapestry fell into decline at the end of the 18C. It has now revived in Mechelen, with the Gaspard de Wit Royal Tapestry Works *(see Mechelen)*, in Oudenaarde *(qv)* and in Tournai *(qv)*, where the group Force Murale, led by Roger Somville and Edmond Dubrunfaut, was created in 1945.

OTHER ART FORMS

Furniture – Items of Gothic furniture carved in oak included tables, benches and chests with linenfold decoration. During the Renaissance, tables and very high-backed chairs were embellished with heavy turned feet. The massive sideboards made in **Antwerp** had two main parts and featured entablatures supported by caryatids, uprights decorated with lions'-heads (the Flemish lion) holding rings in their mouths, friezes and panels which were either moulded or sculpted to depict religious, historical or mythological scenes. Seats and walls were covered in the Spanish style, that is with embossed and painted leather which was produced in **Mechelen** from the beginning of the 16C, taking over from Cordoba. During this period the flanges and brackets of the beams in most of the civic buildings were sculpted. The fireplaces were embellished with Renaissance motifs.
Craftsmen began to use exotic woods from the end of the 16C. Cupboards, which soon took on gigantic proportions, were often veneered in ebony. **Antwerp** produced its famous cabinets in ebony or rosewood, richly encrusted with ivory, mother-of-pearl or tortoiseshell; some are decorated with painted panels from Rubens's studio.
The French taste for flowing lines came into fashion in the 18C; elegant oak presses were produced in **Liège** and **Namur**.
Art Nouveau became very popular under the iron rule of Henry Van de Velde and Victor Horta, especially in the work of Serrurier-Bovy.
Furniture-making is still a flourishing industry in Mechelen and Liège.

Ceramics – The decoration of houses in the Middle Ages gave rise to a high level of production of **ceramic tiles** for walls and floors. Crockery in **glazed stoneware** came from the Rhine region, but also from **Raeren** and, from the 16C, from **Bouffioulx** (near Charleroi) as well. Nowadays the blue sandstone ware from **La Roche-en-Ardenne** is widely appreciated. **Faïence** (tin-glazed earthenware) was first produced in Antwerp in the 16C, based on Italian techniques. Apart from traditional tiles, dishes and apothecary pots were also produced. Ceramics factories were established in the 18C and 19C in Nimy (near Mons), Liège, Namur, Brussels, Tournai and Andenne (the largest centre for faïence ware).
Ceramic tableware is an important manufacturing activity in Belgium (La Louvière) and in the Grand Duchy of Luxembourg.
For **porcelain**, the main centre of production besides Andenne was **Tournai**, where a manufactoring industry was founded in the middle of the 18C. **Brussels** porcelain still has a good reputation.

Glassware – This craft was established in Hainaut in the 2C and made enormous strides in the late 15C, under the influence of Venice, and again in the 17C, owing this time to Bohemian and English influences. At the same time the use of coal as a fuel from the end of the 17C was instrumental in concentrating the production of window panes in the Charleroi basin.
The **Vonêche** crystal glassworks, founded near Beauraing (Namur province) in 1802, was the largest in the French Empire until 1815; **Val St-Lambert** (west of Liège) took over from it after 1826. The Manage glassworks (near Charleroi) is reputed nowadays for the manufacture of perfume bottles.

Lace – While this craft is probably of Venetian origin, Flanders lays claim to the invention of bobbin (or pillow) lace. This is made on a cushion or pillow; threads are held taut by bobbins and manipulated to form a web or a pattern, the work being continually fixed in place with pins.
Lace first appeared during the Renaissance and was designed to ornament clothing. Flemish paintings depict both adults and children in suits decorated with lace at the collar and on the sleeves. This craft was taught to young girls at school and soon became popular. Its popularity increased once Belgium's period of political and religious upheaval had passed, and Flemish lace gained an unequalled reputation in the 17C. The principal centres of production of this period included **Brussels** (mainly needlepoint lace), **Bruges**, **Mechelen** and **Antwerp**.
In the 18C lacemaking reached its peak, with patterns largely incorporating rococo designs and embellishment in particular with floral motifs. Sadly the invention first of machine-made tulle, then the Jacquard loom, had an adverse effect on the popularity of needlepoint lacemaking.
There have been successful efforts to preserve the craft of lacemaking; it is still practised in Bruges and Sint-Truiden. Bobbin lacemaking is once more being taught, and several new centres have sprung up, in particular at Lier, Mechelen and Poperinge. Zele is continuing the tradition of needlepoint lace. There is a centre of contemporary lacemaking in Brussels.

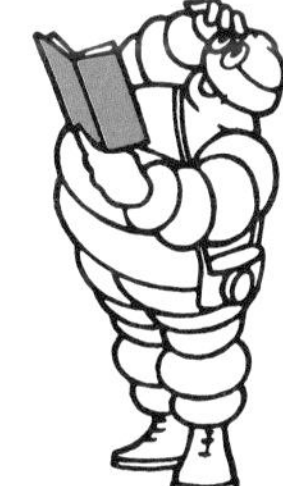

GLOSSARY OF ART AND ARCHITECTURAL TERMS USED IN THE GUIDE

Ambulatory: *illustration I.*

Apse: semicircular or semi-polygonal east end of a church, behind the altar.

Arcade: a line of small counterthrusting arches, usually raised on columns.

Avant-corps: the part of a building which projects obviously from the main body or façade.

Axial (or Lady) chapel: chapel in the main axis of the church (often dedicated to Our Lady, if the church itself is not); *illustration I.*

Bartizan: a battlemented parapet (watch tower); *illustration II.*

Bas-relief: carved or sculpted figures which are slightly proud of their background; low relief.

Bracket: piece of projecting stone or timber supporting a beam or cornice.

Brattice: temporary projecting wooden gallery or parapet used during sieges.

Cantilever: see bracket.

Capital: enlarged uppermost part of a column shaft.

Champlevé enamel: enamel poured into engraved patterns on metal surfaces and then smoothed down to the same level as the metal.

Chancel: the part of the church reserved for the clergy (sanctuary) and cantors (choir), which contains the high altar; *illustration I.*

Chapter-house: room in a monastery where the chapter of canons or nuns meets.

Chevet: French term for the exterior of the apse (the east end); *illustration I.*

Corbel: see bracket.

Crowstepped gable: triangular upper part of a wall which supports the two slopes of the roof and which has stepped edges.

Curtain wall: length of wall or rampart between two towers or bastions; *illustration III.*

Foliated scroll: sculpted spiral ornamentation, decorated predominantly with stylised foliage motifs.

High relief: sculpted relief figures which are proud of their background by more than half their thickness (in between bas-relief and fully detached sculpture).

Lancet arch: a narrow, sharply pointed arch (resembling the head of a lance).

Lantern: a windowed structure at the top of a dome or turret permitting light to enter a building.

Machicolation: a projecting defensive parapet, supported by brackets, with holes in the floor through which missiles etc. can be dropped on the attackers; *illustrations II and III.*

Merlon: solid part of a battlemented parapet between two embrasures.

Moat: a trench, generally filled with water, surrounding and protecting a fortress.

Mullion: a stone upright separating panels in windows, doors or other openings.

Oriel: a bay window cantilevered out from a wall.

Palladian style: door or window openings in sets of three, divided by pilasters or columns and with triangular pediments above the outer two openings and a round-arched lintel above the central one.

Pilaster: an engaged rectangular column.

Pinnacle: apex of a building.

Polyptych: painting or sculpture composed of several hinged panels.

Radiating or apsidal chapel: *illustration I.*

Rood-screen: carved screen separating chancel and nave, generally bearing a large crucifix (rood) and sometimes representations of other figures present at the Crucifixion.

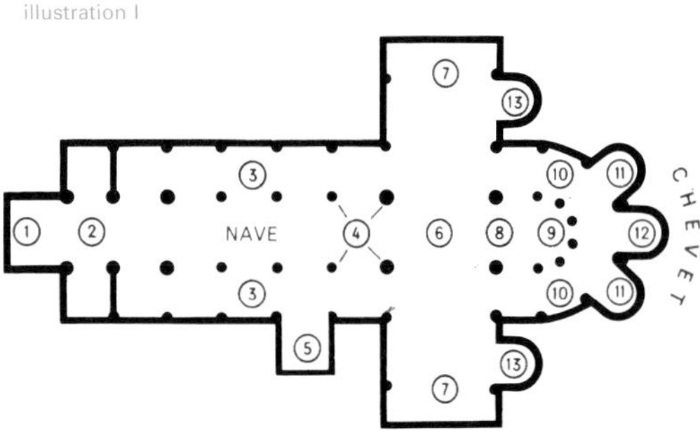

Ground plan. – The more usual Catholic form is based on the outline of a cross with the two arms of the cross forming the transept: ① Porch – ② Narthex – ③ Side aisles (sometimes double) ④ Bay (transverse section of the nave between 2 pillars) ⑤ Side chapel (often predates the church) – ⑥ Transept crossing – ⑦ Arms of the transept, sometimes with a side doorway – ⑧ Chancel, nearly always facing east towards Jerusalem; the chancel often vast in size was reserved for the monks in abbatial churches – ⑨ High altar – ⑩ Ambulatory: in pilgrimage churches the aisles were extended round the chancel, forming the ambulatory, to allow the faithful to file past the relics – Radiating or apsidal chapel – ⑫ Axial chapel. In churches which are not dedicated to the Virgin this chapel in the main axis of the building is often consecrated to the Virgin (Lady Chapel) – ⑬ Transept chapel.

illustration II

Fortified gatehouse: ① Machicolations – ② Watch turrets or bartizan – ③ Slots for the arms of the drawbridge – ④ Postern.

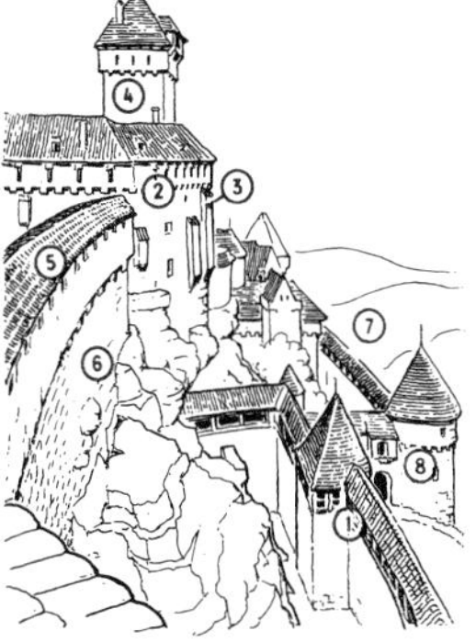

illustration III

Fortified enclosure: ① Hoarding (projecting timber gallery – ② Machicolations (corbelled crenellations) – ③ Barbican – ④ Keep or donjon – ⑤ Covered watchpath – ⑥ Curtain wall – ⑦ Outer curtain wall – ⑧ Postern.

illustration IV

Stalls:
① High back – ② Elbow rest – ③ Cheek-piece – ④ Misericord.

Round (arch etc.): semicircular.

Side aisle: aisle running along each side of the nave at the same height as it.

Stalls: *illustration IV*

Stucco: mixture of marble dust and plaster bound with strong glue.

Transept: *illustration I*

Transept arm: *illustration I*

Tribune: raised platform at one end of a church, reserved for the seat of the bishop or other high-ranking church dignitary.

Triforium: shallow gallery running along the nave and chancel of a church, above the side aisles and below the clerestory.

Triptych: painting or sculpture composed of three hinged panels, which can be closed up.

Watch turret: *illustration II*

MUSIC

Whether in Wallonia or Flanders, Belgium has always been a fertile ground for music. In the 15C and 16C Belgian composers, such as the Mons musician **Roland de Lassus** *(qv)*, were among the foremost in Europe.

In the 17C and 18C, however, first-class musicians were less common; the Liège composer **Grétry** *(qv)* wrote many comic operas, and his Mémoires ou Essais sur la Musique are full of original ideas.

The creation of the Royal Conservatories in 1830 brought about a change for the better. **Fétis**, first director of the Brussels Conservatory, acquired an international reputation with his theoretical and musicological works, as also did Gevaert, who succeeded him in 1871. Among Fétis' students, Edgar Tinel can perhaps be considered the greatest master of religious music in Belgium at the turn of this century.

After a nomadic life as a young virtuoso, **Henri Vieuxtemps**, born in Verviers *(qv)*, became a violin teacher at the Brussels Conservatory in 1871. He founded the Franco-Belgian school for violin with his master Bériot.

The great symphony composer **Paul Gilson** (1865-1942), a student of Gevaert, is one of the figures of contemporary Belgian music who has had the greatest impact on his period. A prolific composer in every genre, he had many disciples, including Jean Absil (1893-1974). Following the example of the Group of Six, founded in Paris in 1918 and headed by Erik Satie, several of Gilson's students formed the Group of Synthesists, with the goal of integrating the contributions of modern music into classical forms.

In 1867 in Antwerp a movement in favour of music with a distinctly Flemish character was born. **Peter Benoit** (1834-1901) took its head. He created the first Flemish School of Music, which became a Conservatory in 1898. As a composer of oratorios in Flemish illustrating themes particular to Flanders, he was often emulated.

Wallonia was no less prolific. **César Franck** (1822-1890), born in Liège and a naturalised French citizen, was a great innovator, for whom fame, however, only came posthumously. His student Guillaume Lekeu died in 1894 without fully realising his potential. Eugène Isaye (1858-1931), the great Liège violinist, and Joseph Jongen are also noteworthy.

Henry Pousseur (born in 1929) is the head of serial music; in 1970 he founded the Wallonia Centre of Musical Research in Liège.

The Queen Elisabeth Music Chapel, founded in 1939, offers Belgian artists and some foreign artists the opportunity to continue their studies after the Conservatory.

LITERATURE

The enormous extent and variety of Belgian literature is virtually unknown outside the country itself. Literary works, in particular those by Flemings, have a pronounced local flavour and are characterised also by an unquestionable originality.

French-speaking Belgium – In earlier centuries the country produced some famous chroniclers: in the 14C, Froissart; in the 15C, Philippe de Commines; and in the 16C, Jean Lemaire de Belges, born in Bavay. In the 18C the cosmopolitanism of the Maréchal de Ligne *(qv)*, a memorialist, was his hallmark.
A highly original and active literary movement has developed in Belgium during the last century. Following the great precursor **Charles de Coster**, author of the celebrated *Légende d'Ulenspiegel* (1867), came the group "La Jeune Belgique" (1881) and a period of upsurge in literary activity from novelists, such as the Antwerp writer **Georges Eekhoud** (1854-1927) and Camille Lemonnier (1844-1913), from poets, such as the Ghent author Van Lerberghe (1861-1907), Max Elskamp (1862-1931), **Georges Rodenbach** (1855-1898), made famous by among other things his novel *Bruges la Morte* (1892). Some writers earned worldwide renown, such as the great poet **Émile Verhaeren** *(qv)* and the Ghent author **Maurice Maeterlinck** (1862-1949), mysterious and melancholy writer of the play *Palléas and Mélisande*, also essayist and Nobel Prize winner in 1911.
From subsequent generations, outstanding writers include: Maurice Carême (1899-1978); **Marcel Thiry** (1897-1977); and Marie Gevers (1883-1975), who has been compared to the French author Colette.
The Mons author **Charles Plisnier** (1896-1952) was a famous novelist and winner of the Prix Goncourt. **Fernand Crommelynck** (1886-1970) was a writer of earthy plays; **Michel De Ghelderode** (1898-1962) was a prolific, audacious playwright.
Maurice Grevisse (1895-1980) wrote *Bon Usage* (1936), and M Joseph Hanse (1902-1992) wrote *Nouveau Dictionnaire des difficultés du français moderne*, both significant reference works in the field of grammar and linguistics.
Writers who have achieved international fame include: the Namur author **Henri Michaux** (1899-1984), who took French nationality; the Liège writer of detective stories **Georges Simenon** (1903-1989), creator of the famous Inspector Maigret in 1930 and author of many analytical novels; the essayist **Suzanne Lilar** (1901-1992); the historian **Carlo Bronne** (1901-1987); and the novelist **Françoise Mallet-Joris** (*b*1930) who lives in Paris.
In the world of the comic-strip **Hergé** (1907-1983), creator of Tintin in 1929, lived to see his albums translated into languages from all over the world. **Folon's** little character in a hat has achieved fame on billboards the world over.
Finally, the songwriter-composer **Jacques Brel** (*Le Plat Pays*) (1929-1978) can be ranked among Belgium's poets.

Tintin by Hergé

Flemish-speaking Belgium – Flemish literature was born in the 12C, and gained momentum first in the 13C with the poetess Hadewijch and the poet and moralist **Jacob van Maerlant** *(qv)*; then in the 14C, with the mystic **Jan van Ruusbroec** *(qv)*, considered to be the father of Dutch prose. Writers who distinguished themselves in the 19C include the Antwerp citizen **Hendrik Conscience** *(qv)*, Romantic author of novels and short stories, and the great Catholic poet **Guido Gezelle** *(qv)*.
In the 20C a number of poets stand out, such as **Karel van de Woestijne** (1878-1929), sensual and mystic, and the modernist Expressionist Paul van Ostaijen (1896-1928). Cyriel Buysse (1859-1932) figures among the novelists, along with **Stijn Streuvels** (1871-1969), who drew his inspiration from the flat southwest countryside (*De Vlaschaard* – The Flax Field); Herman Teirlinck (1879-1967), prolific novelist and dramatist; Willem Elsschot (1882-1960); **Ernest Claes** *(qv)* with his mischievous tales; **Felix Timmermans** *(qv)*; and Gerard Walschap (1896-1989).
After 1930 poetry was dominated by **Jan van Nijlen** (1884-1965); **Richard Minne** (1891-1965); **Karel Jonckheere** (*b*1906); **Anton van Wilderode** (*b*1918); and **Christine D'Haen** (*b*1923).
A second wave of modernism occurred in about 1948, producing talented writers such as the Bruges author **Hugo Claus** (*b*1929), who is a dramatist, novelist (*Het verdriet van België* - The Sorrows of Belgium, 1983) and highly regarded poet; Paul Snoek (1933-1983); and Hugues Pernath (1931-1976).
Contemporary Flemish novelists include **Marnix Gijsen** (1899-1984), writer of philosophical tales; Louis Paul Boon (1912-1979), a writer of realistic, passionate prose and a painter besides; **Johan Daisne** (1912-1978), some of whose works inspired film maker **André Delvaux**; **Hubert Lampo** (*b*1920); Jef Geeraerts (*b*1930), interested by the Belgian Congo issue; Ivo Michiels (*b*1923), whose formal research marked the European avant-garde.
Jean Ray (1887-1964), born in Ghent and who took the pen-name John Flanders, wrote black tales in Dutch and fantasy novels in French, including *Malpertuis* (1943) which was adapted for the cinema in 1972.

Luxembourg – Luxembourg has a few writers in the French language, such as Marcel Noppeney (1877-1966).
A poet expressing himself in the local language of Letzebuergisch, **Michel Rodange** (1827-1876) wrote a version of the animal epic by Van den Vos Reinaerde.

FOLKLORE AND TRADITIONS

See Calendar of Events, p 238.

Folklore in Belgium is extremely important and very much alive. It reflects a happy gregarious people, faithful to the past and its customs. Each major city has its own museum displaying traditions which have been preserved over the years: customs of town, especially of Flemish towns where guilds played a major role, and country; traditions of Flanders in the north and also of Wallonia in the south, influenced to some extent by Picardy. A history which has mixed peoples of diverse origins only served to enrich this heritage, which is especially evident during festivals and holidays. All year long there is a succession of events, of religious or secular origin, which date back many years and evoke legends or ancient mysteries. From the most devout of processions (Veurne Penitents) to the bawdiest of festivities, festivals increase in number or are revived over the years. The slightest pretext is an opportunity for a public gathering or a parade. Everything is organised a long time in advance by the members of different "societies" or brotherhoods, who for several months pour their energies into preparing for the festival. When the big day comes, it is time to dress up in fancy dress, meet old friends, eat well and let the beer flow. Very often the festival or patronal feast *(kermesse or ducasse – see below)* is combined with religious ceremonies.

Carnivals – Carnival-time is celebrated almost all over Belgium. This celebration, probably of pagan origins, takes place around Mardi Gras, or Shrove Tuesday; it was presented by Christianity as a symbol of rejoicing before the period of Lenten fasting and penitence. Twenty days later, Refreshment Sunday represents a break in the austerity of Lent.

The three most famous carnivals in Belgium take place in Binche, Eupen and Malmédy. In Binche renown is due largely to the **Gilles** *(qv)*, who only appear on Shrove Tuesday. However the festivities last four days, and before the Gilles appear there have already been processions of "Trouilles de nouilles" and "mam'zelles". Eupen is well-known for the Rhenish carnival which takes place on Shrove Monday. As for Malmédy, the **"Cwarmê"** *(qv)* is original in incorporating satirical revues and the famous "haguètes" among the costumed figures. Other noteworthy festivals include that at Aalst, with its parade of giants and Bayard the horse, and at Blankenberge.

During Lent – Certain customs have come to be associated with this period, such as the beheading of a goose or rooster by horsemen of the Antwerp region. Refreshment Sunday (Mid-Lent) is celebrated particularly enthusiastically at Stavelot with the **Blancs-Moussis**, amusing figures in huge white hooded garments and with long red noses, who hark back to the period when the Stavelot Abbey monks participated in the carnival. The Chinels, irresistable Punch and Judy characters, parade in Fosses-la-Ville *(qv)*. This festival is also very lively in Maaseik.

A Passion Play (Jeu de la Passion) take place in Ligny; it is a series of tableaux drawn from the Gospels which also make allusions to the modern world. The Spanish left a heritage of penitence during Holy Week, a tradition which is upheld on Good Friday in particular in Veurne, where the famous Stations of the Cross procession takes place, in which hooded penitents participate, each bearing a cross. The same tradition is also upheld in Lessines *(qv)*.

Holy Blood Procession, Bruges

Giants – Many of the parades in Belgium include giants. Although the number of giants has increased since the beginning of this century, the custom itself of including giants dates back to the 15C. The tradition began in Belgium and spread to Spain, owing to the Spanish occupation. The first giant character probably appeared in a religious procession or an "Ommegang", in which he symbolised Goliath or St Christopher. Goliath is in fact still present at the patronal festival *(ducasse)* of Ath, where he is nicknamed Mr Gouyasse. He joins combat with David in a symbolic re-enactment of the Bible story.
Secular characters gradually appeared at these events; even Bayard the horse came to be included, ridden by the four Aymon sons (in Aalst and Dendermonde). Giants appear also in Nivelles (Argayon, Argayonne, their son Lolo and the horse Godet), in Geraardsbergen, in Lier and in Arlon. The more famous giants include: Polydor, Polydora and little Polysorke in Aalst; Cagène and his companion Florentine in Beloeil; Pie and Wanne and their son Jommeke in Tervuren; Count Baldwin IV in Briane; and Alix of Namur. A parade in Heist brings together all 120 giants of Flanders.

Bonfires – These are the Lenten bonfires, at which a dummy is sometimes burned. The most famous bonfire is the **tonnekensbrand** in Geraardsbergen; a cask is set on fire after the throwing of *Krakelingen* biscuits.

Processions – Religious holidays, combining deep piety with secular traditions, are celebrated with processions which often incorporate historical pageants and even bright and colourful carnival parades. In the Middle Ages few people knew how to read, and over the course of the centuries the procession became a way of teaching Biblical themes. In addition to the usual characters representing apostles, prophets or angels, there were also floats on which tableaux vivants illustrated scenes from religious history. Some of these are extremely impressive, such as the **Holy Blood Procession** in Bruges *(qv)*. The faithful would follow the statue or reliquary of the saint across the fields for quite long distances – over 30km - 19 miles in Ronse *(qv)* – praying and singing hymns as they went.

Plays and pageants – Derived from religious and medieval origins, a little similar to the mystery plays, these re-enact old legends during processions. One of the best-known is that in Rutten, which commemorates the death of St Evermeire in the 8C. In Mons, the **Chariot of Gold** (Car d'Or) procession involves the various guilds with their patron saints and statues of the Virgin, with the Chariot of Gold itself bringing up the rear. The "Lumeçon" Combat recalls a pageant dating from the Middle Ages.
Witches and their sabbaths are evoked in Ellezelles, to commemorate the execution of five witches in 1610. In Vielsalm it is the "macrâlles", witches who foretell the future, who are the stars of a comic celebration.
In Wingene, the Brueghel festivals illustrate paintings by the great master.

The Ducasse and the Kermesse – The words *ducasse* (from *dédicace*, meaning a Catholic holiday – one of the most famous *ducasses* is in Ath) and *kermesse* ("church fair" in Flemish) now both designate a town or village patron saint's day. This holiday has preserved aspects of its religious origins (Mass and procession) but now includes traditional pageants, stalls, competitions and sometimes a jumble sale.

Military parades – The first military parades begin at the end of May in the Entre-Sambre-et-Meuse region *(qv)*, and offer an opportunity to admire the resplendent uniforms of the parading troops, in a rigorous military ceremony. One of the most surprising aspects of these parades is the use of Napoleonic uniforms: Zouaves, grenadier guards, dragoons, mamelukes and sappers accompanied by a canteen-keeper.

The May tree – On 30 April, 1 May or during the month of May certain towns, such as Hasselt, Genk and Tongeren in the province of Limburg, solemnly plant a May tree as a symbol of renewal. In Brussels this tree is called the Meyboom or Tree of Joy (planted in August).

Historical pageants – These vividly re-enacted, sumptuous pageants of days gone by breathe new life into past grandeur: in Brussels, the **Ommegang** was once presided over by Emperor Charles V and his court; in Bruges, the Golden Tree pageant *(qv)* recalls the days of the Dukes of Burgundy.

Marionettes – Marionette theatre appeared in Liège in the 19C and was a great success owing to the famous Tchantchès character *(qv)*. The Liège marionette is moved by means of a rod fixed to the top of its head; it is carved out of wood, painted and covered with cloth. The repertoire draws as much on history as on legend and on modern life and is aimed mainly at adult audiences. The theatre founded by Toone in Brussels *(qv)* dates from the same period.
The hero of marionette theatre nowadays is Woltje, who speaks a colourful Brussels dialect. The repertoire has kept its classics (the four Aymon sons, Till Eulenspiegel) while continuing to add new plays.
Other theatres in Antwerp, Ghent and Mechelen perform works in Flemish.

Folklore Museums and Open-Air Museums – Belgium is rich in folklore museums, which are always located in old buildings (hospitals, convents etc.) and evoke traditions which vary from one region to another. For example:
Antwerp: Folklore Museum; **Binche**: International Museum of Carnivals and Masks★; **Bruges**: Folklore Museum★; **Ghent**: Folklore Museum★; **Liège**: Museum of Walloon Life★★; **Mons**: Museum of Mons Life★; **Tournai**: Folklore Museum.
Two large open-air museums exhibit traditional regional architecture: in the Ardennes, the Fourneau St-Michel★★ *(qv)* museum of rural life in Wallonia; in Flanders, the Bokrijk★★ *(qv)* open-air museum.

TOWNSCAPES

Belgian towns, especially Flemish ones, have a characteristic composition related to the autonomy they have as communities, which dates back to the 13C *(see Historical Table and Notes)*. This is reflected by the imposing civic buildings *(see Architecture)*: the belfry, the town hall and the covered market. Towns are imbued with remarkable charm by the canals, the cheerful music of the chimes, the peacefulness of the beguine convents, the welcoming atmosphere of the cafés and *estaminets*.

Market Squares – These are surrounded by the community's principal monuments, including the town hall, the covered market and the belfry. The guild halls with richly sculpted façades decorated with the statue of a patron saint or symbolic animal are to be seen here too.
These squares were once used for punishments in the pillories and executions, as well as for markets and major celebrations, theatre performances, parades and cavalcades with all the attendant pomp and ceremony. The best known market squares are those in Brussels, Bruges, Antwerp and Mechelen.

Chimes – The carillon chimes regularly ring out their melodies, lending a rhythm to town life. Carillons were not always installed in the belfry, but sometimes in the cathedral itself, as is the case in Mechelen and Antwerp. The word "carillon" comes from "carignon", meaning a group of four bells. Carillons were connected to a clock (the first town clock appeared in 1370), and their various chimes were set to play just before the sounding of the hour. They were tapped by hand with a hammer for many years; the first mechanical chimes, made to play by the clock mechanism, were created in the 15C. The discovery of the manual keyboard, used for the first time in 1510 in Oudenaarde, made it possible to increase the number of bells. In 1583 the invention of the pedal board in Mechelen enabled bass stops to be used, thus enriching the variety of sound possible. The art of founding the bells has been refined to a quite remarkable degree, so that most of the major carillons now consist of at least 47 bells. The most famous examples in Belgium are in Mechelen, Bruges, Nieuwpoort, Antwerp, Ghent, Leuven, Florenville. There is a school of campanology in Mechelen.

Jack o' the clocks – From the 14C, belfries were adorned with a clock and jack o' the clocks, metal figures which strike the hours by tapping a little bell with a hammer. Jack o' the clocks are a delightful sight to be found in Kortrijk, Nivelles, Brussels (Mont des Arts), Virton, Lier and Sint-Truiden.

Beguine convents – Beguine convents, often a little off the beaten track and enclosed inside walls, constitute a picturesque little town-within-a-town. Small cottages clustered together around a church and garden house the beguine nuns. The members of these lay sisterhoods observe certain rules governing, for example, mode of dress and attendance of religious services (Mass), but they are not bound by any vows and are entitled to possess money of their own. They are free during the day to pursue their various occupations, but the doors of the beguine convent close at nightfall. The little community is under the direction of a Mother Superior.
The origin of beguine convents is unknown. The first establishment of this type is supposed by some to have been founded by Lambert le Bègue in Liège at the end of the 12C. On the other hand, tradition attributes their creation to Saint Begga, who was the Mother Superior of a convent in Andenne, where she died in 694. By the 13C beguine convents had developed their definitive structure as independent enclosed communities with their own church. In 1566 the protestant "iconoclasts" destroyed many of the beguine convents, which were then rebuilt at the end of the 16C and the 17C.
These quiet, peaceful convents are perhaps the clearest embodiment of the mystic side of Belgium. There are now about twenty of them in the north of the country, and some are still occupied by a small number of beguine nuns (St.-Amandsberg in Ghent) or by religious congregations (the Benedictines in Bruges). For the most part, however, the towns rent the empty houses to the elderly, or sometimes to students, as in Leuven.

Almshouses – Financed by the guilds, these were a sort of sanctuary for the old or the poverty-stricken. They were rows of low, whitewashed brick maisonettes.

Estaminets – *Estaminet* is the Walloon word for a café. These are friendly places where people can meet and have a glass of beer, play cards and gossip. They are also a favourite gathering point for "coulonneux" (homing pigeon enthusiasts). What better place to sit and watch the world go by over a cup of coffee with a cinnamon biscuit (speculaas) or a Belgian chocolate!

FOOD AND DRINK

Belgium

The Belgians are fond of the good life and appreciate the merits of a well-laden table. While a number of dishes reflect French influence, local preparations have successfully withstood being swamped, and the Walloon and Flemish provinces are justifiably proud of their culinary specialities.

Vegetable broth or clear beef or chicken soups *(bouillons)* are usually served at the beginning of the meal.

Ardennes ham or sausage, cold fish, seafood with mayonnaise, shrimp rissoles or eels in a herb sauce may also feature as an hors d'oeuvre.

The main course offers a choice of many regional specialities: rabbit with prunes, Flemish *karbonaden* (braised beef, beer and onions), *oie à l'instar de Visé* (goose boiled then fried in the style of Visé, near Liège) or, in hunting season, a sample of the game with which the Ardennes abounds (hare, venison, young wild boar, mallard duck, pheasant).

Local vegetables include hops shoots (in March) in a mousseline sauce, Brussels chicory baked with cheese and ham, Brussels sprouts and Mechelen asparagus.

There are some delicious varieties of cheese: those from Herve, in particular the pungent, strongly-flavoured Remoudou; Maredsous, similar to the French St-Paulin cheese (mild); cheese from Brussels; and the Flemish Présent cheese.

The mixed fruit, rhubarb or sugar tarts of the Ardennes are mouthwatering. Overijse and the surrounding region are renowned for hothouse grapes, while Limburg produces plums preserved in vinegar syrup. Belgian ice cream is delicious, and of course the excellent reputation of Belgian chocolates, especially the "pralines" (chocolates with creamy or nutty fillings), speaks for itself.

Drinks – Beer is the most common drink in Belgium. Quality French wines can be found in good restaurants. Belgium also produces spirits and liqueurs, for example mandarin orange liqueur, Spa Elixir (a type of Chartreuse), as well as the strong juniper berry gin *(jenever)* from Hasselt, Deinze and Liège, where it is known as *péquet*.

Luxembourg

Particular specialities include: suckling pig in jelly, smoked or raw Ardennes ham, other smoked meats such as smoked neck of pork with broad beans *(judd mat gaardebounen)*. Game is available in season. Kachkéis is a salted handmade cheese. September is the time to taste the local plum tarts. All this is washed down with Moselle wine *(see Luxembourg Moselle Valley)* or beer, which is drunk by most people here. The liqueurs (various types of plum, blackcurrant) are well-known.

Brief gastronomic glossary

Babelutten: hard butter caramels.

Baisers de Malmédy: meringues filled with whipped cream.

Cassis: blackcurrant liqueur

Chicorée or chicon (Witloof): chicory.

Choesels: offal cooked in a Madeira sauce with mushrooms.

Couques (Koeken): in Brussels, sweet, lightly spiced bread; in Dinant, hard gingerbread sweetened with honey.

Cramiques (Kramieken): currant buns.

Craquelins (Krakelingen): buns with a sugary filling.

Doubles: two pancakes filled with Herve or Maredsous cheese.

Escavèche: fried fish preserved in a spicy marinade.
Filet américain: type of steak tartare (raw minced beef).
Filet d'Anvers: portion of smoked beef or horse.
Flamiche: cheese tart made from Romedenne, a local cheese, served hot.
Fricadelles: meat balls.
Friture de la Moselle: fried whitebait.
Herve: soft cheese.
Hutsepot (Hochepot): mixed stew of pork, beef and mutton.
Karbonaden (Stoofvlees): beef braised in beer or water with onions, spices, vinegar and sugar.
Kletskoppen: thin butter biscuits made with almonds and hazelnuts.
Koekoek Mechelen: type of chicken.
Lierse Vlaaikens: plum tarts.
Maitrank: aperitif from Arlon *(qv)*.
Manons: chocolates with a fresh cream filling.
Mastellen: aniseed biscuits.
Mattentaart (Tarte au maton): tart made from fromage blanc, milk and almonds.
Mokken: type of macaroon flavoured with cinnamon or aniseed.
Paling in 't groen (Anguilles au vert): eels sautéed in butter and stewed in a sauce of finely chopped parsley, chervil, sorrel, sage, citronella and onions.
Péquet: strongly flavoured gin from Liège.
Pistolet: small round bun.
Potjesvlees: type of potted meat made from veal, rabbit and chicken.
Potkès (Boulette de Huy): savoury cream cheese.
Remoudou: strong, pungent cheese of the Herve region.
Spantôles: sweet biscuits named after a well-known canon.
Speculaas (spéculos): small biscuit flavoured with brown sugar and cinnamon.
Strikken (Noeuds): biscuits made with butter and brown sugar.
Tarte al djote: cheese tart made from eggs, cardoons (akin to artichokes) and cream, served hot.
Tarte au stofé: tart made from fromage blanc, eggs, almonds and apple purée.
Veianer Kränzercher: small rings of choux pastry.
Waterzooi: type of clear fish or chicken soup.

BEER

Beer is Belgium's national drink. On average, every Belgian drinks 118 litres (about 200 pints) a year. There are nearly 100 breweries in the country and an endless variety of beers. Pale or dark, bitter or sweet, light or strong, there is a Belgian beer for every taste.
Beer was already known about in Antiquity, then later the Gauls started to make it and gave it the name **"cervoise"**. During the Middle Ages brewing beer was a privilege of the monasteries. It spread widely throughout Flanders; indeed the word "beer" might itself be derived from the Flemish "bier".
Aalst and Poperinge are Belgium's main hops-growing regions, and the harvest is brought home in September. There are two signposted tourist routes to enable visitors to explore these regions: one is around Kobbegem ("Hopperoute": "Hops route") and the other is around Poperinge ("Hoppelandroute": "Hops country route").

The brewing process – Barley grains are soaked in water until they germinate. The sprouting grains are then dried, roasted in a kiln and ground to a powder (malt): this is the **malting process**. The **brewing process** turns the starch in the finely ground malt into a sugary juice – the **wort** – by mixing the malt with pure water and hops and cooking it. It is this process which is the most important and characteristic part of beer-making. Brewing actually does two things: as well as turning the barley malt starch into sugar, it draws out the soluble malt substances. The quantity of hops added to the boiling wort affect the degree of bitterness and aromatic quality in the finished beer. **Fermentation**, the final stage, turns the wort into beer; the wort is left in large vats for several days, and yeast added to it to change the maltose sugar into ethyl alcohol and carbonic gas.

Varieties – Three types of beer are produced in this way, depending on variations in the fermentation process:

– **Low fermentation** beers, such as "pilsen"-type (lager) beer. Fermentation and more particularly the aging process take place at a low temperature. The best-known breweries are at Leuven (Interbrew breweries) and Waarloos, south of Antwerp (Alken-Maes breweries).

– **High fermentation** beers. Fermentation takes place at a "high" temperature of 15° to 20°C - 59° to 68°F. Most "special" beers are in this category, and so are the famous "Trappist" beers which are still brewed in the great Cistercian abbeys. These are the beers of Orval, Chimay *(qv)*, Rochefort *(qv)*, Westmalle and St-Sixtus (in Westvleteren).

– **Spontaneous fermentation** beers, which include typically Belgian beers such as gueuze, kriek and lambic. These are made by letting the fermentation take place at its own pace, without the addition of yeast, in huge vats or casks. After being kept for about one to two years the beer is designated a **"lambic"**. Then the beer is drawn off into bottles in which a second fermentation takes place, after which it becomes what is known as a **"gueuze"**. **"Kriek"** is characterised by a red colour and fruity taste, from cherries having been steeped in it at the lambic stage.

Belgium

AALST Oost-Vlaanderen Pop 76 441

Michelin maps 409 fold 3 or 213 fold 5
Town plan in the current Michelin Red Guide Benelux

Aalst, on the banks of the River Dender, was once a commercial town and now has an industrial park grouping together a number of active industrial concerns. Large breweries have grown up in connection with regional hops-growing. Aalst is also a centre for the cut-flower business.

Carnival – The festivities *(see the Calendar of Events at the end of this guide)* begin the Sunday before Shrove Tuesday, with a great parade of giants, including Bayard the horse *(see Meuse/Namur Region)*, and floats, immense papier mâché constructions often political and satirical in theme. On Shrove Monday there is a second parade and the throwing of onions *(ajuinworp)* from the top of the buildings in the Market Square. The festival reaches its peak of excitement on Shrove Tuesday, with the Vuil Jeannetten – men comically dressed as women.

Carnival – Bayard the Horse

SIGHTS

Market Square (Grote Markt) – The statue of **Dirk Martens**, a native of Aalst, stands in the middle of this irregularly-shaped square; it was he who introduced the technique of printing to Flanders (1473).

Old Town Hall (Schepenhuis) – This gracious 15C building was extensively restored in the 19C. Those 13C features which remain are the façades on the right-hand side and at the rear; the latter has a cusped gable and windows surmounted with trefoil arcades.
A charming 16C flamboyant oriel to the right brightens up the main façade.
The tall slender belfry dates from the 15C; it bears the town motto "Nec spe nec metu" ("neither by hope nor by fear") above two recesses containing two warriors, which represent the Count of Flanders and the Count of Aalst; the carillon consists of 52 bells.

Amsterdam Stock Exchange (Beurs van Amsterdam) – This arcaded building dates from the 17C and 18C.
It has a beautiful brick-and-stone façade, with four scrolled pediments and an onion-domed campanile. It once belonged to the Barbarions, members of the **Chamber of Rhetoric**, a literary society which composed and performed songs and theatrical works.

Town Hall (Stadhuis) – This 19C colonnaded building displays a gracious 18C rocaille façade on the far side of the courtyard.

St Martin's Collegiate Church (St.-Martinuskerk) ⊙ – Herman de Waghemakere, a member of the Keldermans family, built this Late Gothic sandstone edifice in the Brabant style.
The nave is unfinished, but the **architectural unit★** consisting of the transept, apse, ambulatory and radiating chapels is quite beautiful.

Interior – The inside of the church has a certain elegant simplicity. Notice the round pillars and leaf-decorated capitals typical of the Brabant style, as well as the lovely side aisles and the openwork triforium balustrade.
A large work by Rubens, *St Roch Patron Saint of the Plague-Stricken*, forms the altarpiece which can be seen in the south transept arm; the frame is said to have been created following a plan of the great master.
Gaspar de Crayer's painting on the left has Rubens-like characteristics.
In the chancel on the north side there is a splendid **tabernacle★** in black and white marble sculpted in 1604 by Jerome Duquesnoy the Elder. The three juxtaposed turrets are decorated with charming statuettes (the Virtues, the Evangelists, the Church Fathers, angels bearing the instruments of the Passion).
The first ambulatory chapel on the south side has an *Adoration of the Shepherds* attributed to Ambrosius Francken; distinctly Italian influences can be detected (the Virgin's very pure and gentle face; the stylised positions of the subjects).
Dirk Martens's tombstone is in the fourth chapel, and the vestiges of delicately, freely drawn late-15C frescoes can be seen in the axial chapel.

Old Hospital (Oud-Hospitaal) ⊙ – *This is in the street leading from the east end of St Martin's Collegiate Church.*
Provisions and supplies used to be delivered here by boat, as the River Dender once flowed just behind the hospital. The restored buildings, which stand around a cloister and a chapel, have been turned into a **museum** of archaeology and regional decorative arts.

AARSCHOT Brabant

Pop 26 079

Michelin maps 409 H 3 or 213 fold 8

The collegiate church bell tower rises over the rest of the little industrial town of Aarschot (pronounced "arskot"), in the **Hageland** region on the banks of the River Demer. The Austrians and Burgundians set about pillaging the town in the 15C, followed by the Spanish in the 16C. Joseph II of Austria had the fortifications razed in 1782. Aarschot also suffered during the two World Wars, but has since risen from its ruins.
Pieter Jozef Verhaghen (1728-1811), who continued the work of the great 17C masters, was born here. His canvases embellish several churches, in particular in Leuven, where he spent the last years of his life.
Aarschot inhabitants are jokingly referred to as "cobblestone beaters", from the time when watchmen doing their rounds reassured town citizens of their presence by tapping their feet on the cobblestones. An amusing "Kasseistamper" statue illustrates this nickname above a fountain near the Market Square.

SIGHTS

Collegiate Church of Our Lady (O.-L.-Vrouwkerk) ⊙ – The chancel of this beautiful church, built of ferruginous sandstone, dates from the 14C, and the nave from the beginning of the 15C. The tower comprising the façade rises to a height of 85m - 279ft (Mechelen: 98m - 321ft), its lower part brightened by alternate use of limestone and sandstone.
On entering there is a strikingly beautiful perspective of the nave; the upward sweep of its slender lines is heightened by the ribbing of the transverse arches. The same colouring as the tower is found in the chancel, which is concealed by a Late Gothic rood-screen. This is surmounted with a 15C triumphal cross and decorated with scenes of the Passion and Resurrection.
The pulpit and the confessionals are in the 17C Flemish baroque style.
The stalls (1515) in the chancel are decorated with satirical carvings (hurdy-gurdyist, Lay of Aristotle, wolf and stork, professions); note also the wrought-iron chandelier (1500) attributed to Quentin Metsys. A painting by P J Verhaghen *(Disciples of Emmaus)* can be seen in a chapel on the south side of the ambulatory. In a chapel on the north side there is a remarkable painting on wood by an unknown 16C master of the Flemish school, the **Mystic Wine-press**. The Seven Sacraments are on the predella. The miraculous statue of Our Lady of Aarschot (1596) is in the north arm of the transept.

Beguine Convent (Begijnhof) – There is a Renaissance house by the church tower. A little further on, a few 17C dwellings stand in a row, all that remains of the beguine convent founded in 1259. The 16C **ducal mills** can be seen to the right on the banks of the Demer; there is an enclosure containing a charming reconstruction of a beguine convent on the left, which is part of a hospice.

St Roch's Tower (St.-Rochustoren) – *On the Market Square.*
The 14C brown sandstone building was used in the Middle Ages as a tribunal. It now houses the tourist office.

Viewpoint – There is a good view of the town and its surroundings from the **Aurelian Tower** (Aurelianustoren), sometimes called the Orleans Tower, the remains of the old fortifications.

Head in the direction of Leuven from the Market Square.

EXCURSION

St.-Pieters-Rode – *8km - 5 miles south. Leave by the Leuven road (N 19), soon afterwards turn left towards St.-Joris-Winge (N 223), then turn right after crossing under the motorway.* **Horst Castle** is a beautiful polygonal construction surrounded by water, flanked by a 14C keep. This, together with the entrance porch, is the only remaining trace of the building which Emperor Maximilian's troops destroyed in 1489. The rest of the castle is in brick with stone string courses and dates from the 16C. The grounds around the castle as well as the nearby lake have been turned into a recreational centre *(fishing and boating in season).*

AISNE VALLEY Luxembourg

Michelin maps 409 J 4-5 or 214 fold 7 – Local map see OURTHE VALLEY

The little river wends its way between wooded slopes until it joins the Ourthe.

FROM EREZÉE BRIDGE TO BOMAL

16km - 10 miles – allow 2 hours

The charming **Aisne Tourist Tramway** ⊙ follows the Aisne's course south from Erezée Bridge up through the rugged valley to the village of Forge.

Wéris – *6km - 3.75 miles north of Erezée Bridge.*
The charming 11C **church** (Église Ste-Walburge) in Wéris is built on slate columns. There is a 16C sculpted tabernacle known as the "théothèque" to the right of the main altar. There are still several megaliths in Wéris, in particular a **dolmen** formed of blocks of local pudding-stone *(northwest heading towards Barvaux, to the left not far from the road).*

The road follows the Aisne Valley.

The enormous sandstone wall of **Roche à Frêne** can be seen on the right. The road then goes through **Aisne**, the village after which the river is named, in which there are hot springs. Bomal is at the confluence of the Rivers Aisne and Ourthe.

★★ AMBLÈVE VALLEY Liège

Michelin maps 409 J4-K4 or 213 folds 22, 23 and 214 folds 7, 8

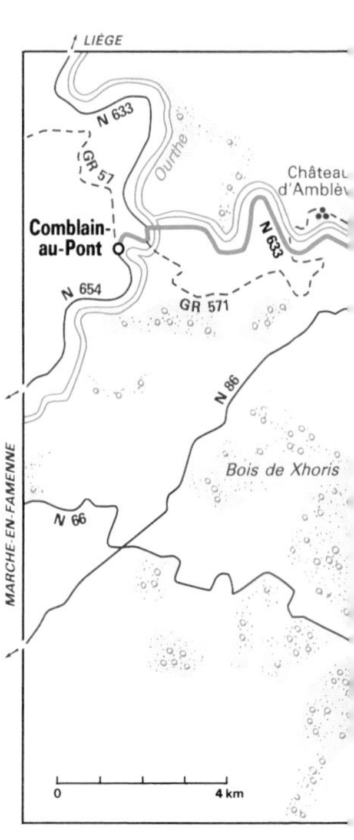

The Amblève rises in the Hautes Fagnes-Eifel nature park *(qv)*.
Winding along an erratic, rustic course at first, the river cuts a wide V-shaped valley further downstream, forming large meanders between sloping banks clad in a thick carpet of green.

FROM STAVELOT TO COMBLAIN-AU-PONT

46km - 28.5 miles – allow 2 hours – local maps see right, Ourthe Valley and Spa.

★ **Stavelot** – *See Stavelot.*

Leave Stavelot and head towards Trois-Ponts.

Level with the Salm confluence the road passes quite near **Trois-Ponts** *(qv)* before reaching **Coo** *(qv)*.

The Congo viewpoint is on the left shortly after **Stoumont**, a village perched high above the Amblève. There is a marvellous **view★** of the valley, so sparsely inhabited and thickly wooded here that in summer it resembles a tropical forest.

From Targnon the road follows the river until this flows into the Ourthe.

Just after Targnon, the N 645 on the left leads up the delightful **Lienne Valley**.

★ **Fonds de Quareux** – A little bridge under the railway line leads *(on foot)* to the edge of the Amblève. The river rushes down here, foaming over enormous chunks of hardwearing quartz which stand out from the surrounding rocky massif.

Nonceveux – This community is on the south bank, tucked inside a meander. The north bank has become a summer holiday resort.
Follow the **Ninglinspo** torrent on foot *(15min; leave from the large car-park on the right, just outside the town)*, to reach the Chaudière (cauldron), a natural basin of reddish stone at the foot of two small waterfalls.

Just before going under the Remouchamps viaduct, there is a glimpse of Montjardin Castle on the left, perched amidst the greenery overlooking the river.

Sougné-Remouchamps – *See Sougné-Remouchamps.*

Amblève Castle once stood on an outcrop downstream from **Aywaille** (pop 8 878). Legend has it that the four Aymon sons *(qv)* stayed here.

The road soon comes to Comblain-au-Pont and the confluence of the Amblève with the Ourthe.

Comblain-au-Pont – *See Ourthe Valley.*

★ ANNEVOIE-ROUILLON DOMAIN Namur

Michelin maps 409 H4 or 214 fold 5 – Local map see MEUSE/NAMUR REGION

The palace and gardens of the Annevoie Domain are a beautiful example of 18C architecture and landscaping.
There is a wonderful floral display including tulips and hyacinths in spring, and roses and begonias in summer.

★★ **Gardens** ⊙ – The estate has belonged to the Montpelliers since 1675. It was at the end of the 18C that one of the members of the family conceived the idea of these gardens flowing with water, compromising between formal French and romantic Italian gardens, which would charm visitors with the sparkling diversity and imaginative design of their groves and fountains. It is pleasant to stroll beneath century-old foliage and admire the Buffet d'Eau (display of fountains opposite the palace), the Little Canal and, after a short climb, the Great Canal, with limetrees edging its banks. Besides these highlights there are also one or two strikingly original baroque garden seats.

Palace ⊙ – The old part (1627) on the right can be recognized by the pattern of pink bricks running just under the edge of the roof. The palace was enlarged in 1775, the same time that the gardens, its perfect complement, were created.
The rooms **inside★** are decorated with 18C woodwork and furniture, as well as family portraits and bouquets, all of which evokes an atmosphere of elegance. The music room in the form of an angle is particularly impressive with its delicate stucco decor by the Italian Moretti brothers; there are also beautiful views of the gardens.

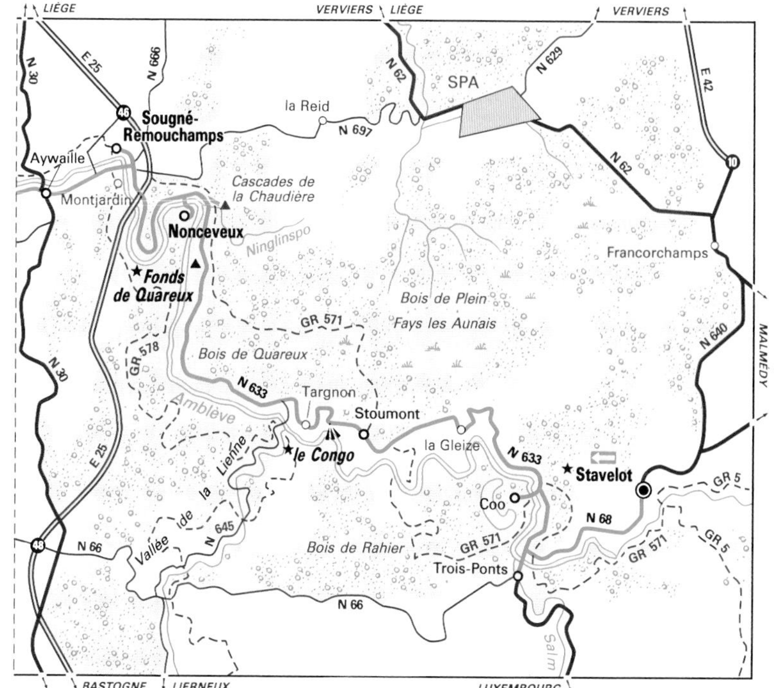

Except when otherwise stated, all recommended town tours are intended as walks.

★★★ ANTWERPEN (ANTWERP) Antwerpen Ⓟ — Pop 473 082

Michelin maps 409 G2, folds 8 and 9 for enlarged inset map, or 213 folds 6 and 7

Antwerp, Belgium's second city, is one of the world's largest ports. It lies on the east bank of the Scheldt, which flows into the North Sea 88km - 54.5 miles to the northwest (the town is linked to the west bank by three tunnels for motorists and one for cyclists and pedestrians).

In sharp contrast to its role as an economic centre, which is perhaps most plainly in evidence in the bustling diamond merchants' district around the central railway station, Antwerp has nonetheless preserved all the charm of Flemish towns in its Old Town, overlooked by the graceful cathedral spire. It is a great pleasure to wander along the narrow streets or through the spacious squares, bordered by houses decorated with crowstepped gables and scrollwork or with tall many-windowed façades. There is the opportunity not only of visiting museums, richly stocked with works of art, or historical houses, in which the interiors served as models for the Flemish masters, but also of discovering theatres, stores (on the Meir and Keyserlei), elegant boutiques (in the pedestrian zone around Schoenmarkt, Komedie plaats, Leopoldstraat), restaurants, markets, antique dealers and art galleries.

Antwerp is the birthplace of a number of celebrities, including the writer **Hendrik Conscience** (1812-1883), author of the historical novel *De Leeuw van Vlaanderen* - The Lion of Flanders (1838) and the painter **Constant Permeke** *(qv)*. The most noteworthy, however, remain the printer **Plantin** *(see Plantin-Moretus Museum below)* and the painter **Rubens** *(see Rubens' House below)*, whose personalities are most strongly evoked by a visit to where they used to live.

HISTORICAL NOTES

Antwerp "owes the Scheldt to God, and everything else to the Scheldt" (Edmond de Bruyn, 1914).

Mysterious origins – The first settlement on the present site dates back to the third century. The name of the town seems to be derived from the word "aanwerpen", which means "alluvial deposits". According to a 16C legend, however, the name comes from the exploit of a Roman soldier, Silvius Brabo. The story goes that Brabo challenged the giant Druon Antigon, who regularly pillaged shipping on the Scheldt, ultimately cutting off the giant's hand and flinging it into the river. This explains why the city's coat-of-arms represents two cut-off hands next to a castle (the Steen); the word "handwerpen" means "to throw a hand".

The golden age (15C-16C) – Antwerp built its first ramparts in the 11C, and began to grow as an economic power in the 13C, specialising in the trade of fish, salt and grain and in the importing of English wool. The Hanseatic League established a branch here in the 15C. Antwerp was already in competition with Bruges, where the port was beginning to silt up.

The 16C decided the town's destiny. At the beginning of the century the Portuguese, who had discovered the Indian trade route, set up a European distribution centre for the spices and precious objects brought back from far-off lands. The first commodities exchange was built in 1515; the town was then under the protection of Emperor Charles V and had a population of more than 100 000. A new stock exchange established in 1531, as well as the use of modern banking techniques (bills of exchange and letters of credit), made Antwerp a world centre of trade, with more than 1 000 representatives of foreign houses of trade setting up home in the city. Printing evolved there in the middle of the century, largely through the efforts of Christopher Plantin. By 1560 Antwerp was Europe's second-ranking city after Paris. This was a golden age too for architecture, with the construction of the cathedral, the butchers' and brewers' guild halls and the Town Hall, and for art, with the Antwerp school represented by Quentin Metsys, Joachim Patinir, Gossaert and Brueghel.

The decline – Under Philip II, uncompromisingly Catholic, the Inquisition led to the Wars of Religion, which put an end to this prosperity. In 1566 the cathedral was ransacked and desecrated by Calvinists, nicknamed "iconoclasts". Harsh repression followed, led by the Duke of Alva, and then in 1576 the Spanish garrison assaulted the town in a terrifying attack of blood and fire; this was the "Spanish fury".
Antwerp's Calvinists had joined the revolt against the Spanish; Alexander Farnese, great-grandson of the pope of the same name and governor of the Low Countries, had to lay siege for a year before he could take the town in 1585. In 1648 the Treaty of Münster closed the Scheldt to traffic; it was not reopened until 1795.

A desirable position – In 1794 the town was in the hands of the French. When Napoleon came in 1803 he immediately realised how strategically well-placed it was – a "cocked pistol aimed at England". He developed the port and had the first dock hollowed out, which is known today as the Bonapart dock or Bonapartedok (**DT**). In 1914 Antwerp resisted the German army from 28 September to 9 October, enabling Belgian troops to fall back to the River IJzer (Yser) at Nieuwpoort *(qv)*. Antwerp's port was fully functional shortly after liberation in September 1944, in spite of the V1 and V2 bombings.

Traditional industry and trade: diamonds – In 1476 Louis de Berken, from Bruges, perfected diamond-cutting; this was to become a major Antwerp industry. The arrival in the 16C of several Jewish families from Portugal gave it a new impetus. The diamond trade, which had had its origins mainly in the Indies up to that time, became virtually a Portugeuse monopoly with Vasco de Gama's discovery of the Indian sea route. Antwerp's craftsmen rapidly won renown. The South African diamond rush began in 1869, while at the same time a great migration of Eastern Jews arrived. Today trading of diamonds is handled by a number of Jewish families which have been established for centuries, as well as by traders from India, Zaïre, and Lebanon, while the cutting of diamonds remains the province of people from Antwerp.

A new growth linked to the port – Antwerp is now the main channel of Belgian trade; it is also a large industrial centre. The port is being expanded *(see the enlarged inset map on* **409** *folds 8 and 9)*, with its centre being pushed north towards the border with the Netherlands. It covers over 13 780ha - 31 579 acres, comprising 127km - 79 miles of waterside, 949km - 590 miles of railway, 1 400ha - 3 459 acres of docks, a large amount of stock handling equipment and enormous storage depots. The building of a large northern dock, the Kanaaldok, has greatly increased mooring capacity. Seven locks *(sluis)* connect the Scheldt with the docks. The Berendrecht lock, opened in 1988, is the biggest in the world: 763 000m^3 - 791 994yds^3 in volume, 500m - 0.4 miles long by 68m - 74yds wide. The Zandvliet lock is almost as large, with a volume of 613 000m^3 - 801 804yds^3.
The volume of traffic through Antwerp's port depends in large part on Belgium's economy, but also on its being a transit point to Germany, France, the Netherlands, Switzerland and Italy. Imports consist of petroleum products, minerals, coal, wood products, grain and raw chemicals; exports are usually fertilisers, cements and metallurgical and chemical products. As for storage, Antwerp has excellent warehouse installations making it a crucial link in the distribution chain. Sizeable industries have developed near the port, dependent on its existence: petroleum refineries, car assembly plants, food industries, ship construction and repair.

★★★ MARKET SQUARE AND CATHEDRAL *time: half a day*

This district is a maze of squares, narrow streets and passages, in which a remarkable number of niches containing Madonnas are to be found; there are more than 300 of them. The many candidates for the sculptors' guild of St Luke produced a proportionally large number of masterpieces.

★ **Market Square (Grote Markt) (FY)** – The cathedral's slender, graceful spire rises above this irregularly-shaped square, which is surrounded by 16C and 17C **guild halls** with very tall façades consisting almost entirely of windows. They are crowned with crowstepped or scrolled gables, often bristling with delicate pinnacles.
Look towards the Town Hall and note the five beautiful guild halls to the right, built mostly in the Renaissance style, dating from the late 16C: the White Angel, with an angel on top; the Coopers' hall, with its statue of St Matthew; the very tall **Old Crossbow**, surmounted with an equestrian statue of St George; the Young Crossbowmen's hall dating from 1500 and the Drapers' hall, with an eagle.

Town Hall (Stadhuis) (FY H) ⊙ – This was built in 1564 by Cornelis Floris de Vriendt. The façade is 76m - 282ft long, and displays a successful combination of Flemish elements (dormers, gables) with those of the Italian Renaissance

Brabo Fountain and the Guild Halls in the Market Square

(a loggia just under the roof, pilasters between the window, niches). The richly decorated central part lightens the austere orderly appearance of the tall mullion windows. The interior was completely remodelled in the 19C.

Brabo Fountain – This spirited work by Jef Lambeaux (1887) depicts Silvius Brabo's legendary gesture of brandishing the giant Druon's hand *(see above)*. The water falls directly onto the square's paving stones.

★ **Vlaaikensgang** (FYZ) – The porch at no 16 of the **Oude Koornmarkt** leads into this pretty little old Antwerp street, which still looks like that of a village.

Return to the Oude Koornmarkt.

Handschoenmarkt (FY 82) – This triangular square surrounded by old houses just in front of the cathedral used to be a glove market. The well is crowned with an elegant wrought-iron canopy, with Brabo on the top preparing to throw the giant's hand. It stood in front of the town hall until 1565, and is attributed to Quentin Metsys, a wrought-ironworker who is said to have become a painter – because of love.

★★★ **Cathedral** (FY) ⊙ – This is the most admirable of all of Antwerp's buildings; it is also the largest in Belgium, standing on almost 1ha - 2.5 acres. Although construction began with the east end in 1352 and was finished as late as 1521, the whole is nevertheless quite harmonious. Several builders succeeded one another: Jacob Van Thienen, Jan Appelmans and his son Pieter, Jan Tac, Everaert Spoorwater, Herman and Domien de Waghemakere and Rombout Keldermans. The cathedral was originally the home of *Our Lady of the Tree*, a statue found on a branch after a Viking invasion. This statue was destroyed in 1580, but a copy still exists in the church of Notre-Dame-du-Sablon in Brussels *(qv)*.

★★★ **Tower** – As is also the case in Mechelen and Ghent, the wonder of the cathedral is the tower. It is 123m - 403ft tall, a miracle of ornamentation and delicacy. The magnificent bell tower crowning it is "clear as a summons, straight and beautiful as a mast, bright as a candle", as wrote Verhaeren. It was built in a century by Pieter Appelmans and Herman and Domien de Waghemakere. It houses a carillon of 47 bells.
The second tower was left unfinished in the 16C. Four people seem to be busily at work at its foot, who, on looking more closely, are revealed to be statues. They were chiselled by Jef Lambeaux (1906) in homage to Pieter Appelmans.
A curious onion dome has topped the transept crossing since the 16C.

Interior – *A brochure indicating where works of art can be found is available at the entrance. Some variation in the position of works of art described below is possible, following restoration work recently carried out on the nave and chancel.*
The inside of the cathedral is exceptionally large, comprising seven aisles, 125 pillars without capitals and a transept 117m - 384ft long by 65m - 213ft wide. There are many remarkable **works of art** contrasting with the cool majesty of the place.
In the central nave, the pulpit sculpted by Michel van der Voort in 1713 is a surprising sight, its effect heightened by flights of stairs crowned with birds and a ring of tumbling cherubs floating beneath a Fame falling from heaven. The basin is supported by four female figures representing the four continents (Europe, Africa, Asia and America).
There are many works by **Rubens**. Above the high altar there is an **Assumption** (1625-26), one of his better representations on this theme, which captivates the viewer with its colourfulness broken up by touches of light. The **Raising of the Cross** (1610) in the north transept, originally intended for St Walburga's Church, is a violent, diagonal composition depicting a wonderfully noble head of Christ; the wildly tortuous postures of the vigorous soldiers throws their muscles into relief. The

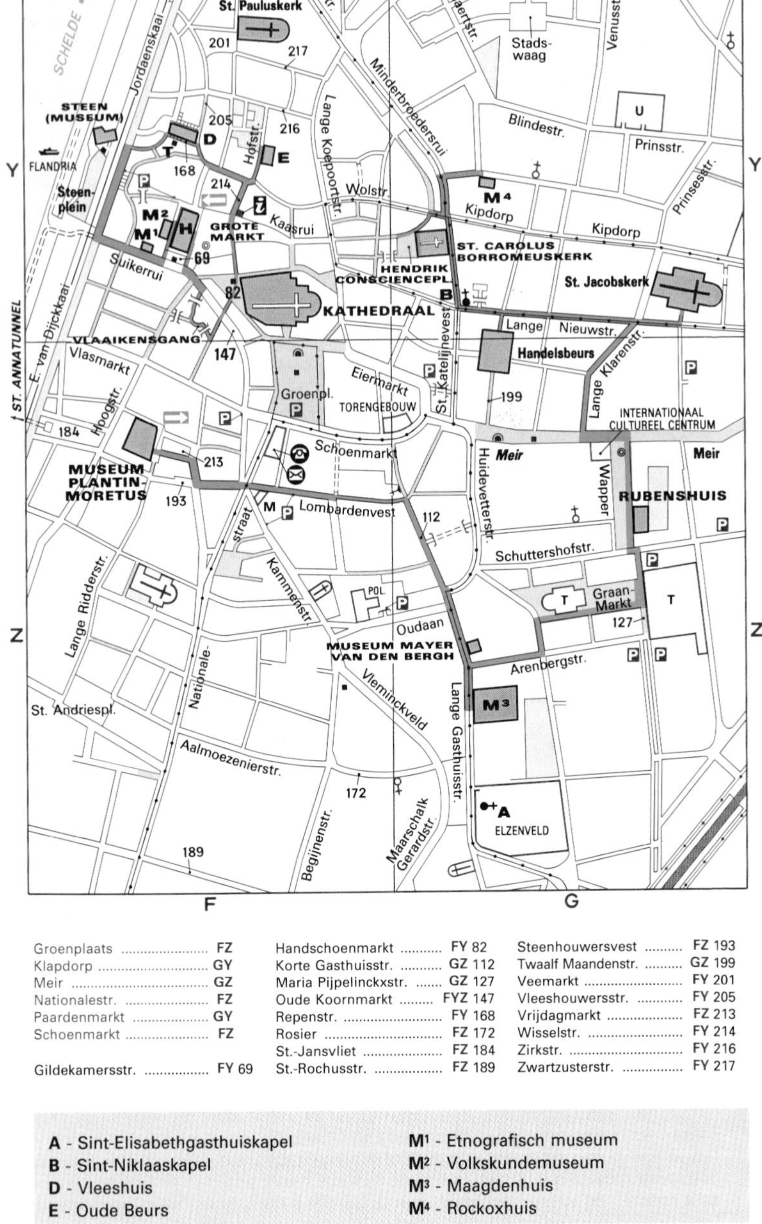

Groenplaats .... FZ	Handschoenmarkt .... FY 82	Steenhouwersvest .... FZ 193
Klapdorp .... GY	Korte Gasthuisstr. .... GZ 112	Twaalf Maandenstr. .... GZ 199
Meir .... GZ	Maria Pijpelinckxstr. .... GZ 127	Veemarkt .... FY 201
Nationalestr. .... FZ	Oude Koornmarkt .... FYZ 147	Vleeshouwersstr. .... FY 205
Paardenmarkt .... GY	Repenstr. .... FY 168	Vrijdagmarkt .... FZ 213
Schoenmarkt .... FZ	Rosier .... FZ 172	Wisselstr. .... FY 214
	St.-Jansvliet .... FZ 184	Zirkstr. .... FY 216
Gildekamersstr. .... FY 69	St.-Rochusstr. .... FZ 189	Zwartzusterstr. .... FY 217

A - Sint-Elisabethgasthuiskapel
B - Sint-Niklaaskapel
D - Vleeshuis
E - Oude Beurs
M¹ - Etnografisch museum
M² - Volkskundemuseum
M³ - Maagdenhuis
M⁴ - Rockoxhuis

Descent from the Cross (1612) in the south transept is more classical in style: the body of the dead Christ and his white shroud stand out against the dark background and the red of St John's clothing; the blond hair of Mary Magdalene is resplendant while the martyred man seems to slip, barely supported, in the arms of a lividly pale Mary. Commissioned by the Harquebusiers' guild, of which St Christopher was patron saint, all the themes in this altarpiece represent the "bearers of Christ": St Christopher, Mary bearing Christ in her bosom during the Visitation, Jesus being held by Simeon during the Presentation in the Temple, and the body of Christ being carried during the Descent from the Cross.
Rubens' **Resurrection** (1612), commissioned by Plantin's son-in-law Moretus, is to the south in the second chapel in the ambulatory. In the third chapel is Quellin the Younger's baroque sarcophagus for Bishop Capello (1676); in the north transept, Frans Francken the Elder's triptych *Jesus among the Doctors* (1586); in the south transept, Murillo's *St Francis*, the *Last Supper* by Otto Venius and the *Marriage at Cana* by Martin de Vos.

Return to the Market Square and take Rue Wisselstraat.

Commodities Exchange (Oude Beurs) (FY E) ⊙ – This dates from 1515. Public administration offices occupy the building today. Behind the classical façade there is a charming paved courtyard surrounded by porticos and overlooked by a watchtower.

★ **Butchers' Guild Hall** **(Vleeshuis)** **(FY D)** – This imposing Gothic building, its tall roof pierced by dormer windows, is to be found in the old port district. Stripes of white sandstone decorate the brick walls, which are framed by delicate turrets. The hall was built for the butchers' guild by one of the cathedral's architects between 1501 and 1504. It now houses a museum of decorative arts from Antwerp, archaeology and numismatology.
Various works are exhibited on the ground floor and first floor beneath the great hall's beautiful Gothic vaulting: silverware, glazed earthenware, wrought-iron-work, 15C statues, the 1514 Averbode altarpiece, panels of 16C Antwerp glazed earthenware tiles representing the conversion of St Paul, antique furniture.
The **musical instrument collection**★, especially the harpsichords for which Antwerp was a renowned manufacturing centre in the 17C (the Ruckers family), is particularly varied.

Take the Repenstraat.

The **"Poesje"**, a famous Antwerp marionette theatre, is in a basement to one side.

★ **"Steen" Maritime Museum** **(Nationaal Scheepvaartmuseum)** **(FY)** – This is in the Steen fortress built after 843 on the Scheldt to defend the new frontier established by the Treaty of Verdun *(qv)*. Having been a prison since the early 14C, the castle was enlarged by Emperor Charles V around 1520, and then restored in the 19C and 20C.
An interesting exhibition traces maritime and river life, with particular reference to Belgium, from its beginnings to today, aided by numerous pictures, models, instruments, sculptures and documents. There is also a department of industrial archaeology (maritiem park) open to visitors where a collection of boats is on display (including the river boat *Lauranda*; temporary exhibitions). In front of the Steen is a statue of the legendary mischievous imp of Antwerp, Lange Wapper.
Traffic on the estuary (500m - 0.4 miles wide at this point) is visible from the **Steenplein** promenade terraces. Boat excursions leave from here for the tour of the port *(see below)*. All along this quay modern houses (Van Roosmalenhuis, on the corner of Goede Hoopstraat and St.-Michielskaai) alternate with older buildings.

★ **Ethnography Museum** **(Etnografisch museum)** **(FY M1)** – There are several communicating houses dating from the 16C to the 19C located on the Suikerrui which house Antwerp's ethnographic collections. Visitors are greeted by the famous statue of the Luba-Hembas' ancestor (Zaïre), to which André Malraux alluded in his "imaginary museum". This statue introduces the African section, organised by theme: precious objects, everyday objects, those used for magic (masks, voodoo dolls). The South Sea Islands section highlights Melanesian tribes, in which ancestor worship and social ranking are important elements: note the drum from the New Hebrides with a vertical slit to symbolise high rank; see also the Asmat (New Guinea) sculptures carved from tree-ferns for funerary rites, such as the magnificent ancestor's post called "bis". In the Americas section on the first floor, there is again this idea of an ancestor's post with the Haida Indians' (Canada) totem pole. A child's kayak nearby evokes Eskimo society, while a number of pre-Colombian earthenware pieces represent South and Central American civilisations; see also the brilliantly coloured Amazonian feather masks. On the second floor the collections are connected with Buddhism and Hinduism. Japan is represented by the 16C statue of Kannon Bosatsu in gilded laquered wood, as well as by paintings depicting "the nine meditations on the impurity of the body". The lamaistic objects include a remarkable 19C map of Lhassa and a unique series of 54 miniatures representing a mandala meditation. On the third floor there are arts and crafts from China (Celadon ware), Japan, Afghanistan and Turkey.

Gildekamersstraat (FY **69**) – This narrow street, its name meaning "guild halls", runs behind the Town Hall and is bordered by beautiful old houses; one of these is a folklore museum.

Folklore Museum **(Volkskundemuseum)** **(FY M2)** – The rich and varied collections are devoted to Flemish popular art. The ground floor concerns life outside the home: street scenes, façades, games, signs, the *kermesse* represented by a marvellous Mortier street organ. The festive atmosphere continues into the stairway with the heads of the giants Druon and Pallas. The first floor handles certain aspects of Flemish daily life: toy collections, reconstruction of an apothecary's, display cases devoted to magic and popular beliefs. The second floor illustrates home life and the community lifestyle so important in Belgium (De Poesje marionette theatre).

★★ FROM THE PLANTIN-MORETUS MUSEUM TO THE ROCKOX HOUSE *time: one day*

★★★ **Plantin-Moretus Museum** (FZ) – This museum occupies 34 rooms in the house and printing house built by the famous printer Plantin and enlarged in the 17C and 18C by Moretus family descendants. This museum provides a fascinating history of humanism and old books in 16C and 17C Netherlands, with arresting decor consisting of beautiful old furniture, tapestries, gilded leatherwork, paintings, well-stocked libraries, collections of typography and drawings, engravings, old manuscripts and valuable editions.

The "Prince of Printers" – Tourangeau having come to Antwerp in 1549, Christopher Plantin became a printer here in 1555 under the sign of the Golden Compasses; this emblem illustrated his motto "Labore et Constantia", the moving point representing work and the fixed point constancy.
The perfection of the publications coming from his sixteen presses (the Estienne family in France had only four) and his reputation for culture and erudition earned him the admiration of the greatest men of his time, including that of Philip II, who

ANTWERPEN

Carnotstr. .... EU 3
Dambruggestr. .... ETU 39
Gemeentestr. .... DU 63
de Keyserlei .... DU 103
Leysstraat .... DU 123
Offerandestr. .... EU 136
Pelikaanstr. .... DU 151
Quellinstr. .... DU 165
Turnhoutsebaan (BORGERHOUT) .... EU

van Aedtstraat .... DT 3
Amsterdamstr. .... DT 4
Ankerrui .... DT 6
Ballaerstr. .... DV 12
Bolivarplaats .... CV 15
Borsbeekbrug .... EX 16
van Breestr. .... DV 19
Brialmontlei .... DV 21
Britselei .... DV 22
Broederminstr. .... CV 24
Brouwersvliet .... DT 25
Brusselstr. .... CV 27
Cassierstr. .... DT 31
Charlottalei .... DV 33
Cockerillkaai .... CV 36
Cuperusstr. .... EV 37
Diksmuidelaan .... EX 43
Emiel Banningstr. .... CV 51
Emiel Vloorsstr. .... CX 52
Emile Verhaerenlaan .... CT 54
Erwtenstraat .... ET 55
van Eycklei .... DV 57
Falconplein .... DT 58
Franklin Rooseveltpl. .... DU 60
Gén. Armstrongweg .... CX 64
Gerard Le Grellelaan .... DX 66
de Gerlachekaai .... CV 67
Gitschotellei .... EX 70
Graaf van Egmontstr. .... CV 72
Haantjeslei .... CDV 79
Halenstr. .... ET 81
Hessenplein .... DT 84
Jan de Voslei .... CX 90
Jan van Gentstr. .... CV 91
Jezusstraat .... DU 96
Justitiestraat .... DV 97
Kasteelpleinstr. .... DV 102
Kloosterstraat .... CU 105
Kol. Silvertopstr. .... CX 106
Koningin Astridplein .... DEU 109
Koningin Elisabethlei .... DX 110
Korte Winkelstr. .... DTU 114
Lange Lobroekstr. .... ET 117
Lange Winkelstr. .... DT 118
Leopold de Waelplein .... CV 120
Léopold de Waelstr. .... CV 121
Londenstr. .... DT 124
Maria-Henriettalei .... DV 129
Mercatorstr. .... DEV 130
Namenstr. .... CV 133
van den Nestlei .... EV 135
Ommeganckstr. .... EU 138
Orteliuskaai .... DT 141
Osystraat .... DU 142
Oude Leeuwenrui .... DT 148
Platinkaai .... CU 153
Ploegstr. .... EU 154
Pluvierstraat .... CU 156
Posthofbrug .... EX 157
Prins Albertlei .... DX 159
Provinciestr. .... EUV 162
Pyckestraat .... CX 163
Quinten Matsijslei .... DUV 166
Rolwagenstr. .... EV 171
Schijnpoortweg .... ET 174
van Schoonhovestr. .... DEU 175
Simonsstr. .... DEV 178
St.-Bernardsesteenweg .... CX 180
St.-Gummarusstr. .... DT 181
St.-Jansplein .... DT 183
St.-Jozefsstr. .... DV 186
St.-Michielskaai .... CU 187
Stuivenbergplein .... ET 196
Viaduct Dam .... ET 202
Visestraat .... ET 204
Volkstraat .... CV 207
Vondelstr. .... DT 208

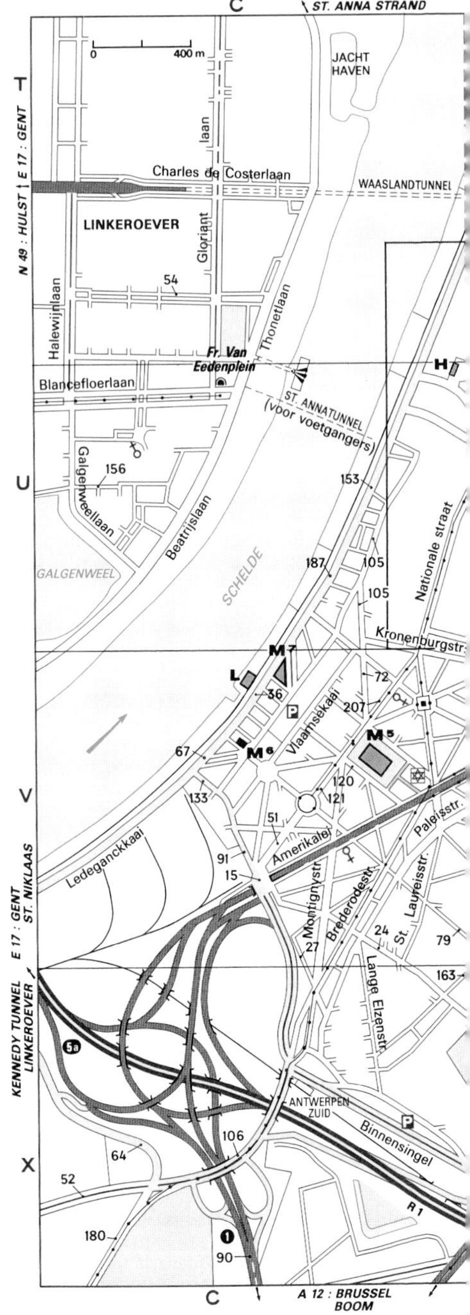

K - Brouwershuis
L - Mini-Antwerpen
M5 - Koninklijk Museum voor Schone Kunsten
M6 - Museum voor Fotografie

made him his official royal printer and granted him the monopoly of sales of liturgical works in Spain and the Spanish colonies. Plantin created the famous Antwerp school of engraving, in collaboration with his friend, the governor and merchant Jerome Cook; Rubens himself would later head this institution. Plantin's greatest typographical success was his **Biblia Regia**, printed in five languages (Hebrew, Syrian, Greek, Latin and Aramaic). He died in 1589.

Museum visit – *Follow the numbering of the rooms.* Visitors are greeted by the welcoming tranquility of the courtyard, surrounded by lead-set stained glass windows framed by Virginia creeper. Go through the large room decorated with portraits by Rubens, then the shop, the proofreading room, Plantin's office and that of Justus Lipsius, Plantin's erudite friend. The presses in the shop date from the 16C, 17C and 18C; they still print *The Happiness of This World*, a poem by Plant The famous *Biblia Regia* is exhibited on the first floor, along with the Gutenberg Bible, of which there are only thirteen copies in the world. The wonderful libraries contain more than 25 000 old works, and the Max Horn Room has almost all of French literature from the 16C, 17C and 18C in magnificently bound first editions. The foundry is on the second floor.

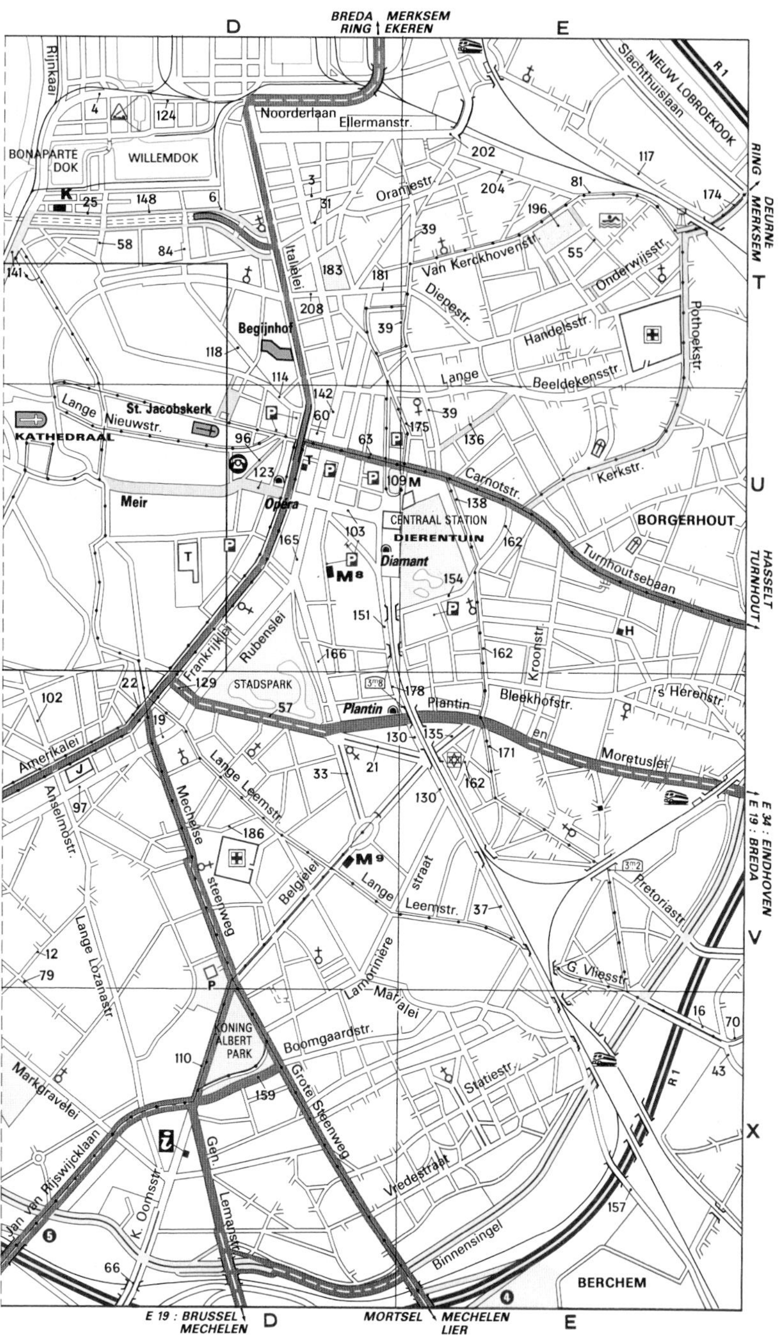

M⁷ - Museum van Hedendaagse Kunst Antwerpen
M⁸ - Provinciaal Diamantmuseum
M⁹ - Museum Smidt van Gelder

★★ **Mayer van den Bergh Museum** (**GZ**) ⊙ – This is in a neo-Gothic house of the early 20C enlarged in 1974. The museum houses a remarkable collection of works of art, assembled in under ten years by the collector Fritz Mayer van den Bergh (1858-1901), who showed real genius in his purchases of medieval sculpture, illuminated manuscripts, ivories, tapestries and paintings.

Ground floor – The two 12C statue-columns from the cloister of Notre-Dame-en-Vaux in Châlons-sur-Marne, France, as well as the 13C altarpiece painted on wood by Simeon and Machilos de Spoleto, can be seen in Room 3. A 15C triptych of *Christ on the Cross* by Quentin Metsys is in Room 4, a testament to this painter's talent; note the beauty and serenity of the landscape contrasted with the people's suffering.

First floor – Beautiful Byzantine and Gothic ivories are exhibited in Room 6. Particularly arresting, however, is the group of *Jesus and St John* sculpted by the master Heinrich von Konstanz (*c*1300), as is also the small Dutch diptych (1400) representing the *Nativity* and *St Christopher* (*Resurrection of Christ* on the other side).

Mad Meg (detail), by Brueghel the Elder

Room 9 is the centrepiece of the museum. The painting **Mad Meg★★** *(De Dulle Griet)* by Brueghel the Elder is an apocalyptic vision of war in remarkable fiery colours. The *Twelve Flemish Proverbs (see illustration p 266)* shows another facet of Brueghel's astounding talent. His son's *Census at Bethlehem* and *Winter Landscape* are here as well.

Maagdenhuis (GZ M[3]) ⊙ – A part of this former orphanage has been turned into a museum. There are many paintings (by Rubens), *St Jerome* by Van Dyck, sculptures and a collection of 16C Antwerp ceramics.

The area between the Maagdenhuis and Rubens' House is pleasant, with peaceful squares and a number of theatres and restaurants.

★★ **Rubens' House (Rubenshuis)** (GZ) ⊙ – Rubens' presence is everywhere in the museums and churches of Antwerp, but can be sensed most strongly in this grand house bought in 1610, a year after he married Isabella Brant. Rubens turned it into a sumptuous palace, after extensive rebuilding and enlarging done and the construction of an immense studio. Having borne him three children his first wife died; four years after her death he married the very young Hélène Fourment. They had five more children who were brought up here.

Pieter Paul Rubens: a painter from Antwerp – Rubens was born in exile near Cologne on 28 June 1577, where his father, an alderman of Antwerp, had been forced to take refuge when suspected of heresy. Rubens first saw Antwerp, in ruins, at the age of 12, after his father's death. He was initially a student of Verhaecht and Van Noort; from 1594 to 1598 he worked in the painter Otto Venius's studio and then he became a master in the Guild of St Luke.

He spent some time in Italy and returned to Antwerp in 1608, when the town was enjoying a period of peace under the Infanta Isabella. This was the apotheosis for Rubens and his school. Flemish and cosmopolitan, Catholic and an unbeliever, masterful and productive, he incarnated the town's spirit of genius. Acting as various sovereigns' official ambassador, he succeeded in combining features of Italianism with the Flemish tradition in painting.

His students and collaborators include the most prestigious names: Jan Brueghel, known as "Velvet" Brueghel; and the three Antwerp painters Jordaens, Van Dyck and Snyders. His influence extended both to sculpture (the Quellins and Verbruggen) and baroque architecture.

He died in Antwerp in 1640, and his remains are in St James's Church.

Tour – The entire house was refurbished in 1946. In the north wing, the Flemish-style living quarters are embellished with old tiles, gilded leatherwork, 17C furniture and numerous paintings (note Rubens' self-portrait in the dining-room). In the south wing, the studio has a tribune from which admirers could contemplate his paintings.

The studio's baroque façade with its philosophers' busts and mythological statuary can be admired from the courtyard. A portico links the two lodges and opens onto a garden through three arches which Rubens reproduced in some of his canvases.

The 17C garden has been redesigned in accordance with period paintings and engravings.

The Meir (GZ) – This is the town's prestigious main thoroughfare. The royal palace, a beautiful 18C rococo building in which a number of sovereigns resided, is on the corner of the Meir (no 50) and the Wapper. The palace is now the International Cultural Centre (exhibitions).

St James's Church (**St.-Jacobskerk**) (GY) – The **interior★** of this Late Gothic church is richly decorated in baroque style. Among the paintings note in particular Otto Venius's *Virgin* in the south side aisle and *The Calling of St Peter* by Jordaens in the ambulatory on the south side.
Rubens' funerary chapel behind the chancel contains one of his last works, the *Virgin and the Saints* (1634); it is said that he depicted himself in St George's armour, the Virgin being Isabella Brant, and Mary Magdalene Hélène Fourment. Jordaens' *St Charles Healing the Plague-Stricken in Milan* hangs in the neighbouring chapel.
The restored Gothic clock, believed to date from the late 15C, is on display in a room at the back of the church.

Stock Exchange (**Handelsbeurs**) (GZ) – This building stands at a crossroads, its glass-paned dome dominating the houses tightly packed around it.
Domien de Waghemakere built the first exchange, which soon became too crowded *(see above)*; he created a new one, which was inaugurated in 1531. It was very active throughout the 16C, but a fire destroyed it in 1858. The architect Schadde rebuilt it in 1872 in the same style, and the present building consists of a hall with superposed galleries, crowned by a superb glazed roof.

St Nicholas's Chapel (**St.-Niklaaskapel**) (GY **B**) – This 15C chapel is home to a marionette theatre (Poppenschouwburg). There is a charming little courtyard, surrounded by old buildings, tucked away behind it.

★ **Hendrik Conscience Square** – This quiet cobbled square blends harmoniously with the surrounding 17C and 19C buildings and the façade of the Church of St Charles Borromeo.

★ **Church of St Charles Borromeo** (**St.-Carolus Borromeuskerk**) (GY) – The beautiful **baroque façade** breaks up horizontally into three classical registers, with a central medallion based on a drawing by Rubens and two offset lantern turrets. The elegant baroque bell tower, on which Renaissance themes are superposed, backing onto the church's east end is the work of Pieter Huyssens.
The Jesuits built the church between 1615 and 1621, and it was initially dedicated to St Ignatius, before taking the name of St Charles Borromeo. The interior is still striking, despite the 1718 fire which destroyed the ceilings painted by Rubens and by Van Dyck in the side aisles. The building is barrel-vaulted and has tribunes communicating with the nave through tall, brightly-lit galleries. The chancel and the Lady Chapel still have their marble ornamentation.
Rubens's *Assumption* and other altarpieces commissioned in 1620 from the artist for the decoration of this church are now in the Museum of Fine Art in Vienna.
There is 18C carved wood panelling running under the arcades; between each confessional guarded by four angels there are medallions tracing the lives of St Ignatius (the south side) and St Francis Xavier (the north side).

Museum – The gallery, funerary crypt and vestry are open to visitors, as well as five rooms of the museum exhibiting collections of antique lace.

★ **Rockox House** (**Rockoxhuis**) (GY **M4**) – Nikolas Rockox (1560-1640), a friend of Rubens and a burgomaster of Antwerp, was an enthusiastic collector of objets d'art.
His 17C restored patrician home is now a museum. *(An audiovisual presentation in English, French and Dutch traces Antwerp's cultural history from 1560 to 1640.)* Note the magnificent furniture (particularly the cupboards called "ribbanken", finely decorated ebony cabinets), the beautiful pieces of ceramic ware, an extensive collection of paintings which includes in particular works by Patinir (Room 1), Van Dyck (two studies of a man's head), Jordaens, Teniers the Younger, Rubens (Room 2), Momper (Room 3), Snyders (*Antwerp Fish-Market*, Room 5) and Pieter Brueghel the Younger (copy of Brueghel the Elder's *Proverbs*, Room 6).

OTHER SIGHTS

Central Antwerp

St Paul's Church (**St.-Pauluskerk**) (FY) – *Entrance on St.-Paulusstraat.*
This Late Gothic church was begun in 1517 and completed in 1639, and is surmounted by a baroque bell tower (1680).
Baroque furnishings and beautiful 17C wooden panels on the confessionals, which are framed by huge expressive figures, richly embellish the majestic **interior★**. Statues surround the chancel, which is narrower than the nave, giving an impression of depth further accentuated by the elevated position of the monumental marble altarpiece. In the north side aisle paintings from the Rubens' school depict the Mysteries of the Rosary. A work by the master himself is to be seen among them, the *Flagellation*, a powerful painting in muted colours. There are two other Rubens works in the transept, dating from about 1609: *Adoration of the Shepherds* (north transept arm) and *Dispute on the Nature of the Holy Sacrament* (south transept arm).

St Elizabeth's Chapel (**St.-Elisabethgasthuiskapel**) (GZ **A**) – This chapel is part of the 13C St Elizabeth's hospital, closed down in 1986 and restored as a cultural centre (Elzenveld). The Brabant Gothic nave, its capitals decorated with curly cabbage-leaf motifs, dates from the early 15C. The chancel is the same length and was added between 1442 and 1460. The black-and-white marble high altar by Artus Quellin the Younger dominates the baroque decoration; above the altar is a statue of the Virgin. Among the works of art note paintings by Godfried Maes and Frans Francken the Younger.

Outside Central Antwerp

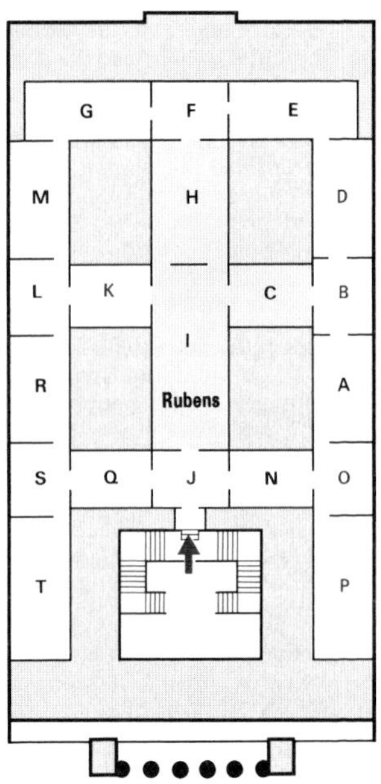

ROYAL MUSEUM OF FINE ART (First floor)

★★★ **Royal Museum of Fine Art (Koninklijk Museum voor Schone Kunsten)** (CV M5) – This 19C building is home to an exceptional collection of paintings, in particular of works by Rubens and Flemish Primitive painters. The façade is an imposing arrangement of Corinthian columns surmounted by a bronze chariot by Vinçotte. The Guild of St Luke collected most of the early art from 1442 onwards. A large collection of modern art is on the ground floor.

First floor (Old Master paintings) – It is interesting to begin in Room N, non-Belgian painters, before following the evolution of Flemish painting. In this room there are several real treasures to be admired: four small panels by **Simone Martini** (14C), including one representing the *Annunciation* executed with a delicacy reminiscent of miniature painting; the famous *Virgin Surrounded by Red and Blue Angels* which **Fouquet** endowed with Agnès Sorel's lovely features; the elegant, serene *Calvary* by **Antello de Messina**; **Jean Clouet**'s splendid portraits, particularly that of the *Dauphin of France*, the son of Francis I; and finally a few works by **Lucas Cranach**, including a *Charity* and an *Eve* which he marked with his unusual insignia (a tiny serpent holding a ring in its mouth).

Room Q is devoted to 15C Flemish Primitives. True masterpieces by the period's greatest painters are here: **Van Eyck**'s *St Barbara*, a meticulously drawn work depicting the saint in front of a Gothic tower still under construction, and the delicately-coloured *Madonna at the Fountain*; **Van der Weyden**'s *Triptych of the Seven Sacraments*, set inside a vast Gothic cathedral with each sacrament personified as an angel bearing a banner, as well as his *Portrait of Philippe de Croÿ*; and the **Master of Frankfurt**'s *Portrait of the Artist and his Wife*, the Antwerp school's oldest known work (1496). Admire also **Memling**'s *Portrait of a Man* and in the neighbouring room (S) three paintings representing *Christ Surrounded by Angel Musicians*.

Rooms R and L are devoted to 16C painting. Works from that period still have the main characteristics of Flemish Primitives but are nevertheless under the Italian influence, as can be seen by **Quentin Metsys**' *Mary Magdalene* as well as his famous *Triptych of the Entombment of Christ*, commissioned by the joiners' guild. **Joachim Patinir**'s little painting in Room L represents the *Flight into Egypt*, an important step in the evolution of landscape painting. **Jan Massys**' *Portrait of Judith* is in the same room, along with an entire series of portraits by **Pourbus**, by Jan Gossaert (known as **Mabuse**), and by the Master of Antwerp. Room M is devoted to the **Brueghels**, especially the more or less faithful copies and imitations of works by Velvet Brueghel executed by his descendants, including *Bridal Dance*. Rooms G, F and E exhibit paintings by Jan Fyt and Martin de Vos.

Room I, devoted to **Rubens**, is reached by going through Room C, in which his preparatory sketches are exhibited. The many compositions showing the master's evolution, such as the *Baptism of Christ* painted in Italy, and the *Venus Frigida* (inspired by the marble crouching Venus in the Vatican), are still classical paintings along with the *Triptych of the Incredulity of St Thomas*. Realism comes to the fore in the bloody *Christ in the Hay*, the heart-rending *Last Communion of St Francis*, in the *Blow of the Spear* and the expressive *Trinity*. Finally, the *Adoration of the Magi* (1624), with its brilliant colours and expressive figures, is one of the summits of 17C Flemish painting. Room H recalls Rubens's collaborators: **Van Dyck**'s distinguished portraits, his Piètas or the large *Calvary* in subtle tones; **Jordaens** and his astonishing scenes of everyday life, such as the *Family Concert*.

Room A exhibits still life paintings and works by painters of animals, including Snyders; his paintings overflow with foods or brim over with fish. Room T displays 17C Dutch paintings, including **Rembrandt**'s *Portrait of a Preacher*.

Ground floor (Modern painting) – This gives a very complete idea of the Belgian school after 1830. Note **Henri De Braekeleer**'s *Man with Chair*, painted in the brewers' guild hall; a large collection of **James Ensor** paintings illustrates the painter's evolution from his first quasi-Impressionist works, representing his friends' and acquaintances' homes, to macabre paintings filled with strange masks and skeletons, such as *Intrigue* (1890) and *Skeletons Arguing Over a Hung Man* (1891). **Rik Wouters**' light-filled paintings, such as the *Woman Ironing*, are examples of Fauvism. The **Sint-Martens-Latem** group is well represented by the Expressionist **Permeke**'s brutal style *(Fisherman's Woman, Snow, Seascape, Pale Clouds)*, the **De Smet** brothers, **Van den Berghe**, **Servaes** (the *Country Life* series) and **Van de Woestijne**. Surrealism is particularly well represented by **Magritte** *(16 September)* and **Delvaux**.

Among contemporary works, note Pierre Alechinsky's large canvas painted in 1964, the *Last Day*, which shows the evolution of his experiences during his period with the Cobra group, reacting against the desolation of the post-war world.

Some of the old warehouses between the Fine Art Museum and the quays have been turned into art galleries or museums (Museum of Photography, Museum of Contemporary Art).

★ **Photography Museum** (**Museum voor Fotografie**) (CV M6) ⊙ – Each step in the history of photography since the "camera obscura" is traced on the first floor, by means of a remarkable collection: daguerreotypes, dark rooms, detective apparatus, spy cameras hidden in walking sticks or in a tie, folding equipment and more modern equipment. The exhibition of work by some of the world's greatest photographers unfolds the history of the art: Atget, Man Ray, Kertesz, Sanders, Cartier-Bresson, Brassaï, Capa, Avedon, Irving Penn, Ansel Adams, etc. The second floor is devoted to stereoscopic photography, illustrated by the "Panorama Kaiser", and to cinema.
Two ground floor galleries, one named after Lieven Gevaert (born in Antwerp in 1868), house temporary exhibitions.

Antwerp Contemporary Art Museum (**Museum van Hedendaagse Kunst Antwerpen-MUHKA**) (CUV M7) ⊙ – An old grain elevator near the Scheldt quays has been converted into a large international exhibition space displaying works of art produced since the seventies.

Mini-Antwerpen (CV L) ⊙ – This miniature reconstruction of Antwerp *(still being completed)* has been set up in an old Scheldt dock shed and is displayed as part of a son-et-lumière presentation. The workshops where new parts of the miniature town are being created are also open to visitors.

★★ **Zoological Garden** (**Dierentuin**) (DEU) ⊙ – This 10ha - 25 acre park lies between the central train station and the Natural History Museum. It was built in 1885, and a statue of its founder astride a camel can be seen above it. The zoo has some rare specimens among its 5 000 animals, such as the white rhinoceros and the okapis (Moorish building). The brightly coloured Egyptian temple (1856) houses elephants, giraffes, ostriches and Arabian oryx. Sculptor Rembrandt Bugatti often came here for inspiration. Nothing in the bird house separates the exotic birds in the bright light from the public below in the shadows. Visitors can see nocturnal animals in their burrows from behind the large windows in the Nocturama. The reptiles live in a beautiful tropical environment. Finally, the planetarium, the aquarium, the Natural History Museum and the Delphinarium *(3 to 4 shows a day)* offer additional attractions.

Middelheim Open-Air Sculpture Museum

★ **Middelheim Open-Air Sculpture Museum** (**Openluchtmuseum voor Beeldhouwkunst**) ⊙ – *Leave by the Karel Oomsstraat* (**DX**)
Vast lawns in Middelheim Park (13ha - 32 acres), shaded with great trees, serve as a backdrop for over 300 sculptures dating from Rodin's day to the present (Maillol, Rik Wouters, Henry Moore, Mari Andriessen, Germaine Richier, Calder, Louise Nevelson, etc.); Realism rubs elbows with Cubism, Surrealism or abstraction. Note Henry Moore's beautiful, ethereal *King and Queen*. There is a pavilion for rotating exhibitions of small or fragile sculptures in wood, metal or clay.

Provincial Diamond Museum (**Provinciaal Diamantmuseum**) (DU M8) ⊙ – This is in the heart of the diamond district near the station. The properties and origin of this crystal are described on the third floor. The weight of diamonds, the hardest known matter, formed at a depth of 150-200km - 93-124 miles at a temperature of 2 000°C - 3 632°F, is calculated in carats. Up to the 18C the stones came from India, but now the principal mines are in South Africa, West Africa and Australia.
The second floor is devoted to industrial use of diamonds and the transformation of the raw stone into a jewel. A 19C diamond workshop has been reconstructed. The history of the diamond in Antwerp is retraced on the first floor.
Precious jewels are kept in the treasure room.

Beguine Convent (**Begijnhof**) (DTU) ⊙ – The houses cluster together in their brick enclosure. The roughly-paved street frames an orchard surrounded by hedges. The church, rebuilt in the 19C, is embellished with Jordaens and Van Noort paintings. Note the *Christ Bound* in the oratory.

Brewers' Guild Hall (**Brouwershuis**) (DT K) ⊙ – Gilbert van Schoonbeke had this house built around 1553 to supply his many breweries in the quarter with water. In 1581 this waterworks building became the seat of the brewers' guild. Visitors can see the refurbished stable, the horse treadmill and the water-raising system, as well as the reservoirs once connected to the canals. The workshop and more particularly the beautiful Council Room are upstairs; this room often figures in Henri De Braekeleer paintings *(qv)*. It is furnished with antiques, there is 17C gilded Mechelen leather on the walls and a beautiful fireplace with twisted columns.

Smidt van Gelder Museum (DV M[9]) ⊙ – This museum is in a refined 18C interior, featuring beautiful furniture and valuable collections (Dutch painting, Chinese porcelain).

Sterckshof Provincial Museum ⊙ – *Scheduled to reopen in 1994. The museum is currently being converted into a silver centre (Zilvercentrum).*

THE PORT

Boat trip on the Scheldt (**Scheldetocht**) ⊙ – This excursion goes down the Scheldt to Kallo and gives an interesting glimpse of Antwerp's industrial development, but it does not go into the dock area.
The boat turns around before the Kallo lock *(sluis)*, which can handle boats of up to 125 000 tons and will soon provide access to a canal (Baalhoekkanaal) linking the western part of the Scheldt to the Netherlands. This canal will be the backbone of a new complex of docks on the west bank, four of which are completed. There is already a variety of industries in this initial area of port extension (6 000ha - 14 826 acres), including a thermal power station.
The boat heads against the current to run along the west bank, with its large chemical industrial plants, and then it comes to little St Anne's beach, the mill and the marina.

Boat tour of the harbour (**Havenrondvaart**) ⊙ – This trip shows the docks where cargo vessels and tankers berth. The industrial complexes, the oil refineries, grain elevators, transfer bridges, dry docks, marine shops and the many reservoirs are most impressive. The port is surprisingly busy during the week.

Lillo-Fort – *15km - 9.4 miles along the east bank of the Scheldt.* The old stronghold of Lillo, surrounded by water, hides a peaceful village behind its wooded entrenchments. The church presides over a charming central square and a little harbour. This is one of the last three villages in the old polders area, evoked by the **Polders Museum** (Polder en zeemuseum).
Doel *(see below)* can be seen from the dyke along the Scheldt.

EXCURSIONS

East of Antwerp – *30km - 18.75 miles round tour - leave Antwerp on Schijnpoortweg* (**ET 174**) *on the map.*

Brasschaat – Pop 34 065. This town has a large recreational centre in an extensive park with swimming pools and a zoo.
The **road** from Braschaat to Schilde is most attractive. Masses of rhododendron blooms border it in May and June, making a marvellous show. This is particularly the case in the Botermelk area, where the swing bridge crosses the Antwerp canal at Turnhout. There are several well-to-do homes tucked amidst the woods and flowers of **'s-Gravenwezel**.

Vrieselhof Provincial Estate – This piece of public property between the Schilde and **Oelegem** offers pleasant walks in a beautiful flower-filled park *(paths indicated)*. The palace in its centre was rebuilt after its destruction in 1914 and now contains a **textile museum** (Textielmuseum) ⊙. Techniques of spinning, weaving and fabric-printing are explained here; there are also exhibitions of lace, costume and contemporary textile art.

West Bank of the Scheldt to Doel – *25km - 15.5 miles. In Amerikalei, take the Kennedy tunnel towards Hulst, then head towards Antwerp-Linkeroever (west bank).*
A little garden strewn with propellers, anchors and buoys near the pedestrian and cyclist tunnel provides an interesting view of central Antwerp with its towering cathedral and skyscraper. A marina tucks itself out of sight further north, along with a little mill and St Anne's beach; to the south a lake is given over to boating and swimming (Galgenweel).

Take the road towards Hulst, then head for Doel.

The road crosses a curious region where the polders traditionally used for raising stock lie next to Kallo's great industrial complexes *(see above)*, for which the ground had to be pumped dry.

Doel – This little village, protected against the Scheldt by an enormous dike, has a tiny fishing port. A windmill stands at the top of the dike. Lillo can be seen directly opposite, its white mill standing out against the trees, and so can the industrial area's smokestacks. A nuclear power plant has been built near Doel.

De Kalmthoutse Heide Nature Reserve and Kalmthout Arboretum – *25km - 15.5 miles to the north. Michelin map 212 fold 15. Leave on Schijnpoortweg* (**ET 174**).

De Kalmthoutse Heide nature reserve (natuurreservaat) lies north of the Antwerp de Kempen region, about 2km - 1.25 miles from the town of Kalmthout near the frontier. It covers 732ha - 1 809 acres of sand dunes, moors covered with heather *(heide)*, pine forests and marshes, inhabited by numerous birds and crisscrossed by indicated footpaths.
The **Kalmthout Arboretum** ⊙ *(located on the N 111)*, dating from 1857, is as much a quiet place for someone who loves walks as interesting terrain for the amateur botanist. Walking in the grounds *(there are no paths – be sure to wear sensible, sturdy shoes)* provides an opportunity to admire a large variety of trees and shrubs, including rare species grouped on an area of 10ha - 25 acres. Besides the many coniferous trees, there are also magnolias, rhododendrons and members of the rose family. The presence of wild species as well lends a particular charm to this very beautifully arranged park.

Join us in our constant task of keeping up-to-date.
Please send us your comments and suggestions.
Michelin Tyre PLC
Tourism Department
The Edward Hyde Building
38 Clarendon Road
WATFORD - Herts WD1 1SX
Tel : (0923) 415000

ARLON Luxembourg P

Pop 23 213

Michelin maps 409 K6 or 214 fold 18
Town plan in the current Michelin Red Guide Benelux

The old town of Arlon, built on a hill, is the provincial capital of Belgian Luxembourg. Under Roman domination it was an important stop (Orolaunum) on the way from Rheims to Trier. Fortified in the late 3C, it still has many Roman remains.
Arlon has suffered from fires and wars over the centuries.

Maitrank – This Arlon aperitif, known locally as May wine, consists of dry white wine flavoured with sprigs of woodruff (asperula), picked before flowering, full-bodied cognac and sugar; it is then served cold with a slice of orange. Since 1954 the Maitrank Brotherhood has organised large popular festivals taking place at the end of May *(see the Calendar of Events at the end of this guide)*.

Viewpoint – The **viewpoint** ⊙ at the top of St Donat's Church, itself on the hill, provides a sight of the town's slate roofs, St Martin's Church, and a panorama across four countries: Belgium, the Grand Duchy of Luxembourg, France and Germany *(orientation tables)*.

★ **Luxembourg Museum (Musée luxembourgeois)** ⊙ – This reorganised museum contains beautiful archaeological and regional ethnographic collections. The remarkable **Gallo-Roman Lapidary section★★** on the ground floor contains above all a unique collection of funerary monuments and fragments of civic architecture from the town itself or the region. These are carved with bas-reliefs either representing mythological (Bacchus, Hercules) or allegorical figures (dancers), or representing domestic scenes providing precise information about daily life in the first three centuries of our era: farmers, schoolmasters, a draper's. Note in particular the magnificent, beautifully expressive **relief of "The Travellers"**, and also the very beautiful Vervicii monument discovered in 1980 (scene of combat between Achilles and Hector).

Relief of "The Travellers"

There is a Merovingian collection upstairs (tombs, jewels), medieval and Renaissance furniture and a 16C altarpiece.

Roman tower; thermal baths – The **Roman tower** ⊙ *(Grand-Place)* was part of a rampart, the structure of which can still be seen by visitors. The rampart was built on a large foundation consisting of fragments of demolished buildings, including the magnificent bas-reliefs which now have pride of place at the Luxembourg Museum. One of these sculptures, representing Neptune, is still in its place in the wall under the tower *(access by metal ladder)*.
One can also see part of the *Relief of "The Travellers"* which is at the museum. There are a few remains of the 4C **Roman baths** ⊙, as well as the 5C foundations of Belgium's oldest Christian **basilica** ⊙, to be found near the **old cemetery** *(Rue des Thermes Romains)* with its beautiful stone crosses.

EXCURSION

★ **Victory Memorial Museum** ⊙ – *6km - 3.75 miles southeast, exit direct from the E 411 motorway.*
Twelve years of research were necessary to create this remarkable collection of **Second World War transport and combat vehicles★★**. Tanks, trucks, cars, ambulances, motorcycles and sidecars manufactured in England, Germany, Canada, the United States, France, Italy, Poland and Czechoslovakia are exhibited in a vast modern building. They are completely restored and in perfect working order, equipped with their weapons, surrounded by soldier-mannequins in uniform. Several scenes have been reconstructed: Rommel in his command-car in North Africa, the Normandy landings, a dance recalling the Liberation, and the Battle of the Bulge in the snowy Ardennes.
A documentary entitled *From Africa to Berlin* is comprised of archive newsreel clips recalling the great moments from 1942 to May 1945.

ATH Hainaut

Pop 23 833

Michelin maps 409 E4 or 214 folds 16, 17

Ath is where the two River Denders meet, extended southward by a canal. Unfortunately, its strategic location earned it the questionable honour of being personally besieged by Louis XIV in 1667. Once taken, the town had the second honour of being the first town that Vauban fortified; he also had a relief map made of Ath, the first of its type (1669). Ath underwent a second French siege in 1745, during the War of Austrian Succession; most of the fortifications were destroyed at this time.
The humanist Justus Lipsius *(qv)* was a student at the old school during the 16C Stone quarries are worked in the surrounding region.

The parade of giants – At the end of August *(see the Calendar of Events chapter at the end of this guide)* the **ducasse★★** (a name coming from the word meaning "dedication" or "consecration") is held with its parades of giants. More than 4m - 13ft tall and weighing more than 100kg – 220lbs, the giants wend their way through the town on Sunday from 10.00 to 15.00, in a merry atmosphere of gaiety and fun. They include Monsieur and Madame Gouyasse (local dialect for "Goliath"); the four Aymon sons *(qv)* riding on Bayard their horse; Samson; Ambiorix *(qv)* and Mam'zelle Victoire, who symbolises Ath itself. St Julian's Church blesses the Gouyasses' marriage at 15.00 the previous day during the Gouyasse vespers; then David and Goliath pitch battle in front of the town hall.

SIGHTS

Market Square (Grand-Place) – The **town hall**, finished in 1624, was the work of **Coebergher** (1557-1634). This astonishing individual was a painter, architect and engineer who introduced pawnshops into Flanders. The waiting hall has a beautiful fireplace and a carved portal.

St Julian's Church can be glimpsed from here; its tall 15C tower, half-destroyed by fire in 1817, still has its corner turrets.

Burbant Tower – This massive square keep is discreetly located near the Market Square. The Count of Hainaut, Baldwin the Builder, had it constructed in 1166. *Access via the narrow little street near the police station.* The surrounding mantle wall, added during the 15C and 16C, was restored and turned into a cultural centre.

Museum ⊙ – *Rue du Bouchain, access via the Esplanade.*
Here one can see two interesting *Entombments*, one dating from 1395 from the nearby town of Mainvault, the other dating from the 16C from St Martin's Church.

EXCURSION

Ath region – *Round tour of 38km - 23.75 miles – local map see above right – leave Ath on the Mons road to the south, head for Irchonwelz, then turn right.*
The region around Ath is devoted to agriculture and stock-raising. The landscape encompasses broad horizons, broken by ranges of poplars, large farms and hamlets.

Moulbaix – The pretty **mill★** (Moulin de la Marquise) ⊙ (1614) is the Hainaut's last working mill. An unusual 19C palace built in the Tudor style is concealed in the great park near the church.

Tongre-Notre-Dame – The 18C basilica is home to a Romanesque Virgin in wood, her rich robes enveloping all but the Infant Jesus's face. This venerated statue is located where the Virgin was said to have appeared in February 1081.

Chièvres – Pop 5 894. This little town belonged to the Egmonts in the 17C; one of the family members was beheaded in Brussels in 1568.
The 15-16C Gothic **church** (Église St-Martin) ⊙ has a bell tower decorated with corner turrets. The church contains beautiful funerary monuments and a 15C lectern.
The 15C **Gavre Tower** is a remnant of the old ramparts; its brick gable can be seen from the church.
The **Ladrerie** is a pretty Romanesque chapel just outside the town *(signposted)* in the courtyard of a Hunelle Valley farmhouse. It was once part of a leper-hospital *(ladrerie)*.

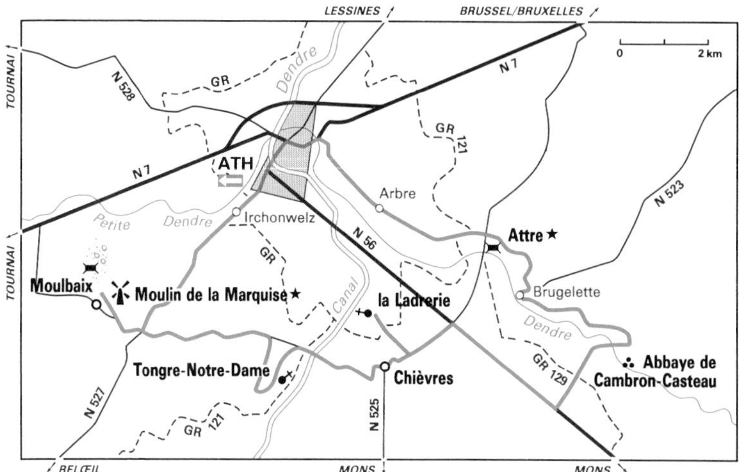

Cambron-Casteau – The Cistercian **Cambron-Casteau Abbey**, founded in the 12C, was one of the country's most prosperous abbeys. It was rebuilt in the 18C, and then destroyed by decree during the French Revolution. Only the ruins now remain. The entrance to the **estate** (domaine) ⏲ *(playground, cafés, restaurants)* is at the end of an avanue of lime-trees. The abbey farm with its curious barn ("charril"), surmounted by a dovecot, is on the right of the entrance to the park. A tall **tower** (56m - 184ft) dominates the park; it was once part of the abbey church's façade. To the left, at the foot of the tower, four Gothic recumbant effigies from an old cloister lie in tombs in recesses in the walls. The gardens are shaded with lime trees, beeches and century-old plane trees. Note the impressive winding **flight of steps** edged with balustrades spanning the Dender, which crosses the park in a canal. The steps lead to vast lakes *(pedalboats, canoes, fishing)*.

★ **Attre** – *See below.*

★ ATTRE Hainaut

Michelin maps 409 E4 or 213 fold 17 – Local map ATH: Excursion (above)

Attre has a delightful palace, which was built in 1752 by the Count of Gomegnies and finished by his son, Chamberlain to Emperor Joseph II. Its remarkably harmonious interior decoration is still intact.

★ **Palace** ⏲ – Four columns from Cambron-Casteau Abbey's rood-screen stand in front of the entrance. Two sphinxes in the form of women frame the doorway. The vestibule also served as a chapel; an altar has been set up in one of the corners. The very decorative handrail of the stairs is said to have been designed by 17C architect Blondel. Many works of art and valuable collections adorn the rooms, including paintings by Snyders; the architect Dewez created the remarkable parquet floors. Lovely 18C paintings attributed to Hubert Robert decorate the panelling of the great room, in which there is also some very fine moulded plasterwork, by the Ferraris. The Archducal Room is hung with the first painted wallpaper ever imported to Belgium (1760); a matching chintz covers the armchairs. Chinese silk hangings decorate the Chinese Room's walls and seats.

Park – The Dender cuts across this very beautiful park. There is a 17C dovecot near the palace. The park's principal point of interest is the artificial rock, 24m - 79ft high, pierced by underground corridors. It was executed for the Arch-Duchess Mary Christine of Saxony, who governed the Low Countries together with her spouse Albert of Saxony. She used the little pavilion at the top as a hunting lodge.

★ AULNE ABBEY Hainaut

Michelin maps 409 G4 or 214 fold 3 – 12km - 7.5 miles southwest of Charleroi

The imposing ruins of **Aulne Abbey** ⏲ stand at the bottom of the verdant Sambre Valley. This monastery, founded in the 7C by St Landelin in a spot surrounded by alders, depended on Lobbes Abbey. A community of Cistercians from Clairvaux settled here in 1147. The abbey was burned down in 1794 and later restored to become the Herset Hospice in 1896; it was named after the founder, who was also the last abbot of Aulne.

Central courtyard – The stables are on the left and frame the 18C arcaded coach-house. Next comes the 18C reception hall of Liège's Prince-Bishops. The guest quarters were at the back, where the abbey palace was before 1767; only a tower remains. Note on the right the late-18C arcades of the abbey palace, as well as the church façade.

Abbey church – An imposing 16C Gothic church is hidden behind a classical façade (1728). It still has its very beautiful chancel and transept; notice the tracery in the window in the south transept arm. The north transept arm leads first to

the vestry, then the 18C chapter-house looking out on what little remains of the cloister; both the vestry and chapter-house had dormitories over them. Take the path on the right to reach the part of the abbey where the old monks lived (on the left) and the infirmary (at the end, on the right). There is a remarkable view of majestic loftiness of the whole church formed by the **east end** and the **transept★★** with immense lanceolate windows.
Go back the same way towards the cloister; there is an 18C refectory on the right, with very pretty vaulting from spherical bricks carried in the centre by flared columns. This was the everyday refectory, called the "lean" one because no meat was eaten here.

★ AVERBODE Brabant

Michelin maps 409 H2 or 213 fold 8 – 9km - 5.5 miles northwest of Diest

The Premonstratensians founded Averbode Abbey in 1134-1135 in a pine forest region, where the three provinces of Antwerpen, Limburg and Brabant meet. Besides traditional activities, the Fathers now run a retirement home as well as a publishing house turning out books and weekly publications. Chamber music concerts are held here every year in the spring.

The Premonstratensians – **St Norbert** was the founder of this Order based on the Augustinian rule. In 1120 he established the first house of the Order at Prémontré, near Laon in France, and it spread rapidly to the old Low Countries where it was a great success. This is still one of Belgium's most important orders, the principal abbeys being Averbode, Park (Leuven) and Tongerlo. The Premonstratensians, or Norbertines, are regular canons. While living in their community, they devote themselves to apostleship, which they conduct mostly in the parishes. They dress in white.

★ ABBEY

Enter the courtyard through the 14C porch, surmounted by a ferruginous sandstone building, decorated with statues in Gothic niches. The prelature at the far end of the courtyard was rebuilt in the 18C style.

★ **Church** – This beautiful abbatial church, built from 1664 to 1672 by Van den Eynde, resembles those in Grimbergen and Ninove. The façade with undulating lines displays the statues of St Norbert on the right and St John the Baptist, patron of the abbey, on the left. The interior has majestic proportions. The chancel, longer than the nave, is separated from it by two altarpieces which once formed the rood-screen. Visitors can glimpse beyond this the richly carved 17C stalls.

Conventual buildings ⏲ – These were burned down in 1942, except for the 18C cloister, the chapter-house and the vestry decorated with beautiful 18C woodwork. Interesting paintings can be seen here: in the cloister the portraits of abbots from the 17C are on view; in the chapter-house, there is a De Crayer.

Conventual cemetery – *Between the church and the road.*
The tomb of **Ernest Claes** and his wife lies here. This Flemish author (1885-1968) was born in Zichem *(qv)* and was especially fond of Averbode Abbey.

BASTOGNE Luxembourg

Pop 11 959

Michelin maps 409 K5 or 214 folds 17, 18

Bastogne is on the Ardennes plateau at an altitude of 515m - 1 689ft. It is a former stronghold of which a 14C tower and the **Trier Gate** (Porte de Trèves), near St Peter's Church, still remain. Louis XIV's troops razed the fortifications in 1688. Bastogne has earned a reputation over the centuries for its excellent Ardennes ham as well as for its walnuts. Ever since General McAuliffe's famous sally in 1944 *(see below)*, the traditional walnut festival in December includes commemorative ceremonies.

The Battle of the Bulge (Battle of the Ardennes: Dec 1944-Jan 1945) and the siege of Bastogne – The Germans sent a counter-offensive against the Allied front on 16 December 1944, led by General Gerd von Rundstedt; he above all wanted to take Antwerp. The element of surprise combined with the stubbornly bad weather (fog and snow) brought the Germans immediate success. General Hasso von Manteuffel headed for the Meuse, forcing the Allies to retreat while leaving their front line in a "bulge" (from which the battle took its name) around Bastogne. The Germans surrounded this area, which the Americans held knowing too well that it had become a strategical key point.
The commanding officer of the US 101st Airborne Division, General Anthony **McAuliffe**, was rudely awakened on the morning of 22 December with an ultimatum from the Germans to surrender or expect a German attack. His terse answer was "Nuts!", and so the siege of Bastogne was decided.
The sky cleared on 23 December, allowing Allied planes to get supplies to Bastogne. By Christmas Day, however, the Germans had advanced as far as Celles *(qv)*; this was as far as they were to get. The Allies threw everything they had into getting the upper hand. US General George Patton's 3rd Army counter-attacked on the southeast flank, and entered Bastogne on 26 December. Allied planes were able to prevent fuel supplies getting to the Germans for their tanks. The US 1st Army reached the North at the beginning of January.
By 25 January, the German army's last desperate attempt to win the upper hand in western Europe was completely defeated.

SIGHTS

The tank gun turrets just outside the town on the main routes mark how closely the Germans surrounded the town in 1944.

Grand-Place (or Place McAuliffe) – There is an American assault tank on display here next to a bust of General McAuliffe. A milestone from the Road to Liberty, which runs from Ste-Mère-Église in Normandy to Bastogne, indicates the route the American troops took.

★ **St Peter's Church (Église St-Pierre)** – This 15C hall-church is in the Flamboyant Gothic style. It has a square tower in front of it (11C-12C) surmounted by a projecting timber gallery.
The church is remarkable **inside★**. The vaulting was painted in 1536 and depicts scenes from the Old and New Testaments, as well as patron saints of guilds and brotherhoods. Note also a baroque pulpit by the sculptor Scholtus; a 16C wood *Entombment*, still somewhat Gothic in style; a Romanesque font with sculpted heads on the corners; and a beautiful 16C chandelier in beaten iron, also called a "crown of light."

★ **Le Mardasson** – *3km - 1.75 miles east.*
A gigantic monument honouring the American soldiers who died in the Battle of the Bulge stands on a hill, where it was put in place in 1950. The final milestone of the Road to Liberty is nearby.

"Le Mardasson" Memorial – The memorial is in the form of a five-pointed star, engraved with the names of the various battalions and the story of the battle.
There is a **panoramic view** from the terraced area at the top over Bastogne and the surrounding area; at each point of the star an orientation table indicates the main episodes of the struggle. The crypt, decorated by Fernand Léger, contains three altars.

★ **Bastogne Historical Center** ⏲ – This imposing building, constructed in the form of a star, is devoted to the Battle of the Bulge. It is home to collections of uniforms and vehicles, and exhibits two reconstructed scenes; one taking place among the German troops, the other among the Americans.
The course of the battle is traced on an illuminated model and small screens *(commentary in several languages)* in the central amphitheatre. Finally, a film composed of sequences actually filmed during the battle is shown in the cinema.

BEAUMONT Hainaut

Pop 6 104

Michelin maps 409 F5 or 214 fold 3

Beaumont is at the junction of several major roads commanding the entrance to the "boot" shape of Hainaut province. It is a small, old town perched on a hill. Delicious macaroons are made here according to a recipe left by one of Napoleon's chefs when the French Emperor stayed in Beaumont on 14 June 1815, on his way to Waterloo.

The Three Auvergnats – "Beaumont town, woe begun,
Come at noon, hung at one."
Such was the fate of three vagabonds from Auvergne, who forced a horserider on the road to Beaumont to carry their heavy bags. Once in the town the stranger revealed his identity: he was Emperor Charles V, come to visit the Low Countries (1549). After holding an open meeting, the Emperor had the three vagabonds hung in the public square.

Salamander Tower (Tour Salamandre) ⏲ – This trace of the 12C fortifications, on a hillside, has been restored and is now home to a museum of local and regional history.
The Croÿ family crest is over one of the doors, along with their motto of "Où que soit Croÿ" ("Wherever Croÿ may be") and the collar of the Order of the Golden Fleece.
There is a charming view of Beaumont from the terraced area at the top, along with a glimpse of the undulating landscape of the Hantes Valley as a backdrop to an old mill. The beautiful park on the site of the fortress destroyed in 1655 belongs to a school.

EXCURSIONS

From Beaumont to Solre-sur-Sambre – *10km - 6.25 miles. Leave the town and head for Mons. Turn left shortly after Montignies.*
A partly Romanesque **bridge** with 13 arches is not far from the ancient Roman road from Bavay to Trier; it spans the River Hantes, forming a dam, in a pretty setting.

Solre-sur-Sambre – There is a 13C-14C **fortress** ⏲ at the foot of the town, partly hidden beyond the shaded moats. The austere façade is composed of a square keep flanked by two great round towers with machicolations and pepperpot roofs.

Rance – *13km - 8 miles south.* Rance is famous for its marble industry and now disused quarry, which once produced red marble of coralline origin. The **National Marble Museum** (Musée national du marbre) ⏲ is in an old public building. Visitors can familiarise themselves here with the origins of this stone, the types of marble most usually found in Belgium, and the techniques used to extract and polish it *(demonstration of polishing technique).*
Rance's **church** is adorned with many works in local marble.

★ BEAURAING Namur

Pop 7 951

Michelin maps 409 H5 or 214 south of fold 5

Beauraing has been a famous site of pilgrimage ever since the appearance of the Virgin to five children from the town, between 29 November 1932 and 3 January 1933.

The sanctuaries – These have increased in number since 1943. There is a statue of the Virgin in the garden, under the hawthorn where the apparitions took place; some of the stones the children kneeled on are set in a pavement nearby. **St John's crypt** is a little further down the street. Max van der Linden's Way of the Cross, executed in colourful naïve-style ceramics, add life to the bare walls of rough stone.

The thick-walled **monumental chapel** is lit by stained glass windows put up in 1963-1964. The glass façade of the nearby concrete religious building designed by architect Roger Bastin overlooks the esplanade and its series of steps. Bastin's work comprises the **great crypt** and the **upper church** which can hold 7 000 worshippers as well as accommodate the ill or handicapped via a special entrance ramp.

★★ BELŒIL Hainaut

Pop 13 338

Michelin maps 409 E4 or 213 fold 16

Belœil castle has belonged to the princes of Ligne since the 14C. The most illustrious member of the family was **Maréchal Charles-Joseph de Ligne** (1735-1814). This man of war, "the Prince Charming of Europe" renowned for his famous remark "Chaque homme a deux patries: la sienne et puis la France" (Every man has two countries – his own and France), was also a man of letters, author of the famous *Mémoires* (Memoirs) and *Coup d'oeil sur Belœil* (A Glimpse of Belœil), a work in which he wittily described the castle and its gardens.

Belœil Castle

★★ **Castle** ⏲ – There was a fortress here as early as the 12C, but the castle was rebuilt in the 16C and extensively modified in the 17C and 18C, producing an elegant residential palace.

The main building, burnt down in 1900, was rebuilt on the same foundations. The wings and the entrance lodges, with mansard roofs, have remained intact and date from the end of the 17C.

The palace is a marvellous museum, containing **splendid collections**★★★, although it has managed also to retain a residential character. Valuable furniture, remarkable tapestries (Brussels, Lille, Beauvais, Gobelins), paintings (including Oudry, Nattier, Fragonard, Canaletto), sculptures and porcelains adorn the various rooms. The many family mementoes, including a multitude of portraits, also evoke the European history of the 17C, 18C and 19C. Certain rooms contain Maréchal de Ligne's personal effects, particularly the mementoes given to him by Marie-Antoinette and Catherine the Great of Russia.

The library contains over 20 000 books. The three large paintings in the Ambassadors' Hall illustrate the high points in the life of Prince Claude-Lamoral I de Ligne, who was ambassador to the King of Spain, Philip II, and Viceroy of Sicily in 1669.

The **chapel** in the wing leading into the palace contains religious objets d'art and a collection of coral sculptures brought back from Sicily by Prince Claude-Lamoral I. A show with animated puppets in the little theatre evokes moments from Maréchal de Ligne's life.

★★ **Gardens** ⊙ – Prince Claude-Lamoral II designed the gardens in the 18C with the advice of French architect Chevotet, a disciple of Le Nôtre; the prince's son, Prince Charles-Joseph, enlarged it with an English style garden.
The gardens are arranged along the axis of a marvellous view several miles in length, the **Grande Vue★★★**, which leads to the **Great Neptune Basin** covering a 6ha - 15 acre area. The basin, the bowers, the green arbours, the many groves alternating with the many lakes all make an enticing setting for a stroll.

Minibel – *Access by the little shuttle train or by foot, crossing the park.* Visitors walk around among scale (1:25) reconstructions of Belgium's best-known sights: Brussels Town Hall, Antwerp station, Bouillon Castle, the Grand-Hornu etc., as well as the Battle of Waterloo in miniature.

EXCURSION

Aubechies Archaeological Site (Archéosite d'Aubechies) ⊙ – *6km - 3.75 miles west on the N 526, then turn right at Ellignies.*
After years of productive excavation in Aubechies and the surrounding area, archaeologists have reconstructed the various types of dwellings which succeeded one another from the Neolithic period until the Gauls. The way of life of our ancestors is easy to imagine during a visit to the six wood-and-clay houses with their furnishings and utensils. The first, vast buildings were in fact communal dwellings; single-family homes appeared from the Bronze Age onwards.
The **Romanesque house** (end of the 11C-early 12C) is at the heart of the village of Aubechies, beyond the Scaldian Romanesque **church**; it was built according to the plan of a 2C villa and now contains the findings of excavations of Gallo-Roman sites.

★ BINCHE Hainaut

Pop 32 820

Michelin maps 409 F4 or 214 fold 3
Town plan in the current Michelin Red Guide Benelux

Binche lies at the heart of Hainaut province, on an escarpment which was once encircled by a loop of the River Samme. It is a calm village, still ringed by its fortified enclosure (12C-14C); the curtain wall has 27 towers.
The town suffered in 1554 under the troops of Henry II, King of France, adversary of Emperor Charles V.
Binche's economy is based on local trade, crafts for making the carnival costumes, and the off-the-peg clothes industry.

★★ **Carnival** – Events are organised from January onwards: rehearsals for the drum-corps, followed by four Sundays when the future "Gilles" can be seen wearing their "apertintailles" (belts with bells).
The "trouilles de nouilles" ball takes place during the night of the Monday before Quinquagesima Sunday.
From 10.00 onwards on **Quinquagesima Sunday** hundreds of people in fancy dress dance to the music of violas, hand-organs, accordions and tambourines. The afternoon is marked by a parade of 1 500 Binche dancers. Monday is the day for groups of young people.

The Gilles – Shrove Tuesday, or Mardi Gras, is the only day when people "play the Gille" in Binche. A "Gille" is any native Binche male citizen who has never left the town since his birth. The legendary Gilles appear any time from dawn onwards. Large or small, they all wear a linen costume decorated with heraldic lions, trimmed with ribbons and brilliantly white lace, with two humps, one on the chest and one on the back. Wearing a belt of bells, clogs on their feet, they brandish a bundle of sticks ("ramon") to ward off the spirits of darkness. Like the Pierrots, Sailors and young beribboned Country-Folk, they can be seen in the streets of the town dancing slowly to the rhythm of a tambourine on their way to join their brotherhood. At about 10.00 they dance on the market square (Grand-Place), wearing wax masks with green spectacles.

Gilles

They parade through the town in the afternoon, sporting their magnificent ostrich-feather hats weighing 3kg-7lbs, delving into a basket for oranges to throw at and to the people they know (the windows along this route have been protected with grilles).
This is followed by the **rondeau** dance on the Grand-Place, which is by this time packed with people.
The same thing takes place at 19.00, by the light of flares, and ends in a glorious fireworks display. The Gilles dance all night, escorted by the town's inhabitants. Tradition has it that the Gilles may drink nothing but champagne.
In 1872 these customs were linked to the celebrations given in August 1549 by Mary of Hungary, governor of the Low Countries, in honour of her brother Emperor Charles V, who had come to present his son, the future Philip II, to the country's nobility. The present Gilles are said to be descendants of the Indians, crowned with ostrich plumes, who suddenly appeared before the emperor in honour of his recent conquest of Peru.
In fact Binche's carnival dates back at least as far as the 14C. The Gille is a serious figure cloaked in ritual. His customs – the dance of masked men (women are excluded), the giving of oranges (bread used to be given), the bearing of the "ramon", the belt of bells – are all very distant in origin, dating back to the time when the dance had a religious and magical meaning.

★ OLD TOWN

time: allow 1 hour 30min

Market Square (Grand-Place) – This is the site of the Gothic **town hall** (hôtel de ville), which was modified in the 16C by Mons sculptor and architect Jacques Du Broeucq; the onion dome was added later.

Go on foot and take the narrow street to the right of the town hall.

Follow the ramparts to the right around St George's Tower; this offers the best view of the town – from the south.

Return via the Posty (postern).

St Andrew's Chapel (Chapelle St-André) ⊙ (1537), in the old cemetery on the left, contains sculpted modillions vividly illustrating the Dance of Death.

St Ursmer's Collegiate Church (Collégiale St-Ursmer) ⊙ – Note the beautiful Renaissance rood-screen on the other side of the porch. There is a 15C *Entombment* inside the church.

Town park (Parc communal) – A gilded bronze statue at the entrance represents a Gille. The park was developed from the ruins of a palace that Du Broeucq built in 1548 for Mary of Hungary. This imposing building, destroyed in 1554, crowned the ramparts at the southernmost end of the town. There are beautiful views from the top of these fortifications.

★ **International Carnival and Mask Museum (Musée international du Carnaval et du Masque)** ⊙ – This is in an old 18C Augustine school near the collegiate church. The museum collections take the visitor from carnival to carnival, from festival to festival, through many countries.
The **mask collection★★**, with examples from all over the world, demonstrates the extent to which human imagination and creativity has been inspired by this art form in any age and any place: from the festival costumes of the South Sea Islands and the Amazon, to the astonishing masks from North America (Red Indians) and Africa, to the theatre masks of Asia and the often macabre masks of Latin America.
Another part of the museum takes us to Europe's winter festivals and carnivals in Austria, Poland, Romania, Switzerland, Italy, Spain, France, not to mention the mascarades of Austria, the Czech and Slovac Republics, ex-Yugoslavia and Bulgaria.
A large part of the museum is set aside for Wallonia's traditional carnivals, especially that of Binche, completed by an audiovisual presentation in several languages as well as explanations of the origins and details of the Gilles' strange costume.
Each year there is an exhibition on a more particular theme concerning the mask or the carnival.

EXCURSIONS

★★ **Mariemont Domain (Domaine de Mariemont)** – *10km - 6.2 miles northeast. Leave Binche on the N 55 in the direction of Brussels, and then turn left at Morianwelz.*
In 1548 the governor Mary of Hungary entrusted Du Broeucq with building the palace to which she would give her name. Henri II destroyed it in 1554, as he did the one in Binche, and it was rebuilt and enlarged by Archdukes Albert and Isabella.
Charles of Lorraine built a second palace in the 18C, of which the ruins can still be seen in the park; this burnt down during the struggles of 1794.
The Warocqué family, a dynasty of industrialists, transformed the grounds in the 19C and bequeathed them to the State in 1917, along with a large collection. This is exhibited today in a building constructed *c*1970 at the highest point of the park, to replace the Warocqué mansion destroyed by fire in 1960.

★ **Park** ⊙ – The ruins of the old palace can still be seen in this beautiful 45ha - 111 acre park; many sculptures by Belgian artists such as Victor Rousseau, Constantin Meunier and Jef Lambeaux are on display, as well as Rodin's Burghers of Calais.

★★ **Museum** ⏲ – This museum's rich archaeological and artistic collections are pleasantly displayed.
Works of art from great civilisations are on the first floor. Egyptian (note the colossal head of a Ptolemaic queen), Greek (a Mariemont ephebe) and Roman antiquities (Boscoreale fresco) and **Far Eastern arts** (enamels, lacquerwork, jades and Chinese porcelains) are particularly well represented.
Gallo-Roman and Merovingian archaeology is below ground level, as are the history of the Mariemont Domain and a large collection of **Tournai porcelain**.
The second floor is devoted to contemporary exhibitions.
The museum has a valuable **library** ⏲ of manuscripts, beautifully bound works, etc.

Bonne-Espérance Abbey ⏲ – *6km - 3.75 miles south on the N 55, in the direction of Merbes-le-Château, then Vellereille-les-Brayeux.*
A school now occupies this old Premonstratensian *(qv)* abbey, which Odon, a disciple of St Norbert, founded in 1126. A majestic 18C façade dominates the main courtyard. The abbey church's 15C Gothic tower is to the right.

Enter by the central doorway.

Pause to admire the beautiful oak double staircase in the hall. A door hidden beneath it leads to the cloisters.
The **cloisters**, modified in the 18C, have kept their Gothic vaulting; the refectory has some particularly notable 18C decoration. The whole complex is completed by a beautiful chapter-house.
The **church** was built on the exact location of the 13C structure constructed by Laurent Dewez. It dates from the 18C and is neo-classical. The interior is characteristic of this style, with Corinthian columns and barrel vaulting decorated with stuccowork. The north transept chapel contains a Virgin with Child, a miraculous 14C statue in white Avesnes stone with a warm smile and finely executed dress. The 1768 organ case at the back of the nave comes from Affligem Abbey.

***Michelin Green Guides** are regularly revised.*
Use the most recent edition to ensure a successful holiday.

★ BLANKENBERGE West-Vlaanderen — Pop 16 285

Michelin maps 409 C2 or 213 fold 2
Town plan in the current Michelin Red Guide Benelux

This small fishing port has become a large, well-organised seaside resort with a large variety of activities. Some of Blankenberge's main attractions include a casino (Kursaal), a large pier (Pier) and a marina.
The resort is certainly not averse to festivals *(see the Calendar of Events at the end of the guide)*; its carnival is particularly lively. The **port festivities** in May are well-known for the folklore-filled parade followed by dances performed for the public.
The blessing of the sea with a Mass held on the beach takes place in July; the altar is on a boat with a mast in the form of a cross.
There is a famous procession of floral floats in August.

St Anthony's Church (St.-Antoniuskerk) – This was built to replace the Church of Our Lady, destroyed by a storm during the winter of 1334-1335; the present one was inaugurated in 1358. It has been modified on several occasions. The interior is adorned with beautiful 17C and 18C works of art: altarpieces, communion bench, a confessional, a pulpit, an organ.

Blankenberge Pier

EXCURSION

Wenduine; De Haan; Klemskerke – *13km - 8 miles southwest.*

Wenduine – The highest of the dunes (Spioenkop) west of the town has a viewpoint at its top, which offers an interesting perspective of the beaches, the string of dunes and the resort with its old town hall rebuilt in the Flemish style. Note the small post windmill.

De Haan – Pop 9 803. This is a charming, flower-bedecked resort (De Haan-Centrum). The villas cluster in wooded surroundings with footpaths criss-crossing the dunes nearby.

Klemskerke – This is a pretty village in the region of the polders. **St Clement's**, a hall church (the nave and side aisles are all the same height), houses 17C woodwork: benches, confessionals. A post windmill stands nearby.

Fancy a trip to the seaside? Belgian beaches include Blankenberge, De Haan, Knokke-Heist, Koksijde, Nieuwpoort, Oostduinkerke, Ostend, De Panne and Zeebrugge.

BLATON Hainaut

Michelin maps 409 D4 or 213 fold 16

Blaton lies in a valley sunk between two heather-covered slopes (the Grande and the Petite Bruyère); three canals supply the town with water.

All Saints Church (Église de Tous-les-Saints) – A tall 13C tower with a 17C onion dome dominates the outline of this church, one of the oldest in Hainaut province. It has retained its solid Romanesque pillars, which bear the thrust of quadripartite vaulting constructed on an oblong plan. The sober-looking nave is supported by thick columns with capitals decorated with crockets and stylised foliage in Tournai stone. Note the Gothic statues in the niches to the right of the entrance.

EXCURSIONS

Stambruges – *5km - 3.25 miles east on the Mons road. Take the motorway and turn right.* The **Sea of Sand** (Mer de Sable), a sandy clearing among the pines and birches, is in the middle of the forest.

Bon-Secours – *7.5km - 4.5 miles west.*
Bon-Secours is simultaneously a place for a pleasant stay and a site of pilgrimage. The basilica, at the top of a hill on the Franco-Belgian border, is neo-Gothic (1885) and contains a Madonna venerated since 1606.
A beautiful forest extends to the east and south, crossing partly into French territory to enclose the Château de l'Hermitage.

★★ BLÉGNY-TREMBLEUR Liège

Michelin maps 409 K3 or 213 fold 23

Around the Blégny-Trembleur coal mines lies the Trimbleu tourist complex (complexe touristique), including a small train and various installations: a cafeteria, a self-service restaurant, a playing-field, etc.
The Blégny-Trembleur mines, the last in the Liège coal basin, have since their closure in 1980 been kept in working order to demonstrate the miner's way of life to visitors. The monks of Val-Dieu Abbey were already exploiting the surface coal in the 16C; the present shafts appeared during the course of the 19C. Women and children worked there; horses were lowered into the galleries to pull carts, sometimes staying there until the end of their lives.

The mine and the mining process – The mine consists of two shafts to ventilate the galleries, which descend on eight levels to a depth of 530m - 1 739ft. The mining shafts strike out from each gallery, cut parallel to the path of the coal vein which descends at the steepest angle. These veins could be mined until they were only 30cm - 12 inches in diameter. The miners worked in three eight-hour shifts. The morning shift was responsible for cutting, which consisted of getting the coal loose with a jackhammer; the afternoon shift involved propping work, that is, putting in pit props with wooden billets or metal shores. The night shift was responsible for backing (filling in holes with rubble) or caving (further hollowing out the rocky roof).

TOUR ⏲ *time: 2 hours 30min*

The tour is made even more interesting and poignant by the fact that the guide is one of the old miners, describing their working conditions.

Mary Shaft (Puits Marie) – The pit's surface installations can be visited as they were when they were used until 1980. They consist of the lamp works, the bath and shower rooms, the compressor station where air was compressed for the ventilation and the jackhammers, and the sawmill where the pit props were made.

Pit Number 1 (Puits no 1) – The 45m - 148ft high concrete tower was rebuilt during the last World War. The carts climbed halfway up to reach the sorting station, and the stones were put in the spoil heap.
The **underground installations** are reached by descending from this pit. The mine lift stops in a gallery 30m-98ft underground, and metal stairs lead along a passage, following a vein, to reach the next gallery 60m-196ft underground. The deafening sound of the ventilation system and the jackhammer worked by the guide, the narrowness of the passage with water gurgling through it in which the miners had to lie down to work – all this combines to give a vivid idea of the miserable conditions in which the "gueules noires" ("black faces") laboured without a break for 8 hours at a stretch. They were liable to suffer from silicosis, rheumatism and deafness from a very early age; added to this were the dangers of pit-gas explosions, rock slides and pockets of water that could suddenly break into floods.

ADDITIONAL SIGHT AT THE "TRIMBLEU" TOURIST COMPLEX

Tourist train (Train touristique) ⏲ – This little train travels through the valleys and orchards of the Herve region to reach **Mortroux** and its **Museum of Regional Life** (Musée de la vie régionale) ⏲; techniques for the handmade production of Herve specialities, such as pear or apple syrup, cheese and butter, are demonstrated.

★ BOKRIJK PROVINCIAL DOMAIN Limburg

Michelin maps 409 J3 or 213 fold 10

These grounds once belonged to Herkenrode Abbey; they lie today around a late-19C palace, covering 550ha - 1 359 acres, including 150ha - 371 acres of woodland and 40ha - 99 acres of lakeland.

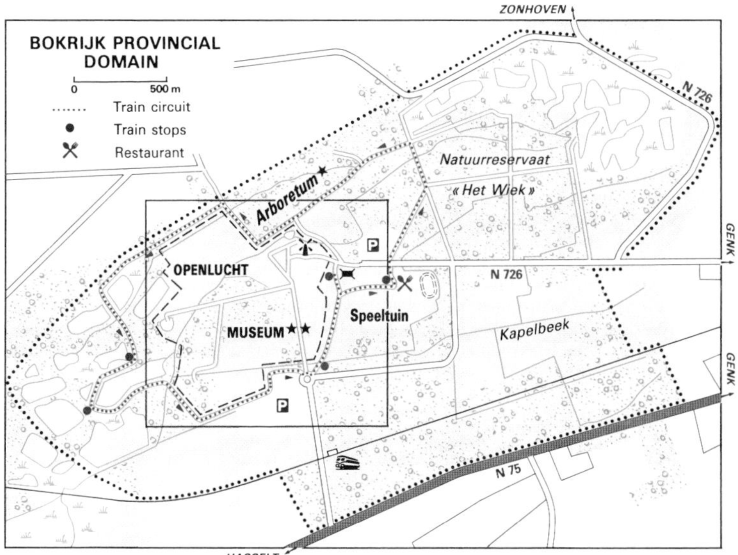

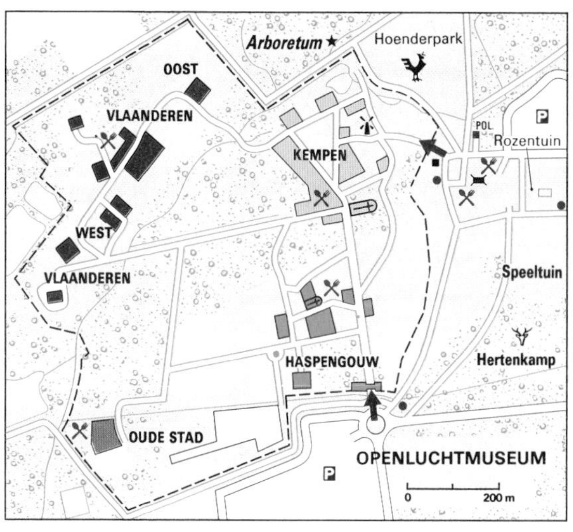

Attendant

TOUR

★ **Recreation Grounds** – Besides the central **park** (Speeltuin), comprising a playground, a sports field and a rose garden, there is also a **nature reserve** (Het Wiek Natuurreservaat) set up around a ring of lakes, a **deer enclosure** (Hertenkamp), a remarkably well-maintained 10ha - 25 acre **arboretum★**, as well as several restaurants. A small train (autotrein) enables visitors to travel from one side of the park to the other.

★★ **Open-air museum (Openluchtmuseum)** ⏲ – This consists of reconstructions of a hundred or so buildings on a 90ha - 222 acre area, serving to illustrate Flemish provincial life of days gone by. There are four sectors, three of which are rural and one of which is urban. Each rural section corresponds to a cultural region. The unfertile heather-clad heathland of the **Kempen** region *(qv)* is represented by a reconstructed village: the civic buildings (church, inn) are around a triangular square. A southern Limburg village inspired the section devoted to the undulating, fertile countryside of the **Hesbaye** and **Meuse** regions (Haspengouw en het Maasland); it has a more "closed-in" look to it than the Kempen village does. The farmhouses of fertile **Lower Belgium** (Oost-Vlaanderen, West-Vlaanderen) are not grouped in a village. They come from a variety of regions in East and West Flanders, which is why they are so different. The historical Antwerp houses (15C-18C) in the urban section (De Oude Stad) were both reconstructed and rebuilt.

★ BOUILLON Luxembourg — Pop 5 396

Michelin maps 409 I6 or 214 fold 16 – Local map see SEMOIS VALLEY
Town plan in the current Michelin Red Guide Benelux

A fortress's severe-looking mass on a rocky spur looks down on the little capital of the **Semois Valley** *(qv)*. The old slate roofs of the town crowd at the river's edge, where it forms a big loop.

The Duchy of Bouillon – Bouillon grew around the fortress standing in a key position on one of the great routes into Belgium.
The name recalls that of **Godefroy de Bouillon**, who successfully ended the first Crusade (1096-1099) by taking Jerusalem. He had sold his duchy to the Prince-Bishop of Liège before leaving in 1096.
Evrard de La Marck, Prince of Sedan, was one of the governors of the Duchy of Bouillon in the 15C. His descendents laid claim to the ducal title until it was inherited in 1594 by the Viscount Henri de La Tour d'Auvergne, father of the famous French Marshal General Henri de Turenne *(see Michelin Green Guide Dordogne)*.
Louis XIV confiscated the castle, then later returned it to the family; Vauban was in charge of its fortification.
The town was just on the border between France and the principality of Liège, but showed such an independent spirit that Vauban commented that it certainly had a strong awareness of its tiny sovereignty.
Bouillon became a centre for liberal tendencies in the 18C, holding a strong appeal for the Encyclopaedists; the printer Pierre Rousseau produced many of Voltaire's and Diderot's works here.

SIGHTS

★★ **Castle** ⏲ – This is Belgium's largest remaining trace of medieval military architecture. Its existence is recorded as early as the 10C. Three 17C stone drawbridges, separated by small forts, defended the castle entrances. *Follow the numbered arrows.*

Bouillon Castle

After the third bridge climb Vauban's staircase; this has very pure lines and was built without either cement or mortar. Visitors can then see the "primitive room" ("salle primitive") with its enormous 12C walls, then the 13C Godefroy de Bouillon Room hollowed out of the rock, which contains a large cross sunk into the floor and carved with images depicting the castle's history.
Go out into the main courtyard. The **Austria Tower** (tour d'Autriche) was restored in 1551 by the Prince-Bishop of Liège, George of Austria; from it there are magnificent **views★★** of the fortress, the meander of the River Semois, the town and the old bridge to the north. It is possible to return to the entrance by going through the torture room, where various instruments of torture have been re-created, the dungeons and the great underground passage which was both a means of reaching other parts of the castle and a warehouse. The cistern and the 54m - 177ft deep well are indications that water was not in short supply here.

★ **Ducal Museum (Musée Ducal)** ⊙ – The **History and Folklore section** is in a charming old-fashioned 18C house; it recaptures the past of the Dukes of Bouillon as well as the folklore and crafts of the region. There is a reconstruction of an Ardennes home (early 19C bedroom and kitchen) and of Pierre Rousseau's workroom.
A weaver's and a sabot-maker's workshops can be seen in the attic.
The **Godefroy de Bouillon section** is in a home restored by a court advisor; it recalls the Middle Ages and the time of the Crusades. In addition to the mementoes brought back by Crusaders, a model evokes an attack on the castle, and a miniature model of the Bouillon fortress gives an excellent idea of its power in the 12C.

EXCURSION

Cordemoy Abbey (Abbaye de Cordemoy) – *3km - 1.75 miles west along a narrow road.*
Follow the bank of the deep and narrow River Semois, beyond the old **Gothic bridge** (Pont de la Poulie).

Our Lady of Clairefontaine Abbey (Abbaye Notre-Dame-de-Clairefontaine) stands in a pretty setting. It was built in 1935 in the neo-Gothic style. It perpetuates the memory of a Cistercian abbey founded near Arlon by Ermesinde, daughter of the Count of Luxembourg; this abbey was burnt down in 1794.

★★★ BRUGGE (BRUGES) West-Vlaanderen — Pop 117 653

Michelin maps 409 C2 or 213 fold 3

In winter moonlight, this is the *Bruges la Morte* fêted by Georges Rodenbach in his novel; the town seems to come straight out of the Middle Ages, with brick houses bearing the wear marks of centuries, noble-looking buildings, churches with clear, melodious chimes. Bruges lies close to the black waters of the canals, where swans swim gracefully. The town undergoes a metamorphosis during the summer and festivals, but even then its silent, mystical side can be discovered near the beguine convent and the Minnewater.
The great Flemish poet **Guido Gezelle** (1830-1899) was born and died in Bruges. Priest and teacher, he spent his free time writing poetry. He sings of the Flanders that he discovered in the course of his travels, which inspired him to write a lot of beautiful verse.

★★★ **The Holy Blood Procession** – *Photograph p 31.* On Ascension Day at 15.00 the Holy Blood reliquary is borne through the streets in a procession. The clergy precedes it, accompanied by innumerable religious brotherhoods and groups in costume, some of which represent biblical scenes from the original sin of Adam and Eve to the Passion of Christ; others represent the return from the second Crusade, with Thierry of Alsace.
The **Golden Tree Pageant** (Cortège de l'Arbre d'Or) takes place every five years in Bruges. This recalls the pomp and ceremony of the Burgundian period *(next parade in August 1996).*
The **Canals Festival** (Reiefeest) ⊙ takes place every three years in August.

HISTORICAL NOTES

Like most of the towns in northern Flanders, little is known of Bruges's relatively late origins. Count Baldwin of the Iron Arm built the castle in the late 9C to protect the coast which was under continuous attack from the Normans.

The sea, source of wealth – Bruges was already a flourishing city when Robert the Curly-haired made it the capital of his duchy in 1093. The River Reie linked the port to the Zwin estuary. The town, like many others in Flanders, manufactured cloth; indeed, by the 12C it was a large import centre for the English wool needed for this activity. It headed the Hanseatic League of London, an association grouping several towns trading with England. Damme was built at this time; owing to its location on the Zwin estuary, it served as an outer harbour.
Bruges soon began a great exchange market, selling Flemish cloth and buying fish and wood from the Scandinavians, amber and fur from the Russians, wines from the Spanish, gold cloth from the Lombards, and silks and other Eastern products from the Venetians and Genoese.
By the 13C Bruges was one of the most active members of the powerful **Hanseatic League**, an association of northern European towns, with Lübeck as capital, that monopolised trade with Scandinavia and Russia. The Minnewater received

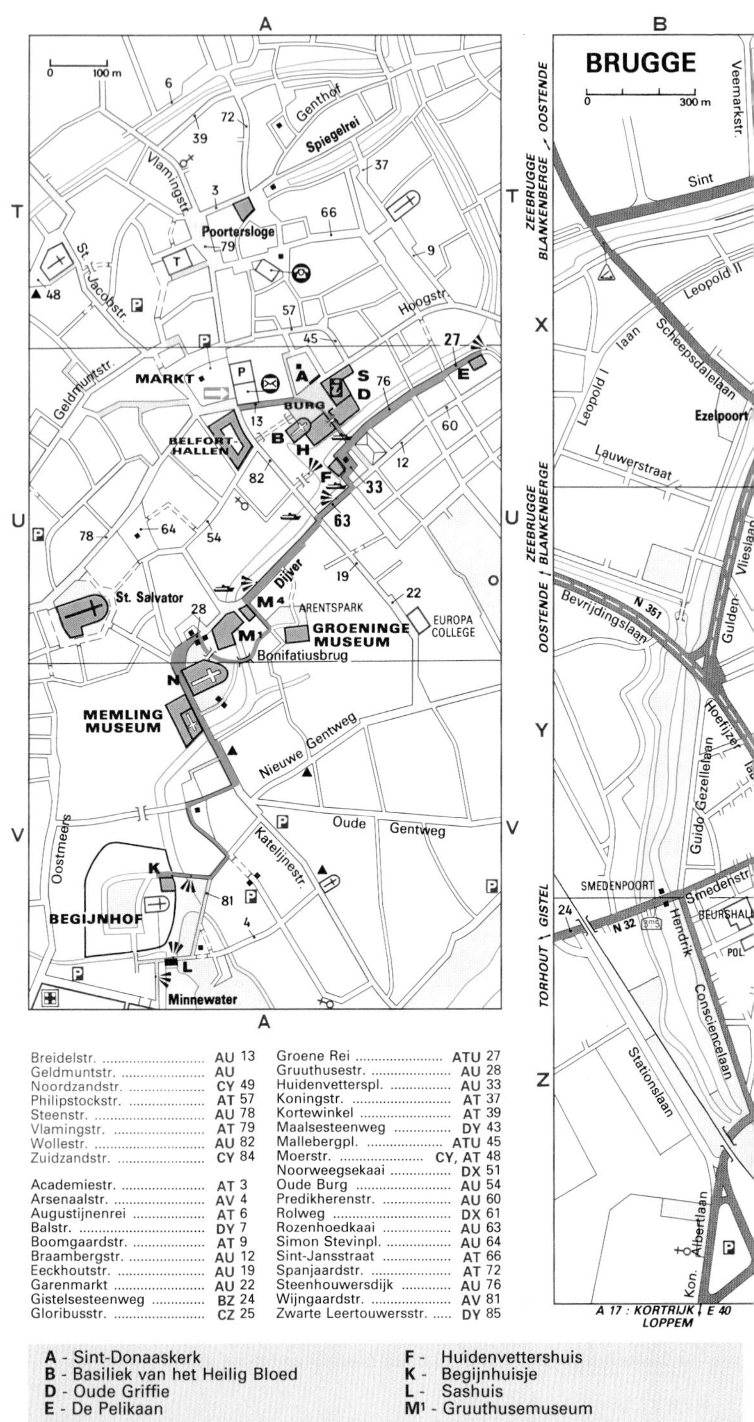

150 vessels daily. Commercial wealth was accompanied by artistic activity in the town: St John's Hospital was enlarged, as was the St Saviour's Church; the belfry, the covered market and the Church of Our Lady were built. Bruges also constructed a fortified enclosure, of which four gates still remain.
The town hall was built at the end of the 14C, then in the 15C a characteristic **architectural style** developed: tympana above rectangular windows, all the openings sometimes framed by an elegant ogee moulding.
Europe's first stock exchange was held in Bruges, in the open air.

Princely receptions – Conflict began in Flanders in 1280 between patricians, who supported the King of France ("leliaerts", or partisans of the fleur-de-lis), and the **clauwaerts** ("people with claws", referring to those of the lion of Flanders).
Philip the Handsome took the opportunity of annexing Flanders. During the Joyful Entry (1301) his wife, Queen Joan of Navarre, cried out when she saw the richly dressed citizens of Bruges who had come to greet her, "Je me croyais seule reine, j'en vois des centaines autour de moi (I thought I alone was queen, but I can see hundreds of them around me)!" The people grew angry upon seeing the luxury

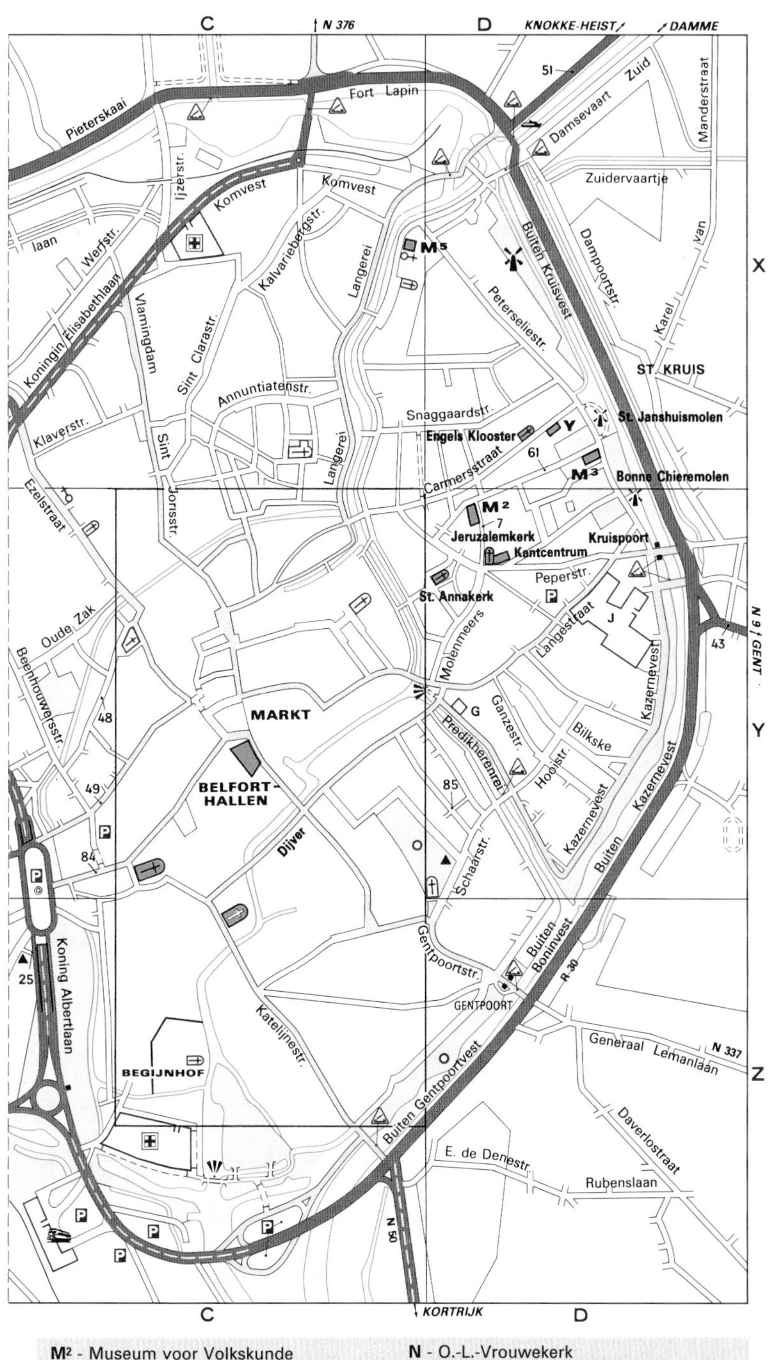

M² - Museum voor Volkskunde
M³ - Guido Gezellemuseum
M⁴ - Brangwynmuseum
M⁵ - Museum O.L. Vrouw ter Potterie

N - O.-L.-Vrouwekerk
S - Paleis van het Brugse Vrije
Y - Schuttersgilde St. Sebastiaan
▲ - Godshuizen

of this reception, which they were expected to pay for. At dawn on 13 May 1302 the clauwaerts, led by Pieter de Coninck, massacred the French garrison. These were the **"Bruges Mornings"**, a revolt bringing about the Flemish general uprising and the Battle of the Golden Spurs *(see Kortrijk)*.
The Dukes of Burgundy began to spend more and more time in Flanders in the 15C. Philip the Good received his fiancée Isabella of Portugal in Bruges, in January 1429. The reception was unforgettably sumptuous: "Even in the smallest house of the town they were drinking from silver vessels." Philip founded the Order of the Golden Fleece during the marriage celebrations.

Flemish primitives in Bruges (15C) – Bruges is the cradle of Flemish painting. It was here that **Jan van Eyck** (born in Maaseik) executed the *Adoration of the Mystic Lamb* which adorns St Bavo's Cathedral in Ghent. Van Eyck uses marvellous colours in the famous polyptych, and abandons golden backgrounds and conventional buildings, creating a realistic landscape with a startling sense of depth. He was also a distinguished portraitist. His genius is on show elsewhere in Bruges: the *Madonna with Canon Van der Paele* is one painting as remarkable

for the richness of the décor as for the treatment of the portrait of the donor. His follower, **Petrus Christus** (died *c*1473), is the painter of the famous *Portrait of a Young Girl* in Berlin's Dahlem Museums *(see Michelin Green Guide Germany)*.
Hugo **Van der Goes** (*c*1440-1482) worked in Ghent and ended his days near Brussels *(qv)*, but his last and greatest work, *Death of the Virgin*, can be seen in Bruges. The composition's reflectiveness and emotional intensity is unusual.
Hans **Memling** (*c*1435-1494) is to Bruges what Rubens is to Antwerp. Memling was of German origin, born near Mainz, but he settled in Bruges in 1465 after a stay in Cologne and perhaps also in Brussels. He completed a number of commissioned works, including some for St John's Hospital, for the town magistrates, as well as for wealthy foreigners; the most important of these are still in Bruges. The serenity of his paintings sets him apart from his contemporaries; this, combined with his warm palette and perfect details, renders his works both charming and intense. He is the painter of gentle Madonnas, feminine figures that are calm, even ethereal. His paintings are often considered more idealistic than those of Van Eyck.
Gérard David (*c*1460-1523) was born in Oudewater, in Holland; he came to Bruges in 1483. David was a student of Memling, and faithfully perpetuated his style, never abandoning the gravity and characteristic precision of his master's works *(Baptism of Christ)*.
His Renaissance followers include **Adriaan Isenbrant**, from Haarlem; the Lombard **Ambrosius Benson**; **Jan Provost**, originally from Mons; and **Pieter Pourbus** from Gouda (The Netherlands). These were the last great talents of the Bruges school, although a few anonymous painters should be cited as well: the Master of the Legend of St Ursula and the Master of the Legend of St Lucy.

"Sleeping Beauty" – Bruges' decline began in the late 15C, due largely to the silting up of the Zwin and the decline in the clothmaking industry. Antwerp soon took Bruges's former position. Nevertheless, the town revolted against Maximilian of Austria in 1488 and took him prisoner; in 1520 it made a great show of receiving Emperor Charles V, an event organised by the painter Lancelot Blondeel.
The fury of the 16C Protestant "iconoclasts", the bands of "Geuzen" revolting against Spanish rule, and later, the French invasion in 1794, brought about the town's collapse and the destruction of many great buildings.

Renewal – Great construction projects were undertaken in the late 19C. The building of a breakwater at Zeebrugge *(qv)* linked by an 11km - 7 mile canal (finished in 1907) to Bruges's new port brought a certain degree of activity back to the town.
The installations were destroyed during the two World Wars. Since their reconstruction in 1950 new industries have sprung up along the inner basin and the Baudouin Canal: glass works, mechanical constructions, chemical products, television assembly plants.
Bobbin lace, a traditional Bruges craft, is well-known.
Europa College (**AU**) (1949) makes the town an important centre of education.

★★★ HISTORICAL CENTRE AND CANALS *time: 2 days*

Visiting Bruges by night (from early May to the end of September) is an exceptional experience; the town, the canals and the old ramparts all take on an arresting appearance under the floodlights.

★★ **Market Square (Markt)** (**AU**) – Life in Bruges centres on the Market Square, bordered with houses with crowstepped gables, old guild halls and the market building, overlooked by the town belfry. The statue of Pieter de Coninck and Jan Breydel recall the heros of the 1302 revolt *(see above)*.
The canal led to the Market Square until the 18C; it was here that the boats used to berth.

★★★ **Belfry and covered market (Belfort-Hallen)** (**AU**) – These form a magnificent group of weathered, brick buildings.
The **belfry** ⊙ is the most imposing in Belgium. The massive tower dates from the 13C, but the corner turrets were added in the 14C, and the final octagonal storey at the end of the 15C. Above the entrance porch, a few statues frame the balcony, from where new laws used to be proclaimed. The climb up to the top of the belfry *(366 steps)* includes a visit to the second-floor **treasury**; the town seal and charters are behind beautifully wrought-iron grilles. The **carillon** ⊙ is higher up, consisting of 47 bells which chime every quarter hour. Finally, the remarkable **view**★★ from the top looks out over all of Bruges and its surroundings.
The **covered market** was constructed at the same time as the belfry, and enlarged in the 14C and 16C; it forms a four-sided space around a pretty courtyard. The south wing arcades are home to a flower market; note the old wooden façades just opposite.

★★ **Burg Square** (**AU**) – This is named after the castle (Burg) built by Baldwin of the Iron Arm. Four of Bruges's main buildings surround this square: from right to left, the Holy Blood Basilica, the Gothic town hall, the Renaissance court record office, and opposite, the old law courts.
One side of **St Donatian's Church** (St.-Donaaskerk) (**AU A**) still remains; the church was built *c*900 in the Carolingian style and then destroyed in 1799.
Horse-drawn carriages for hire wait here ⊙.

★ **Holy Blood Basilica** (Basiliek van het Heilig Bloed) (**AU B**) ⊙ – Housed inside is a reliquary of the Holy Blood of Christ, brought back by Thierry of Alsace, Count of Flanders, from the Holy Land on his return from the second Crusade.

The Romanesque 12C **lower chapel**★, or St Basil's Chapel, was built by Thierry of Alsace. It has kept its early character, as can be seen by the massive cylindrical pillars. Note the Romanesque bas-relief of the Baptism of Christ; this is the reverse side of the typanum over the door leading to a chapel on the right. There is a wooden Virgin dating from 1300 in the south side aisle. The **Chapel of the Holy Blood** is reached first by going through a beautiful independent doorway in a transitional Late Gothic-Renaissance style, then by taking the graceful 16C spiral staircase with low vaulting. The chapel, originally Romanesque, was altered in the 15C; it is now decorated with 19C mural paintings.
There is a little **museum** ⏲ beside the chapel. It contains the reliquary of the Holy Blood (1617), a prodigious example of goldsmithing, in which the relic is borne during the famous processions. There are also two magnificent triptych side panels by Pieter Pourbus representing members of the Holy Blood brotherhood.

Town Hall (Stadhuis) (**AU H**) ⏲ – This was built at the end of the 14C in the Late Gothic style and was restored in the 19C. The façade is unusual not only for its rich decoration, but also for its loftiness, accentuated by three turrets.
The panelled **Gothic Room** ⏲ upstairs has panelled ogive vaulting, decorated at the junction of the arches with beautiful pendant keystones.

Old Court Record Office (Oude Griffie) (**AU D**) – This now houses the Justice of the Peace. The Renaissance façade has harmonious lines, with three graceful scrolled gables.

Freeman of Bruges Mansion (Paleis van het Brugse Vrije) (**AU S**) – This was built in the neo-classical style in the 18C, on the location of the old Freeman of Bruges building (1520) which was part of the Burg. A vestige looking out over the canal still remains. In the 14C the Freeman of Bruges was a councillor overseeing the region surrounding the town. In the **Freeman of Bruges Provincial Museum** ⏲ the **chimneypiece**★ from the 16C alderman's bedroom is on display; Lancelot Blondeel directed its execution after having prepared the plans for it. The chimneypiece is in the Renaissance style in black marble and oak, and is decorated with an alabaster frieze telling the story of Susanna and the Elders. The upper part depicts several Flemish sovereigns: Emperor Charles V is in the centre, his sword upraised.
The handholds above the hearth made it possible for the aldermen to balance themselves while their boots dried.

Take the little passage of Blinde Ezelstraat.

By turning around the visitor can admire the beautiful window over the arch, as well as the gables and turrets of the Freeman of Bruges Mansion.

Take the Steenhouwersdijk.

Groene Rei (**ATU 27**) – To the right of this shaded quay stands **Pelican House** (De Pelikaan) (1714) (**AU E**), a low building with tall dormers and with the emblem of a pelican. This used to be a hospital for the poor *(see Additional Sights below)*. At the far end of the wharf there is a beautiful **view** of the canal, the belfry and the spire of the Church of Our Lady.

Tanners Square (**Huidenvettersplaats**) (**AU 33**) – This is a charming square which contains a little column bearing two lions.

Rozenhoedkaai (**AU 63**) – This quay ("Rosary Quay") offers some of the most characteristic **views**★★ of Bruges. The pretty **tanners' guild hall** (Huidenvettershuis) (1631) (**AU F**) stands near the basin; a turreted house is next to it. The high roof of the Holy Blood Chapel can be seen beyond, and the haughty-looking belfry is to the left.

Dijver (**AU**) – The **bridge of St John of Nepomuk** (St J. Nepomucenusbrug) is topped with a statue of the patron saint of bridges. There is a splendid **view**★★ at the end of the lime-tree shaded wharf: the old bridge, the porch of the Gruuthuse Museum and then the tower and spire of the Church of Our Lady.

Rozenhoedkaai and the Belfry

The flea market spreads its stalls here on Saturday and Sunday afternoons *(March to the end of October)*.

★★★ **Groeninge Museum (Stedelijk Museum voor Schone Kunsten)** (AU) ⊙ – This museum is noted for the admirable masterpieces by Flemish primitives which it contains; the first exceptionally interesting five rooms come one after another, and are devoted to the Bruges school.
In room one there are two fine works by **Van Eyck**: the *Madonna with Canon van der Paele* is striking for the brilliance of its colours, its luminous atmosphere and its fine details. The canon's portrait is remarkable – Van Eyck doesn't overlook a single wrinkle, or a single wart. As for the *Portrait of Margaret Van Eyck*, he evokes the slightly surly middle-class dignity, the sense of duty and the piety of his wife. The work representing *St Luke painting the Virgin* is an old copy of a panel by Rogier Van der Weyden.
Van der Goes is represented in room two; he is a painter who depicts fleeting expressions and movements in his portraits and religious scenes. His *Death of the Virgin*, an exceptional, intensely dramatic painting, is on show.
Memling's *Moreel Triptych*, depicting St Maur, St Christopher and St Giles with mysticism, inner peace and contemplation, is perhaps the painter's greatest masterpiece.
Two anonymous painters from Bruges are in room three: the Master of the Legend of St Lucy and the Master of the Legend of St Ursula.
Works by **Gérard David** are hung in room four: the two great panels of the *Judgement of Cambyses* (or the Story of the Unjust Judge); and the splendidly coloured triptych entitled the *Baptism of Christ*.
Room five contains Hieronymus Bosch's strange and stunning *Last Judgement*, while rooms six and seven are devoted to Jan Provost and Pieter Pourbus, who is represented by some remarkable portraits and a *Last Judgement*. The exhibition of Flemish Impressionist and contemporary Belgian painting (Delvaux, Magritte, Broodthaers) completes the museum collection.

Cross the little street to go into the Arentspark.

Gruuthuse Museum sleighs and carriages can be seen behind glass opposite the Brangwyn Museum *(see below)*.
Cross the humpbacked St Boniface's Bridge (Bonifatiusbrug) (AUV) which is in a wonderful **setting**★★. The bust of Luis Vives evokes this 16C Spanish humanist who spent the end of his life in Bruges.

Pass between the Gruuthuse Museum and the north side of the Church of Our Lady.

★★★ **Memling Museum** (AV) ⊙ – This is in the old 12C St John's Hospital. A little cloister, where a few pieces of furniture and an **apothecary's** from the 17C can be seen to the right of the entrance. The old sickrooms contain works of art and objects illustrating the hospital's history.
Memling's works are exhibited in the **church**:
The **Reliquary of St Ursula** is undoubtedly the most famous of Memling's works. The highly detailed images describe the life and martyrdom of St Ursula and her companions, the 11 000 virgins: their arrival in Cologne, then Basle and Rome; their return to Basle with the Pope, then to Cologne, where the Huns put the saint and her companions to death. On the end panels of the reliquary, the Virgin and St Ursula shelter the virgins under their mantles. Three other works surround the reliquary, including two capitals.
The **Mystic Marriage of St Catherine** represents the Infant Jesus slipping a ring onto the saint's hand while St Barbara is deeply engrossed in reading a book. The two patron saints of the hospital are also depicted; the beheading of St John the Baptist, and St John the Evangelist on the island of Patmos. Memling reaches the height of grandeur with this highly symbolic triptych, completed in 1479. Some people believe that St Catherine and St Barbara depict Mary of Burgundy and Margaret of York.
The 1479 **Adoration of the Magi** is an important work if only for the perfect beauty of the Virgin with her lowered eyes, and the youthful handsomeness of the black king Balthazar.
The **Lamentation** triptych (or the *Descent from the Cross*) was executed in 1480 on the request of the priest Adrien Reyns, who appears on his knees in the inside right leaf; St Barbara is on the inside left leaf. This saint was very popular at the time, and was venerated for her protection against sudden death and the plague
The perturbing **Sambeth Sibyl**, diaphonous and enigmatic, is in the chapel. The **Martin van Nieuwenhove** diptych, with the portrait of the donor and the **Virgin with Apple**, was painted in 1487 and has wonderfully sophisticated lines and tones.

★★ **Beguine Convent (Begijnhof)** (AV) – The "beguine convent of the vine" was founded in 1245 by Margaret of Constantinople, Countess of Flanders. The peaceful close is reached by going through a beautiful classical door near the canal. The 17C church and the nuns' white buildings are grouped around a vast green rectangle of lawn, brightened by a scattering of jonquils in the spring and planted with large trees. The Benedictines who took the place of the beguine nuns nevertheless wear the same costume.

Beguine House (Begijnhuisje) (AV K) ⊙ – A little cloister with a brick well is accessed by going through the kitchen and rustically-furnished rooms.
The nearby bridge provides a beautiful **view** of the charming **lock house** (sashuis) (AV L) in front of the **Minnewater**, one of the old harbour's docks; this is the famous Lake of Love. A tower remaining from the old fortifications can be seen to the right. There is a story behind the swans swimming in these calm waters: in 1448

Beguine Convent, Bruges

the citizens of Bruges imprisoned Maximilian of Austria and beheaded his councillor, Pierre Lanchais. Once freed, as the councillor's crest featured a swan, Maximilian ordered the citizens of Bruges to keep swans on the town canals from that day forward ever more, to pay for their crime.

★★★ **Boat trip** (**Boottocht**) ⊙ – *Landing stages (aanlegplaatsen) are indicated on the town plan.*

This is one of the best ways for tourists who are pressed for time to enjoy Bruges. For others, this is an indispensable – and relaxing – complement to the visit on foot. The boats generally reach the beguine convent to the south and the Spiegelrei to the north.

At the far end of the **Spiegelrei**, or Mirror Quay, stand the statue of Van Eyck and the 15C Bourgeois Lodge (Poortersloge) (**AT**), flanked by a turret and home to the State archives. A stone bear (town symbol) is tucked in a niche *(not visible from the boat)*. The old city tollhouse (Tonlieu), dating from 1477, is on the other side of the little square.

ADDITIONAL SIGHTS

★ **Gruuthuse Museum** (**Gruuthusemuseum**) (**AU M**[1]) ⊙ – The Gruuthuse mansion was originally used for handling "grut", a mixture of flowers and dried plants combined with barley for brewing beer. This vast 15C residence, built of warm red-toned brick, houses a Museum of Decorative Arts at the far side of the main courtyard. The beautiful interior, featuring splendid fireplaces, is very well-kept; here the past lives on through the thousand or so old Flemish objects, many from Bruges: very beautiful furniture, sculptures, tapestries, musical instruments, weapons. Note the 1520 bust of **Emperor Charles V**★ as a young man in the first room. Louis van Gruuthuse's wooden oratory leads directly to the chancel of the Church of Our Lady.

Bust of Emperor Charles V, attributed to Konradt Meit, Gruuthuse Museum, Bruges

★ **Church of Our Lady** (**O.-L.-Vrouwekerk**) (**AV N**) ⊙ – This building dates for the most part from the 13C. The most remarkable feature is the lofty brick **tower**★★, 122m - 400ft tall.

Michelangelo's splendid white marble **Virgin and Child**★★ is on the altar at the far end of the south side aisle.

Chancel ⊙ – The mausoleums of Charles the Bold and his daughter Mary of Burgundy are here. The Gothic **tomb**★★ of Mary of Burgundy, who died at the age of 25 *(see Torhout)* was designed by Jan Borman in 1498; the recumbent effigy with the youthful face, the graceful neck and the long delicate hands with their tapering fingers is quite remarkable *(photograph p 73)*. The base is decorated with the crests of her ancestors.

The Renaissance monument to Charles the Bold dates from the 16C. Van Orley's *Calvary* decorates the high altar. Several funerary vaults decorated with frescoes were discovered beneath the chancel; Mary of Burgundy's original tomb was found to be among them.
The funerary chapel of Pierre Lanchais is in the ambulatory, containing the beautiful *Virgin of Seven Sorrows*, a 16C Isenbrant masterpiece; there is also a *Christ on the Cross* by Van Dyck. A 15C tribune in sculpted wood leads to the Gruuthuse Museum.

★ **Brangwyn Museum (Brangwynmuseum)** (AU M4) – This late 18C town house is home to a beautiful collection of old Bruges landscapes (17C-19C) as well as large collection of lace.
Works by the English decorative painter and engraver **Frank Brangwyn** (1867-1956), who was born in Bruges, are upstairs. Brangwyn was apprenticed to William Morris and was an official war artist during the First World War. He won an international reputation for his skilled draughtsmanship and his flamboyant compositions.

Church of Jerusalem (Jeruzalemkerk) (DY) – The curious lantern tower of this church can be seen from the corner of Balstraat. The church was built in the 15C by the Adornes family, merchants from Ghent. Pieter Adornes obtained a plan of the Church of the Holy Sepulchre during a pilgrimage to the Holy Land, which he used as a model.
The instruments of the Passion can be detected on the altarpiece of the altar in the nave. The stained glass windows date from the 16C and represent members of the Adornes family. The 15C recumbant effigies of Anselme Adornes and his wife are in the centre of the nave. The tomb of Christ has been reconstructed in the crypt.
The **Lace Centre** (Kantcentrum) (DY) is next to the Church of Jerusalem; it aims to preserve the delicate art of bobbin lacemaking.

★ **Folklore Museum (Museum voor Volkskunde)** (DY M2) – The museum entrance is at 40 Rolweg, at the sign of an *estaminet* (café) called the "Black Cat" (Zwarte Kat). The folklore and traditions of West Flanders is evoked in these charming old almshouses which the cobblers' guild built in the 17C; there are collections of everyday objects, tools, the reconstruction of a domestic interior, and a shop.

Kruispoort (DY) – There are several sights to be seen around the Kruispoort district, in amidst the ramparts.
Three post **windmills** stand on the ramparts to the north. The first, **Bonne Chieremolen** (DXY) was brought here in 1911 from Olsene. The second, **St.-Janshuismolen** (DX), dates from 1770.
The **Guido Gezelle Museum** (Guido Gezellemuseum) (DX M3) is nearby, in the house where the poet was born.
The beautiful 16C and 17C architectural ensemble in Camersstraat, the **St Sebastian Archers' Guild Hall** (Schuttersgilde St.-Sebastiaan) (DX Y), has preserved portraits of the guild's "kings" and a collection of silver.
The **English convent** (Engels Klooster) (DX) is in the same street; the domed chapel dates from the 18C.

St Saviour's Cathedral (St.-Salvatorskathedraal) (AU) – This imposing Gothic brick building, flanked with a 99m - 325ft high tower, rises above a shady square The tower foundations were laid in the 10C. Later, the construction burnt down several times and was not completed with the chancel chapels until the 16C. The pinnacle of the tower was finished in the Romanesque style in the 19C.
Inside, the nave is supported by tall, slender clustered columns. The 13C triforium and clerestory windows are surmounted by walls which were rebuilt in the 15C.
The cathedral is richly decorated. At the far end of the nave is the late 17C baroque rood-screen, crowned by a beautiful statue of *God the Father* by Artus Quellin. The organ case above it dates from 1719. The pulpit was sculpted in 1785 by H Pulinx. Coats of arms of knights of the Golden Fleece decorate the 15C stalls; the thirteenth chapter of this Order was held here in 1478. Brussels tapestries from 1725 hang above.

Treasury (Schatkamer) – *Access via the south transept arm.* In addition to a few liturgical objects, there are some interesting paintings. Note Dirk Bouts's *Martyrdom of St Hippolytus*; the left panel of this triptych is attributed to Van der Goes.

St Anne's Church (St.-Annakerk) (DY) – The interior of this church was built in the Gothic style in the 17C. It was embellished with beautiful baroque furnishings: rood-screen, panelling and confessionals, pulpit, etc.

Ostend (or Donkey) Gate (Ezelpoort) (BX) – This stands in a pretty, shady setting at the far end of a canal; swans glide on the peaceful surface of the waterway.

Almshouses (Godshuizen) *(see key on town plan)* – There were many almshouses in Bruges from the 15C-18C; they were a sort of shelter, financed by the guilds, for the elderly and those in poverty. They are generally in rows of low, white-washed and rather modest-looking brick houses. Each dwelling's façade consists of a door and a window with a tall dormer over it.
In addition to Pelican House *(see above)* and the little houses of the Folklore Museum *(see above)*, do not miss the houses in Gloribusstraat (CZ 25), Moerstraat (AT 48), Zwarte-Leertouwersstraat (DY 85), Nieuwe Gentweg (AV) and Sinte-Katelijnestraat (AV).

Museum Onze-Lieve-Vrouw ter Potterie (**CDX M**[5]) ⏲ – The old 13C hospice of Our Lady of Pottery is at 79 Potterierei; its role was similar to that of St John's Hospital. Although it still serves as an old people's home, part of it is now a museum: the sickroom, the 14C-15C cloister, the passage to the richly decorated little baroque church. Exhibits include 15C, 16C and 17C furniture, paintings, Flemish books of hours and objects evoking religious life and the veneration of the miraculous Virgin known as Our Lady of Pottery.

EXCURSIONS

Plan of the conurbation in the Michelin Red Guide Benelux.

★ Damme – *7km - 4.3 miles northeast.*

Access by boat ⏲ – Damme can be reached by boat in season. *Departure from Noorweegse kaai landing-stage* (**DX 51**) *northeast of Bruges.*
The road runs along the Napoleon canal (built in 1812). The trees, bowed slightly by the wind, are reflected in this beautiful stretch of water. *See Damme for description of the town.*

St.-Michiels – *3km - 1.8 miles south.*

Boudewijnpark ⏲ – This park is attractive for many reasons. Two magnificent **barrel-organs**, one called De Senior (1880) and the other called De Condor, are exhibited in the great restaurant hall.
An enormous **astronomical clock**, the **Heirmanklok** ⏲ is in an equally enormous building. This mechanism, built by Edgar Heirman, is finely decorated and has many lively automata to delight the visitor.
The **Dolfinarium** ⏲, facing the park entrance, puts on shows featuring dolphins and seals.

Tillegembos – These woods cover 44ha - 108 acres, and include signposted footpaths and a pond beside which stand a typical inn and an old mill driven by animals in traction (rosmolen).

Loppem – *7km - 4.3 miles south.*

Palace (Kasteel) ⏲ – Loppem's neo-Gothic palace, commissioned by the Baron and Baroness Charles van Caloen, was designed by London architect Edward Walby Pugin (1834-1875) and Baron Jean Béthune, who was also architect of Maredsous Abbey *(see Molignée Valley)*. King Albert and his family stayed there in October and November 1918. It was here that the sovereign promised to establish universal suffrage and the "conversion to Flemish" of Ghent University. An interesting collection of works of art can be seen in the palace: paintings, especially from the 16C and 17C; glazed earthenware (faïences); porcelain, etc. Among the Dutch and Flemish school paintings, note *De Burg te Brugge* (Bruges Burg Square), executed in the early 17C. Jan van Caloen's collection is exhibited upstairs: about sixty religious sculptures (13C-16C) of various origins (Netherlands, France, Italy, Spain, Germany).
There is a **maze** (doolhof) ⏲ in the park.

Zedelgem – Pop 19 992. *10.5km - 6.5 miles south. Leave Bruges on the N 32* (**BZ**).

After crossing the A 10, **St Andrew's Abbey** (Zeven-Kerken) comes into view on the right. The buildings of this great missionary centre surround a basilica with seven shrines which was built at the beginning of this century.

Turn right at the next crossroads.

St Laurence's Church (St.-Laurentiuskerk) at Zedelgem has a remarkable 11C-12C **font**★. It rests on a richly carved base, with four columns supporting the basin which is decorated with scenes in relief on all its sides. St Nicholas is represented on the four corners.

Male – *5km - 3.1 miles east on the N 9* (**DY**).

Castle (Kasteel) ⏲ – Since 1954 the canonesses of St Trudo have lived in the enormous castle at Male, surrounded by moats; it was once the residence of the Counts of Flanders.
The Knights' Hall and the church, rebuilt in 1965, are open to visitors.

Mary of Burgundy's Tomb

★★★ BRUSSELS (BRUSSEL/BRUXELLES) Brabant Pop 970 501 (conurbation)

Michelin maps 409 G3, enlarged inset map on folds 21 and 22, or 213 fold 18

Brussels is the capital of Belgium, the royal residence and the seat of the European communities (EC, Euratom, ECSC) and of NATO. This very busy city incorporates a world of contrasts: the linguistic contrast between the Walloon and Flemish communities, not to mention the European functionaries who often speak in English; the contrast between urban Brussels, with its grand avenues offering wide-ranging views and opening onto monumental buildings, and its mazes of little streets lined with gabled houses; the contrast between its immense parks and the modern districts with their tall tower blocks such as the **World Trade Center**; last but not least, the contrast between the city's commercial function and its role as a cultural centre. Brussels has an highly active intellectual life and is home to museums of world renown, a large number of theatres and other entertainment halls. Music has a special place here, due in part to the famous **Queen Elizabeth Competition** (piano, violin, composition, singing) in the spring. The **Europalia Festival** *(odd-numbered years)* involves arts and culture from other European countries.

Finally, under the patronage of Gambrinus, King of Beer, Brussels holds sway as a city of comfort and good cheer.

Since Brussels is bilingual, both French and Flemish names feature on signposts etc., however, for reasons of space, only the French names for sights are given in the text below and on the town and conurbation plans.

St Hubert Arcades

Brussels Conurbation – It is under this name that nineteen communities have been grouped since 1971; that in the centre, Brussels, covers the greatest area.

The **Brussels Community** consists principally of the "pentagon" formed by a belt of wide avenues and the Laeken district. The area inside the "pentagon" is divided into two parts: the **Lower City**, which stretches into the Senne River Valley (now covered over) and includes the Grand-Place and the centre of commercial activity; and the **Upper City**, on the Coudenberg and the other hills near Brussels Park, which includes the Palais Royal, the Parliament, the high-level ministries and the Law Courts (Palais de Justice).

The suburbs to the north and west, near the port and the canals, are highly industrialised; those to the east and south, on the other hand, are attractive residential areas with large parks.

HISTORICAL NOTES

Uneventful Middle Ages – Brussels emerged at the end of the 10C when Charles, Duke of Lower Lotharingia, settled there. He had a castle built on a small island (Ilot St-Géry) in the River Senne. It was a marshy site, and the settlement was named Bruocsella, a Frankish word meaning "the house of the marshes".

Brussels became a trading stopover point between Cologne and Flanders during the growth period of the clothmaking industry. St Michael's Church, a sign of the town's prosperity, was built on a hill; it became a collegiate church in 1047. It was then placed under the patronage of St Gudula, the virgin whose piety triumphed over the devil who extinguished her lantern while she was at prayer. The first ramparts were built in the 12C.

A new fortified enclosure was built from 1357 to 1379. This was destroyed on the orders of Napoleon, and its location is now marked by the ring of avenues known as the Petite Ceinture. Only one gateway, the Porte de Hal to the south, remains of the original seven fortified entries.

Conflicts throughout the Middle Ages divided craftsmen and merchants, but the community as a whole remained loyal to its prince.

15C Brussels turned to the arts, influenced by the merchant class and the Dukes of Burgundy. A magnificent Town Hall (Hôtel de Ville) was built, decorated by the paintings of Rogier Van der Weyden (destroyed in 1695). Many fountains adorned the streets. Brussels tapestry-makers produced marvellous works of art at the end of the century *(see Introduction: Tapestry)*.

The woes of the capital of the Low Countries – In the 16C the town celebrated the arrival of Emperor Charles V, crowned in St Gudula's in 1516. The governor, Mary of Hungary, settled in Brussels in 1531, and the town gradually replaced Mechelen as the central seat of government of the Low Countries. Emperor Charles V abdicated in Coudenberg, handing over sovereignty of the Low Countries to his son Philip II.

Philip II drew Brussels into the religious strife of the 16C. The merchant class rebelled against the Spanish rule symbolised by the Duke of Alva. The **Count of Egmont** and his companion, the Count of Hornes, died on the scaffold in 1568. Egmont was the military governor of Flanders and was condemned for having supported the Count of Hornes and William of Nassau in the Low Countries revolt against Philip II. Goethe made him the hero of a tragedy (1787) which bears his name; the work was later staged, set to Beethoven's music, in 1810.

In 1575 the town, which had shaken off Spanish rule, was recaptured by Farnese, Duke of Parma. The War of the Augsburg League was waged in 1695, and the French Field Marshal Villeroi laid Brussels to siege on the orders of Louis XIV, who hoped to free besieged Namur in this way. Now only ruins remain of the town centre, although an extensive reconstruction project has been carried out. Governor Charles of Lorraine did a great deal to embellish Brussels. In 1795 Brussels came under French rule and was made the seat of the Dyle département. In 1815 the city once more became the capital of the Low Countries, an honour it was to share alternately with The Hague for 15 years.

A place of welcome – Brussels has attracted foreign citizens, both passing visitors and long-term residents, for many years. Often the latter were political or artistic exiles seeking refuge, for example Proudhon, Victor Hugo, Karl Marx and Paul Verlaine (who shot his lover Rimbaud, who had threatened to leave him, quite near the Grand-Place, and for this was imprisoned in the Amigo, then later at Mons). In recent years there have been increasing problems caused by the rising population density, as first people from other parts of Belgium, then immigrants from all over the world flocked to the 19 Brussels communities. It is estimated that more than a quarter of the inhabitants of the Brussels conurbation are now of foreign extraction.

The capital of Belgium – After the 1830 Revolution, marked by the **"Days of September"** in Brussels, the Belgian provinces separated from Holland and became independent. The kingdom of Belgium was established with Brussels as capital; **King Leopold I** entered the city ceremoniously on 21 July 1831 (21 July has been a national holiday ever since). The city has grown considerably since 1830, with a particular spurt at the turn of the century. The free University was founded in 1834. Europe's first railway began operating in 1835, running from the Gare de l'Allée Verte (Brussels-Mechelen). The Congress Column was erected in 1859 to commemorate the National Congress which established Belgium's first constitution.

King Leopold II undertook several urban projects. Anspach oversaw the building of the great central avenues; several parks were created, including Laeken. A number of imposing buildings arose, including:

– the Palais du Cinquantenaire with its arcade, the Tervuren Museum, linked by the Avenue de Tervuren;

– the Basilica of Koekelberg, completed in 1970 and accessed by the grandiose Avenue Léopold-II.

The list of other notable buildings is endless, but includes: the Museum of Ancient (15C to 19C) Art, the Bourse, the Théâtre de la Monnaie, the Law Courts (Palais de Justice). The façade of the Palais Royal dates from this period.

Expansion after the First World War – The building of the **Junction**, a semi-underground railway line linking the Gare du Midi to the Gare du Nord which was inaugurated in 1952, transformed the district in between the Upper and Lower City: new architectural projects such as the Banque Nationale and the government's administrative district (1958), and the creation of the Mont des Arts in a modernistic architectural setting.

The various Palais du Centenaire had already been built in the exhibition grounds on the Heysel plateau for the 1935 **World Fair**. The Atomium and the **Petite Ceinture tunnels** were built for the second World Fair in 1958.

A plethora of civic and private construction has contributed to the city's modernisation since then: the Royal Library (1969), the European district of Berlaymont (1970), the Central Post Office and the administrative sections of the City of Brussels (1971).

The Forest-National sports and entertainments stadium (1970) in Forest can hold 7 000 spectators (variety, music hall). The ultra-modern, well-equipped medical faculty of the Catholic University of Leuven *(qv)*, which also has a hospital, was built in Woluwe-St-Lambert.

Finally, the vast shopping centre known as the Brussels International Trade Mart was inaugurated in 1975 in Heysel.

Brussels develops a new look – Nowadays, outside the "sacred island" ("îlot sacré") of the Grand-Place and the old buildings preserved there, Brussels is implementing extensive reconstruction projects.

Huge tower blocks have been erected west of the Gare du Nord, including the **World Trade Center** (**FQ**) and the Manhattan Center. The National Theatre is housed in the skyscraper known as the Centre International Rogier on **Place Rogier** (**FQ 213**). City 2 (**FQ**), a shopping centre in nearby Rue Neuve is partly underground, and includes eight cinemas.

Brussels is currently pouring its energies into preserving its architectural heritage and has undertaken the renovation of existing old buildings.
A project to improve the public transport system is also underway to complete urban development. The current underground railway and tramway network covers 40km - 25 miles and is continuing to expand. Belgium's great artists have been commissioned to decorate the underground stations.

Traditions – The people of Brussels are faithful to their traditional folklore festivals: **Ommegang** *(see below)*, the planting of the Meyboom *(see Introduction: Folklore and Traditions)* as well as the open-air markets, including especially the bird market on the Grand-Place, the antiques and book market on Place du Grand-Sablon *(see below)*, and the flea market on Place du Jeu-de-Balle.

★★★ GRAND-PLACE *time: 1 hour 30min*

This vast town square admired by so many visitors is unique. One sight of the flower market in the early morning hours during summer, or of the evening illuminations throwing the stunning gilded ornamentation of the buildings into sharp relief, or of the bird market on Sunday morning will be enough to captivate anyone. Every two years a Carpet of Flowers covers the cobblestones of the Grand-Place for a few days in August *(see the Calendar of Events at the end of this guide)*.

The Guild Halls – These were built after the Spanish destroyed the town in 1695 and then restored in the 19C; their beautiful baroque façades surround the Grand-Place. In general, three orders are superposed on them: Ionic, Doric and Corinthian. The whole is then surmounted with scrolled gables and decorated with sculptures, gilded motifs and flame ornamentation.
Every year in July, during the aristocratic **Ommegang** procession *(see the Calendar of Events at the end of this guide)*, the Guilds have places of honour, along with the Serments (armed troops) and the Chambers of Rhetoric. The majestic parade, with hundreds of flags fluttering in the wind, evokes the 1549 ceremony in the presence of Emperor Charles V and his sister Eleanor of Habsburg, widow of Francis I.
Walk round the Grand-Place anti-clockwise to see:

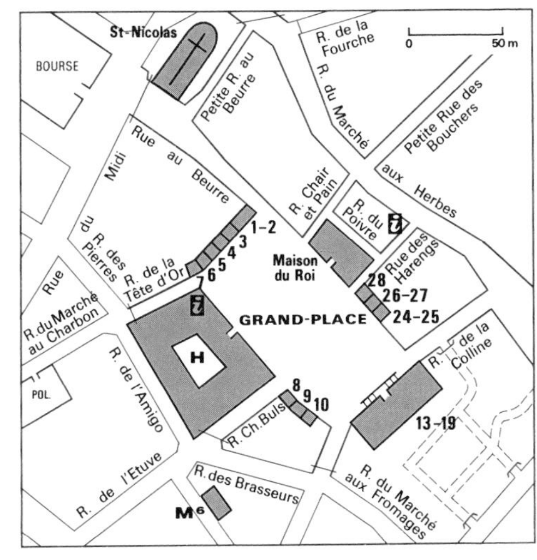

1-2 King of Spain Hall (Le Roi d'Espagne), or the Bakers' Hall, topped with a dome and a gilded weather vane representing Fame.

3 Wheelbarrow Hall (La Brouette) for the Tallow Merchants' Guild.

4 Sack Hall (Le Sac) for the Coopers' Guild.

5 Wolf Hall (La Louve) for the Archers' Guild. This has a sculpture representing Romulus and Remus being suckled; on the second storey there are four statues; Truth, Falsehood, Peace and Discord. On top there is a gilded phoenix.

6 Horn Hall (Le Cornet) for the Boatmen's Guild. Its gable is in the form of a frigate's poop.

7 Fox Hall (Le Renard) for the Drapers' Guild. A sculpted frieze runs above the first storey. On top is a statue of St Nicholas.

H Town Hall (Hôtel de ville) *(see below)*.

8 Star Hall (L'Étoile). The Everard 't Serclaes memorial by Dillens beneath the arcade will ensure happiness for those whose hands touch the statue.

9 Swan Hall (Le Cygne) for the Butchers' Guild.

10 Golden Tree Hall (L'Arbre d'Or) for the Brewers' Guild. Part of this is occupied by Belgium's Breweries Confederation. It is surmounted by a statue of Charles of Lorraine. The **Brewery Museum** (Musée de la Brasserie) ⊙ is in the cellars, including a reconstruction of a 17C brewery and all the equipment for preparing beer.

13-19 Dukes of Brabant Hall (Maison des ducs de Brabant). This imposing façade (1698), surmounted by a beautiful carved pediment and an attic storey in the Italian Palladian style, conceals six guild halls. A row of busts representing the Dukes of Brabant decorates the pillars.

24-25 Golden Boat Hall (La Chaloupe d'Or) for the Tailors' Guild.

26-27 Pigeon Hall (Le Pigeon) for the Painters' Guild, where Victor Hugo stayed in 1852.

28 The Amman's Garret (La chambrette de l'Amman). The "amman" was a magistrate representing the Duke of Brabant.

Carpet of Flowers on the Grand-Place

Town Hall (Hôtel de ville) (H) ⊙ – *Illustration p 21.* This pure Gothic town hall dates from the 13C and 15C. At the beginning of the 15C it consisted of no more than the south wing and the belfry; the present Lions' Staircase was then the main entrance. The slightly shorter north wing was added to enlarge it. The whole is dominated by a tower built by Van Ruysbroeck, a marvel of elegance and sturdiness (96m - 315ft), crowned with a gilded copper statue of St Michael.
Note the beautiful Brussels tapestries inside, especially those in the Maximilian Room.

King of Spain Hall (Maison du Roi d'Espagne) – This was rebuilt in the 19C, based on plans dating from 1515. This was the old Bakers' guild hall, then the Duke's residence, but in fact no king has ever stayed here.
The **Museum of the City of Brussels** (Musée de la ville de Bruxelles) ⊙ is housed here and exhibits works of art tracing the city's history and its many local artistic industries. Among the 15C and 16C paintings and altarpieces located on the ground floor, admire the peaceful *Wedding Procession* attributed to Pieter Brueghel the Elder, and the *Saluzzo Altarpiece*, a masterpiece dating from the early 16C. Among the Brussels tapestries is the outstanding representation of the legend of Notre-Dame-du-Sablon (1516-1518). The porcelain and silver collections contain beautiful examples of Brussels decorative art. Note the eight prophets from the Town Hall's porch, in the room devoted to Gothic sculpture.
The city's growth and various transformations over the centuries are illustrated on the first floor by means of paintings, engravings, photographs and other objects, including a model of 13C Brussels. The second floor exhibits the many outfits which have been given to the Manneken Pis.

★★ THE SABLON AND MONT DES ARTS DISTRICTS

time: half a day

Leave from the Grand-Place and follow the route on the town plan overleaf.

Rue de L'Étuve is lined with gabled houses, as are all the nearby quaintly-named streets.

★★ **Manneken Pis** (JZ) – *Illustration p 93.* The Manneken Pis fountain, also known as Little Julian, was sculpted by Jerome Duquesnoy the Elder in 1619 and supplied the district with water. This dimpled little boy (manneken: little man), whose unselfconscious gesture has a certain cheeky charm, is said to symbolise the Brabant people's lively sense of humour and their vitality. The custom of giving him an outfit may have been established for reasons of decency, or more probably to honour Brussels most famous and "oldest citizen". The donors range from Louis XV, who presented him with his first outfit, a beautiful French costume, to the Military Police, who presented him with a uniform. The entire country has taken part in compiling his wardrobe, which takes up an entire room of the Museum of the City of Brussels *(see above)*.

The walk passes beside the **Anneessens Tower** (tour d'Anneessens) (**JZ C**), a remnant of the 12C fortifications. Anneessens, who represented the tradesmen in the revolt against the Austrian government, is said to have been imprisoned here before his execution in 1719.

Église Notre-Dame-de-la-Chapelle (JZ) ⊙ – This church is on the outskirts of the colourful Marolles district. While the 13C transept is in the Romanesque style, most of the building is characteristic of Brabant Gothic art; note in particular the exterior alignment of the side gables and the tower porch.
Painter Pieter Brueghel the Elder was buried in this church in 1569; his epitaph on black marble, surmounted by a copy of a work by Rubens called *Christ Giving the Keys to St Peter*, is above the confessional in the third chapel of the south side aisle. There is an interesting triptych executed by Henri de Clerck in 1619 in the second chapel in the north side aisle. In the third chapel, note the beautiful **wooden statue★** of St Margaret of Antioch (*c*1520). The Spinola marble funerary monument, dating from 1716, is in the chapel south of the chancel.

★ **Place du Grand-Sablon** (JZ 112) ⊙ – This is the chic square of Brussels, surrounded by old façades, antique dealers' shops and elegant restaurants.

BRUXELLES BRUSSEL

Adolphe-Max (Bd) .... JY 3
Anspach (Bd) .... JY
Beurre (Rue au) .... JY 19
Etuve (R. de l') .... JZ 88
Fripiers (R. des) .... JY 105
Grand-Sablon (Pl. du) ..... JZ 112
Ixelles (Chée d') .... KZ 129
Marché-aux-Herbes (R. du) JY 168
Marché-aux-Poulets (R. du) .... JY 169
Midi (R. du) .... JYZ
Neuve (Rue) .... JY
Toison d'Or (Av. de la) ... KZ 238

Albertine (Pl. de l') .... JZ 4
Assaut (R. d') .... JY 10
Baudet (R.) .... KZ 15
Bouchers (Petite rue des) .... JY 24
Bouchers (R. des) .... JY 25
Bourse (Pl. de la) .... JY 27
Chêne (R. du) .... JZ 39
Colonies (R. des) .... KY 43
Comédiens (R. des) .... KY 45
Commerce (R. du) .... KZ 46
Croix-de-Fer (R. de la) .... KY 52
Duquesnoy (Rue) .... JYZ 66
Empereur (Bd de l') .... JZ 84
Ernest Allard (R.) .... JZ 87
Fossé-aux-Loups (R.) ...... JY 99

Impératrice (Bd de l') ...... JY 124
Joseph Lebeau (R.) .... JZ 142
Laeken (R. de) .... JY 151
Louvain (R. de) .... KY 163
Montagne (Rue) .... JY 178
Petit Sablon (Sq. du) ...... JZ 195
Presse (R. de la) .... KY 201
Princes (Galeries des) .... JY 205
Ravenstein (R.) .... KZ 207
Reine (Galerie de la) .... JY 210
Roi (Galerie du) .... JY 214
Rollebeek (R. de) .... JZ 217
Sainte-Gudule (Pl.) .... KY 222
Trône (R. du) .... KZ 241
Ursulines (R. des) .... JZ 243
Waterloo (Bd de) .... KZ 255
6 Jeunes Hommes (R. des). JZ 268

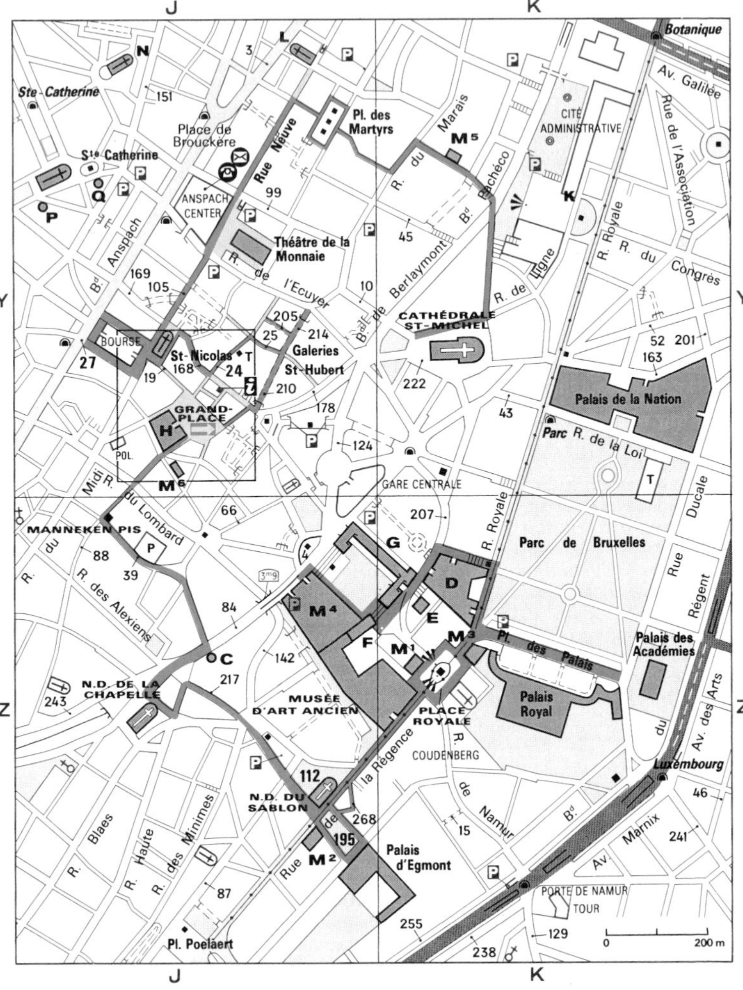

C - Tour d'Anneessens
D - Palais des Beaux-Arts
E - Hôtel Ravenstein
F - Appartements de Ch. de Lorraine
G - Palais de la Dynastie
K - Colonne du Congrès
L - Eglise du Finistère
M1 - Musée d'Art moderne

M2 - Musée instrumental
M3 - Musée Bellevue
M4 - Bibliothèque Royale Albert 1er
M5 - Centre belge de la Bande dessinée
M6 - Musée du Costume et de la Dentelle
N - Eglise St-Jean-Baptiste-au-Béguinage
P - Tour de l'ancienne église
Q - Tour Noire

★ **Église Notre-Dame-du-Sablon** (JZ) – This beautiful Flamboyant Gothic church was originally the chapel of the Crossbowmens' guild. The story goes that in 1348 a woman from Antwerp, Baet Soetkens, saw a statue of the Virgin in a dream; she brought it to Brussels in a small boat (Notre-Dame-du-Sablon: Our Lady of the Sands) and presented it to the crossbowmen. This sanctuary became a site of pilgrimage and had to be enlarged in about 1400; the work was concluded in 1550 with the main doorway. The "sacrarium", a small richly-decorated structure to house the Holy Sacrament, was adjoined to the apse in 1549.
Inside, the chancel is marvellously high and airy; delicate twinned columns rise between the tall stained glass windows. The pulpit dates from 1697. The south transept arm is embellished with a beautiful rose window. The side aisle chapels are connected with one another in true Brabant fashion; their lower arches, like those of the chancel, are decorated with historiated spandrils. A copy of the statue of *Our Lady of the Tree (see Antwerpen: Cathedral)* is in the Lady Chapel.

The **Tours and Taxis (or Tassis) sepulchral chapel** is near the chancel; this is the family of Austrian origin that founded the international postal system in 1516. The décor in black and white marble is the work of Lucas Faydherbe. The white marble statue of St Ursula is by Jerome Duquesnoy the Younger.
Magnificent tapestries attributed to Bernard Van Orley illustrate the legend of Notre-Dame-du-Sablon; they were meant to decorate the side aisles. One is on show in the Brussels city museum, the other in the Royal Museums of Art and History *(photograph p 26)*.

★ **Square du Petit-Sablon** (JZ 195) – This square is surrounded by columns bearing 48 charming bronze statues representing the trades of Brussels. Fraikin's statues of the Counts of Egmont and of Hornes stand in the square itself, as well as statues of great 16C humanists. The **Palais d'Egmont** (JKZ), also known as the Palais Arenberg, is on the southeast side; international receptions are held here. Attractive old houses have been restored in Rue des Six-Jeunes-Hommes to the north. The **Museum of Musical Instruments** (Musée instrumental) (JZ **M**[2]) *(qv)* is on the edge of the square, on the corner of Rue de la Régence.

★★★ **Royal Belgian Museums of Fine Art (Musées royaux des Beaux-Arts de Belgique)** (JKZ) – These consist of the Museum of Ancient (15C to 19C) Art and the Museum of Modern Art (**M**[1]) *(see below)*.

★ **Place Royale** (KZ) – This elegantly proportioned, Louis XVI style square is at the summit of the Coudenberg; it is part of the district transformed at the end of the 18C by Charles of Lorraine. The square was built by the French architects Guimard and Barré and is overlooked by a church (Église St-Jacques-sur-Coudenberg). There is a statue of Godefroy de Bouillon standing in the centre, from which there is also a beautiful view of the Mont des Arts gardens and the Law Courts.

Place des Palais (KZ) – This is a vast esplanade, dominated by the **Palais Royal** ⊙. The curved, colonnaded façade of this palace was built under Leopold II; a flag flying from the roof indicates that the sovereign is on Belgian soil. The sumptuous **Throne Room★** inside, dating from 1872, is decorated with gorgeous chandeliers. The **Palais des Académies** dating from 1823 is to the east of the square; this was once the residence of the Prince of Orange.
The **Palais des Beaux-Arts** (KZ **D**) stands discreetly to the west of the square, on the other side of Rue Royale. Victor Horta built this between 1921 and 1928, during a period of many large and important cultural events (exhibitions, concerts, cinema, theatre).

★ **Bellevue Museum (Musée Bellevue)** (KZ **M**[3]) ⊙ – This is in the old Bellevue mansion and features beautiful collections of everyday 18C and 19C objects. The display includes furniture, porcelain and cosmetic accessories. Two rooms on the ground floor house the Coeur Boyadjian museum in which a collection of hearts of all shapes and sizes is on display.
The museum also exhibits on the second floor comprehensive documentation on the Belgian royal family from 1831 to the present.

Brussels Park (KYZ) – This was where the Dukes of Brabant once hunted. In the 18C it was turned into a French style garden, peopled with statues.

Ravenstein Mansion (Hôtel Ravenstein) (KZ **E**) – This mansion dating from the 15C and 16C is on Rue Ravenstein, beyond Place Royale. Note the façade with its turret.

Apartments of Charles of Lorraine (JZ **F**) ⊙ – The palace of Charles of Lorraine, with its neo-classical façade, stands on the northwest side of Rue du Musée; this is actually the only surviving wing of the building constructed under this governor of the Low Countries. Work was carried out from 1756 to 1780, on the site of the old Nassau Mansion. The Print-room of the Royal Library is on the ground floor. A monumental staircase leads to the first floor; note the statue at its foot, representing Hercules Vanquishing the Erymanthian Boar (1770) by Laurent Delvaux. Do not miss the marvellous round drawing room decorated with a marble floor – the rose-shape uses 28 different Belgian marbles – or the five restored rooms looking out onto Rue du Musée; the floodlights of the Museum of Modern Art can be seen.

Albert I Royal Library (JZ **M**[4]) ⊙ – This library was founded in the 15C during the reign of the Dukes of Burgundy. It has been open to the public since 1839 and was transferred to Mont des Arts in 1969. The magnificent collection consists of three million volumes available for consultation: manuscripts and printed material, prints and drawings, maps and plans, coins and medallions.
The building encloses the **Nassau Chapel**, also known as St George's Chapel, which is a remnant of the old Nassau Mansion. This Flamboyant Gothic structure dates from 1520, and is now used for temporary exhibitions.

Book Museum (Musée du Livre) ⊙ – A little room is home to precious manuscripts and printed material. There are also reconstructions of Emile Verhaeren's study at St-Cloud near Paris, Michel de Ghelderode's study in Schaerbeek, as well as a room devoted to the memory of Henry Van de Velde and his friend Max Elskamp.

Printing Museum (Musée de l'Imprimerie) ⊙ – A series of machines and printing-presses are exhibited, dating from the late 18C to the early 20C; they illustrate the history of printing (typography, copperplate engraving, lithography, offset) and the art of bookbinding and gilding.

Palais de la Dynastie (JKZ **G**) – This can be seen on the other side of the Mont des Arts gardens; the **Palais des Congrès** is in one wing. There is a jack o'the clocks above the arcade.
There is a beautiful view of the town hall spire from the top of the gardens, and also of the rows of houses rebuilt in the Flemish style.

Return to the Grand-Place.

★★ WEST OF THE CATHEDRAL *time: half a day*

Leave from the Grand-Place.

★ **St Hubert Arcades (Galeries St-Hubert)** (JY) – *(Photograph p 74).* This elegant classical building stands at the far end of the Rue du Marché-aux-Herbes; the façade is decorated with pilasters and a central triumphal Renaissance motif embellished with statues. The motto "Omnibus omnia" ("all for all") is the only trace of the former Goldsmiths' Guild Hall demolished to make way for the St Hubert Arcades built by Jean-Pierre Cluysenaar in 1846.
The **King's Arcade** (Galerie du Roi) and the **Queen's Arcade** (Galerie de la Reine), with a classical structure on three levels, are covered by round-arched glazed vaulting supported on a delicate metal framework.
These galleries house luxury boutiques and elegant tea shops.
The Queen's Arcade crosses the Rue des Bouchers, with its many restaurants, into the King's Arcade, from which shortly afterwards the **Princes' Arcade** (Galerie des Princes) leads off to the left, and which opens onto Rue de l'Écuyer through a large façade echoing the architectural themes of the square.

Return to Rue des Bouchers.

Petite Rue des Bouchers (JY 24) – The famous **Toone marionette theatre** ⊙ *(see Introduction: Folklore and Traditions in Belgium)* is in this tiny street crowded with tourist restaurants.

Place de la Bourse (JY 27) – The most imposing building on this square is the Bourse, which dates from 1871.
Behind the Bourse, surrounded by old houses, stands little **St Nicholas's Church** (Église St-Nicolas) ⊙ in Rue au Beurre. Inside, the chancel is out of line with the nave; notice the canvas attributed to Rubens, the *Virgin with Sleeping Child.*

Théâtre de la Monnaie (JY) – This was rebuilt by Poelaert in 1856 and was the scene of a historic event on 25 August 1830. During a production of Auber's *La Muette de Portici*, while the famous aria on love of one's homeland – *"Amour sacré de la patrie"* – was being sung, the audience broke into a rebellion that was the prelude to the "Days of September" *(see Historical Notes above).* The extensive renovation project carried out in 1986 under the architect C Vandenhove has managed successfully to incorporate a post-modern section, which has a blue frieze emphasising the cornice of the neo-classical building. In the entrance hall the brightly coloured, flowing forms on the ceiling by S Francis constrast sharply with the spartan lines of the floor by S Lewitt. The renovation has adapted the theatre to meet modern technical standards.

Historium ⊙ – *In the Anspach Center* (JY). A series of paintings with wax figures enables visitors to retrace the great events of Belgium's history since Caesar and the Conquest of Gaul.

Rue Neuve (JY) – This is a busy pedestrian shopping precinct.

Place des Martyrs (JKY) – This urban complex designed in 1775 has unfortunately been left to decline, however, restoration work is currently under way. At the centre of the square is Willem Geefs's 1838 monument dedicated to those who died in the 1830 Revolution.

★ **Belgian Centre for Comic Strip Art (Centre belge de la Bande dessinée) (KY M5)** ⊙ – This is in the magnificent Art Nouveau building designed by Victor Horta in 1903 for the Waucquez stores.
The entrance hall is vast, lit from overhead by the reflections from a huge mirror, making the interior look like a public square. A bookshop, a library and a restaurant have been installed around the hall, and a monumental stone staircase with an ironwork balustrade leads up to the museum collections.
An exhibition on the mezzanine explains the various stages of making a comic strip (scenario, drawing, colouring, printing) as well as "the treasury", which is home to more than 3 000 original plates from the greatest comic strips, exhibited in rotations of 300. An area is devoted to the actual production process of a comic strip. On the first floor, beneath the immense mirror, the **Museum of Imagination** beckons the visitor into the world of the great heros of Belgian comic strips and their creators: Tintin (Hergé), Gaston Lagaffe (André Franquin), Spirou (Rob Vel), Bob and Bobette (Willy Vandersteen), Blake and Mortimer (Edgar Pierre Jacobs), Lucky Luke (Morris), Boule and Bill (Roba), etc.
The Centre for Comic Strip Art is also an important location for temporary exhibitions.

★★ **St Michael's Cathedral** (KY) ⊙ – Situated on the heights of the Treurenberg (Mount of Tears), the old collegiate church of SS Michael and Gudula has shared the title of cathedral of the Mechelen-Brussels archdiocese with the cathedral of Mechelen since 1962. This beautiful Gothic building, the "nave anchored at the heart of Brussels", was built over several periods: the chancel dates from the 13C, the nave and side aisles from the 14C and 15C, the towers from the 15C. The radiating chapels were added in the 16C and 17C. The façade's two lofty, powerful towers were built by Van Ruysbroeck.
Leaving from the east end, where the Brabant Gothic style made its first appearance, brings the visitor to the porch of the south transept arm. This is surmounted by a statue of St Gudula dating from the 15C.

Interior – *The chancel is currently undergoing restoration and therefore cannot be seen.* The Brabant style nave is sober and impressive in appearance. There are 17C statues of the twelve apostles against the columns. The baroque pulpit, by Hendrik Frans Verbruggen, represents Adam and Eve being driven out of the Garden of Eden.

Note the difference between the 14C south side aisle, supported by columns, and the 15C north side aisle, striking for the seeming weightlessness of its ribbed vaulting. The chancel has great purity of line and a well-proportioned triforium with alternating supports, one strong, one weak. The mausoleum with a lion on top of it is that of the Dukes of Brabant (1610).

The **stained glass windows★** are marvellous. The tribune at the far end of the nave is decorated with a brilliantly coloured (with rich blues and greens) *Last Judgement*, dating from 1528. The transept is lit through two sumptuous 16C stained glass windows in a beautiful design (architecture, perspective, relief), executed using cartoons by Bernard van Orley; that in the north transept arm represents Emperor Charles V and Isabella of Portugal, while the other in the south arm depicts Louis II, King of Hungary, with his wife Mary, the sister of Emperor Charles V. Wonderful 16C stained glass windows decorate the Chapel of the Holy Sacrament north of the chancel. Others from the 17C decorate in true Rubens spirit the Lady Chapel to the south of the chancel; they depict episodes from the life of the Virgin and, below these, portraits of the donors.

The axial chapel, or Maes Chapel, contains a splendid alabaster altarpiece (1533) and a *Virgin and Child* (*c*1500), also in alabaster.

Excavations *(crypt)* have brought to light in the nave the remains of a Rheno-Mosan church, as well as the walls of an 11C Romanesque church. White flagstones in the nave trace the outline of the Romanesque church, and glass tiles allow visitors to see the remains for themselves.

Return to the Grand-Place.

★★★ ROYAL BELGIAN MUSEUMS OF FINE ART

These consist of the Museum of Ancient (15C to 19C) Art and the Museum of Modern Art; the central buildings of these two museums are connected with each other inside.

★★★ **Museum of Ancient (15C to 19C) Art (Musée d'Art Ancien)** (JKZ) – This is housed in a classical building built by Alphonse Balat between 1876 and 1880, which has been expanded with the addition of a modern wing. The museum is world-renowned for its collection of marvellous works by Flemish Primitives and famous masterpieces by Brueghel the Elder and Rubens.

15C-16C – This exhibits some real treasures by the Flemish school as well as by the French, German, Dutch, Italian and Spanish schools. One of the oldest paintings is the *Life of the Virgin*, executed by an anonymous Limburg master (*c*1400). The work of the Tournai painter Rogier **Van der Weyden** is represented by: portraits of *Antoine, great bastard of Burgundy* and of *Laurent Froimont*, both marvels of simplicity; and a magnificent *Pietà* (Room 12), its drama heightened by a reddish background light. Also in this room is a work by Van der Weyden's master, the Tournai painter **Robert Campin**, who is thought by some scholars to be the **Master of Flémalle**: his *Annunciation*, which was a variation of the central panel from the *Merode Triptych* exhibited in The Cloisters, New York. It is remarkable for the colours, the gentleness of the Virgin's face and the precise detail with which the various objects have been portrayed. Van Eyck makes his influence felt in *Pietà*, one of the rare works by his student, **Petrus Christus**. The two panels of the *Judgment of Emperor Otto*, one of the major masterpieces by **Dirk Bouts**, were commissioned in 1468 for Leuven's town hall as "paintings of justice"; in fact they depict a miscarriage of justice. Works on display by the Bruges artist **Hans**

The Annunciation by the Master of Flémalle

BRUXELLES BRUSSEL

Midi (Bd du) .... ES
Baudoin (Bd) .... EQ 16
Bienfaiteurs (Pl. des) ...... GQ 21
Brabançonne (Av. de la) GR 28
Colonel Bremer (Pl.) .... GQ 42
Dailly (Pl.) .... GR 55
Edouard de Thibault (Av.) .... HS 72
Europe (Bd de l') .... ES 90
Frans Courtens (Av.) .... HQ 102
Froissart (R.) .... GS 106
Gén. Eisenhower (Av.) .... GQ 108
Hal (Porte de) .... ES 114
Henri Jaspar (Av.) .... ES 117
Herbert Hoover (Av.) .... HR 118
Industrie (Quai de l') ...... ER 126
Jan Stobbaerts (Av.) ...... GQ 133

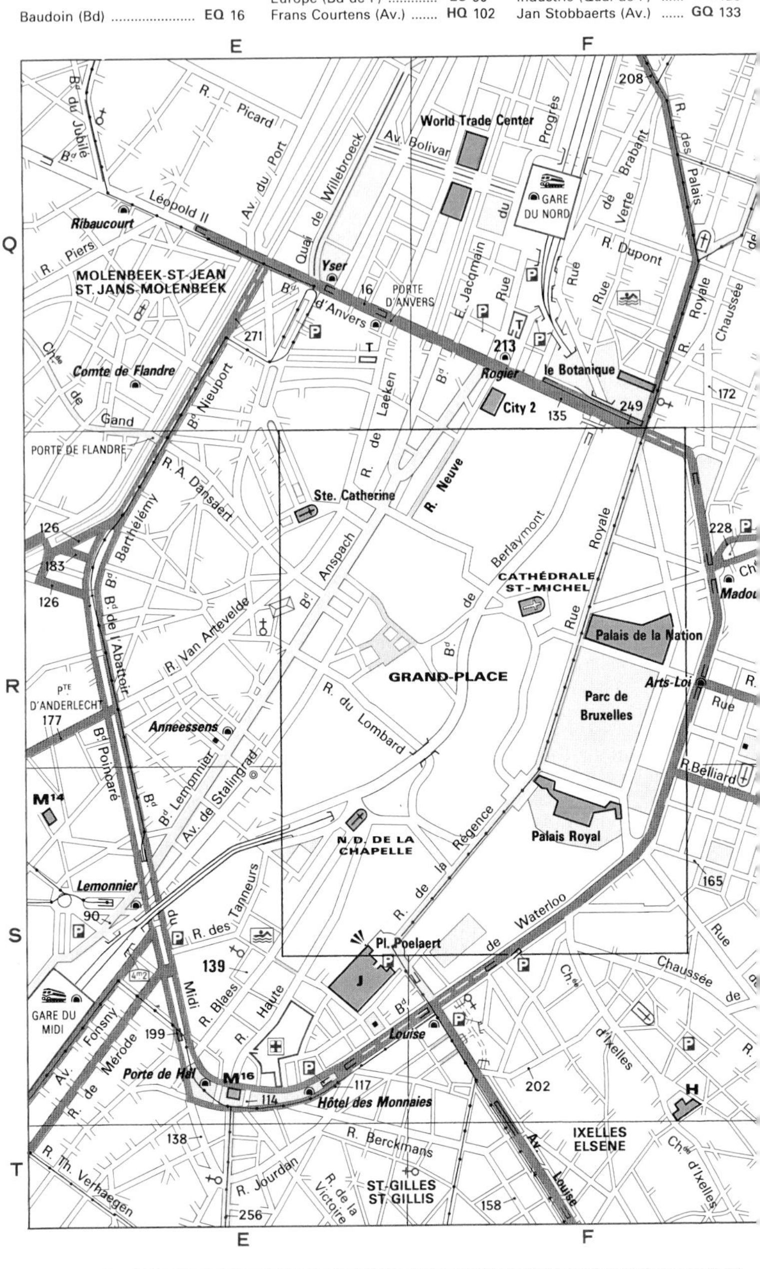

M^7 - Musées royaux d'Art et d'Histoire
M^7 - Autoworld
M^8 - Musée royal de l'Armée et d'Histoire militaire

Memling include the tender *Virgin with Child* and the *Martyrdom of St Sebastian*, with a beautiful background depicting a Flemish town. **Hieronymous Bosch** is represented by a *Calvary with Donor*, in which the landscape consists of chromatic nuances, and by a studio copy of his famous triptych, the *Temptation of St Anthony*. *Virgin with Child (photograph p 24)* by **Hugo van der Goes** is on display, a magnificent work with a slightly cold feel to it from the colours chosen by the artist. The *Madonna with Milk Soup* by **Gérard David**, the last of the of the great Primitive painters, has a striking intimacy. **Quentin Metsys** still shows the main characteristics of the Flemish Primitives, but is affected by Italian influence, foreshadowing Antwerp Mannerism; examples of his work include the triptych of the *Lineage of St Anne* and several paintings of the *Virgin with Child*. **Jan Gossaert**, also known as Mabuse, portraitist and court painter, reveals a different facet of his art here with *Venus and Cupid*, one of the first works in Flemish painting to feature a mythological subject. There is also a panel of the *Altarpiece of the Holy Cross Brotherhood* by **Bernard Van Orley**, painter to Margaret of Austria.

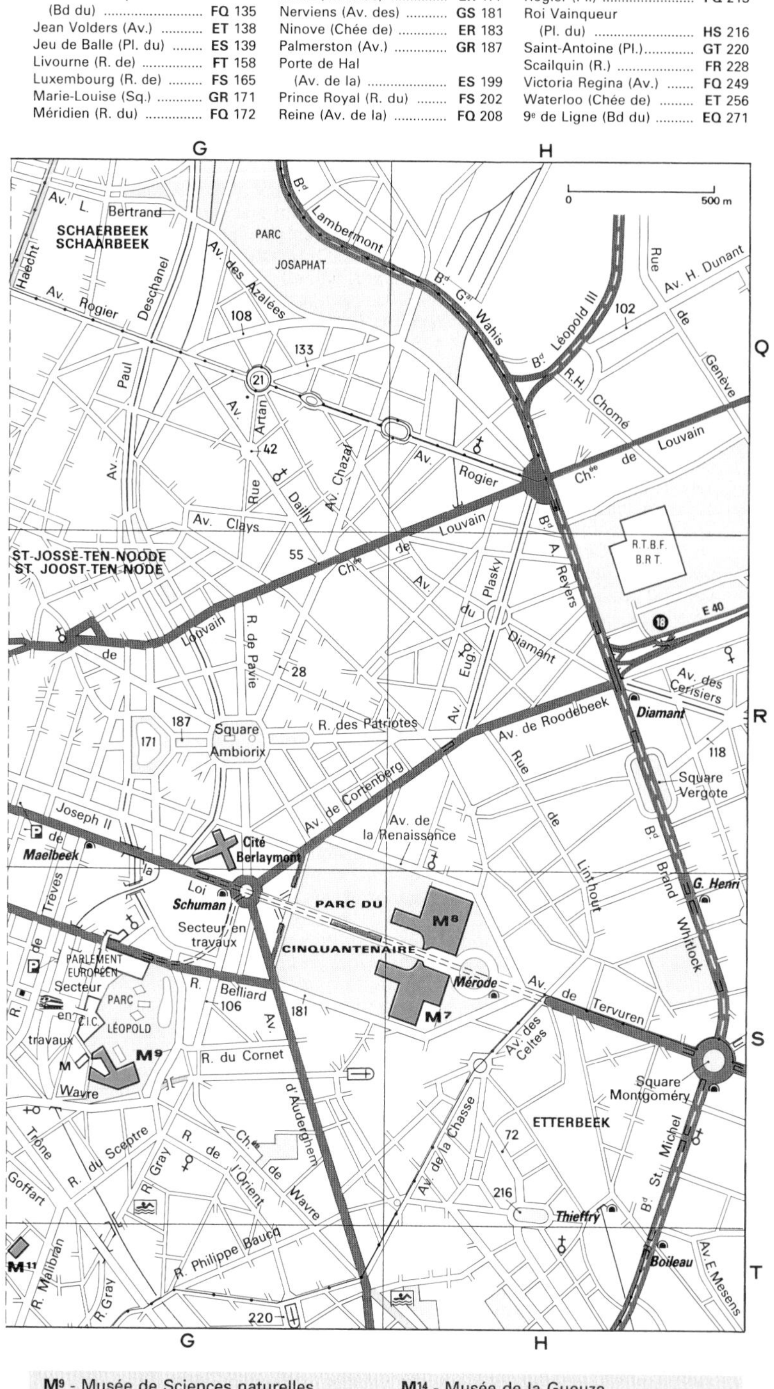

M9 - Musée de Sciences naturelles
M11 - Musée communal d'Ixelles
M14 - Musée de la Gueuze
M16 - Porte de Hal

Room 31 is a veritable shrine to the work of **Brueghel the Elder**. Several of his masterpieces are collected here and bear witness to the range of his talent and style. The *Fall of the Rebel Angels* shows the influence of Hieronymous Bosch on Brueghel at the beginning of his career. Use of irony, realism of detail, serenity of landscape, all of which are characteristic of Brueghel, are particularly evident in the famous *Census at Bethlehem* and *Fall of Icarus*, an unusual painting in which some people claim to see alchemical symbols.

The rooms reserved for the **Delporte Legacy** (1973) include a Dutch Primitive panel, *Calvary and Resurrection*, the pretty round panels by Grimmer representing the *Seasons* and a lovely work by Brueghel the Elder, *Winter Landscape with Skaters*.

17C-18C – The works of this period are gathered in the rooms around the great hall in the renovated galleries. **Rubens** is represented by very high quality paintings: his talent for large religious works is revealed in *Adoration of the Magi*, with its beautiful colours, the *Ascent to Calvary* and the *Martyrdom of St Lievin*, as well as more personal works such as the famous *Negro Heads* and the *Portrait of*

Hélène Fourment, radiating mischievousness and charm, in Room 52. A good deal of space is also devoted to **Jacob Jordaens**; several of his works are on display in Room 57: the *Satyr and Peasant*; *Allegory of Fertility*, a lively painting with a pointed sensuality; *The King drinks*; *Susanna and the Elders*. There are also good works by Cornelis De Vos, Anthony Van Dyck, David Teniers, Frans Hals, and this exceptional collection is completed by works by Dutch landscape and genre painters.

19C – *Ground floor*. This section displays works (paintings, sculptures and drawings) from neo-classicism, Romanticism, Realism and Luminism (*Linen Harvest* by Emile Claus), also from Symbolism, represented in particular by **Fernand Khnopff** (*Memories*, and the enigmatic *Caresses*). Interesting works from the French school (Gauguin, Seurat, Signac, Vuillard, Monet) and the famous *Death of Marat*, painted in 1793 by Jacques-Louis David, are also exhibited here.
An entire room is devoted to **James Ensor**, who was the bridge figure between the 19C and the 20C (*Lamplighter*, 1880; *Scandalised Masks*, 1883; *Skeletons Arguing over a Red Herring*, 1891).

★★ **Museum of Modern Art** (KZ M1) ⊙ – This museum was inaugurated in 1984 and consists of two parts. The building with the main entrance on Place Royale is also used for temporary exhibitions (3 floors). The Museum of Modern Art itself is an underground building, designed by the architects R Bastin and L Beek, who sank it down eight floors around a well of light. It houses permanent collections of 20C sculptures, paintings and drawings (from Fauvism to contemporary art).
The tour begins on level -2 in the agora, in which a large sculpture by Richard Long (*Utah Circle*, 1989) and paintings by Alan Charlton and Alan Green are displayed.
Level -3 is also devoted to contemporary art; striking statues by **Georges Segal** (figures in plaster moulded on the models themselves) as well as works by Anselme Kiefer (*Bérénice*, 1989), Henry Moore, Pol Bury, Nam June Paik and paintings by Francis Bacon and Gaston Bertrand.
Going down through the various levels makes it possible to follow the evolution of artistic movements such as Fauvism, Expressionism, Abstract art, La Jeune Peinture Belge, Cobra, Phases, Surrealism, Groupe Zéro, etc. Other particularly interesting works include those by **Rik Wouters** (*Lady with Yellow Neckband*, 1912; *Flute Player*, 1914), a very beautiful group by **Leon Spilliaert** (*Lady in Hat*, 1907; *Bather*, 1910; *Woman on a Dyke*, 1908), the representatives of the second school of Sint Martens-Latem (**Constant Permeke**, **Gust De Smet** and **Frits Van den Berghe**); the Belgian Futurists (Troyer, Schmalzigaug and Baugniet), Abstract art (Joseph Peeters and Victor Servranckx) and the members of Cobra (**Pierre Alechinsky, Karel Appel**). The works by **Paul Delvaux** (*Night Trains*; *Pygmalion*; *Public Voice*) and **René Magritte** bear witness to the importance of Surrealism in Belgium, as great as that of Symbolism in the 19C. A room is devoted to each of these artists. The Georgette and René Magritte Room regroups works which were part of collections (*The Man of the Sea*, *Midnight Marriage*, *Empire of Lights*, 1954), as well as those bequeathed to the museum by the artist's widow (*Black Magic*, *Pebble*, *Arnheim Domain*). Note also works by Chagall, Wilfredo Lam, Hans Hartung, Joan Miró, Max Ernst, Paul Klee, Giorgio de Chirico, Arman, Fontana, Piene etc.
Level -8 is devoted to contemporary art, with works by Belgian (Michel Mouffe, Dan van Severen, Bernd Lohaus, Jan Vercruysse, Walter Swennen, Jef Geys, Jan Fabre, Panamarenko, J Charlier) as well as foreign artists (Dan Flavin, Don Judd, Ulrich Ruckriem, Anne and Patrick Poirier, T Cragg). One room is given over to Marcel Broodthaers (*Red Mussels Casserole*, 1965; *Museum of Modern Art, Eagles section*, 1971).

ADDITIONAL SIGHTS *town plans on p 78 and pp 82-83.*

★★ **Museum of Musical Instruments** (**Musée instrumental**) (JZ M2) ⊙ – Only part of the collection, which consists of 6 000 instruments dating from the Bronze Age to the present, is exhibited. Wind instruments are on the ground floor, including saxophones, the invention of Dinant native Adolphe Sax. The first floor is the domain of keyboard instruments: virginals and spinets, very much in vogue from the 17C onwards, and harpsichords signed by famous names (Ruckers in Antwerp) and sometimes magnificently decorated; these were replaced in the 19C by the piano. On the second floor the string instruments include harps, lutes and violins. There is also Joachim Tielke's beautiful viola da gamba (1701), marvellously decorated. The museum also has non-European instruments (Indian, Indonesian: the gamelan) and some from European folk art.

Congress Column (KY K) – Designed by Poelaert and inaugurated in 1859, this monument commemorates the National Congress which proclaimed the Belgian constitution on the day after the 1830 Revolution. Willem Geefs's statue of Leopold II stands at its top. Two lions guard the tomb of the Unknown Soldier at the foot of the monument.
There is an interesting overall view of the city from the "Esplanade" between the buildings of the government administration district.

Palais de la Nation (KY) ⊙ – This was built under Charles of Lorraine. It stands north of Brussels Park and was restored after a fire in 1883.
It is the seat of the Chamber of Representatives and of the Senate; the **Senate Conference Room★** (Salle des Séances du Sénat) is particularly finely decorated.

Église du Finistère (JY L) – This church is home to the statue of Our Lady of Finistère.

Église St-Jean-Baptiste-au-Béguinage (**JY N**) ⏲ – This church (dedicated to St John the Baptist) stands in a quiet district. It has a façade in three main parts in the Flemish baroque style (1676), attributed to Lucas Faydherbe.
The interior is beautifully proportioned, with baroque decoration on the Gothic structures. The entablature above the large arcades is very regular; it rests on the heads of winged angels at the points where the arches meet.
There is a figure of St Dominic throwing Heresy to the ground beneath the pulpit dating from 1757.
Note the marvellous paintings by the Brussels artist **Van Loon** and various Flemish artists.
The beguine convent, which once held as many as 1 200 nuns, disappeared in the 19C.

St Catherine's Church (**JY**) is nearby. It still has the **tower** (**JY P**) from the old church, in addition to the **Black Tower** (Tour Noire) (**JY Q**), which was actually once part of the town's first fortified enclosure.

Costume and Lace Museum (**Musée du Costume et de la Dentelle**) (**JY M**[6]) ⏲ – This museum is devoted to the various crafts related to costume-making from the 17C to the 20C: Brussels lace, embroidery, trimmings.

Place Poelaert (**ES**) – This is located at the top of Galgenberg ("Mount Gallows"), once the site of the town gallows. The square is overlooked by the immense **Law Courts** (Palais de Justice) (**ES J**) ⏲ designed by Poelaert and built between 1866 and 1883. There is an extensive view from the terrace, of the Lower Town and the Marolles district with Notre-Dame-de-la-Chapelle.

Porte de Hal (**ES M**[16]) – This gateway is the only trace of the 14C fortifications. It has been restored recently and now houses a **folklore museum** ⏲, which displays folk art and dolls. Temporary exhibitions are also organised here from time to time.

Place du Jeu-de-Balle (**ES 139**) – A **flea market** (marché aux puces) ⏲ is held here on this large square at the heart of the **Marolles district**.

Botanical Gardens (**Le Botanique**) (**FQ**) ⏲ – The French-speaking community of Belgium has its cultural centre here amidst the immense greenhouses of the botanical gardens; facilities include a library, a restaurant, cinemas, theatres, exhibition spaces etc.

THE CINQUANTENAIRE *town plan on pp 82-83*

Cinquantenaire Park (**GHS**) – This was created in 1880, at the time of the fiftieth anniversary of Belgium's independence. A great building stands in it, the Palais du Cinquantenaire, its two wings joined by a monumental arcade designed by architect Girault (1905). Two halls with metal roof frameworks, dating from 1888, stand behind it. The north wing and hall contain the Army Museum, the south hall the Autoworld exhibition; the south wing contains the Royal Museums of Art and History.

★★★ **Royal Museums of Art and History** (**Musées royaux d'Art et d'Histoire**) (**HS M**[7]) ⏲ – The Nerviens Wing was added in 1966 to the Kennedy Wing. The collections are extremely rich, especially in works from Antiquity and the decorative arts.

Antiquities (Western Asia, Greece, Rome, Egypt) – *Kennedy Wing.* Western Asian civilisations are evoked on the ground floor (Palestine, Cyprus, Mesopotamia). A **model of Rome** can be seen on the mezzanine, showing the capital of the Roman Empire in the 4C, executed at a scale of 1:400 *(recorded commentary available with lighting).* The first floor is devoted to **Rome** (bronze by Septimus Severus), **Etruria** and **Greece**. The famous **Apamea mosaic** in the centre of the great inner courtyard is a fabulous scene of hunters fighting wild beasts. This flooring, created in 539, was excavated by a Belgian team from a banqueting hall in Apamea, a Syrian town destroyed by the Persians in 612. The second floor is devoted to **Egypt**: note the **Book of the Dead** in the north gallery; the reconstruction of the mastabas, tombs with historiated walls; the **Lady of Brussels**, an archaic statue going back to 2 650 BC; and the very beautiful low relief representing Queen Tiy, wife of Amenophis III.

Islamic and Byzantine art – *Nerviens Wing, access from the mezzanine of the Kennedy wing.* Ceramics, arms, miniatures, rugs and Persian and Turkish metalwork are gathered here in a beautiful collection. Cases containing icons, pieces of Russian or Greek gold- and silverwork in the Byzantine style, are on show in the nearby rotunda.

Decorative arts – *Nerviens Wing, access from the mezzanine of the Kennedy Wing and the Islamic and Byzantine art section.*
Decorative arts in Belgium are displayed in a marvellous exhibition of pre-Romanesque sculptures, gold- and silverwork (12C Tienen font), 12C ivories, ceramics (Tournai), 16C and 19C pewter, lace, textiles and embroidery *(first floor).*
The Mosan Room houses a treasure trove of ecclesiastical objets d'art, including the **Stavelot portable altar** (*c*1150) in brass and champlevé enamel, and some beautiful ivories.
The **tapestries** vie with each other in the delicacy of their execution and the splendour of their colours: the 14C *Shearing of the Sheep*, wonderfully detailed, from a Tournai workshop; and the 16C *Legend of Herkenbald*, the *Legend of Notre-Dame-du-Sablon (photograph p 26)* and the moving *Descent from the Cross*, woven with gold.
Jan Borman's *St George* (1493) stands out among the wooden **altarpieces** because of the intensely life-like figures.
There is some extremely valuable **furniture** on display.

India and Southeast Asia – *Nerviens Wing, first floor, access from the Islamic and Byzantine art section.* This section illustrates the arts, religions and traditions of India (13C Civa Nataraja bronze), Cambodia (drums and ceramics), Indonesia (models of dwellings, marionettes), Thailand and Tibet (painted banners).

Ancient Belgium – *Nerviens Wing, access from the Decorative arts section.* Excavated objects dating from the Palaeolithic Age to the Carolingian period, and reconstructions (tombs, potter's oven, hypocaust).

Royal Museum of the Army and Military History (HS M8) ⏲ – This museum illustrates the country's military history from 1789 to the present, exhibiting a rich collection of uniforms, decorations, arms and pictures. The armoured tank section exhibits Belgian vehicles (dating back to 1935) as well as models from other countries (the ex-USSR, Great Britain, the United States, France). The Air and Space section, in a large hall, has about a hundred planes. The Nieuport, a small French plane, served during the First World War, while the Spitfire and the Hurricane, both of them English, date from the Second World War.

★★ **Autoworld** (HS M7) ⏲ – Since 1986 some 450 vehicles, mostly cars, have been on display beneath the high glass roof of the south hall of the Palais du Cinquantenaire. While the exhibitions include some of the most beautiful models from the De Pauw collection, which used to be in the Manhattan Center Museum, as well as members of the Royal Veteran Car Club, most of the vehicles are from the prestigious **Ghislain Mahy collection.**

Born in Ghent in 1901, Mahy managed to collect more than 800 vehicles (running on steam, electricity or petrol) over a period of forty years. They were often in pitiful condition, but they were always brought back to life in the collector's repair shop; there are now about 300 cars in perfect working order. Mahy bought the first car in 1944: a 1921 Ford. The collection came to include many American cars, such as the little 1917 Cadillac – worth comparing with that of 1928; then those in the De Pauw collection *(ground floor, left)* dating from the 1930s and 50s. There are also many other famous makes (Buick, Chevrolet, Chrysler, Oldsmobile, Packard) and some that are less well known (Black, Detroit Electric, Willys-Overland). Particularly fine examples of English car manufacture include the makes of Bentley, Daimler, Humber, Jaguar and Rolls-Royce – note the magnificent 1921 Silver Ghost. French vehicles include the 1896 Léon Bollée minicar, a 1908 Renault 14, a 1911 Delaunay-Belleville, a 1920s Delage and a 1935 Hispano-Suiza. German car manufacture is represented by the names of Adler, Mercedes, Horch and Opel, and Italian by Alfa-Romeo, Fiat and Lancia. The Belgian makes deserve particular attention: examples from Belga Rise, FN, Fondu, Hermes, Imperia, Miesse, Nagant and Vivinus are on display, not forgetting of course the famous **Minerva**.

Minerva mascot

Antwerp citizen Sylvain de Jong first built cycles, then motorcycles; this museum contains his 1902 prototype for the Minerva. Although the line initially consisted of only three models (2, 3 and 4 cylinders), it expanded quickly until the 1930s. By 1911 the factory had 1 600 workers; in 1912 electric lights were an option on their automobiles, and then by 1914 electric ignition followed; by 1922 all four wheels had brakes. The firm acquired a solid reputation for enormously comfortable, superb quality automobiles, with almost noiseless engines. By 1930 Minerva had a range of cars from 12 to 40hp. The golden age of the luxury car was drawing to a close, however, and customers were turning to less expensive makes. In 1934 the Minerva company went bankrupt. The museum has about fifteen Minervas. The oldest one, dating from 1910, belonged to the Belgian Court under King Albert. The most luxurious is a 1930 model (40hp), which could travel up to as fast as 140km - 87 miles per hour.

Natural Science Museum (**Institut Royal**) (GS M9) ⏲ – The highlight of the museum is its collection of **iguanodon skeletons**★. In 1878 the well-preserved bones of 29 of these reptilian dinosaurs were discovered in a Bernissart mine, in the western part of the country; the animals were herbivores from the Cretacious period, and the species is long since extinct.

Ten skeletons about 10m - 33ft long have been reconstructed, while others are exhibited as they were found, lying in the sand. Other rooms present the life cycle of the invertebrates, a spider vivarium, meteorites, some crystals and the skeleton of a whale.

Cité Berlaymont (GR) – This X-shaped complex of buildings at the Schuman roundabout constituted the working quarters of 5 000 "Europeans", or EC officials. However, the premises have now been emptied, as the 1967 building failed to meet official safety standards.

THE OTHER BRUSSELS COMMUNITIES

To the east: Woluwe-St-Lambert and Woluwe-St-Pierre

Chapel of Marie-la-Misérable (DM) – This charming chapel was built in 1360 in honour of a pious young girl who refused a young man's advances and was subsequently accused by him of theft and buried alive. Miracles occurred on the site of her death.

An old post **windmill** (moulin à vent) (DL R) stands in a wood not far to the north *(access via Avenue de la Chapelle-aux-Champs).*
The 18C **Malou Palace** (DM), now a cultural centre, stands overlooking a pond in a vast park to the south.
The pretty setting of the **Mellaerts lakes** area (DN) in **Woluwe-St-Pierre** is very popular in the summer.

To the south: St-Gilles and Ixelles

These two communities south of the town, beyond the Porte Louise, constitute a residential area. **Avenue Louise** was created in the middle of the 19C to link Cambre woods with the centre of the town; it is now home to elegant fashion boutiques and antiques shops. The Louise Arcade is a modern version of the St Hubert Arcades. This district has a number of Art Nouveau buildings; the most beautiful example is Victor Horta's house.

★ **Horta Museum** (BN M10) – The museum was set up in the two narrow houses that architect Victor Horta built between 1898 and 1901 as his home and workshop. He wrote in his Memoirs: "People should please realise that I drew and created the design for each piece of furniture, each hinge and door-latch, the rugs and the wall decoration ..." This enormous amount of work resulted in a marvel of harmony and elegance, a remarkable tribute to Art Nouveau as a style in which glass and iron play the leading role and in which curves and inverse curves are combined so gracefully. The **staircase**★ is one of Horta's most beautiful creations: the lightness of the metal structure is accentuated by the golden light diffused by the glazed ceiling and the reflections from the multitude of mirrors *(see photograph p 229).*

★ **Ixelles Community Museum (Musée communal d'Ixelles)** (FGT M11) – This contains an excellent collection of 19C and 20C paintings and sculptures, in which famous Belgian and French artists are represented. The display includes a sketch by Dürer, *The Swan*, and original posters by Toulouse-Lautrec (the museum has 29 of them). Some rooms are devoted to a variety of temporary exhibitions.

★ **Abbey of Notre-Dame-de-la-Cambre** (CN S) – This old Cistercian abbey rises south of the Ixelles lakes. It now houses the Higher Institute of Architecture and Decorative Arts and the National Geographic Institute.
The beautiful **main courtyard**, with the abbey building flanked by pavilions at the corners and outbuildings in a semi-circular layout, forms a very harmonious 18C ensemble. The **church** dates from the 14C and contains a marvellous **Mocking of Christ**★ by Albert Bouts in the nave; a Stations of the Cross by Anto Carte (1886-1954); and, in the north transept arm, the 17C reliquary of St Bonifacius, the Brussels citizen who became bishop of Lausanne and died in the monastery in the 13C.
The vaulting in the chapel south of the chancel rests on brackets carved with human figures and symbolic animals.

★ **Cambre Woods** (BCN) – This wooded area is an oasis of greenery, in which undulating countryside encloses an excellent lake for boating.

Constantin Meunier Museum (BN M12) – *Rue de l'Abbaye.* This is in the residential area of the artist's (1831-1905) old workshop; alternately sculptor and painter, he devoted himself to depicting the world of work.

Ixelles Community Centre (FST H) – This was the summer residence of La Malibran. The famous singer married the Belgian violinist Bériot in 1836 and died the same year after falling from a horse.

University (Université Libre de Bruxelles) (CN U) – Part of this university, which was founded in 1834, is east of the woods. Another campus is near Ixelles cemetery.

Ixelles Cemetery (CN) – This is the burial place of, among others, French General Georges Boulanger (1837-1891), who took refuge in Brussels after his attempted coup d'état, and committed suicide in 1891 on the tomb of his mistress (Marguerite de Bonnemains, avenue 3). There is a statue of Till Eulenspiegel on the tomb of Charles de Coster (avenue 1).

Watermael-Boitsfort

St Clement's Church (CN) – This has preserved a certain rural air, with its nave and 12C Romanesque tower.

Garden-Cities of "Le Logis" and "Floréal" (CN) – *Near Square des Archiducs.* Built between 1921 and 1929, these were a model for Belgian low-income housing policies. At the end of April or the beginning of May there is a magnificent show of pink Japanese cherry blossoms in flower.

BRUXELLES
BRUSSEL

Alfred Madoux (Av.) .... DN 6
Antwerpselaan .... BK 9
Broqueville (Av. de) .... CM 30
Charleroi (Chée de) .... BM 34
Charroi (R. du) .... AN 36
Croix-du-Feu (Av. des) ...... BK 54
Delleur (Av.) .... CN 57
Demosthène Poplimont (Av.) BL 58
Edith Cavell (R.) .... BN 67
Edmond Parmentier (Av.) . DM 69
Emile Bockstael (Bd) .... BL 75
Emile Bossaert (Av.) .... AL 76
Emile Vandervelde (Av.) . DM 82
Fonsny (Av.) .... BN 94
Foresterie (Av. de la) .... CN 96
France (R. de) .... BM 100
Frans van Kalken (Av.) ... AN 103
Gén. Jacques (Bd) .... CN 109
Henneaulaan .... DL 115
Houba de Strooper (Av.) . BK 121
Houzeau (Av.) .... BN 123
Jacques Sermon (Av.) ..... BL 130
Jean Sobieski (Av.) .... BK 136
Jules van Praet (Av.) .... BK 144
Louis Schmidt (Bd) .... CN 162
Madrid (Av. de) .... BK 166
Mérode (R. de) .... BN 174
Meysse (Av. de) .... BK 175
Paepsem (Bd) .... AN 186

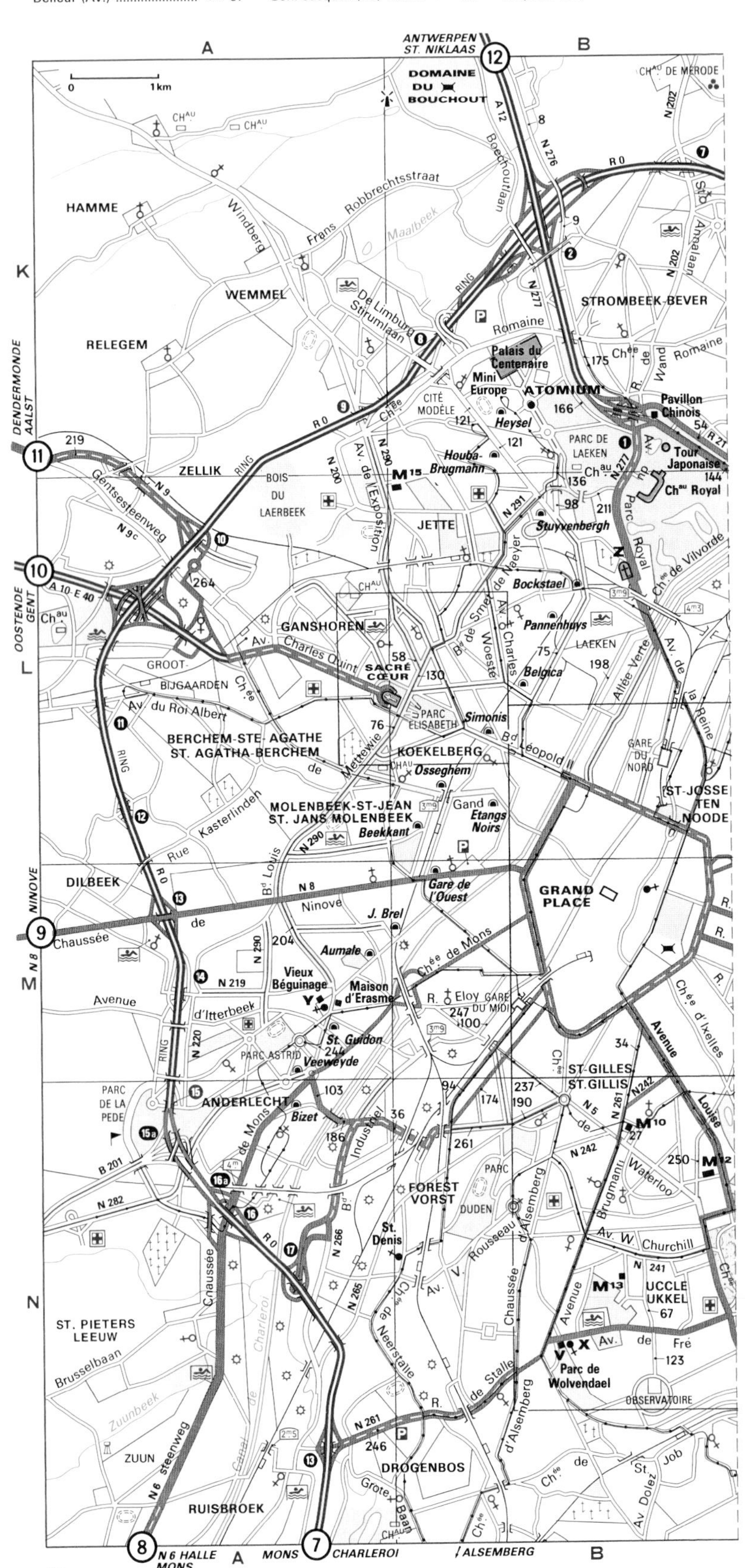

Parc (Av. du)	BN 190	Triomphe (Bd du)	CN 240	M[10] - Musée Horta
Parkstraat	CK 192	Veeweyde (R. de)	AM 244	M[12] - Musée Constantin Meunier
Plaine (Bd de la)	CN 196	Verlengde (R.)	AN 246	M[13] - Musée van Buuren
Port (Av. du)	BL 198	Vétérinaires (R. des)	BM 247	M[15] - Demeure abbatiale de Dieleghem
Prince-de-Liège (Bd)	AM 204	Vleurgat (Chée de)	BN 250	R - Moulin à Vent
Robiniers (Av. des)	BL 211	Vuurkruisenlaan	CK 252	S - Abbaye N.-D.-de-la-Cambre
Romeinsebaan	AK 219	Wezembeek (Av. de)	DM 259	V - le Cornet
Stationlei	CK 231	W. Ceuppens (Av.)	BN 261	X - Église orthodoxe russe
Stockel (Chée de)	DM 232	Zuiderlaan	AL 264	Y - Collégiale des Sts-Pierre-et-Guidon
Tervuren (Chée de)	DN 235	2e Rég. de Lanciers (Av. du)	CN 265	Z - Église N.-D.-de-Laeken
Th. Verhaegen (R.)	BN 237			

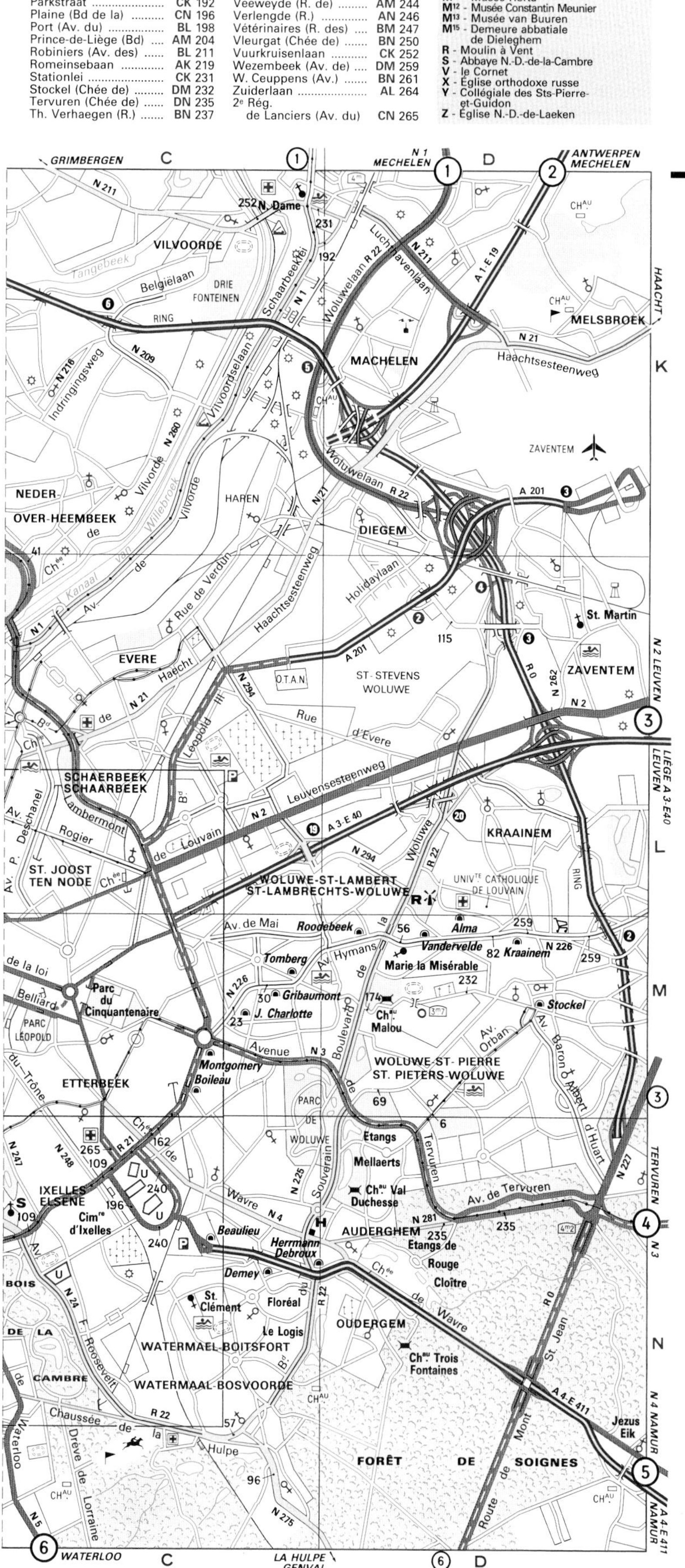

Uccle

★ **David and Alice Van Buuren Museum** (BN M13) ⏲ – *41 avenue Léo-Errera.* David van Buuren's house, built in 1928, is a worthy setting in which to exhibit part of the collection which belonged to this amateur art enthusiast. There is a version of Brueghel the Elder's **Fall of Icarus**, as well as landscapes by Hercules Seghers and Patinar, still-life paintings by Fantin-Latour, several paintings by Permeke, a series by Van de Woestyne, and also sculptures by Georges Minne and Delft ceramic ware. The gardens are charming, with a Heart Garden and a **maze** containing symbols evoking the Song of Songs.

Wolvendael Park (BN) – This vast park (10ha - 25 acres) is a pleasant spot for a stroll.
At the edge of the park is the **Cornet** (BN V), a charming inn from 1570, in which Eulenspiegel *(see Damme)* is said to have stayed. The **Russian Orthodox Church** (BN X) nearby, a charming white building surrounded by silver birches, was built in the shape of a Novgorod church.

Forest

St Denis's Church (ABN) ⏲ – This charming Gothic building, at the foot of the hill, not far from the famous Forest-National *(see Historical Notes above)*, is where the tomb of St Alène lies (12C). Only the entrance doorway remains of what was once a large abbey, founded in 1102.

Auderghem

Auderghem Community Centre (CDN H) – This complex, but nonetheless elegant building, which houses a cultural centre, stands at the crossroads of Chaussée de Wavre and Boulevard du Souverain, forming a section of the Grande Ceinture. There is an old priory (now a restaurant) slightly east of the picturesque **Rouge Cloître lakes** (DN). The painter Hugo van der Goes *(qv)* stayed here until his death in 1482. There are painting exhibitions in the abbey outbuildings.
Not far from here in the woods south of the Wavre road, stand the remains of the 14C castle, **Château des Trois Fontaines** (DN).
A vast park to the north surrounds **Château de Val Duchesse** (DN), where the Treaty of Rome was drawn up, and the 12C St Anne's Chapel.

To the west: Anderlecht

★ **Erasmus's House (Maison d'Erasme)** (AM) ⏲ – The "Swan", built in 1468 and enlarged in 1515, was one of the houses of the Anderlecht chapter where members of the community and their illustrious guests were lodged. In 1521 the most famous of these gave his name to the house: Erasmus (1469-1536).
Behind the brick walls of the shady close, there are five rooms furnished with Gothic and Renaissance furniture; the light that penetrates there is subdued, and seems to evoke the spirit of the "prince of humanists".
Crossing the ground floor, brings the visitor to the rhetoric chamber, then the chapter-house containing old master paintings such as Hieronymous Bosch's superb *Epiphany*, **Erasmus's study** with its simple writing desk *(photograph p 208)*, and the portraits of the philospher by Quentin Metsys, Dürer and Holbein (copy). The 16C statue at the foot of the staircase represents Erasmus as a pilgrim.
The **white room** upstairs, once a dormitory, contains valuable first editions, including the first edition of *In Praise of Madness*, and engraved portraits of Erasmus and his contemporaries.

Collegiate Church (Collégiale des Sts-Pierre-et-Guidon) (AM Y) ⏲ – This beautiful Late Gothic church, dedicated to St Peter and St Guy of Anderlecht, dates from the 14C and the 15C, its spire from the 19C.
Once inside, there are traces of frescoes (*c*1400) in a chapel to the south; these illustrate the life of St Guy, a labourer who died in 1012, greatly venerated as the patron saint of peasants and the protector of horses. The late-11C crypt contains the tombstone of St Guy.

Old Beguine Convent (Vieux Béguinage) (AM) – This was founded in 1252, rebuilt in 1634, and has since been restored.

Gueuze Museum (ES M14) ⏲ – *56 Rue Gheude.* This is where visitors can discover how this traditional Brussels beverage is made.

Koekelberg

★ **National Basilica of the Sacred Heart (Sacré-Coeur)** (ABL) ⏲ – This was begun in 1905, consecrated in 1951 and finally completed in 1970. The dome of this immense brick, concrete and stone building rises to 81m - 266ft above the Koekelberg summit.
Inside, the walls of brick and golden-yellow terracotta enclose a vast space; the transept is 108m - 354ft long. Notice especially the **Ciborium** above the high altar. It is surmounted by a calvary and four bronze angels, kneeling, executed by Harry Elström. The many **stained glass windows** diffuse a multi-coloured light inside the church; those in the nave were created based on cartoons by Anto Carte. There is a huge figure of Christ by Georges Minne in the chancel of the Holy Sacrament. It is possible to climb up to the **gallery-walkway** ⏲ and to the top of the **dome** ⏲, from where there is a panoramic **view** of Brussels.
At the foot of the basilica is Elizabeth Park.

To the north: Jette

Dieleghem Abbey (Demeure abbatiale de Dieleghem) (ABL M[15]) – This is the only vestige of an 11C abbey, which now houses the **National Museum of Historical Figurines** ⊙ in beautiful Louis XVI rooms. This is a rich collection of figurines illustrating historic scenes, for the most part military, from Antiquity to the present.

Laeken

Church of Our Lady of Laeken (BL Z) ⊙ – Poelaert built this church in the neo-Gothic style. It contains the royal family's tombs (crypt) and a much venerated 13C *Madonna*. The Gothic chancel of the old church can be seen in the cemetery.

Laeken Royal Palace (Château Royal) (BL) – Located in the eastern section *(not open to the public)* of Laeken Park, this is the everyday residence of the Belgian sovereigns. The façade, rebuilt in 1902 by the architect Girault, can be seen beyond the entrance gates. There is a monument opposite, in the public park, in memory of Leopold I.
The Belvédère Pavilion, the residence of Prince Albert of Liège and Princess Paola, is discreetly placed not far from this royal monument.
The **Laeken Royal Greenhouses** ⊙ are to the north of the royal estate; their architectural décor is splendid, and from a botanical point of view they are magnificent, but they are only rarely open to the public. The greenhouses were built towards the end of the last century (1874-93) by the architect, Balat. A number of galleries and pavilions containing exotic plants link the two main axes, the iron church *(not open to the public)* and the marvellous Winter Garden. The dimensions of this greenhouse are awesome (57m - 187ft interior diameter and 25.6m - 83ft high). It is quite simply a palace of glass, iron, cast iron and steel, a bold synthesis of technical and aesthetic prowess. The **Japanese Tower** ⊙ is an imitation of a Buddhist temple from the 1900 World Fair in Paris.

Chinese Pavilion (Pavillon Chinois) (BK) ⊙ – This elegant building opposite the Japanese Tower is another survivor from the 1900 World Fair; it now houses beautiful collections of porcelain ware and objets d'art from 17C, 18C and 19C China and Japan *(exhibited in rotation)*.
The nearby **fountain** is a reproduction of the famous Neptune Fountain in Bologna by Flemish sculptor Giambologna (Giovanni Bologna).

Heysel

★ **Atomium (BK)** ⊙ – A reminder of the 1958 World Fair, the 102m - 335ft high Atomium dominates the Heysel plateau. It is a symbol of the atomic age, representing a molecule of iron crystal enlarged 165 billion times. The structure, made of steel sheathed in aluminum, consists of 9 spheres 18m - 59ft in diameter, linked by tubes 29m - 95ft long and 3m - 10ft in diameter, through which it is possible to walk. Four of these spheres contain the Biogenium exhibition, "medicine on the move". The major breakthroughs of medicine, microscopy, genetics, cellular biology, virology and immunology are the main subjects handled through models and photographs, research equipment and computer technology.
A lift leads to the uppermost sphere, from which there is a panoramic view of Brussels.

The **Bruparck** stretches away from the foot of the Atomium. This vast area contains Mini-Europe *(see below)*, the Kinepolis with 24 cinemas, an Imax room with a 600m^2 – 6 458ft^2 screen, the Océade (a hall for water sports) and The Village, a group of cafés and restaurants.
The **Palais du Centenaire** can be seen further away to the north in the Parc des Expositions, which was created for the 1935 International Fair.

Mini-Europe (BK) ⊙ – All the EC countries are represented here by models (at a scale of 1:25) of buildings with a socio-cultural, historic or symbolic value. The exhibition in this 2.5ha - 6 acre park thus includes among other examples the Athens Acropolis, Danish constructions from the Viking period, the 15C Leuven Town Hall, a copy of the severe 16C Escurial monastery which Philip II had built in northwest Madrid, the 17C houses along the canals of Amsterdam, and the English town of Bath, the work of the 18C architects John Wood Sr and Jr etc. There are also a few contemporary creations in the park, such as the Ariane rocket, the TGV and a Jumbo-ferry.

EXCURSIONS

★★ Soignes Forest

59km - 37 miles southeast. Leave on ④ on the plan of the conurbation pp 88-89.

★ **Tervuren** – Tervuren **Park★**, lying northeast of Soignes Forest, was once a highly prized area for hunting; its attraction now lies in its carefully attended lawns and beautiful lakes. From the 13C to the 19C a glorious succession of castles, palaces, manor-houses and gardens made it an impressive sight. *Main entrance to the park for those in cars via Place de l'Église.*

★★ **Royal Museum of Central Africa (Musée royal de l'Afrique Centrale)** ⊙ – *Entrance in Route de Louvain.*
In 1897 King Leopold II of Belgium organised an exhibition in the Palais Colonial on the Congo, featuring the flora, fauna, art and ethnology of those faraway lands. It was such a success that it became a permanent museum, for which architect Girault constructed the current building with its Louis XVI façade from 1906 to 1910.

The museum collections display a vast overview of Africa. The sculptures and other ethnographic exhibits represent various ethnic groups and, in particular, the two main centres of production of this form of artistic expression: Central Africa, especially the Belgian Congo or later Zaïre, and West Africa. The museum is also an important scientific research centre on the African continent.

Tour – Enter through the **rotunda**, from which there is a beautiful view of the park. The **great gallery** and a few other rooms leading off from it to the right contain a remarkable selection of African objects and works of art. In the part of the gallery to the left of the rotunda the collections are exhibited by ethnographic theme (hunting, agriculture, craftmanship or social events, such as marriage or death); in the part to the right the objects are arranged by geographic area (Zaïre, north Angola, Rwanda and Burundi). There is a variety of amazing sculptures in wood, ivory, stone and metal (especially in Room 4). There is also a marvellously rich collection of jewels and accessories (Room 6). The rest of the tour provides interesting glimpses of Africa's colonial history (Livingstone and Stanley have a place of honour among the great explorers), of the African mountain landscape of Ruwenzori at various zones of altitude, as well as of the region's zoology (enormous dioramas), geology and mineralogy.

Return to the centre of Tervuren and follow the signs to the Arboretum.

★ **Arboretum** ⊙ – Tervuren's geographical arboretum, created in 1902, takes up part of Capucins woods. Tree species include those from temperate climates, classified by region: oaks, elms, ashes, birches and coniferous trees, and some exotic varieties. Note the huge resinous trees from the Pacific (sequoias and Douglas firs).

Jezus-Eik – Walkers often stop at this spot, known as Notre-Dame-au-Bois ("Our Lady in the Wood") by French-speakers, to rest a little and enjoy a Brussels speciality: bread spread with fromage blanc, flavoured with onions and radishes.

★★ **Soignes Forest (Forêt de Soignes)** (DN) – This superb forest, known as **Zoniënwoud** to Flemish-speakers, extends over a 4 380ha - 10 823 acre area. It was once part of the ancient **charcoal-burners' forest** in the area west of the Ardennes forests, in which wood charcoal was produced in Roman times. Magnificent beech trees grow thickly in this undulating countryside which once rang with the cries of hunters. Deep in the valleys, there are many traces of abbeys and their estates. One such valley is **Groenendael** (Groenendaal), in a beautifully romantic **setting**★ dotted with lakes which was widely reputed from the 14C to the 18C for its abbey. The great mystic Jan Van Ruusbroec, also called "the Admirable", lived here during the 14C. Besides major roads, there are many footpaths and bridle paths, and a few cycle paths, which offer the opportunity of a pleasant ramble.

La Hulpe – Pop 7 016. Stately houses and castles are widely scattered among the hills in this area. The 220ha - 544 acres of the **Solvay estate**, which once belonged to the family of the industrialist Solvay, were bequeathed to the State.
The magnificent **park**★★ ⊙ with its many lakes is overlooked by a **manor-house** *(not open to the public)* dating from 1840, which has been converted into a cultural centre.

Genval Lake – Brussel's inhabitants often come here at the weekend. The stretch of water is large enough to accommodate a variety of water sports; the wooded areas on the shores of the lake are a lovely setting for walks.

Rixensart Palace ⊙ – This is an imposing 17C square brick building in the Renaissance style, with turrets at the corners.
The estate has belonged to the Merode family for over a century; one of the family, Félix de Merode, was a member of the 1830 provisory government. One of his daughters married Montalembert, the famous French Catholic writer. Inside, there are beautiful tapestries (Beauvais, Gobelins), French paintings (Valentin, Nattier) and a collection of arms brought back from the Egyptian campaign by the French mathematician Monge.

Beersel Fortress

Waterloo

19km - 11.75 miles south. Leave on ⑥ on the plan (pp 88-89). See Waterloo.

Beersel and Huizingen

16km - 10 miles south. Leave on ⑦ on the plan.

Beersel – Pop 21 747. This market town has a beautiful brick **fortress**★ ⊙ built between 1300 and 1310. It has been restored to its former beauty following late-17C engravings.
It is a very romantic-looking place, surrounded by a ring of moats, in which the machicolated watchpaths are reflected, along with the three watch turrets and crowstepped gables.

Huizingen – Its **provincial recreation area** ⊙ covers 90ha - 22 acres. It is carefully maintained, a real oasis of greenery at the heart of an industrial region.

Gaasbeek

12km - 7.5 miles southwest.

Gaasbeek palace and grounds★ ⊙ – Gaasbeek palace, which stands at the edge of valleyed grounds, was extensively restored in the late 19C and now houses a well-stocked museum. The whole estate was bequeathed by its owner in 1921, and has belonged to the Flemish community since 1981. The famous Count of Egmont *(qv)* spent the last three years of his life here.
The **museum** has preserved beautiful furniture, a great number of antique exhibits and magnificent **tapestries★** (Tournai, 15C, Brussels, 16C and 17C), including the five episodes of the story of Thomas (main staircase). The archives room has preserved Rubens's will. There is a view from the terrace that brings to mind the works of Brueghel the Elder, who came to paint this Payottenland region, particularly at St.-Anna-Pede; the church from this region can be identified in one of his paintings.

Meise

14km - 8.75 miles north.

★ **Bouchout Domain (Domaine du Bouchout)** (BK) ⊙ – This estate lies south of Meise, with magnificent **gardens** surrounding the **castle** (14C to 17C). This is where Empress Charlotte died, sister of Leopold II and widow of Maximilian, Emperor of Mexico. The castle makes a pretty picture, its crenellated towers reflected in the calm waters of the old moat.
The park is occupied by the **National Botanical Garden**, particularly notable for the **Plantenpaleis★★** ⊙. There is a signposted route leading through the world of tropical and subtropical plants in these well-maintained pavilions. Classification by geographical region does nothing to alter the beauty of the luxuriant plant-life.

Grimbergen

16km - 10 miles north. On the A 12 until Meuse, then turn right.

Premonstratensian abbey church – This is one of the most interesting examples of baroque architecture and ornamentation in Belgium (1660-1725). It was never actually completed. The chancel is very long and extends into a square tower. The interior owes its majestic proportions to the height of the vaulting and of the cupola. It has preserved its sumptuous furnishings, most notably four **confessionals★** on which allegories and characters from the Old and New Testament are alternately depicted, sculpted by the Antwerp artist Hendrik Frans Verbruggen. The 17C **stalls** are interesting. The church is also home to 15 paintings by Flemish old masters (17C-18C). The **large sacristy** (1763) north of the chancel is decorated with remarkable panelling; on the ceiling, there are grisailles dedicated to St Norbert, founder of the Order, and a fresco.
There are beautiful 17C paintings in the small vestry.

Vilvoorde

12km - 7.5 miles north. On the N 1.

Church of Our Lady (N. Dame) (CK) ⊙ – This Gothic church has magnificent baroque **stalls★** (1663) in carved wood which came from Groenendael Abbey *(see Soignes Forest above).*
The 17C pulpit is by Artus Quellin the Younger.

Zaventem

10km - 6.25 miles east. On the Chaussée de Louvain; then turn left.

St Martin's Church (St. Martin) (DL) – This houses an interesting Van Dyck painting of *St Martin Dividing His Cloak.*

Manneken Pis

CANAL DU CENTRE Hainaut

Michelin maps 409 F4 or 214 folds 2-3

The Canal du Centre was constructed between 1882 and 1917 to link the Meuse basin with that of the Scheldt and create a direct line of communication between Germany and France. The greatest problem was reducing the 90m - 295ft difference in height between the two basins. This was finally resolved by the building of 4 canal lifts and 6 locks which are still operational.
After the passing of the law of 9 March 1957 requiring major Belgian canals to meet European standards (a capacity for 1 350-ton vessels), this canal was given a new layout and the hydraulic lifts and locks were replaced with the Strépy-Thieu boat lift.

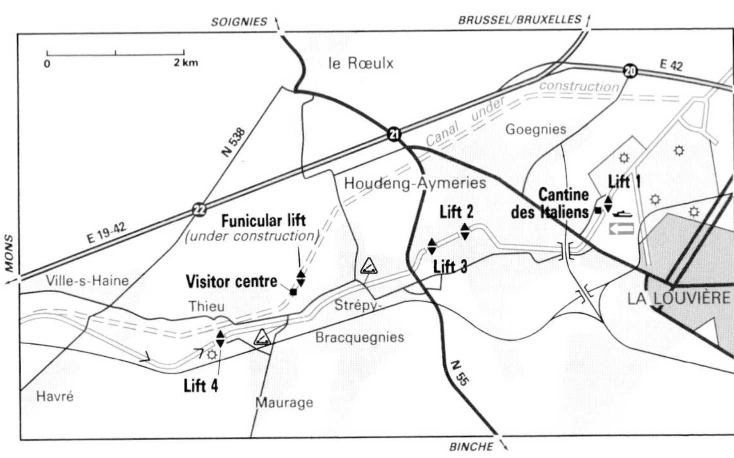

★ **The hydraulic lifts** (ascenseurs hydrauliques) – These beautiful metal structures were designed by a London firm and built by the Cocherill factories; they were actually put in place between 1888 and 1917. The principle is very simple: the barges take their places in two basins filled with water, one in the upper part of the canal and the other in the lower part. The two containers, which are fixed to enormous pistons, constitute a sort of hydraulic balance. The addition of extra water into the upper container makes it sink, while the principle of counter-balanced vessels makes the other rise.

Strépy-Thieu boat lift (ascenseur à bateaux) – It was decided to construct a canal bridge leading to an enormous funicular lift, as a complement to the new layout of the Canal du Centre. There is a model and a film in the **visitor centre** (pavillon d'accueil) ⏲ giving an idea of the size, technical details and execution of the pro-

Hydraulic lift on the Canal du Centre

ject since 1982. The project chosen to resolve the problem of the 73.25m - 240ft difference in height in the canal's new route will result in impressive dimensions: 110m - 361ft high, 130m - 426ft long, and 75m - 246ft wide; the weight being transferred to the ground is 300 000 tons. Two steel tubs, 112m - 367ft by 12m - 39ft, suspended by cables and balanced by counterweights, can independently go up or down in 6-7 minutes. Only 4 minutes will be necessary for a barge to get completely beyond the drop. Therefore, in 1994 or 1995, the date for the scheduled opening of the new system, the current waterway, which can only let pass 300-ton boats in 5 hours, will be replaced so that it can handle 1 350-ton boats in 2 hours.

Boat trip to visit the lifts ⊙ – *2 hour 30min trip; departure from the Cantine des Italiens.*

This pleasant trip on the canal edged with trees and houses makes it possible to imagine the life of the sailors: the passage through the hydraulic lifts, the turning or lift bridge, manipulated by the bridgemen or lockmen. The landing-stage is near the **Cantine des Italiens**, workmen's living quarters built in 1945 to receive Italian workers. Taking lifts 2 and 3 makes it possible to see how they work; in the machine room near lift 3 one can see how very highly-compressed water is used to work the pistons. This visit can be completed by taking lift 1 to the **exhibition** ⊙ devoted to canal lifts throughout the world.

CHARLEROI Hainaut

Pop 208 021 (conurbation)

Michelin maps 409 G4 or 214 fold 3

Town plan in the current Michelin Red Guide Benelux

Charleroi is a major intersection of a number of main roads and railway lines; it is also near the coal-mining basin and is one of the metropolises of the Belgian economy. Its busy streets, its shops, its liveliness all make the capital of the "Pays Noir" (Black Country) an attractive city.

Two main districts lie at the heart of this sprawling city: the **upper city**, crowded around the modern belfry in the south; and the **lower city**, the commercial section, lies what was once an island in the Sambre, but where part of the river's course has been filled in.

Military past – In 1666 the government of the Spanish Low Countries, worried by Louis XIV's ambitions, had the village of Charnoy turned into a fortress; in homage to the Spanish king Charles II, it was renamed Charleroi. Louis XIV captured the fortified town in June 1667. Vauban reinforced the ramparts of the upper town, then built the lower town to maintain economic activity. Industry (glass works) was attracted to the region by its coal supply. Charleroi became the prize at stake in many a hard fought battle until 1868, when the ramparts were converted into boulevards. The town was captured by Jourdan in 1794 and served as a base first for the army of the French Republic, then for Napoleon's troops.

The Battle of Charleroi took place in 1914 (21-23 August), during which the French failed in their attempt to block the Germans from crossing the Sambre on the 21 August; Charleroi fell. Nevertheless the German advance was stalled momentarily, until the French troops, almost surrounded, were forced to retreat on the evening of the 23 August, just before German reinforcements arrived on the 24.

Industry – Industry has been attracted here mainly because of the coal: first the glass-makers from 1577 onwards, then metallurgy (founderies, manufacture works for nails, wire and rolled sheet-metal), which made particularly good progress from the early 19C. Nowadays, the iron, steel and glass industries are still very much present, but manufacturing has diversified into electric, electromechanical, chemical, pharmaceutical, printing and other industries. Two institutes of higher education train specialised technicians and engineers.

The canal from Charleroi to Brussels links the Sambre to the Scheldt via Brussels and the maritime canal. The Sambre then flows into the Meuse at Namur.

The Entre-Sambre-et-Meuse processions – The towns and villages in the region to the south of Charleroi between the rivers Sambre and Meuse hold particularly large numbers of war memories. They also feature prominently in the Belgian calendar of folkloric events, because of the military processions – **"marches"** – that have been held here since the 17C.

These are probably an echo of the troubled period of reforms, when religious processions were flanked by armed rural militias; these highly military-seeming displays now honour local patron saints.

On the day of the festival it is virtually a small army which parades through the streets, sometimes escorting the statue of a saint. The regimental "sappers" come first, then the drum corps, the fifes and the brass band; then come the soldiers armed with guns, firing volleys into the air, with soldiers on horseback and even canteen-keepers. Since Napoleon, the uniform of the First Empire has been extremely popular.

About forty towns organise military processions *(see Introduction: Folklore and Traditions)*; the St Roch procession at **Ham-sur-Heure** has more than 700 people, including the "Mons volunteers of the 1789 Brabant Revolution" *(see Turnhout)*. The longest procession, 35km - 28 miles long, involving 5 000 people, is in **Gerpinnes**. A small **Museum of Entre-Sambre-et-Meuse Folklore Processions** ⊙ in this village exhibits the marchers' military costumes. The **Fosses-la-Ville** procession is as rare as it is splendid, taking place only every 7 years *(see Namur: Excursions)*.

Outside the area between the Sambre and the Meuse, the Mary Magdalene procession in **Jumet** *(4km - 2.5 miles north of Charleroi)* is interesting too. This is the oldest in all of Wallonia, dating back to the year 1380; it has an unusual variety of costumes.

THE UPPER CITY *time: 1 hour*

Belfry (Beffroi) – Like the town hall of which it is part, the belfry was built between 1930 and 1936. With a height of 70m - 230ft it rises above the many busy streets which converge in a star-shape at Place Charles-II. The **Museum of Fine Art** ⏲ is in the town hall; exhibits include works by François-Joseph Navez (1787-1869), who studied with David, Pierre Paulus, Magritte and Delvaux.

Place du Manège – This great square is where part of the open-air market is held every Sunday. Round it, the Palais des Expositions (1954) houses exhibitions, and the Palais des Beaux-Arts (concert and entertainment hall) is the home of Belgium's French Community Choreographic Centre.

★ **Glass Museum (Musée du Verre)** ⏲ – *10 boulevard Defontaine, near the Palais de Justice.*
The premises of the National Institute of Glass can be recognised by the reddish tinted glass of the windows. The exhibition is remarkable. It presents the art of glass-making and various techniques, from their origins to the present, in an interesting way *(recorded 40-minute commentary in several languages)*. The permanent exhibition downstairs provides a look at Belgian glass products as well as a chance to see the temporary exhibitions.

Charleroi archaeological museum – A room downstairs in the basement of the Glass Museum recalls the region's Roman and Merovingian past, through the craftsmanship of the pottery and earthenware excavated in the Sambre basin.

EXCURSIONS

Mont-sur-Marchienne – *3km - 1.75 miles south. Access via the Porte de la Villette exit on the ring road, or the Mont-sur-Marchienne exit on the R 3 ring road.*
The **Photography Museum**★ ⏲ is in an old neo-Gothic Carmelite convent. The history of photography can be retraced by going through the rooms surrounding the old cloister. The visitor can follow the development of this art from its beginnings not only by seeing the changes in equipment (from the camera obscura and the daguerreotype to holography), but also by looking at the evolution in photographic art. Work by the world's greatest photographers illustrates this evolution. The museum aims to be a "living" institution, and has a library of more than 2 000 volumes on photography, in addition to organising temporary exhibitions all year long; these feature very fine work which is later published.

Sambre Valley – *26km - 16 miles. Leave Charleroi by taking the N 53 in the direction of Beaumont. When 5km - 3 miles from the centre, turn towards Montignies-le-Tilleul and reach Landelies by crossing the N 579, then the Sambre.*

Upstream from Landelies the Sambre River flows through a green, steep-walled valley, a setting which is greatly appreciated by anglers and ramblers alike.

★ **Aulne Abbey** – *See Aulne Abbey.*

Follow the road to reach Gozée.

There is a beautiful view of the ruins from above the abbey.

Gozée – It is worth taking a look at the **Zeupire Stone** (pierre de Zeupire) *(on the left near a large café when heading towards Beaumont)* on the way through. This is a pinkish limestone megalith weighing 20 tons which is thought to be the only trace left of an ancient cromlech.

Turn back and take the N 59.

Thuin – *See Thuin.*

Lobbes – Pop 5 316. The famous abbey, like that of Aulne, was founded in the 7C by St Landelin; it stood near the Sambre, but was destroyed in 1794.
The **collegiate church of St Ursmer** is at the top of the hill, where it replaced a funerary church built by St Ursmer in about 713. The present one dates back to the Carolingian period, and was enlarged in the 11C; the chancel and crypt are Romanesque, as are the porch and the west tower, which seem influenced by the Mosan school. A tower was added above the transept crossing in the 19C.
Notice the tombs of St Ursmer and St Erasmus in the crypt. The pillars here were reworked in the 16C.

★ CHIMAY Hainaut

Pop 9 527

Michelin maps 409 F-G5 or 214 fold 13

The little town of Chimay is at the foot of the "Hainaut boot", on the southern edge of the vast forest of Rance. One of its best-known features is the palace, of which there is a lovely view from the Eau Blanche bridge. The palace recalls the 14C author **Froissart**, who wrote some famous *Chroniques*, as well as Mme Tallien.

The Princess of Chimay – **Mme Tallien**, born Theresa Cabarrus, was one of the most beautiful women of her time. In 1805 she married for the third time, taking as her husband the Prince of Chimay François-Joseph, and so spent the rest of her otherwise turbulent life (1773-1835) in the calm of the palace.
Having been saved from the Bordeaux scaffold by the proconsul Tallien, she was moved to a Paris prison. From there she inspired Tallien to overthrow Robespierre, earning herself the name of Notre-Dame-de-Thermidor. Tallien married her shortly thereafter.

Palace ⊙ – This first belonged to the Croÿ family; then, in 1804, it passed to Riquet de Caraman, a descendant of the Riquet who built the Midi Canal in the 17C and a relative of the famous French politician and orator, Count Mirabeau. It was partially destroyed by a fire in 1935 and rebuilt according to old plans in the late Renaissance style. Its bluish limestone façade is somewhat subdued at the far end of a vast esplanade.

Inside, there is a drawing room with a terrace overlooking the Eau Blanche Valley from a height of 16m - 53ft. There are two portraits in this room which recall Mme Tallien: one by Gérard, the other painted when she was older. Her first son Joseph had the charming rococo theatre built in 1863 which is richly decorated with gilded stuccowork; it is a replica of the one at Fontainebleau (southeast of Paris). La Malibran was among the many artists invited here.

The chapel, with pretty, depressed vaulting, contains the banners of Louis XI; these came from the Carrouges château in Normandy. (Louis XI himself captured Chimay in 1447).

The baptismal robe of the King of Rome and various Napoleonic memorabilia are on display in a small living room.

Collegiate Church **(Collégiale des Sts-Pierre-et-Paul)** ⊙ – This 16C church built in limestone blocks still has its beautiful 13C chancel. There is a remarkable recumbant effigy of Charles de Croÿ, chamberlain and godfather to Emperor Charles V (died in 1552), as well as four plaques in memory of illustrious members of the Chimay family. Note also the interesting 17C stalls and a triumphal cross (*c*1550), the Latin epitaph of the chronicler Froissart, in the first chapel on the south side upon entering the church. Froissart was also canon at Chimay and died there in 1410. A monument can be seen on the square where members of the Chimay family are represented, including Mme Tallien and her husband, wearing a cape.

EXCURSIONS

★ **Virelles Lake** **(Étang de Virelles)** ⊙ – *3km - 1.75 miles northeast.*

This nature reserve covers a 100ha - 247 acre area. The much frequented lake is surrounded by woods and is one of the largest natural stretches of water in Belgium. It is possible to get a meal, or to hire pedal craft and games for children at the rest area.

Abbey **(Abbaye Notre-Dame-de-Scourmont)** – *10km - 6.25 miles south via Bourlers.*

Founded in 1850, this is now occupied by Trappist monks. The sobre-looking buildings stand around a central courtyard, where the church's bare façade can be seen (1949).

The monks make a delicious, dark, fruity beer known by the name of "Trappiste de Chimay".

Cheese made with beer, and Chimay special brew "Grande Réserve"

COO Liège

Michelin maps 409 K4 or 214 fold 8 – 8.5km - 5.25 miles west of Stavelot – Local map see AMBLÈVE VALLEY

This lively holiday resort (ski slopes at Wanne and Brume) is in a mountain setting. It is well known for its magnificent **waterfall★**, where the seething, foaming waters of the Amblève pour down with a thunderous roar. *Floodlighting every evening.* In the 18C the Amblève formed a long meander at this point, which erosion had caused almost to form a complete circle. Could the Stavelot monks have had the idea of piercing the rock to complete the work that Nature had already begun? In any case, a waterfall eventually formed as a result of the drop in level.

Lancre Mountain – There is a broad **panorama★** of the Amblève Valley from the tower built at the summit of this mountain *(access by chairlift).* The Coo-Trois-Ponts electric pumping installations can also be seen, where the meander known as the Tour de Coo, contained by two dikes, forms the lower basin. At night, as is the case in Vianden *(qv)*, the pumps draw the water back up to the upper reservoirs of Brume so that extra energy supplies can be produced for periods of peak consumption.

★ COURTRAI See Kortrijk

COUVIN Namur

Pop 13 021

Michelin maps 409 G5 or 214 fold 14

Couvin's rows of slate roofs can be seen along the shaded quays lining the Eau Noire river. Overlooking the town is a limestone crag (Falize), on which a castle once stood, destroyed by Louis XIV in 1672. This is an increasingly popular holiday town at the heart of a region ideal for walks *(signposted)* and river-fishing. Couvin is also famous for its cuisine: *poulet à la Couvinoise* (Couvin chicken), *escavèche* (fried fish dish) etc.
Foundery-work is a very old activity in the region. There is an exhibition of firebacks at the Eau Noire Founderies.
In 872 the Benedictines from the abbey of St-Germain-des-Prés in Paris evangelised the region; this is why the main street is named Faubourg St-Germain.

Cavernes de l'Abîme ⊙ – These caves (abîme: abyss) were once inhabited by prehistoric man and were also used as a refuge during the Roman period and the Middle Ages. An audiovisual presentation on Belgian prehistory is shown in one of the most impressive of the caves. A small museum complements the presentation. There is a pretty view of Couvin from the top of the stairs outside.

Round tour of 17km - 10.5 miles to the west of Couvin – *Take the N 99 and turn left at Pétigny.*

★ **Neptune Caves** (Grottes de Neptune) ⊙ – *5km - 3.25 miles from Couvin.* The Eau Noire river, so called because of the black rock at the bottom of its course, disappears underground in the Adugeoir chasm before reappearing near Nismes. It is possible to visit three superposed galleries with their beautiful, well displayed concretions. While the Eau Noire has not flowed in the upper gallery for centuries, it fills the middle course during flood periods. It is possible to take a pleasant boat trip in the lower part of the caves, where the subterranean river flows; the visitor can admire a spectacular underground **waterfall**. The end of the trip is enhanced by an exceptional son-et-lumière show.

Return to Pétigny, take the N 99 again and turn left towards Nismes.

Nismes – The Eau Noire, after having gone through the Neptune Caves, reappears above ground here and flows into the Eau Blanche to form the Viroin. Nismes is a popular summer holiday resort. There are many geological curiosities in the surrounding limestone area, including the **Fondry des Chiens** *(access by Rue Orgeveau)*, the most impressive of these twisting abysses, bristling with monoliths, which crisscross the plateau east of the town. There is also a beautiful view of the surrounding countryside from here.

Mariembourg – This little town is named after Mary of Hungary, the governor of the Low Countries who had it built in 1542. The geometrically laid-out town was fortified (no traces remain today) and faced the Place de Maubert-Fontaine on French territory opposite. Mariembourg was reputed to be impregnable, but was captured in 1554 by the King of France Henri II *(see Binche)*, forcing Emperor Charles V to create Philippeville *(qv)*. Mariembourg was recaptured by the Spanish in 1559 and then yielded to the French a century later. It remained French until 25 July 1815, the date on which the town defenders were forced to capitulate to the Prussians, although they were granted full war honours for their courage.
Mariembourg is the departure point for the **Three Valleys Railway** (Chemin de fer des Trois Vallées) ⊙, a tourist train that heads for Treignes through the picturesque **Viroin Valley**; it also goes through the Eau Blanche Valley on its way to Chimay.

Excursion in the French border region – *20km - 12.5 miles south.*
The wild region of moors and forests near the French border is known as the **Pays des Rièzes et des Sarts**. The forest *(rièzes)* areas, where the soil is poor, are partly used for raising livestock. The region's butter and cheese is well known and widely appreciated.

Take the Rocroi road, then the N 964, before turning towards Brûly-de-Pesche.

Brûly-de-Pesche – In a wood near a spring, on the site of a traditional pilgrimage in veneration of St Méen, **Hitler's bunker** (Abri d'Hitler) ⊙ is to be found. Hitler made this place his general headquarters from 6 June to 4 July 1940, directing the French campaign from here together with his staff. The small concrete bunker was built in great haste.

Cul-des-Sarts – A **regional museum** (Musée des Rièzes et des Sarts) ⊙, evoking local traditional life, is in a little half-timbered house with a thatched roof.

★ DAMME West-Vlaanderen

Pop 10 482

Michelin maps 409 C2 or 213 fold 3 – 7km - 4.3 miles north of Bruges

The pretty little town of Damme, which has a slightly melancholy feeling about it owing to the decline in its importance, is on the old Zwin estuary. It served as Bruges's outer harbour, and it was for this reason that the town's history has always been so strongly influenced by Bruges's own history. All sorts of merchandise went through here, although Damme specialised particularly in the wine trade. The marriage of Charles the Bold and Margaret of York was celebrated here with great pomp and ceremony in 1468; but by the end of the 15C, Damme was already suffering from Bruges's decline.
One of the earliest Flemish writers, **Jacob van Maerlant** (*c*1225-late 13C) came from here, as did **Till Eulenspiegel**. Eulenspiegel was the hero of the picaresque novel (1867) by Charles de Coster *(qv)* and waged continual conflict against the tyranny of Emperor Charles V and Philip II.

SIGHTS

★ **Town Hall (Stadhuis)** ⊙ – This dates from the 15C and was restored in the 19C; the town market used to have its stalls on the ground floor here.
The fine façade, with its watch turrets and flight of steps, is decorated with pretty statues supporting historiated corbels, executed with a mixture of mischievous verve and charm. There is a niche in which Charles the Bold is holding out a wedding ring to his fiancée, Margaret of York.
There are still magnificent carved beams inside. One of the figures is said to represent the writer Jacob van Maerlant.

Church of Our Lady (O.-L.-Vrouwekerk) ⊙ – This dates from the 13C and 14C. The apse, between the flat chevets of the two side chapels, has beautiful lancet windows. Many of the town's inhabitants left at the beginning of the 17C, when Damme had been forced to end its port activities and was turning itself into a fortress; it was at this time that the church was considered too big, and the nave was demolished. The ruins still have a gallery of Tournai-style triplet windows. A series of late-13C wooden statues representing the apostles can be seen inside; note also the baroque altarpiece against the north wall, a *Christ of Miracles* carried in religious processions, such as that of the Holy Blood in Bruges.
The tall square **tower★** ⊙, which has lost its spire, is remarkable. It overlooks a charming little square shaded by lime trees with the great roofs of the hospice along its edge. There is a **view** of the town from the top of the tower: hills mark the location of the 17C fortifications. The coast can be seen in clear weather.

St John's Hospital (St.-Jans Hospitaal) ⊙ – This was founded in the 13C, then later enlarged and turned into a hospice. It is possible to visit the chapel and the **museum**, where furniture, paintings, faïences, liturgical objects and sculptures (statuette of St Margaret of Antioch) evoke the rich past of the hospital and the town.

Till Eulenspiegel Museum (Tijl Uilenspiegelmuseum) ⊙ – This is near the Town Hall in a picturesque, double-gabled 15C house called De Grote Sterre (The Great Star); books, drawings, paintings and stained glass windows depict Till and his entourage.

Mill (De Schellemolen) ⊙ – This mill on the banks of the canal has been restored and is operational, grinding grain.

★ DENDERMONDE Oost-Vlaanderen — Pop 42 446

Michelin maps 409 F2 or 213 fold 5

Dendermonde is in a strategic position on the confluence of the Dender with the Scheldt (Dendermonde: mouth of the Dender). Louis XIV was forced to abandon his siege of the town in 1667 because of a flood brought about by the town's inhabitants. "Accursed town!" he cried, "I would need an army of ducks to capture you!"
Dendermonde suffered badly in September 1914 after Antwerp's surrender. Every year *(see the Calendar of Events at the end of this guide)* there is a parade of giants held here. The parade with Bayard the horse, ridden by the four Aymon sons *(qv)*, is organised every ten years *(see the Calendar of Events at the end of this guide)*. Legend has it that this illustrious horse was drowned in the Scheldt at Dendermonde, on Charlemagne's orders.

SIGHTS

Market Square (Grote Markt) – This still has its old charm even though part of it has been rebuilt; there are two important buildings worth taking a look at here.

Town Hall (Stadhuis) – This former cloth market was rebuilt in the Flemish Renaissance style after the First World War; all that remained of the original was the square 14C belfry with its corner turrets.
There is a pretty view of the Dender (Oude Dender) from behind the Town Hall.

Municipal Museum (Stedelijk Oudheidkundig Museum) ⊙ – This museum is located in a former meat market (vleeshuis) dating from 1460. It is flanked by an octagonal turret. Collections concerning the town's archaeology and history are exhibited in a pretty medieval setting.

★★ **Church of Our Lady (O.-L.-Vrouwekerk)** ⊙ – This is on a spot surrounded by chestnut trees that can be seen from the museum's rear façade. It was built in the 13C and 14C, and is surmounted by an octagonal tower above the transept crossing which is a blend of Gothic, Brabant and Scaldian styles.
There is a beautiful collection of **works of art★** inside. Note the Romanesque font in the south side aisle, in blue Tournai stone, the sides decorated with symbolic pictures concerning baptism. The main events of the life of St Paul the Apostle are on the two friezes. He is depicted among the other apostles on the sides of the basin. Two paintings by Van Dyck can be seen nearby: a *Calvary* and an *Adoration of the Shepherds*.
Admire another *Adoration of the Shepherds*, attributed to the 16C Flemish painter Herri met de Bles. The north transept arm and the chancel still have 15C and 17C frescoes.

Beguine Convent (Begijnhof) – *Access via the Brussels road (Brusselsestraat) and then to the right.* Tall 17C houses stand around the inner courtyard. There are little **museums** ⊙ at nos 11, 24 and 25.

DEURLE Oost-Vlaanderen

Michelin maps 409 D2 or 213 fold 4 – 11km - 6.75 miles southwest of Ghent

Deurle, on the edge of the Leie in the region dear to the Flemish Expressionist painters of St.-Martens-Latem *(qv)*, stands half-hidden by the green foliage of the many flower-bedecked villas.

Gustave De Smet Museum ⊙ – The house to which Ghent artist Gustave (Gust) De Smet (1877-1943) retired to paint from 1935 to his death has become a museum. The workshop and the interior are both unchanged and contain many works by this artist from the second group of St.-Martens-Latem artists.

Léon De Smet Museum ⊙ – This house was built in 1969 by the last companion of Léon De Smet (1881-1966), Gust's brother. It still has the painter's furniture and everyday objects that he reproduced in his paintings. About twenty of his paintings and drawings are exhibited.

Mevrouw Jules Dhondt-Dhaenens Museum ⊙ – This long white brick building next to the Léon De Smet Museum was built in 1969. It offers a good overview of Flemish Expressionism, which developed from the Latem school of art, with great masters like Permeke (*Lady in the Green Hat, Golden Landscape*), Van den Berghe, Gustave De Smet (*Twilight, Farm, Shooting Gallery*) and the tragic mysticism of the precursor Albert Servaes (*Executioner, The Passion, The Tomb, Resurrection*).
This collection is completed by a few sculptures and an exhibition room.

★ DIEST Brabant Pop 21 512

Michelin maps 409 I3 or 213 folds 8, 9

Diest lies in a bend formed by the Demer and is a peaceful community surrounded by a fortified enclosure of ramparts, some of which still are still standing.
Like Breda in the Netherlands, Dillenburg in Germany, and Orange in France, Diest was the fief of the **House of Orange**, of which the most famous member was William of Nassau or **William the Silent** (1533-1584), who led the revolt of the Netherlands against Spain. Heir to his cousin René of Chalon, Prince of Orange born at Diest, he founded the Orange-Nassau dynasty to which the present Queen Beatrix of the Netherlands belongs. Philip-William, William's eldest son, was buried in the Church of St Sulpitius and St Dionysius.
Jan Berchmans died here in 1621 at the age of 22; he became the patron saint of the young (born in the house at no 24 in the street of the same name).

SIGHTS

Market Square (Grote Markt) (**AZ 7**) – This is surrounded by interesting 16C and 18C houses as well as containing the 18C town hall. The church stands in the middle of the square.

Church of St Sulpitius and St Dionysius (St.-Sulpitius en St.-Dionysiuskerk) (**AZ**) ⊙ – This church was built from the 14C to the 16C in the Brabant style; the various stages of construction can be seen from the type of stone: local ferruginous sandstone (chancel, nave) and white stone (unfinished 16C tower). The church has a large carillon.
There is an openwork triforium inside, as well as interesting **works of art**★. The beautiful 18C woodwork – pulpit, organ cases – is also noteworthy. The choir **stalls** with their amusing misericords representing the capital sins and the proverbs are interesting; note also the 17C tabernacle with niches decorated in the Italian style; the 16C triptych, *Adoration of the Magi*; the 13C *Virgin with Child* (Sedes Sapientiae).
The church treasury is in a room behind the chancel.

★ **Community Museum** (Stedelijk Museum) (**AZ H**) ⊙ – This is in the town hall crypts *(right-hand door under the flight of steps)*. The medieval setting shows the museum off to its best advantage. A 15C **Last Judgement** painted on wood is exhibited under the 14C red sandstone Gothic vaulting; there is also a *Virgin with Child* from 1345 in marble, which came from the beguine convent; and 15C and 16C armour.
The next room, clearly of Romanesque influence, with the brick cupolas supported by short pillars, is an old seigneurial brewery; the wells still exist. Notice the 15C chandelier in deerhorn, gold and silver. The guild rooms and the aldermen's chamber, with their carved furniture and statues, and the gold- and silverwork cases containing beautiful 17C and 18C **guild chains of office** complete the collection.

Guild chain of office

DIEST

Botermarkt	AZ 2	St Jan Berchmansstr.	AZ 17	Koestraat	BZ 81
F. Moonsstraat	AZ 5	Delphine Alenuslaan	AZ 3	Overstraat	BY 14
Grote Markt	AZ 7	Ed. Robeynslaan	BZ 4	Pesthuizenstraat	BY 15
Ketelstraat	AZ 12	Graanmarkt	BZ 6	Refugiestraat	AY 16
Koning Albertstr.	BY	Guido Gezellestr.	BZ 8	St. Jansstraat	BZ 18
		H. Verstappenplein	BZ 9	Schotelstraat	AZ 19
		Kattenstraat	BZ 10	Vestenstraat	BY 21
				Wolvenstraat	BY 22

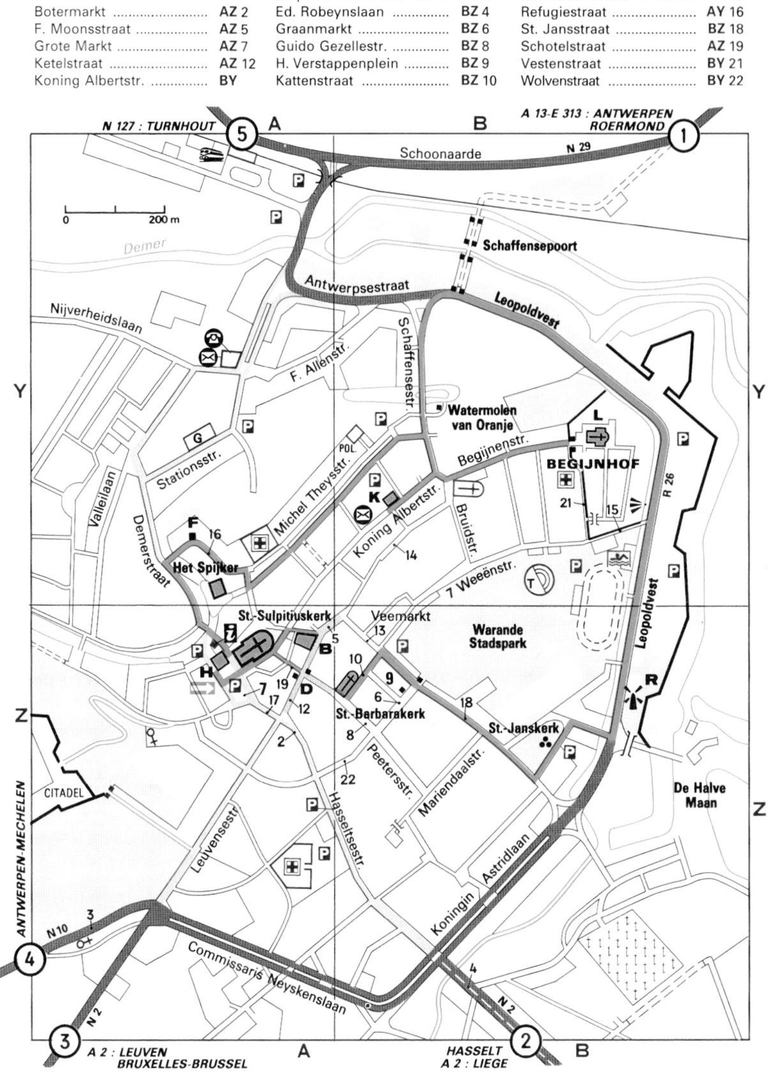

Cloth market (**AZ B**) – This dates from the 14C. The façade was rebuilt in the 19C; a 15C cannon called the Holle Griet was placed nearby.
Go around the building to see the old façade.

There are two picturesque 15C **corbelled houses** (**AZ D**) at the crossroads of the nearby pedestrian streets.

Almshouses – By walking a little way along Demerstraat visitors will be able to see the 16C **Tongerlo abbey almshouses** (Het Spijker) (**AY**) on the right, near a canal. The 15C **Averbode** almshouses (**AY F**) are a little further along, half-hidden amidst foliage.

To get to the beguine convent by car, go along Michel Theysstraat.

★ **Beguine Convent** (**Begijnhof**) (**BY**) – This beguine convent founded in the 13C is one of the largest in Belgium. Visitors enter through a beautiful 1671 baroque door, with a niche sheltering a *Virgin with Child*.
The houses, with gables and niches, date from the 16C to the 18C. It is possible to visit one at no 5 Engelen Conventstraat (main street).
The Brabant Gothic style **church** (**BY L**) ⏲ has beautiful woodwork; note the pulpit dating from 1671 with its remarkably graceful statues, and the finely worked chancel parclose screen, from the same period. There are interesting statues.
Stop to admire the gables of the two old breweries at nos 72 and 74 Koning Albertstraat (**BY K**); they are carved into brewer's tools.

House of Orange Watermill (**Watermolen van Oranje**) (**BY**) – This 16C mill stands in the shade of a weeping willow. With its crowstepped gable reflecting in the nearby canal, it makes a very pretty picture.

Schaffen Gate (**Schaffensepoort**) (**BY**) – This gateway was pierced into two successive 19C fortified enclosures.

Leopoldvest (**BYZ**) – This boulevard runs along the ramparts (vest: rampart), providing a pretty **view** of the beguine convent, its gardens extending behind the brick enclosure, with the high roofs of the closely packed houses beyond.
The **Lindenmolen** (**BZ R**) comes into sight next, a standard sort of 18C wooden mill which came from the nearby village of Assent. The surrounding area has been turned into a recreation area *(huge bathing area surrounded by sand)* called **De Halve Maan**.

Ruins of St John's Church (**Ruïnes van de St.-Janskerk**) (**BZ**) – The ivy-covered red sandstone ruins of the Gothic chancel stand in the middle of a square.

H. Verstappenplein (**BZ 9**) – The main entrance to **Warande Park** can be seen from this square; located on the hill where the castle once stood, this is where the Princes of Orange once hunted. Their palace, dating from 1516 and flanked with a turret, is opposite.

Church (**St.-Barbarakerk**) (**BZ**) ⊙ – This baroque church has sumptuous 17C carved wooden confessionals. One of these forms the base of the pulpit.

EXCURSION

Round tour of 37km - 23 miles – *Allow 2 hours. Leave on ① on the map and turn left.*

Tessenderlo – Pop 14 209. **St Martin's Church** (St.-Maartenskerk) has a beautiful **rood-screen★** from the early 16C, its three finely sculpted arcades resting on six pillars. Eight large statues of the Evangelists and the Church Fathers stand in the arches. Little figures in medieval costume enliven the four medallions which surmount the arches, depicting scenes from the Life of the Virgin and, above this but beneath the openwork canopies, scenes from the Life of Christ. The font was sculpted in the 12C.

★ **Averbode** – *See Averbode.*

Zichem – Ernest Claes *(qv)* was born in this small market town. The church has a beautiful 16C triptych illustrating the Life of St Eustace, the patron saint. The stained glass window over the high altar, dating from 1397, is the oldest in the country.

Scherpenheuvel – Pop 20 382. At the summit of a mountain which reaches 77m - 253ft in altitude is Belgium's national site of pilgrimage in veneration of the Virgin. A candlelight procession takes place in the afternoon of the Sunday following All Saints' Day.
Coebergher *(qv)* built the basilica between 1609 and 1627. It has seven sides and is topped by a baroque dome, which marks the advent of this style in Belgium. It stands in the centre of a geometric urban layout, with seven avenues converging on it. A tall square tower rises behind it.
Six brightly coloured paintings by Van Loon, depicting the *Lives of St Anne and the Virgin*, are in the radiating chapels.

DIKSMUIDE West-Vlaanderen — Pop 15 211

Michelin maps 409 B2 or 213 folds 1, 2

Diksmuide was a port and a clothmaking town in the Middle Ages; it was destroyed in 1914, then bombarded again in 1940. It was rebuilt, like Ypres, in the Flemish style. Diksmuide was one of the strategic points in the Battle of the Yser *(see Nieuwpoort)*. The name of the town is tied to the memory of Belgian soldiers and French marines under Admiral Ronarc'h who put up a heroic resistance against all the odds from 16 October to 10 November.

SIGHTS

Beguine Convent (**Begijnhof**) – *Go past the church porch and turn left at the Vismarkt.*
This has been rebuilt to look like the old convent. The white houses are arranged around the well, on either side of a charming chapel with tall gables.

Yser Tower (**IJzertoren**) ⊙ – This tower is 84m - 275ft tall. It rises on the opposite bank of the IJzer (Yser), in memory of the heros of the Battle of the Yser. It bears the letters A.V.V.-V.V.K., for the motto: Alles voor Vlaanderen, Vlaanderen voor Kristus (All for Flanders, Flanders for Christ).
There is a beautiful **panorama★** from the top *(lift)* which looks out on Diksmuide and the winding IJzer (Yser). In clear weather it is possible to see, from right to left: the belfries of Bruges, Ostend, Nieuwpoort; and the Flemish peaks – De Rode and De Zwarte Berg *(orientation table)*.
The **museum** of the Battle of the Yser is on the first floor.

Trench of Death (**Dodengang**) ⊙ – *3km - 2 miles northwest on the west bank of the IJzer.*
For four years (1914-1918) Belgian soldiers resisted the German advance in these trenches; here they were only a few yards away from the lines of the German troops, which had managed to cross the IJzer (Yser) in October 1914 *(see Nieuwpoort)*.
An orientation table on the first floor of the building locates the strategic points. Visitors can then go through the two long corridors of the trenches, with parapets made of bags of earth reproduced in concrete.

★★ DINANT Namur

Pop 12 158

Michelin maps 409 H5 or 214 fold 5 – Local maps see overleaf and MEUSE/NAMUR REGION – Town plan in the current Michelin Red Guide Benelux

Dinant lies in a remarkable **setting★★** in the Meuse Valley. The massive solidity of the citadel and the onion-domed bell tower of the collegiate church dominate the town; Dinant, with its blue-roofed houses, covers the 4km - 2.5 miles between the river and the rock face.
This is a well-known tourist centre. Dinant's name is the origin of the French word **dinanderie**, the art of melting and beating copper and brass, which has been practised here since the 12C. Dinant has another speciality: *couques*, honey cakes baked in decoratively carved wooden moulds.

Joachim Patinir (or Patenier) was born here in the late 15C. This painter inserted biblical scenes into vast landscapes recalling those of the Meuse valley. As for **Adolphe Sax** (1814-1894), it is to this Dinant citizen that we owe ... the saxophone.

A turbulent past – Dinant always was in conflict with Bouvignes, as well as Namur, Liège and the Dukes of Burgundy, all rivals in copper- and brass-smithing. The town was destroyed for this reason in 1466, by Charles the Bold. Owing to Dinant's strategic position in the Meuse Valley, it also witnessed a succession of conquering armies. In 1554 these were the troops under the King of France, Henri II; in 1675 and 1692, they were those of Louis XIV.
This is also one of the towns that suffered the most in Belgium during the World Wars. In 1914 Dinant was sacked by the Germans: 1 100 homes were burned and 674 civilians were shot. In 1940 and 1944, it was bombed and partly burned.

Boat trips ⏲ – *Landing stage opposite the Town Hall.*

Collegiate church and citadel, Dinant

SIGHTS

★ **Citadel (Citadelle)** ⏲ – *Access by cable car, on foot (408 steps) or by car (the N 936, Sorinnes road).*
A castle was built here in 1051. The Bishop of Liège rebuilt it in 1523; the French destroyed it in 1703. Its present appearance dates from the Dutch occupation (1818-1821).
The citadel has been turned into a **museum**. The past of both the town and the citadel are recalled here through objects, reconstructions, and a small weapons museum. There is a very pretty **view★★** from the top of the walls, 100m - 328ft above the Meuse: the collegiate church, Bayard Rock, the Meuse Valley, and Bouvignes.

★ **Cave (Grotte la Merveilleuse)** ⏲ – *West bank of the Meuse, Philippeville road.*
The large numbers and beautiful white colour of the concretions in this cave are its most distinguishing feature.

★ **Bayard Rock (Rocher Bayard)** – This rock needle stands 1km - 0.75 miles south of the town *(on the N 95)*. It is said that this is the one that Bayard the famous horse *(qv)* split with one blow of his hoof as he escaped from Charlemagne. In days gone by there was just a narrow path, which was enlarged in 1661, then again in 1698, for the troops of Louis XIV.

Mont-Fat Park ⏲ – The **Mont-Fat Tower**, which can be reached by chairlift, stands in the centre of this tourist park; there is a vast panorama of Dinant and the Meuse Valley to be seen from the terrace.

Prehistoric Cave (Grotte de Mont-Fat) ⏲ – This prehistoric dwelling on a slope became a temple to Diana in Roman times; it is adorned with concretions.

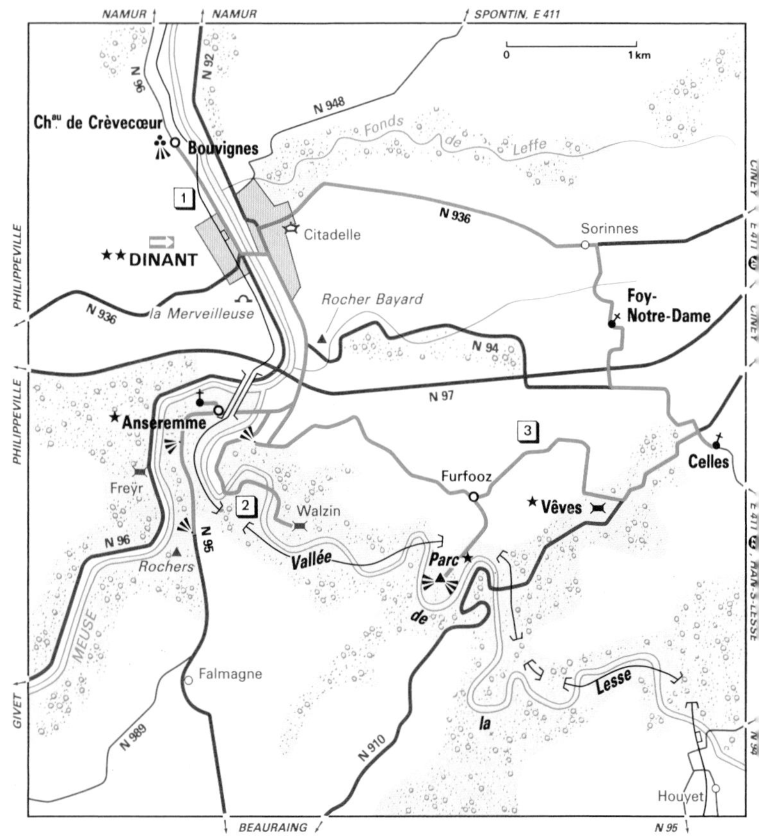

EXCURSIONS

1 Bouvignes – *2km - 1.25 miles north on the N 96.*
This town has been fused with Dinant. The ruins of Crèvecoeur ("Heartbreak") Castle dominate Bouvignes; it was thus named after being razed by the troops of the King of France, Henri II, in 1554. **Herri met de Bles**, the marvellous landscape painter who continued in Patinir's *(see above)* vein, was born here; he had the particularity of hiding a little owl in his paintings *(see Namur)* which he put there as his signature.

Spanish House (Maison espagnole) – This building with scrolled gables and Renaissance windows stands on the Grand-Place. It is named after the period in which it was built (16C) and was once the Town Hall. It is now home to the **Museum of Local History** ⊙, which contains the treasure of St Lambert's Church.

St Lambert's Church (Église St-Lambert) ⊙ – This dates from the 13C and 16C. It has been restored and has some interesting works of art: the 16C *Christ Bound* and the 17C pulpit and lectern.
The remains of an 11C castle are next to the church.

Crèvecoeur Castle – *Access on the Sommière road (4km - 2.5 miles) or up a flight of stairs.* A vestige of the fortifications, a gate, can be seen from the stairs. There is a beautiful **view**★★ from the castle of the town, the church, and the Spanish House, as well as of the Meuse Valley and Dinant on the horizon.

★ **2 Anseremme and Down the River Lesse** – *4.5km - 2.75 miles south of Dinant on the N 95.*

★ **Anseremme** – This little town, stretching along the river's right bank to join Dinant, is a well-situated tourist centre at the confluence of the Lesse with the Meuse. Note in particular the 16C **St John's Bridge** over the Lesse; and to the south in Old Anseremme, a 15C **priory** *(private property)* and its church surrounded by a cemetery.

Lesse Valley – *4km - 2.5 miles.* A very narrow road goes through the steep-sided, verdant Lesse Valley, continuing to the rocky spur where Walzin Castle stands.

★ **Down the River Lesse** ⊙ – It is possible to go down the Lesse River by canoe or a boat with a guide, from Houyet to Anseremme. Houyet can be reached by train from Anseremme, or by bus.
Cross the Lesse where it flows into the Meuse. There is a viewpoint in a hairpin bend near a café; this, the Freÿr Viewpoint, provides almost a **bird's eye view**★ of Freÿr Château gardens *(see Freÿr Château)*. Further along, admire the **broad view**★ from the next viewpoint of the valley, with the Freÿr crags in the foreground and the château in the background.

3 Furfooz; Vêves; Celles; Foy-Notre-Dame – *Round tour of 30km - 18.75 miles. Head south from Dinant on the N 95 and take the Furfooz road on the left*
The road climbs and soon comes to a road on the right; a few yards from the fork there is a pretty **view**★ down over Anseremme.

Furfooz – **Furfooz Park**★ ⊙ lies in an area of calcareous cliffs 500m - 0.3 miles south of the village, in a loop of the Lesse. The river has in fact cut an underground bed which has been explored since 1962. *Follow the signposted route.*
The site, a natural fortress, has been occupied since the 10C. The reconstructed Roman baths built on a hypocaust, the ruins at the top of the plateau (from which there is a beautiful sight of the Lesse Valley, wooded here) bear witness to this. The promontory is pitted with caves in which traces of prehistoric habitation have been found.

Vêves – An elegant **castle**★ ⊙, with a keep and narrow pepper-pot roofs, stands out against the woods and overlooks the hamlet. Since the 12C it has belonged first to the Beaufort line, then to that of the Counts of Liedekerke Beaufort.
As one of its lords participated in the 1466 siege of Dinant, the fortress was destroyed by the town's citizens. It was immediately rebuilt, then modified in the Renaissance, and again in the early 18C. There is an arched gallery surmounted with half-timbering in the courtyard. 18C French furniture and family mementoes decorate the carefully restored interior.

Celles – This village is in a pretty valley. A German tank at the north entrance to the community marks the extreme limit of the 1944 German advance *(see Bastogne)*. The 11C **Romanesque church of St-Hadelin** is an excellent example of the Mosan style, with the massive tower-façade flanked by two turrets, the exterior decoration of Lombard columns, the half-domed vaulting of the apse.
Inside there are lovely 17C grisailles with vivid portraits; 13 stalls, the oldest in Belgium; and above all, the superb 16C **tombstone**★ in black Dinant marble, with Louis de Beaufort and his wife on either side of a calvary. The church still has two 11C crypts.

Foy-Notre-Dame – A statue of the Virgin was found in an old oak tree in Foy in 1609. Its miraculous gifts were recognised by the Prince-Bishop of Liège, and the village became an important pilgrimage site.
The church dates from 1623. There is Louis XIII panelling inside and a remarkable coffered **ceiling**★ in wood, decorated with 145 17C paintings by the Stilmant brothers and Guillaume Goblet, all Dinant artists. These were given to the church by pilgrims, and represent the *Lives of the Virgin and of Christ*, the *Evangelists*, the *Doctors of the Church* and the *Saints*.

Return to Dinant via Sorinnes. This route passes near the citadel (see above).

★ EAU D'HEURE DAMS Hainaut-Namur

Michelin maps 409 G5 or 214 fold 3 – 32km - 20 miles south of Charleroi

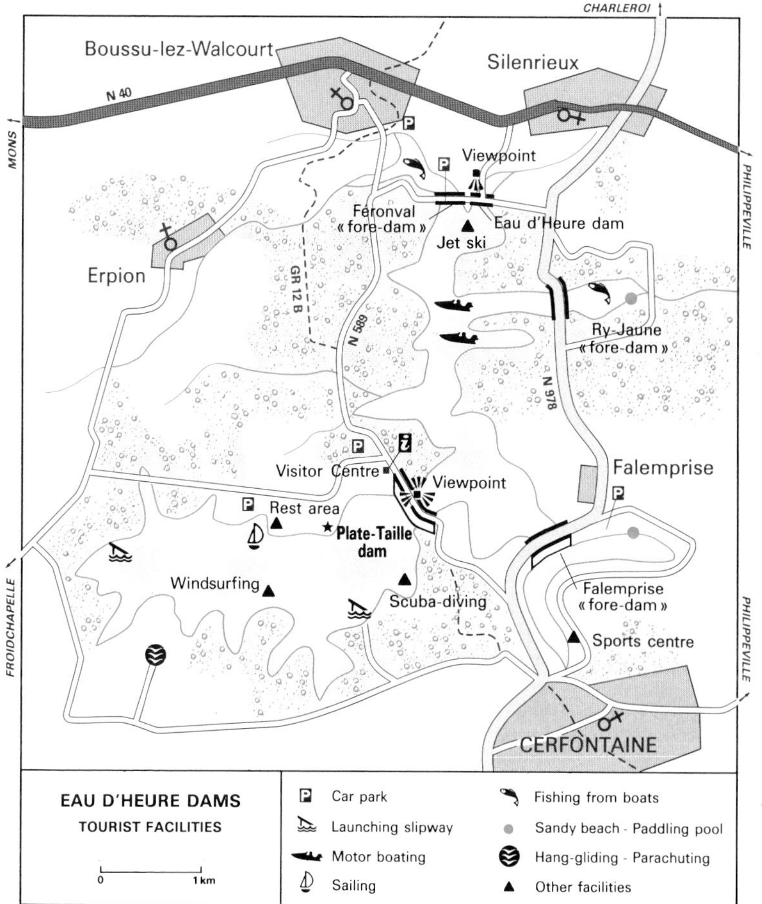

This well-watered, undulating countryside was chosen for a series of reservoirs meant to supply the River Sambre as well as the Charleroi Canal; the water volume for the canal has been insufficient since it was made to meet the international boat volume standards.
Two great dams have been created: Eau d'Heure, a great rock-fill dam with a crest 250m - almost 0.25 miles long; and Plate-Taille, which has a hydro-electric plant. Plate-Taille is higher but insufficiently supplied so that it has to be filled by pumps during the night, using the Eau d'Heure turbo-pumps.
Three "fore-dams", Féronval, Ry-Jaune and Falemprise, were built to make the larger projects easier to carry out; they have also made it possible to create a new road network.
An extensive programme of tourist development is in progress on the lake shores, for various types of lodging, sports and amusements.
The area is crisscrossed with more than 100km - 62 miles of footpaths.

★ **Plate-Taille Dam** – *Access on a large road from Boussu.*
This was built in 1977, and is the largest dam in Belgium. It is a gravity dam and has a crest 790m - 0.5 miles long. The reservoir itself covers an area of 351ha - 867 acres and has a capacity of 68.4 million m^3 – 2 416 million ft^3 of water; it is used for sailing and underwater diving. A **viewing tower** 107m - 351ft high has been built on the crest.

Visitor Centre – There are audio-visual presentations on the dams and aquariums with regional fish.

The Practical Information section at the end of the guide lists:

- ***local or national organisations providing additional information;***
- ***events of interest to the tourist;***
- ***admission times and charges for the sights.***

ENGHIEN Hainaut

Pop 10 019

Michelin maps 409 F3 or 213 fold 17

Enghien is on the linguistic border, and was the fief of the Arenberg family. The castle was demolished in the 19C. Only the **gardens** ⏲, created from 1630 to 1665 by Charles d'Arenburg, are left.

Capuchin Church ⏲ – *Access via the Ninove road and then via Rue des Capucins on the left.*
This 1615 building has a beautiful Renaissance mausoleum in a chapel; it was created by Emperor Charles V's sculptor, Jean Mone, for Guillaume de Croÿ. On the high altar, there is an ebony and ivory altarpiece (1616) framing an *Adoration of the Magi*; 51 of the figures are portraits of Arenburg family members.

St Nicholas's Church (Église St-Nicolas) ⏲ – This vast Gothic church is on the Grand-Place; it has a carillon in which 51 bells have been restored.
Modern stained glass windows by Max Ingrand can be seen inside, as well as statues from the 15C to the 17C, a 15C font, and, in the Chapel of Our Lady of Messines, a beautiful 16C altarpiece of the Life of the Virgin.

Jonathas's House (Maison de Jonathas) – This 16C dwelling includes a 12C Romanesque keep. There is a small **tapestry museum** (musée de la Tapisserie) ⏲ recalling that Enghien had large workshops from the 15C to the 18C. A series of 16C Enghien "verdures" (tapestries representing trees or foliage) is exhibited.

EUPEN Liège

Pop 16 959

Michelin maps 409 L4 or 213 fold 24
Town plan in the current Michelin Red Guide Benelux

Eupen lies on a slope of the Vesdre Valley, near the Hautes Fagnes *(qv)*. It is a large industrial town with factories scattered all along the river.
Eupen dates from the 18C, a period when its beautiful patrician houses were built by rich Ghent wool merchants attracted to the Vesdre's waters. **St Nicholas's Church** with its amusing green onion-domed towers and exuberant baroque altars also is from this time.
A German dialect is spoken in Eupen, as it belonged to Germany for a century and only became part of Belgium in 1925, like Moresnet, Malmédy and St-Vith.

★★ **Carnival** *(see the Calendar of Events at the end of this guide)* – The carnival is in the true Rhineland spirit, and preparations are under way for it from mid-November. On the Saturday before Lent His Madness the Prince appears, crowned with pheasant feathers. The children's parade takes place on the Sunday afternoon. The festivities reach their high point on the eve of Shrove Tuesday with the Rosenmontag (Rose Monday) Procession.

Eupen Town Museum ⏲ – *At no 52, Gospertstrasse.* This is in a picturesque 17C house and features watch- and clock-making, the town history, the development of fashion, as well as a silver- and goldsmith's workshop and a collection of Raeren potteries *(qv)*.

EXCURSIONS

★ **Vesdre Dam** *(signposted: Talsperre) – 5km – 3.25 miles. Leave Eupen heading southeast on the N 67 and turn left.*
This dam is upstream from the town, at the confluence of the Vesdre and the Getzbach. It was inaugurated in 1950 and is one of the largest projects of this type in Belgium, along with Gileppe dam and the Eau d'Heure dam complex.
This is a gravity dam, more than 63m - 207ft tall and nearly 410m - 0.25 miles long, and 55m - 180ft thick at the base. It has a capacity of 25 million m^3 – 883 million ft^3.
It was meant, like Gileppe dam, to supply water to the Eupen area as well as the Liège area. It is equipped with a water-processing plant and a small electric power station. Sailing is permitted on the reservoir (Vesdre Yacht Club) but motorboats, fishing and swimming are forbidden.

Viewpoint – The visitor can contemplate the lake and its surrounding of Hertogenwald forests (spruces, birches).

Henri-Chapelle – *11km - 6.75 miles northwest on the N 67; then the N 3 on the left.*
An **American cemetery** is about 4.5km - 2.75 miles north of Henri-Chapelle, in Vogelsang-Hombourg. The remarkably well-maintained site blooms with roses and rhododendrons. Here lie 7 989 American soldiers, who died in the Ardennes or in Germany from 1944-1945. White marble crosses or monuments carved with the Star of David form circles converging at the monument. There is a little **museum** inside; the story and the maps of the end of the campaign are carved into the marble.
There is a **panorama**★ from the terrace opposite the cemetery of the Herve plateau, the fields edged with hedgerows, and the undulating countryside which is well inhabited despite its open look.

★ **Triple Milestone (Drielandenpunt)** – *18km - 11.25 miles north on the N 68.*
After having left the N 68 at Kettenis, the road crosses Walhorn and then Astenet, where the little sanctuary in memory of Catherine of Sienna is located. After Kelmis-La Calamine, it reaches Gemmenich via the Moresnet-Chapelle shrine to the Virgin, with its monumental calvary in a leafy setting. From there a winding road leads to the wooded plateau on which the borders of the Netherlands, Belgium and Germany meet. The border of the little neutral territory of Moresnet was also here until 1918; it is now part of Belgium. This is also the highest point in the Netherlands, at 321m - 1 053ft in altitude.
There is a beautiful **panorama**★ of the region at the top of the **Baldwin Tower**, a tall metal construction; it reveals the urban area of Aachen and the forests of the German Eifel, as well as Maastricht on the horizon in a setting of wooded hills.
There is a beautiful **viewpoint**★ 500m - 0.3 mile further on the Vaals (Netherlands) road; the German plain and Aachen can be seen on the right.

★★ FOURNEAU-ST-MICHEL Luxembourg

Michelin maps 409 J5 or 214 fold 6

Fourneau-St-Michel is in the green and fertile Masblette Valley, between two wooded hills. The Benedictines once occupied this lovely valley. In the 18C the last abbot of St-Hubert, Nicolas Spirlet, founded a metallurgy centre here. In 1966 this spot became the property of the province, and it was decided to set up several museums.

Museum of Walloon Country Life, Fourneau-St-Michel

★★ **Museum of Walloon Country Life** **(Musée de la Vie rurale en Wallonie)** ⏲ – *This can be accessed through two different entrances. Allow 3 hours for this pleasant outing, with a stop for refreshment at the 18C Prêvost inn or at the Tahons inn (playing field).* This open-air museum, covering 40ha – 99 acres, consists of old rural dwellings representing the different Walloon regions. They are scattered along a touring itinerary about 2km – 1.25 miles long. A school can be seen here, a chapel, a printers', tobacco sheds, a washhouse, a craftmen's house. A large traditional Ardennes building is home to the **Ardennes Draught-Horse Museum** (musée du Cheval de trait ardennais) as well as an exhibition of the instruments that this powerful working animal used to pull.

★ **Iron and Ancient Metallurgy Museum** **(Musée du Fer et de la Métallurgie ancienne)** ⏲ – *Time: allow 1 hour.*
This was once the blacksmith's house; it is now a museum of the metallurgy of days gone by and the various associated craftmen's techniques. Apart from objects made of this metal (firebacks, irons, locks, religious objects, traps, etc.) there are also craftmen's tools on display (for nail-making, forges, coopering, cart-making). The tall furnace and the forge with its different types of bellows help to explain how iron was obtained in the 18C and 19C.

P. J. Redouté Museum ⏲ – This is in another part of the blacksmith's home, and is devoted to Pierre-Joseph Redouté, the "Raphaël of flowers", born in 1759 in St-Hubert, and his brother Henri-Joseph, who did the illustrations for *Description of Egypt.*

LES FOURONS See VOERSTREEK

★ FREŸR CHÂTEAU Namur

Michelin maps 409 H5 or 214 fold 5 – Local map see MEUSE/NAMUR REGION

The estate is in a superb **setting★★** beside the road running along the Meuse; this elegant scene contrasts with the rough crags on the opposite bank, which plunge down to the river *(see Meuse/Namur Region).*

★ **Château** ⏲ – This was built from the 16C to the 18C, then restored in 1972; the style is Renaissance Mosan and Louis XV.
The tour takes the visitor through a series of rooms with beautiful woodwork and fireplaces, decorated with 17C and 18C furniture. Louis XIV was received here during the siege of Dinant in May 1675 and again in October for the signing of the Treaty of Freÿr; in 1785 the governor of the Netherlands, the Archduchess Mary-Christine, was also here.
A great vestibule is decorated with paintings representing hunting scenes (Snyders' workshop); the beautiful wrought-iron balustrade on the balcony took its inspiration from the decoration of Place Stanislas in Nancy, France.

★ **Gardens** ⏲ – French-style gardens were designed in 1760 by the Counts of Beaufort-Spontin with inspiration from Le Nôtre's work; they run parallel to the river, laid out in three terraces decorated with pools. The lowest one, in which lime trees have been planted, also has a collection of 33 **orange trees** in pots; some of these are three hundred years old. Others are surrounded by tall hedges, which form a **maze**.
A pavilion at the highest point of the garden, near Frédéric Hall, overlooks the entire estate; it was decorated inside by the Moretti brothers, as at Annevoie-Rouillon *(qv).*

Freÿr Château and Cliffs

GEMBLOUX Namur

Pop 18 850

Michelin maps 409 H4 or 213 folds 19, 20

Gembloux, an agricultural and horticultural town, was famous for its Benedictine abbey. This was founded in the 10C and became a great centre of cultural influence. The monk **Sigebert**, who died in 1112, left an important World Chronicle concerning the period of 381 to 1111.
The abbey estate was abolished during the French Revolution, and since 1860 the building has been occupied by an agricultural sciences faculty.
The town has several traces left of its 12C ramparts.

Abbey – This architectural ensemble was constructed by Dewez from 1759 to 1779. Admire the beautiful arrangement of the **main courtyard**, at the far end of which the old abbey palace can be seen; the sculpture on the pediment recalls the abbot's powerful position as Count of Gembloux. The cloister has been restored; it provides access to a Romanesque room, the only trace left of the medieval abbey.
The old 18C abbey **church**, now a parish church, is nearby.

Bailli House (Maison du Bailli) ⊙ – This old 12C "fortified house" was extensively modified in the 16C. It is now the town hall. The first floor houses a museum on the local way of life.

Corroy-le-Château

EXCURSIONS

Corroy-le-Château – *5km – 3.25 miles southwest.*
This 13C **feudal castle**★ ⊙ is surrounded by woods and casts its reflection in the moats spanned by a stone bridge. The layout imitates the royal castles of Philippe-Auguste and it still has a quite military feel to it with the seven cylindrical towers and the little additional castle.
The interior has been extensively altered over the course of the centuries. The Gothic chapel was restored in the 19C. The apartments are decorated with marble, painted canvases, some of which depict Flemish festivals, and 17C and 18C furniture. There is a beautiful collection of "jolités" (little painted boxes) from Spa.

Grand-Leez – *8km – 5 miles northeast on the Namur road, then turn left.*
The Defrenne **mill** (moulin) dates from 1830 and is the only operational mill left in the province of Namur; it grinds wheat. It is shaped like a truncated cone, with a rotating cap.

Gentinnes – *12km – 7.5 miles. Take the Charleroi road, then turn right.*
A training centre for prospective missionaries, belonging to the congregation of the Pères du St-Esprit (similar to the Montfort Fathers), has been in Gentinnes since 1904.
The **Kongolo Memorial** is a chapel built in 1967 in memory of the 21 Belgian missionaries from this order who were massacred in 1962 during a revolt in Kongolo in Zaïre. Their names are carved on the façade as well as those of the 196 other victims, religious or lay, Catholic or Protestant.

The chapter on art and architecture in this guide gives an outline of artistic creation in the region, providing the context of the building and works of art described in the sightseeing section.

This chapter may also provide ideas for touring itineraries.

It is advisable to read it before setting out.

GENK Limburg

Pop 61 217

Michelin maps 409 J3 or 213 fold 10
Town plan in the current Michelin Red Guide Benelux

Genk is on the edge of the Kempen region, conveniently close to the Albert Canal and two motorways. It is Limburg's most important industrial centre, owing to the three coal mines north of the town and the two large industrial areas south of it. Genk is also a prosperous city, with three modern shopping centres and the **Limburghal** (1979) where conventions and exhibits are organised.
The town also has the **Molenvijver**, superb public gardens of 15ha – 37 acres including a small lake and a watermill, as well as recreation parks such as the Kattevennen, or sports areas such as Kattevenia. On a little outcrop, a sombre-looking brick church (1954) with lofty vaulting can be seen.

EXCURSIONS

De Maten Nature Reserve (Natuurreservaat) ⊙ – *2km – 1.25 miles. Hasselt road, then left after the railway bridge.*
A marshy area stretches between the heathland of the hills, in which a string of lakes is home to numerous aquatic birds *(footpaths).*

Zwartberg – *6km – 3.75 miles north on the N 76.*
The 30ha – 74 acre **Limburgse zoo★** ⊙ is home to more than 4 000 animals, including large colonies of bears, monkeys and birds.

De Mechelse Heide Nature Reserve – *7km – 4.5 miles northeast on the N 75, then the N 763 toward Maasmechelen.*
This is an immense clearing (400ha – 988 acres) in the forest, revealing a magnificent landscape of heather-covered moors *(heide)*; heather is one of the rare traces left of primitive Kempen vegetation. *Footpaths signposted.*

★★★ GENT (GHENT) Oost-Vlaanderen Ⓟ

Pop 230 822

Michelin maps 409 E2 or 213 fold 4

Ghent is the spiritual citadel of Flanders, a university town, the second-ranking Belgian port and a great industrial centre, in short, a hub of great vitality. It is crisscrossed by canals and waterways, built as it is on numerous islets at the confluence of the Rivers Leie and Scheldt.
Emperor Charles V (1500-1558) was born here, and Ghent is indeed steeped in history and crammed with historical buildings. Furthermore, between the cathedral and Gravensteen castle, it reveals the poetic, intimate atmosphere of its old districts and its quays.
The many famous Ghent citizens include the great writer in the French language, **Maurice Maeterlinck** (1862-1949).

Boat trips ⊙ – Trips (rondvaart) are organised on the canals and the River Leie *(see Excursions below).*

HISTORICAL NOTES

Ghent was one of the last havens of paganism in Gaul. St Amand, who came to evangelise the town in the 7C, was thrown into the Scheldt. Ghent later developed around two monasteries: St Peter's, founded by St Amand; and the future abbey of St Bavo, near the Leie.
A stone fortress was built in about 1000, on the location of the present Gravensteen Castle, which became the centre of a third urban settlement.
At the end of the 12C the clothmaking industry was flourishing. The city formed a single unit and gained important privileges; the wealthy merchant class built fortified stone homes called "stenen". In the middle of the 12C St John's Church was built, now known as the St Bavo's Cathedral.
Count Philip of Alsace, wishing to make a show of his precedence over the powerful cloth merchants, had the castle rebuilt in 1180.

Incessant conflict – Before long Ghent succumbed to fierce internal conflicts; as in Bruges, the wool workers, supported by Count Guy of Dampierre, rose in 1280 against the patricians, defended by the King of France *(see Bruges).* In the 14C during the Hundred Years War, the situation developed into a battle against France. The Count of Flanders Louis of Nevers supported the King of France against England. As this blocked the importing of English wool to Flanders, the citizens of Ghent rose in revolt. They chose **Jacob Van Artevelde** as their leader, who sided with the English, and he became the figurehead of the Flemish towns.
Van Artevelde was assassinated by the dean of the weavers' guild in 1345, but his son Philip managed to impose the supremacy of Ghent throughout Flanders. Finally, however, the Flemish were defeated by the French at the Battle of Westrozebeke in 1382 *(see Kortrijk).*
In the 15C, Ghent, under the rule of the Dukes of Burgundy, rose against Philip the Good who wanted to impose a new tax on the townspeople (1452). The citizens of Ghent were defeated at Gavere *(18km – 11 miles southwest)* and surrendered (1453). The town rebelled again against Charles the Bold in 1469, and in 1477 against Mary of Burgundy who had to grant new privileges to the Low Countries. By the end of the century the clothmaking industry was in decline. Nonetheless, Ghent had become the main storage centre for Europe's grain, and thus assured itself a new prosperity.
In the 16C the citizens rose once more against Emperor Charles V, who had himself been born in Ghent, refusing to pay heavy taxes. Charles V responded with the **Caroline Concession** (1540) which stripped the commune of its privileges.

Religious strife was disrupting the community's way of life by the end of the century. The Duke of Alva put down a revolt by Calvinist iconoclasts in 1567, but the Protestants reacted strongly; four days after the Antwerp "Spanish Fury" *(see Antwerpen)*, Philip II was forced to concede the famous **Pacification of Ghent** (1576) which liberated the 17 Low Countries provinces of Spanish troops.
The town became a Republic in 1577, having revolted against the Spanish, but it was recaptured by Farnese in 1585. **Louis XVIII** took refuge in Ghent in 1815 in the old 18C Hane Steenhuyse mansion (*47 Veldstraat* **EZ A**). This is known as the "flight to Ghent".

From decline to renewal – Ghent's economic decline worsened during the 17C. The 1648 closure of the Scheldt was a fatal blow to its commercial and industrial activities. However, Ghent was annexed to France in the early 19C and grew more prosperous through the cotton-weaving techniques developed by Ghent native **Lievin Bauwens**. He introduced the mule-jenny, an English method of spinning thread mechanically. Ghent spun and wove linen as well, since the waters of the Leie, as in Kortrijk, were excellently suited for retting flax. Textile industry has remained very important for Ghent's economy.
The 33km – 20.5 mile long canal from Ghent to Terneuzen has linked the **port** to the west stretch of the Scheldt since 1827. In 1968 it could handle 80 000-ton vessels, and its international cargo traffic reached 25 million tons in 1990. There are installations for the transhipment of cereal cargoes all along the canal; new industries which have appeared include: metallurgy, chemical products, petroleum products, automobile parts. The Sidmar steel works complex is in the north port area near the ore ship docking installations. It produces about 3.5 million tons of steel per year.
Ghent has also developed a prospering local horticultural industry (especially east of the town) which has earned it the name "city of flowers". A large proportion of production is exported.
The town organises the world famous **Ghent Floral Festival** at the Flanders Festival every five years *(the next will be in 1995)*.

★★★ OLD TOWN *time: half a day*

Illuminations ⏲ create a magical atmosphere for an evening stroll.

★★ **St Bavo's Cathedral (St.-Baafskathedraal) (FZ)** ⏲ – This stands on the location of the 12C St John's Church; a few traces of the old church can be seen in the present crypt. When Emperor Charles V had the Abbey of St Bavo *(see Additional Sights below)* destroyed to build the Spanish palace, he ordered the church to take the name Collegiate Church of St Bavo. It became a cathedral in 1561.
The cathedral was built in stages and shows diverse influences – elements of French Gothic (the chancel), Brabant Gothic (the tower), Late Gothic (the nave); nevertheless, it gives an overall impression of harmony and solemn grace.
The remarkable **tower**, on the west side of the church, is also the entrance, as is the rule in Brabant Gothic architecture. There is an extensive **view** of Ghent and its surroundings from the top ⏲ of the tower.
The majestic effect of the **interior** is somewhat diminished by the neo-classical marble choir screen, decorated with 18C grisailles, which disrupts the beautiful arrangement of the nave. The lofty chancel in Tournai stone, slightly raised in relation to the nave, dates from the 14C. It was enlarged in the 15C by five radiating chapels and surmounted with a triforium.
A certain rhythmic regularity is added to the ambulatory by marble columns and finely worked doors.
The plain sandstone and brick nave dates from the 16C and harmonises well with the elegant Late Gothic balustrades and the densely-ribbed vaulting.
This cathedral contains many valuable works of art, including the extraordinary *Mystic Lamb*.

★★ **Polyptych of the Adoration of the Mystic Lamb** ⏲ – *In a chapel to the left upon entering.*
This polyptych, a marvel of painting, has had many an adventure.
It was donated to the church by Joos Vijd, and was solemnly placed in an ambulatory chapel in 1432. Philip II wanted to take possession of it, the Protestants wanted to burn it in 1566, Emperor Joseph II had the paintings of Adam and Eve

Polyptych of the Adoration of the Mystic Lamb (detail), Jan van Eyck

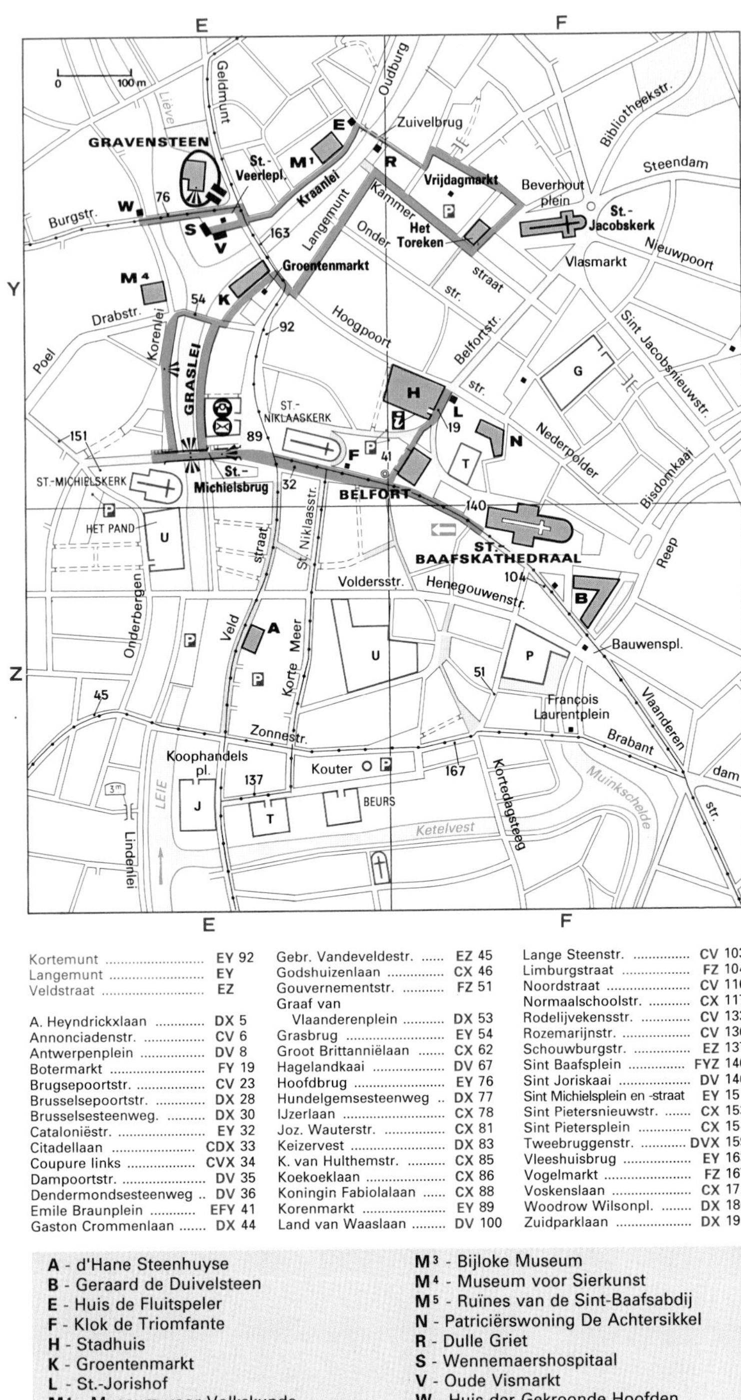

Kortemunt	EY 92	Gebr. Vandeveldestr.	EZ 45	Lange Steenstr.	CV 103
Langemunt	EY	Godshuizenlaan	CX 46	Limburgstraat	FZ 104
Veldstraat	EZ	Gouvernementstr.	FZ 51	Noordstraat	CV 116
		Graaf van Vlaanderenplein	DX 53	Normaalschoolstr.	CX 117
A. Heyndrickxlaan	DX 5	Grasbrug	EY 54	Rodelijvekensstr.	CV 133
Annonciadenstr.	CV 6	Groot Brittanniëlaan	CX 62	Rozemarijnstr.	CV 136
Antwerpenplein	DV 8	Hagelandkaai	DV 67	Schouwburgstr.	EZ 137
Botermarkt	FY 19	Hoofdbrug	EY 76	Sint Baafsplein	FYZ 140
Brugsepoortstr.	CV 23	Hundelgemsesteenweg	DX 77	Sint Joriskaai	DV 146
Brusselsepoortstr.	DX 28	IJzerlaan	CX 78	Sint Michielsplein en -straat	EY 151
Brusselsesteenweg.	DX 30	Joz. Wauterstr.	CX 81	Sint Pietersnieuwstr.	CX 153
Cataloniëstr.	EY 32	Keizervest	DX 83	Sint Pietersplein	CX 154
Citadellaan	CDX 33	K. van Hulthemstr.	CX 85	Tweebruggenstr.	DVX 159
Coupure links	CVX 34	Koekoeklaan	CX 86	Vleeshuisbrug	EY 163
Dampoortstr.	DV 35	Koningin Fabiolalaan	CX 88	Vogelmarkt	FZ 167
Dendermondsesteenweg	DV 36	Korenmarkt	EY 89	Voskenslaan	CX 172
Emile Braunplein	EFY 41	Land van Waaslaan	DV 100	Woodrow Wilsonpl.	DX 186
Gaston Crommenlaan	DX 44			Zuidparklaan	DX 193

A - d'Hane Steenhuyse
B - Geraard de Duivelsteen
E - Huis de Fluitspeler
F - Klok de Triomfante
H - Stadhuis
K - Groentenmarkt
L - St.-Jorishof
M1 - Museum voor Volkskunde
M2 - Museum voor Schone Kunsten
M3 - Bijloke Museum
M4 - Museum voor Sierkunst
M5 - Ruïnes van de Sint-Baafsabdij
N - Patriciërswoning De Achtersikkel
R - Dulle Griet
S - Wennemaershospitaal
V - Oude Vismarkt
W - Huis der Gekroonde Hoofden
Z - Oude Begijnhof van St.-Elisabeth

removed as he found them shocking, and the French Directoire had it sent to Paris where it remained until 1815. It then lost several of its panels which were exhibited in the Museum of Berlin. It was put back together again in 1920, but the panel of the Righteous Judges was stolen in 1934; it has been replaced by a copy since 1941. The polyptych was first entrusted to the French during the Second World War, but the German authorities transferred it to Austria, where American troops found it in 1945 in a Styrian salt mine near Altaussee. The work took its place once more in the chapel chosen by the original donor, but was moved again in 1986 to a more secure location where viewing it would be easier. It is now exhibited in a chapel which has been converted into a fortified vault. The identity of its executor(s) has supplied endless material for discussion: is it the work of **Jan Van Eyck** *(qv)* alone? Or are we to believe the Latin inscription on the polyptych's frame, which says it was begun by Van Eyck's older brother Hubert, although no other painting by this artist is known? In any case, the colossal work depicts no fewer than 248 figures illuminated by a light shining from the right; the technique and the style are magnificent. The painting also bears witness to the Christian ideals of the Middle Ages.

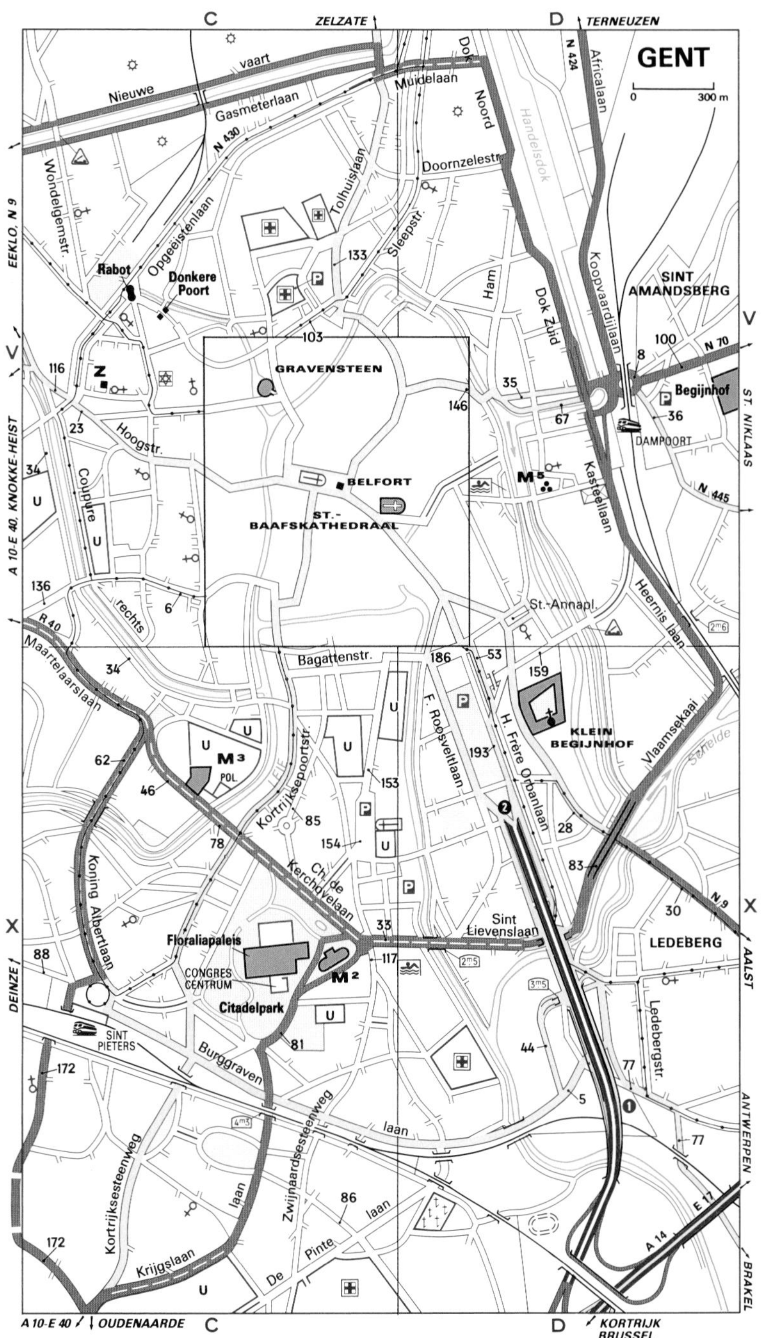

The **paintings on the lower section** depict the Mystic Lamb on an altar surrounded by angels; approaching the altar from either side of the Fountain of Life in front of it are the Knights *(photograph p 37)* and the Righteous Judges, from the left, and the Hermits and Pilgrims, from the right. In the background the Virgins are gathered on the right, and the Martyrs and Confessors on the left.

The landscape is bright, the vegetation precisely detailed; botanists have identified 42 species of plants and flowers.

In the **upper section** we see Christ Triumphant, enthroned as the Great High Priest; to the left of him are the Virgin, a choir of angels, and Adam; to the right, St John the Baptist, a group of angel musicians, and Eve. The vivid realism of the figures and the decorative beauty of the fabrics are stunning.

When closed the panels represent the Annunciation in the centre, the Prophets and the Sibyls above, and St John the Baptist, St John the Evangelist and the donors, Joos Vijd and his wife Elisabeth Borluut, below.

Cathedral furniture and works of art – The baroque "truth pulpit" (*qv*) with its marble statues is by Laurent Delvaux.

Hendrik Frans Verbruggen made the high altar in the chancel in the baroque style; it depicts the *Apotheosis of St Bavo*. The mausoleum of Monsignor Triest (1654) by Jerome Duquesnoy the Younger is left of the chancel; the figure's weary expression is striking.

The altarpiece of **Jesus Among the Doctors** (1751), by Frans Pourbus the Elder is in the first ambulatory chapel to the south. Many famous figures feature in it, including Emperor Charles V in the lower left corner. There is a **Vocation of St Bavo** (1624) in the tenth ambulatory chapel, painted by Rubens; the artist represented himself as a convert in a red cloak.

★ **Crypt** – This has the same ground plan as the chancel above it. The oldest part (1150) is marked out in black tiles on the floor. 15C and 16C naïve ex-votos are painted on the pillars and the Romanesque vaulting. There is also a valuable treasury in the crypt: a silver reliquary of St Macaire signed by Hugo de la Vigne (1616), a 9C gospel-book and a necrological scroll describing monastic life in the Middle Ages. Do not miss the remarkable **Calvary triptych**★ painted by Justus van Gent, a major work executed by the artist in 1466, before he left for Italy. The influence of Van Eyck and Van der Weyden is very clear (group of holy women in front of the cross). This work is striking for the subtlety of the colours often acid in tone.
The 13C castle known as **Gerard the Devil** (Geraard de Duivelsteen) (**FZ B**) is behind the east end of the cathedral. This austere medieval dwelling was restored in the 19C and belonged to a Ghent lord of this name.

★★★ **Belfry (Belfort) and Cloth Hall (Lakenhalle) (FY)** ⏲ – The belfry's striking shape (91m - 298ft), topped with a gilded copper dragon, symbolises the medieval power of the guilds of Ghent. This was built in the 13C and 14C and has frequently been remodelled and restored. It is attached to the 15C **Cloth Hall**. The carillon contains 52 chimes.

Inside the belfry, the room called "Secret" once contained the archives; there is a statue of a wild-looking man-at-arms, the only survivor of the four who once decorated the belfry's corners. Upstairs, a few historical mementoes and the carillon keyboard are worth a visit.
There is a beautiful view of the town from the upper platform. It was here that, while viewing the city, King Francis I of France said to Emperor Charles V: "How many Spanish skins would be needed to make a glove (*gant* in French, which sounds the same as the French name for Ghent, *Gand*) of this splendour?"!
Walk around the belfry to see the classical door (1741) of the **old prison** embellished with the "the man who suckles", the **mammelokker**. This baroque low relief is a symbol of Christian charity: Cimon, an old Roman condemned to die of hunger, is given the breast by his daughter. A bell called **the Triumphant** (Klok de Triomfante) (**EY F**) is in the square, at the foot of the belfry. This is the successor of the bell which once was in the belfry and bore this legend: "This bell is called Roland; when it is set ringing, it sends a storm throughout the country."

Town Hall (Stadhuis) (FY H) ⏲ – Two distinct styles can be seen. Building was begun in 1518 after plans by Waghemakere *(qv)* and Keldermans; the work was interrupted in 1535, however, and resumed 60 years later.
The **Keure House** on the right, decorated with a corner turret, is in a flowery 16C Gothic style; the chapel, a little balcony (for proclamations) and a flight of steps stand out on the north façade.
The left part, dating from the 17C, took its inspiration from the Renaissance; this is the **Parchons' House**, for aldermen responsible for settling disputes.
Inside, part of the Keure House is open to visitors: the hall of justice with its labyrinth pavement, which leads onto the balcony from which the Pacification of Ghent was proclaimed; a chapel roofed with beautiful Gothic vaulting; the Throne Room upstairs with Renaissance vaulting.
The old crossbowmen's guild hall (1478), **St.-Jorishof** (**FY L**), is opposite the town hall; it is now occupied by a hotel.

Go past St Nicholas's church to reach St Michael's Bridge.

St Michael's Bridge (St.-Michielsbrug) (EY) – There is a stunning **view**★★★ of the old town's historic buildings and façades. Turn round to admire the line of St Nicholas's towers, the belfry and St Bavo's.
From the centre of the bridge, the view to the south reveals: the apse of St Michael's and the old 15C Dominican convent next to St Michael's, which is now a university building (Het Pand); and to the north: the crenellations of Gravensteen castle and, in front of it, the houses of the Graslei and Korenlei quays.

★★★ **Graslei (EY)** – *Stand on the Korenlei for a good view of the group of façades.*
Ghent's port was once here. The Graslei is edged with 12C to 17C houses, in a very pure architectural style. The most interesting of these, from left to right, are:
- the 16C Masons' House, with a tall stone façade crowned with graceful pinnacles;
- the first Grain Weighers' House (15C);
- the large Romanesque Scaldian style Store House, which was a warehouse for grain taken as an in-kind customs duty payment;
- the tiny Toll House, where the customs officer was lodged;
- the second Grain Weigher's House (1698);
- the Free Boatmen's House; the doorway is surmounted with the figure of a ship, and the wonderful façade is crowned with a gable with gently flowing lines, which dates from 1531.

Return to the Graslei.

Vegetable Market (Groentenmarkt) (EY) – The **meat market** (**K**) with its many crow-stepped dormer windows, dating from 1404, rises on the left.

Friday Market (Vrijdagmarkt) (FY) – This enormous marketplace was the scene of many historical episodes. The sovereigns of Flanders came here to speak to the people; weavers and wool workers fought bloody battles here in May 1345.

Graslei

The house with the turret, on the far side of the marketplace, is **Het Toreken**; it dates from 1480 and belonged to the tanners' guild.
More to the east, the three towers of **St James's Church** (St.-Jacobskerk) can be seen; the two towers are Romanesque, but one had a sandstone roof with crockets added to it in the 15C. The central statue is of Jacob Van Artevelde.

Mad Meg (Dulle Griet) (EFY R) – This little 15C cannon was placed near a bridge over the Leie.

Kraanlei (EY) – Interesting houses can be seen here, in particular that of the Paper-Kite, also known as the **Flute Player's House** (Huis de Fluitspeler) (**E**); this is next to another one with low reliefs representing works of mercy.

★ **Folklore Museum** (Museum voor Volkskunde) (**EY M1**) ⏲ – This is in the cottages and Gothic chapel of the **Alyn Children's Hospice**, founded in the 14C. The inner **courtyard★**, together with the delightful white houses and their tall dormer windows, makes a pretty picture.
The museum evokes Flemish popular arts and traditions. Among the forty or so rooms, there are remarkable reconstructions of shops (grocer's, *estaminet*, apothecary's), domestic interiors, craftmen's workshops (cobbler, wax-taper maker, wood-turner) which serve to recall life in Ghent in *c*1900. The museum also has temporary exhibitions and a **theatre** ⏲ with traditional Ghent marionettes.

St.-Veerleplein (EY) – This square was once used for executions. Today it is surrounded by old houses; the **Wennemaershospitaal** (**S**), a hospice, with a façade dating from 1564; and the old baroque **fish market** (oude Vismarkt) (**V**) dating from 1690, with beautiful high reliefs representing Neptune and the rivers Leie and Scheldt.

★★ **Gravensteen, Castle of the Counts of Flanders (EY)** ⏲ – The castle, built in 1180 by the Count of Flanders Philip of Alsace on the site of an older keep, was radically restored in the early 20C. At the time there was nothing left but a few ruins occupied by a spinning mill. Its architecture takes its inspiration from the Crusaders' strongholds in Syria. The crown of the curtain wall has oriels, watch turrets and merlons, all of which are reflected in the waters of the Liève.
Inside the curtain wall, it is possible to visit the watchpath (notice the twin Romanesque openings on the east wall of the keep). Note the beautiful rooms of the counts' palace, one of which received the seventh chapter of the Order of the Golden Fleece in 1445, presided over by Philip the Good; they now contain a collection of instruments of torture, recalling that the castle was also a prison for many years.
From the top of the keep there is an absolutely beautiful **view★** of Ghent and its surrounding area.
Go round the keep to enter the building which contained the old stables, as well as the double-naved crypt with ogive vaulting, which contains a well.
On leaving the castle there is the **House of the Crowned Heads** (Huis der Gekroonde Hoofden) (**W**) just at the beginning of the Burgstraat; it is decorated with medallions with busts of the counts of Flanders.

Gravensteen

★★ MAJOR MUSEUMS *time: allow half a day*

★★ **Fine Art Museum (Museum voor Schone Kunsten)** (CX M[2]) ⊙ – This large museum is on the edge of Citadelpark, which surrounds the **Floral Festival Palace** (Floraliapaleis). It houses rich and interesting collections of ancient and modern art from the 15C to the 20C. While some sculptures and the Brussels tapestries are well worth a visit, it is the paintings in particular that stand out.

Ancient painting *(left wing)* – The collection of old masters includes the delightful *Madonna with Carnation* by Van der Weyden and the two paintings by **Hieronymous Bosch** that deal with the same theme, that of good versus evil. The first, **St Jerome**, is a work from his early years. The foreground of the painting represents evil, with the saint at prayer surrounded by terrifying objects and a menacing natural landscape; in the background, the peaceful landscape represents good. The **Bearing of the Cross**, one of the great painter's last works, reveals an extraordinary modernism in the way the mass of bloated, demonic faces is depicted, with Christ's serene one in the centre. Christ himself is between two diagonals: one symbolises evil with the beam of the cross and the face of the bad thief on the lower right; the other links the face of the good thief with St Veronica withdrawing with the shroud.

Adriaan Isenbrant's *Virgin and Child* has a strikingly beautiful landscape. The work of 16C Ghent artist Gerard Horenbaut, known especially as a miniaturist, is represented here by portraits.

The works of Pieter Brueghel the Younger and Roland Savery come next, then an admirable *Portrait of a Woman* by Pourbus the Elder, then some works by Rubens, a *Study of Heads* by Jordaens of unusual vigour, Gaspar de Crayer's *Study of a Young Moor's Head, Emmaus's Disciplines* and a *Portrait of Jean-Pierre Camus* by Philippe de Champaigne, a *Bittern* by Fyt and a portrait by Frans Hals.

The works by Antwerp painter Joachim Beuckelaer (1530-1574), gathered in another part of the museum, depict realistic representations of markets and kitchens.

Modern painting *(right wing)* – The collection is extensive, displaying in particular paintings by the Belgian artists Ensor, Evenepoel *(Spaniard in Paris)*, Spilliaert, Emile Claus, Van Rysselberghe *(Reading)*, as well as by the French artist Rouault and the Expressionists Kokoschka, Kirchner and Rholfs.

A few rooms have been devoted to paintings by the first St.-Martens-Latem group *(qv)* with Minne, Van de Woestijne, De Saedeleer; and by the second one, that is Permeke, Gust De Smet, Servaes.

Works from the 19C French school are in a room together: Géricault with his remarkable *Portrait of a Kleptomaniac*, Corot, Courbet, Fantin-Latour, Daubigny, Théodore Rousseau.

Museum of Contemporary Art (Museum van Hedendaagse Kunst) – This museum, inaugurated in 1976, is in the same building. It is devoted to movements of contemporary art presented in a series of temporary exhibitions. Cobra, hyperrealism, minimal art, conceptual art, pop art and all contemporary movements are represented, as well as forerunners such as René Magritte, Paul Delvaux and Victor Servranckx.

★★ **Bijloke Museum** (CX M[3]) ⊙ – The old Bijloke Cistercian abbey was founded in the 13C. This remarkable group of brick buildings dates from the 14C to the 17C, and contains a museum of archaeology and history.

Inside the conventual buildings there are beautiful rooms in which old Ghent interiors have been reconstructed; large **collections of decorative art** are exhibited in the galleries of the cloister (ironwork, copperware, bronze, potteries and ceramics), costumes and arms.

The marvellous 14C **refectory** on the first floor has a large coffered vault and frescoes, one of which represents the Last Supper. There is a beautiful recumbant effigy in Tournai stone in the centre; this is of a Ghent lord who died in 1232.

The Guild Room, once the dormitory, has magnificent 18C **candelabra** in carved wood, symbolising the different professions.

Two rooms on the ground floor are devoted to various military brotherhoods in Ghent.

While crossing the little gallery looking out on a second courtyard, notice the refectory's gable, delicately sculpted with moulded bricks.

In the 17C abbesses' house, beautiful 17C fireplaces were installed from the town hall.

There are wonderful silver insignia of the town musicians (15C and 16C) in the room on the Ghent community.

ADDITIONAL SIGHTS

★ **Little Beguine Convent (Klein Begijnhof)** (DX) – This calm enclosed community was founded in 1234 by Joanna of Constantinople; it has not changed since the 17C and four beguine nuns still live here. The charming brick houses, with little gardens and whitewashed walls, surround the church and two meadows.

Museum of Decorative Arts (Museum voor Sierkunst) (EY M[4]) ⊙ – The elegant rooms in the old 18C Coninck mansion is home to beautiful furniture grouped by period, tapestries and objets d'art which reproduce the atmosphere of a patrician home of the past. Certain rooms are decorated with painted canvas panels. The **dining room** (Room 7), with its painted ceiling, woodwork, furniture and Chinese porcelains, makes a particularly elegant 18C ensemble. A new wing contains modern furniture.

St Bavo's Abbey Ruins **(Ruïnes van de St.-Baafsabdij)** (DV M5) – The abbey was founded in the 7C and rebuilt in the 10C.
In 1540, having proclaimed the Caroline Concession *(qv)*, Emperor Charles V turned the abbey into a citadel. It was demolished in the 19C.
Nothing remains of the abbey buildings but the gallery of a Gothic cloister, the beautiful Romanesque wash-house, the twinned Romanesque windows, the chapter-house and above all the vast 12C **refectory★**, with its magnificent timber ceiling shaped like a ship's hull. It contains Romanesque frescoes and a large collection of gravestones. There are also many Romanesque and Gothic stones in the cellars.

Old Beguine Convent of St Elizabeth **(Oude Begijnhof van St.-Elisabeth)** (CV **Z**) – This large beguine convent, like the small one, was founded in 1234. When it became inadequate for their needs in the 19C the nuns abandoned it to settle in St.-Amandsberg *(see below)*. All that now remains is a narrow picturesque street, the **Proveniersterstraat**, near St Elizabeth's Church; there are also three pretty gabled houses not far from the church porch which have been well-restored.

The Begijnhoflaan leads to the **Rabot** (CV) from the north. This 1489 fortified sluice has pointed roofs and crowstepped gables; it was once a lock beneath which the Liève disappeared to flow underground. Not far from here is the **Donkere Poort**, the only trace of the palace (Prinsenhof) where Emperor Charles V lived.

Patrician House **(Patriciërswoning De Achtersikkel)** (FY **N**) – This mansion, with its turrets and arcaded courtyard, forms part of a pretty 16C setting, in a little street near the cathedral (Biezekapelstraat).

EXCURSIONS

St.-Amandsberg – *Return to the Land van Waaslaan (***DV 100***). The entrance to the beguine convent is at no 53.*

The Large Beguine Convent (Begijnhof) (**DV**) – In 1874 this succeeded the old beguine convent of St Elizabeth *(see above)*, from which it took its name. This is an immense enclosure with the traditional look of beguine convents. A neo-Gothic church stands in the middle. A few nuns still live here. The **museum** gives a glimpse of the beguine nuns' way of life.

Lochristi – Pop 16 970. *9km – 5.5 miles northeast on the N 70.* The cultivation of begonias (flowering in summer) and azaleas predominates in this important agricultural centre.

★ **Laarne** – *13km - 8 miles eastwards. Leave on the N 445 and turn left towards Heusden.* Magnificent properties can be seen along this road before reaching Heusden. *Description of Laarne Castle under Laarne Castle.*

Eeklo – Pop 18 989. *20km – 12.5 miles northwest on the N 9.* Eeklo has a pretty Renaissance **town hall**, with gables, dormers and brightly-coloured shutters.

The 16C **Watervliet** church, 29km - 18 miles north on the N 456, near the border with the Netherlands, has a beautiful 15C triptych painted on wood, and interesting baroque furniture.

Along the River Leie **(Leiestreek)** – *22km - 13.75 miles. Leave on the Koningin Fabiolalaan, near the station (St.-Pietersstation) (***CX***).*
The banks of the Leie have inspired many a painter. The name of the little town of **St.-Martens-Latem** has a permanent place in the history of art.
At the end of the 19C a group of artists formed around sculptor Georges Minne, who had lived in the village since 1897: Gustave Van de Woestijne (1881-1947), the landscape painters Van den Abeele (1835-1918) and Valerius de Saedeleer (1867-1941).
Their research ended, after the war, in the very marked Expressionism of the second St.-Martens-Latem group, of which the forerunner was **Albert Servaes** (1873-1967). The principal representatives were **Constant Permeke** (1886-1952), the head; **Gustave De Smet** (1877-1943) and **Frits Van den Berghe** (1883-1939).

There is no road which actually follows the course of the Leie; a **boat trip** is the best way to discover the countryside along its banks.

Afsnee – The charming Romanesque church here, with its east end on the banks of the Leie, is often made the subject of paintings.

St.-Martens-Latem – Pop 7 948. The area around this village near the Leie, like that of Deurle, is very much frequented by people from Ghent. A 15C wooden windmill can be seen on the left from the road crossing the village.

Deurle – *See Deurle.*

On leaving Deurle the route initially follows the Leie (pretty view on the left), before crossing a bridge and revealing a beautiful **view** of the river running lazily between rich green meadows.

Ooidonk Palace (Kasteel van Ooidonk) – This 16C palace is in a meander of the Leie, near the village of Bachte-Maria-Leerne; it replaced a medieval fortress, inhabited by the lords of Nevele and demolished during the Wars of Religion.
The present palace, surrounded by water and a wooded estate, is still inhabited. It is characteristic of the hispano-flemish style, with crowstepped gables and onion-domed towers. The interior was reworked in the 19C and includes a beautiful suite of apartments. Among the 16C portraits are those of Philip of Montmorency, Count of Hornes and owner of the palace, and that of the Count of Egmont. Both were beheaded in Brussels in 1568.

Deinze – Pop 25 614. This small industrial town was built on the banks of the Leie. There is a beautiful **church** dedicated to Our Lady (Onze-Lieve-Vrouwekerk). It dates from the 13C and is an excellent example of Scaldian Gothic (triplets, tower above the transept crossing). A work by Gaspar de Crayer can be admired inside: *Adoration of the Shepherds.*

A little further along, the white building of the **Museum of Deinze and the Leie Region** (Museum van Deinze en Leiestreek) ⊙ can be seen through the trees. The St.-Martens-Latem group is well represented in the collections of paintings and sculptures by Ghent-Kortrijk regional artists. Note: the *Beetroot Harvest* by Emile Claus, *Marshy Landscape* by Saedeleer and the works of A Saverys, A Servaes, Van de Woestijne, G Minne, Van Rysselberghe, Van den Abeele and R Raveel. The museum also includes an archaeology and folklore section.

★ GERAARDSBERGEN Oost-Vlaanderen

Pop 30 133

Michelin maps 409 E3 or 213 fold 17

The name of this town evokes its lofty **location**★ on a hillside, overlooking the River Dender. It is famous in the world of cycle racing because of the terrible hill called the "Geraardsbergen wall".

Geraardsbergen has a very large match factory. Mattentaart (fromage blanc tart) is a town speciality.

SIGHTS

Market Place (**Grote Markt**) – St Bartholomew's Church stands on this square, along with the 19C town hall with its toothed gables and corner turrets. The little Manneken Pis against it is said to be the oldest in Belgium (1455).

A Gothic fountain, called the Marbol, in the centre of the square dates from 1475.

St Adrian's Abbey (**St.-Adriaansabdij**) – *Follow the road (Vredestraat) left of the town hall, then Abdijstraat to the right.*

A Benedictine monastery was founded here in 1081. The 18C abbey buildings were transformed into a **museum** ⊙, with old paintings and furniture from Geraardsbergen's St Bartholomew's Church and Ghent's Hane Steenhuyse mansion. A park has been created around a lake *(fishing).*

Oudenberg – *Access by car by the Zonnebloemstraat.*

A pilgrims' chapel was built at the top of this mountain, at an altitude of 111m - 364ft; there is a beautiful view of the surrounding countryside from here.

The **Krakelingenworp** festival takes place here, or "sugar bun throwing" *(see the Calendar of Events at the end of this guide).* A folkloric procession (800 participants) begins to climb the hill at 15.00. When they reach the top, 8 000 sugar buns called "Krakelingen" are thrown out over the crowd and the local celebrities must drink little live fish from a silver goblet. In the evening, a cask is set on fire during the **Tonnekensbrand**. The origin of this event, which is thought to be very old, is still a mystery.

★★★ GHENT See Gent

GRAND-HORNU Hainaut

Michelin maps 409 E4 or 214 fold 2

Hornu is a coal-mining town in the Borinage region near Mons which has an architecturally-designed industrial complex, the Grand-Hornu, which was built between 1814 and 1832. This complex is a remarkable example of how workplace and home can be designed to make a unified whole, as had been done at the salt-works at Arc-et-Senans in France 25 years earlier.

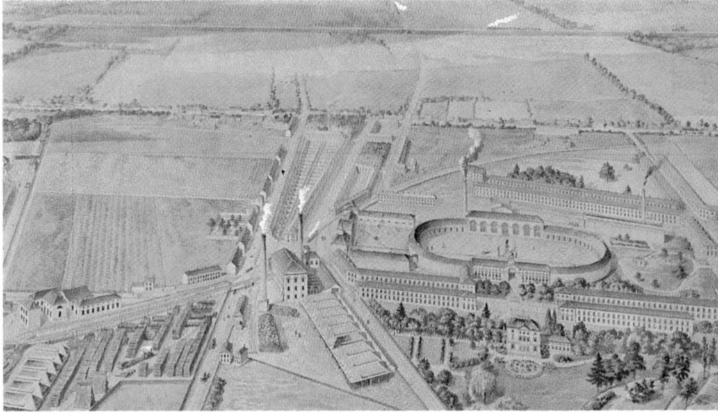

Panoramic view of the use of the Grand-Hornu area *c*1900

The founder of Grand-Hornu, the industrialist **Henri de Gorge** (1774-1832), assigned the design of the complex to architect Bruno Renard, who conceived the site in the neo-classical style very much in vogue at the time. This can be seen from the use of arcades, pediments and half-moon windows. In addition to the industrial complex, 425 houses, exceptionally comfortable for the period, were built for the workers.
Grand-Hornu ceased its activites in 1954, and was abandoned for several years. In 1969 a royal decree condemned it to demolition. Then in 1971 a Grand-Hornu architect, Henri Gucher, bought the ruins of the site and undertook its restoration. Since 1989 the Grand-Hornu has been the property of the Province of Hainaut.

TOUR ⏲

The tour takes visitors first into a closed courtyard bordered on the left by old stables converted into art galleries (doors sculpted by Félix Roulin); on the right is the barn for storing hay. Then there is an oval courtyard surrounded by arcades and brick buildings, which is where the workshops once were (these are now used as offices). The main workshop on the left made steam-run machines; the pillars which used to support domes on pendentives can still be seen here. The administrative building is hidden behind a pedimented façade. The workers' 425 houses are arranged around the factory in rectilinear streets to form a rectangle. The community consisted of 2 500 people in 1829.

HAKENDOVER Brabant

Michelin maps 490 H3 or 213 fold 20 – 3km - 2 miles east of Tienen

This very old village is famous for its pilgrimages. The most spectacular one is the great procession of the Divine Redeemer *(see the Calendar of Events at the end of the guide)*, accompanied by men on horseback. This wends its way through the meadows and fields already sown with seed which, despite being trampled on by the crowds, still apparently produce rich harvests.

Church (Kerk van de Goddelijke Zaligmaker) ⏲ – The foundation dates from 690. It has conserved a tower and part of the transept which are both Romanesque; the chancel itself was built in the 14C. The nave was enlarged in the 18C. A famous Brabant **altarpiece★** on the high altar is in wood and dates from 1400; it depicts in a lively yet elegant way the miraculous construction of the church, in thirteen scenes. Three virgins undertook the construction of the church in the 7C; angels demolished it during the night. The thirteenth day after Epiphany a crow showed the virgins where they should build the church. They took 12 workers, and a thirteenth one came to join them, who was no other than Christ. It was in this way that the church was completed.

★ HALLE Brabant

Pop 32 370

Michelin maps 409 F3 or 213 fold 18
Town plan in the current Michelin Red Guide Benelux

Since the 13C the town has been consecrated to the cult of the Black Virgin, the object of a famous pilgrimage: the procession at Whitsun with its historical pageant *(see the Calendar of Events at the end of the guide)* is the main procession, followed by those on the first Sunday of September and the first Sunday of October.
The carnival *(on Refreshment Sunday)* is famous.

★★ BASILICA *time: allow 45 min*

This was built in the 14C. Its layout, without a projecting transept, is a good example of early Brabant Gothic style. There is a powerful-looking square **tower** ⏲ surmounted by little bell towers at the corners and, since 1775, also by a baroque lantern. There is a little 15C baptistery on the south side, projecting from the main body of the basilica, with a bulbous roof. The carillon installed in 1973 contains of 54 chimes.
Note the **south doorway** and its *Virgin with Child* surrounded by angel musicians; a little further on, there is a little door depicting the *Coronation of the Virgin*. The harmoniously proportioned east end and the sides of the building are decorated with superb historiated corbels and a double series of balustrades.

Interior – The elegant nave has a triforium with Flamboyant Gothic tracery; above the porch, the wall is pierced with a double series of openings that also are Flamboyant Gothic. There are many wonderful **objets d'art** to be admired, as well as the beautiful sculptures.
The font *(chapel south of the tower)* dates from 1466; executed in brass, it has sumptuously decorated covers with apostles, horsemen (St Martin, St George, St Hubert) and a group representing the *Baptism of Christ*. Ten apostle statues from 1410 are in the chancel, inspired by the art of Claus Sluter, the famous sculptor to the Dukes of Burgundy in Dijon. The famous Black Virgin is enthroned in the middle. The sprandrils of the arches in the ambulatory are sculpted into remarkable scenes (15C).
An altarpiece in the Trazegnies chapel, which juts out from the basilica along the north side aisle, represents the Seven Sacraments; this was executed in the Italian Renaissance style by Jean Mone, sculptor to Emperor Charles V. Note also the

tiny recumbant effigy of Joachim, the son of Louis XI, in a chapel north of the chancel; the boy died in 1460, while his father, still Dauphin, was in hiding in Genappe *(7km - 4.75 miles east)*

Treasury ⏲ – The most beautiful items from the treasury are in the crypt, bearing witness to the generosity of illustrious donors. Particularly beautiful examples include two Brussels monstrances, one dating from the 15C and donated by Louis XI, the other from the 16C, donated by Henry VIII.

ADDITIONAL SIGHTS

Market Square (Grote Markt) – The **town hall** near the basilica was built in the early 17C in the Renaissance style; it was restored in the 19C, and now displays a harmonious façade. A statue of the cellist **Adrien-François Servais** (1807-1866), born in Halle, stands in the middle of the square. Servais was an international success – Berlioz called him the Paganini of the cello – and he was also the solo cellist of Leopold I.

Southwest Brabant Museum ⏲ – This is in an old 17C Jesuit school, and reflects the regional way of life life of the past: objects found in excavations, old tools, baskets made in Halle in the 17C and 18C, Huizingen porcelain, etc.

EXCURSION

Rebecq – Pop 9 088. *10km - 6.25 miles southwest on the N 6, then a road to the right.*
A **tourist train** ⏲ pulled by a little locomotive links the old Rebecq station to Rognon station in the Senne Valley.
Exhibitions are organised in the **Arenberg Mill** on the Senne.

★ HAN-SUR-LESSE Namur

Michelin 409 I5 or 214 fold 6

There is a mass of calcareous rock, crossed by two rivers, at the heart of the **National Park of Lesse and Lomme**; Han-sur-Lesse is famous for its magnificent cave and its animal reserve.

SIGHTS

★★★ **Han Cave (Grotte de Han)** ⏲ – *The entrance to the cave is in the reserve, and can only be reached by tramway. The return trip is made on foot (400m - about 0.3 mile).*
About a third of the giant calcareous cave cut by the Lesse over a 10km - 6.25 mile distance can be visited as part of a tour. This cave served as a refuge from the end of the Neolithic period to the 18C. It is very humid, with a temperature of 12°C - 54°F; gigantic concretions have formed, 4cm-1.5in per century, such as the graceful **Minaret** stalagmite. Certain galleries, used since 1856, have been blackened by torches. The **Chamber of Wonders** (Salle des Mystérieuses) nevertheless has all the magic of a crystal palace. The imposing **Chamber of Weapons** (Salle d'Armes), 50m - 164ft across, is crossed by the Lesse and features a son-et-lumière show. It is just before the **Dome Chamber** (Salle du Dôme) which is 129m - 423ft high, and the **Chamber of Draperies** with its spiky ceiling vault of marbled stalactites.
Large barges go down the subterranean stretch of the Lesse and emerge into daylight through the **Han Hole** (Trou de Han).

Museum (Musée du Monde souterrain) ⏲ – This museum exhibits the results of regional excavations, mainly those conducted in the Han Cave at the bottom of the river or on the banks: Neolithic shaped and polished flints; a remarkable collection of pottery; tools; arms; ornaments, some in gold from the Bronze Age (1100-700 BC); buckles from the Iron Age; a fragment of an **official diploma★** belonging to a Roman veteran, consisting of two bronze tablets; and various Gallo-Roman, Merovingian and medieval objects.

★ **Safari** ⏲ – A **wild animal reserve** is in a magnificent estate of 250ha - 618 acres, where the Lesse is swallowed underground. It contains animals from the Ardennes forests (deer, stags, boars) and, in a vast open area, the main wild animals that once lived in the region: bisons, brown bears, ibex, chamois , wolves, tarpans (small wild horses) and wild oxen (this extinct animal was "recreated" by breeding).
The Lesse disappears in the **Belvaux chasm** under a rocky arch of Mt Boine, to re-emerge at Han Hole.

EXCURSION

Lavaux-Ste-Anne – *10km - 6.2 miles west on the Dinant road.*
The **feudal castle**, surrounded by moats fed by the Wimbe, looks like a fortress; it is still flanked at the corners by three massive 15C towers with onion domes, and a 15C keep. The watchpaths linking the towers made way for a U-shaped main residential building in the 17C and 18C.
The **Museum of Hunting, Game, Falconry and Nature** ⏲ is inside. Stuffed animals, hunting trophies and documentation on European animals are on display.

HASSELT Limburg Ⓟ

Pop 65 861

Michelin maps 409 I3-J3 or 213 fold 9

Hasselt lies within the Kempen and Hesbaye regions. Since 1839 it has been the principal city of Belgian Limburg, when a treaty signed in London divided the province, a former duchy, between Belgium and the Netherlands. It is a busy city, growing ever more so with the region's increasing industrialisation. An excellent gin-like spirit flavoured with juniper-berries (geneva) is made here *(see below)*. The Hasselt district includes no less than nine makers of this spirit, locally known as "witteke" (little white).

The town depended on the bishopric of Liège from the 14C to the 18C, although it did rise in revolt from time to time, for instance in the 16C when Hasselt's Protestants took part in the religious disturbances breaking out against the prince-bishops.

The Flemish peasants revolted in 1798 against the French occupiers who were pillaging the country and selling church properties as "national property". This revolt, called **Boerenkrijg**, ended in a bloodbath; the monument on Leopoldplein (Z) recalls that in Hasselt a thousand men died.

In 1959 Hasselt was endowed with a modern cultural centre *(via Kunstlaan, Z **32**)*. The diocese of Hasselt was founded in 1967 and covers the province of Limburg. The University of Limburg was founded in 1968 east of the town.

Hendrik van Veldeke – The first poet in the Dutch language not to remain anonymous was born near Hasselt in the 12C. Hendrik van Veldeke died after 1210, and a statue in his memory stands in the little park at the corner of Dorpsstraat and Thonissenlaan.

Festivals – Every seven years in August *(see the Calendar of Events at the end of the guide)* the Madonna Virga Jesse, patron saint of the town, is honoured by a large religious procession, presided over by Hasselt giant De Langeman or Don Christophe.

A folklore festival takes place every year on 30 April on the Market Square: the Meieavondviering. The May tree is brought there in a procession, then planted while witches dance, and dummies representing the bad season are burned. Then Hasselt songs ring out, especially the Meiliedeke.

HASSELT

Street	Grid
Botermarkt	Y 7
Demerstr.	Y
Diesterstr.	YZ 8
Grote Markt	Z
Havermarkt	Z 18
Hoogstr.	Y 22
Koning Albertstr.	Z 27
Ridder Portmanstr.	Z 39
Badderijstr.	Y 2
Dorpstraat	Y 10
Kapelstr.	Z 23
Kempischesteenweg	Y 24
Kolonel Dusartpl.	Y 26
Koning Boudewijnlaan	Y 28
Koningin Astridlaan	Y 30
Kunstlaan	Z 32
Lombaardstr.	Y 34
Maastrichtersteenweg	Y 35
Maastrichterstr.	YZ 36
de Schiervellaan	Z 43
St. Jozefstr.	Z 44
Windmolenstraat	Z 50
Zuivelmarkt	Y 51

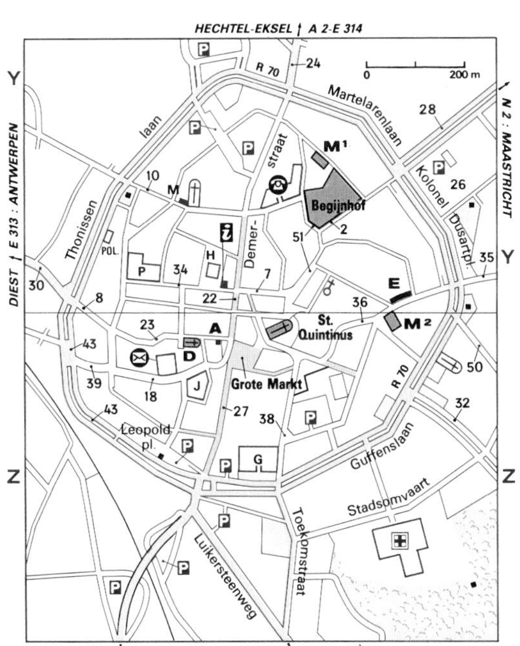

SIGHTS

Market Square (Grote Markt) (Z) – A half-timbered house dating from 1659, now housing a chemist's, is named after its sign **Het Sweert** (Z **A**), the Sword. **St Quentin's Cathedral** (St.-Quintinuskathedraal) (Z) is nearby, its presence marked by a squat 13C tower topped by an 18C spire. The nave and side aisles were built in the 14C and gradually enlarged with the chancel, the side chapels, then the ambulatory.

Church of Our Lady (O.L.Vrouwkerk) (Z **D**) – This 18C church contains works of art sculpted in marble from the Cistercian Herkenrode Abbey *(5km - 3 miles northwest of Hasselt)*. The abbey was founded at the end of the 12C, abolished in 1797, and its church was destroyed in the 16C by a fire. The **high altar** is the masterpiece of Liège sculptor Jean Delcour, who died in 1707 *(see Liège)*; the statues of St Bernard and the Immaculate Conception are also works by Delcour. The two **mausoleums** in the transept for the abbesses of Herkenrode were created by two artists; the one on the right *(Christ in the Tomb)* by Artus Quellin the Younger (1625-1700), the one on the left *(Resurrection of Christ)* by Laurent Delvaux (1696-1778). The 14C Virga Jesse, the origin of the septennial procession, is exhibited in the chancel.

★ **Gin Museum** (**Nationaal Jenevermuseum**) (**Y M**[1]) – The gin, or more specifically geneva, museum is in the farm-house of an old convent, which was turned into a geneva factory in 1803. This was in service until 1939. The museum has taken up geneva manufacture again, using 19C processes. This gin-like spirit is known as *jenever* to Flemish speakers and *genièvre* to French speakers, although it more often than not has its own local name from region to region. There are apparently over a hundred Belgian genevas.

Geneva, a malt wine made with a base of barley and rye, has been made in Flanders since the 16C. Sprouted barley is put on the perforated floor of a kiln to dry it. Then the barley and rye malt is ground to release the starch, and the mix (2/3 rye and 1/3 barley malt) is left to steep at about 63°C - 145°F, which lets the enzymes transform the starch into sucrose. By adding yeast the sugars turn into alcohol, and the whole is distilled to separate wort and alcohol; a second distillation of this rough geneva produces the malt wine with the taste that varies according to the quantity and type of flavourings (juniper berries, for example) which are added during the second distillation.

A numbered tour programme takes the visitor via the old ox stables to get to the kiln. On the ground floor there is the impressive steam machine that runs the millstones and the macerator. The 19C distillation set-up can still be made to operate. The exhibited collections in the old house concern geneva's history, packaging and advertising done by the manufacturers. The tour ends with a tasting session.

Beguine Convent (**Begijnhof**) (**Y**) - The garden is still bordered by rows of 18C beguine houses, with a little courtyard in front of them. They are in the Mosan style, with brick walls intersected with stone courses; they are now occupied by the provincial administrative offices. A modern building is home to the **Provincial Museum of Modern Art** (Provinciaal Museum voor Moderne Kunst) which organises exhibitions of international contemporary art. Moss-covered ruins and a few sculpted stones are the only traces left of the church destroyed by a 1944 bomb attack.

Stellingwerff-Waerdenhof Museum (**YZ M**[2]) – The collections in this museum illustrate the history and artistic life of the town of Hasselt and the old Loon county. Besides the liturgical objects, including the world's oldest monstrance dating from 1286, there are some marvellous Art Nouveau ceramics from the Decorative Ceramics Manufacturers founded in 1895, a collection of signs and some 19C and 20C paintings.

Abbey of Herkenrode Almshouse (**Y E**) – This beautiful 18C transitional Gothic-Renaissance building is now occupied by government administration; in times of trouble, this was a refuge for the Cistercians of Herkenrode.

EXCURSIONS

Round tour northeast – *42km - 26 miles – allow 3 hours. Leave on Kempischesteenweg* (**Y 24**) *and turn right after the bridge over the Albert Canal.*

★ **Bokrijk Provincial Domain** – *See Bokrijk Provincial Domain.*

Go round the grounds to the east.

The route soon crosses magnificent heather-covered hills, characteristic of the Kempen, then passes the recreation park of **Hengelhoef**, before reaching the road from Houthalen to Zwartberg.

Kelchterhoef – This is a great wooded recreation ground dotted with lakes *(fishing)* where an old half-timbered abbey farmhouse has been turned into an inn.

Head east to reach Zwartberg.

Zwartberg – *See Genk Excursions.*

Genk – *See Genk.*

The way back to Hasselt takes visitors past **De Maten nature reserve** *(qv).*

Heusden-Zolder; 't Fonteintje; Molenheide – *59km - 37 miles north. Leave via Koningin Astridlaan* (**Y 30**) *and turn right after going under the motorway.*

Heusden-Zolder – The **Zolder International Motor Racing Track** is south of the town near the **Bolderberg** (alt 60m - 197ft). It is 4.19km - 2.6 miles long, and is an important competition centre where the Belgian Grand Prix Formula 1 is run when it is not held at Francorchamps.

The Heusden-Zolder coal mine is the last one still in operation in Belgium.

't Fonteintje – This is a **recreation area** east of Koersel-Beringen, surrounded by pines. There is a view of the Kempen from the top of the **tower** (uitkijktoren).

Molenheide – This 180ha - 445 acre recreation park is north of Helchteren-Houthalen. It is located in the woods and has many resources. The **game park** (wilden wandelpark) lets wild animals (deer, stags, etc.) live at liberty. The park also provides many opportunities for sports (swimming, tennis, bicycles for hire).

★★ HAUTES FAGNES Liège

Michelin maps 409 L4 or 213 fold 24

The Hautes Fagnes region lies between Eupen and Malmédy, a wind-swept and desolate plateau with peat bogs and fields of flying bent (a smooth, herbaceous grass with a purplish blue panicle) stretching as far as the eye can see, broken up by the dark masses of planted spruce and clumps of deciduous trees (beech, oaks, birches). This region is now practically deserted, but it was once densely inhabited; traces have been found of a road, the Via Mansuerisca, which dates back to the 7C.

Nature reserve ⊙ – *Photograph p 14*
The Hautes Fagnes State Nature Reserve was created in 1957. It covers over 4 200ha - 10 378 acres, providing complete protection for flora, fauna, soil and countryside within its boundaries. Most peat bogs fall within the limits of the reserve. The plateau is not very high, but its harsh climate makes it possible to propagate several species of mountain animals and plants, even from quite far north. There are two dangers threatening the peat bogs. Firstly, being trampled on regularly stops their development and will ultimately lead to their destruction. This is why it is forbidden to leave the authorised signposted footpaths. Secondly, fire is absolutely fatal to this environment, and unfortunately occurs here all too often. Extreme caution is strongly recommended, especially in the dry season *(red flags = no admission).*

Nature park – Since 1971 the park has been part of the **Hautes Fagnes-Eifel nature park**. This includes the Robertville and Bütgenbach lakes in Gileppe and Eupen, and the Our and Eifel Valley, which leads into the German Nordeifel nature park. The whole area is called the **Deutsch-Belgischer Naturpark**, and covers a territory of 2 400km^2 - 5 930 acres, of which 700km^2 – 1 730 acres are in Belgium. To the south, it joins the Germano-Luxembourg nature park.

SELECTED SIGHTS

Botrange Nature Centre ⊙ – A vast, warm, well-lit building in pale wood greets visitors to the Hautes Fagnes. It houses an information centre, exhibitions, audio-visual presentations, and also a bookshop.

Signal de Botrange – 694m – 2 277ft. This beacon marks the highest point in Belgium. Together with the Baraque-Michel survey station this occupies the centre of this somewhat convex plateau of bleak and marshy countryside sprinkled with shaggy tufts of white-plumed cotton grass.
There is a far-ranging panorama *(orientation table)* from the top of the **tower** ⊙. On a clear day the **view★** is especially far-reaching to the northeast; the moors beyond the conifers, broken up by trees, stretch as far as Germany towards Roetgen and Aachen.

★ **Nature discovery path** – *1 hour 15min on foot, preferably in rubber boots. The beginning of the path is opposite the Signal de Botrange on the other side of the road.*
This pleasant walk follows the boarding over the peat bogs, making it possible to appreciate the immensity of the landscape extending to the horizon on all sides, as well as to discover birds and the plants of this region in close up: rowans, bilberry bushes, heather, birches, conifers.

Baraque-Michel – This is a land-surveying station (1886-1888) at an altitude of 675m – 2 214ft. The University of Liège has set up a scientific study station on nearby **Mt Rigi**.

HERENTALS Antwerpen

Pop 24 316

Michelin maps 409 H2 or 213 fold 8

Herentals was once a flourishing clothmaking town and has kept a few mementoes of its past, especially the south and east gateways from its 14C fortified enclosure.

SIGHTS

Town Hall (Stadhuis) – This is in the middle of the elongated market square and used to be the clothmakers' guild hall. Dating from the 16C, it was built in brick and sandstone and is surmounted with a tiny belfry with a carillon. The **Fraikin museum** ⊙ is on the top floor and contains a collection of plaster works by sculptor Charles Fraikin, born in Herentals (1817-1893).

St Waudru's Church (St-Waldetrudiskerk) ⊙ – This Brabant Gothic church still has its 14C square central tower. There is interesting furniture inside. The **altarpiece★** represents the *Martyrdom of St Crispin and St Crispinian*, patron saints of cobblers and tanners; Pasquier Borremans sculpted this in wood in the early 16C. Other interesting works include stalls sculpted in the 17C, and 16C and 17C paintings by Ambrosius and **Frans Francken the Elder**, who was born in Herentals, and Pieter Jozef Verhaghen (18C). Note the Romanesque font.

Beguine Convent (Begijnhof) ⊙ – *Access via Kraikinstraat and Begijnenstraat.*
This was founded in the 13C and was very prosperous. However the "iconoclasts" destroyed it in 1578, and it had to be rebuilt. The houses surround a garden, in which there is a charming Gothic church (1614).

EXCURSION

Round trip 65km - 40 miles to the northeast

Geel – Pop 32 228. The town earned a reputation for its colony of harmless mentally ill people, who are boarded out with local families. This special function of Geel is said to have arisen after the decapitation of the Irish princess St Dympna by her father, who had been driven mad by the devil.

St Dympna's Church (St.-Dimpnakerk) ⏲ can be seen on leaving the town towards Mol. This Late Gothic church has sumptuous furnishings: in the chancel, a beautiful black marble and alabaster **mausoleum★** dating from the 16C, by Antwerp artist Cornelis Floris; an altarpiece (1513) on the high altar illustrating the life of the saint; a late-15C Brabant altarpiece in the south transept arm representing scenes of the Passion; a 14C altarpiece in the first chapel of the ambulatory, showing the twelve apostles.
A little building against the church tower, called the Chamber of the Ill, has a pretty Renaissance façade.

Mol – Pop 30 412. Mol is reputed for its National Centre of Nuclear Studies, created in 1952. The **Church of St Peter and St Paul** (St.-Pieter-en-Pauluskerk) has a thorn from Christ's crown, in honour of which a procession (H. Doornprocessie) is held every year. A **pillory** stands near the church.

Jakob Smits (1855-1928), who lived in the village of **Achterbos**, is the great Kempen painter. The old presbytery in the neighbouring village of **Sluis** has been converted into a **museum** (Jakob Smits Museum) ⏲.

Ginderbuiten – The modern church (St.-Jozef Ambachtsman), built by Meekels, is most interesting.

Zilvermeer – These large provincial recreation grounds in the pine forests north of Sluis enclose two lakes: one is for swimming and boating, the other is for sailing.

Postel Abbey (Abdij Postel) – This is a Premonstratensian *(qv)* abbey, founded in the 12C by the Floreffe monks in the middle of a pine forest. The 18C buildings are flanked by a Renaissance tower with a carillon (concerts). The Romanesque **church** dates from the 12C and 13C, and was modified in the 17C. Organ concerts are given here. In summer the new room is used for chamber music concerts.

Kasterlee – Pop 15 785. This is the great tourist centre of the Antwerp Kempen region, located in the middle of a pine forest.
There is a pretty **windmill** to the south, opposite the little British Second World War cemetery abundantly decorated with flowers. Further south, on the River Nete, there is a watermill that has been turned into a restaurant *(signposted: "De Watermolen").*

Papekelders Viewpoint (Toeristentoren) ⏲ – *Shortly before the railway just outside Herentals, turn right towards the Bosbergen Wood and continue on foot.*
A 24m - 74ft viewpoint tower at the wood's highest point (altitude 40m - 131ft) provides a panorama of the region.

★★ HUY Liège — Pop 17 971

Michelin maps 409 fold I4 or 213 fold 21

Huy (pronounced "oo-ee") is a charming little village huddled at the foot of its collegiate church and its fortress, at the confluence of the Meuse and the Houyoux. In days gone by Huy's inhabitants boasted that they possessed four marvels: "li pontia", the bridge (Gothic, rebuilt in 1956); "li rondia", the collegiate church's rose window; "li bassinia", the market square fountain; "li tchestia", the fortress.
Huy was part of the Liège province from 985 to 1789. Its strategic location has meant that in its history there have been about thirty sieges and a long series of destructions.
The town produced famous Mosan goldsmiths in the 12C: **Renier de Huy**, creator of the font in St Bartholomew's church in Liège *(see Liège)*; and Godefroy de Claire, also known as **Godefroy de Huy**. Pewter has been a local speciality since the 7C.
In 1095 **Pieter the Hermit** preached to the First Crusade here. He ended his days in the convent of Neufmoustier, where he was buried in 1115. His mausoleum (1857) is inside the cloister ruins to the north of Rue de Neufmoustier *(access via Avenue Delchambre).*

Boat trips on the Meuse ⏲ – Trips are organised on the stretches of water around Huy.

SIGHTS

★ **Collegiate Church of Our Lady** **(Collégiale Notre-Dame)** (Z) ⏲ – This is a vast 14C Gothic church. Flamboyant Gothic flourishes can be noted in the clerestory, which was finished at the end of the 15C. An imposing tower adorned with a beautiful **rose window** ("li rondia"), 9m - 30ft in diameter, precedes the main body of the church. The apse is flanked by two square towers, very unusual in Belgium.
The nave and side aisles inside are lofty, harmonising with the chancel lancet windows rising 20m - 66ft high; they are decorated with modern stained glass to replace that destroyed in 1944. The vaulting was rebuilt in the 16C and painted with Renaissance arabesques. A Romanesque crypt lies under the chancel.

★ **Treasury** ⊙ – Apart from some interesting wooden statues of saints dating from the 14C to the 16C, there is a rich collection of Mosan gold- and silverware. This includes most particularly the four magnificent **reliquaries** from the 12C and 13C: those of the town's patron saints St Domitian and St Mengold, created by Godefroy de Huy, are unfortunately quite damaged; the reliquary of St Mark (probably from the 13C), with its remarkable lively little figures whose fluid lines are highlighted with champlevé enamel; and the reliquary of the Virgin (*c*1265), with repoussé figures against a very richly decorative background.

Fabri medallion "The Tree of Life", Treasury of the Church of Our Lady

Bethlehem doorway – *Go along the south side of the nave.*

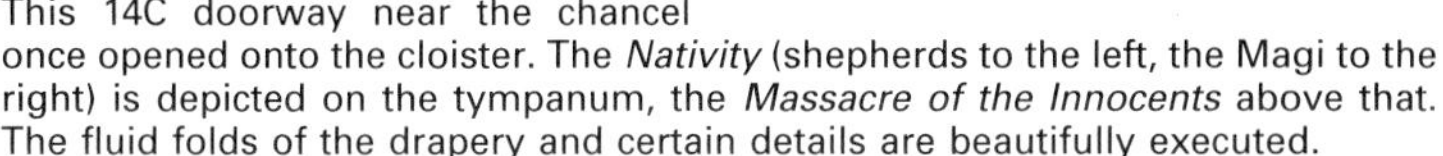

This 14C doorway near the chancel once opened onto the cloister. The *Nativity* (shepherds to the left, the Magi to the right) is depicted on the tympanum, the *Massacre of the Innocents* above that. The fluid folds of the drapery and certain details are beautifully executed.

Oultremont hospice – The **tourist office** is in this brick building, built in the 16C by Canon Gérard d'Oultremont, at the foot of the citadel. Note the beautiful tower-staircase. The Mosan Renaissance **Batta House** (maison de Batta) (**Z A**) is opposite on the far bank.

★ **Fortress** (Z) ⊙ – *Access by foot or by cable car going to the Sarte.* The fortress was built from 1818 to 1823 by the Dutch, on the site of the old prince-bishops' castle ("il tchestia"), demolished in 1717. This was a prison for hostages and Resistance members from 1940 to 1944. More than 7 000 people have been imprisoned here.
An indicated route leads visitors through the dungeons, the interrogation room and the military museum. From the glacis there is a splendid **view★★** over the old town, the Meuse and its surroundings; the Tihange nuclear power station (1975) to the northeast can also be seen.

Market Square (**Grand-Place**) (Z) – The beautiful 18C **fountain** (**B**), "li bassinia", stands in front of the elegant town hall, which dates from 1766. The fountain is surmounted with bronze figures dating from 1406 and 1597.
Charming little twisting streets lead to the museum, via **Place Verte** with the pretty Gothic church of St Mengold.

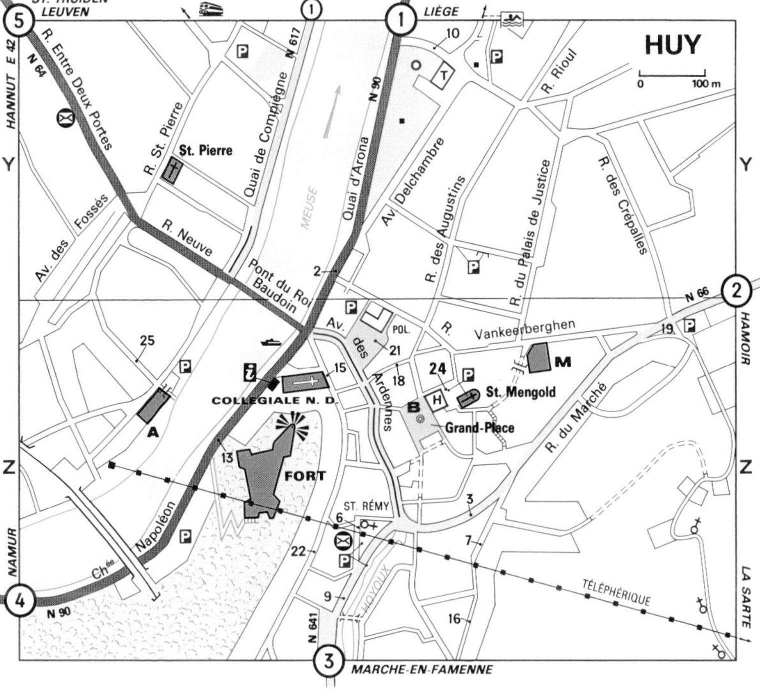

Neuve (R.)	Y	Condroz (Av. du)	Z 3	Reine (r. de la)	Z 16
Pont (R. du)	Z 15	Foulons (R. des)	Z 6	St Denis (Pl.)	Z 19
Rôtisseurs (R. des)	Z 18	Haut-Chêne (R. du)	Z 7	St Séverin (Pl.)	Z 21
St Pierre (R.)	Y	Hoyoux (Av. du)	Z 9	Sous-le-Château (R.)	Z 22
		Joseph Lebeau (Av.)	Y 10	Verte (Place)	Z 24
Autrebande (Quai d')	Y 2	Namur (Quai de)	Z 13	Vieux Pont (R. du)	Z 25

★ **Town Museum (Musée communal)** (Z M) ⏲ – This is in the buildings and cloiste of the old 17C monastery. The museum has large local history and folklore col lections: a regional interior decorated with a beautiful sandstone fireplace datin from 1621; archaeological finds; prints of the town; ceramics made in Huy in th 19C; pewter ware; and liturgical objects, including a 13C Christ called the "**hand some God of Huy**".

St Peter's Church (Église St-Pierre) (Y) – Romanesque font decorated with sym bolic animals (lion, dragon).

La Sarte – The **playing fields** ⏲ just where the cable car arrives also have a chil dren's playground.

EXCURSIONS

Amay – Pop 12 693. *8km - 5 miles east following the Meuse on the N 617.*

St George's Collegiate Church – This was originally Romanesque, then restored in th 18C. It is home to beautiful pieces of Mosan goldsmithing: the **reliquary**★ in silve and gilded copper of St Ode and St George, created in about 1230 *(north transep arm)*; and a **Merovingian sarcophagus*** *(beneath the chancel)* bearing the inscriptio of Santa Chrodoara, but which could in fact be that of St Ode. There is a littl **Town Museum of Archaeology and Religious Art** (musée communal d'Archéologie an d'Art religieux) ⏲ in the cloister. **Flône Abbey**, dating from the 17C and 18C, stand between the rock face and the Meuse about 2km - 1.25 miles from Amay. Ther is a beautiful 12C Romanesque font in the church.

★ **Château de Jehay** ⏲ – *12km - 7.5 miles east.* This makes a very romantic picture with façades in a white and brown stone checkerboard pattern reflecting in the moat's water. The building dates from the 16C and is a beautiful example of a Mosan fortified manor-house, but occupation of the site actually dates back quite a long way. Archaeological excavations have unearthed traces of a lakeside city 10 000 years old. The present owner of the castle, a sculptor and an archaeologist, has redesigned the gardens. There are marvellous **collections**★ inside including furniture, tapestries, porcelain and gold- and silverware. Note in particular in the smoking-room: a beautiful collection of silver- and goldware; a complete Koran on a single roll of paper; a human head shrunk by the Jivaros; in the library: a Brussels tapestry based on Teniers; and in the Queen Anne drawing room: a rare 18C harpsichord The **Museum of Archaeology and Speleology** (Musée archéospéléologique) ⏲ is in the 13C cellars. It exhibits certain items found under the castle's courtyard, including exhibits of fossilised bone.

Château de Jehay

★ IEPER (YPRES) West-Vlaanderen

Pop 35 099

Michelin maps 409 B3 or 213 folds 13, 14

Ypres, virtually flattened during the First World War, was rebuilt after the war. I was one of the most powerful Flemish towns in the 13C, together with Bruges and Ghent.

HISTORICAL NOTES

A great clothmaking town (12C-13C) – Founded in the 10C, Ypres would have had a population of 40 000 by *c*1260. The markets and St Martin's Church were built at about this time. Ypres sided with England in the Hundred Years War in the 14C, which meant it had the English wool it needed to continue clothmaking as a result, it suffered reprisals from the King of France. This was the beginning of the town's decline, when Bruges replaced it on the international market. Ypres suffered from local problems too; the conflicts between the upper class and craftsmen later put the power in the hands of the artisans, especially after the Battle of the Golden Spurs in 1302 *(see Kortrijk)*.

The decline of the town was accelerated first by an epidemic in 1316, then by the destruction in 1383 of the workers' suburbs during the siege by the people of Ghent and the English. By the 16C repression had given way to religious strife; many clothmakers left the country altogether. Ypres became an ecclesiastical town in 1559, when it was made the seat of a new bishropic (which was abolished in 1801); several convents were built. One of the bishops was the famous Jansenius *(qv)*.

A fortified site (17C-18C) – Its strategic location unfortunately made Ypres the victim of several sieges, and caused it to change hands on numerous occasions. The French captured the town in 1678 and Vauban surrounded it with ramparts. Under the reign of the Habsburgs, Ypres constituted the southern edge of a vast empire and had its fortifications further reinforced.
The ramparts were demolished in 1852, and have since been turned into walkways.

The Ypres Salient (1914-1918)

Who will remember, passing through this gate,
The unheroic dead who fed the guns?
Who shall absolve the foulness of their fate -
Those doomed, conscripted, unvictorious ones?
(Sassoon, On Passing the New Menin Gate, 1918)

The town of Ypres was completely destroyed by the First World War, although it subsequently managed to rise from its ashes and revive its commercial activites (textiles and other industries). After the flooding at Nieuwpoort *(qv)* the Germans concentrated their attacks in October 1914 on the Ypres region, one of the "bulges" in the German line of attack. The town was the focus of bloody battles for the next four years, during the continuing struggle to capture the salient to the east of the town, held by British troops. As was the case on the River IJzer (Yser), the front hardly moved an inch, in spite of all the Germans' efforts – not least their use of a lethal new weapon, poison gas, in Steenstraat (north of Ypres) in April 1915.
British troops suffered horrendous casualties during their offensive in 1917, which won them Passchendaele at the cost of thousands of lives. After a major German offensive planned by Ludendorff in the spring of 1918, which gained them some new ground (including Passchendaele once more), the Germans were finally thwarted in Merkhem to the north by Belgian troops, and in the Heuvelland (Flanders mountains – *see Excursions below*) by the British and the French. The Allied counter-attack began in September and finally resulted in the liberation of Belgium by October and the Armistice of 11 November. More than 300 000 Allies, including 250 000 British soldiers, died during these battles. The countryside around Ypres is nothing but a vast necropolis; there are over 170 military cemeteries.

The touring programme indicated with hexagonal signs, "Route 14-18", makes it possible to discover the sites and military cemeteries northeast of the town.

★ CLOTH HALLS (LAKENHALLE) (ABX) *time: allow 30 min*

These were finished in 1304, but destroyed during the First World War. They were carefully rebuilt in sandstone in the original primitive style.
They are in the form of a long rectangle surrounding two narrow courts. Seen from the market square (Grote Markt Albert I) they have a façade of 133m – 436ft in length, broken by a very beautiful square belfry flanked with four turrets. Stuffed toy cats are thrown from the belfry's second floor during the **Cat Festival**, which takes place every three years *(see the Calendar of Events at the end of this guide)*. This festival dates back to the 10C; the cats at that time were very much alive, and this was considered a challenge to the devil and witchcraft. Since 1955 the event has been preceded by a great procession of cats.

Cat Festival, Witches' Parade

IEPER

Boterstraat	AX 8
Diksmuidestr.	BX
G. de Stuersstr.	AX
Grote Markt	BX 9
Meensestr.	BX 26
Rijselsestr.	BXY
Tempelstr.	AX 38
Adj. Masscheleinlaan.	BX 2
Arsenaalstr.	AY 4
A. Stoffelstr.	BX 5
A. Vandenpeereboompl.	AX 6
Bollingstr.	BX 7
Hoge Wieltjesgracht	BX 10
J. Capronstr.	AX 12
J. Coomansstr.	AX 14
Kalfvaartstr.	BX 15
Kanonweg	BY 17
Kauwekijnstr.	BX 18
Lange Torhoutstr.	BX 22
Maarschalk Fochlaan	AX 23
Maarschalk Frenchlaan	BX 24
Meenseweg	BX 27
de Montstr.	AY 29
Oude Houtmarktstr.	BX 30
Patersstr.	AX 31
Poperingseweg	AX 32
Rijselseweg	BY 33
Stationsstraat	AXY 35
Surmont de Volsbergestr.	ABX 36
Wateringsstr.	BY 40

The halls are beside the **Nieuwerk** (**BX H**), an elegant Renaissance building dating from 1619, intended to house the town hall.

Ascent of the Belfry ⊙ – From the top there is a good view over the town and the cathedral *(264 steps)*.

Memorial Museum (Herinneringsmuseum) ⊙ – There are many documents on the First World War and on the Battle of the Salient on the first floor of the cloth halls. A display case is devoted to Guynemer, a French flying captain shot down in Poelkapelle *(9km – 5.6 miles on ① on the map)* in 1917.

ADDITIONAL SIGHTS

Hotel-Museum Merghelynck (**BXY M1**) ⊙ – This building dating from 1774 was destroyed in 1915 and rebuilt in 1932; luckily its collections were saved from the disaster. The beautiful furniture and objets d'art (paintings, porcelain) complement the refined 18C beauty evoked by the reconstructed rooms.

OCMW Museum (**BX M2**) ⊙ – This is in the chapel of the **Belle Hospice**, with its beautiful Renaissance panels. The collection consists of antique furniture and works of art: sculptures, silver- and goldwork, paintings (including the *Virgin and Donors*, from 1420, a beautiful composition with a gold background).

Menin Memorial Gate (Menenpoort) (**BX**) ⊙ – The walls of the memorial bear the names of 54 896 Britons who died during the battles preceding 16 August 1917. The bugles of the fire-fighting corps play the Last Post every evening at 20.00.

St Martin's Cathedral (St.-Maartenskathedraal) (**ABX**) – This was destroyed during the war, but rebuilt in its original style (13C-15C).
Admire the 16C polyptych on the right upon entering, and the 17C alabaster statues on the left, which crown the parclose screen of the baptistery chapel.

St George's Memorial Church (**AX F**) ⊙ – This Anglican church built in 1929 now commemorates the British military personnel who died during both World Wars. The furniture and the decoration were provided thanks to the generosity of donors from Great Britain and the Commonwealth.

EXCURSIONS

Bellewaerde Park – *5km - 3 miles east. Leave on ② on the map.*
The road goes past the Menin Gate and several military cemeteries, notably the **Hooghe Crater Cemetery** on the right, which contains over 6 800 British tombs.

In **Bellewaerde Park** ⊙ visitors can wander among antelopes, ostriches, deer, llamas and zebras; they can take a safari-tram to cross the area reserved for tigers and lions, see a show given by an elephant, and take a boat ride through an African landscape having passed beneath a magical waterfall and much more.

Tyne Cot Military Cemetery – *10km - 6.25 miles northeast on the N 332.* This British cemetery is the largest in the region. There are 11 856 white tombstones standing out against the beautifully kept lawn, arranged around the tall "Cross of Sacrifice". The curving semi-circular wall enclosing the cemetery bears the names of almost 35 000 soldiers who disappeared after 16 August 1917. This site, from which there is a beautiful view, overlooks the surrounding countryside.

The village of **Westrozebeke** to the northeast (13km - 8 miles) recalls a 14C battle *(see Kortrijk: Battle of the Golden Spurs).*

Heuvelland – *17km - 10.5 south on the ③ on the map; take the N 331 on the right.*

Kemmelberg – This wooded mountain (altitude 159m - 522ft) is a part of the chain of Flanders mountains which extend along part of the border. Very violent battles raged in the region until April 1918, at the beginning of the major German offensive.
The climb up this small mountain reveals some interesting views of the countryside. There is a neo-Gothic **tower** ⊙ from which there is an good panorama. An obelisk on the south slope marks the **French ossuary** where more than 5 000 unknown soldiers are buried.

Cross the N 375.

Rodeberg – This mountain reaches an altitude of 143m - 469ft; together with Zwarteberg (Mt Noir) in France it is a very busy tourist centre. A little windmill is to be found here.

★★ KNOKKE-HEIST West-Vlaanderen   Pop 31 340

Michelin maps 409 C1 or 213 fold 3
Town plan in the current Michelin Red Guide Benelux

Heist, Duinbergen, Albert-Strand, Knokke and Het Zoute together constitute essentially a single seaside resort, renowned for its elegance and what are considered the most beautiful towns on the coast, particularly Het Zoute.
The resort offers a wide variety of entertainment. A folklore market takes place in **De Bolle Centre** *(not far from Heist station)* on Thursday afternoons in July and August. Large exhibitions are organised every year in the **casino** and the **Scharpoord Cultural Centre** (Ontmoetingscentrum, *Meerlaan 32*), which is also used for conventions.
The resort is also extremely well equipped for sports enthusiasts *(golf, swimming pools, archery, stadium, gymnasium)*, an artificial lake (Zegemeer) and a thalassotherapy institute. A tramway provides a shuttle service between Knokke and De Panne *(qv)*.

Walks ⊙ – There are several pleasant routes for a walk starting from the station. The signposted **Flower Walk** (Bloemenwandeling) covers 8km - 5 miles and leads along willow-shaded avenues past well-to-do Zoute villas hidden in beautiful gardens. Several of the walks in the surrounding area lead through green countryside scattered with pretty white farmhouses with red-tiled roofs.

SIGHTS

Casino (Kursaal) – There is a beautiful Venetian crystal chandelier in the central hall. A bronze statue (1965) by Zadkine, entitled *The Poet*, stands in front of the building.

★ **Het Zwin** – The Zwin, an arm of the sea which is now silted up, lies between the resort town and the Belgian-Dutch border; it once served the ports in Sluis, Damme and Bruges.
This is a world of channels, tides and salt meadows, surrounded by dunes that isolate it from the sea and dikes that protect the countryside from flooding.
The Zwin was turned into a **nature reserve** ⊙ (150ha - 370 acres, of which 25ha - 62 acres are in the Netherlands) and is home to some interesting flora and fauna. Part of the reserve (60ha - 148 acres) is open to the public.
The best times to visit are spring, for the birds, and summer, for the flowers. Indeed from mid-July to the end of August the "sea-lavender of the mud-flats", the flower of the Zwin, forms a marvellous pink carpet.
Before beginning the walk, it is worth visiting the aviaries and the enclosure: storks nest and ducks splash about here, and it is possible to observe birds that come from the reserve itself. There is a view of the entire reserve from the top of the dike, which can be reached by crossing the woods.
The innumerable species living in the Zwin include terns, long-legged wading birds such as the avocet with its fine curved beak, ducks such as the red-beaked sheldrake and several migrating birds such as the grey plover and various species of sandpiper.

Michelin maps 409 A2 or 213 fold 1

This site, which embraces the sea resort of **Koksijde-Bad**, also includes the highest dune of the Belgian coast, the **Hoge Blekker** (33ha - 108ft) (**BX**).
Among the many events in Koksijde, the large **flower market** ⊙ is interesting, as are the fishermen's folkloric festival and a procession "in homage to Flemish painting" *(see the Calendar of Events at the end of this guide)*.

SIGHTS

Dunes Abbey (Duinenabdij) (**BY**) ⊙ – This was founded in 1107 by the Benedictines and became Cistercian in 1138. The abbey reached its apogee in the 12C, then declined and was finally destroyed by the "iconoclasts" in 1566 *(see Introduction: Historical Table)*.
Archaeological excavations carried out since 1949 have revealed certain **remnants**, which reveal the majestic lines of the abbey church. The cloister still has pretty corbels; the beautiful sandstone columns which belonged to the chapter-house and the lay-brothers' refectory still exist.
The products of the excavations are exhibited in the **museum** (**M**2). These collections concern, in addition to archaeology, history and regional flora and fauna (dioramas).
There is a wooden post **windmill** (Zuid Abdijmolen) (**AY**), dating from 1773, near Dunes Abbey.

Church (O.L.V.-ter-Duinenkerk) (**BX**) ⊙ – This modern church, which was built in 1964, is north of the abbey. It has great fluidity of line, in which arc-shapes predominate The undulating form of the roof and its navy-blue colour recall sea waves, and the beige colour of the brick walls reflects that of the nearby dunes. The stained glass windows diffuse an iridescent light inside.
The crypt *(access from outside)* contains a relic of St Idesbald, who was abbot of Dunes Abbey in the 12C.

Paul Delvaux Museum (**M**1) ⊙ – *In St.-Idesbald.* It is possible to follow the artist's development through the paintings, water-colours and drawings collected by the Paul Delvaux Foundation and exhibited here.
Paul Delvaux was born in 1897 in Antheit, a province of Liège, but executed a large part of his work in Koksijde. His post-Impressionist works are on display here, and his Expressionist ones, up to the Surrealist paintings in which he developed a highly personal style.
Certain subjects were particularly interesting to the artist: stations, compare for example *View of the Leopold Quarter Station* (1922) and *Forest Station* (1960); and above all women, whom he liked to represent more or less naked against a backdrop of Greek or Roman temples.

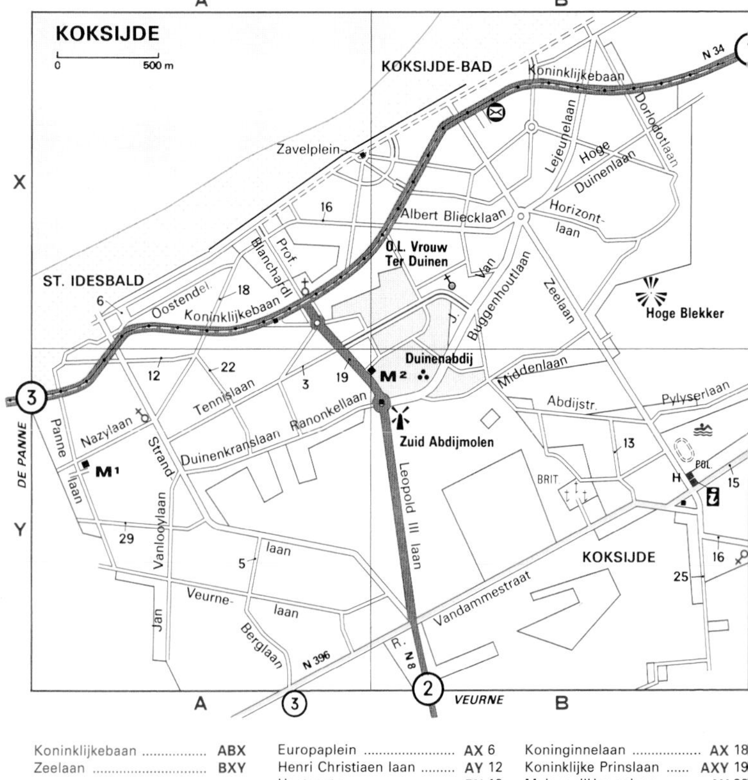

Koninklijkebaan	ABX		Europaplein	AX 6		Koninginnelaan	AX 18	
Zeelaan	BXY		Henri Christiaen laan	AY 12		Koninklijke Prinslaan	AXY 19	
			Hostenstr.	BY 13		Majoor d'Hoogelaan	AY 22	
Brialmontlaan	AY 3		Houtsaegerlaan	BY 15		Veurnestr.	BY 25	
Dageraadstr.	AY 5		Kerkstraat	BY 16		W. Elsschotlaan	AY 29	

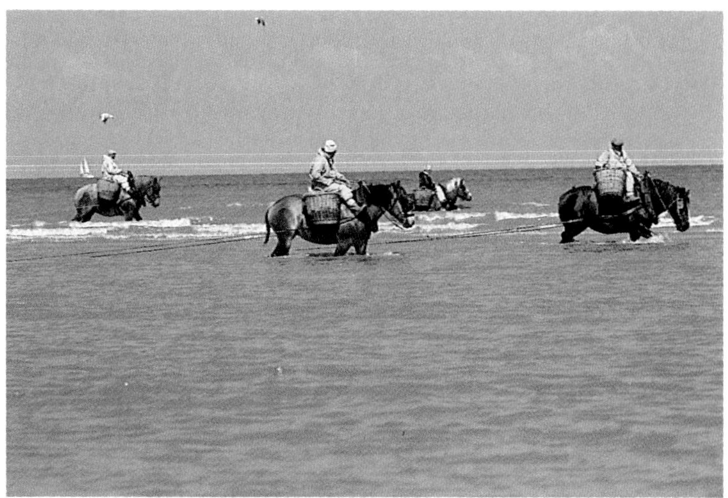

Fishing on horseback for shrimps

EXCURSIONS

Oostduinkerke – *4.5km - 2.75 miles east. Leave on ① on the map.*
A few people still fish on horseback for shrimps on the beach of **Oostduinkerke-Bad**. At low tide the horse, which has replaced the mule, pulls a heavy drag-net and heads into the water up to its chest. Each year the Shrimp Festival *(see the Calendar of Events at the end of this guide)* takes place with a parade on Sunday. Here, as well as in De Panne, the width of the beaches is ideal for the pursuit of landsailing (SYCO club).

St Nicholas's Church (St.-Niklaaskerk) ⊙ – This brown brick church, built in 1954, has great pointed roofs. Arcades join it to a massive square tower reminiscent of that of Lissewege *(see Zeebrugge Excursion).*
Yellow tones predominate inside, contrasting with the bluish colour of the flag-stones. The originality of the building comes from the absence of any chancel and the series of closely spaced lancet arches which spring up from below ground level.

National Museum of Fishing (Nationaal Visserijmuseum) ⊙ – *Pastoor Schmitzstraat 5.*
The museum is in a modern building. There is a beautiful collection of boat models, marine instruments and paintings by artists who worked in Oostduinkerke *c*1900, such as **Artan**, the Belgian painter born in La Haye (1837-1890). A typical fisherman's house was built beside the museum, with the north façade protected from the wind by a very low roof; a 1920 tavern was also constructed here. A lifeboat and a shrimp boat have been placed in the courtyard.

Florishof Folklore Museum ⊙ – *Koksijdesteenweg 24.*
This includes a reconstruction of a regional interior, workshops (lacemaker's, sabot-maker's, etc.), a chapel, a grocer's, a farm and a small school.

Ten Bogaerde Farm – *4km - 2.5 miles south on ③.*
This farm, a beautiful brick unit that once belonged to the Dunes Abbey, is to the right of the road. The monumental barn, comparable to that of Ter Doest *(see Zeebrugge Excursion)*, is now in ruins.

★ KORTRIJK (COURTRAI) West-Vlaanderen — Pop 76 279

Michelin maps 409 C3 or 213 fold 15
Town plan in the current Michelin Red Guide Benelux

Kortrijk, through which the River Leie flows, is a dynamic business centre at the heart of a growing industrial area. Its pedestrian streets and luxurious boutiques are a major attraction throughout the local region. **Roland Savery** (1576-1639) was born in Kortrijk. He was a remarkable painter of flowers and landscapes with animals. Savery worked in Prague for the Emperor Rodolph II, travelled in the Alps to observe the nature and then ended his days in Utrecht. His art is very similar to that of Velvet Brueghel.

HISTORICAL NOTES

A prosperous town – Kortrijk has existed since the Roman period (a 1C Gallo-Roman cemetery was discovered in Molenstraat in 1959), but its zenith came in the 15C with the flourishing of its cloth trade. Wool-weaving soon gave way to linen-making, because of the Leie; the soft water of this river was ideal for retting flax. Kortrijk became famous for making linen, and damask linen became its speciality. Kortrijk has remained an internationally renowned textile centre (carpets, upholstery, ready-to-wear clothing).
There are several other expanding sectors: metallurgy, iron and steel works, gold- and silverwork, oils, wood, chemical industries, construction.

The **Hallen** *(access by Doorniksewijk to the south)* is a modern architectural complex, dating from 1967, for conventions, exhibitions and concerts. It bears witness to the town's industrial and cultural development, which also plays an important role in education, notably because of the university (K.U.L.) campus *(see Leuven)*.

The Battle of the Golden Spurs – On 11 July 1302 a battle took place under the very walls of Kortrijk (near to the present Groeningelaan) which marked the Flemish struggle against the hegemony of the King of France. This battle had much to do with the actual formation of Belgium.

Philip the Handsome's French horsemen were defeated by the craftsmen of Ypres and Bruges, under the command of Pieter de Coninck *(see Brugge)*. The golden spurs collected from the field of battle by the victors carpeted the vaults of the Church of Our Lady until 1382, when they were taken by the victorious French army who had just defeated the Flemish in the Battle of Westrozebeke *(qv)*.

It was at this time that the Duke of Burgundy Philip the Bold is said to have taken the jack o' the clocks statues crowning the belfry and presented them to the Church of Our Lady in Dijon, France. A symbolic restitution took place on 23 September 1961; Manten and his wife Kalle now stand once again at the top of the belfry.

SIGHTS

Market Square (Grote-Markt) (CDZ) – This is the commercial hub of the town with a great number of pedestrian streets.

Belfry (Belfort) (**CZ**) – This dates from the 14C. The belfry stands in the middle of the market square and is topped with five pointed turrets and the famous jack o the clocks statues at the very pinnacle.

The imposing tower of the 15C **St Martin's Church** (**DZ C**) can be seen east of the square.

Town Hall (Stadhuis) (**CZ H**) ⊙ – The town hall has a restored Late Gothic façade; the statues, refurbished in the 19C, represent the Counts of Flanders.

The modernised interior still has magnificent rooms. The **Aldermen's Room**★ (Schepenzaal) on the ground floor is decorated with a remarkable stone chimneypiece in the Late Gothic style (1527), with alcoves containing statues of the Virgin and regional town patron saints. The ends of the beams on the ceilings are decorated with picturesque coloured scenes featuring Justice, a crowned woman, as the principal character.

The **old Council Room**★ (Oude Raadzaal) on the first floor also has a chimneypiece from 1527, decorated with three tiers of sculpture: at the top, the virtues; in the middle, on either side of Emperor Charles V, the vices; at the bottom, idolatry and the capital sins.

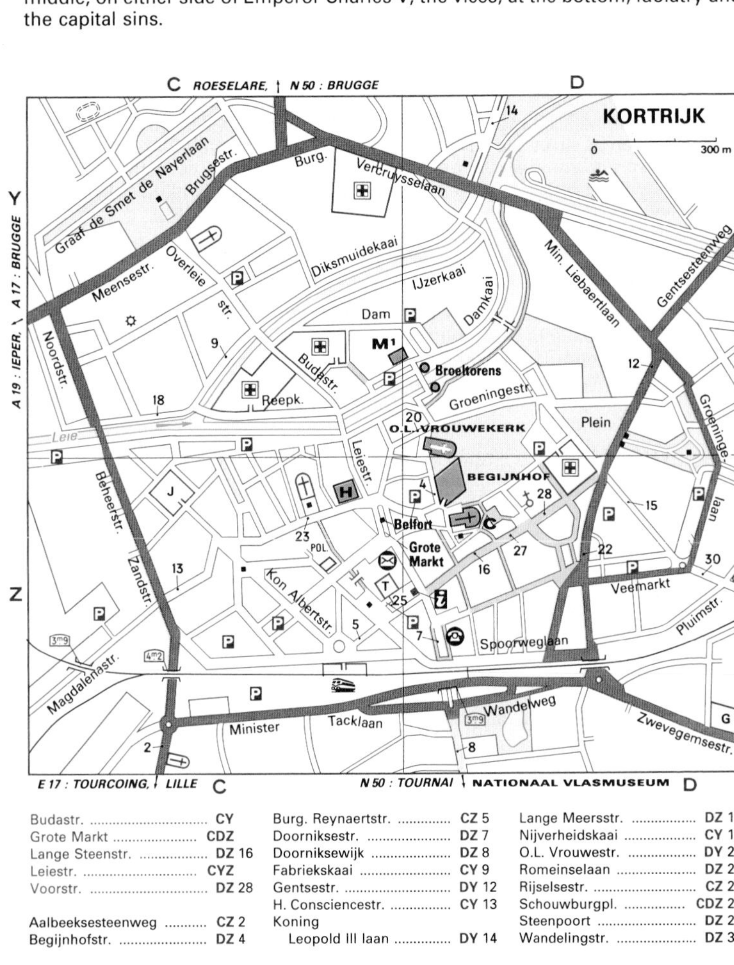

Budastr.	CY	Burg. Reynaertstr.	CZ 5	Lange Meersstr.	DZ 15
Grote Markt	CDZ	Doorniksestr.	DZ 7	Nijverheidskaai	CY 18
Lange Steenstr.	DZ 16	Doorniksewijk	DZ 8	O.L. Vrouwestr.	DY 20
Leiestr.	CYZ	Fabriekskaai	CY 9	Romeinselaan	DZ 22
Voorstr.	DZ 28	Gentsestr.	DY 12	Rijselsestr.	CZ 23
		H. Consciencestr.	CY 13	Schouwburgpl.	CDZ 25
Aalbeeksesteenweg	CZ 2	Koning		Steenpoort	DZ 27
Begijnhofstr.	DZ 4	Leopold III laan	DY 14	Wandelingstr.	DZ 30

Beguine Convent, Kortrijk

The sculptures on the ceiling beams here represent very picturesque scenes depicting the evil influence of woman over man, for example the illustration of the Lay of Aristotle (medieval poem) in which the philospher is being ridden by a woman.

★ **Beguine Convent** **(Begijnhof)** (DZ) – This is a charming little village between the churches of St Martin and Our Lady, with a surprising tranquillity amidst the hustle and bustle of the surrounding district.
The beguine convent, founded in 1238, was richly endowed by the Countess of Flanders, Joanna of Constantinople; a statue of her is on display here. The present 41 cottages date from the 17C. The Superior's House (no 27) is distinguished by double gables. A small **museum** ⊙ evokes the atmosphere of the past.

★ **Church of Our Lady** **(O.-L.-Vrouwekerk)** (DY) ⊙ – The towers of this church look out over the picturesque little streets. Baldwin of Constantinople founded it in the 13C, and the poet Guido Gezelle *(qv)* was vicar in the 19C.
The 14C chapel of the Counts of Flanders opens onto the south side of the ambulatory, and has arches with curious sculpted spandrils. It is home to an alabaster **statue of St Catherine**★ (1380) attributed to Beauneveu; the drapery is extraordinary. A beautiful Van Dyck canvas, **The Raising of the Cross**★, is in the north transept arm; Rubens' influence is plainly at work in it.

Broel Towers **(Broeltorens)** (DY) – These remain from the old fortifications Louis XIV destroyed in 1684. They protected the bridge over the Leie (rebuilt after the First World War). The south tower dates from the 12C, the north one from the 13C.

Town Museum **(Stedelijk Museum)** (CY M[1]) ⊙ – This well-arranged museum has a beautiful collection of ceramics, silver, old objects, sculptures and an interesting series of paintings from the 16C to the present; note Roland Savery's *Pillaging of a Village*.

★ **National Linen Museum** **(Nationaal Vlasmuseum)** ⊙ – *Etienne Sabbelaan 4. Via Doorniksewijk south of the map.*
The National Linen Museum is in a 19C farm originally intended for producing linen, one of Flander's most important activities, especially in the Leie region.
The successive steps in producing linen as well as the development of this industry up to the use of the first machines (*c*1900) are evoked by paintings or life-size dummies dressed in traditional costumes demonstrating each activity. A wing of the building is devoted to growing the necessary plants and working the linen, the other to crafts for domestic purposes.
Reconstructed interiors demonstrate the various steps – breaking, stripping, hackling, spinning and finally the weaving of linen.

EXCURSION

Rumbeke – *18km - 11 miles northwest towards Roeselare.*
A beautiful park (Sterrebos) surrounds **Rumbeke palace** ⊙.
The palace dates from the 15C and 16C, and its many turrets, including one with an onion dome, and gables jut out into the skyline. Baldwin of the Iron Arm, who came to carry off Judith, daughter of the King of France, Charles the Bald, took refuge here in 862. Following this incident he became king of the territory of Flanders, and also became the first count.

★ LAARNE CASTLE Oost-Vlaanderen Pop 11 349

Michelin maps 409 E2 or 213 fold 5

The grey walls of **Laarne Castle** ⊙ are flanked with stone-roofed towers and a turreted keep, rising up from the moat which surrounds it. The castle was built in the 12C to defend Ghent and was modified in the 17C. The main courtyard and present entrance, which is preceded by a stone bridge and surmounted by a loggia, date from this period.
The **interior** has been furnished to recreate the atmosphere of a 17C palace. Large pieces of Antwerp and French furniture are arranged around the rooms, which have beautiful chimneypieces. The walls are hung with marvellous tapestries. Two of these date from the 16C and come from Brussels. They were made based on cartoons by B van Orley and belong to the series known as *Hunts of Maximilian*. Note on the ground floor the Renaissance vaulting in the gallery overlooking the inner courtyard. On the first floor there is a lovely 16C tapestry depicting the life of a lord. Finally, visitors should not miss the 15C-18C European **silver collection★** donated by M Claude Dallemagne.

LESSINES Hainaut Pop 15 905

Michelin maps 409 E3 or 213 fold 17

Lessines is on the banks of the River Dender, in the middle of a region cultivating medicinal plants (especially in Deux-Acren). The town has famous open-pit **porphyry mines** *(not open to the public)* to the east.
The painter **René Magritte** was born here in 1898.

Lessines and its festivals – Good Friday is when the **Penitents' Procession** takes place, which dates back to the 15C. The **Cayoteu 1900** festival takes place on the third Sunday in August; in the morning the "cayoteux" (name given to quarry workers) work porphyry in the streets, and in the afternoon there is a procession of giants, led by one incarnating "El Cayoteu".
The **Historical Festival Pageant** takes place during the first weekend in September and commemorates the 1553 victory of Sebastian de Tramasure over the bands of pillaging English and Dutch who tried to capture the town. More than 600 people participate in fancy dress.

Hospital (Hôpital Notre-Dame à la Rose) ⊙ – This hospital was founded in 1242 by Alix de Rosoit, lady-in-waiting to Blanche of Castille. The buildings were reconstructed in the 16C, 17C and 18C in the Flemish Renaissance style around Gothic cloisters. The hospital is now a museum housing 16C and 17C paintings, pewters, porcelains. The materials to make "helkiase" can be seen in the infirmary; this was a cream to heal wounds, invented by Sister Marie-Rose Carouy in the late 19C.

EXCURSION

Ellezelles – *11km - 6.75 miles west.* 3km - 1.75 miles beyond the village **Wild Cat mill** (De Kattenmolen) ⊙ stands on the top of a hill 115m - 377ft in altitude. This picturesque wooden post mill dates from 1751.

★★ LEUVEN Brabant Pop 85 947

Michelin maps 409 G-H3 or 213 fold 19

Leuven is the seat of a famous university. It stands on the banks of the River Dijle, and a number of beautiful historical religious buildings and an admirable town hall stand as reminders of its illustrious past.

HISTORICAL NOTES

Leuven's first castle was captured by the Vikings, who were defeated in turn soon afterwards by Arnold de Carinthie (891). A new one was built in the 11C by Lambert I the Bearded, Count of Leuven; this was to form the root of the town's development.
Leuven was the capital of the Duchy of Brabant, favoured by its site at the far end of the navigable part of the Dijle, and its position on the route linking the Rhineland to the sea. It became an important clothmaking town. A rampart was built in the 12C, of which a few traces remain, especially in **St.-Donatus Park** (**Z**). In the 13C a fortress was built to the north on **Cesarsberg** (**Y**).
The **Joyous Entry**, a charter of Brabant's liberties to which all new sovereigns had to swear fealty, was signed in Leuven in 1356 and was effective until 1789. Leuven then surrounded itself with a second fortified enclosure, about 7km - 4.25 miles long. However, violent conflicts pitted the clothmakers' guilds against the aristocracy, and a great riot broke out in 1378, culminating in the capture of the town hall. The aristocrats who had taken refuge there threw themselves from the windows. With its cloth trade ruined by civil war, Leuven suffered under competition from Brussels. Nevertheless, under the Burgundian domination several large buildings (the town hall was built at the end of the 15C) and a university were added to the town.
Leuven developed its commercial activities in the 18C, especially the brewing of beer, an art going back to the 14C. There is a large **brewery** ⊙ open to visitors.

When Leuven was sacked and burned in 1914, 1 800 houses and the university library were destroyed. In 1940 the university was set on fire and the town heavily bombed; in May 1944 Allied bombs also damaged the town. However, Leuven's rise from the ashes was rapid.

The Catholic University of Leuven – The "Alma Mater" was founded in 1425 on the initiative of Pope Martin V and at the request of John IV, Duke of Brabant. This soon became one of the most prestigious institutions in Europe. In 1517 Erasmus founded the Three Languages College, where Hebrew, Latin and Greek were taught, and which served as a model for the Collège de France in Paris. The University withstood the religious strife of the 16C and remained a steadfast champion of orthodoxy for many years. Several illustrious figures are associated with it: one of its rectors, the preceptor of Emperor Charles V, became Pope Adrian VI (1459-1523); in the 16C, Justus Lipsius *(see Excursion below)* taught here; then Mercator *(see Sint-Niklaas)*; and in the 17C, **Jansenius** (1585-1638). After the death of Jansenius, the *Augustinus* was published in 1640 in Leuven, a work condemned by the Pope in 1642 but which was to give birth to the Jansenist movement.
The University built up a magnificent library which was seriously damaged in the two World Wars.
The Catholic University of Leuven has been split since 1968. The French-speaking university, or Université Catholique de Louvain (U.C.L.) is in Louvain-la-Neuve *(qv)*. The Flemish Katholieke Universiteit Leuven, called **K.U. Leuven**, has 25 000 students, including about 2 000 from abroad.

Dirk Bouts – Dirk Bouts ranks highly among the 15C Primitive painters. Having studied in Brussels at Van der Weyden's studio, this Haarlem-born (Dutch) artist settled in Leuven in 1450, where he became the official painter in 1468. His masterpiece, the *Last Supper*, can still be admired in St Peter's Collegiate Church. While the sparseness and sobriety of his composition reflects Van der Weyden's influence, his works nevertheless have a style of their own: impassive expressions of the subjects, rich colours, meticulously painted décor.
Dirk Bouts died in Leuven in 1475. Both his sons, Dirk and especially **Albrecht**, inherited his talent.

Quentin Metsys was born in Leuven in 1466; this remarkable portraitist settled in Antwerp and died there in 1530.

★★ TOWN HALL (STADHUIS) (Z H) ⏲ *time: allow 45min*

Mathieu de Layens built this in the mid-15C in the late Gothic style, under the Duke of Burgundy Philip the Good. It needs to be studied at a distance to appreciate the vertical lines of this stone reliquary, elegantly carved with gables, turrets and pinnacles, dormers, and almost 300 alcoves sheltering 19C statues. The alcove corbels are decorated with small picturesque naive scenes that illustrate biblical stories.
Inside several works by Constantin Meunier are exhibited in a hall. There are three rooms, one after the other, the last two of which are particularly richly decorated. Otto Venius's *Resurrection of Christ* can be admired in the Louis XVI room with the painted ceiling. The large and small Gothic rooms on the first floor have oak ceilings, on which the archstones of the vaulting are decorated with scenes from the Old and New Testaments. Note also in the large room the 16C beams, with the corbels carved into biblical scenes.
A café and a small beer museum are to be found in the **cellars** (Raadskelder)

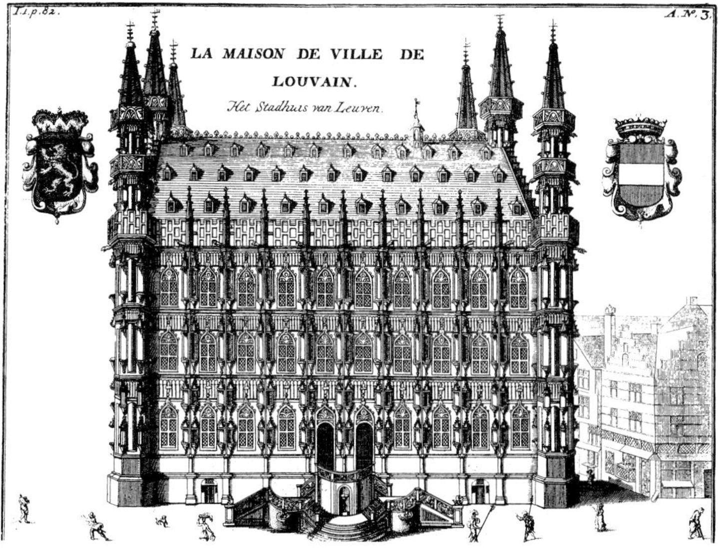

Town Hall, engraving by Jacques Harrewyn

ADDITIONAL SIGHTS

★ **St Peter's Church** (**St.-Pieterskerk**) (Z) – This was built in the 15C, in the Brabant Gothic style, on the site of a Romanesque church.

The 16C façade was intended to have three tall towers, according to Joost Metsys's bold plans; the ground was unstable, however, and it remained unfinished.

The **interior** has a particularly lovely effect with the pure lines of the Gothic nave; enormous pillars meet the vaulting in a single sweep. There are two storeys, and a triforium extended by many tall lancet windows.

The 18C pulpit is exuberantly baroque; St Norbert is seen struck by lightning at the foot of a rock set amidst spiky palm trees.

Before reaching the chancel the visitor will notice the three delicate arches of the **rood-screen**★ (1499), on which the dominant feature is a wooden Christ. The *Sedes Sapientiae*, a 1441 *Virgin with Child*, patron of the University of Leuven, is in the north transept arm.

★★ **Museum of Religious Art** (Museum voor Religieuze Kunst) ⏲ – The ambulatory and chancel contain pieces from the treasury as well as magnificent paintings.

Dirk Bouts's **Last Supper**★★ (1468) is a calm, luminous masterpiece of a marvellous simplicity. Depth and delicacy of brush stroke are combined with a varied palette. The painter, who represented himself standing to the right in a red hat, put the emphasis on the mystery of the Eucharist rather than on Judas's treason. Four richly-coloured biblical scenes on the leaves of the altarpiece prefigure the institution of the Sacrament. The *Triptych of the Martyrdom of St Erasmus* shows the executioner winding out the impassive saint's entrails with a winch.

A small copy of the Van der Weyden triptych, *Descent from the Cross*, was painted in 1440; the original is in the Prado, Madrid.

A remarkable 13C wooden **Head of Christ**★, called "of the Tortured Cross", was damaged by fire in 1914; the face is especially moving.

A superb **tabernacle**★ stands in the chancel. The lace-like openwork of the tower was executed in Avesnes stone by Mathieu de Layens (1450). The 15C stalls are carved with satirical subjects.

The Romanesque crypt was a sepulchre for the Counts of Leuven; their 16C mantles and chasubles are on display.

Naamsestraat (Z) – Several of the university colleges are along this street.

University halls (Univeriteitshalle) (**Z U**[1]) – In 1425 the University settled in these drapers' halls built in the 14C. A new floor was added in the 17C, and then the whole was rebuilt after its destruction in 1914.

It now houses the University Administration.

Pope's College (Pauscollege) (**Z U**[2]) – Founded by Pope Adrian VI, this vast 18C building has two wings and a severe-looking façade with a portico around the main courtyard.

St Michael's Church (St.-Michielskerk) (**Z B**) – This was designed by Father Hesius in the 17C; the splendid baroque **façade**★ is harmoniously proportioned, with lines flowing in a beautiful upward movement.

★★ **Large Beguine Convent** (**Groot Begijnhof**) (Z) – This beguine convent, founded in about 1230, first consisted of the district near the church. In the 17C it was enlarged to cover the impressive area of 6ha - 15 acres; it is the largest beguine convent in Belgium. The university bought it in 1962 and restored it as closely as possible to its original state. They have since provided accommodation for students; the last nun died in 1988.

This is a very beautiful group of buildings, crisscrossed by two arms of the Dijle, behind a boss-bricked wall. The houses in brick and white stone have small gates surmounted with arches; sometimes, as in the Spanish district, there are little alcoves with statues. Some of the dwellings have gardens. While some of the richer nuns had their own homes – the Sint-Pauwel House (1634) at Middenstraat 65 is an example – others shared a convent.

The Gothic **church** is sobre-looking; it has no tower, no transept and no ambulatory. The apse is lit through a beautiful double-lancet window. The decoration of the interior dates from the 18C.

★ **Vander Kelen-Mertens Town Museum** (**Z M**) ⏲ – The Vander Kelen-Mertens family mansion, which is now a museum with marvellous art collections, is accessed through a baroque door at the Savoy College.

Four rooms on the ground floor have been restored in the 19C style. The ceramics section displays European faïence ware as well as Japanese and Chinese porcelain. There is a collection of wonderful stained glass.

The fine art section contains works by painters Van der Weyden and Metsys (born in Leuven) and P J Verhaghen (who died here).

The 11C *Sedes Sapientiae* stands out among the sculptures, as does a late 16C altarpiece. The collection gives an idea of Brabant's great productivity in the 15C and 16C.

The **University Library** (**Z U**[3]) is nearby. Built in 1927 after the old library was destroyed (1914), this is an enormous neo-Gothic building crowned with a tower imitating that of the Giralda in Seville. The building was damaged by fire in 1940 but has been restored.

St Gertrude's Church (**St.-Gertrudiskerk**) (Z) ⏲ – This has a beautiful 15C tower built by Jan van Ruysbroeck, architect of the Town Hall in Brussels; the tower is surmounted by an openwork stone spire. Inside there are some interesting 16C wooden **stalls** carved with biblical scenes.

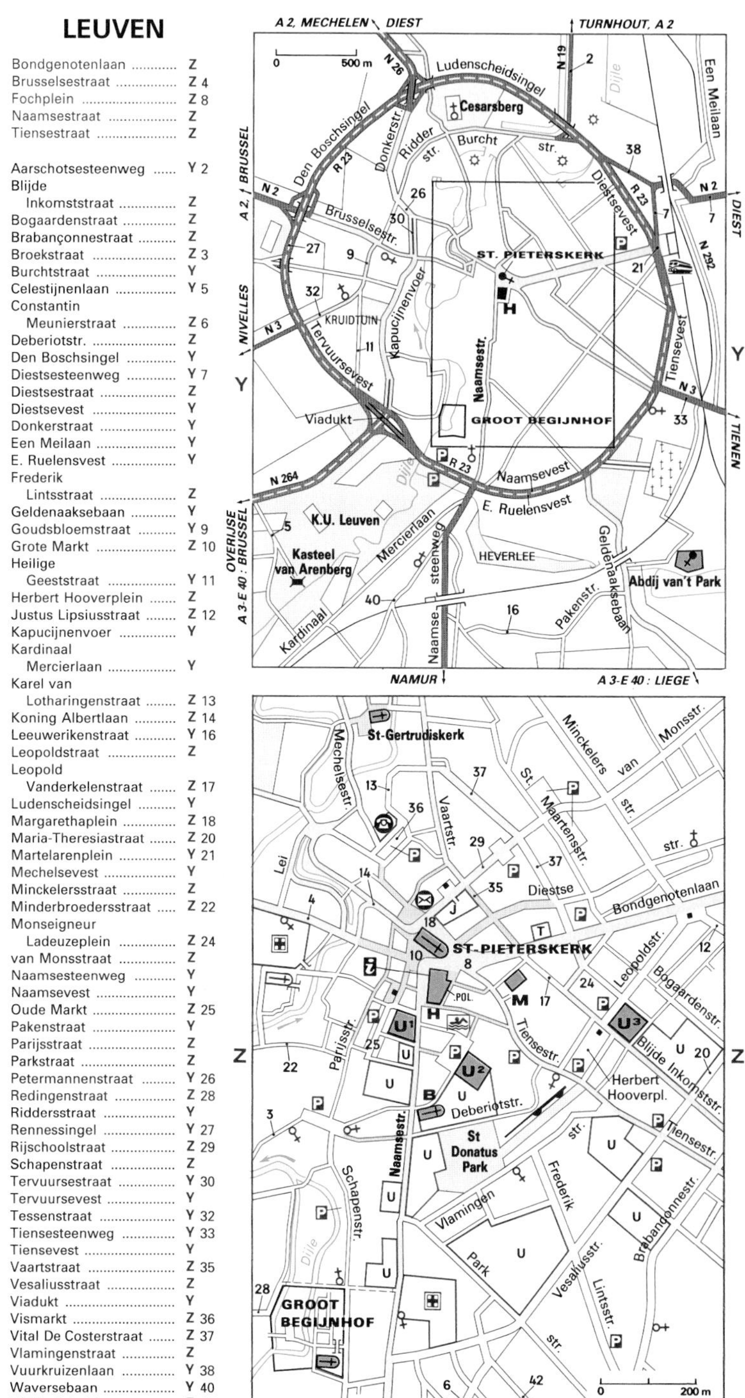

Park Abbey (Abdij van 't Park) (Y) – *In Heverlee. Leave on the Geldenaaksebaan and turn left after the railway bridge.*

The 16C-18C buildings of this Premonstratensian *(qv)* abbey stand on the edge of small lakes fed by the Molenbeek; the abbey was founded in 1129 by Godfrey I the Bearded. After going past several dilapidated doorways, then a water mill and a farmhouse, the road leads to the prelate's courtyard, guarded by two stone lions. The guided tour of the abbey buildings offers plenty of opportunity to admire the **ceilings**★ of the refectory (1679) and the library (1672), which are adorned with stucco high reliefs by Jean-Christian Hansche. The Romanesque church was transformed in 1729, and the baroque interior was decorated with several canvases by P J Verhagen (in the chancel and tribune).

Arenberg Castle (Kasteel van Arenberg) (Y) – *In Heverlee.*

This immense, early 16C castle *(not open to the public)* has an imposing dormer-crowned façade flanked by two onion-domed towers. It stands at the far end of a wide lawn and belongs to the university. The **science faculties** are in the grounds of the surrounding estate (120ha - 296 acres).

EXCURSION

IJse Valley – *25km - 15.5 miles southwest. Take the N 264 and take the N 253 on the left towards Overijse.* The road soon passes through pleasant countryside with rows of graceful poplars.

Korbeek-Dijle – **St Bartholomew's Church** ⊙ has a superb sculpted wooden **altarpiece**★ (1522) with expressive figures and painted side panels; it takes as its subject the martyrdom and cult of St Stephen.

't Zoet Water – *3km - 1.75 miles from Korbeek-Dijle.* This pretty wooded site (the name means "Gentle Waters") has five small lakes in succession which are popular with tourists *(horse-riding, fishing, boating, recreation park).* The Spanish house, a remnant of the 16C manor-house, has been converted into a restaurant; its image is mirrored in one of the lakes.

The road enters the valley of the IJse, a tributary of the Dijle, at Neerijse.

Huldenberg – The first **greenhouses for grapes** come into view at this point. The regional cultivation of vines in heated greenhouses began in 1865; this is widely practised throughout the IJse Valley and around Duisburg (Germany).

Overijse – Pop 23 389. **Justus Lipsius** (1547-1606) was born here, the humanist who taught at Leuven and was a friend of Plantin *(qv).*
Overijse, the heart of the wine region, organises grape festivals every year *(see the Calendar of Events at the end of this guide)*, occasions of great rejoicing.

Hoeilaart – Pop 9 300. Hoeilaart was built on hillsides where the smallest plot of land is occupied by a greenhouse; it is for this reason that it is nicknamed the "glass town". The great Harvest Festivals take place during the third weekend of September.

★★ LIÈGE Liège Ⓟ — Pop 199 020

Michelin maps 409 J4 (enlarged inset map folds 17 and 18) or 213 fold 22
Town plan in the current Michelin Red Guide Benelux

Liège is at the confluence of the Meuse and the Ourthe, lying in a valley surrounded by hills. The third-ranking city of Belgium, it is a major economic and commercial centre. Liège is an important river port and benefits from its position at the intersection of major transport routes and its proximity to both the Netherlands and Germany. During the glorious events of its past it has evolved into a cultural centre rich in churches and museums. Perhaps the most striking feature of Liège is its liveliness, arising from the character of its inhabitants who are renowned for their warmth, hospitality and light-hearted irreverence for authority. This reputation is enhanced by the many students from the Sart Tilman campus, who by night fill the cafés, bars and small restaurants of the "carré" (the area between Rues du Pot-d'Or, St-Adalbert, St-Gilles and Boulevard de la Sauvenière). During the day the lively atmosphere is transferred to the shopping precincts around Place St-Lambert and between Feronstrée and the Meuse. On Sunday mornings everyone from Liège heads for the **Batte Market** (**FY**) on the Maastricht and Batte quays, where a huge variety of items is on offer: antiques, poultry, household appliances, etc.

Viewpoints – To get an idea of the city's extended layout along the Meuse go to the **Citadel** (**DW**) *(by car, or on foot: 373 steps up Beuren Mountain)* where an orientation table gives an overall **view**★★ or at **Cointe park** (**CX**), where there is a **view**★ near the orientation table.

HISTORICAL NOTES

It is thought that Liège was founded in 705 after the assassination of St Lambert, Bishop of Tongeren and Maastricht. St Hubert built a chapel in honour of this saint which rapidly became a great pilgrimage site. In 721 it was decided to turn it into a bishopric, but it was only from the 10C that the importance of the town really began to grow.

The ecclesiastical principality (10C-18C) – At the end of the 10C the bishop **Notger** converted his territories into a principality, covering land from the Holy German Empire and corresponding to two-thirds of the present Wallonia. The history of this region was to be little more than a long series of battles; those led by princes to uphold their autonomy, and those led by subjects against their prince.
Liège was granted certain privileges in 1316 and again in 1343. However, these were taken away in 1408 after the principality's communities rose in revolt. Charles the Bold crushed another revolt and had the town razed in 1468, sparing nothing but the churches. As it happens, he later repented and presented Liège with the beautiful reliquary in the treasury of St Paul's Cathedral.
In the 15C savage William de la Marck, called "the Wild Boar of the Ardennes" because his followers wore boarskins, terrorised the principality and eventually killed Prince-Bishop Louis de Bourbon (1482) with his own hands.

Reliquary
of Charles the Bold,
St Paul's Cathedral

The town recovered its prosperity during the reign of Evrard de la Marck (1506-1538). On his death the battle between the prince-bishop's followers and opponents broke out again.
In the 18C Liège threw itself into the Age of Enlightenment and welcomed the Revolution of 1789. The rule of the prince-bishops ended in 1794, and the town became French territory, then Dutch, until 1830.
In August 1914 the heroic resistance at the citadel and the circle of strongholds (including **Fort Loncin** ⊙, of which the ruins can be seen 8km - 5 miles north of Liège) made it possible for the Belgian and French troops to join forces and consolidate their position. More then 1 500 V1s and V2s fell on Liège between 1944 and 1945.

A major centre of art – The Mosan school began to develop under Notger. This distinguished itself especially from the 10C to the 11C with beautifully executed ivories; then in the 12C and 13C it began producing wonderful masterpieces in gold and silver, in enamels and most particularly in cast iron, copper and brass. **Lambert Lombard** (1505-1566) excelled in both painting and architecture during the Renaissance. **Jean Delcour** (1627-1707), influenced by Italian art and sometimes called the Bernini of Liège, was the most productive sculptor of the 17C. His innumerable statues with their flowing drapery, including graceful Madonnas, decorate the town's churches and fountains.
Architecture came into its own in the 16C and the 18C. The classical style triumphed but local particularities were retained, such as the use of brick lightened by white stone string courses and window mullions in stone. The great period of Liège cabinet-making was in the 18C; decorative furniture carving is still done from a single solid block.
Music flourished with composers such as **André-Modeste Grétry** (1741-1813), **César Franck** (1822-1890) and violinist **Eugène Ysaïe** (1858-1931).
Literature made illustrious progress as well, with novels by **Georges Simenon** (1903-1989), who evoked his native city in several of his works.
Folklore is also an important part of Liège life; there are three marionette theatres. The best-known character since the turn of the century has been **Tchantchès**, the incarnation of the good-natured Liège soul.

Economic growth – Owing to coal deposits, discovered in the 12C, many blacksmiths plied their trade in Liège from the 14C onwards. The town earned a reputation for armour-making.
Liège underwent massive industrial development in the 19C, favoured by its location on a large navigable waterway and near a rich coal seam. Tall furnaces and heavy industries sprang up on the banks of the Meuse. Europe's first locomotive was built here, and the Bessemer process for steelmaking was tested. The National Factory of Herstal Arms was founded in 1889.
Industrial growth was interrupted by the two World Wars, which hit Liège hard. Nevertheless, the building of the **Albert Canal** (1939) to link the Meuse and the Scheldt made Liège Europe's third-ranking inland port. A tanker port was constructed between 1951 and 1964. Nowadays, metalworking remains one of the region's most important activities: iron and steel, heavy metals, the treatment of non-ferrous metals, especially zinc (Seraing). There are chemical and plastics industries, glass-making (Val-St-Lambert), cement works and rubber manufacturing.

★★ OLD TOWN *time: half a day*

Leave from **Place St-Lambert** (**EY 138**), centre of Liège's shopping district, where St Lambert's Cathedral once stood. It is currently undergoing major construction work.

★ **Palace of the Prince-Bishops (Palais des Princes-Évêques)** – This was built *c*1000 by bishop Notger, and was completely rebuilt from 1526 on the orders of Prince-Bishop Erard de la Marck. The main façade was replaced after the fire in 1734, and the left wing dates from the last century. The building is now occupied by local administration and the law courts.
The **large courtyard**★★ is surrounded by arcades with raised arches and sixty massive yet elegant columns with entasis, surmounted by richly ornamented capitals. The variety of decoration on the columns is extraordinary. The **small courtyard**, which can be seen from the window of a corridor, seems more intimate.

★ **Perron** (EY A) – The perron is perched on a monumental Delcour fountain on the Place du Marché directly opposite the stately 18C Town Hall, which conceals a beautiful façade at the back. At the top of the perron, the Three Graces are holding aloft a pine cone and a cross. This monument, the most famous of its kind in Belgium, was erected in 1697 on the site of the old one destroyed in a storm. Initially the emblem of episcopal jurisdiction, the perron became a symbol of civil liberty. It was for this reason that it was stolen in 1468 by Charles the Bold and transferred to Bruges. It was not returned until 1478.

Hors-Château – This street dating from the 11C was named after the fact that it was situated outside the fortified enclosure (hors-château: outside the castle).

★★ **Museum of Walloon Life (Musée de la Vie wallonne)** (EY) ⊙ – This museum, devoted to Walloon ethnography and folklore, is in an old Minorite monastery. It is a magnificent 17C Mosan Renaissance style architectural ensemble, where brick and stone are beautifully combined. The museum evokes life in the past through reconstructed interiors, workshops and traditional family scenes and by displaying regional arts and popular beliefs. Note the "nail oaks" in the room devoted to witchcraft, to which the sick would nail their clothing to heal themselves of their illnesses. An exceptional collection of sundials and a remarkable series of Liège marionettes are on the second floor. The museum also has a **marionette theatre** ⊙ and a room on dialects.

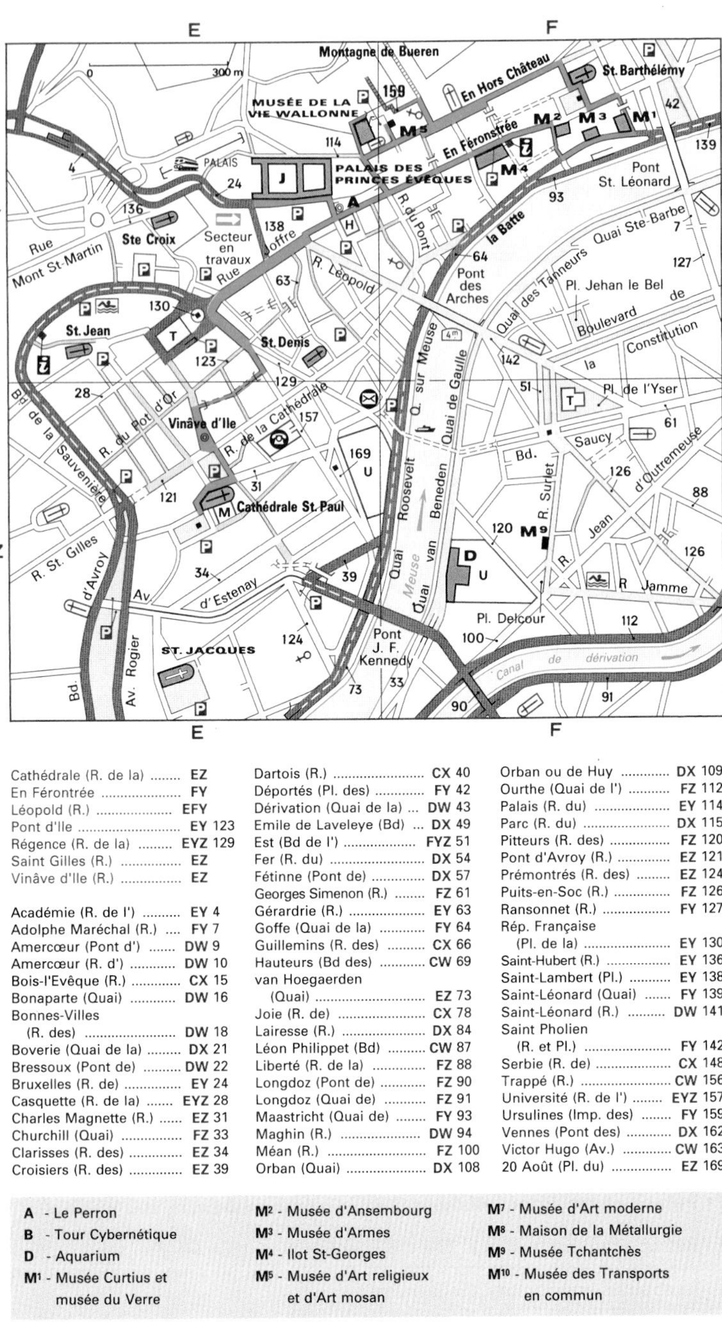

★ **Museum of Religious and Mosan Art** (**Musée d'Art religieux et d'Art mosan**) (**FY M5**) – The museum collections trace the evolution of religious art in the Liège diocese since the early Middle Ages and include several masterpieces. Mosan Romanesque art is represented by numerous sculptures and pieces in gold and silver: the **Évegnée Madonna**, a very early (late 11C) statue; the **Rausa Christ**, a 13C wooden sculpture showing the transition from the Romanesque (seated effigy) and the Gothic (softness of the facial characteristics and the folds of the garments). Among the Gothic paintings note the **Virgin and Butterfly**, a rare 15C work from the Mosan school, and the marvellous **Virgin with Donor and St Mary Magdalene** (1475), attributed to the Master of St Gudula. The wooden **Berselius Madonna**, executed in 1530 by Swabian artist Daniel Mauch, shows a wriggling Infant Jesus and saucy cherubs playing among the skirts of a beautiful Madonna.

Turn left from Rue Hors-Château, towards the Montagne de Bueren stairway, then turn left into Impasse des Ursulines.

Impasse des Ursulines (FY 159) – This is named after the religious community of nuns from the **old beguine convent of the Holy Spirit**; the beautiful half-timbered façades of the convent can be seen from the street. An old post stage has been moved next to it and houses a reconstruction of violinist Eugène Ysaïe's studio.

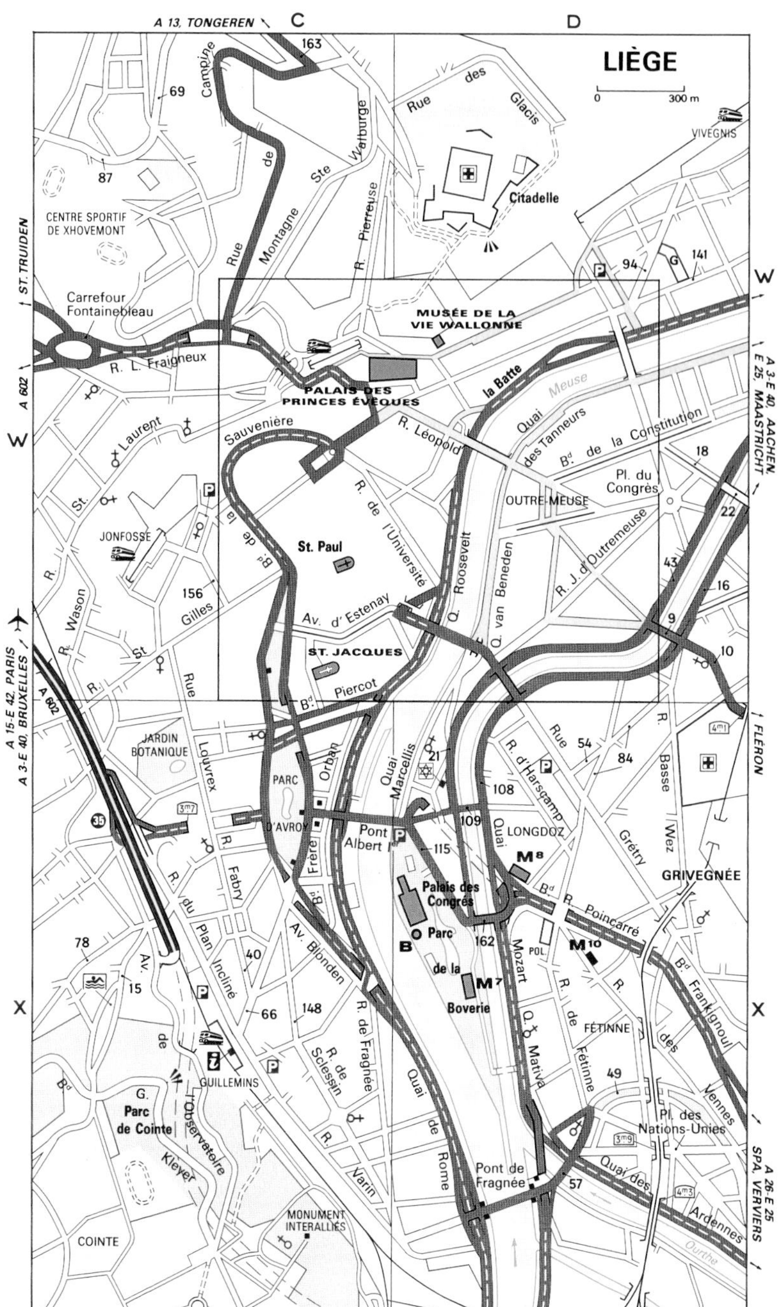

St Bartholomew's Church (**Église St-Barthélemy**) (**FY**) – This Romanesque church has a massive avant-corps surmounted with two towers, very characteristic of the 12C Rhineland-Mosan style. There is a brass **font★★★** executed by Renier de Huy from 1107 to 1118 for the Church of Notre-Dame aux Fonts *(illustration p 20)*. It originally rested on 12 oxen (only 10 remain), symbolising the apostles. The basin has five scenes depicted on it, the main one being the baptism of Jesus in the Jordan; the others represent the Preaching of St John the Baptist; the Baptism of the Catechumens; the Baptism of Cornelius the Centurion; and that of the philosopher Crato. High-relief figures stand out against the smooth background. The great fluidity of their stances and their highly stylised forms elevate them to a level of sculptural perfection reminiscent of the art of Antiquity.

★ **Curtius Museum and Glass Museum** (**Musée Curtius et Musée du Verre**) (Archaeological and Decorative Arts Museums) (**FY M**1) – This tall aristocratic house dates from the early 17C. Jean Curtius, a rich commissary to the Spanish armies, had it built in the Mosan Renaissance style. It now houses valuable collections. It contains in particular three remarkable Mosan works: the **Notger Gospel-book★★★** (Évangéliaire de Notger), an ivory dating from *c*1000 that is decorated with 12C champlevé enamels and copper plaques added later on; the **Dom Rupert Madonna**, a 12C sandstone sculpture which still has a Byzantine look about it; and the **Mystery of Apollo**, a 12C carved stone tympanum.

The Glass Museum at the far end of the courtyard has a large **collection of glass objects★**, about 9 000 items, dating from the origins of glass-making to the present.

★ **Arms Museum (Musée d'Armes) (FY M3)** ⏲ – This museum is contained in a beautiful 18C town house. From 1800 to 1814 this was the seat of the Ourthe *préfecture;* Napoleon stayed here in 1803 and 1811. The museum displays to great advantage an exceptionally rich collection of portable arms, mainly firearms from the Middle Ages to the present, as well as a large collection of Napoleonic medals and decorations.

★ **Ansembourg Museum (Musée d'Ansembourg)** (Archaeological and Decorative Arts Museums) (**FY M2**) ⏲ – The contents of this beautiful 18C town house combine to give it the sophisticated atmosphere of the period: ceilings decorated with stucco, walls covered with Mechelen leather, Oudenaarde tapestries, furniture characteristic of Liège cabinet-making, and a kitchen adorned with Delft tiles.

En Féronstrée (FY) – This street is named after the "férons", or blacksmiths, who worked here in the Middle Ages.

Ilot St-Georges (FY **M4**) – The **Museum of Walloon Art** ⏲ exhibits its collections in a very original modern building. This museum is devoted to the works by painters and sculptors from Hainaut, the Namur region, Luxembourg, Liège and Walloon Brabant and Brussels, who were part of the great European art movement from the 16C to the present. Among the many artists represented by works there are Lambert Lombard, Léonard Defrance, Antoine Wiertz, Félicien Rops, Henri Evenepoel, Constantin Meunier, and for the 20C, Anto Carte, Pierre Paulus, Léon Navez, Louis Buisseret (all four from the Nervia group), Pol Bury, Jo Delahaut, René Magritte and Paul Delvaux. There is also a room for temporary exhibitions.

Vinâve d'Ile (EZ) – There is a Delcour *Virgin with Child* above the fountain in this square, in the heart of the pedestrian shopping district.

St Paul's Cathedral (Cathédrale St-Paul) (EZ) – This Gothic cathedral has three lofty naves and a triforium, containing works by Delcour *(St Peter and St Paul, Christ in the Tomb)*, a pulpit carved by Willem Geefs in the 19C, and a remarkable treasury.

★★ **Treasury** ⏲ – The **reliquary of Charles the Bold★★** is in a room in the cloister. The piece is in gold embellished with enamels, and was given by the Duke in 1471; he is represented on it next to St George, whose face is identical to his. The majestic silver-gilt bust **reliquary of St Lambert** dates from 1512; it is 1.5m - 5ft tall, on a greatly worked base (scenes of the saint's life). Two 11C ivories, one Byzantine and the other Mosan, are also noteworthy.

ADDITIONAL SIGHTS

West Bank

★★ **St James's Church (Église St-Jacques)** (EZ) ⏲ – The west end of this Flamboyant Gothic church still has part of a Romanesque narthex; this is a trace of the 11C Benedictine abbey church that once stood here. An interesting Renaissance façade, executed by Lambert Lombard, was added to the north porch. There is a 1380 low relief beneath the porch, depicting the *Coronation of the Virgin.*

Inside, the sumptuous architectural decoration is awe-inspiring. The **nave vaulting★★** with its many ribs creates prismatic "compartments", in which medallion portraits are painted. There is a carved keystone at each intersection of the ribbing. Great statues in painted limewood, works by Delcour for the most part, are fixed along the line of columns. The chancel was decorated in an extraordinarily rich Flamboyant ogival style, with 16C stained glass windows donated by the town's great families.

An altarpiece, with a 15C Pietà incorporated into its centre is in the chapel north of the chancel; there is also a 16C Immaculate Conception nearby in the transept. A superb 17C organ case rests on a tribune at the far western end of the nave.

Vaulting in St James's Church

St Denis's Church (**Église St-Denis**) (EY) – This church was founded in the 10C by Notger and now stands at the heart of the shopping district. It has been modified several times, but still has the foundation of a large 12C avant-corps. The interior was modified in the 18C. An early 16C wooden Brabant style **altarpiece**★ in the south transept arm illustrates the Passion of Christ with a crowd of figures. The predella, dating from somewhat later, represents the life of St Denis (Dionysius).

St John's Church (**Église St-Jean**) (EY) ⊙ – The shape of this church – an octagon surmounted by a cupola – was inspired by Aachen Cathedral. It was built in the late 10C by Prince-Bishop Notger. The avant-corps was erected in *c*1200 and the nave rebuilt in the 18C. The rotunda and the chancel inside were decorated in the neo-classical style at the end of the 18C.
There is a 13C Calvary in the vestry, with beautiful wooden **statues**★ of the Virgin and St John. There is a magnificent Virgin with Child, or **Sedes Sapientiae**★, in a side chapel; this was carved in wood in about 1220, with remarkably fluid drapery and a delicately feminine face.
Openwork was added to the cloisters in the 16C, and more modifications were made in the 18C. The south gallery still has a beautiful 16C vault, the ribbing and liernes forming graceful rose patterns.

Church of the Holy Cross (**Église Ste-Croix**) (EY) ⊙ – This is a hall church, with three equally high naves, dating from the 13C and 14C; the avant-corps is Romanesque. Its particularity is that it has two chancels opposite each other, with that to the west now used for baptisms.
The **treasury** ⊙ has precious liturgical ornaments and some gold- and silverware. One of its most valuable exhibits is a symbolic bronze key given by Pope Gregory II to St Hubert in 722. There is also a 12C triptych reliquary in gilded repoussé brass, attributed to Godefroy de Huy.

East Bank

Parc de la Boverie (DX) – This park is at the extreme south end of the island, watered by the Meuse on one side and by the canal on the other.
The **Palais des Congrès**, its long façade reflected in the water, is near the **cybernetic tower** (B) 52m - 170ft high, designed by Nicolas Schöffer, on which the motion of pale mobiles reflects atmospheric changes. There is a **Museum of Modern Art** (M7) in the centre of the park.

Metallurgy Centre (**Maison de la Métallurgie**) (DX M8) ⊙ – Here, in enormous 19C workshops are a Walloon forge with a tall 17C coal-burning furnace and two huge 18C "makas" (hydraulic hammers). The traditional work of Liège's "férons" or ironworkers is exhibited: plaques or firebacks and andirons.
The history of energy is illustrated in another room through a rich collection of machines, models and motors.

★ **Aquarium** (FZ D) ⊙ – This beautiful aquarium belongs to the university's Institute of Zoology. Visitors can admire fish from all over the world in the 26 tanks on the lower level.
On the first floor there is an interesting collection of madrepores which were brought back from an expedition to the Great Barrier Reef in Australia.

Tchantchès Museum (**Musée Tchantchès**) (FZ M9) ⊙ – This museum, at the heart of the Outre-Meuse district, belongs to an association called the Free Republic of Outre-Meuse; this is devoted to Tchantchès (Walloon name for "Francis"), the popular hero of the Liège marionette theatre. The museum has the costumes which have been given, and a collection of marionettes from the Imperial Old Royal Theatre. It is possible to attend **puppet shows** here ⊙.
A Tchantchès monument stands on Yser Place at the far end of Rue Surlet. There are several niches containing Christ- or Madonna-figures in the nearby streets. The Potales Festival takes place on August 15.

Liège Public Transport Museum (DX M10) ⊙ – *9 rue Richard-Heintz.* Refurbished trams and buses have been put here in a great shed.

EXCURSIONS

Boat trips (FZ) ⊙ – A cruise is organised on the Meuse and the Albert Canal, from Liège to Maastricht.

★★ **Blégny-Trembleur** – *20km - 12.5 miles northeast, in the direction of Aachen. See Blégny-Trembleur.*

Sart Tilman – *10km - 6.25 miles south.* The **University of Liège** holds an area of 740ha - 1 828 acres on this wooded plateau; this is a centre of metallurgical research. The 17C Colonster Palace at the eastern edge of the estate has been turned into a conference centre and houses the Simenon Foundation (the writer's archives, manuscripts and library).
The park also has an open-air museum.

Chaudfontaine – Pop 20 195. *10km - 6.25 miles towards Verviers.* Chaudfontaine has been a popular Vesdre Valley spa since the late 17C. Its hot springs (38.6°C - 101.4°F), the only ones in Belgium, are used to treat rheumatism. Chaudfontaine also has an open-roofed hot-spring pool and a **casino** with miniature golf.
The 17C restored **Maison Sauveur** ⊙ in the hot-springs park is home to the tourist information centre.

Aigremont Castle ⊙ – *16km - 10 miles west, on the E 40 motorway, leaving at junction 4.*
Aigremont Castle is located, like that of Chokier, on the top of a sheer cliff overlooking the Meuse; it is said that this castle was built by the four Aymon brothers. During the 15C it was one of the lairs of William de la Marck. The castle was rebuilt in the early 18C, in brick and stone.
The interior is adorned with beautiful 18C furnishings. The most beautiful decorative feature is the stairwell with its *trompe l'oeil* frescoes reproducing the architecture of an Italian palace. The walls of the kitchen are decorated with Delft tiles representing more than 1 000 different patterns.
There is a pretty French-style garden on the terraces.

Neuville-en-Condroz and St-Séverin – *27km - 16.75 miles southwest, in the Dinant direction.*

Neuville-en-Condroz – This is home to the Ardennes American cemetery. A magnificent, well-tended park precedes the memorial and the lawn where 5 310 Americans are buried; these men died during the Second World War, most of them in the Battle of the Bulge. All the white gravestones are arranged in the form of an immense Greek cross. Maps carved inside the memorial describe the famous battle.

St-Séverin – The **church★** in this small town is a harmonious 12C Romanesque building that was once a priory of Cluny Abbey (Burgundy, France). Moreover, the tower at the octagonal transept crossing is inspired by the "Blessed Water" (eau bénite) bell tower at Cluny. The beautiful architectural balance of masses can be appreciated more fully from the presbytery garden. The ceiling of the central nave, the transept vaulting and the chancel are all the same height; those of the apse and the transept chapels are much lower. The décor in the great nave is discreet: an alternance of columns and groups of small coupled columns and pillars, and above this, twisted twinned columns.
The late-12C stone **font★** is original; the basin, supported by 12 small coupled columns surrounding a central shaft, is sculpted with back-to-back lions; there is a head, of Syrian inspiration, at each of the four corners.

Visé – Pop 17 175. *17km - 10.5 miles north on the E 25.*
Visé is a popular tourist centre on the banks of the Meuse; the town is well-known for its gastronomic speciality, goose prepared with a garlic sauce. Visé is also proud of its three guilds – the crossbowmen's, the arquebusiers' and the free arquebusiers' – who can be seen parading on holidays. The town has many tourist facilities: a cultural centre, a playing field, a nature reserve and Robinson Island.

Collegiate Church – The **reliquary of St Hadelin★** is in the south transept arm. This is a 12C Mosan work in repoussé silver. The gables, from an older reliquary (1046), represent on one side Christ crushing the asp and the basilisk (mythological beast), and on the other side Christ crowning the two friends Saint Remaclus and Saint Hadelin. Some of the side panel scenes, illustrating the life of St Hadelin, are attributed to Renier de Huy. St Hadelin was the founder of Celles monastery in Dinant in the 7C; the community moved to Visé in the 14C.

★★ LIER Antwerpen — Pop 30 856

Michelin maps 409 G2 or 213 fold 7

Many tourists, writers and artists have been drawn here by the atmosphere, the walks, the historical buildings and old façades of this town lying within both the Antwerp Kempen and Brabant regions. Lier still has its 16C ramparts, which have been turned into walkways and edged with a canal.
The well-known people born here include the artist Van Boeckel (1857-1944), who worked chiefly with iron; the portrait painter Opsomer (1878-1967); the writer **Felix Timmermans** (1886-1947); and the great clock and watch maker, Zimmer (1888-1970).
"Lierse Vlaaikens", or Lier tartlets, are a delicious local speciality.

★★ ST GOMMARUS' CHURCH (ST.-GUMMARUSKERK) (Z) *time: 45min*

This Brabant Gothic church was built between the 14C and the 16C, the Keldermans and the Waghemakeres *(qv)* taking part in the construction. The massive square tower, ending in a restored octagonal bell tower, has a 45-chime carillon.
There is a good view of the whole of the exterieur from near the north transept arm. Philip the Handsome married Joanna of Castille here in 1496.
The **interior** has some beautiful keystones, and the floor is paved with gravestones. The thick columns with great statues of the apostles leaning against them, the openwork of the triforium are characteristic of Brabant style. There are some interesting works of art to see.
The magnificent white stone **rood-screen★★**, Flamboyant Gothic despite its late date of 1536, is the work of Mechelen sculptors. Statues of the Evangelists and the Church Fathers (re-executed in 1850) are displayed on columns; scenes from the Passion stand out against the rich decoration. The turret was added in 1850.
The church has a beautiful collection of stained glass windows. A 15C **window★** in the south side aisle depicts the *Coronation of the Virgin* in a medallion; the fluidity of the drawing recalls the art of Van der Weyden. Maximilian presented the church with three of the stained glass windows in the chancel during his 1516 visit; one of them shows him with his wife, Mary of Burgundy.

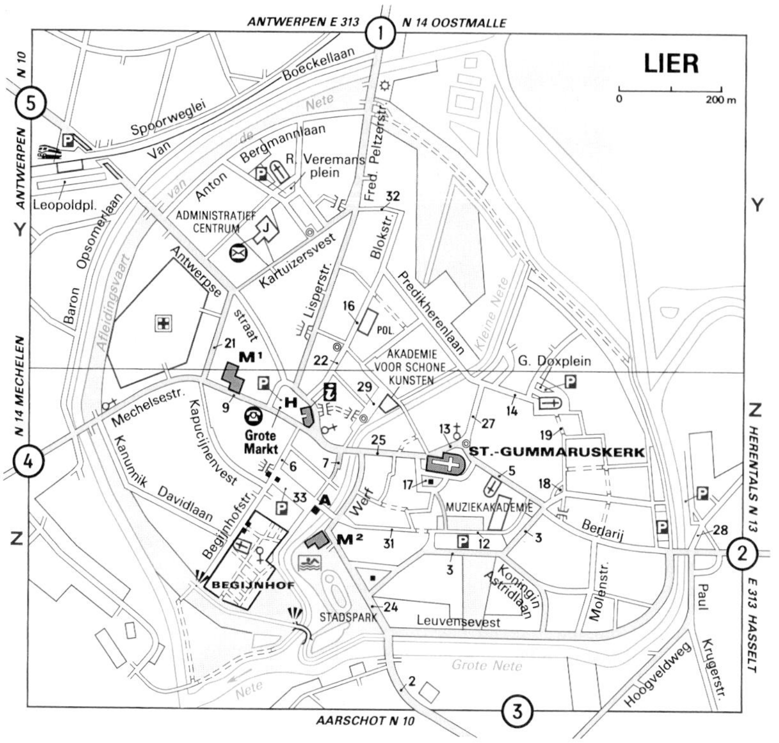

Antwerpsestr.	Y	Felix Timmermansplein	Z 7	Kolveniersvest	Y 21
Berlaarsestr.	Z 5	Fl. Van Cauwenberghstr.	Z 9	Koning Albertstr.	YZ 22
Berlarij	Z	Gasthuisvest	Z 12	Netelaan	Z 24
Grote Markt	Z	Heilige Geeststr.	Z 13	Sint-Gummarusstr.	Z 27
Rechtsestr.	Z 25	de Heyderstr.	Z 14	Veemarkt	Z 28
		Huibrechtstr.	Y 16	Vismarkt	Z 29
Aarschotsesteenweg	Z 2	Kard. Mercierplein	Z 17	Volmolenstr.	Z 31
Arthur V.D. Poortenlaan	Z 3	Kluizeplein	Z 18	Waterpoortstr.	Y 32
Eikelstraat	Z 6	Kluizestraat	Z 19	Zimmerplein	Z 33

The chancel stalls (1555) are sculpted into picturesque patterns. The copper lectern in the centre of the chancel dates from the 17C; the baroque pulpit is the work of three artists, including Artus Quellin the Elder. A triptych is exhibited in the first ambulatory chapel to the north; the leaves, representing St Clare and St Francis, are said to be by Rubens. The *Colibrant Triptych*, the *Marriage of the Virgin*, is attributed to Goswyn van der Weyden, grandson of Rogier (1516). Notice also in the south transept a triptych dating from 1612 by Otto Venius, Rubens's master (*Descent of the Holy Spirit*).

Once a year *(see the Calendar of Events at the end of this guide)* the 17C reliquary in repoussé silver, containing the relics of St Gommarus, is carried through Lier's streets in a procession.

ADDITIONAL SIGHTS

Zimmer Tower (Zimmertoren) (Z A) ⏲ – Two traces of the original 14C fortifications stand on the Zimmerplein: the **Prisoners' Gate** (Gevangenenpoort) and the Zimmer Tower, once the Cornelius Tower.

On the front of the tower is the astonishing **astronomical clock★** created in 1930 by Zimmer of Lier; it has 11 different dials and two spheres, the earth and the moon, in the place of numbers. Every day at noon there is a sequence of automata on the right side of the tower. The **astronomical studio** inside the tower has 57 dials showing the lunar cycle, the tides, the zodiac and the main cosmic phenomena. Another astronomical clock, the **Wonderklok**, can be visited in the tower's neighbouring pavilion; this has 93 dials and 14 automata; Zimmer's workshop is also open to visitors.

★ **Beguine Convent (Begijnhof) (Z)** – This was founded in the early 13C and modified in the 17C. A monumental Renaissance portal marks the entrance; this dates from the late 17C and has a statue of St Begga at its top. There is a beautiful view from here of the Prisoners' Gate and the belfry.

Astronomical Clock on the Zimmer Tower

Inside the enclosure the houses, some with gardens half-hidden behind low walls, crowd together by narrow paved streets along which there is a Stations of the Cross. The church has a 17C Renaissance façade topped with 18C scrolling and a lantern turret. The random arrangement of the roofs and lantern turrets looks quite picturesque.

Market Square (Grote Markt) (**Z**) – The **town hall** (Stadhuis) (**H**) in the centre is an elegant 18C structure; the windows containing more than 3 900 panes of glass are flanked by a slender Gothic **belfry** (1369). This is surmounted with four corner turrets and has a carillon. The structure itself is a remnant of the old drapers' guild hall. Several old guild halls surround the square, where a market is held every Saturday. Near the belfry the butchers' guild hall, with its gables and perron guarded by two heraldic lions, is used for exhibitions (tentoonstelling).

Wuyts-Van Campen-Baron Caroly Museum (**YZ M**[1]) ⊙ – This possesses a good painting collection from the 16C to the present. Brueghel the Younger, Velvet Brueghel and Rubens feature among the Flemish painters; visitors should not miss **Frans Floris**'s truly remarkable group portrait of the **Van Berchem family**. Also not to be missed are paintings from the Dutch (Van de Velde, Jan Steen), Spanish (Murillo) and French (Poussin, Le Lorrain) schools, and 19C and 20C Belgian paintings (Ferdinand De Braekeleer, Tytgat, Opsomer).

Timmermans-Opsomer House (Timmermans-Opsomerhuis) (**Z M**[2]) ⊙ – This museum is devoted to contemporary Lier artists.
The **Van Broeckel** forge regroups, under a flowery chandelier, the works of art of the famous iron craftsman.
The reconstructed painter's studio belonging to Baron **Opsomer** exhibits landscapes *(Lier Beguine Convent)* and many portraits (Albert I, Félix Timmermans, Opsomer himself).
There are several rooms upstairs devoted to the Flemish writer Félix **Timmermans**, who was also a painter and creator of humourous drawings; some of his most famous works are recalled: *Tales of the Beguine Convent*, *Twilight of Death*, **Pallieter** (1916, a powerful, spirited book) and *Peasants' Psalms*.
Another room contains works and mementoes of the musician Renaat **Veremans** (1894-1969), author of *Vlaanderen* (Flanders), a well-known popular song.

LOMMEL Limburg — Pop 26 973

Michelin maps 409 I2 or 213 fold 9

Lommel's best-known feature is the large German military cemetery in the pine forests a few miles south of the town.

German military cemetery – German soldiers who fell in Belgium during the Second World War, and some who died in East Germany or during the First World War, lie in this 16ha - 40 acre enclosure.
There is a basalt calvary built above the crypt in front of the cemetery; this stands 6m - 20ft high. Almost 20 000 crosses (one cross for every two graves) are in rows. They stand out against the heather carpet, scattered with pines and birches, divided by strips of lawn.

Kattenbos Nature Reserve (Natuurreservaat) – This is part of the **Lower Kempen Park** (Park der Lage Kempen), together with the Pijnven Forest near Eksel to the south and the Holven Forest to the east near Overpelt. This park covers an area of 12 000ha - 29 652 acres spread throughout the province of Limburg.
A wooden post windmill (1809) stands near the road north of the far side of Kattenbos. This is the starting point for several signposted footpaths leading through the pine forest.

★ LOUVAIN-LA-NEUVE Brabant

Michelin maps 409 G3 or 213 fold 19 – 7km - 4.3 miles south of Wavre

Since Charleroi was founded in 1666, Louvain-la-Neuve has been the only new town to be founded in Belgium. Designed for 35 000 inhabitants, it extends over the **Ottignies-Louvain-la-Neuve** (pop 21 665) community.

French Catholic University of Leuven (U.C.L.) – Since the 1968 split in the Catholic University (founded in Leuven, in 1425), the French-language University has been in Louvain-la-Neuve. The medical students are the only exception; their faculty is in **Woluwe-St-Lambert** (Brussels), on the site of **Louvain-en-Woluwe**. The transfer took place from 1972 to 1979. The U.C.L. has about 18 300 students, 14 000 of whom are in Louvain-la-Neuve.

Town and gown – Louvain-la-Neuve is an original idea, being not only an urban centre but also a university town.
It is divided into four parts – **Hocaille**, **Biéreau**, **Bruyères** and **Lauzelle** – but the intermingling of shops, homes and faculties makes the division less apparent.
The **urban centre** in the heart of the town was conceived as a busy place reserved exclusively for pedestrians; the railway, motor traffic and car parks have been banished underground.
A high-tech park was created for science companies and research laboratories as well as the Cyclotron complex. The natural site itself was respected. The buildings are on four hills of the Lauzelle plateau which overlook the little valley of the

river Malaise; this has been covered over with a layer of concrete to bear the weight of the central town streets and buildings, including the University's central building, the **University Halls of Residence**.

Contemporary architecture serves urbanism here, taking its inspiration from medieval towns and keeping everything on a human scale. Narrow streets, small squares, stairs, buildings that are set back, all create an element of surprise and avoid monotony. Bricks and small white cobblestones predominate.

Several decorative elements have appeared since the town was created: a fountain (Place de l'Université), the work of a student; and murals, including R Somville's great fresco (400m² - 478yds²). Its colours of blue, white, grey and red brighten a wall of the University Halls on the Rue des Wallons side. There is a T Bosquet mural in the underground railway station depicting a 16C university town, with enlarged versions of Paul Delvaux's paintings of railway stations.

A motorway (Brussels-Namur) provides access to the town, as does the railway; a line off the Brussels-Namur line ends in the underground station. Maps and information are available in the information centre (follow the signs marked "REUL").

Louvain-la-Neuve Museum ⌚ – *Place Blaise Pascal.*

The collections include Egyptian, Greek and Roman antiquities, sculptures and masks representing African and South Sea primitive art, religious art (sculptures including a 16C *Christ and the Triumphal Entrance into Jerusalem*), porcelain, etc. The **Charles Delsemme legacy★** came to the museum in 1990; it represents the same universal quality. "By its diversity, its transcendence, this collection forms the desired whole", wrote the donor in his testament. Note: a Japanese theatrical mask, a Renaissance female figure, Picasso drawings, Delvaux and Magritte paintings.

MAASEIK Limburg

Pop 20 987

Michelin maps 409 K2 or 213 fold 11

Maaseik is on the bank of the Meuse, at the extreme northeast of the Limburg Kempen region. This town is said to be the birthplace of the **Van Eyck** brothers, Jan *(qv)* and Hubert.

Maaseik's carnival procession (halfvastenstoet) about halfway through Lent draws a considerable crowd *(see the Calendar of Events at the end of this guide).* The town still has some vestiges of fortifications built in 1672 under Louis XIV. **Boat trips** ⌚ are organised on the Meuse.

SIGHTS

Market Square (Grote Markt) – This vast rectangular square, shaded by lime trees, is surrounded by 17C and 18C houses; their narrow windows are often embellished with little squares of glass held in place with lead.

The town hall (stadhuis) to the north is in a beautiful 18C bourgeois home. A statue of the brothers Jan and Hubert Van Eyck stands in the centre.

Museactron ⌚ – *Lekkerstraat 5.*

The Museactron regroups three museums. The collections of the **Regional Archaeological Museum** include regional archaeology and the history of the town: prehistoric objects, some objects from the Roman period (a Roman doctor's instruments), and some from the Middle Ages. An overhead passageway links this museum to **Belgium's oldest apothecary's**, where the atmosphere of the past is perfectly reconstructed. The **Bakery Museum** (Bakkerijmuseum) is in the cellars.

Bosstraat – There are old houses all along this street.

The De Verkeerde Wereld (the World in Reverse) House, an old brick building, is at no 7. There is a half-timbered medieval house on the corner of the Halstraat. The house at no 19 has a white façade (1621), projecting on arches, a feature common to this region. The Stenen Huis (Stone House), or the Drossaardshuis (Bailiff's House), is at no 21; the façade here is classical and more sober-looking.

St Catherine's Church (St.-Catharinakerk) – This dates from the 19C. The vestry is home to a remarkable **treasury** (kerkschat) ⌚; most of the items it houses come from the old Aldeneik Abbey *(see below).* Note St Harlinde's gospel-book dating from the 8C, which is said to be the oldest book in Belgium, and a 10C silver-gilt reliquary.

Aldeneik – *2km - 1.25 miles east.*

The **church** ⌚ of Aldeneik is the old abbey church of an 8C monastery founded by St Harlinde and St Relinde. It was enlarged in the 12C, and a Gothic chancel was added in the 13C. Restoration work was carried out in the 19C. The church still has its Romanesque central nave decorated with mural paintings. There are Merovingian (8C) sarcophagi.

★ MALMÉDY Liège

Pop 10 246

Michelin maps 409 L4 or 214 northwest of fold 9 - Local map see SPA Excursions

Malmédy, on the River Warche, is in a picturesque **setting★**. It lies in the middle of a hollow surrounded by steep wooded hills; the town itself is at an altitude of 340m - 1 115ft. Skiing is possible in the surrounding area: at **Ferme Libert** (north on the Bévercé road; downhill and cross-country skiing) and at **Ovifat**, near Robertville (downhill skiing). Malmédy's paper works and tanneries are well-known. "Baisers de Malmédy" ("Malmédy kisses") are a delicious local cake.

Together with Stavelot, the town formed an abbey principality until 1794. Malmédy, where the Walloon dialect is spoken, was Prussian from 1815 to 1925 *(see Eupen)*. The town was destroyed in December 1944 by an air attack. The French avant-garde poet Guillaume Apollinaire stayed in Malmédy in 1899. A monument was built in 1935 on the old Francorchamps road.

★ **Carnival** – *See the Calendar of Events at the end of this guide.* Malmédy's very popular "Cwarmê" is one of the merriest carnivals in Belgium. The town practically boils over for four days. On Saturday afternoon a humourous procession accompanies the "Trouv'lê", a sort of carnival king who is enthroned at the Town Hall. Sunday is the day of the great parade after which the "banes corantes" ("bands of running people") pursue the public. Steer clear of the **"haguètes"**, who have an Austrian eagle emblazoned on their backs and wear a bihorn hat embellished with feathers, and, most importantly, who are armed with long hinged pincers! On Monday short satirical sketches in the local dialect are performed in the streets.

Cathedral of SS Peter, Paul and Quirinus (Cathédrale Sts-Pierre-Paul-et-Quirin) ⌚ – This was once a Benedictine abbey church dating from 1782. The façade is framed by two towers. This was the Eupen-Malmédy diocese cathedral from 1921 to 1925. Inside, the furniture is particularly interesting (carved 18C pulpit, late 17C confessionals), as is the artwork: the 17C Delcour Madonna in the north transept arm, the St Quirin reliquary in gilded wood dating from 1698. Also noteworthy are the silver bust-reliquaries of St Gereon and his companions, Roman soldiers (18C).

EXCURSIONS

Robertville – *10km - 6.25 miles northeast.*

Robertville is part of the Hautes Fagnes-Eifel nature park *(qv)*. This town is renowned above all else for its arch gravity **dam**, built in 1928, which overlooks the Warche from a height of 55m - 180ft. The reservoir forms a 62ha - 153 acre **lake★** which supplies Malmédy with drinking water and runs an electrical power station in Bévercé. The lake is surrounded by a dense forest and offers many possibilities for sports enthusiasts *(fishing, boating, yachting, swimming, diving)*. There is a beautiful view of the reservoir from just outside Robertville.

★ **Reinhardstein Castle** ⌚ – *Access via a path starting from the dam, or on the first road on the left after the dam (signs), then 800m - 0.5 mile on foot after the car park.*

Reinhardstein Castle

The keep, surrounded by walls and standing on a rocky spur in the magnificent setting of a coniferous forest, seems to suggest that the centuries have left it unmarked. It exudes the air of a fortress still ready to defend against invasions. However, in the early 1960s there was nothing on this site but ruins. Professor Overloop brought about a resurrection by rebuilding the castle according to 17C engravings depicting the fortress at the height of its splendour. At that time it was the property of the Metternich family. The rooms with their stone walls and flagstone floors are decorated with old furniture, tapestries, armour and works of art. The Knights' Hall and the chapel are particularly eye-catching.

Bütgenbach – Pop 4 992. *15km - 9.3 miles east.* This dam (1928-1932) is also on the Warche. It has a vast 120ha - 296 acre reservoir, and is also a great tourist centre *(swimming, sailing, boating, pedal boats, fishing, tennis, wind-surfing etc.)*.

Round trip south – *13km - 8 miles – Leave on the Stavelot road. Take a little road on the left before the viaduct, then a road on the right.*

★ **Falize Rock** – This is a magnificent needle of rock providing almost a bird's-eye view of the Warche Valley. A spire on the opposite height marks the location of Wavreumont Abbey, founded in 1950 by Benedictines from Leuven.

Bellevaux-Ligneuville – This village in the upper Amblève Valley still has a pretty half-timbered house, the Maraite House (1592), which is typical of the region.

Return to Malmédy via Hédomont.

Faymonville – *11km - 6.75 miles southeast.* A very old legend has led to the inhabitants of this village being known as "Turks". This name is reflected in the great carnival parade of Shrove Monday.

★★ MECHELEN Antwerpen

Pop 75 514

Michelin maps 409 G2 or 213 folds 6, 7.
Town plan in the current Michelin Red Guide Benelux

This is an ecclesiastical town, the residence of Belgium's archbishop. Mechelen is quiet and a bit old-fashioned with its old houses bordering the squares and the Dijle quays. The town is dominated by the magnificent St Rumbald's Tower with its famous carillon.
The traditional art industries still exist here: lace, tapestry. It was a Mechelen workshop that produced the tapestry Belgium presented to the United Nations in 1954; this was originally for New York's United Nations Building, but was given in 1964 to NATO in Paris. Mechelen is also an important centre of furniture-making.
It should also be noted that brewing has its own place in the town's activities. Lastly, the region is known for its market gardens (asparagus).

Mechelen carillons – In the Middle Ages Mechelen's bell-casters were already well-known. Nevertheless, Mechelen had an Amsterdam bell-caster, Pieter Hemony, create a carillon in 1674 for St Rumbald's Tower; in the late 19C the exceptionally virtuoso carillon-player Jef Denyn made these chimes famous. He founded a school in 1922 and his students play throughout the world.
The first carillon at St Rumbald's (restored) consisted of 49 chimes; a second set with the same number of chimes was added in 1981; the total weight of these two groups is 80 tons.
Carillon concerts ⊙ are given in St Rumbald's, at the church of Onze-Lieve-Vrouw-over-de-Dijle, or at the Busleyden Mansion *(see below)*.

HISTORICAL NOTES

Mechelen was a lakeside community in prehistoric times, and seems to have been evangelised in the 8C by St Rumbald from Ireland. It belonged to the prince-bishops of Liège who surrounded it with a fortified enclosure.
Owing to its location on the Dijle, the town had a port, and trade prospered, especially with the advent of clothmaking. Mechelen gained a second set of ramparts in about 1300.

The golden age – Mechelen belonged to the Count of Flanders in the 14C, then later came under the rule of the succession of the Dukes of Burgundy; this was the beginning of its most illustrious period. Charles the Bold established his Court of Accounts (combining those in Lille and Brussels) and the Parliament of Burgundian Estates here in 1473; the Parliament became the **Grand Council** in 1503, acting as a supreme court until the French Revolution.
The town reached its high point under **Margaret of Austria**, Emperor Charles V's aunt who governed until his majority, then under Emperor Charles V himself from 1519-1530. The highly cultivated princess loved the arts and surrounded herself with her period's greatest intellects: philosophers Erasmus and Thomas More, historian Lemaire de Belges, musicians Pierre de la Rue and Josquin Des Prés, and painters Gossaert and Van Orley.
Margaret also constructed many buildings. Mechelen architect Rombout Keldermans built a palace for her.

From the 16C to the present – The Court moved to Brussels in 1531. While the Grand Council remained in Mechelen, the town's period of stardom was over, except for its religious significance. It has been an archbishopric since 1559 (a title shared with Brussels since 1961); Mechelen's prelate therefore became the Low Countries' archbishop. The cardinal of Granvelle, Philip II's minister, was the first one.
The Spanish set fire to the town and massacred the inhabitants in 1572.
Nevertheless, by the 17C and the 18C Mechelen lace achieved its most widespread renown. Baroque furniture was produced in prolific quantities. The incomparable virtuosity of Mechelen sculptors such as **Lucas Faydherbe** (1617-1697), Rubens' student, or **Theodoor Verhaegen** (1700-1759), Faydherbe's student, became famous.
Cardinal Mercier amply illustrated the spirit of the city during the First World War by showing a quite extraordinarily heroic spiritual strength in the face of the invading forces.

THE HEART OF THE TOWN *time: 2 hours*

★ **Market Square** **(Grote Markt)** **(ABY 26)** – *Illustration overleaf.* The cathedral's imposing tower overlooks this square from the northwest; otherwise, beautiful 16C and 18C façades, with crowstepped or scrolled gables, line the square. A statue of Margaret of Austria stands in the middle.

★ **Town Hall** **(Stadhuis)** **(BY H)** – This is to the east of the square, occupying three adjacent buildings.
The Late Gothic **Grand Council Building** on the left was begun in the early 16C. It remained unfinished until the late 19C, when it was completed according to Rombout Keldermans' original plans. Emperor Charles V's effigy is recognisable in a niche. The building has housed the town hall since 1913.
The central façade is actually that of the uncompleted 14C belfry; there are corbelled turrets at the top.
The former **cloth hall** (to the right) is also from the 14C, although the gable was added in the 17C.

Aldermen's House (Schepenhuis) (**AY A**) – The late 14C "old palace" is a rather isolated building set somewhat back to the southwest; the town archives are here.

Postgebouw (**AY**) – This extensively restored mansion used to be the town hall.

★★ **St Rumbald's Cathedral (St.-Romboutskathedraal) (AY)** ⊙ – This Gothic building is remarkable for its grandiose tower alone, as wide as the nave itself. Graceful pinnacles decorate the side aisle buttresses and elegant gables adorn the east end.

St Rumbald's Cathedral

★★★ **The tower** – This tower, considered the most beautiful in Belgium, forms the façade and porch; it measures 97m - 318ft in height. Begun in 1452, it was intended to reach the surprising height of 167m - 548ft, but the project was stopped in 1521. The Keldermans architectural dynasty directed the construction; the awesome proportions combine with powerful, yet subtle vertical lines to create an unforgettable impression. Vauban called this the eighth marvel of the world. There are two carillons here *(concerts: see the Calendar of Events at the end of the guide).*

Interior – Enter throught the south portal, which opens beneath a tall window with flamboyant tracery and a delicately arched pediment. The interior is surprisingly large (99m - 325ft long, 28m - 92ft high) but is nevertheless harmonious. The 13C central nave is 13m - 43ft wide, and has six bays. 17C statues of the apostles stand against stout cylindrical pillars to separate the bays. After the 1342 fire, the cathedral was embellished with an ambulatory and an apse with seven radiating chapels. The north side aisle chapels appeared between 1498 and 1502. Michel Vervoort's 18C pulpit displays a rocaille fig tree where Adam and Eve are hiding themselves, and many animals carved in full motion; a huge Christ dominates the scene of St Norbert's conversion.
Note among the **works of art** a moving Van Dyck *Crucifixion* in the south transept arm; the dull colours and the sorrowing figures of Mary and Mary Magadalene, as well as of the unrepentant thief, are particularly expressive. Lucas Faydherbe made the black-and-white marble altar. Artus Quellin the Younger is said to have made the communion bench; this delicately executed work in white marble is in the Holy Sacrament chapel, at the far end next to the tower. Cardinal Mercier's mausoleum is in the the north side aisle in a chapel near the transept; he died in 1926.

Leave from the north transept arm.

Notice the painting on the left; it depicts the inside of this metropolitan church in 1775.

Take the Wollemarkt leading to a small bridge; there is a delightful **view**★ **(AY F)** to the left of the 16C **Sint-Truiden abbey refuge (AY D)**. The crowstepped pediment and the pinnacle stand out against the tall trees, while the pink brick walls seem to plunge into the canal. At the end of the Schoutetstraat the old Tongerlo abbey refuge's restored buildings (15C) house a tapestry factory.

★ **Gaspard De Wit Royal Tapestry Works (Koninklijke Manufactuur van Wandtapijten) (AY M¹)** ⊙ – The aim of the works is to preserve the Flemish tapestry-making tradition. Theodoor De Wit founded this in 1889, and it bears his son's name. Gaspard De Wit (1892-1971) was an artist and painter as well as an internationally famous weaver. He invented the "numbered cartoon", a black-and-white card with the design reproduced in outlines only, with the blocks of colour numbered.
The guided tour goes through the workshops for restoring old tapestries or creating new ones. All work is done by hand, as in the past. Several beautiful rooms serve as decor for the beautiful tapestry collection hung here. The evolution of the art of tapestry from about 1500 to the present can be retraced; there is also some illustration of the difference between various manufacturers *(see Introduction: Tapestry).*

Return to the little bridge and take the covered passageway opposite.

St John's Church (St.-Janskerk) (BY) ⊙ – This 15C church has baroque furnishings and more particularly a 1619 Rubens triptych, the *Adoration of the Magi.* The central panel is a remarkable composition in two parts, one dark, the other light. The subtlety of the colours, the contrast between the Virgin's soft profile and the softened expression of the kings' faces turned towards that of the blond Infant, make this panel an exceptional work. Rubens's first wife, Isabella Brant, posed for the Virgin's face.

To get to Frederik de Merodestraat go round the north side of the church.

Busleyden Mansion (Hof van Busleyden) (BY M²) – This 16C brick mansion was built for one of Emperor Charles V's councillors. It stands at the far end of a courtyard adorned with lawns and lined with arcades, overlooked by a turret. The carillon school and the municipal museum are to be found here.

Reach the Veemarkt (meat market) and Befferstraat.

Church of St Peter and St Paul (**St.-Pieter-en-Pauluskerk**) (**BY**) – This has a beautiful restored façade.

Margaret of Austria's Palace (**Law Courts**) (**BY J**) – Rombout Keldermans built this in the early 16C; it became the law courts in 1796. The Renaissance buildings are still influenced by the Gothic, as can be seen around the pretty arcaded courtyard.

ADDITIONAL SIGHTS

Iron Avenue (**IJzerenleen**) (**AY**) – This long avenue, used for a market, is named after the iron balustrades along it which used to protect the 16C canal. There are some beautifully restored façades.

Zoutwerf (**AZ**) – Along this quay there are many beautiful façades, especially that of **Salmon House** (De Zalm) (**AZ K**), built in the 16C for the fishermen's guild. The stone of the façade above the door represents a golden salmon.

Brussels Gate (**Brusselsepoort**) (**AZ**) – This is the only remaining trace of the 14C fortifications; the gate is framed by two 17C towers with pointed roofs.

Church (**Kerk van O.-L.-Vrouw over de Dijle**) (**AZ**) ⊙ – This church has a Rubens triptych, *The Miraculous Draught of Fishes*, commissioned by the fishermen's guild.

Haverwerf (**AY**) – On this quay, three picturesque **old houses** (**AY E**) remain near a little bridge opposite the Fish Market (Vismarkt): St Joseph's House, with a scrolled gable; Devil's House, in wood with caryatids; and Paradise House, with tympana depicting Adam and Eve.

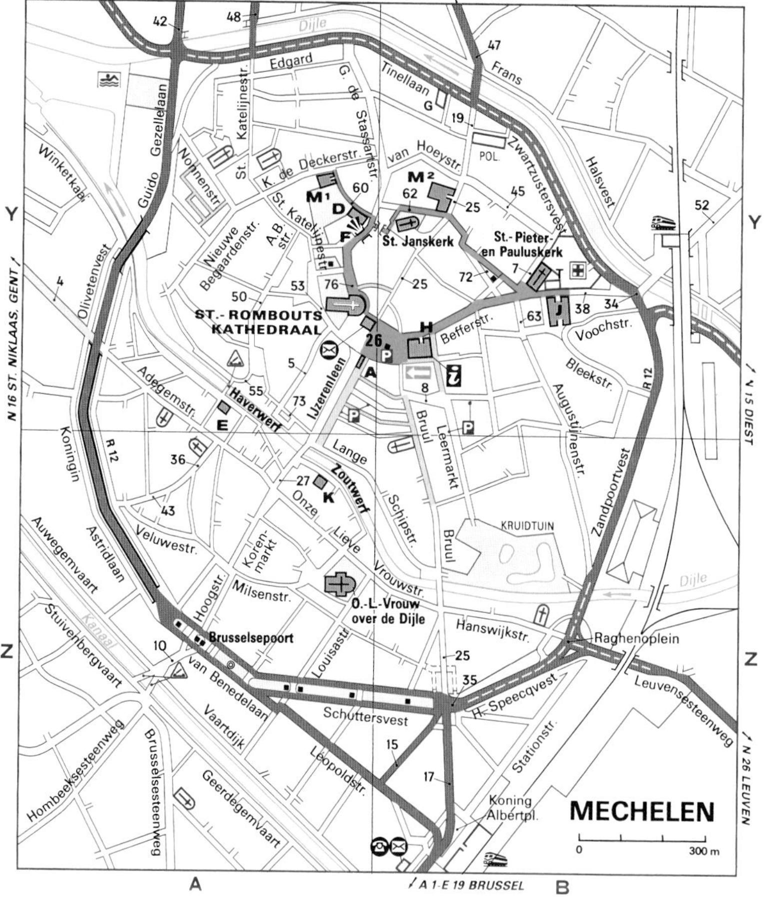

Botermarkt .... BY 8
Bruul .... BYZ
Consciencestr. .... BZ 17
Grote Markt .... ABY 26
Hoogstr. .... AZ
Korenmarkt .... AZ
IJzerenleen .... AY
O.L. Vrouwstr. .... ABZ

Battelsesteenweg .... AY 4
Begijnenstr. .... AY 5
Blokstr. .... BY 7
Brusselsepoortstr. .... AZ 10
Colomastr. .... BZ 15
Frederik de Merodestr. .... BY 19
Gr. van Egmontstr. .... BZ 25
Guldenstr. .... AZ 27
Hoogstratenplein .... BY 34
Kardinaal Mercierplein .... BZ 35
Karmelietenstr. .... AZ 36
Keizerstr. .... BY 38
van Kesbeeckstr. .... AY 42
Korte Penningstr. .... AZ 43
Lange Heergracht .... BY 45
Liersesteenweg .... BY 47
Maurits Sabbestr. .... AY 48
Melaan .... AY 50
Nekkerspoelstr. .... BY 52
Onder den Toren .... AY 53
Persoonshoek .... AY 55
Schoutetstr. .... AY 60
St.-Janstr. .... BY 62
St.-Pietersberg .... BY 63
Veemarkt .... BY 72
Vismarkt .... AY 73
Wollemarkt .... AY 76

EXCURSIONS

Fort Breendonk ⏲ – *12km - 7.5 miles west via Willebroek.*
This fort, a national memorial, was built between 1906 and 1914 to complete Antwerp's defences. Although bombarded in 1914, this was the last Antwerp fort to surrender to the Germans. The Belgian Army chose it in May 1940 to be the general headquarters (King Leopold III stayed here), but the German advance pushed the troops back to the coast, forcing them to abandon the fort. The Nazis turned it into a "reception camp" which was in reality a concentration camp; about 4 000 people were imprisoned here, some of whom were later deported.
A signposted tour, and recordings of survivors' accounts at certain places on it, serve to take the visitor through the prisoners' rooms, the torture room, the huts used for living and sleeping quarters, the execution enclosure and the scaffold for the condemned. The little museum's documentation evokes the two World Wars, life in the Breendonk camp, and in other similar Nazi installations.

From Mechelen to Elewijt – *12km - 7.5 miles, leaving on Leuvensesteenweg* **(BZ)**.

Muizen – The **Plankendael zoological garden★★** ⏲ is a vast park of about a hundred acres to the south. It is planted with flowers and trees and provides a home for nearly 1 000 animals. There are species of rare birds and of those in danger of extinction, aviaries of exotic birds, and lakes with large colonies of aquatic birds.

Hofstade – This immense recreation park consists of almost 150ha - nearly 371 acres that include two lakes and an ornithological reserve.

Elewijt – **Het Steen Castle** ⏲, to the west, is where Rubens spent the last five years of his life (1635-1640). It still has a pretty north façade with crowstepped gables, as well as a 13C keep.

Keerbergen and Tremelo – *23km - 14.25 miles east, leaving by the Nekkerspoelstraat* **(BY 52)**.

Keerbergen – Pop 10 215. This is a pleasant vacation spot in the Brabant Kempen region; luxurious villas are tucked amidst the pine forest.

Tremelo – Pop 11 241. The **Father Damien museum** (Pater Damiaanmuseum) ⏲ is now in the house where the missionary (1840-1889) was born. He died caring for Hawaii's lepers on Molokai Island. A collection of his personal belongings and an audio-visual presentation in several languages retrace his life.

★★ MEUSE/NAMUR REGION Namur

Michelin maps 409 H5, H4, I4 or 213 folds 20, 21 and 214 fold 5

The source of the Meuse is in France at an altitude of 409m - 1 342ft. The river crosses Belgium and the south of the Netherlands, travelling 950km - 590 miles before flowing into the North Sea.

The Meuse in the Namur Region – The Meuse is at its most picturesque as it crosses the province of Namur. Its powerful course cuts a path to drop 300m - 984ft in altitude, and it continues to drop as it heads north. The river, like most of those in Belgium, flows initially from south to north; when it reaches Namur it suddenly bends to the east, flowing along the corridor it encounters there.
The variety of landscapes is a result of the types of soil. Shale-covered, wooded slopes alternate with hard rocks (calcareous, sandstone); the bare stone is a channel for the river, which cuts magnificent escarpments, narrow blades or fine needles, or the many deep grottoes. All this variety of relief is frequented by rock-climbing enthusiasts.
Quite a few barges use the parts of the river made to accommodate 1 350-ton vessels (international standard) downstream of Givet, and in the area from Hermalle-s/s-Huy to Liège, handling 2 000-ton boats.

The four Aymon sons – Ever since Renaud de Montauban's medieval verse-chronicle, the exploits of Renaud, Alart, Guichard and Richard, forced to flee the wrath of Charlemagne, whose beloved nephew had been killed by Renaud, on their magnificent **horse, Bayard**, have given rise to many other tales. The four sons of Duke Aymes of Dordogne took refuge only briefly in the Ardennes, along the Meuse, but numerous places evoke their legend locally, especially along the Meuse in the Namur region.

Boat trips, see Dinant, Huy, Namur.

★★ 1 FROM HASTIÈRE-LAVAUX TO NAMUR

80km - 50 miles - allow 1 day - local map overleaf

The imposing rocky cliffs and the ruins of a number of castles on top of them give this route has a romantic atmosphere. The very presence of these ruins underlines the strategic importance of the valley. It lies on a traditional line of north-south traffic, unfortunately therefore having attracted several invasions; one of the most disastrous of these was in 1554, when King of France **Henri II** was fighting Emperor Charles V.
The valley is more densely inhabited than the surrounding plateaux (Condroz to the east, Entre-Sambre-et-Meuse to the west). Straggling villages lie at the foot of the wild, rocky walls, while villas, inns and cafés crowd along the riverside.

Hastière-Lavaux – The **Pont d'Arcole caves** (grottes) ⊙ *(Rue d'Anthée)* have five galleries adorned with concretions; there is also a deep well with the underground river running at its bottom. The upper gallery has delicate stalactites, some of them an extraordinarily pure white.

Cross to the south bank of the river.

Hastière-par-delà – The **Church of Our Lady** is near the Meuse; it is actually the remains of a priory in the Mosan Romanesque style (1033-1035), except for the Gothic chancel. It has certain points in common with St Hadelin's at Celles *(qv)*: the large gate-tower, the pilaster strips, the nave with a wooden-ceiling, the great arcades on square pillars.
The 13C stalls were carved into greatly varied designs. The font dates from the 14C. The Romanesque **crypt** contains two Merovingian sarcophagi.

Return to the north bank.

Waulsort – This is a little tourist centre in a pleasant location. The great Waulsort abbey was founded in the 11C; the former abbey palace is all that now remains. The river bed closes in shortly after this, and beautiful rough grey rock faces plunge steeply into the Meuse on the opposite bank. These are the famous **Freÿr cliffs★** (rochers), the domain of the Belgian Alpine Club rockclimbing school.

★ **Freÿr Château** – *See Freÿr Château.*

Before long, the Viel Anseremme priory comes into view standing among beautiful trees in a bend in the river.

★ **Cave (Grotte la Merveilleuse)** – *See Dinant.*

★★ **Dinant** – *See Dinant.*

Cross the river to the east bank and head south; after Bayard Rock, follow the road along the river to Anseremme.

★ **Anseremme** – *See Dinant: Excursions* 2.

Return to Dinant and cross back to the west bank of the Meuse.

Bouvignes and Crèvecoeur Castle – *See Dinant: Excursions* 1.

The ruins of the **Géronsart tower** and those of **Poilvache Castle** ⊙ can be seen on the opposite bank at a height of 125m - 410ft above the Meuse, above Houx village. The people of Liège destroyed the castle in 1430, and vegetation has invaded it ever since; legend says that the four Aymon sons built it. It was initially called the Emerald Castle, then this 10C fortress acquired the name of Poilvache (literally "cowhide") in the 14C, as a result of a trick used in a war: the besieged castle occupants had slipped out to find cattle to eat and were captured by the people of Dinant, the latter dressed themselves in their prisoners' clothes, while others covered themselves with animal skins and hid themselves amidst herds of cows; in this way they managed to enter the castle. The **Molignée Valley★** *(qv)* leads off to the west of Anhée.

Cross to the east bank of the Meuse, towards Yvoir.

Yvoir – Once a metal-producing town, this is now a popular resort appreciated for the island, now a **recreation centre** ⊙. It is possible to go caving and pot-holing nearby to the north. The **Nature Oasis** ⊙ south of Yvoir is an estate devoted to Belgium's flora and fauna, and includes botanical gardens, a castle, a farm with dioramas, an enclosure containing deer, boar, wild sheep etc. The "breeding farm" shows the visitor a butterfly's development from egg to chrysalis; butterflies can be seen in their natural environment in a special garden (450m^2 - 92yds^2).

Take the steep road (N 937) away from the river's course upon leaving Yvoir.

★ **Spontin** – *See Spontin.*

Crupet – This village lies between two valleys; there is a lovely **manor-house** (12C and 16C) surrounded by water.
It is essentially a powerful square tower with an oriel on one side; there is also a corner turret and a half-timbered covered watchpath. The Carondelet family lived here until 1621, and indeed the crest of this Franche-Comté family is on the pediment of the entrance porch. These lords' gravestones are in Crupet's **church** left of the entrance; the lords themselves are depicted in stiff ceremonial clothing.

Return to the Meuse and cross to the west bank just outside Godinne.

★ **Annevoie-Rouillon** – *See Annevoie-Rouillon Domain.*

There is a pretty **view★** of Godinne's priory a few miles along from Annevoie; this is a charming 16C structure adjoining a 16C church with a Gothic chancel.

Take the Lustin road by going over the next bridge.

★ **Frênes Rocks (Rochers)** ⊙ – There is a beautiful **view★** of the Meuse Valley and Profondeville from the viewpoint at the top of the rocks *(access through the café).*

Return to the west bank.

★ **Profondeville** – Pop 9 431. This charming tourist centre is pleasantly located in a Meuse riverbend. The Frênes Rocks stand on the opposite bank.

Wépion – This town is renowned for its strawberry farms; the imposing **Néviaux Rocks** are on the opposite river bank.

Reach Namur (qv) on ⑥ on the map, which arrives at the foot of the citadel.

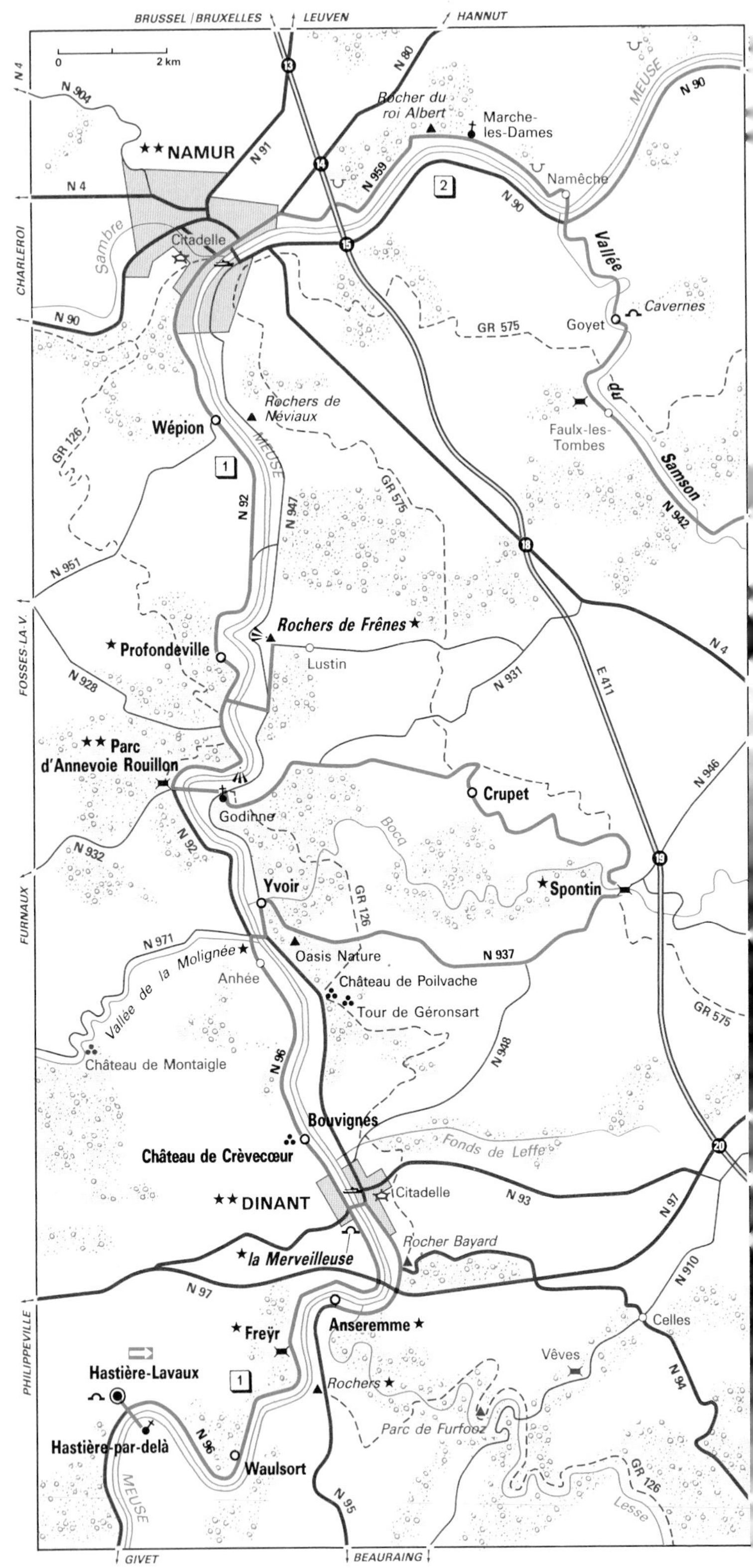

Constantly revised ***Michelin Maps****, at a scale of 1:200 000, highlight towns cited in the* ***Michelin Red Guide Benelux*** *for their hotels or restaurants, and indicate which towns in the Red Guide are accompanied by a town plan.*

Michelin *makes it so easy to choose where to stay and to find the right route.*

Keep current ***Michelin Maps*** *in the car at all times.*

★ 2 FROM NAMUR TO ANDENNE

35km - 22 miles – local map opposite

The Meuse expands and the valley widens from here. Although from time to time stubbornly hard rock can still be seen, the slopes are generally less steep. There are many active limestone and marble quarries along the riverbanks.

★★ **Namur** – *See Namur.*

Leave Namur on ② on the map and head along the Meuse's north bank.

King Albert Rock (Rocher du roi Albert) – Rocks rising 70m - 230ft above the Meuse are to the left. It was here that **King Albert I** fell to his death on 17 February 1934, during a rock-climbing excursion. A cross halfway up marks the place where his body was found. The surrounding forest has become a **national park** and a little **museum** shows the gifts made by pilgrims to this site.

Marche-les-Dames – The Cistercians founded the **abbey** (abbaye Notre-Dame-du-Vivier) in the early 13C; the Little Sisters of Bethlehem now live here. The abbey buildings date from the 13C and the 18C.

Cross the Meuse at Namêche and take the N 942 south towards Gesves.

Samson Valley – This is a green and picturesque valley.

Goyet – The **caverns** ⏲ give an idea of the way of life in prehistoric cave dwellings; other **caves** ⏲ nearby have beautiful concretions. A 19C **castle** shortly before Faulx-les-Tombes is a convincing imitation of a medieval fortress.

Turn back and return to the Meuse Valley; follow it to Andenne.

Andenne – Pop 22 841. This little town began with the monastery founded in about 690 by St Begga, Charlemagne's great-great-great grandmother. The monastery became an aristocratic chapter of secular canonesses.

The **War of the Cow** began in Andenne. A peasant had stolen a cow from a wealthy man in Ciney, and was recognised at the Andenne fair while he was trying to return the cow to the owner. He was arrested and hung in Ciney. The Count of Namur came to revenge his serf's death, aided by the people of Luxembourg, and they laid siege to the town. Liège's prince-bishop, sovereign of Ciney, called on Dinant for help. The war lasted two years and raged through the Condroz region.

St Begga's Collegiate Church (Collégiale Ste-Begge) – This was built in the 18C based on Dewez's plans, replacing the monastery's seven churches. The saint's blue stone Gothic tomb is here *(chapel north of the chancel)*. The church **museum** ⏲ contains the canonesses' treasure: paintings, sculptures, manuscripts and the finely worked reliquary of St Begga (about 1570-1580).

This guide, which is regularly revised, is based on tourist information provided at the time of going to press. Improved facilities and fluctuations in the cost of living make changes inevitable.

★ MODAVE CASTLE Liège

Michelin maps 409 I4 or 214 fold 6

The first thing that strikes visitors on their arrival at the castle is the size of the buildings, but at this point there is no indication of how remarkable the site overlooking the Hoyoux is. Certain parts of the castle (the keep) date back to the 13C; but for the most part the Count of Marchin, who restored it between 1652 and 1673, is responsible for the way it looks today. After him it belonged to the Liège prince-bishop, the Duke of Montmorency, and other families, before the Compagnie Intercommunale Bruxelloise des Eaux (Brussels Local Water Authority) acquired it in 1941. The purchase was necessary for the water reservoir, now supplying Brussels, on the castle's estate. Rennequin Sualem's hydraulic wheel, a model for the Marly machine, was constructed here in 1667.

Tour ⏲

A great main courtyard precedes the classical façade. The rooms inside are elegantly furnished. Note **Jean-Christian Hansche**'s extraordinary stuccos: those in the guards' room represent the Count of Marchin's genealogy with their family crests; those in the Hercules apartment depict the hero's Labours. There is a beautiful **view★** over the Hoyoux Valley from the terrace of the Duke of Montmorency's room. The bedroom of the Duchess of Montmorency, who owned the castle in the late 18C, is upstairs. A model of the hydraulic wheel is in the cellars.

EXCURSION

Bois-et-Borsu – *7km - 4.3 miles southeast.* The **Romanesque church in Bois** ⏲ still has its beautiful late 14C-early 15C **frescoes★** illustrating the Coronation of the Virgin, the Life of Christ and the legends of St Lambert and St Hubert. They are on the vaults and walls of the chancel and nave.
The village of Ocquier is about 3.5km - 2 miles from Bois-et-Borsu; its grey stone houses cluster around the Romanesque church of St Remaclus.

★ MOLIGNÉE VALLEY Namur

Michelin maps 409 H5 or 214 folds 4, 5 – Local map see MEUSE/NAMUR REGION

The Molignée is a small river with a charming valley; the river wends its way between meadows and wooded slopes before it joins the Meuse. Villages of blue stone houses follow on from one another, and there are several abbeys on the hillsides.

FROM ANHÉE TO FURNAUX *24km - 15 miles – allow 4 hours*

Montaigle Castle - This ruined fortress is on a rocky outcrop; Henri II destroyed it in 1554.

Turn left at the old Falaën station.

Falaën fortified farm (**Château-ferme de Falaën**) ⏲ – Surrounding moats and a drawbridge once defended this 17C building in brick and limestone. It forms a square with a lofty tower at each corner. Inside there is a small museum on brotherhoods, with temporary exhibitions.

Maredsous Abbey ⏲ – The Benedictines founded this in 1872. It is a vast neo-Gothic ensemble on a wooded plateau overlooking a valley. The monks engage in a great variety of activities besides their usual hours of prayer: teaching, computer technology, theological research, the hotel trade, cheesemaking, a bookshop etc.

Maredret – This village, also with an abbey, specialises in crafts.

Ermeton-sur-Biert – The old castle overlooking this densely wooded area has become a convent.

Turn right after the station and go under the railway.

Furnaux – The church has a magnificent **font**★ from about 1135-1150. Four lions support the Mosan Romanesque basin, decorated with scenes from the Old and New Testament, in particular the Baptism of Christ.

*The **Michelin Maps** for this region are shown in the diagram on the outside back cover of the guide.*

The text refers to the maps which, owing to their scale or coverage, are the clearest and most appropriate in each case.

★ MONS Hainaut Ⓟ

Pop 91 650

Michelin maps 409 E4 or 214 fold 2
Town plan in the current Michelin Red Guide Benelux

Mons is both the capital of Hainaut province, a status which is emphasised by its magnificent belfry, and the commercial hub of the **Borinage** mining region near the French border. The steep old streets, with elegant 17C and 18C homes along them, are quite charming.

Sculptor and architect **Jacques Du Broeucq** (*c*1510-1584) was born here in the 16C, as was the musician **Roland de Lassus** (1532-1594). The French poet **Paul Verlaine** was imprisoned in Mons from 1874 to 1875 for having shot his friend Rimbaud *(qv)*, and wrote the *Romances sans parole* and a few fragments of *Sagesse* here. Novelist and poet **Charles Plisnier** (1897-1952) was born at Ghlin *(4km - 2.5 miles west)*.

Mons has been the location since 1971 of a four-faculty State University. The town also has a Polytechnic School, a Catholic Faculty of Economic Sciences and an International Interpreters School.

Lake Grand Large to the north offers many recreation activities.

A brief history – Mons, as the etymology of its name reveals (mons/bergen: mountain), grew up around a high point of land. It developed around a fortress and monastery founded by St Waudru in the 7C. The Counts of Hainaut built a castle on the location of this fortress.

The town bathed in a period of prosperity in the Middle Ages and under Emperor Charles V, due largely to its clothmaking activities. It was besieged several times, however, especially in the 17C and 18C, because of its strategic position. Louis XIV captured the town in 1691, and in fact the architectural style of most of the houses dates from this period.

In 1792 in **Jemappes** *(5km - 3 miles west)* Dumouriez won a victory against the Austrians, temporarily making the country French.

For the British Empire, Mons was a true symbol of the First World War. It was at its walls that General French held Von Kluck's German troops at bay for 48 hours. The Canadians finally liberated the city at dawn of 11 November 1918, after three days of fierce combat.

SHAPE, the top command of European Allied forces, settled on Maisières and Casteau territory in the northeast in 1967.

The Lumeçon – Each year the Procession of the Chariot of Gold *(see below)* takes place, with fanfares, bells and banners; the Lumeçon takes place on the market square, a combat ending with St George winning over the Dragon, all to traditional music.

See the Calendar of Events at the end of this guide.

★★ ST WAUDRU'S COLLEGIATE CHURCH (COLLÉGIALE STE-WAUDRU) (Z) ⏲ *time: 1 hour*

This Brabant Gothic church was built by the aristocratic chapter of St Waudru canonesses between 1450 and 1686, under the direction of Mathieu de Layens *(qv)*. The exterior is imposing but somewhat squat, as the planned tower-façade was never finished. Twenty-nine chapels surround the architectural ensemble.

Interior – *Access through the south doorway.*

This contains a great quantity of furnishings.

The vast nave (108m - 354ft long) has pillars rising in a single sweep up to the brick vaulting.

Jacques Du Broeucq's 16C Italian Renaissance alabaster **rood-screen** was demolished in 1797; its fragments are distributed throughout the church (chapels, transept arm, main altar).

A 16C silver and stone Virgin with Child is in the last north side aisle chapel *(on the right when entering)*. The **Chariot of Gold** (Car d'Or), a 1780 carriage for the 19C reliquary shrine of St Waudru during the annual procession, can be seen near the first chapel.

A Du Broeucq Christ giving Blessing is on the wall of the south side aisle's third chapel; this beautiful work is in alabaster.

Du Broeucq alabaster statues surround the **chancel**; those representing the Virtues are particularly graceful.

Beautiful 16C and 17C stained glass, some presented by Maximilian of Austria, embellishes the clerestory windows.

The Chariot of Gold in St Waudru's Collegiate Church

There is a 16C (upper part) Gothic stone altarpiece in the first chapel to the south in the **ambulatory**; in the tenth chapel, white stone statues of St Michael (15C) and St Waudru (16C); in the twelfth chapel, a beautiful Du Broeucq black marble and alabaster altarpiece, a lovely statue of Mary Magdalene over it; below, the altar front has an Entombment inspired by Jean Goujon.

Treasury (Trésor) ⏲ – This has interesting religious art objects: wooden statues; liturgical ornaments; works in gold and silver, including a 13C-14C finely worked silver-gilt reliquary of St Vincent, and a piece of Parisian metalwork of St Elias, dating from 1396.

ADDITIONAL SIGHTS

★ **Belfry (Beffroi)** (Y) – *Illustration p 23.* This was built at the highest point in the town, in the charming castle square, from which there are beautiful glimpses of the surroundings, including the 12C ruins of the **Count of Hainaut's castle** and the 11C Romanesque chapel of St Calixte. The baroque **belfry** (1662) is 87m - 285ft high, with onion domes. There are 49 chimes in the carillon.

Town Hall (Hôtel de ville) (Y H) ⏲ – This stands on the Grand-Place, and was built in 1458. Construction was halted, for lack of money, when Charles the Bold died in 1477; it was continued in the 16C and 19C. The beautiful Gothic façade has a bell tower, framed by two 17C pavilions with scrolled pediments.

Near the main door is the cast iron figurine of a monkey, known as the "Singe du Grand-Garde". The origins of this monkey are a mystery. His head has been polished by the many hands touching it for good luck.

Notice the 15C sculpted keystones, depicting justice, under the porch.

There are many rooms inside from many different periods, decorated with beautiful furniture and tapestries. The beams in the Gothic room on the first floor rest on beautiful sculpted corbels. The Gothic vault (17C) from St George's chapel is in the next room; temporary exhibitions are held here.

Mayor's Garden (Jardin du Mayeur) (Y F) – This garden is a pretty complement to the old buildings behind the town hall; one of them, the old pawnshop, is now home to the Centenaire museums. The Ropieur Fountain, sculpted by Gobert, represents a little boy spraying fountain water on those who pass.

MONS

Capucins (R. des) .... Z
Chaussée (R. de la) .... Z 6
Grand Rue .... Z
Havré (R. d') .... Z
Pte Guirlande
(R. de la) .... Z 35

Athénée (R. de l') .... Z 2
Bootle (Pl. de) .... Y 3
Chartriers (R. des) .... Z 5
Claude de
Bettignies (R.) .... Y 7
Clef (R. de la) .... Z 8
Clercs (R. des) .... Z 9
Coupe (R. de la) .... Z 13
Dolez (Bd) .... Z 14
Échelles (R. des) .... Y 17
Enghien (R. d') .... Y 18
Étampes (R. d') .... Y 19
F. Roosevelt
(Square) .... YZ 20
Frère Orban (Av.) .... YZ 21
Fripiers (R. des) .... Z 22
Gades (R. des) .... Y 23
Gaillers (R. des) .... Y 24
Grosse Pomme
(R. de la) .... Z 26
Houdain (R. de) .... Z 27
Houssière (R. de la) .... Y 28
M. Bervoets (R.) .... Y 30
Notre-Dame
Débonnaire (R.) .... Y 31
Telliers (R. des) .... Y 37
Tour Auberon (R. de la) . Y 40
4 Fils Aymon (R. des) ... Y 41

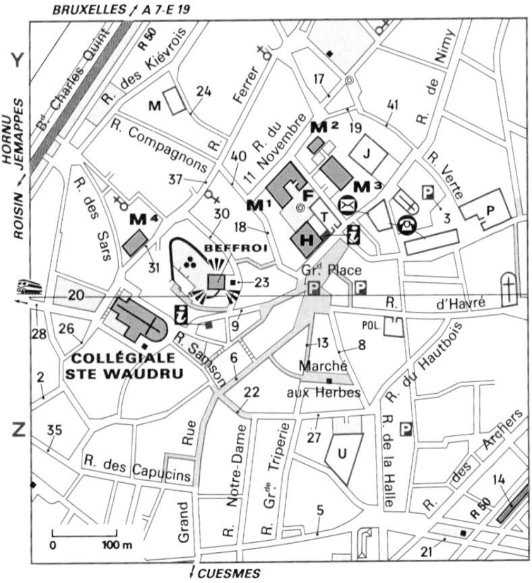

Centenaire Museums (Musées du Centenaire) (Y M1) – These museums, built for the centenary, are in the old 17C pawnshop; they include a War Museum, a Numismatics Museum and most particularly a **Ceramics Museum** with more than 3 600 works from between the 17C and the 20C. Note especially those from Delft, St-Amand-les-Eaux (France) and Brussels.

★ **Museum of Life in Mons (Musée de la Vie montoise)** (Y M2) – The Jean-Lescarts building stands alone at the far end of a garden; it can be reached by a set of stairs. It is a charming building dating from 1636, which used to be the convent's infirmary.
The museum evokes regional history and traditions through its furniture, its simple decoration, the collections and documentation.

Fine Art Museum (Musée des Beaux-Arts) (Y M3) – Art works from the 16C to the present are exhibited in rotation; large temporary exhibitions are held here every year.

Le Vieux Logis (Chanoine-Puissant Museums) (Y M4) – Canon Puissant, a great art lover, installed rich collections in this little 16C house before his death in 1934: antique furniture, a carved wooden Renaissance ceiling, statues, metalwork and drawings.

EXCURSIONS

Cuesmes – *3.5km - 2 miles south. Leave from Grand-Rue.*

Van Gogh's house is in a pretty, rural spot; the artist lived here with a family of miners, the Descrucqs, in 1879 and 1880. He came in December 1878 to preach in the Borinage district; he began drawing the countryside and the miners' life in Cuesmes. His re-created room and a documentation room where an audio-visual presentation is shown are open to visitors.

Grand-Hornu – *See Grand-Hornu.*

Blaugies – *20km - 12.5 miles southwest of Mons.*
There is a little 15C polychrome wooden altarpiece in the **church**, representing an *Entombment* in an animated composition. There is also a 12C font, with images of dragons biting bunches of grapes.

Roisin – *30km - 18.5 miles southwest of Mons.*

Verhaeren's house is north of the village, near **Caillou-qui-bique**. The writer lived here with his wife Martha during the last years of his life (1900 to 1916). The little **Verhaeren museum** in the Caillou inn courtyard includes a reconstruction of the poet's study.

★★ NAMUR Namur

Pop 103 131

Michelin maps 409 H4 or 214 fold 5 – Local map see MEUSE/NAMUR REGION

This town has been a prime military site, owing to its location at the confluence of the Sambre and the Meuse, spanned by the beautiful Jambes Bridge. The enormous citadel spread over Champeau Hill dominates the scene, while Namur itself is laid out around its many churches. It is now a prosperous city, where trade and administration are the main activities, in addition to tourism. Its university (Facultés universitaires Notre-Dame-de-la-Paix), founded in 1831, has a good reputation.

A city often under siege – The history of Namur province is one of war. The city itself was often under siege because of its strategic position. As early as the Roman period, Caesar pursued the Aduatuci tribes here. In 1577 Don Juan of Austria captured the castle, and from the 17C onwards assaults followed thick and fast.

The 1692 siege led by Vauban in Louis XIV's presence had a great impact. The capture of Namur was celebrated in grandiloquent odes by Boileau and Racine, historiographers of the Sun King, and even in works by his official court painter, Van der Meulen. Vauban reinforced the fortifications, but Namur was recaptured again in 1695 by William III of Orange.

In 1746 the armies of Louis XV attacked the city, which was then handed over in 1748 to Austria; Emperor Joseph II demolished the fortifications.

The Revolutionaries took Namur in 1792, but they were forced out in turn by the Austrians the following year. The last siege, in 1794, ended in favour of the French.

After Waterloo in 1815 Grouchy's rear guard in Namur valiantly protected most of the field marshal's retreating forces heading for the Meuse and Givet-Charlemont Valleys. The Dutch rebuilt the citadel in 1816.

Owing to the belt of fortifications built in the late 19C, Namur was able to put up a heroic resistance against the enemy during the First World War. Nevertheless the town was eventually invaded, then pillaged and partly burned down on 23 August 1914. Namur was captured in May 1940 and bombarded several times until 1944.

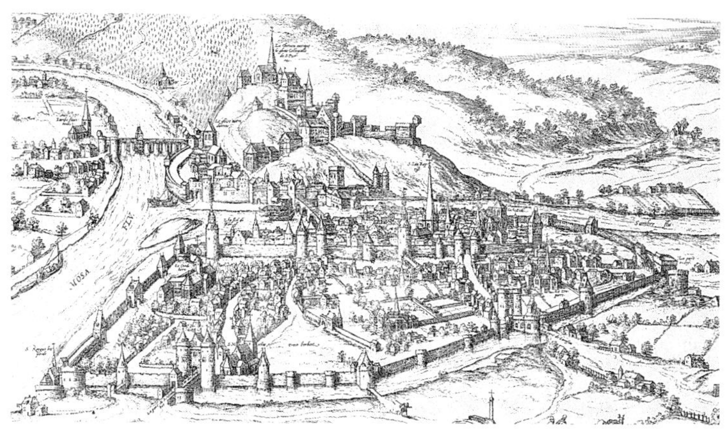

Namur, engraving by Frans Hogenberg

Festivals – Every year traditional folklore groups are on display at the **Wallonia festivals** *(see the Calendar of Events at the end of this guide)*. The **stilt-walkers**, whose existence has been traced back to the 15C, dress up in 17C costume and fight each other on stilts. The Canaris battalion distinguished itself during the Brabant Revolution.

Boat trips on the Meuse ⊙ – Boat trips are organised on the Meuse to Dinant and Wépion.

★ CITADEL (BZ) *time: 1 hour 30min*

Access via the Route Merveilleuse (1.5km - 1 mile) or by cablecar ⊙ leaving from the foot of the Citadel.

Route Merveilleuse – The **Joyeuse Tower** (**BZ**), a trace of the counts' old castle, is on the right as the road climbs.

A terrace, northeast of a rocky spur at a bend in the road, affords a magnificent **panorama★★** over the valley of the Sambre and the Meuse. A little road, not far on the left, heads down to Namur, overlooking its slate roofs and many bell towers. The road then leads to the **keep** (donjon), passing between two of the old castle's **towers** (**BZ A**) and crosses the moat separating the keep from the Mediane fortress.

Fortified estate ⊙ – The late 15C and 16C Mediane bastion was reinforced in 1640 by another, the Terra Nova, built by the Spanish. A wide moat separates them. A visit to the estate reveals the complex defensive architecture of each bastion, from both the outside *(recorded commentary)* and the inside, with a tour *(guided)* of the two underground areas.

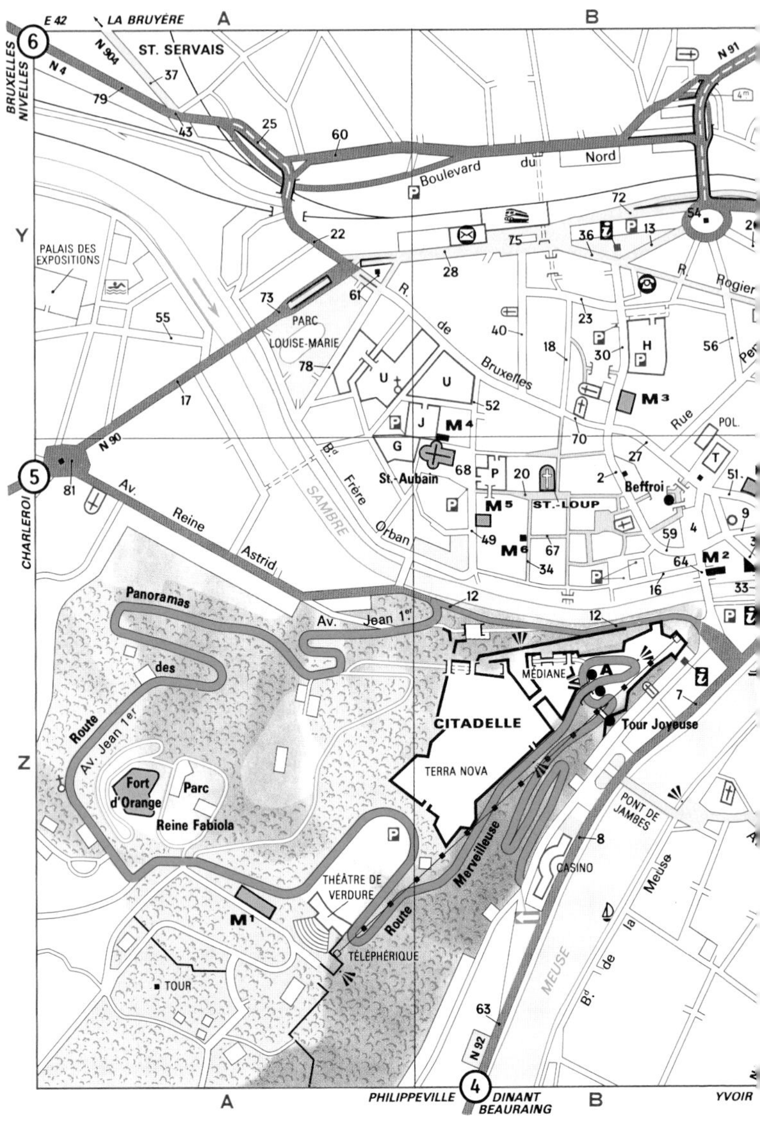

Provincial Forest Museum (Musée provincial de la forêt) (**AZ M**[1]) ⏲ – This museum, surrounded by beautiful trees, is a chance to discover the forest's flora and fauna. A large diorama with sound effects of the Ardennes Forest is particularly captivating.

Exotic insect collections are on display upstairs; the butterflies are really remarkable.

Fort d'Orange – This fortress is near the **Reine-Fabiola amusement park** (**AZ**). The fortress was built in 1691 to protect the Terra Nova bastion; the Dutch partly rebuilt it in 1816.

Route des Panoramas (**AZ**) – This winding road heads down through the woods to the town centre.

★ CITY CENTRE *time: half a day*

★ **Archaeological Museum (Musée archéologique)** (**BZ M**[2]) ⏲ – This is in the beautiful 16C building where the meat market once was. The exhibitions display the results of excavations in the province, itself particularly rich in Roman and Merovingian antiquities.

There are magnificent examples of 1C-7C jewellery and glassware.

The **Cultural Centre** (Maison de la Culture) (**BZ B**), built in 1964, is behind the museum.

Oignies Treasury (Le Trésor d'Oignies) (**BZ K**) ⏲ – The very rich Oignies priory **treasury★★** is in one room; it was fortunately saved from the 1940 bombings. The display includes delicate early 13C Mosan metalwork by the monk **Hugo d'Oignies**: gospel-books, reliquaries, etc. The delicacy of his workmanship is remarkable, especially the medallions on a black background in the filigree and leaf decoration, on which tiny hunting scenes can be discerned.

Just past the theatre, **St James' Tower** (tour St-Jacques) comes into sight on the left; it has an octagonal bell tower on top and has been used as a **belfry** (**BZ**) since the 18C.

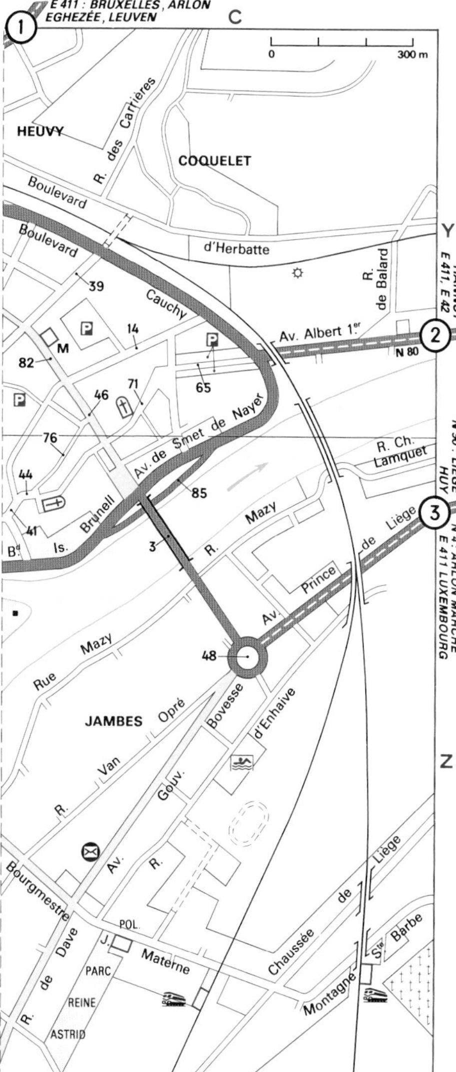

NAMUR

Ange (R. de l')	BZ 2
Fer (R. de)	BY 30
Marchovelette (R. de)	BZ 59
St Jacques (R.)	BYZ 70

Ardennes (Pont des)	CZ 3
Armes (Pl. d')	BZ 4
Baron L. Huart (Bd.)	BZ 7
Baron-de-Moreau (Av.)	BZ 8
Bas-de-la-Place (R.)	BZ 9
Bord-de-l'Eau (R. du)	ABZ 12
Borgnet (Rue)	BY 13
Bourgeois (R. des)	CY 14
Brasseurs (R. des)	BZ 16
Cardinal-Mercier (Av.)	AY 17
Carmes (R. des)	BY 18
Collège (Rue du)	BZ 20
Combattants (Av. des)	AY 22
Croisiers (R. des)	BY 23
Croix-du-Feu (Av. des)	AY 25
Dewez (Rue)	BCY 26
Emile-Cuvelier (R.)	BYZ 27
Ernest-Mélot (Bd.)	BY 28
Fernand-Golenvaux (Av.)	BCZ 31
France (Pont de)	BCZ 33
Fumal (Rue)	BZ 34
Gare (Av. de la)	BY 36
Gembloux (Rue de)	AY 37
Général-Michel (Rue)	CY 39
Godefroid (Rue)	BY 40
Gravière (Rue de)	CZ 41
Hastedon (Pl. d')	AY 43
Ilon (Pl. d')	CZ 44
J.-B. Brabant (Rue)	CY 46
Joséphine-Charlotte (Pl.)	CZ 48
Joseph-Saintraint (R.)	BZ 49
Julie-Billiard (R.)	BZ 51
Lelièvre (Rue)	BY 52
Léopold (Pl.)	BY 54
Léopold II (Av.)	AY 55
Lucien-Namèche R.)	BY 56
Merckem (Bd de)	AY 60
Omalius (Pl. d')	AY 61
Plante (Av. de la)	BZ 63
Pont (Rue du)	BZ 64
Reine Elisabeth (Pl.)	CY 65
Rupplémont (Rue)	BZ 67
St-Aubain (Pl.)	BZ 68
St-Nicolas (R.)	CY 71
Square-Léopold (Av. du)	BY 72
Stassart (Av. de)	AY 73
Station (Pl. de la)	BY 75
Tanneries (Rue des)	CYZ 76
Vierge (Rempart de la)	AY 78
Waterloo (Chaussée de)	AY 79
Wiertz (Pl.)	AYZ 81
1er-Lanciers (R. du)	BY 82
4 Fils Aymon (Rue des)	CZ 85

★ **Museum of Ancient Arts of the Namur Region (Musée des Arts anciens du Namurois)** (BY M3) – The museum is in the **Hôtel de Gaiffier d'Hestroy**, an elegant 17C mansion, which contains beautiful collections of local medieval to Renaissance works of art.

The collection of gold- and silverware is particularly rich; there are some beautiful Mosan reliquaries.

There are many sculptures in stone (fonts, tombs) as well as in wood (altarpieces, statues), and worked copper, bearing witness to the interest in artistic production in the Namur region. Stop and admire also the four beautiful landscapes by Herri met de Bles *(qv)* from the early 16C.

★ **St Loup's Church (Église St-Loup)** (BZ) – This used to be a Jesuit collegiate church and is now a school (Athénée Royal). It is a remarkable baroque building, built from 1621 to 1645 from the design plans by Pierre Huyssens.

Ringed columns, surmounted by a red and white marble entablature, support sandstone vaulting richly decorated in high-relief. Note also the lovely furniture.

St Auban's Cathedral (Cathédrale St-Aubain) (BYZ) – This classical domed building was built in 1751 by the Italian architect Pizzoni. It is on the site of the old collegiate church of St Auban, founded in 1047.

There are beautiful works of baroque art inside, coming for the most part from the region's churches and abbey, such as the Rubens school paintings above the stalls, originally from St Loup's Church.

The old 18C bishop's palace is opposite the cathedral and is nowadays occupied by the provincial government.

★ **Diocesan Museum and Cathedral Treasury** (BYZ M4) – Located south of the cathedral, the museum has a beautiful collection of religious objects: a precious crown-reliquary, enamel discs decorating it (*c*1210); the portable altar decorated with ivory plaques (11C-12C); the arm-reliquary of St Adrian (*c*1235); the statue of St Blaise (*c*1280) in silver gilt; the Mosan Virgin (*c*1220); a rare series of 16C-18C glassware; gold- and silverware; and sculptures.

★ **Musée de Croix** (BZ M5) ⏲ – This museum is in an elegant 18C Louis XV style town house. There are many rooms to visit, in which the decoration integrates perfectly with the architecture: ceilings garnished with stuccoes, woodwork (panelling, doors, main staircase), and St Rémy marble fireplaces.
Note the many high-corniced armoires, decorated with rocaille inset panels, that are typical of Namur cabinet-making. There are also interesting pieces of regional art (paintings, sculptures, faïence, glass, gold- and silverwork).

Félicien Rops Museum (BZ M6) ⏲ – This museum is devoted to the illustrious satirical cartoonist (1833-1898): lithographies, etchings *(Sataniques)*, drawings and paintings.

EXCURSIONS

Franc-Waret – *12km - 7.5 miles northeast. Leave on ② on the map.*
The **castle** ⏲, an imposing 18C building surrounded by moats, is flanked with two wings at an angle. A turret and a square tower, traces of the 16C construction, are hidden at the back. Inside, admire the main staircase with two spiral flights, the rooms decorated with beautiful pieces of furniture, the Flemish and French paintings (Largillière portrait), 17C Brussels tapestries based on designs by P Coecke and F Boveman, and the porcelain collection.
The visit ends in a beautiful vaulted room.

From Namur to Fosses-la-Ville. *18km - 11 miles west. Leave on ⑥ on the map.*

Floreffe – Pop 6 534. This **abbey** ⏲ overlooking the Sambre was founded in 1121 by the Premonstratensians *(qv)*, and was rebuilt in the 17C and 18C.
It was enlarged by a long concrete construction in 1964; a small seminary now occupies this vast building.
The main courtyard opens onto a terrace bordered with 18C buildings. A 17C tower and portico building can be seen beyond the garden.
The **abbey church** (13C-18C), flanked by a tower, is 90m - 295ft long. In the 18C, Dewez transformed the inside into the neo-classical style. The immense chancel includes remarkable **stalls**★ executed by Pieter Enderlin from 1632 to 1648. He represented about forty figures, most of them from religious orders, on the upper panels. The eight cherub musicians or singers decorating the end-pieces are particularly noteworthy.
The 13C mill-brewery below the abbey has been turned into an inn.

Fosses-la-Ville – Pop 7 981. This town of the Entre-Sambre-et-Meuse region *(qv)* was founded around a monastery in the 7C; it underwent several sieges, especially in the 17C.
St Feuillen collegiate church, rebuilt in the 18C, still has its late-10C Romanesque tower. The stalls were carved in 1524, the late-16C sculptures include an *Entombment*, and a late 16C bust-reliquary of St Feuillen. A "crypt" stands east of the church, built outside the principal building in 1086. It is the only one of its kind still existing in Belgium.
The **"Petit Chapitre"**, a museum-gallery next to the church, was once the summer residence of the Liège prince-bishops; it contains a **collection of traditional dolls** ⏲ (poupées folkloriques).
Lilette Arnould made the costumes of the 800 figurines by hand; characters from Belgian folklore can be recognised, such as Till Eulenspiegel *(qv)*, Tchantchès *(qv)*, the "Gilles" of Binche, the **Chinels** and the participants in St Feuillen's impressive military march *(see below)*. Fosses is well-known for its festivals *(see the Calendar of Events at the end of this guide)*: first the carnival-like **Chinels** procession, a sort of tongue-in-cheek Punch and Judy show; and the St Feuillen military march *(see Charleroi)* which takes place every seven years on the last Sunday in September *(next procession in 1998)*.

NIEUWPOORT West-Vlaanderen

Pop 9 297

Michelin maps 409 B2 or 213 fold 1

This is an old stronghold at the mouth of the River IJzer (Yser) which was rebuilt after 1918 in the Flemish style. Nieuwpoort has an active fishing fleet and a large fresh fish auction (minque).
As in Ostend, the harbour channel is protected by two long dikes extending far into the sea and bearing two piers. Square fishing nets or dipping nets hang on the west pier *(for hire)*.
Nieuwpoort is also a seaside resort **(Nieuwpoort-Bad)** and a water sports centre; the marina has a capacity for 3 000 boats.

The Battle of the Yser – The Nieuwpoort region was the scene of this terrible wartime episode. In August 1914 the Germans invaded first Belgium, then France. When Maréchal Joffre stopped them at the Marne, they immediately attacked Antwerp *(qv)*, leaving the Belgian troops just time to evacuate and retrench themselves west of the River IJzer (Yser), around King Albert. They were backed up by French and British troops.
The Germans assaulted the last bastion of Belgian territory on 16 October: they succeeded in crossing the IJzer (Yser) at Tervate, north of Diksmuide.
As the Allied forces still had not arrived, the Belgians opened the sluice gates of the Veurne-Ambacht canal at Nieuwpoort on 28 October. The subsequent flooding of the surrounding polders immediately halted the German advance.
The front line then settled itself south of Diksmuide until the end of the war, and the Germans turned to the Ypres salient *(see Ieper)*.

SIGHTS

Church (**O.-L.-Vrouwekerk**) – The tower was built in 1951, and contains a 67-chime **carillon** that can be heard twice a week and during **concerts** ⊙.

King Albert I Monument (**Koning Albertmonument**) ⊙ – This equestrian statue of the king, surrounded by a circular monument, is near the IJzer Bridge. There is an interesting **view** from the top over Nieuwpoort, Ostend, the IJzer, six locks in a fan-shape and the countryside beyond the polder region *(orientation table).*

Municipal museums (**Musea**) – The town hall was rebuilt after the war as was the market (stadshalle). The **K.R. Berquin Museum★** ⊙ is on the first floor, in a large timber-framed room. The region's history and folklore is attractively presented. Note the diptych attributed to Lancelot Blondeel representing the port at the end of the 15C. There is a little **Ornithological Museum** (Museum voor Vogels en Schaaldieren) ⊙ on the ground floor of the **town hall** *(side entrance)*; there is a large diorama of birds and shellfish in their natural seashore environment.

De IJzermonding ⊙ – This nature reserve extends north of the resort, beside the mouth of the River IJzer (Yser).

NINOVE Oost-Vlaanderen

Pop 33 385

Michelin maps 409 F3 or 213 fold 17

Ninove was renowned for its 12C Premonstratensian *(qv)* abbey, of which the beautiful **abbey church** (17C-18C) ⊙ remains. *Entrance through side door on the right.*

This has the same design as the Grimbergen church, and has a remarkable collection of **woodwork★**. There are two splendid confessionals at the far end of the church, one of which is attributed to Theodoor Verhaegen (18C, north side) and is decorated with relief figures in a refined baroque style. The same style is to be found in the side aisle panelling, executed by the same sculptor.

The stalls, dating from 1635, are for their part more sober and elegant in style. Note the graceful 18C marble lectern, decorated with cherubs, which is in the chancel.

★ NIVELLES Brabant

Pop 22 779

Michelin maps 409 G4 or 213 fold 18

Nivelles, rebuilt after the war, is a pretty and welcoming town with a famous collegiate church.

A brief history – Nivelles was one of the cradles of the Carolingian dynasty. It developed around an abbey dedicated to St Peter, founded in about 650 by Itta, the wife of Pepin the Elder (Mayor of the Palace of the Austrasian kings) and by their daughter, St Gertrude. This saint later became the first abbess of a religious sisterhood.

Ramparts were built around the town in the 12C; some of the towers still remain, such as the Simone Tower in Rue Seutin. The abbey was turned into a chapter-house of canons and canonesses under the guidance of an abbess.

It was not long before the canonesses, all of noble blood, acquired a sumptuous way of life. The abbey was very powerful until its suppression in 1798.

The collegiate church was ravaged and more than 500 houses burned down in May 1940, but the town rebuilt itself. It now depends economically on various activities (metallurgical construction, paper mills) grouped in an industrial park.

Traditions – The **Tour de Sainte Gertrude** Procession *(see the Calendar of Events at the end of this guide)* takes place in autumn. The parade stretches over 14km - 8.5 miles up hill and down dale; a 15C cart, drawn by six horses, carries the reliquary of the saint. As the procession wends its way back it is joined by the giants (Argayon, Argayonne, their son Lolo and Godet the horse) as well as a group of canonesses in 17C dress. The local hero is the jack o' the clocks, Jean de Nivelles. There is some doubt about where he came from. The character he represents has no relation to Jean de Nivelle, the son of Jean de Montmorency, who is evoked by the popular French song "Cadet Rousselle".

The local speciality is a succulent cheese and vegetable tart, served hot, known as "tarte al djote".

SIGHTS

★★ **St Gertrude's Collegiate Church** (**Collégiale Ste-Gertrude**) ⊙ – This is an Ottonian Empire Romanesque abbey church, which was consecrated in 1046 by Emperor Henri III. The nave is very long (102m - 335ft), and there are two transepts. The layout of two opposing chancels is, in fact, the architectural expression of the Holy Empire's double nature, the complementary elements of the emperor and the pope. The east chancel is raised, over a crypt with ribbed vaulting. The west chancel, representing imperial authority, is comprised in the building's 12C avant-corps.

This late-Romanesque **avant-corps** has an impressive solidity. It consists of an apse, two chapel galleries, a vast high hall (19m - 63ft) called the "Imperial Hall", and an octagonal bell tower. The restoration of this western ensemble, which has a total of eight remarkable cupolas, was completed in 1984.

The two doorways to the avant-corps are decorated with 12C Romanesque sculptures: St Michael is on the right doorway on entering, the story of Samson is on the left.
The highest transept gable on the church's south side, called St Peter's Gable, is decorated with Romanesque arches.

St Gertrude's Collegiate Church

Interior – The size and the simplicity are striking. The nave was covered with ogive vaulting in the 17C. Restoration gave it back its original look while protecting it with a concrete ceiling made to look like wood. Note the graceful *Virgin of the Annunciation*, a 15C wooden statue, also the 18C oak and marble "truth pulpit" *(qv)* representing the Samaritan woman at Jacob's well by Laurent Delvaux (some of the statues are by him as well), the beautiful Renaissance stalls and the 16C altarpiece in marble and alabaster. There is a 16C brass cupboard in the east chancel, above St Gertrude's mausoleum. A modern reliquary by F Roulin has replaced the magnificent 13C St Gertrude's reliquary destroyed in the May 1940 fire.

Crypt and archaeological basement – An 11C groin-vaulted crypt is beneath the east chancel. The archaeological basement is under the nave and consists of the ruins of the five churches, from the 7C to the 10C, which preceded the Romanesque one. The first Merovingian church (about 650) held the remains of St Gertrude and her parents in its cellars. The last, a Carolingian church from the 10C, contains the tomb of Ermentrude, the granddaughter of Hugh Capet.

Cloisters – These 13C cloisters are a trace of the chapter of canons and canonesses who gradually replaced the monks and recluses of the early times; only the north side, however, is still entirely authentic.
The **Saintes Gate**, near the collegiate church, commemorates the twinning of Nivelles with the town of Saintes (Charente-Maritime, France).

Museum of Archaeology, History and Folklore ⊙ – *27 Rue de Bruxelles.*
This museum displays interesting collections of regional art in an 18C house. Particularly noteworthy are the four stone statues from the collegiate church's Gothic rood-screen *(ground floor)* and a beautiful collection of baroque terracottas by the sculptor Laurent Delvaux (1696-1778). Archaeological, prehistoric and Gallo-Roman collections are on the second floor.

Dodaine Park – *South of the town.*
A flower-bedecked garden around a pond and a small lake is a beautiful setting for this park which is also well-equipped with sports facilities.
Following Avenue de la Tour-de-Guet west towards the motorway gives a sighting of the **Tourette**, a charming 17C building, on the right.

EXCURSIONS

Ronquières – *9km - 5.25 miles west.*
This charming village is well-known for its pretty view of the Charleroi Canal, along which there are some remarkable technological installations.
The **Ronquières inclined plane★** ⊙, constructed in 1968, is 1 432m - 4 698ft long; it makes it possible for boats to transfer easily across a drop in the level of the canal of 68m - 223ft. Two containers 91m - 298ft long, filled with water, each with a 5 200-ton counterweight, can transport a 1 350-ton boat, or four 300-ton barges, from one canal reach to another, by running along on a series of 236 rollers 70cm - 28in in diameter. The whole installation is completed upstream by a canal bridge 300m - 984ft long and a **tower** 150m - 492ft high.
An exhibition inside the tower includes a film explaining the inclined plane, seen in the winch room. The upstream installations can be seen closer up by going out on the third floor. There is an audio-visual presentation on the Hainaut region on the second floor.
The visit can be completed by a **tourist boat ride** ⊙ along the canal as far as Ittre. *Departure from the foot of the canal reach.*

Bois-Seigneur-Isaac; Braine-le-Château – *12km - 7.5 miles north.*

Bois-Seigneur-Isaac – The decoration in the 16C chapel (chapelle du Saint Sang) in the **abbey** is baroque; note Laurent Delvaux's sculptures *(Entombment)* on the main altar. The Gothic vaulted vestry still has a reliquary containing a piece of sacred cloth stained with Christ's blood; this has become an object of pilgrimage. The 18C Bois-Seigneur-Isaac **manor-house** ⊙ opposite the abbey is an enormous building which houses some valuable collections.

Braine-le-Château – Pop 7 728. The castle, surrounded by water, is near a water mill (exhibitions); it belonged to the Counts of Hornes.
Maximilien de Hornes had the pillory set in place on the neighbouring market square in 1521; he was Chamberlain to Emperor Charles V. His alabaster mausoleum, by Jean Mone, is in the church.

★★ OOSTENDE (OSTEND) West-Vlaanderen — Pop 68 370

Michelin maps 409 B2 or 213 fold 2 – Town plan in the current Michelin Red Guide Benelux

There are two Ostends: one is the elegant seaside resort, the other is the fishing port, the ferry link with England (Dover, Folkestone) and the hydrofoil station for Dover.
The **seaside resort** stretches between the **casino** (Kursaal) (**CY**), opened in 1953, and the Thermae Palace Hotel, along the Albert I Promenade bordering the beach; this area is popular with surfers.
The old **fishermen's district** is near the harbour mouth and outer harbour; it consists of crisscrossing narrow streets, cut off to the south by the marina's docks. A large park, the **Marie-Hendrikapark** to the south, has several small lakes for boating and fishing enthusiasts.
Ostend's famous oysters are matured in an 80ha - 198 acre basin, the Spuikom, southeast of the town.
The Siege of Ostend during the Eighty Years War is still famous. The story goes that Archduchess Isabella had vowed never to change her shift until the town was taken. The siege lasted three years (1601-1604); it is for this reason that the word "isabelle" here refers to unidentifiable shades of colour.
The first Belgian sovereigns enjoyed staying in Ostend; Queen Louise-Marie ended her days here in 1850.

Intrigue, by James Ensor

James Ensor (1860-1949) – Born in Ostend of an English father and a Flemish mother, this solitary genius rarely distanced himself from his native town and was recognised only much later by his contemporaries as one of the greatest painters of the late 19C.
Ensor painted initially in dark tones, then later his palette brightened. Between 1883 and 1892 he used violent colours and a technique already tending towards Expressionism to illustrate macabre or satirical subjects which met with little public success. Ensor created an imaginary fantastic world, peopled with masked characters and skeletons, a squirming carnival atmosphere that paved the way to Surrealism.
His most representative work is *Entrance of Christ into Brussels* (1888), exhibited in the Malibu Museum, California.

Festivals – In 1896 James Ensor was one of the promoters of the **"Dead Rat Ball"**, a name chosen in memory of a Montmartre café called "The Dead Rat", frequented by Cœcilia Club members. This elegant annual philanthropic event *(see the Calendar of Events at the end of this guide)* takes place on a Saturday in the casino; men dressing up in women's clothes and wearing masks on a chosen theme are the main feature. Among the other annual events, the Blessing of the Sea with a historical procession is interesting, as are the festivals of Belgium Kites International and Ostend Jazz festivals *(see the Calendar of Events at the end of this guide)*.

OOSTENDE

Street	Grid
Adolf Buylstr.	CY 2
Alfons Pieterslaan	CZ
Kapellestr.	CZ
Vlaanderenstr.	CY 30
Edith Cavellstr.	CZ 4
Ernest Feyspl.	CZ 6
Filip Van Maestrichtpl.	CZ 8
Graaf de Smet de Nayerlaan	CZ 9
Groentemarkt	CY 10
Hendrik Serruyslaan	CZ 13
Kanunnik Dr. Louis Colensstr.	CZ 14
Koninginnelaan	CZ 18
Nieuwpoortse steenweg	CZ 22
Oesterbankstr.	CZ 24
Sir Winston Churchill Kaai	CY 27
Stockholmstr.	CZ 28
Wapenpl.	CY 32
Warschaustr.	CZ 33
Wellingtonstr.	CZ 35
Wittenonnenstr.	CY 36

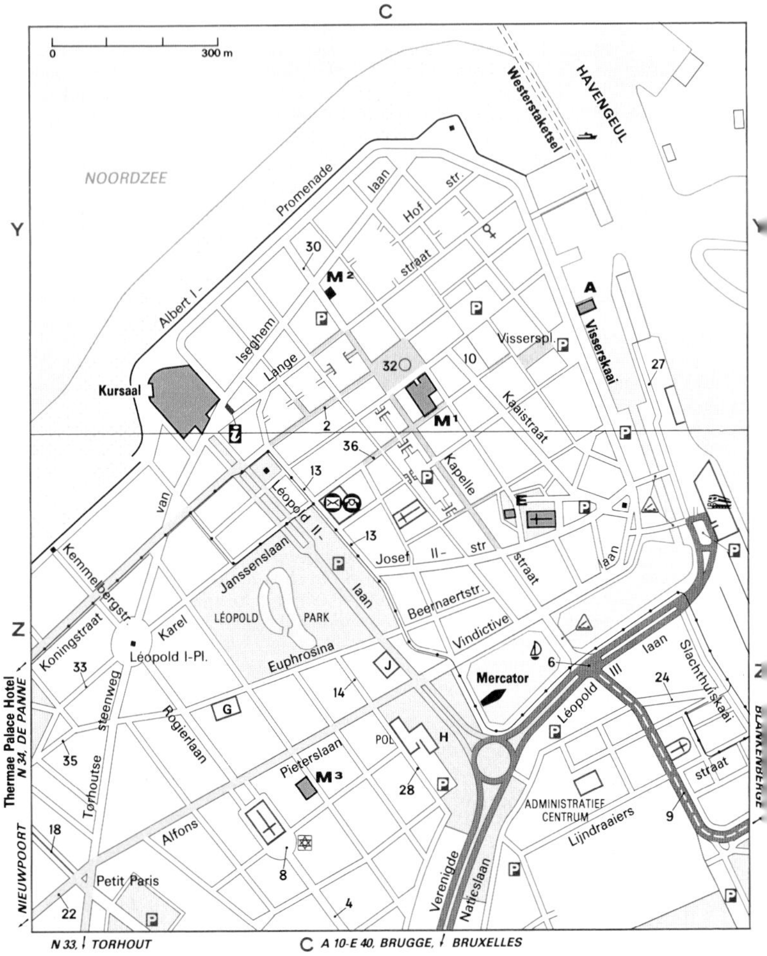

SIGHTS

Visserskaai (Fishermen's Quay) (CY) – There is a virtually uninterrupted line of restaurants along this quay. The fishing port can be seen from here, as can the large fresh fish auction, the **"minque"**, beyond the harbour mouth; the selling of fish and shellfish here makes a picturesque scene.

West Pier (Westerstaketsel) (**CY**) – This is one of the two jetties on either side of the harbour mouth, or "havengeul". From here there is a view of the beach and the movement of the boats and ferries. At the far end, fishermen set up their dipping nets; square nets suspended on winches.

North Sea Aquarium (Noordzeeaquarium) (**CY A**) ⊙ – This consists of small tanks of North Sea fish and shellfish, and collections of shells.

Festival and Cultural Centre (Stedelijk Feest- en Kultuurpaleis) (CY M1) – This overlooks the Wapenplein, the town's main square, and contains two museums.

Fine Art Museum (Museum voor Schone Kunsten) ⊙ – *Second floor.* Romantic to post-Impressionist Belgian paintings. Artists with works on show include Ensor, Spilliaert, Musin and Van Rysselberghe.

De Plate Museum of Local History (Heemkundig Museum) ⊙ – *First floor.* This is devoted to regional history and traditions (banners, old Ostend society medals). Ostend's maritime vocation is evoked particularly strongly by the reconstruction of a fishermen's café.

James Ensor's House (James Ensorhuis) (CY M2) ⊙ – The inside of Ensor's home has been reconstructed and turned into a museum. The entrance is through a seashell shop once run by his aunt and uncle; the painter's workshop is on the second floor.

Mercator Sailing Ship (Opleidings-zeilschip) (CZ) ⊙ – This white three-master, once an officers' training school for the Belgian merchant navy, has been here in this marina since 1964. Although still in working order, the Mercator, which crossed the world's seas 41 times in its career from 1932 to 1962, is now home to a naval museum. There are several objects and photographs recalling its participation in scientific missions, including bringing back gigantic Easter Island statues or the mortal remains of Father Damien *(qv)*.

Modern Art Museum (**Provincial museum voor Moderne Kunst**) (**CZ M3**) ⊙ – This museum exhibits Belgian paintings, sculpture, ceramics and graphic art, on the various floors of a former cooperative. The collections *(exhibited in rotation)* give an idea of modern and contemporary artistic movements.
Expressionism is represented by the St.-Martens-Latem artists *(qv)*. Among the more recent movements on display are abstract art, Pop art and conceptual art. The works of Panamarenko (1940-) and Jan Fabre are classed with contemporary art. The museum also organises temporary exhibitions taking national or international themes.

Church of St Peter and St Paul (**St.-Petrus-en-Pauluskerk**) (**CZ E**) – This church was built in 1905 in the neo-Gothic style and contains the mausoleum of Queen Marie-Louise.
The **Peperbus**, the bell tower of an 18C church destroyed by fire, is nearby.

EXCURSIONS

Stene – *3km - 2 miles south on the N 33.*

St Anne's church (St.-Annakerk), entirely white, has a prettily proportioned exterior and a rustic interior decoration. Only the north side aisle existed in the 14C; the nave and the south side aisle were added in the 17C.
The presbytery to the south was added in 1764, and it has since been restored.

Jabbeke – Pop 11 887. *17km - 10.5 miles east on the A 10 – E 40, then taking junction 6.*

★ **Provinciaal Museum Constant Permeke** ⊙ – Permeke (1886-1952) had this house, the Four Winds (Vier Winden), built in 1929 and lived here for more than 20 years. It now contains the artist's works from the beginning of his career onwards: his post-Impressionist period (*Landscape*), as well as his Cubist (*About Permeke*) and Expressionist periods (*Sower, Dark Sea, Maternity, Daily Bread*) and, more recently, *Unfinished Landscape* (1951). The museum has almost all of Permeke's sculpture, some of which is exhibited in the garden (*Niobe, The Sower*).

Gistel – Pop 9 920. *9km - 5.5 miles south on the N 33.* The **St Godelive Procession** *(see the Calendar of Events at the end of this guide)* takes place each year in this commercial centre. The **church** houses the sepulchre of this saint, whose name means "beloved of God". Godelive was married against her will to a lord called Bertulf; she was later killed and her body thrown into a well in 1070.

Ten Putte Abbey *(3km - 2 miles west of Gistel)* was founded around this well. The well itself can be seen, in a charming enclosure of white walls and a welcoming garden; the cellars where the saint is said to have been imprisoned are under the stairs. She also is said to have accomplished a miracle on the spot where the chapel now stands. The saint is represented on a little 16C triptych in the abbey church (1962); she can be recognised by her attribute, four crowns.

The towns and sights described in this guide are indicated in black lettering on the local maps and town plans.

★★ ORVAL ABBEY Luxembourg

Michelin maps 409 J7 or 214 folds 16, 17

This abbey, tucked away in the Forest of Gaume *(see Virton)*, was founded in 1070 by Benedictines from Calabria in southern Italy. By the 12C it had become one of the most famous and the richest of Europe's Cistercian monasteries.

Legend and history – The name of the abbey ("Orval" means "valley of gold") and its arms (in silver representing an azure rivulet from which a ring with three diamonds is emerging) recall the following legend: Countess Mathilda, the Duchess of Lorraine and the abbey's protectress, lost her wedding ring in a spring, but it was miraculously returned to her by a trout.
The Church of Our Lady was built at the end of the 12C in the Gothic style, with nonetheless some remaining traces of Romanesque. It was modified in the 16C and the early 17C. The abbey had to be rebuilt in 1637 after being burned and pillaged by Field Marshal Chatillon's troops. The monastery was so prosperous in the 18C, however, that new construction was undertaken by the architect Dewez. Hardly had this work been finished when General Loyson's soldiers laid waste to it (1793). The abbey was sold in 1797.

The new monastery – The restoration of the monastery was undertaken in 1926 by the Cistercian monks of the Abbey of Sept-Fons in the Bourbonnais region (Auvergne, France). It was completed in 1946 on the spot where the 18C buildings stood. It is plain yet elegant, in a warm golden stone, following the traditional Cistercian layout.
The façade of the new abbey church, upon which a monumental Virgin and Child has been inscribed, is in front of the retreatants' courtyard; it has a great purity of line.

The Ruins ⏲ – *time: 1 hour – follow the numbered tour.* After a film projection on monastery life *(20min)*, the tour embarks on a discovery of the ruins dating from the Middle Ages to the 18C. The Gothic ruins of the **Church of Our Lady** (église Notre-Dame) stand near the Mathilda Fountain, set amidst the greenery. The rose window in the north arm of the transept, the Romanesque capitals, and the Gothic and Renaissance pillars are remarkable. The tomb of Wenceslas, the first Duke of Luxembourg, is in the chancel. This chancel, with a flat Cistercian east end, was judged too small in the 17C, and an apse was added. The tour then visits the cloisters, rebuilt in the 14C, and the 18C cellars. There is a garden of medicinal plants in front of the museum of the monks' pharmacy.

★★ OSTEND See Oostende

★ OUDENAARDE Oost-Vlaanderen

Pop 27 018

Michelin maps 409 D3 or 213 fold 16
Town plan in the current Michelin Red Guide Benelux

This Flemish town, rich in history and historic buildings, stands on the banks of the Scheldt. **Adriaen Brouwer**, the painter of Flemish peasant life, was born here. Oudenaarde is a centre for the textile industry; its brown ale is also famous.

Oudenaarde tapestries – In the 15C high-warp tapestry began to replace the declining cloth industry in Oudenaarde. The town became a great centre of tapestry-making in the 16C and 17C, specialising in *verdures*, in which flowers and plants constitute the main part of the composition.

HISTORICAL NOTES

Baldwin IV, Count of Flanders, built a fortress here in the early 11C. Oudenaarde was repeatedly attacked by the people of Ghent in the 14C and 15C, who lost their famous cannon known as "Dulle Griet" here; the cannon is now in Ghent near the Vrijdag Markt. In 1521, Emperor Charles V besieged Oudenaarde during his conquest of his kingdom's French enclave, the Tournai region. He was charmed by Johanna Van den Geenst here, by whom he had a daughter, **Margaret of Parma**, who governed the Low Countries from 1559 to 1568.

Oudenaarde underwent many other sieges. The worst was that of 1684, led by the Maréchal d'Humières, commanding Louis XIV's troops. The best known date in the town history, however, is 11 July 1708, which is when Marlborough completely crushed the French army.

★★★ TOWN HALL (Stadhuis) (YZ) ⏲

Hendrik van Pede built this from 1526 to 1530, taking his inspiration from several of the region's town houses, indeed there are strong similarities between this building and others (Brussels, Leuven). The town hall overlooks the vast **market square** (Grote Markt) (Z). The old 13C cloth market is nearby.

The town hall is Late Gothic in style, already exhibiting hints of baroque. Its lightness of line and its rich yet exquisitely tasteful ornamentation contribute in large part to its charm. Arcades support a projecting belfry, with a statue of an armed man on top, "Hanske de Krijger" (John the Warrior); lovely slender pinnacles decorate the corners. In front of the façade the fountain adorned with dolphins was financed by Louis XIV.

Once inside, admire the beautiful fireplace and carved wood of the door drum panelling (16C) in the **Council Room** by Van der Schelden; the "listener" responsible for noting the assembly's debates used to sit in the little lodge above this. Notice also some picturesque paintings by **Adriaen Brouwer**.

ADDITIONAL SIGHTS

St Walburga's Church (St.-Walburgakerk) (Z A) – The east end of this large church stands west of the market square; its beautiful tower is 90m - 295ft high.

Margaret of Parma's House (Z B) – This is southwest of the market square and features tall crowstepped dormers; to the left is 11C **Baldwin tower (Z D)**.

Beguine Convent (Begijnhof) (Z) – This dates from the 13C. The simplicity of the chapel is very appealing.

★ **Church (O.L.-Vrouwekerk van Pamele) (Z)** ⏲ – This beautiful 13C church was built by Arnould de Binche; it is typical of Scaldian Gothic architecture *(qv)*. Inside, there are three naves and a transept with an ambulatory, which is rather rare in Belgium. Two tombs, one from the early 16C and the other from the early 17C can be seen on the other side of the west façade.

Tapestry Museum and Restoration Workshop (Wandtapijtenmuseum en restauratieatelier) (Z M) ⏲ – **Lalaing House**, with a white façade decorated in rococo style overlooking the Scheldt, exhibits some of Oudenaarde's *verdure* tapestries. There is also a workshop where old tapestries are restored and modern creations are woven.

OUDENAARDE

Beverestraat .... Y 4
Broodstraat .... Z 9
Grote Markt .... Z
Hoogstraat .... YZ 17
Krekelput .... Z 23
Nederstraat .... YZ 35
Stationsstraat .... Y
Tussenbruggen .... Z 40

Aalststraat .... Z
Achterbrug .... Z 2
Achter de Wacht .... Y 3
Baarstraat .... Z
Bekstraat .... Y
Bergstraat .... Z
Bourgondiëstraat .... Z 7
Burg .... Z 10
Dijkstraat .... Y
Doornikstraat .... Z
Fortstraat .... Y
Gevaertsdreef.................. Y
Jezuïetenplein .... Z 18
Kasteelstraat .... Z 21
Kattestraat .... Y
Louise-Mariekaai .... Z 26
Margaretha van Parmastr. Z 32
Marlboroughlaan .... YZ
Matthijs Casteleinstr. .... Z
Minderbroedersstr. .... Z 33
Parkstraat .... Y
Prins Leopoldstraat .... Y
Remparden .... Z
Tacambaroplein .... Y 38
Voorburg .... Z 42
Wijngaardstraat .... Y 46
Woeker .... Y

EXCURSION

From Oudenaarde to Waregem – *15km - 9.3 miles northwest. Take the N 459 towards Deinze.*

In **Kruishoutem** (Pop 7 269), the **Veranneman Foundation** (Stichting) ⊙ *(2 Vandevoorde-weg, on the Waregem road then to the left)* is both an art museum housing contemporary paintings by Mathieu, Permeke, Vasarely, Hartung, Wunderlich, Mara, Raveel, Botero, Arman, Bram Bogart and Vic Gentils, and a temporary exhibition centre. There are sculptures in the park by Dodeigne, Niki de St-Phalle, Vasarely, Gilioli, Schöffer, Antes, Rickey, Caro, Nigel Hall, Liberman, Niizuma and Vari.
The 17C **Kruishoutem castle** *(not open to the public)*, surrounded by moats, has corners reinforced with four onion-domed towers; it stands in the middle of a great park.

Waregem – Pop 34 250. Flander's popular obstacle course race which takes place on the Gaverbeek race course is a great crowd-puller *(see the Calendar of Events at the end of this guide)*.

★ OURTHE VALLEY Liège-Luxembourg

Michelin maps 409 J4, J5, 213 fold 22 or 214 fold 7

The Ourthe winds its way across the various northeast-southwest folds in the Ardennes plateau, cutting a deep course into it, before spreading its banks in the plains, such as the Famenne, then flowing into the Meuse at Liège.
A footpath (GR 57), 170km - 106 miles long, crosses the valley, running from Angleur near Liège to Houffalize in the province of Luxembourg.
The Ourthe Valley can be divided into two parts: the **Upper Ourthe**★★ before La Roche-en-Ardenne *(see La Roche-en-Ardenne)* and the **Lower Ourthe**★ between La Roche-en-Ardenne and Liège.

★ THE LOWER OURTHE

From La Roche-en-Ardenne to Liège

95km - 59 miles – allow 1 day

★ **La Roche-en-Ardenne** – *See La Roche-en-Ardenne. Time: 1 hour.*

Between La Roche-en-Ardenne and Liège the Ourthe flows through a delightful, tranquil valley, here and there bordered with rough escarpments, elsewhere with calcareous rock hollowed out into caves (Hotton, Comblain).

The road follows the Ourthe until Melreux. After Hampteau, a road on the left leads to the Hotton caves.

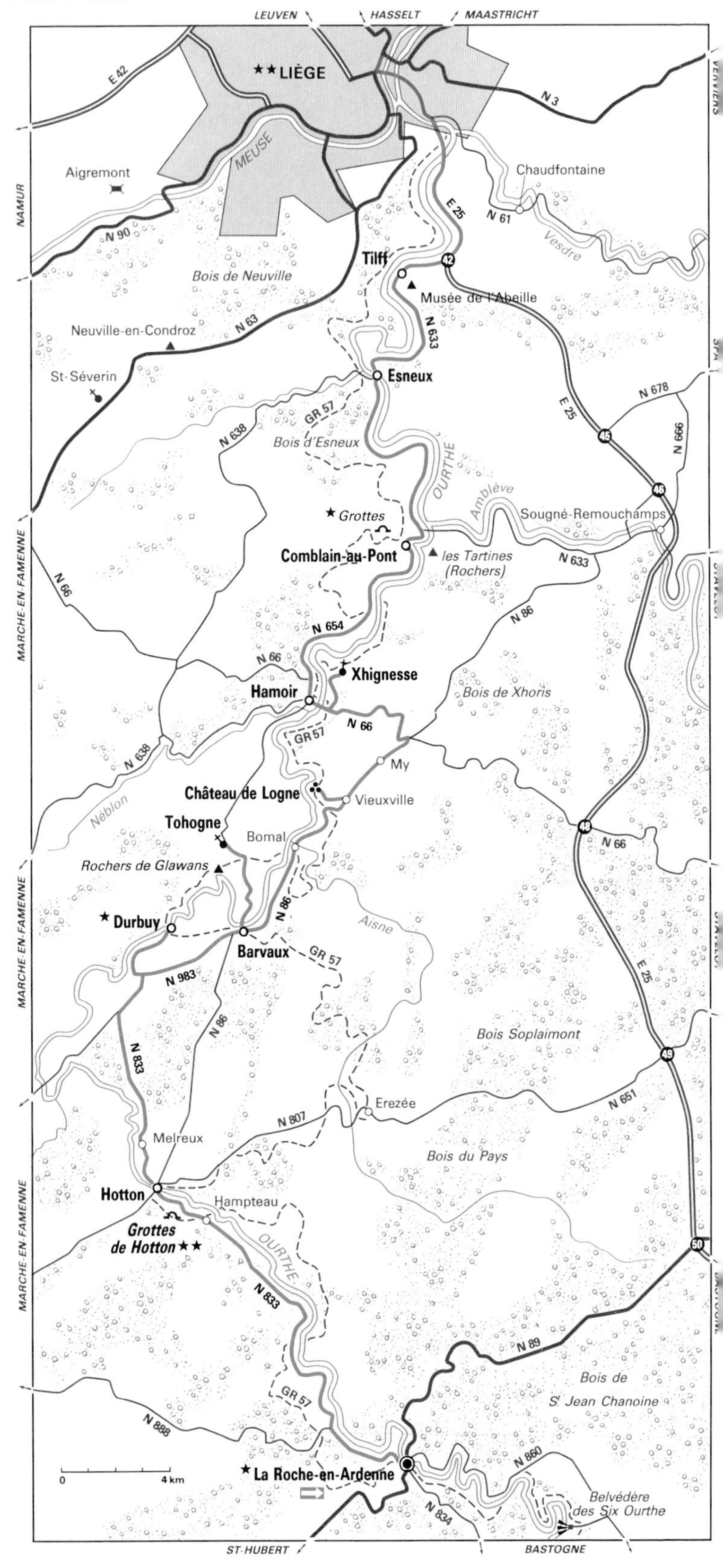
LEUVEN
HASSELT
MAASTRICHT
LIÈGE
E 42
N 3
MEUSE
NAMUR
Aigremont
N 90
Chaudfontaine
N 61
E 25
Vesdre
Tilff
Musée de l'Abeille
Bois de Neuville
Neuville-en-Condroz
N 63
N 633
St-Séverin
Esneux
GR 57
N 638
Bois d'Esneux
N 678
N 666
OURTHE
Amblève
Sougné-Remouchamps
Grottes
Comblain-au-Pont
les Tartines (Rochers)
N 633
MARCHE-EN-FAMENNE
N 66
N 86
N 654
N 66
Xhignesse
Hamoir
Bois de Xhoris
N 66
GR 57
N 638
My
Château de Logne
Vieuxville
Néblon
Tohogne
Bomal
N 66
Rochers de Glawans
Durbuy
N 86
Aisne
Barvaux
GR 57
N 983
E 25
N 86
N 833
Bois Soplaimont
Erezée
N 651
N 807
Melreux
Bois du Pays
Hotton
Hampteau
Grottes de Hotton
OURTHE
N 833
N 89
Bois de St Jean Chanoine
GR 57
N 888
N 860
4 km
La Roche-en-Ardenne
Belvédère des Six Ourthe
N 834
ST-HUBERT
BASTOGNE

★★ **Hotton Caves** ⏲ – Part of these caves, which were formed by a river gradually cutting a course underground, was discovered between 1958 and 1964. Only the Cave of the Thousand and One Nights (grotte des Mille et Une Nuits) at the end of the explored network is open to the public. There is a great variety of concretions in the series of narrow rooms (temperature 12-16°C - 54-61°F). The delicacy of their shapes – from transparent macaroni-shapes, to eccentrics, and undulating draperies – is remarkable, but it is the splendour of their natural colours which is particularly captivating: the pure white of the calcite, with red, brilliant orange, and delicate rose-pink from traces of iron. In the Friendship Gallery (Galerie de l'Amitié) this fairytale effect is accentuated by the clear light reflected from the pools. The route through the caves takes in a balcony 28m - 92ft over a chasm, in which the roar of a distant waterfall (at the far end of the Spéléo-Club passageway) can be heard.

Hotton – Pop 4 288. The slate-roofed houses of this typical little town in the Famenne plain *(qv)* are lined up along the Ourthe, which has an island midstream at this point.
There is an 18C watermill upstream on the Érezée road. A dam containing a reservoir is downstream from the bridge.

★ **Durbuy** – Pop 8 564. The road rejoins the Ourthe again near Durbuy. The town is in a beautiful forested region, one of the Ardennes' most pleasant places for a stay. This tiny settlement, promoted to the rank of town in 1331, was the world's smallest town with fewer than 400 inhabitants until it was fused with other communities in 1977. Durbuy has preserved its old character with its maze of medieval streets and the 17C castle, the old bridge and the half-timbered wheat market. The charm of its streets and stone houses, where many craftsmen and artists live, combines well with the natural beauty of the site, at the foot of a rocky spur from which a spectacular geological fold, the Falize, can be seen.

Barvaux – This is another tourist centre in the valley of the Ourthe, which runs along the foot of the famous **Rochers de Glawans** (cliffs) downstream from here.

2km - 1.25 miles after Barvaux, take a road on the left for Tohogne.

Tohogne – This village has a well-restored **Romanesque church** in which there are works of art on display, including a 13C Mosan font and a 14C calvary.

Return to the N 86.

Beyond Bomal, where the River Aisne *(qv)* flows into the Ourthe, there is a pretty **view**★ of the valley, which is narrower here because of a rocky outcrop, beyond which the ruins of Logne Castle can be seen.

Logne Castle (Château de Logne) ⏲ – This was initially the property of the Stavelot monks, then of the powerful La Marck family. This "eagle's eyrie" was one of the first fortresses adapted for firearms. It was destroyed in 1521 on the orders of Emperor Charles V. The objects found during excavations inside the fortified enclosure are exhibited at the **Bouverie Farm** (ferme de la Bouverie) ⏲ in Vieuxville. The village of Logne is an important tourist centre for sports enthusiasts.

Turn left after My.

Hamoir – Pop 3 293. This is a small community on the banks of the Ourthe. A statue of Jean Delcour *(qv)* stands in the central square; he was born here in 1627. The town hall is in a charming 17C manor-house, hidden on the left bank in a pretty park.

Xhignesse – *Round tour of 4km - 2.5 miles from Hamoir.* The Mosan Romanesque church of St Peter has a remarkable apse decorated with blind arcades, surmounted with niches.

Comblain-au-Pont – Pop 5 085. This town is on the confluence of the Ourthe and the Amblève, overlooked by an impressive cliff called the Tartines ("Sandwiches"), so called because the rocks look as if they have been cut into slices *(see Amblève Valley)*.
Comblain's **caves**★ (grottes) ⏲ are 1km - 0.75 mile to the west on a little hill.

Esneux – Pop 12 571. This little town is arranged in tiers up a slope tucked in a coil of the Ourthe River.

Tilff – Tilff has a **Bee Museum** (Musée de l'Abeille) ⏲ in an old castle farm. There is interesting documentation on apiculture, collections of equipment, and hives (in some of them, the bees can be seen at work) as well as some literature on the biology of bees.

★★ **Liège** – *See Liège.*

DE PANNE West-Vlaanderen — Pop 9 552

Michelin maps 409 A2 or 213 fold 1
Town plan in the current Michelin Red Guide Benelux

De Panne is a resort town on the border with France, very popular with French tourists.
Its **beach**★ reaches 250m - 820ft in width in certain places at low tide, and is particularly well adapted for landsailing (zeilwagen). *Illustration p 277.*
Near the beach is the **monument to King Leopold I**, marking where Belgium's first sovereign landed in 1831, coming from England after stopping at Calais.
Queen Elizabeth stayed here during the First World War, while King Albert was in Veurne.

EXCURSIONS

Westhoek – Part of the dunes lying around De Panne to the west, the Westhoek, is a State nature reserve and covers 340ha - 840 acres up to the border. **Guided walks** ⏲ are organised.
Five signposted footpaths ranging from 1.6km - 1 mile to 2.4km - 1.5 miles in length cross the Westhoek. While sea reeds or shrubs (climbing willow, sea-buckthorn, common elder) cover the dunes, there is a bare open space in the middle, sometimes called the Sahara.

Oosthoek – This municipal nature reserve lies on a 61ha - 150 acre area of dunes and woods southeast of De Panne.

Adinkerke – *3km - 1.75 miles south.* Adinkerke is near the **Meli** ⏲, a 30ha - 74 acre recreation park; its main theme is the bee (exhibition on bees, animals, attractions, fairytale village).

PHILIPPEVILLE Namur

Pop 7 089

Michelin maps 409 G5 or 214 fold 4

Founded in 1555 by Emperor Charles V to oppose Mariembourg, fallen to the French *(see Couvin)*, this fortified place was called Philippeville in honour of the emperor's son, the future Philip II. In 1659 it fell into French hands; during the Revolution it was called the "Republican star".
Only a few underground installations and an old powder magazine remain of the fortifications dismantled in 1860. An audio-visual presentation at the tourist reception centre relates the history of Philippeville and its fortifications.

Underground installations ⏲ – The old powder magazine, now the **Chapel of Our Lady of the Ramparts**, still has its thick walls which used to house a ventilation system.
Part of the 16C and 17C underground galleries extending for 10km - 6.5 miles under the town is open to visitors.

POPERINGE West-Vlaanderen

Pop 19 372

Michelin maps 409 B3 or 213 fold 13

Poperinge is an old clothmaking town, which became the centre of the hops-producing region *(see Introduction: Food and Drink – Beer)* from the 15C onwards; it is proud of its three beautiful Gothic churches.
Every three years in September the **Hops Festival** *(see the Calendar of Events at the end of this guide)* takes place with a picturesque procession. The hops fields stand out from the rest of the gently undulating landscape, owing to the tall posts up which the plants are growing.

SIGHTS

St Bertin's Church (Hoofdkerk St.-Bertinus) – *Vroonhof.*
This 15C hall-church has a particularly beautiful 17C rood-screen, embellished with statues of Jesus and the Apostles; also note the 18C pulpit, and the richly decorated baroque confessional.

National Hops Museum (Nationaal Hopmuseum) ⏲ – *Gasthuisstraat 71.*
This museum is in an old public weighing station (stadsschaal) where, until 1968, the hops were weighed, selected, dried and pressed. Tools, machines, photographs and audio-visual presentations illustrate the cultivation and processing of hops.

Church of Our Lady (O.-L.-Vrouwekerk) – *Casselstraat.*
This 14C hall-church, flanked by a tall tower with a stone spire, contains a wonderfully sculpted wooden communion bench.

St John's Church (St.-Janskerk) – *St.-Janskruisstraat.*
This building, with a massive tower similar to the bell tower of St Bertin's, has beautiful 18C woodwork and a much venerated statue of the Virgin which is borne along in an annual procession on the first Sunday of July.

Weeuwhof – *St.-Annastraat, via Gasthuisstraat.*
A little porch surmounted by a statue of the Virgin leads into this 18C hospice, or "widows' courtyard", with picturesque cottages standing neatly around a flower garden.

EXCURSIONS

Lyssenthoek Military Cemetery – *3km - 1.75 miles south.*
More than 10 000 soldiers from the First World War, including many British men, lie in this impressive, flower-bedecked enclosure.

Haringe – *11km - 6.75 miles northwest.*
The inside of **St Martin's Church** (St.-Martinuskerk) has a certain rustic charm. The organ was made by the Ghent craftsmen Van Peteghem in 1778.

REDU-TRANSINNE Luxembourg

Michelin maps 409 I5-6 or 214 fold 16

Lying in a magnificent undulating region of wooded countryside, the village of Redu is home to a European space station for satellite telemetry and telecommands.

A book-worm's village – Redu is a paradise for lovers of old books. About thirty booksellers have opened shops here; the village comes alive with crowds of people during those ideal periods for reading books – in the summer and at the weekends.
A few antique dealers and restaurants have opened here as well.

★ **Euro Space Center** ⊙ – *Situated near the E 411 motorway at junction 24.*
The latest audio-visual techniques have been used to present the great adventure of outer space: film projections of space missions on show in the auditorium, a holoramic explanation of the future Columbus space laboratory, a description of the history of astronomy and black holes in the planetarium, tours of several spaceships and rockets, including full-scale models of Ariane 4 and 5, and to finish, the Space Show, which induces the powerful sensations of being caught in the middle of a terrible spaceship battle by means of mobile seats. This is also a training centre for young people wishing to learn about space (sessions lasting several days).

REULAND Liège

Michelin maps 409 L5 or 214 fold 9 – 15km - 9.3 miles south of St-Vith

This is a picturesque village in the south of the Liège province in the Ulf Valley. It is overlooked by the ruins of its 11C fortress.
There is a delightful **view★** from the keep of the white houses, with their heavy slate roofs, clustered around the onion-domed bell tower. Reuland is in the Hautes Fagnes-Eifel nature park *(qv)*.

★ **LA ROCHE-EN-ARDENNE** Luxembourg Pop 3 967

Michelin maps 409 J5 or 214 fold 7 – Local maps see OURTHE VALLEY and Excursions overleaf – Town plan in the current Michelin Red Guide Benelux

Long wooded spurs separated by deep valleys converge on this famous tourist centre, famed for the beauty of its **setting★★**, in a loop of the Ourthe River.
The river forms a wide stretch of water here *(canoeing, pedal-craft)*. Several signposted footpaths (120km - 74.5 miles) have been set up in the area around La Roche.
The town was rebuilt after it had been destroyed in 1944.
"Roche kisses", cream-filled meringues, are a speciality rivalled only by the delicious fruit or sugar tarts. The local blue sandstone ware is also famous.

SIGHTS

Castle ⊙ – *Access via a flight of stairs opposite the town hall.*
The romantic-looking ruins of this imposing 11C castle are on the extreme tip of the rocky **Deister** spur, bristling with ancient fir trees, overlooking the town.
The fortifications were reinforced after Louis XIV's siege in 1680. The castle was then demolished in the 18C on the orders of Joseph II.

La Roche-en-Ardenne

Blue Sandstone Ware Pottery ⊙ – *Rue Rompré, via Place du Bronze.*
Sandstone ware, a speciality of La Roche, is made here; the engraved design is highlighted in blue.
The tour includes a visit to the old potter's wood kiln, the turning and decorating workshops as well as the museum about the production process.

Chapel (Chapelle Ste-Marguerite) – *Follow the Ourthe River towards Houffalize and take the road that climbs up to the left.*
The chapel is on the hill of the Deister, above the castle.
A viewpoint higher up can be reached by a little path following the crest of the spur; there is a superb **panorama**★★ of the town.

Deister Park of "Nature and Health" ("Nature et Santé") – *Follow the road beyond the Chapelle de Ste-Marguerite up to the top of the hill.*
The 15ha - 37 acre **Forest Park**, ideal for long walks, lies on the Deister Plateau.

EXCURSIONS

★★ **Upper Ourthe Valley** – *Round tour of 36km - 22 miles – allow 4 hours – local map below.*

The eastern Ourthe, which rises near the village of Ourthe on the border with Luxembourg, and the western Ourthe, which rises at Ourt, a village south of St-Hubert, converge to form the River Ourthe near Nisramont. Upstream from La Roche-en-Ardenne, the river is more like a torrent, gushing through wild and beautiful countryside.

Leave La Roche-en-Ardenne and head southeast towards Bastogne.

The road climbs the slopes up to the plateau, from which there is an open view of the rolling countryside.

Turn left towards Nisramont.

★ **Nisramont Viewpoint** (Belvédère) – 2km - 1.25 miles after the village of Nisramont, there is a car park to the right of the road; from here there is a marvellous **view**★ of the Ourthe and its dam (the lake formed by the two Ourthes) against a green backdrop of coniferous trees.
A signposted walk (no 1) near the neighbouring tower-viewpoint offers a beautiful view of the Hérou's magnificent rocky crest.

Cross the bridge over the Ourthe and turn left to Nadrin.

A **marble sculpture** to the left of the road represents a stylised portico in the form of a menhir. This is the work of Portuguese sculptor Joao Charters de Almeida, created in 1991 on the occasion of Europalia Portugal.

★★ **Six Ourthes Viewpoint** (Belvédère) – A **tower** ⊙ was built at the foot of the Hérou, a schist crest 1 400m - 4 593ft in length. From the top of the tower *(120 steps)*, an impressive panorama unfolds to the gaze over the wild beauty of this countryside so typical of the Ardennes. The winding River Ourthe has cut a serpentine valley around wooded spurs, often disappearing behind hillocks and then reappearing to sparkle again in the sun; the viewpoint is named after these "many" Ourthes.

★★ **The Hérou** – This awesome outcrop of land, hidden beneath luxuriant vegetation, is crisscrossed by pleasant signposted footpaths, including the GR 57. Its rocky ground appears suddenly to view as the cliff dropping sharply down to the river to the east *(allow 30min Rtn to be within sight of the cliff)*. At the foot of the Hérou the river runs through a wild landscape. This spot is popular with rock-climbing schools.

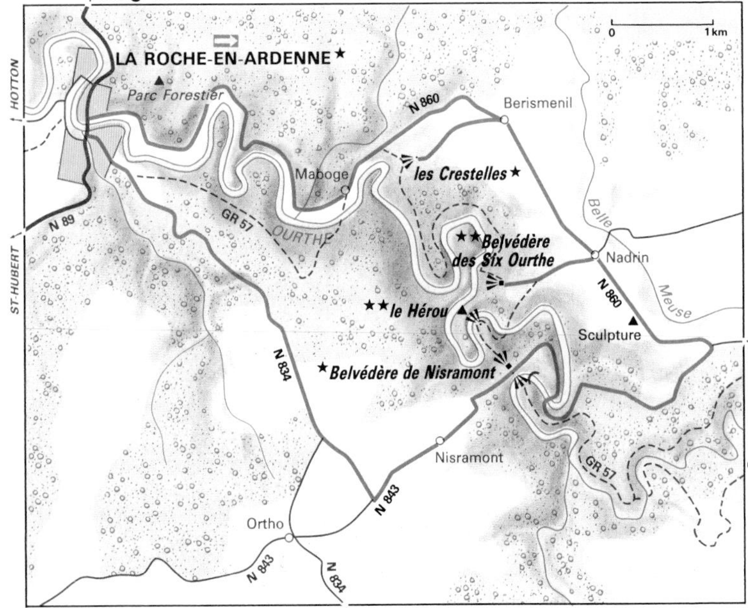

Return to Nadrin, then turn left towards Berismenil. At the second left in Berismenil, head towards Crestelles.

★ **Crestelles Viewpoint** – This is a remarkable viewpoint over the River Ourthe 200m - 656ft below. It is a departure point for hang-gliders and delta-gliders.

Return to the N 860. Go through Maboge (pretty view from the bridge), then return to La Roche-en-Ardenne.

★ **Lower Ourthe** – *See Ourthe Valley.*

Houffalize – Pop 4 190. *25km - 15.5 miles east on the N 860.*
This busy holiday location lies at the heart of the Ardennes, at an altitude of 370m - 1 214ft. Its **setting**★ in the green valley of the east River Ourthe is most attractive. The town was destroyed during the Battle of the Bulge *(qv)* in 1944, and has since been rebuilt. The roads arriving from the south and the west afford pretty views over the slate roofs.

A number of Touring Programmes is given at the beginning of the guide.

Plan a trip with the help of the preceding Map of Principal Sights.

★ ROCHEFORT Namur

Pop 11 055

Michelin maps 409 I5 or 214 fold 6

This little town on the edge of the Lesse and Lomme national park *(qv)* is a good base for holidays and excursions into the surrounding region.
The famous Trappist beer of Rochefort is made by the monks at the Abbey of St Rémy 2km - 1.25 miles from here; the famous marble quarries of St Rémy were also worked nearby.
In August 1792 La Fayette, his life in danger for having defended Louis XVI, left the army and fled. With Chateaubriand he was sheltered at 8 Rue Jacquet before being arrested by the Austrians. Nearby is a monument in La Fayette's honour.

★★ **Cave (Grotte)** ⊙ – This cave, worked for its marble since 1870, was originally cut by the Lomme and has a more rugged appearance than that of the Han; its temperature (8°C - 46°F) is also cooler. The first concretions unfold to view at the end of the manmade passage of non-porous marble. To the sound of music, a play of lights picks the strange chaotic formations out of the shadows. The current course of the underground river and its successive riverbeds can be seen further below. The little Hall of Arcades is hollowed out 80m - 262ft beneath Beauregard Castle.
The **Hall of the Sabbath** is the most impressive one in terms of size: 65m - 213ft by 125m - 410ft; a glowing airballoon allowed to float up to the roof gives an idea of the great height (85m - 278ft). The visit returns via an artificial gallery opening onto a pretty view of the Lomme Valley.

EXCURSIONS

Grupont – *10km - 6.25 miles southeast.*
Grupont has a picturesque **Spanish House** (Maison espagnole), also called the Burgomaster's House; it is half-timbered and cantilevered out, and it dates from 1590.

Chevetogne – *15km - 9.3 miles northwest.*

Chevetogne Monastery (Monastère) – An ecumenical community, celebrating the liturgy with Latin and Byzantine rites, settled here in 1939 in a 19C château. This **Eastern Orthodox Church** (église orientale) (1957) was built in the Novgorod Byzantine style; it is a square brick building, with a vast narthex surmounted by a little cupola on a drum base.
The walls and vaulting inside are covered with frescoes: in the narthex, scenes from the Old Testament; in the nave, scenes from the life of Christ. An effigy of Christ the Pantocrator dominates the cupola. The iconostasis, which serves to define the sanctuary space, is decorated with icons: the main ones, representing Christ and the Virgin and Child, are on each side of the Royal Doors. The small shop can be accessed from the church; there are beautiful copies of old orthodox religious objets d'art on display.

★ **Valéry Cousin Provincial Estate** ⊙ – This vast recreation park in a wooded setting with flowers surrounds a château and a string of lakes. It is very well-equipped for sports and other leisure activities and walks *(signposted paths).*

Lessive – *6km - 3.75 miles southwest, via Eprave.*
The **Belgian Earth Station of Satellite Telecommunications** (Station terrienne belge de télécommunications spatiales) ⊙ is set in the midst of woods south of the little village of Lessive. Equipped with three antennae and an impressively large radio relay tower, this has been the link since 1972 between outer space and the national telecommunications network.
The guided tour of the site is completed by an exhibition on current and future communications technology, a museum on past telephone and telegraph communications, and a film on launching a satellite into space.

From Rochefort to Marche-en-Famenne – *12km - 7.5 northeast on the N 86.*

Hargimont – **Jemeppe Castle** was built in the 17C around a massive 13C keep.

Waha – This village has a charming sandstone **Romanesque church** dedicated to St Stephen, which was consecrated in the year 1050.
There is a graceful 16C bell tower on top of the 12C tower; the square shapes are superposed in an imaginative way. The plain interior, with its massive pillars, houses some interesting works of art. Several gravestones can be seen under the porch. There is a beautiful Late Gothic (16C) calvary over the triumphal arch. The font in the south side aisle (1590) is decorated with four carved heads. The church's consecration stone from 1050 can be seen mounted on one of the pillars. Reliquaries, old books and missals, chasubles, etc. are exhibited in a display case. The church also has some beautiful statues of popular art: St Nicholas (15C), St Barbara (16C), and St Roch, in polychrome wood (17C).

Marche-en-Famenne – Pop 15 224. This is the capital of the Famenne. In 1577 Don Juan of Austria, governor of the Low Countries, signed the Perpetual Edict here which confirmed the Pacification of Ghent *(qv)*, freeing the country of Spanish troops.

Jannée Castle – *19km - 12 miles north on the N 949, N 929 and N 4.*
Jannée Castle, surrounded by its park, dates back to the 12C; reconstructions in the 17C and 19C have given it its current appearance. The 18 rooms open to the public evoke life in the past. There are old copper utensils in the kitchen. The drawing rooms on the ground floor and the bedrooms were decorated with taste; the furniture includes some Louis XV cupboards and a Mosan Louis XV desk. Note also the porcelain and the portraits of the owner's family.

RONSE Oost-Vlaanderen — Pop 23 997

Michelin maps 409 D3 or 213 fold 16

Ronse is set amidst the hills of the **Flemish Ardennes**, near the linguistic border.
The **Zotte Maandag** (Crazy Monday) festivities take place the Saturday after Epiphany; the stars of this great popular holiday are the masked characters called the "Bommels". The **Fiertel** takes place on Trinity Sunday, with a procession in honour of St Hermes; the reliquary is carried along a route 32.6km - 20.25 miles long.

St Hermes Collegiate Church (St.-Hermes Collegiaal) – The present church dates from the 15C and 16C; the south transept arm is devoted to the cult of St Hermes. The church stands above a beautiful **crypt★** (1089) of Romanesque origin which is absolutely vast, containing 32 pillars. Despite a restoration in the 13C and a Gothic style extension (16C) to the east end, the style of the whole is quite harmonious. Two side doors, which have been blocked off, recall the original purpose of the place: in the Middle Ages this was a site of pilgrimage to the relics of St Hermes on display here. This saint was invoked against mental illness in Ronse.
The beautiful house (17C-18C) next to the church belonged to the canon of the St Hermes chapter (Museum of Folklore).

EXCURSION

From Ronse to Kluisberg – *15km - 9.3 miles west.*
There is a pretty view of the town from the gardens north of Ronse (Park de l'Arbre).

Take the N 60 towards Oudenaarde, then turn left towards Kluisberg at the top of the hill.

Hotond Mill (Hotondmolen) stands to the right of the road near an inn, at an altitude of 150m - 492ft; from the top of this squat building there is a vast panorama of the region and of the Kluisberg *(orientation table)*.

Kluisberg – This mountain peak, known as **Mont de l'Enclus** to French-speakers, at an altitude of 141m - 463ft, is just on the linguistic border and that of the Oost-Vlaanderen and Hainaut provinces. It is covered with conifers and is much appreciated as a location for a holiday.

ST- See also SINT-

★ ST-HUBERT Luxembourg

Pop 5 591

Michelin maps 409 J5 or 214 fold 16

The houses of St-Hubert nestle around the basilica, on a plateau at the heart of the Ardennes Forest, at an altitude of 435m - 1 427ft. The basilica was the site of large pilgrimages to St Hubert, patron saint of hunters as well as butchers. There is a beautiful **view** of the basilica's chevet when approaching from the east.
Painter **Pierre Joseph Redouté** was born here (1759-1840), the "Raphaël of Roses". A museum is devoted to him at Fourneau-St-Michel *(qv)*. Each summer the **Juillet Musical** organises concerts in the town and the surrounding area, as part of the Wallonia Festival.

The saint and his legend – One Good Friday in 683 AD, **Hubert**, son-in-law of the Count of Leuven, was hunting in the forests. The dogs led a chase after a great stag with ten points on its antlers. The animal was on the point of being caught when it turned and a blinding image of Christ on the Cross appeared between its antlers. A voice then reproached St Hubert for his immoderate love of hunting, and told him to seek out his friend Lambert, bishop of Tongres-Maastricht, to be instructed in prayer and ministry.
In Rome Hubert learned of Lambert's martyrdom and was offered the vacant bishopric by the Pope. Hubert refused it, protesting his unworthiness. An angel then descended from the heavens to give him a white stole, symbol of the bishop's office, woven with gold by the Virgin herself.
Once he had become bishop of Maastricht, Hubert transferred the episcopal see to Liège *(qv)*.

Town of hunters – Each year on the first weekend of September, the **International Days of Hunting and Nature** take place. Hunting horns sound from Saturday afternoon onwards. On Sunday, after a solemn mass and the blessing of the animals, a great historical procession takes place in the afternoon, recounting the story of St Hubert and the history of the abbey. More than 500 people participate. On **3 November**, St Hubert's Day, the Solemn Eucharist is followed by the blessing of animals, then various festivities.

★ ST HUBERT'S BASILICA ⊙ *time: 30min*

This old Benedictine abbey church was founded in the 7C. The relics of St Hubert were transferred here in the 9C, drawing many pilgrims here ever since. Several buildings have succeeded each other on this spot, and only the crypt remains of the original Romanesque church. The present Brabant Gothic church was rebuilt in 1526 after a fire (go around the church to the south to see this Flamboyant Gothic part), but the façade was modified in the 18C; for this reason the two towers and the façade, with the pediment depicting the miracle of St Hubert, are baroque.

★★ **Interior** – This is imposing, being 25m - 82ft high and consisting of five naves; it has the layout of a pilgrimage church, with an ambulatory and radiating chapels. The initial impression is made by the colours of the brickwork, a combination of pink, grey and ochre stone under brick vaulting dating from 1683.
Willem Geefs's (1847) mausoleum of St Hubert, in the north transept arm, depicts a slightly haughty, majestic figure. There are beautiful, delicately worked **stalls** (1733) in the chancel; their panels depict the lives of St Hubert *(to the right)* and St Benoit *(to the left)*. The high altar Virgin is from the school of Liège sculptor Delcour. The Holy Stole woven with gold, dating from the 10C, is in the south transept arm on the St Hubert altar. An altarpiece with 24 Limoges enamels painted after Dürer's Passion is in the first chapel of the ambulatory; it suffered at the hands of the Huguenots.
The Romanesque **crypt** under the chancel contains abbots' tombs; their faces have been polished by pilgrim's hands. The vaults are from the 16C.
Admire the baroque organ before going out.

The Abbey Palace – *On the left side of the square facing the basilica.*
Built in 1728, this palace with an elegant façade and a pediment decorated with foliage now houses the province's Cultural Affairs offices. Exhibitions are organised here. There is some very beautiful woodwork inside.

EXCURSIONS

★★ **Fourneau-St-Michel** – *See Fourneau-St-Michel.*

Game Park (**Parc à gibier**) ⊙ – *2km - 1.25 miles north.*
Deer, boar, moufflons (wild sheep), etc. can be observed along three signposted routes.
The road goes through beautiful forests of beech and resinous trees: first, King Albert's Forest, then St Michael's.

Poix Valley – *9km - 5.5 miles until Smuid.*
This peaceful rustic valley has a little river which is a tributary of the Lomme. There is a half-timbered house near a lake, to the left of the road, 3km - 1.75 miles from St-Hubert.

★★ SEMOIS VALLEY Luxembourg-Namur

Michelin maps 409 J6, I6, H6 or 214 folds 15, 16

The River Semois (or Semoy in France) is a tributary of the Meuse and rises near Arlon; it runs initially through a marshy depression called the "Belgian Lorraine", then meanders sinuously beyond Florenville through the schist outcrops of the Ardennes massif.

★ 1 FROM CHINY TO BOUILLON

65km - 40 miles – about half a day – local map below

Chiny – Pop 4 614. The Semois, in cutting a course around Chiny, winds for a time through the Ardennes forests.
Its valley becomes deeper and narrower, and the wild scenery is best appreciated from a boat.

★ **Boat trip from Chiny to Lacuisine** ⊙ – *8km - 5 miles. Landing-stage west of village, downstream from St-Nicolas Bridge.*
The boat trip *(1 hour 15min)* takes the Paradise gorge, leaving the Écureuil (squirrel) slope and Pinco Rock to the right, and the Hât Rock to the left. The return trip can be made on foot *(45min)* through the woods, following the marked paths (promenade no 6).

Lacuisine – The turbulent waters calm down here; the river flows quietly through meadows. An old watermill can be seen.

★ **Viewpoint over the Semois Gorge** – *2km - 1.25 miles north. Take the Neufchâteau road; then 800m - half a mile north of the fork for Martué, just after going past a road on the left, take the path on the right.*
Follow the white and orange markings in the woods *(15min walk)* to get to a promontory with a bench; there is a **view** down onto the wild wooded area where the river meanders, often covered with white flowers.

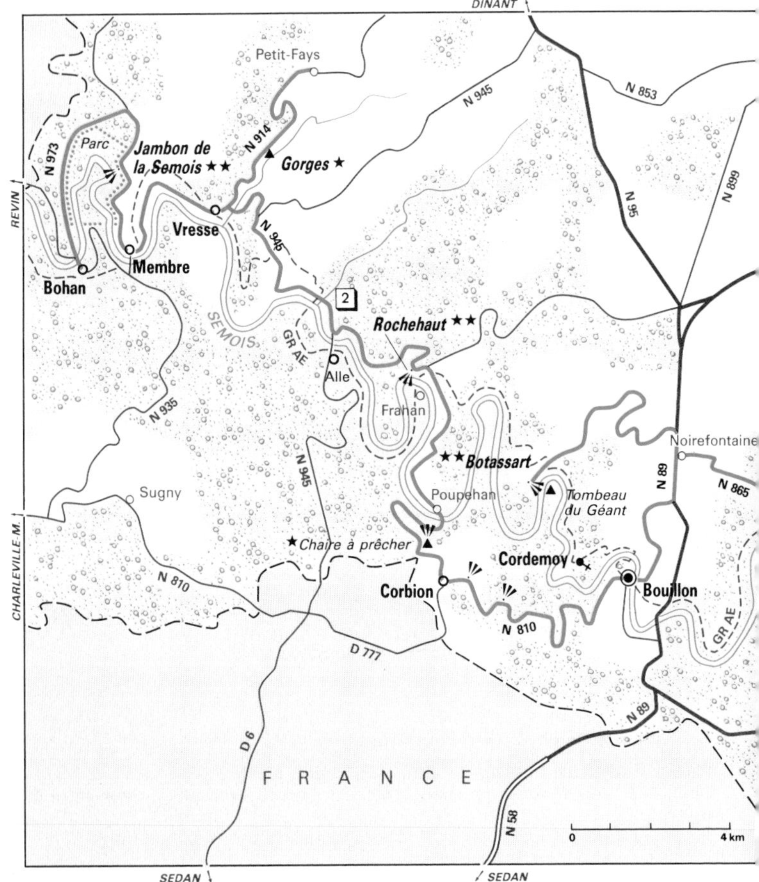

Florenville – Pop 5 650. This is a tourist centre, good as a base for excursions, near the border; it is perched on a spot overlooking the Semois Valley.
From the terrace behind the east end of the church (alt. 351m - 1 151ft; *orientation table*) the valley can be seen cutting a great curve in the vast cultivated plain.
The church, destroyed in 1940, has been rebuilt. The tower had a 48-chime carillon added in 1955.
From the **viewpoint** ⊙ at the top, there is a **view** of the slate roofs, the great Semois Valley and the surrounding countryside *(220 steps)*.

★ **Chassepierre Viewpoint** – This viewpoint (metal globe symbolising peace) is 5km - 3 miles from Florenville, offering a beautiful view of the village's slate roofs and the houses crowding on a rocky outcrop near an onion-domed church (1702); the River Semois meanders through a plain not far off.

Beyond Ste-Cécile, turn right towards Herbeumont.

Before crossing the river, notice the road to the old priory of Conques (18C) on the right; in the Middle Ages this priory was a dependent of Orval Abbey. It is now a hotel.

Herbeumont – Pop 1 404. The ruins of the 12C castle stand on the top of a hill. It was destroyed by Louis XIV's troops.
There is a magnificent **view**★★ from the top of the river's double meander encircling the **Knight's Tomb** (Tombeau du Chevalier). It is thus named for its shape, which is similar to that of medieval tombs; it is in fact a long wooded spur around which the Semois makes a loop, through a magnificent landscape *(photograph overleaf)*.

Follow the river on arriving in Mortehan. Then, on climbing, notice the pretty views of the wild and undulating landscape before the bend on the right. 2km - 1.25 miles on from a viewpoint near the **Dampiry Rocks** (Roches), there is another **view**★ of a beautiful loop in the Semois River.

2km - 1.25 miles after Dohan, take the Hayons road on the right.

Just after Hayons, there is a pretty **glimpse**★ of the River Semois and the valley in wide wooded countryside.

Saut des Sorcières (Witches' Leap) – This is in fact a series of little cascades between lakes.

Return to the N 865. The road passes via Noirefontaine to Botassart.

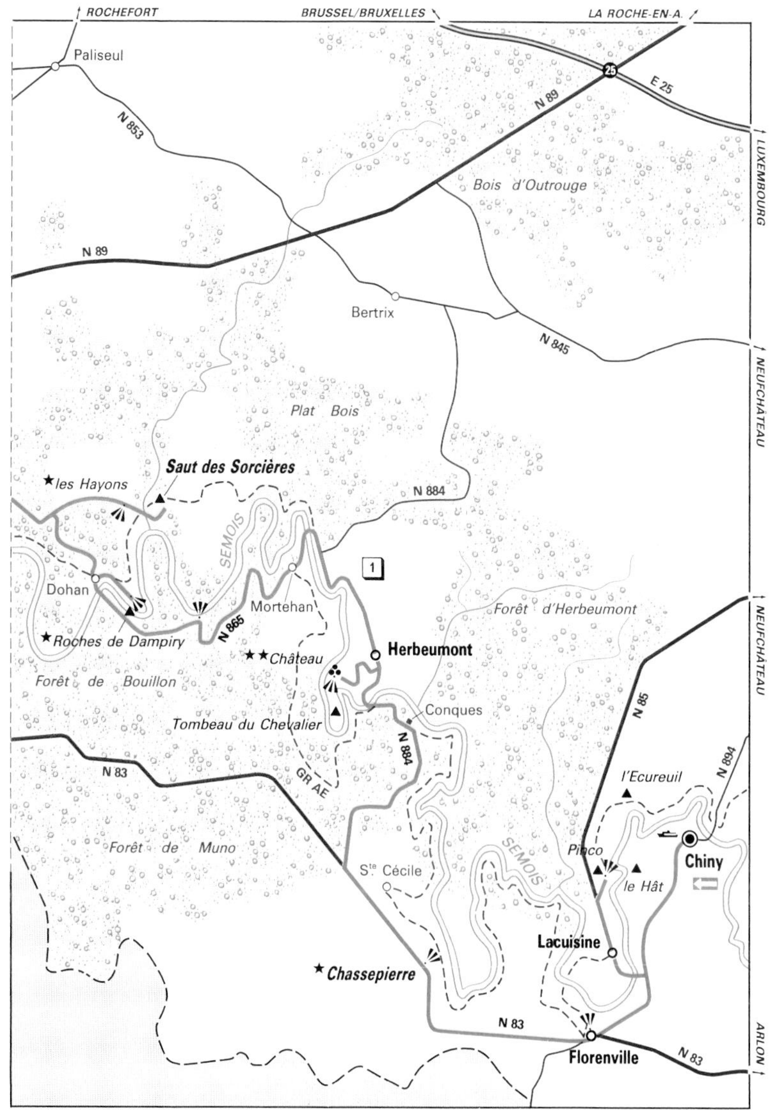

Knight's Tomb, Herbeumont

Botassart – There is a remarkable **view**★★ 2km - 1.25 miles beyond the hamlet, from the viewpoint with a telescope; this is one of the most typical and well-known views of the Semois. The river makes a magnificent loop around a long wooded hill called the **Giant's Tomb** (Tombeau du Géant) because the steep slopes, like those of the Knight's Tomb, resemble the sides of a sarcophagus. The pale-coloured land around it is pasture-land.

Turn back to take the road down to Bouillon

★ **Bouillon** – *See Bouillon. Time: 1 hour.*

★★ 2 FROM BOUILLON TO BOHAN

53km - 33 miles – about half a day – local map previous page

★ **Bouillon** – *See Bouillon. Time: 1 hour.*

Leave Bouillon on the Corbion road, beyond the tunnel.

There is a viewpoint 5km - 3 miles along the road with a view of Cordemoy Abbey *(see Bouillon: Excursion)*. Then 3km - 1.75 miles further, enjoy the panorama of the wooded crests, notably the Giant's Tomb, encircled by the meanders of the river.

Corbion – Reached by a path, the **Pulpit Rock** (*signposted:* Chaire à prêcher) is a natural viewpoint in the form of a church pulpit. The **view**★ encompasses a broad panorama of Poupehan, a well-situated village on a slope overlooking the Semois.

Rochehaut – There is a pretty **view**★★ from this hanging village; the river runs near a promontory surrounded by meadows; the houses of the village of Frahan are spread across the slopes.

Alle, on the opposite bank, is situated at the neck of an old meander which has now been truncated by the river course.

Take the Petit-Fays road on the right.

★ **Petit-Fays Gorges** – The road climbs along these rugged gorges thickly covered in vegetation.

Vresse-sur-Semois – Pop 2 639. The road rejoins the Semois here, at the confluence of the Petit-Fays. Vresse was once an important centre of tobacco-growing owing to the perfect type of soil – dry on the surface and damp deeper down. This is now a spot for holiday-makers and artists. The **Museum of Tobacco and Folklore** ⌚, situated in the tourist and cultural centre (exhibitions of paintings), describes the cultivation and use of tobacco; there is also a pipe collection.
Typical wooden **tobacco-drying sheds** can be seen here and there on the way to Bohan.

Membre – **Bohan-Membre Park** starts near this village. It covers 177ha - 437 acres and is crossed by the Semois and surrounded by a scenic road.

In Membre, turn right.

The road climbs rapidly. 3km - 1.75 miles further on there is a beautiful **view**★★ from the spot called **Jambon de la Semois**, a narrow wooded spine around which the Semois forms a very tight loop.

Bohan – This little tourist centre is near the border.

Respect the life of the countryside
Drive carefully on country roads
Protect wildlife, plants and trees

SINT-NIKLAAS Oost-Vlaanderen

Pop 67 941

Michelin maps 409 F2 or 213 folds 5, 6
Town plan in the current Michelin Red Guide Benelux

The capital of the **Waas** region is a commercial and industrial centre, specialising in textiles (hats). A large market has been held here on Thursdays since the 16C.

SIGHTS

Market Square – This is one of the largest in Belgium, covering 3.19ha - 7.8 acres. Some Flemish Renaissance houses stand to the east; from left to right, **Parochiehuis** (1663), which used to be the parish house, then the town hall; **Cipierage** (1662), once a prison; and next to the post office, **Landhuis** (1637), once used by the Waas regional government.

St Nicholas's Church (St.-Niklaaskerk) ⊙ (13C-18C) is set back from the square. It contains statues by Lucas Faydherbe and a Christ attributed to Duquesnoy.
The present town hall is neo-Gothic (1876).
Parklaan Avenue leads to the beautiful **municipal park**, in which the lake surrounds an extensively restored 16C palace.

Town Museum (Stedelijk Museum) – This exhibits various collections at different addresses.

Waas Region Historical Museum (Historisch Museum van het Land van Waas) ⊙ – *Zamanstraat 49.* The regional history, folklore and craftmanship sections are in an old patrician home.
A modern building was added for other sections. A large room is devoted to the geographer **Mercator**, born in Rupelmonde *(12km - 7.5 miles southeast of St.-Niklaas)* in 1512. He was the inventor of a new technique of cartographic representation, called "Mercator's projection", in which the surface of the earth is projected on a cylinder, the meridians becoming completely parallel. The two globes, terrestrial and celestial, that he completed for Emperor Charles V in 1541 and 1551, are on display; also the first edition of his Atlas (1585); and a second edition of the Atlas edited in Amsterdam by the Flemish geographer Hondius, based on Mercator's maps. A second room is for the paleontology and archaeology sections.

★ **Music box and gramophone section** (Afdeling "Van Musiekdoos tot grammofoon") ⊙ – *Regentiestraat 61-63.* This houses a remarkable collection including a great variety of cylindrical phonographs, record players and mechanical music instruments. The guided tour explains the development of these instruments and gives visitors the chance to hear some of them.

Historical collections (Cultuurhistorische collecties) ⊙ – *Regentiestraat 61-63.* The **"Barbierama"** has preserved four hair salons from the turn of the century (Art Nouveau and classical styles) as well as many objects used in the past by barbers, surgeons and hairdressers.

International Ex-Libris Centre ⊙ – *Regentiestraat 61.* Comparable to a library, this centre has a collection of nearly 120 000 ex-libris (16C-20C), drawn by 5 500 different artists of diverse origins.

Fine Art Salons (Salons voor Schone Kunsten) ⊙ – *Stationsstraat 73.* The salons of a private townhouse (1928), which once belonged to a textile manufacturer, contain paintings (Artans, Rops, Evenepoel), sculptures, furniture and objets d'art from the 16C to the 20C.

EXCURSION

Scheldt and Old Scheldt – *Round tour of 35km - 22 miles. Allow 2 hours (tour of Bornem Castle not included). Leave St.-Niklaas southeast on the N 16.*

Temse – Pop 23 827. On the edge of the Scheldt, this little town specialises in shipbuilding. From the quay near the church a wide river can be seen, with a dike on the opposite bank. A metal bridge – the longest in Belgium (365m - 0.25 mile long) – spans the Scheldt.

Follow the N 16 and turn right after 5km - 3 miles towards Bornem. Follow the signs to Kasteel Bornem.

Bornem Castle (Kasteel Bornem) ⊙ – This imposing neo-Gothic castle (1883-1895) was designed by architect H Beyaert, on the site of a fortress dating back to the 11C. The rooms open to the public contain family portraits, Chinese porcelain and antique furniture. The right wing is inhabited by the Count of Bornem, John de Marnix de Sainte-Aldegonde. The most illustrious member of the Marnix family was **Philips Marnix van Sint-Aldegonde** (*c*1538-1598), a Calvinist writer and diplomat, and an ardent defender of William the Silent *(qv)*. He was the author of the national anthem of the Netherlands. A museum in the castle outbuildings houses a beautiful collection of European and American harnesses.

Reach St.-Amands by going via Zavelberg and Mariekerke.

St.-Amands – Pop 7 274. A terrace overlooks the Scheldt, which here cuts a large meander in a green and fertile setting. The poet **Émile Verhaeren** (1855-1916) lies buried nearby, behind the church, in a black marble tomb near his wife Martha; the church tower "is mirrored in the muddy waters".
It was in Rouen, France, where he had just held a conference, that Verhaeren died, crushed by a train. He was born in St.-Amands, and was the author of *All Flanders*; he always sang the praises of the Scheldt. A few verses, notably extracts from his *Hymn to the Scheldt*, are engraved on his tomb; a statue of the ferry-man who inspired his poem stands nearby. The old ferry-man's house (Het Veerhuis) has been reconstructed on the esplanade. The house where the writer was born is at 69, E Verhaerenstraat, the main street.

Take the road to Mariekerke again and follow the banks of the Scheldt towards Weert.

Before long the **road★** runs along by the Old Scheldt (Oude Schelde), once a tributary of the River Scheldt. Bornem Castle *(see above)* can be seen on the opposite bank. Here lies a picturesque marshy area, crisscrossed by canals surrounding orchards or fields covered with poplars, willows and reeds. Asparagus cultivation and basket-making are the principal activities of this watery region. **Weert** is the centre, very popular with tourists on Sundays.

The road ends at the N 16 leading back to St.-Niklaas.

SINT-TRUIDEN Limburg

Pop 36 846

Michelin maps 409 I3 or 213 fold 21

St.-Truiden, in the heart of the **Hesbaye** (Haspengouw) fruit-growing region well-known for its cherries, is a town that developed around a 7C abbey founded by St Trudo. St.-Truiden is on the great road from Cologne to Bruges, and was a prosperous merchant town in the 13C. Festivities take place in April when the trees in the orchards are in bloom.

SIGHTS

Market Square (Grote-Markt) (B) – This vast square is overlooked by the town hall and the Gothic collegiate church of Our Lady, surmounted by a 19C tower.

Old Town Hall (B H) – This imposing but gracious building, with a brick façade striped with bands of white stone, is flanked by a 17C belfry containing a 41-chime carillon *(concerts)*. The perron at the foot of the belfry dates from 1596. The massive Romanesque bell tower of old St Trudo's Abbey is behind the town hall.

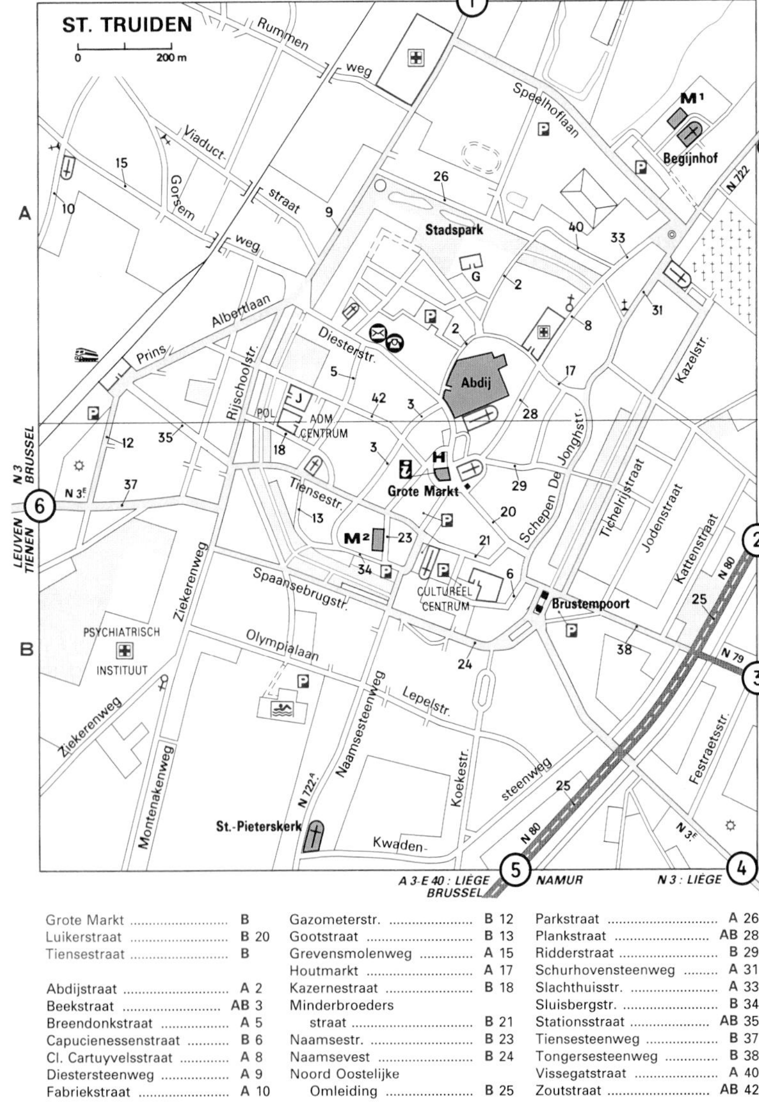

Grote Markt B
Luikerstraat B 20
Tiensestraat B

Abdijstraat A 2
Beekstraat AB 3
Breendonkstraat A 5
Capucienessenstraat B 6
Cl. Cartuyvelsstraat A 8
Diestersteenweg A 9
Fabriekstraat A 10
Gazometerstr. B 12
Gootstraat B 13
Grevensmolenweg A 15
Houtmarkt A 17
Kazernestraat B 18
Minderbroeders straat B 21
Naamsestr. B 23
Naamsevest B 24
Noord Oostelijke Omleiding B 25
Parkstraat A 26
Plankstraat AB 28
Ridderstraat B 29
Schurhovensteenweg A 31
Slachthuisstr. A 33
Sluisbergstr. B 34
Stationsstraat AB 35
Tiensesteenweg B 37
Tongersesteenweg B 38
Vissegatstraat A 40
Zoutstraat AB 42

Abbey (Abdij) (A) – Benedictines occupied the abbey until 1794; from 1839 to 1972 the little seminary of the Liège bishopric settled here. The abbey buildings are nowadays essentially occupied by schools. An 18C porch (on the pediment: St Trudo healing a blind woman) leads into the main courtyard; on the left, a Louis XVI building houses the Imperial Hall (Keizerszaal), with ceiling frescoes dating from the 18C. The wall decoration as well as the staircase are from later alterations.

Beguine Convent (Begijnhof) (A) – Founded in 1258. Its 16C, 17C and 18C Mosan houses surround a rectangular square, in the middle of which is a church.

Church ⊙ – This has been turned into a museum of religious art. It dates from the 13C and 15C, and has 38 restored mural paintings, executed from the 13C to the 17C. Note the pulpit, the confessional, the sculptures and the liturgical ornaments.

Studio Festraets (A M1) ⊙ – This contains most notably an **astronomical clock** built by the town clock-maker. When the hour strikes, Death and a parade of medieval professions appear.

Brustem Gate (Brustempoort) (B) ⊙ – These are the underground traces of the old (15C) fortifications razed by Louis XIV's troops.

St Peter's Church (St.-Pieterskerk) (B) – Like St Gingolph's Church, this is remarkable because of its walls in contrasting colours (ochre and brown). This 12C building is a fine example of the Mosan Romanesque style; it has a wide doorway with a bell turret and is closed off by three apses, the main one bearing a gallery with colonnettes.
The three naves have groined vaulting.

Lace Exhibition (Kanttentoonstelling) (B M2) ⊙ – This is in the Ursuline convent, once the refuge for Averbode Abbey. This exhibits St.-Truiden's spool-made lace, the technique having been brought back into use since 1964, with great originality.

Town park (Stadspark) (A) – A pretty park with a number of lakes.

EXCURSIONS

Borgloon and Colen Abbey (Klooster van Kolen) – *12km - 7.5 miles east. Leave on ③ on the map.*

Borgloon – This was once the Loon county capital; the town bears the county's name. It has a charming 17C Mosan Renaissance town hall with arcades, flanked by a tower; note the statue of the Virgin in a corner niche.

Take the Kerniel road northeast, and turn left before Kerniel.

Colen Abbey (Klooster van Kolen) ⊙ – This old Croisiers convent, an order founded in 13C Belgium, is now occupied by the Cistercians.
The vestry contains the **reliquary of St Odile** (1292). The painted wood panels, of the Mosan school, depict the legend of the saint, which replicates that of St Ursula *(qv)*. The panels were unfortunately cut up in the 19C. The vestry's Liège furnishings, in the Louis XV style, are remarkably elegant. It is also possible to visit the church, decorated in the 18C.

Kortenbos – *6km - 3.75 miles northeast. Leave on the N 722.*
The basilica of Our Lady has a richly decorated baroque interior. The nave has 17C oak panelling, integrated with confessionals decorated with heavy twisted columns.

Zepperen – *3km - 1.75 miles east on ② on the map.*

St Genevieve's Church (St.-Genoveva) dates from the 15C and 16C and has a 12C tower at its entrance. Inside, in the south transept arm there are several mural paintings dating from 1509, representing the Last Judgement, St Christopher and the Life of St Genevieve.

★ SOIGNIES Hainaut

Pop 23 567

Michelin maps 409 F4 or 213 fold 17

The town was built around an abbey founded in about 650 by St Vincent. In honour of this saint, the Grand Tour takes place on Whit Monday *(see the Calendar of Events at the end of this guide)*; there is a large procession over 12km - 7.5 miles which ends in a historical parade.

★★ ST VINCENT'S COLLEGIATE CHURCH *time: 45min*

Building began in about 965 with the two opposite ends, narthex and chancel, in the Carolingian style, it was continued in the 11C in the Scaldian Romanesque style *(qv)*; the tower-porch was finally finished in the 13C. It is a forbidding stone building, soberly decorated with pilaster-strips and dominated by two heavy towers. Its Latin cross layout is arranged around the transept's square courtyard, which is decorated with pinnacles. On the church's south side, there are the 15C St Hubert's Chapel and the remains of some early 13C cloisters, with visible timberwork (lapidary museum).

Inside *(entrance via the north side aisle)*, the nave (20m - 66ft high) is comparable to that in Tournai; it is impressive with its great arches with double-rolled mouldings and its vast tribunes opening onto arcades of the same dimensions. Only the side aisles are vaulted.

The furnishings are interesting. There is a beautiful 14C Virgin giving suck on the "ambo", a sort of rood-screen masking the chancel. The richly decorated choir stalls date from 1676; here too admire the reliquary of St Vincent, and his head reliquary from the 19C. A 15C stone **Entombment** with expressive faces can be seen in the ambulatory.

Treasury ⏲ – This houses precious liturgical ornaments.

The enclosure of the **old cemetery** (vieux cimetière) near the church *(access via Rue Henry-Leroy)* has become a park; there is a Romanesque chapel (archaeological museum), a calvary, funerary monuments and gravestones.

EXCURSIONS

Horrues – *4km - 2.5 miles northwest.*

St Martin's Church, a pretty little 12C Romanesque building, has a 13C chancel and a 15C sculpted stone Gothic altarpiece, which depicts the life of St Hubert.

Ecaussinnes-Lalaing – Pop 9 406. *15km - 9 miles east.*

An imposing **fortress** ⏲ perched on a crag overlooks the town and the River Sennette. It was built in the 12C, but was later partially modified and enlarged with square and round towers.

The vast rooms, with carved chimneypieces adorned with heraldic coats-of-arms, constitute a museum. The display includes furnishings, works of art and collections of porcelain and glass.

The Virgin with Child in the chapel is attributed to the 14C Valenciennes artist Beauneveu. The kitchen still looks much as it did in the 15C.

Since 1903 a festival supper for the unmarried, called the matrimonial "goûter", has taken place on Whit Monday in the market square of Ecaussinnes at the foot of the castle.

Le Rœulx – Pop 7 762. *8km - 5 miles south.*

The **palace** ⏲ of the Princes of Croÿ, a resplendent successor to the 15C fortress, has an elegant, classical 18C façade in brick and stone, perforated by numerous windows. Many notable guests have stayed here: Philip the Good, Emperor Charles V, Philip II, Maria de' Medici.

Inside there are rooms with groined vaulting (arms room, dining room) which remain from the 15C and 16C constructions. The collections are interesting: antique furniture, historical mementoes, objets d'art, porcelain, master-paintings (by Van Dyck, Van Loo). The vast park has some magnificent trees and a beautiful rose garden.

SOUGNÉ-REMOUCHAMPS Liège

Michelin maps 409 K4 or 213 south of fold 23 – Local map see AMBLÈVE VALLEY

Remouchamps is a pleasant holiday location on the banks of the Amblève, where a festival in honour of the daisy is celebrated on the last weekend in June.

★★ **Cave (Grotte)** ⏲ – *Illustration p 15.* Discovered in 1828 and arranged for visiting in 1912, it offers the opportunity of an interesting trip, returning by boat, through galleries scoured out of the rock by the Rubicon, a tributary of the Amblève.

The circular entrance was once a prehistoric shelter; a wide corridor leads to a precipice from which a staircase descends to the river.

Pass a frozen waterfall, petrified natural dams *(gours)* in the Grand Gallery (20m - 66ft high), make the descent to the Rubicon beneath the vault of sparkling stalactites, admire the "Cathedral" measuring 100m - 328ft by 40m - 131ft with beautiful crystal concretions, before reaching the Bridge of the Titans. This is where the path goes down to the landing stage and the visit continues by boat for about 1km - 0.75 mile through strangely coloured vaulted rock walls to the Precipice Chamber.

EXCURSION

From Sougné-Remouchamps to Tancrémont – *11km - 6.75 miles north.*

Deigné-Aywaille – The **Monde Sauvage Safari Park** ⏲ is in Deigné. Elephants, hippopotami, zebras, camels and gazelles live at large; visitors may see them by taking a car or a little train. The section consisting of the enclosures and islets is visited on foot. The park also has a pool with seals, a children's animal farm with a playground and an aviary of exotic birds.

Banneux-Notre-Dame – This has been the international pilgrimage site of the Virgin of the Poor, since the eight apparitions to 11-year-old Mariette Beco during the winter of 1933. The Miraculous Spring, the Stations of the Cross and the chapels are dispersed throughout the neighbouring pine forest.

Tancrémont – A chapel, a pilgrimage site, has a beautiful wooden **statue**★ of Christ which is the object of great veneration. This statue was discovered buried in the earth in about 1830; it depicts a crowned Christ in a robe that seems to be of Eastern influence, and dates back to the 12C.

★ SPA Liège

Pop 9 967

Michelin maps 409 K4 or 213 fold 23 – Local map see AMBLÈVE VALLEY
Town plan in the current Michelin Red Guide Benelux

Spa is in one of the most beautiful regions of the Ardennes, amidst wooded hills, which take on marvellous hues in the autumn. It is a **spa town★★** of some renown. Its clear waters are iron-bearing, bicarbonated and slightly sparkling; they are used primarily for baths and for drinking in the treatment for cardiac, rheumatoid and respiratory problems. The town specialises in "jolités", little painted wooden boxes.

A lengthy past – Spa's waters have been known about since the Roman period. From the 16C on the "bobelins" (those taking the cure, from the Latin "bibulus": he who is a great drinker) became innumerable. Crowned heads such as Margaret of Valois (Queen Margot), Christine of Sweden, Peter the Great (whose name was given to the oldest source, or "pouhon"), and writers such as Marmontel and Victor Hugo came here.

During the First World War the German Emperor William II established himself here with his staff, and it was here that he abdicated in 1918. Two years later the Spa conference brought the Allies and the Germans together for an armistice commission.

The present spa town – Spa has many springs; besides the Pouhon Pierre-le-Grand and the Pouhon Grand-Condé, there are also the Géronstère, the Sauvenière, Groosbeek, Barisart, the Tonnelet and the Spa-Reine, which has non-sparkling water.

The **spa town architecture** of the late 19C and early 20C is particularly well represented. There are some lovely examples of neo-classical and rocaille, the use of metal frameworks and great painted frescoes. The most beautiful examples are the **bath installations** built from 1862 to 1868, the **Pouhon Pierre-le-Grand** ⊙ inside a neo-classical pavilion (1880), and the **Casino**, with the current building (1919) which replaced the "Redoute" built in the 18C.

Spa the holiday resort – The many sports, artistic and cultural activities, the pleasant signposted walks, **guided tours** ⊙, and the interesting excursions into the surrounding area make Spa an excellent spot for a holiday. **Lake Warfaaz** *(2.5km - 1.5 miles northeast)* is appreciated by those who love water sports. Moreover, skiing and tobogganning are popular winter sports at Thier des Raihons *(to the south)*.

Among the many events, note the **autumn music season**, the **Spa Theatre Festival** *(see the Calendar of Events at the end of this guide)* and important temporary exhibitions.

SIGHTS

Spa Town Museum (Musée de la Ville d'eau) ⊙ – *Avenue Reine Astrid 77 B.*
This is in the central building of a royal villa which belonged to the Queen Maria-Henrietta, a Habsburg princess and second Belgian queen, who died in 1902. A rich **collection of "jolités"★** evokes the history of the spa in the decoration on the painted wooden boxes, which actually represent different buildings in Spa from the 17C onwards.

Horse Museum (Musée du Cheval) ⊙ – *In the stables of the Maria-Henrietta villa.* This museum recalls the prestigious "equestrian past" of Spa, which was a stopping place for some of Europe's most beautiful teams of horses, and which organised the first races.

★ **Promenade des Artistes** – *Leave on the Sauvenière road (N 62).*
The town of Neubois, where Emperor William II established his headquarters in 1918, is on the left. Turn left onto the Fontaines road at the crossroads by the **Source de la Sauvenière** spring. The **Source de la Reine** is in the woods on the left. About 1.3km - 0.75 mile on from the crossroads a little stream called the Picherotte flows down to Spa. The path which follows this steeply sloping little valley, scattered with rocks and shaded by magnificent trees, is called the Promenade des Artistes.

Continue along the Fontaines road to reach the **Source de la Géronstère**.

EXCURSIONS

Forest Museum (Musée de la Forêt) ⊙ – *6km - 3.7 miles south in Berinzenne.*
This museum is in a restored farm at the heart of the Spa forest; it introduces the visitor to various aspects of nature: vegetation, flora, local trees (various woods), a geological exhibition, the forestry professions. Fauna are also presented in large dioramas reproducing the animals' natural environment in the Ardennes (deer, lynxes, wolves, foxes, etc.)

Sart – *5km - 3.25 miles northeast on the N 629.*
The Place du Marché is embellished with a perron, symbol of liberty in the Liège region; it is overlooked by a church with a 15C tower, as well as austere-looking stone houses.

Franchimont Castle and Theux – 8km - 5 miles northeast on the N 62.

Franchimont Castle ⊙ – Set on a hill overlooking the Hoëgne Valley, the ruins of Franchimont ("mount of the Francs") hark back to the Liège prince-bishops who lived here during summer from the 16C onwards. It also recalls the 600 proud men massacred in 1468 by Charles the Bold's troops, as they tried to defend the approach to Liège.

The haughty walls of the keep were protected by the pentagonal fortified enclosure with casemates at each angle.

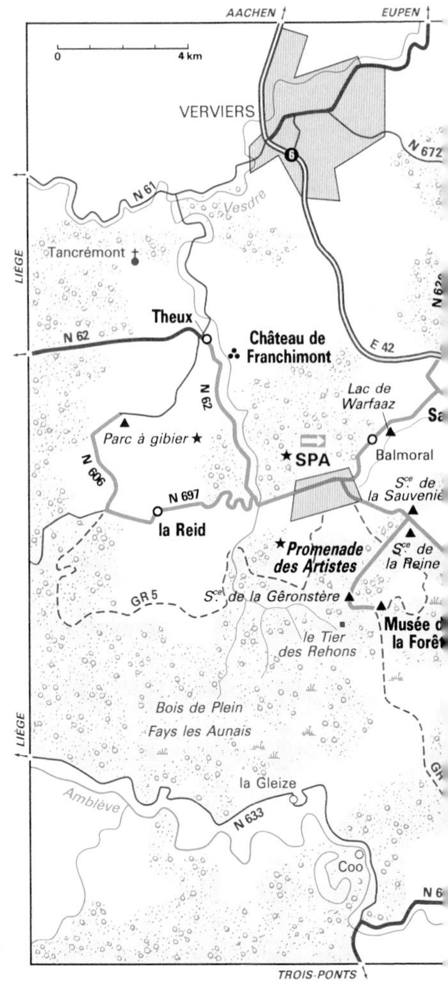

Follow the numbered tour (explanatory plaques).

There is a pretty view of Theux from the chapel.

The building with the tea room and restaurant houses a historical museum.

Theux – Pop 9 788. A 17C and 18C town hall and old houses surround the square, in which there is an 18C perron, with a pine cone at its top.

The restored **Church of SS Hermes and Alexander** ⊙ is nearby. There was originally a Merovingian chapel on the site, then a Carolingian church with a west tower, the vestiges of which have been found; in about the year 1000 a Romanesque nave was built here, followed by a fortified northern tower shortly thereafter; it now has a covered watchpath. The chancel, dating from about 1500, is Gothic.

Notice the sculpted Gothic holy-water basins in the porch. The interior is quite particular: with the three naves separated by tall arcades on pillars; this is the only hall-church with a flat Romanesque ceiling still in existence between the Loire and the Rhine. The ceiling of the central nave was decorated in the 17C with 110 coffers painted with characters and scenes from the Life of Christ. The *Virgin of Theux* (from the late 15C) is in the chapel north of the chancel, and the Romanesque font is interesting, with dragons and four heads on the corners.

La Reid – *5km - 3.25 miles west on the N 62, then take the N 697.*

A **game park**★ (parc à gibier) ⊙ has been created west of the village. It is in a beautiful forest setting, in which the main species of Ardennes fauna are on show, as well as a few rare specimens of various origins: Dabowsky deer from Poland, yaks from Tibet, racoons from America.

★ **Round tour from Spa** – *75km - 47 miles – allow 2 hours. Michelin map 214 folds 8-9.*

Leave on the N 62 southeast in the direction of Malmédy.

Francorchamps – This village is known for its national speed track 7km - 4.3 miles long, south of the town. Each year important speed tests take place. A small modern church is also interesting.

Take the speed track to reach Stavelot.

This **route**★ goes through magnificent countryside.

★ **Stavelot** – *See Stavelot.*

From Stavelot to Malmédy take the Francorchamps speed track once more; this runs through a very pretty setting. The village of **Rivage** is located in the hills on the left, which are still dotted with traditional half-timbered farmhouses.

★ **Malmédy** – *See Malmédy.*

Robertville and Reinhardstein Castle★ – *See Malmédy: Excursions.*

The road, after Robertville, crosses the Hautes-Fagnes plateau (qv). At Jalhay, turn right to reach Gileppe Dam (see Verviers: Excursions).

Return to Spa by taking the N 629 north and going through **Balmoral**, a suburb with luxurious villas half-concealed amidst the green hills.

Gourmets...

The introductory chapter of this guide describes the countries' gastronomic specialities.

*Every year the **Michelin Red Guide Benelux** offers an up-to-date selection of good restaurants.*

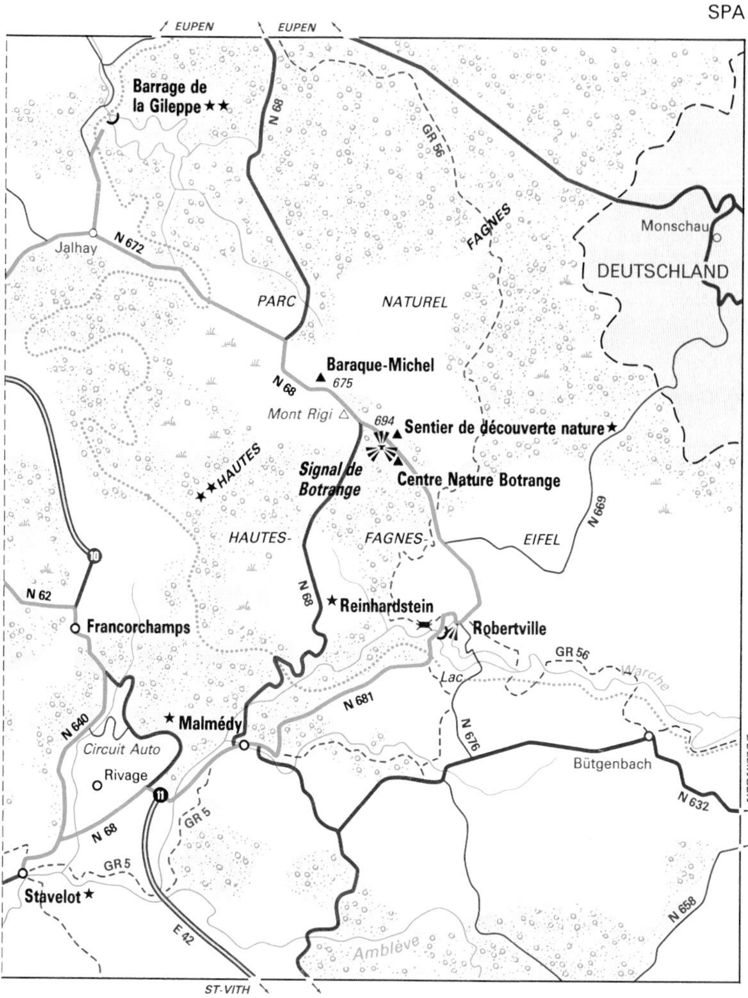

★ **SPONTIN** Namur

Michelin maps 409 I5 or 214 fold 5 – Local map see MEUSE/NAMUR REGION

Spontin, in the Bocq Valley, is well-known for its castle and its mineral water springs. These supply a bottling plant which produces 30 million bottles of mineral water (sparkling and non-sparkling) annually as well as sodas and fruit syrups.

★ **Castle** ⏲ – This is surrounded by the flowing waters of the Bocq and is a remarkable example of Belgian medieval architecture. It shows the development of a seigneurial home from the 12C to the 17C. Starting life as a simple keep in the 12C, it was enlarged into a fortress in the 14C, then restored at the end of the 16C in the Renaissance style and embellished with pink bricks and pepperpot roofs. The outbuildings were added in 1622, outside the moats, and surround the present main courtyard. The old keep can be seen in another courtyard which also contains an elegant wrought-iron well canopy by Van Boeckel (19C). The austere rooms in the old main building, with their thick walls, sandstone floors, Gothic chimney-pieces and Louis XIII woodwork, are a sharp contrast to the apartments.

The south part was decorated in the neo-Gothic style in the 19C.

Spontin Castle

★ STAVELOT Liège

Pop 6 209

Michelin maps 409 K4 or 214 fold 8 – Local maps see AMBLÈVE VALLEY and SPA

Stavelot is at the heart of a magnificent area of the Ardennes. It still has old houses, some of them half-timbered.

The town grew up around an abbey, founded by **St Remaclus** in the 7C, at the same time as that at Malmédy; it soon adopted the Benedictine discipline. Stavelot became the seat of an ecclesiastic principality, in rivalry with Malmédy. Against the will of Liège's prince-bishops, the prince-abbots lived in perfect independence and had no authority but that of the Empire. Nevertheless, Stavelot was incorporated into the Ourthe *département* in 1795.

The French poet Apollinaire spent the summer of 1899 in Stavelot; a medallion on the side façade of the Hôtel du Mal Aimé, 12 Rue Neuve, marks where he stayed.

The town suffered extensive damage in December 1944 *(see Bastogne)*.

Two summer events take place in the abbey, Vacances-Théâtre and the Festival of Chamber Music *(see the Calendar of Events at the end of this guide)*.

★★ **Carnival** – Every year *(see the Calendar of Events at the end of this guide)* Stavelot watches more than 1 500 participants parade during the Laetare Rag procession. The parade has a great many floats and is enlivened by hundreds of **Blanc Moussis**, characters with long red noses and enormous white hooded costumes.

SIGHTS

Place St-Remacle – The **Perron Fountain**, dating from 1769, symbolises the town's liberty, as it does in Liège.

Old Abbey – Remnants include the abbey church and Romanesque tower; the porch is 16C. Around the main courtyard, rebuilt in the 18C, are the conventual buildings, which are now occupied by the town hall and museums. The old 18C monks' refectory is decorated with stuccowork, making an elegant setting for the festival's chamber music concerts. The cellars are used for theatre.

Museum ⊙ – This is in the wing of the outbuildings. The **Regional Religious Museum** ⊙ has some interesting works of art (14C to 19C): a recumbant Christ attributed to Delcour, a 16C painted statue, metalwork and liturgical vestments.

Regional history is evoked by objects found in excavations on the location of the old abbey church as well as firebacks, models (abbey church, Logne castle), seals, portraits, and the reconstruction of a printing works.

The **Tannery section★** on the uppermost floor has some literature *(recorded commentary)* on this local activity, which ended in 1947.

Three rooms have been arranged for temporary exhibitions; they display collections of modern and contemporary Belgian art (Degouve de Nuncques).

Guillaume Apollinaire Museum ⊙ – A little museum on the first floor of the town hall is devoted to the poet, with a reconstruction of his bedroom.

Spa-Francorchamps Speed Track Museum ⊙ – An exhibition has been created in the vaulted cellars of the old abbey; it presents the history of the speed track *(see Spa: Excursions)* from 1896 to today. Models of the victorious automobiles and motorcycles, photos and posters recall the great moments of the famous racing track.

Reliquary of St Remaclus (detail)

St Sebastian's Church (**Église St-Sébastien**) – This church was built in the 18C and has an interesting **treasury** ⊙. The monumental 13C **reliquary of St Remaclus★★**, of the Mosan school, is in gilded metal highlighted with filigree and enamels, and is surrounded by statuettes: St Remaclus, St Lambert, the Apostles (fashioned in a more archaic style); on the ends, Christ and the Virgin; on the roof, scenes from the New Testament.

Note the 17C bust-reliquary of St Poppo, once the abbot of Stavelot; scenes from the life of the saint are on the socle.

Rue Haute – *At the far end of Place St-Remacle, up and to the right.*

This is one of the most picturesque streets in Stavelot. It leads to a charming little square with an old fountain and several old houses, half-timbered or with wooden façades.

THUIN Hainaut

Pop 14 231

Michelin maps 409 F4 or 214 fold 3

Thuin is the capital of the **Thudinie** region, on a pretty **site★** spreading over a hill separating the Sambre from the Biesmelle. It is overlooked by its tall square belfry (17C-18C), once the collegiate church tower.
Thuin was initially a possession of the Abbey of Lobbes *(qv)*, then was made part of the Liège principality in 888; the bishop Notger fortified the town in the 10C.
The St Roch military march takes place in Thuin in May *(see the Calendar of Events at the end of this guide)*, a parade which dates back to 1654. A speciality of Thuin is "spantôles", biscuits named after a canon captured from the French in 1554.

SIGHTS

Place du Chapitre – There is an interesting **panorama** of the winding Sambre Valley, the Lower Town with its port and boats, and the picturesque town of Lobbes with the collegiate church on the summit of a mountain.
The post office is not far from the square, in Grand-Rue, occupying what used to be the Lobbes Abbey refuge (16C, restored).

Midi Ramparts – Follow the placard marked "Panorama" in Grand-Rue, then take a picturesque little street running along the 15C ramparts and church chevet. The **Notger tower** can be seen on the left, the only remaining trace of the ramparts built by the prince-bishop.

Hanging gardens – *Leave the town by car in the direction of Biesme.*
There is a pretty **view** of Thuin's terrace gardens from the park (Parc du Chant des oiseaux) on the right; also of the ramparts and the belfry, overlooking the Biesmelle Valley.

TIENEN Brabant

Pop 31 753

Michelin maps 409 H3 or 213 fold 20
Town plan in the current Michelin Red Guide Benelux

Tienen is in the agricultural region of **Hageland** ("hedge country"). It used to be a drapers' town and is now a centre of trade. It is at the intersection of communications links and is also an important sugar industry centre, with a refinery capable of producing up to 200 000 tons of sugar annually.

SIGHTS

★ **Church (O.L.-Vrouw-ten-Poelkerk)** ⏲ – This stone Brabant-style building stands on the huge market square. The 13C chancel is plain and harmonious, with a ring of chapels, each with a decorated gable; the nave, however, was never built. The 14C transept has a square-section, onion-domed bell tower above it. There used to be a small lake nearby – hence the church's name (Our Lady of the Lake) – which has been drained, but a spring remains and is the site of a pilgrimage. The beautiful deepset **doorways★** by Jean d'Orsy date from 1360; note the amusing little characters carved on the bases of the alcoves. The 14C Virgin which decorated the central doorway was moved into the church and is now over the main altar.

Het Toreke Town Museum (Stedelijk Museum) ⏲ – This is in an old 16C prison, in the courtyard of the Justice of the Peace. The collections (ceramics, metalwork, archaeology) illustrate the history of the town.

Wolmarkt – The restored Flemish Renaissance style **Van Ranst houses**, on the right at nos 19 and 21, are particularly lovely.

St Germanus's Church (St.-Germanuskerk) – Built on the top of the hill, this church is at the heart of the old centre of the town near the Veemarkt (livestock). In the 12C it was a four-towered Romanesque basilica.
The two towers of the avant-corps were built around 1225; they are typical of Mosan Romanesque art. Since the 16C they have framed a massive tower, which had a 54-chime carillon added to it in the 18C that can be heard during **summer concerts** ⏲. The interior is Gothic. Near the central altar copies of the Romanesque font exhibited in the Cinquantenaire Museum in Brussels can be seen. There is a beautiful bronze lectern in the chancel. Note the 15C *Miraculous Christ of the White Ladies* in the south transept chapel. In the north one, there is a Pièta, the breast pierced by seven swords.

EXCURSION

From Tienen to Jodoigne – *13km - 8 miles southwest.*

Hoegaarden – Pop 5 546. This town is well-known for its pale beer. A little folklore museum (Bier- en Streekmuseum) in the attic of the 17C house **'t Nieuwhuys** ⏲ *(2 Ernest Ourystraat)*, once an inn during the Roman period, contains objects concerning local history. There is also a beer cellar (kelder) open to visitors.

Jodoigne – Pop 9 603. Once a stronghold on a slope of the Gette Valley, Jodoigne is an important agricultural market.
St Médard's Church, built in the late 12C, is in a transitional style; it is flanked to the west by a massive square tower. The **apse** is harmonious, with a double row of windows with arcades supported by slender twinned columns. The apse is framed by two apsidal chapels isolated from the chancel. The chancel itself has slender twinned columns with capitals. Note the reliquary of St Médard in an alcove of the north transept arm, behind a grille.

★ TONGEREN Limburg

Pop 29 553

Michelin maps 409 J3 or 213 fold 22

Together with Tournai this is the oldest town in Belgium, and one of the richest in traces of the past. It is in the **Hesbaye** (Haspengouw), a gently undulating region of orchards.

A great Roman community – Tongeren was originally a camp established by Caesar's lieutenants, Sabinus and Cotta; their legions were massacred nearby by **Ambiorix**, the Eburon chief, who raised a number of the Belgian Gauls against Caesar's armies in 54BC. Under Roman occupation the developing town was called **Atuatuca-Tungrorum**, and became a stopping place on the Roman road from Bavay to Cologne. It actually covered a much greater area at the time, as shown by the remains of a late 1C rampart which have been found 4km - 2.5 miles away; traces also exist on the Legioenenlaan to the West. The barbaric invasions in the late 3C were so hard on the community that it drew into itself in the early 4C, into a fortified enclosure of which some traces have survived. St Servais was the first bishop of Tongeren in the 4C, but as a measure of security the episcopal see was then moved to Maastricht. Gradually, under the protection of the Liège principality, Tongeren began to grow again. It organised an administrative system and built a third fortified enclosure in the 13C.

Statue of Ambiorix

★★ BASILICA OF OUR LADY (O.L.-VROUWEBASILIEK) (Y) ⊙

time: 2 hours.

A statue (1866) of Ambiorix stands in the market square, in which the 18C town hall is also to be found. Pause to admire the impressive outline of the old collegiate church of Our Lady, a beautiful Gothic (13C-16C) building with a striking unfinished west front tower (carillon).

Interior – *Go along the south side of the church and enter through the little doorway.* There is a beautiful Romanesque (11C) painted wooden Christ beneath the porch. The 13C nave is supported by cylindrical pillars, which themselves have capitals with crockets. The graceful triforium is surmounted by a covered passageway. On the west side, beneath the rood-screen, there is a beautiful door dating from 1711; the 18C organ above it has been restored.

The most interesting works of art are in the chancel. The beautiful early 16C Antwerp wooden **altarpiece★** on the high altar represents the Life of the Virgin; note also the great paschal chandelier and the lectern, with the metalwork executed in 1372 by a Dinant coppersmith.

A painted **statue★** of Our Lady of Tongeren, carved in walnut (1479), is in the north transept arm.

Concerts ⊙ are given in the basilica.

TONGEREN

Grote Markt	Y
Hasseltsestraat	Y 12
Maastrichterstraat	Y
St Truidenstraat	Y 42
Achttiende-Oogstlaan	Y 2
Clarissenstraat	Y 4
Corversstraat	YZ 5
Eeuwfeestwal	Y 6
Elisabethwal	Z 9
Hasseltsesteenweg	Y 10
Hondsstraat	Y 14
Luikerstraat	Z 15
Looierstraat	Z 17
Minderbroederstraat	Z 19
Moerenstraat	Y 20
Momberstraat	Z 23
Muntstraat	Z 24
Nevenstraat	Y 25
Piepelpoel	Y 27
Pleinstraat	Y 28
Pliniuswal	Y 30
Predikherenstraat	Y 31
Regulierenplein	Z 34
Riddersstraat	Y 35
de Schiervelstraat	Y 37
St. Catharinastraat	Y 38
St. Jansstraat	Z 39
St. Maternuswal	Y 41
Stationslaan	Y 44
Vermeulenstraat	Y 46
11 Novemberlaan	Y 47

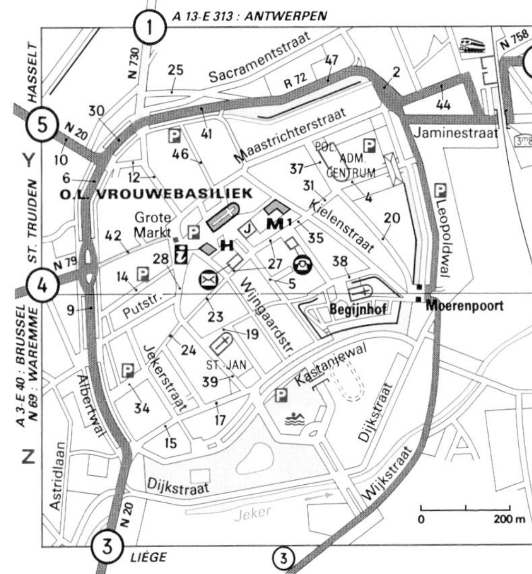

★★ **Treasury** (**Schatkamer**) – Among the exhibited treasures, notice the gospel-book covered with an 11C ivory plaque (calvary); a 6C ivory diptych (St Paul); a 6C Merovingian clasp in gold; a 14C monstrance-reliquary of St Ursula with an enameled base; the reliquary-triptych of the Holy Cross (12C) in silver-gilt highlighted with enamels; a Head of Christ in wood (11C); the reliquary of the Martyrs of Trier (13C); and the reliquary of St Remaclus (15C), decorated with paintings.
Every seven years *(see the Calendar of Events at the end of this guide)* about a hundred priests wearing old liturgical vestments carry the reliquaries from the treasury along in a procession.

★ **Cloisters** – The cloisters are charming. In them, single and twinned colonnettes alternate; there are interesting capitals on the row near the entrance. Gravestones have been set against the walls.

ADDITIONAL SIGHTS

Provincial Gallo-Roman Museum (**Provinciaal Gallo-Romeins Museum**) (**Y M**[1]) ⓥ – This is a collection of the objects found during excavations in the Limburg region, which date from prehistoric times to the Merovingian period. The Gallo-Roman section is particularly interesting in its evocation of the town's past. Notice the beautiful sculpture of the Roman warrior crushing two men with serpent's tails.

Moerenpoort (**YZ**) – This 14C gate from the medieval ramparts is also the east entrance to the beguine convent, which has been turned into a **Museum of the Town's Military History** ⓥ. A room is devoted to the town militias. There is a view of the beguine convent, the town and the collegiate church from here.

Beguine Convent (**Begijnhof**) (**Z**) – Founded in the 13C, this convent was closed down during the French Revolution. The Onder de Linde courtyard to the west still has a striking appearance with the gardens and the round-arched doorway. A Gothic church with interesting furnishings is to be found at the heart of the beguine convent.

Town Museum (**Stedelijk Museum**) (**Y H**) ⓥ – Paintings, engravings, sculptures, literature on the history of Tongeren.

EXCURSION

Alden Biesen – *10km - 6.25 miles on ① on the map.*
The Teutonic Order founded the **Alden Biesen commandery** (Old Rushes) north of **Rijkhoven** in 1220. The present buildings were built or modified between the 16C and the 18C. The castle is an imposing four-sided building, flanked by towers and surrounded by moats. Louis XV attended a Te Deum in the church in 1747 to give thanks for the Lawfeld (Lafelt) victory over the Austrians.
There is a small exhibition in the gallery beside the church.

TONGERLO Antwerpen

Michelin maps 409 H2 or 213 fold 8

The famous Premonstratensian *(qv)* **abbey** is to the west of the town. It was founded in about 1130, then abandoned at the end of the 18C and partly destroyed. It was occupied once more in 1840 and has been rebuilt.
After going through the porch surmounted by three alcoves (14C), visitors enter the **courtyard**, with the farm (1640) and the tythe barn (1618) which is now used for an exhibition on the abbey and its inhabitants. The **Prelacy** has a beautiful classical façade from 1725.
There is an ebony reliquary (1619) in the 19C **abbey church**; it contains the relics of St Siard, invoked by farmers, young mothers and children. This is also the site of a pilgrimage *(see the Calendar of Events at the end of this guide)*.

★ **Leonardo da Vinci Museum** ⓥ – *Access via the Prelacy.*
In a glass and concrete building there is an immense canvas, a copy of the **Last Supper** that Leonardo da Vinci painted on the convent wall in Milan between 1495 and 1498. This faithful copy is surprisingly good, and was executed less than 20 years later. The Last Supper was bought in 1545 and occupied the abbey church for many years. It has been through numerous ups and downs and was badly damaged during a fire in 1929. It has been carefully restored in Belgium, and the emotional response it provokes in the viewer is as strong as ever. Early music and a well-chosen commentary heighten the dramatic intensity of the moment as Christ says, "One of you will betray me"; only Judas is outside the golden light reflected on each face.
There is a beautiful view in the garden in front of the museum of the rear façade of the Prelacy and the graceful 1479 turret, once the watch turret.

Admission times and charges for the sights described are listed at the end of the guide.

Every sight for which there are times and charges is identified by the symbol ⓥ in the middle section of the guide.

TORHOUT West-Vlaanderen

Pop 17 975

Michelin maps 409 C2 or 213 fold 2

Torhout was a prosperous town in the 12C with a well-renowned fair.

St Peter's Church (**St.-Pietersbandenkerk**) ⊙ – Rebuilt after having been bombed in 1940, this has a pretty octagonal Romanesque bell tower with a carillon. Models inside show the church's evolution.

Town Hall (**Stadhuis**) – This is a harmonious building dating from 1713; widely spaced pilasters are aligned under a high roof.

Wijnendale Castle is 3km - 1.75 miles west of Torhout, a composite building (11C-19C) surrounded by moats. This was built in the 11C and became the favourite residence of the Counts of Flanders.
Mary of Burgundy met with her fatal fall from a horse in the surrounding woods.

★★ TOURNAI Hainaut

Pop 67 669

Michelin maps 409 D4 or 213 fold 15

Tournai is a peaceful bourgeois city on the banks of the Scheldt, overlooked by the five towers of its cathedral. It is at the heart of an essentially agricultural region and has had a prestigious past. Together with Tongeren, this is the oldest town in Belgium.
One after the other the Romans, French, English and Austrians made this an important artistic centre. Unfortunately, the May 1940 bombings ravaged Tournai and destroyed most of its old houses.
People from Tournai speak a dialect of the Picardy region.

HISTORICAL NOTES

The cradle of the French monarchy – Tournai was already an important city at the time of the Romans. In the 3C St Piat converted the town to Christianity; it then came under Salian Frank domination in the 5C. This was followed by the Merovingian dynasty: Childeric died here in 481 and **Clovis**, who made Tournai an episcopalian see, was born here in 465.
The kings of France always considered Tournai the cradle of their monarchy, and the town bore the royal fleur-de-lys in its arms. Napoleon later adopted Childeric's symbol, the bee, for his own.
Philippe-August visited the town in 1187 and won the bishop suzerain to his side. The 12C and 13C were great periods of construction, of which a few Romanesque houses, religious buildings and some parts of the second fortified enclosure remain.
Tournai remained faithful to France during the Hundred Years War. The town, called the "Chambre du Roy" (King's Chamber), was isolated in a Belgium won over to the English cause. The citizens of Tournai were invited by Joan of Arc to come to Charles VII's consecration in Rheims (1429) by calling them "gentils loiaux Franchois" (kind loyal Frenchmen). When she was taken prisoner, Tournai sent her a pouch filled with gold to ease her captivity.

A centre of great artistic progress – Already well-known in the Merovingian period for its gold- and silversmiths, the town became a very important artistic centre in the late Middle Ages. With the 13C reliquary of St Eleuthère, the craftsmen of Tournai once more distinguished themselves in metalwork; and in the 15C they were the respected rivals of Mosan art.
The use of local stone in the architecture of the 12C onwards gave birth to a flourishing new school of sculpture: in the 15C, fonts and funerary monuments were cut in the very finely grained grey-blue stone, or sometimes in imported white stone.
In the 15C **Robert Campin** was born in Tournai (died in 1444). A contemporary of Van Eyck, he is thought by some scholars to be the **Master of Flémalle**, the anonymous author of a group of works discovered here in about 1900. The charm of his art lies in its colours, the precision with which he depicts interiors and their furnishings, and the sense of serenity evoked by his pictures.
In more serious subjects a more dramatic mode of expression is evident, which brought Robert Campin closer to his student **Rogier de La Pasture**, better known as **Van der Weyden**. This artist was born in Tournai (1399-1464) and became the official painter of the City of Brussels in 1436.
His touching compositions are full of mysticism, while his neat precise drawing also contributes towards remarkable portraits. His Madonnas, with their soft oval faces and wide foreheads, have often been imitated.
The high-warp **tapestry** of Tournai supplanted that of its rival Arras as well as the other Flemish workshops. It was admired throughout Europe, characterised by vast borderless compositions, with many figures and a highly stylised manner *(see Introduction: Art – Tapestry)*.

A disputed stronghold – From 1513 to 1519, Tournai fell into the hands of Henry VIII, King of England, who had a fortified district built there, with a keep known as **Henry VIII Tower**.
The town then came under the rule of the Emperor Charles V and lost many of its privileges. Prey to religious troubles, Tournai, under the heroic command of **Christine de Lalaing**, held out for two months in 1581 against Alexander Farnese's siege.

The town again became part of France under the reign of Louis XIV from 1667 to 1709. The fortifications were reinforced and bastions added to the 13C ramparts by Vauban. The many brick and stone houses date from this period, with their large windows and overhanging roofs. A few are still standing despite the bombing of 1940, especially on Quai Notre-Dame ⊙.

Tournai then became the seat of the Flemish Parliament, representing the sovereign's justice. It fell into the hands of the Austrians after the Utrecht Treaty, was returned to the French after the Battle of **Fontenoy** (1745) *(8km - 5 miles east)*, then back to the Austrians in 1748.

In the 18C, Tournai underwent a Renaissance of the coppersmithing industry and tapestry-making.

The porcelain works, founded in 1751 by François-Joseph Peterinck, were very much in vogue at this time. Soft porcelain was made here with rich colours and a great variety of decoration, in which the Chinese style played a great part. The works finally closed in 1891.

Folklore and traditions – Tournai is among the Belgian towns where traditions are still very important.

During the festival of the Nativity of Our Lady *(second Sunday in September at 15:00)*, which dates back to the Great Plague of 1090, the reliquary of St Eleuthère *(qv)* and pieces from the cathedral treasury are carried along in a procession.

The days on which the four parades take place *(see the Calendar of Events at the end of this guide)* combine publicity and folklore with fifteen giants, with such figures as Childeric and Louis XIV, a carnival parade, a procession of floral floats and a festival of military music.

★★ CATHEDRAL OF OUR LADY (CATHÉDRALE NOTRE-DAME) (AZ)

time: 1 hour 30min

The most striking and most original of Belgium's religious monuments stands in the centre of Tournai not far from the belfry. It influenced a great number of churches in the town itself and, since the diocese of Tournai once covered most of Flanders, its influence spread throughout the Scheldt Valley, giving birth to Scaldian art *(qv)*. The effect of the gigantic proportions of the outside of this building (134m - 440ft long, 66m - 216ft wide at the transept) and of the massive forms of its five famous towers is most impressive.

The five **towers**, each one different, stand at the transept crossing; the oldest, in the centre, is supported on the pillars of the crossing itself.

The nave and the arms of the transept, which have semi-circular ends, date from the 12C. The slender Gothic chancel, which is taller than the nave and almost as long, replaced the Romanesque chancel in the 13C. *Photograph p 19.*

The Place P E Janson gives one of the best views of the cathedral as a whole.

Detail of a stained glass window: beer tax

Porte Mantile – This side door is named thus to commemorate St Eleuthère's healing of blind Mantilius on this spot; the door still has some remarkable Romanesque sculptures.

Continue walking round the chevet of the church.

Porte Capitole – This is Romanesque and resembles the Porte Mantile, except that it is unfortunately in very bad condition. The archivolt is supported by two knights with a shield.

Go through the "False Doorway", the arch linking the cathedral with the bishop's palace.

Main façade – This was altered in the 14C and masked in the 16C by a modified **porch**, on which there are three tiers of sculptures: at the bottom, 14C high reliefs, including three scenes depicting the story of Adam and Eve; above that, 16C bas-reliefs, with the Tournai procession *(see above)* to the left, and the conflict between Sigebert and his brother Chilperic to the right; at the top there is a row of apostles and saints dating from the 17C. There is a beautiful 14C statue of the Virgin on the central pillar; it was restored in 1609 and is venerated under the name of Our Lady of the Sick (Notre-Dame des Malades).

Interior – This is a vast space containing ten bays. The central nave is four storeys high, with great triple-rolled arcades supported on short pillars with beautifully carved capitals. Above that, the tribunes are surmounted by a triforium of

round arches. The uppermost level is lit by tall clerestory windows. The 18C vaulting was replaced with a wooden ceiling. A rood-screen executed in 1572 by Cornelis Floris cuts off the perspective down the central nave.
The **south side aisle** wall is covered with epitaphs.
Note the **capitals** on the pillars of the nave: plant decoration (1: bunches of grapes), animals (2: horses), human figures, often rather fantastic (3: a falling man).
In St Louis' Chapel, or the Chapel of the Holy Sacrament, there is a Jordaens *Crucifixion* and finely carved 18C wooden panels from an abbey (five scenes: Life of St Benedict and St Ghislain).
Crowned by a tall lantern (Anglo-Norman influence), the **transept** is magnificent in size and splendour, creating the effect of a "cathedral intersecting a cathedral". The layout is very original; each transept arm ends in a semi-circle around which an ambulatory runs with tribunes, blind triforiums and windows above it. This order of four tiers echoes that of the nave.
The transept has traces of frescoes and late-15C stained glass windows by Arnould de Nimègue.
The frescoes (4) in the **south transept arm** represent celestial Jerusalem, and the windows depict the struggle between Sigebert and his brother Chilperic, the origin of the bishops' temporal power (further up, episcopal privileges such as the tax on beer are depicted) *(photograph previous page)*.
The **rood-screen** is the work of sculptor Cornelis Floris de Vriendt; it is a magnificent piece of Antwerp Renaissance art, with different coloured marbles finely chiselled into a rich decoration. The medallions and superposed panels represent episodes from the Bible and the Gospels, with certain of them prefiguring others (for example, Jonah being swallowed by the whale and the Entombment of Christ, to the right).
The **chancel** (1243) is very long and has six bays; its delicacy contrasts to the somewhat austere solidity of the nave. French influence is manifest (Soissons).
The **ambulatory** called the "carolle" (from Old French "caroler", meaning to walk in a round) ends in five radiating chapels. In the first side chapel to the south (5) note the *"Maidens'" Reliquary* (1572); then, in the next chapel (6), Rubens' *Purgatory* as well as several gravestones; in a little chapel (7) there is a *Raising of Lazarus* by Pourbus the Elder and a painting by Coebergher; in the axial chapel (8) there are *Scenes from the Life of the Virgin* by Martin de Vos, somewhat Italian in style. The following chapels still have a series of funerary monuments and gravestones from the 14C and 15C Tournai school.
The vestiges of the frescoes (9) in the **north transept arm** narrate the life and marriage of St Margaret. Here the stained glass windows represent the separation of the Tournai diocese from that of Noyon in France, to which it had been attached in the 7C.
Among the **north side aisle** capitals, admire the swans (10); the imaginary animals (11); a woman being devoured by a monster (12) and on the other side (13), visible only under the porch, Fredegonde and Chilperic, and some birds drinking (14).

★★ **Treasury** ⊙ – Among the many valuable works of art contained in the treasury (15), notice in particular: an *Ecce Homo*, a painting on wood by Quentin Metsys; a reliquary of a piece of the True Cross called the *"Byzantine Cross"*, of 5C or 6C Eastern origin (gold and precious stones); a lovely French-inspired late-13C Madonna in ivory; the **Reliquary of Our Lady** (1205) in silver and gilded copper, by Nicolas de Verdun, decorated with marvellously formed relief figures beneath sumptuous arcading and medallions depicting the Life of Christ.
In the Chapel of the Holy Spirit a long **tapestry** illustrates in 14 panels the life of St Piat, the apostle of Tournai, and that of St Éleuthère, the first bishop of Tournai. This was woven in Arras and donated in 1402 by a former chaplain of the Duke of Burgundy.

TOURNAI

Chapeliers (R. des) .... C 6
Cordonnerie (R. de la) ...... C 14
Gallait (R.) .... C 20
Grand Place C
Puits-d'Eau (R. des) .... C 33
Royale (R.) .... BY

Athénée (R. de l') .... BY 2
Becquerelle (R. du) .... AY 3
Bourdon-St Jacques (R. du) .... C 4
Childeric (R.) .... BY 7
Clairisses (R. des) .... C 8
Clovis (Pl.) .... BY 10
Crombez (Pl.) .... BY 12
Curé-N.-Dame (R. du) .... C 15
Delwart (Bd) .... AY 17
Dorée (R.) .... AZ 18
Hôpital-Notre-Dame (R. de l') .... C 23
Lalaing (Bd) .... AZ 25
Léopold (Bd) .... AY 26
Marché-aux-Poissons (Quai du) .... C 27
Montgomery (Av.) .... AZ 29
Notre-Dame (Quai) .... C 30
Paul-E. Janson (Pl.) .... C 31
Poissonsceaux (Q. des) .. BZ 32
Pont (R. de) .... BYZ 34
Quesnoy (R. du) .... BY 35
Saint-Piat (R.) .... BZ 38
Sainte-Catherine (R.) ...... BZ 39
Tête-d'Argent (R.) .... C 42
Volontaires (R. des) .... BY 44
Wallonie (R. de la) .... C 45

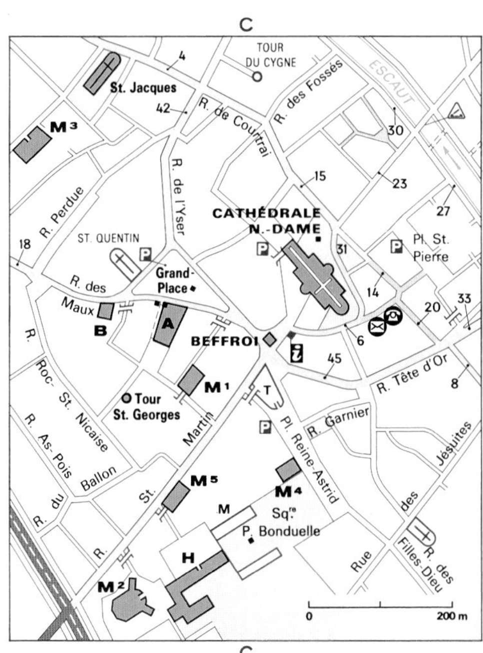

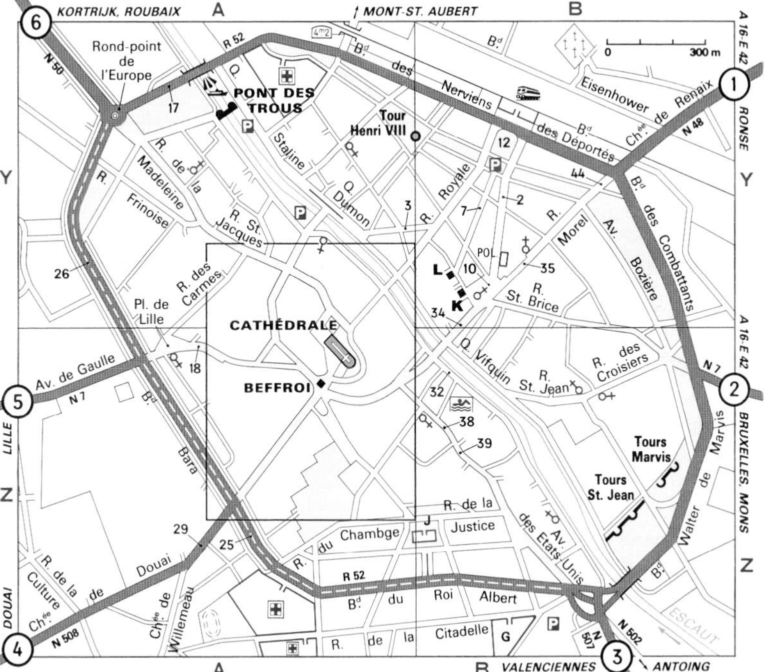

The **Reliquary of St Éleuthère** (1247) is decorated with a profusion of extraordinarily delicate statues of the apostles set against a background of filigree, enamels and gems. Christ and St Éleuthère, who is holding the cathedral in his hand, are represented on the gable-ends. The panelling of the chapter-house has been elegantly and finely chiselled to depict the Life of St Ghislain.

Note also a sculpture representing Aquarius, part of the zodiac which once adorned the 12C Romanesque porch.

ADDITIONAL SIGHTS

★ **Belfry (Beffroi) (C)** – This is the oldest in Belgium. The base dates from the 12C, the upper parts were rebuilt in 1391 after a fire. From the first floor there is an interesting **view** of the cathedral; there is also a good **view** from the top (72m - 236ft high, 256 steps) of the city. The 43-chime carillon gives beautiful concerts *(the belfry is currently undergoing restoration work)*.

★ **Fine Art Museum (C M2)** – This museum was designed by Art Nouveau architect **Victor Horta** *(qv)* who gave it a star-shaped floor plan and a façade with a curving surface plane. It is surmounted by a bronze group by Guillaume Charlier called "Truth, Empress of the Arts". The museum houses among other things a collection of Impressionist works from the Brussels patron of the arts H Van Cutsem.

Among the series of **old paintings★** certain stand out, such as Rogier Van der Weyden's *Virgin with Child*, Gossaert's *St Donatius*, Hell Brueghel's *Fowler*, an interpretation of a work by Brueghel the Elder, and some delicate landscapes by Velvet Brueghel.

There is a didactic display of works throughout the world by Rogier Van der Weyden, using photographs in the same format of the original canvases.

There are 17C Jordaens canvases, and one room is devoted to the paintings of Tournai Romantic Louis Gallait.

Two of Manet's famous compositions stand out among the Impressionist works: *Argenteuil* (1874) and *At Father Lathuille's* (1879). Works by Seurat, Monet and Fantin-Latour are on display in the same room.

19C and 20C Belgian painting is well represented (Ensor, Emile Claus, Henri de Braekeleer), as is sculpture (Charlier, Rousseau). The museum also has a large collection of drawings (Van Gogh, Toulouse-Lautrec). The sculpture in front of the left side of the museum is by Georges Grard.

The elegant building (1763) next to the museum is the **abbey palace** of what was once St Martin's Abbey; it now contains the town hall offices.

Tapestry Museum (C M4) ⊙ – The elegant façade of this museum overlooks Place de la Reine Astrid. The museum evokes an activity which flourished in Tournai from the 15C to the 18C. Tournai tapestry-making reached a peak between 1450 and 1550, and the tapestries exhibited from this period show the main characteristics: varied subjects (history, mythology, heraldry) executed in bright colours with very elegant threadwork. Numerous figures in 15C costume rival each other in magnificence in these lively, crowded compositions in which several scenes are superposed, as in the **Battle of Roncevaux** or **Famine in Jerusalem.**

A large part is also left for modern tapestry with the "Moral Force" group from the 1940s (Louis Delfour, Edmond Dubrunfaut and Roger Somville) as well as contemporary tapestry where the play of textures is often a kind of sculpture. Temporary exhibitions complete this tapestry presentation.

The museum also has a workshop where tapestry-makers can be seen at work.

Market Square (**Grand-Place**) (C) – This square is in fact triangular and is overlooked by the cathedral towers. The belfry stands at one end, and St Quentin's Church at the other. There is a statue of Christine de Lalaing in the middle.

The square was destroyed in 1940, but has had some beautiful houses rebuilt around it, such as the town hall, once the clothmakers' hall (1610) (**C A**), built in a transitional style from Gothic to baroque; further to the right, there is a beautiful brick house (**C B**).

Folklore Museum (C M1) ⊙ – The collections exhibited in the "Tournai House" (façades from 1673) bring to life the popular arts and traditions of Tournai, as well as evoking daily life in about 1850.

There are interesting reconstructions on the ground floor: *estaminet*, "balotil" (hosier's) workshop, farm kitchen, weaver's shop; as well as some historical literature. On the second floor, there is a model of 17C Tournai, which is a reproduction of one executed for Louis XIV.

St George's Tower is nearby (**C**), an element of the initial 12C town fortifications.

Museum of Decorative Arts (C M5) ⊙ – This has a large collection of porcelain from the royal and imperial works established in Tournai in the 18C. Note the service with the bird-motifs based on work by Buffon.

Museum of History and Archaeology (C M3) ⊙ – This is in what used to be the pawnshop built by Coebergher in the 17C. The history of the region is evoked by excavated objects from the Frankish and Roman periods. Note the 3C-4C **Gallo-Roman lead sarcophagus★** excavated in 1989 in a street near the museum, a glass feeding-bottle, as well as a **Roman well** dug out of the trunk of a hollow tree.

★ **Pont des Trous** (AY) – There is a beautiful **view★** of this bridge from the neighbouring bridge (boulevard Delwart), of the more austere side of the bridge with the cathedral silhouetted in the distance. The Pont des Trous is a remnant of the second fortifications of the 13C; in 1948 it was raised 2.4m - 8ft to ease access for river traffic.

Romanesque houses (**BY K**) – Near St Brice's Church, two houses have restored late-12C façades. They constitute a rare example of secular Scaldian Romanesque architecture *(qv)*, with windows divided by slender central columns and aligned between two stone string courses.

There is a Gothic house further along (13C-15C) (**BY L**), which develops the principles seen in the Romanesque houses.

Marvis Towers (BZ) **and St John's Towers** (BZ) – These four towers, traces of the 13C fortifications, overlook pretty gardens on Boulevard Walter de Marvis.

Henry VIII Tower (ABY) ⊙ – This powerful 16C tower built while Tournai was in the hands of Henry VIII of England now houses an **arms museum**.

St James's Church (**St-Jacques**) (C) – The style of this building is transitional from Romanesque to Gothic, the porch is surmounted by a thick square tower with turrets. An arcaded gallery runs along outside the nave; inside, this gallery makes a bridge over the transept crossing. It has some beautiful openwork and is extended into the nave by a triforium.

EXCURSIONS

Antoing Castle ⏲ – *6km - 3.75 miles southeast on the N 502.*
A few vestiges of the 12C fortified enclosure, the 15C keep and the Renaissance façade recall the ancient origins of this castle, rebuilt in the 19C in the neo-Gothic style. A part of the outbuildings was lent to the Jesuits when they were forced to leave France; Charles de Gaulle was their student from 1907-1908. The **chapel** still has a rich collection of sculpted gravestones, particularly those of the de Melun family (early 15C). From the top of the **keep**, there is a beautiful **view** of the region. The rooms of the keep (Gothic furnishings) are open to visitors.

Mont-St-Aubert – *6km - 3.75 miles to the north.*
This hill attains a height of 149m - 488ft and has become a holiday centre. There is a beautiful **panorama**★ of the fields of Flanders from the cemetery near the church. Tournai and the cathedral can just be seen to the south, behind the trees; the conurbation of Roubaix-Tourcoing can be seen to the west.

Brunehault Stone – *10km - 6.25 miles on ③ on the map; at the Hollain exit, turn right.*
Near the ancient Roman road or "Brunehault road" going from Tournai to Bavay, the Brunehault stone can be seen; it is a trapezoidal menhir 4.5m - 15ft high, similar to the Zeupire stone *(see Charleroi: Excursions).*

Leuze-en-Hainaut – Pop 12 879. *13km - 8 miles east on ② on the map.*
The vast **collegiate church of St Peter** was built in 1745 on the site of the old Gothic church destroyed by fire.
The plain nature of the outside is a contrast to the majesty of the interior. Note the beautiful 18C woodwork in particular; the Louis XV panelling; the confessionals sculpted with different motifs; the pulpit under which St Peter in chains is represented; the organ case.

TROIS-PONTS Liège

Pop 2 174

Michelin maps 409 K4 or 214 fold 8

This is a picturesque village, well situated on the confluence of the Salm and the Amblève; it makes a pleasant point of departure for excursions.

EXCURSIONS

Salm Valley – *13km - 8 miles to Vielsam.*
This pleasant country valley was once a principality under the rule of the Princes of Salm and dependent upon the Duchy of Luxembourg. The River Salm flows rapidly along a winding course through a deep steep-sided valley; the road, edged with beautiful trees, runs alongside the river.

Grand-Halleux – The **Monti estate** ⏲ is nearby. *When leaving Grand-Halleux, take a road on the left and follow the signs.* This estate has a vast forest in which the fauna of the Luxembourg Ardennes thrive (various types of deer, boar, wild sheep).

Vielsalm – Pop 6 772. The Macralles (witches') Sabbath takes place on the evening of 20 July in a wood near the town. The next day it is followed by the Bilberry Festival.

★ **Panorama Tour (Circuit des Panoramas)** – *44km - 27.3 miles.*
This signposted tourist route consists of two great loops; it winds through the hills, offering extensive panoramas and views of the Amblève here or the Salm there.
The **"Wanne loop"** to the southeast *(23km - 14.25 miles)* follows the lower course of the Salm *(see above).* The road leaves the forest near Henumont before going down and then up again to Wanne, in the midst of pretty landscapes. The road soon reaches Aisomont; a ski slope (Val de Wanne) has been created to the right, just before this village. Now head down to Trois-Ponts.
Climb to the west by taking the **"Basse-Bodeux loop"** *(21km - 13 miles)* between the Salm and Baleur Valleys (towards Basse-Bodeux), then turn left towards Mont-de-Fosse. After St-Jacques, Fosse and Reharmont, one crosses the N 651 to reach Haute-Bodeux. A little before Basse-Bodeux, turn left. The road crosses a beautiful forest near two of the upper basins of the power station, filled by pumping *(see Coo).* Return to Trois-Ponts by going down through the hamlet of Brume.

TURNHOUT Antwerpen

Pop 37 584

Michelin maps 409 H2 or 213 fold 8 or 212 fold 16

Turnhout is the main town of the Antwerp Kempen region; it is also an industrial and commercial centre. It was part of the Brabant province from the 12C to the 18C; Emperor Charles V made it a seigneury which he gave to his sister Mary of Hungary. After the Treaty of Münster in 1648, Turnhout became a fiefdom held by the Orange-Nassau dynasty until 1753.

The Battle of Turnhout in October 1789 has remained famous; it made it possible for the **Brabant Revolution** to rid the country of the Austrians for a short while. By the end of 1790, however, they occupied the country again.

The town specialises in making playing cards.

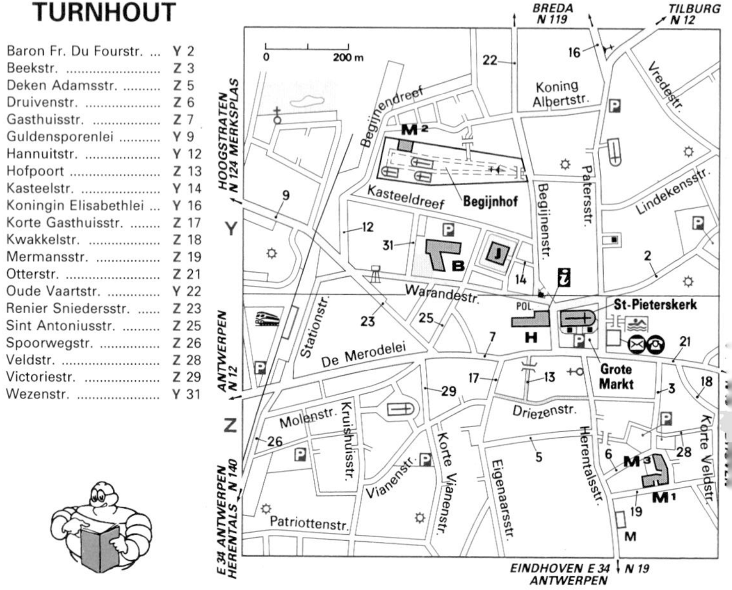

SIGHTS

Market Square (Grote Markt) (Z) – St Peter's Church (St.-Pieterskerk) ⊙ is in the centre; it dates from the 15C and the 18C. It contains an interesting 19C pulpit, stalls dating from 1713 from the old Corsendonk priory (in Oud-Turnhout, east of the town) and baroque confessionals from 1740.

The neo-classical town hall was inaugurated in 1961.

Castle of the Dukes of Brabant (Kasteel "Hertogen van Brabant") (Y J) – This solid, four-sided construction surrounded by water dates from the 13C and the 17C. In the Middle Ages it was a hunting lodge for the Dukes of Brabant, who were attracted by the game in the Kempen Forest. Mary of Hungary, who divided her time between Turnhout and Binche, made it into a sumptuous residence. The castle is now occupied by the law courts.

A modern **cultural centre (Y B)**, De Warande, was built nearby in 1972.

Taxandria Museum (Z M1) ⊙ – In a patrician 16C house, this museum is devoted to the archaeology, local art and folklore of the Kempen region, which was called Taxandria in the Ancient world.

There are rich collections (Merovingian buckles) and an interesting reconstruction of a Kempen kitchen.

Beguine Convent (Begijnhof) (Y) ⊙ – Founded in the 14C and rebuilt in the 16C and 17C after a fire, this is a charming enclosure in which the houses are arranged around a small triangular square; the baroque church stands there. In the house at no 56, there is a small **museum** ⊙ **(Y M2)** devoted to life in the convent.

Playing Cards Museum (Nationaal Museum van de Speelkaart) (Z M3) ⊙ – An old playing cards factory has been turned into a museum devoted to this industry, practised in Turnhout since 1826. Besides the old machines having served to make or print the cards, there is a rich collection of card games from all over the world, the oldest dating from about the year 1500.

Windmill (Windmolen) *(via Otterstraat,* **Z 21**) – This pretty windmill was built in 1848 and has been restored. It is called "De Grote Bentel."

EXCURSIONS

Hoogstraten – Pop 15 460. *18km - 11 miles northwest.* Michelin map 212 fold 16.
A great avenue planted with lime trees crosses this area, overlooked by the magnificent tower-gate of its church, **St Catherine's** (St.-Catharinakerk) ⊙, in brick striped with white stone. It was rebuilt after its destruction in 1944, and remains most imposing at a height of 105m - 344ft.

The church is the work of Rombout Keldermans *(qv)* in the 16C.

Beautiful 16C stalls can be seen inside in the chancel; the tomb of Antoine de Lalaing and his spouse Elisabeth de Culembourg, by Jean Mone, is also here. Note too the wonderful 14-16C stained glass windows and the series of tapestries.

Beguine Convent (Begijnhof) – This was probably founded at the end of the 14C, and was rebuilt after having burned in 1506.
It is a modest enclosure with low, simple houses surrounding a shaded lawn. The 17C baroque church has an elegant porch.

Baarle-Hertog – Pop 2 090. *14km - 8.5 miles north.* Michelin map 212 fold 16.
Baarle-Hertog is a village on Dutch territory. In the 12C the village of Baarle was divided into two. One part fell to the Duke of Brabant (Baarle-Hertog); the other was attached to the Breda seigneury and named **Baarle-Nassau** when Breda became the fiefdom of the Nassau family at the beginning of the 15C.
Each community now has its own town hall, church, police station, school and post office, and the border established in 1831 scrupulously respected community boundaries. However, except for the market square, which is definitely part of the Netherlands, the limits of the two territories get very confused. The Belgian church can be recognised by its characteristic onion dome; but it is less clear to which country the houses belong. Mind you, a close look at the plaques bearing the house numbers will help, since these are marked with the national colours.

VERVIERS Liège

Pop 53 665

Michelin maps 409 K4 or 213 fold 23
Town plan in the current Michelin Red Guide Benelux

Verviers is in the Vesdre Valley near the Hautes Fagnes *(qv)*; it is a large industrial town that once specialised in textiles.
It has few old historical monuments, as it was only recognised as a town in 1651. To the south the upper town consists of a well-to-do district, with expensive houses pleasantly situated amidst a setting of green foliage.
Verviers is the birthplace of the violinist **Henri Vieuxtemps** (1820-1881). Henri Pirenne, author of a *History of Belgium* in seven volumes, was also born here (1862-1935).
Verviers' delicious gingerbread is famous.

Town Hall (D H) – This elegant 18C building is on a hill. It has many windows, highlighted with subtle ornamentation, and a perron *(see Liège)* in front of it.

★ **Museum of Fine Art and Ceramics** (D M1) ⊙ – Established in an old 17C hospice, this contains rich collections of porcelain, Belgian and foreign glazed earthenware (faïence), old Raeren pottery and paintings and sculptures from the 14C to the 19C: Cornelis de Vos's *Portrait of a Child*, with a lace head-dress rather like a halo, and a panel by Pieter Pourbus depicting many characters. Liège engravings from the 16C to the present are kept in a chest of drawers. Upstairs, there is a collection of contemporary (Tytgat, Magritte) and non-representational works.

VERVIERS

Brou (R. du) ... C 4
Crapaurue ... D
Martyr (Pl. du) ... C 28
Saint-Laurent (Pont) ... C 37
Spintay (R.) ... C
Verte (Pl.) ... C

Carmes (R. des) ... D 6
Chêne (Pont du) ... C 9
Coronmeuse (R.) ... D 10
Harmonie (Av. de l') ... C 22
Lions (Pont aux) ... D 25
Maçons (Quai des) ... D 27
Ortmans-Hauzeur (R.) ... D 30
Palais de Justice (Pl. du) ... D 31

Paroisse (R. de la) ... D 33
Raines (R. des) ... D 34
Récollets (Pont des) ... C 36
Sommeville (Pl.) ... D 39
Sommeville (Pont) ... D 40
Théâtre (R. du) ... C 42
Thier-Mère-Dieu (R.) ... D 43
Tribunal (R. du) ... D 45

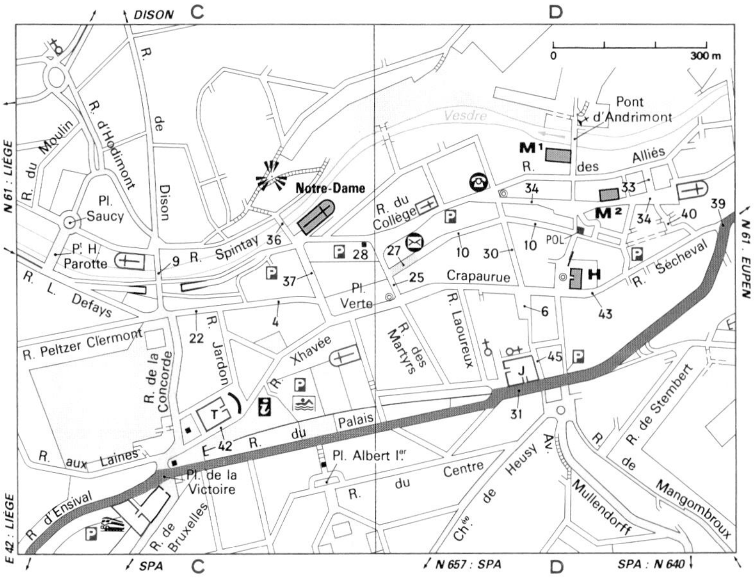

Museum of Archaeology and Folklore (D M2) – This museum occupies an 18C townhouse, containing furniture of various styles (Louis XIII and Charles X), and contains a Dutch suite (in the Grand Salon) and mementoes of the violinist Henri Vieuxtemps; on the first floor, a Liège Louis XV drawing room; on the second floor, objects unearthed in excavations in the region. An interesting **lace*** collection is displayed in drawers, with photographic enlargements making it possible to appreciate the delicacy of the work.

Wool Museum (**Musée de la Laine**) – *8, route Séroule; take Chausée de Heusy* (D) – Three rooms of the State Higher Industrial Institute exhibit tools, engravings and other documents on the subject of working with wool, thread and cloth before 1800.

Church of Our Lady (**Église Notre-Dame**) (C) – This church was rebuilt in the 18C, and has been since the 17C the site of a pilgrimage to the Black Madonna of the Recollects, a statue which, folllowing an earthquake (1692), was discovered in a strangely modified posture.

EXCURSIONS

** **Gileppe Dam** – *13km - 8 miles east on the N 61.*
The dam was built on this confluent of the Vesdre, between 1869 and 1876, and made higher between 1967 and 1971. It is 62m - 203ft high, 320m - 1 049ft long on a rock base of 235m - 771ft; its capacity doubled and rose to 27 million m^3 – 954 million ft^3. It supplies both drinking and industrial water to the region.
There is a splendid **view**** of the wooded valley, the lion dominating the crest of the dam and the reservoir, which covers more than 120ha - 296 acres *(sports activities forbidden on the lake and its shores).*

Limbourg – Pop 5 249. *7.5km - 4.5 miles east on the N 61.*
Perched on a rock above the town of Dolhain, which lies in the Vesdre Valley, Limbourg was the capital of a duchy until the 13C; after the Battle of **Worringen** in 1288, Limbourg was attached to Brabant and shared its fortunes until the end of the 18C. An important stronghold, Limbourg was besieged many times, notably by Louis XIV.
The ramparts, the old Gothic church of St George, the quiet streets and the central paved square, planted with lime trees, make a very picturesque scene.

From Verviers to Val-Dieu – *15km - 9.3 miles north. Leave on the E 42. At Battice, take the N 627, then turn right to Charneux. At Charneux, go towards Thimister and turn left 1km - 0.5 mile after a small bridge.*

Croix de Charneux – This great concrete cross was built on a hill 269m - 882ft high, from which there is a beautiful view of the region. The dome from an observation post (1932-1935) remains nearby; this was the Battice fort that defended Liège.

Continue north to arrive at Val-Dieu.

Val-Dieu Abbey – This is in the charming Berwinne valley. The abbey was founded in about 1216, and has been occupied by the Cistercians since 1844. The vast courtyard of the abbey farm is in front of the guest quarters (1732), to the left of which extend the abbey buildings and church. Rebuilt in 1934, this still has a Gothic chancel. There are beautiful Renaissance stalls inside.

* VEURNE West-Vlaanderen Pop 11 249

Michelin maps 409 B2 or 213 fold 1

Veurne's historical monuments are grouped around a magnificent market square, where the luxury of Flemish decoration is tempered by a slightly solemn dignity typical of Spanish influence. Indeed, it was during the reign of the Archdukes Albert and Isabella, a period of prosperity, that most of the monuments were built. Veurne was a stronghold in the 9C, then it grew larger and enclosed itself within fortifications in the 14C. Vauban modified the fortifications, which were later razed (1783) under Emperor Joseph II. The town was the headquarters of the Belgian army in 1914 during the Battle of the Yser. It was heavily bombed during both World Wars.
A large flower market is held annually on Whit Monday *(see the Calendar of Events at the end of this guide)*; in August, the "Anno 1900" Festival takes place, with events featuring old costumes and demonstrations of crafts from the past.

** **Procession of the Penitents** – *See the Calendar of Events at the end of this guide.* Every year the Sodality Brotherhood, founded in 1637, organises a parade through the town, consisting of floats where groups represent the life and death of Christ, followed by about two hundred penitents dressed in a sombre sackcloth robe with cowls over their heads, barefoot and carrying a heavy cross. Georges Rodenbach evokes them in *Le Carillonneur.* The Sodality Brotherhood also participates in a Stations of the Cross in the streets every Friday evening during Lent, every evening during Holy Week and on Maundy Thursday at midnight.

Procession of the Penitents

★★ MARKET SQUARE (GROTE MARKT) *time: 2 hours*

Veurne's quite vast market square is surrounded by beautiful monuments and old houses surmounted with imposing gables, pediments and cornices, most of them dating from the early 17C.

Town Hall (Stadhuis) (H) – This was built in 1596 (left part) and 1612 (right part) in the Flemish Renaissance style, with a double pedimented façade and an elegant loggia, and also has a little onion-domed turret with a staircase in it.
The walls inside are lined with magnificent **leather★** from Cordoba (reception room) or from Mechelen (council and marriage room).
The school room is embellished with blue velvet from Utrecht.
Note also the 18C furniture, and paintings including a still life attributed to Paul de Vos *(qv)*. The audience chamber of the old law courts, which communicate with the town hall, is also generally open to visitors.

Old Law Courts (Landhuis) – Once a castellany (1618), this building was inspired by the Antwerp town hall. Behind the old law courts stands the **belfry** (1628) (**A**), mainly Gothic in style but with a baroque top section.

St Walburga's Church (St.-Walburgakerk) – *Access via a small street to the right of the old law courts.*
The first church, destroyed by the Norsemen, was rebuilt in the 12C in the Romanesque style. A new building, begun in the 13C with ambitious plans, was never completed. Only the chancel was finished, and it is particularly impressive, being 27m - 88ft in height with numerous flying buttresses; in the 14C the base of a tower (**E**) was built in the neighbouring square. The Romanesque part of the church was renovated in the 20C.
Inside, the proportions are harmonious and impressive. Notice the Flemish Renaissance stalls (1596), a pulpit by H Pulinx (1727) representing the vision of St John in Patmos, 18C organ and rood-screen; 17C Flemish paintings.
The fortress built by Count Baldwin of the Iron Arm was built in the square west of the church. North of the market square, note the group of **five houses**, with beautiful gables adorned with heavy windows with pilasters (**F**).

Noordstraat – In 1906 the Austrian writer Rainer Maria Rilke stayed in the old Inn of the Noble Rose, Die Nobele Rose (1572), which is now a bank. Opposite, a small monument (**B**) has been raised to commemorate the Nieuwpoort lock that flooded the German advance during 1914 *(see Nieuwpoort)*.

Spanish Pavilion (Spaans Paviljoen) – This 15C building on the corner of the market square and Ooststraat was the town hall until 1586. It was the Spanish officers' quarters in the 17C.

Old Meat Hall (Oud Vleeshuis) – This meat hall, built in 1615, has a pretty façade. It is restored and is now houses the town library.

Guard House (Hoge Wacht) – At the far end of the market square, to the south, an arcaded house built in 1636 was once the home of the old guard corps. The side façade looks onto the apple market (Appelmarkt) where St Nicholas's church stands.

St Nicholas's Church (St.-Niklaaskerk) – This is overlooked by a beautiful massive brick **tower** ⊙ dating from the 13C; it contains one of the oldest Flemish clocks, the Bomtje (1379). It is a hall-church inside, with three equally high naves. An interesting triptych (1534) on the main altar represents the Crucifixion; some scholars attribute this to Van Aemstel, brother-in-law to Pieter Coecke, while others believe it to be by Van Orley.

EXCURSIONS

Lo – *15km - 9.3 miles southeast.* This little town still has a gateway and flanking turrets from the 14C ramparts. The beautiful 14C **hall-church**, surmounted with a crocketed spire, was partly reconstructed in 1924. There are interesting 17C and 18C furnishings inside.

From Veurne to Izenberge – *12km - 7.5 miles south.*

Wulveringem – **Beauvoorde Manor-house** (kasteel) ⊙ was built in the 16C and 17C on the site of a derelict castle. It is a charming building with crowstepped gables, surrounded by water and hidden behind the great trees of the park.
The interior was decorated by its last great owner, Arthur Merghelynck *(qv)*: 17C woodwork, rich collections of old furniture and objets d'art (paintings, ceramics).

Izenberge – **Bachten de Kupe Open-Air Museum, "Village of the Past"** ⊙ consists of two sections: the Houtland Farm and the Village Square have been reconstructed with various rural buildings containing old agricultural equipment from the province of West-Vlaanderen. A third section is being set up. There is an interesting Gothic church, with beautiful old woodwork inside; note also the little 17C pilgrimage chapel nearby.

★★ VILLERS-LA-VILLE Brabant — Pop 7 800

Michelin maps 409 G4 or 213 fold 19

The wonderful **ruins** of Villers-la-Ville **Abbey**, north of the town, are the largest in Belgium.

★★ **Abbey ruins** ⊙ – St Bernard laid the foundations of the abbey in 1147. The church and cloisters, however, were not built until 1198 and 1209. Both the Spanish and the Geuzen (Flemish and Dutch lesser nobility who initiated the revolt against Spanish rule) ransacked the convent in the 16C, and it was enclosed within fortifications in 1587. In 1789 the Austrians sacked the buildings, which had been occupied by the French since 1795.
The old 13C **watermill** across from the ruins, on the Thyle, has been turned into a restaurant.

Follow the indicated tour.

Main courtyard – This has a border of 18C buildings now in ruins; the abbey palace is on the right.

Cloisters – These are immense; they were modified in the 14C then the 16C, and have a certain elegant solidity, with the arcades surmounted by an oculus.
The surrounding buildings are typically Cistercian: to the east is the **chapter-house**, altered in the 18C; nearby is the 13C recumbant effigy of Gobert d'Aspremont; above, the dormitories which were altered in the 18C; to the south, the calefactory, the refectory (perpendicular to the cloisters) and the kitchen; to the west, the storerooms with the lay-brothers' dormitories above them, which were sleeping up to 300 by the 13C.

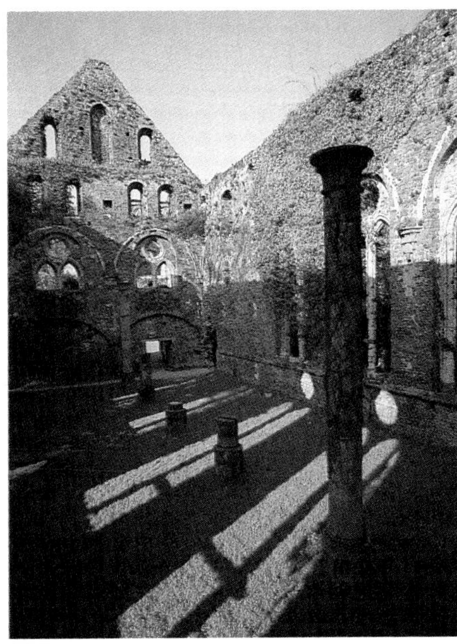

Refectory, Villers-la-Ville Abbey Ruins

Church – Originally built in the early 13C, this collapsed in 1884. It was sober in style, both impregnable-looking and yet moving, as befitted a Cistercian building. The apse and the transept were lit by oculi in the style of the Ile-de-France (Paris region) school, creating an original effect.
Come out of the church by the façade to visit the 13C **brewery**, then go around the east end to go through the 17C and 18C **abbey quarters**.

Church of the Visitation ⊙ – This has two beautiful Brabant **altarpieces** from the 15C and 16C illustrating the Life of the Virgin and the Life of the Infant Jesus; also, a 17C pulpit, a Christ Entombed from 1607, portraits of the Villers abbots and the 17C funerary monuments of the Marbais seigneurs. The eleven modern stained glass windows are signed by F Crickx and G Massinon.

VIRTON Luxembourg

Pop 10 563

Michelin maps 409 J7 or 214 fold 11

Virton, a picturesque locality in the far south of Belgium, is the capital of the **Gaume**, a region where the climate is more temperate than in neighbouring Ardennes. In contrast to the other eastern regions, a romance dialect is spoken in Gaume.

Gaume Museum (Musée gaumais) ⊙ – *Rue d'Arlon.*
This regional museum is in the old Recollects' convent, which has a jack o' the clocks and is devoted to local archaeology and ethnography. There are reconstructed interiors (Gaume kitchen) and craftsmen's workshops on display. Among the collections of industrial folk art, note the pieces of ornamental cast iron (firebacks, andirons) recalling that Gaume was once widely reputed for its forges.

EXCURSIONS

Montauban – *10km - 6.25 miles north. Take the Arlon road, then, in Ethe, a road to the left towards Buzenol.*
South of Buzenol, near the old forges on the edge of the stream, this wooded promontory about 340m - 1 115ft high was occupied in prehistoric times, the Roman period and the Middle Ages. Vestiges of various fortifications can be seen here.

Museum of Roman Sculpture (Musée des Sculptures romaines) – This includes a number of Gallo-Roman bas-reliefs discovered on the site. The most famous one represents the front part of the "vallus", the Celtic harvesting machine described by Pliny the Elder. A lifesize model was reconstructed based on a bas-relief in the Arlon Luxembourg Museum with a man working a "vallus".

From Virton to Torgny – *9km - 5.5 miles south on the Montmédy road. Turn right at Dampicourt.*

Montquintin – The village is perched on a crest more than 300m - 984ft high. Near the church, a farm from 1765 contains the **Museum of Peasant Life** (Musée de la Vie paysanne) ⊙. This represents traditional rural architecture, thereby evoking life in Gaume in the past. Besides the living quarters, it is possible to visit the barn and the stable, with rural vehicles and agricultural equipment in the hayloft.

Return to the Malmédy road, then turn right towards Torgny.

Torgny – This is the southernmost locality in Belgium.
In this flower-bedecked village the houses are built of a slightly golden stone, sometimes rough-rendered, with roman-tiled roofs. They stand in rows on the open slopes of a valley where the particularly temperate climate permits the cultivation of vines.

VOERSTREEK (LES FOURONS) Limburg

Pop 4 172

Michelin maps 409 K3 or 213 fold 23

This is an enclave of Limburg in the province of Liège, a green and fertile region where little rivers like the Voer, the Gulp and the Berwinne cut winding valleys through pleasant wooded hills, grassy pastures and orchards.

St.-Martens-Voeren (Fouron-St-Martin) – Note the church, with its Romanesque tower, and the 18C palace, which has been converted into a cultural centre, Het Veltmanshuis.

St.-Pieters-Voeren (Fouron-St-Pierre) – Near a lake stand the beautiful buildings of the old **Commandery** *(not open to the public)* of the Teutonic Order. This was founded in 1242 and rebuilt in the 17C.

WALCOURT Namur

Pop 15 532

Michelin maps 409 G5 or 214 fold 3

This old, picturesque little town is on the site of a former stronghold.
Each year *(see the Calendar of Events at the end of this guide)* there is a procession in honour of Our Lady of Walcourt, which completes an entire circuit of the town's perimeter in what is called the **"Grand Tour"**. It is accompanied by a **"military march"** *(see Charleroi)* in which the escort dress as Napoleonic soldiers or zouaves and play fifes and drums.
In the middle of the day, a theatre sketch (Jeu scénique du Jardinet) is enacted around a birch tree, commemorating the miracle of the statue of the Virgin, which is said to have fled the basilica when it burned down in the 13C and to have been later found in a tree.

★ **St Maternus's Basilica (Basilique St-Materne)** – This is at the top of a hill, on the location of a Mosan Romanesque building of which the lower section of the avant-corps and the Gothic church still remain; the church was built between the early 13C and the early 16C.
It has an amusing 17C bell tower with an onion dome (rebuilt in 1926).
The plain **interior**, consisting of five naves in grey stone and brick, is richly furnished. The remarkable white stone **rood-screen★** (1531) is said to have been donated by Emperor Charles V; the structure is Gothic but the Renaissance decoration abounds with statues, medallions and ornamental foliage. A 16C calvary is at the top.
The very simple stalls dating from the 16C have misericords carved with satirical motifs. The statue of Our Lady of Walcourt is in the north transept arm. This 10C Virgin in Majesty is one of the oldest in Belgium. The statue is in wood covered with silver plates.

★ **Treasury** ⊙ – This is in the presbytery and includes valuable works of art: a 15C monstrance, a 14C silver Virgin, a little 13C turret-reliquary, and most particularly a 13C reliquary-cross with a delicate decoration typical of the style of the famous goldsmith Hugo d'Oignies *(qv)*.

★ WATERLOO Brabant

Pop 26 870

Michelin maps 409 G3 or 213 fold 18

Thou fatal Waterloo.
Millions of tongues record thee, and anew
Their children's lips shall echo them, and say -
"Here, where the sword united nations drew,
Our countrymen were warring on that day!"
And this is much, and all which will not pass away.
(Lord Byron)

It was at Waterloo on 18 June 1815 that the Allied Anglo-Dutch forces, under the command of the Duke of Wellington, and the Prussians, under Gebhard Leberecht von Blücher, put an end to the Empire-building of Napoleon, thereby turning over a new page in European history.

The battle – Wellington's and Blücher's armies were marching on France, spearheading the attempt by the allied coalition (Great Britain, Prussia, Austria, Russia) to put a stop to Napoleonic domination of Europe. Napoleon advanced to meet them with the cunning scheme of attempting to crush each army separately, before they had time to join forces. On 14 June Napoleon stopped at Beaumont *(qv)*. Two days later, he won a victory against Blücher at **Ligny** *(northeast of Charleroi)*, a victory which nonetheless cost him dearly in lives of men and failed to rout the Prussian army. Napoleon's Maréchal Ney had meanwhile managed to do no more than hold the British at bay in Quatre-Bras.

Butte du Lion

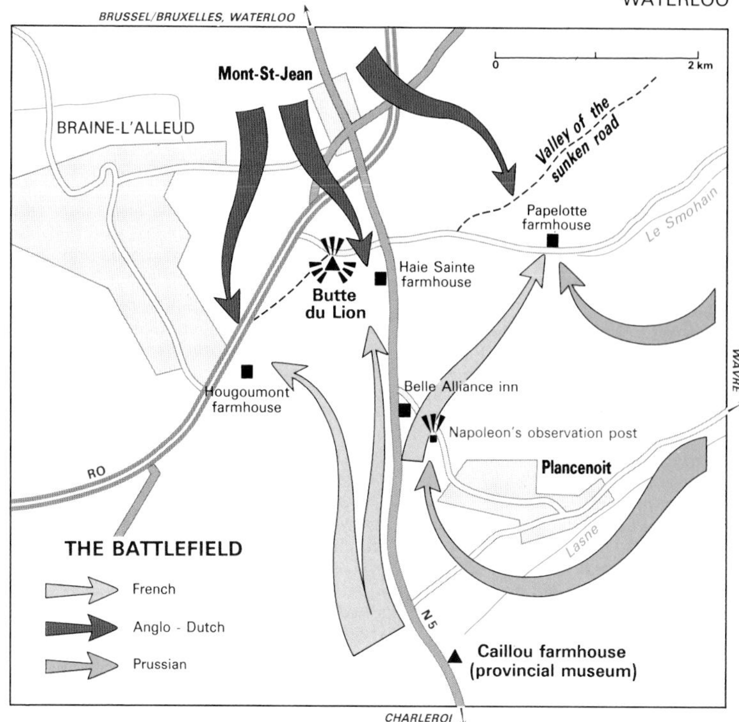

On 17 June Napoleon left to meet Wellington. He arrived on the Mont St-Jean plain during the night and established his headquarters at the **Caillou farmhouse**. Wellington, whose troops were encamped near Mont St-Jean, had set up his headquarters at **Waterloo**.

On 18 June bad weather delayed the arrival of some of the French troops, so the battle did not begin until almost noon, a delay which was to be vital to the final outcome of the battle, as it would give the Prussian troops time to rejoin their allies at Waterloo.

While the French artillery and Napoleon's observation post were positioned on top of the hill by **Belle Alliance inn**, British and French troops engaged each other until nightfall in bloody combat by the **Hougoumont farmhouse**. This was one of three farmhouses which were key positions to be won by any army trying to gain possession of the Mont St-Jean. After hours of fierce skirmishing, the French troops gave up the assault and fell back. The focus of the battlefield then shifted to the **Haie Sainte farmhouse**, which was eventually won by the French after a vicious struggle, and then on to the **Papelotte farmhouse**. At about 16.00, beneath a leaden sky, French troops plunged into the famous **valley of the sunken road** ("chemin creux"), in which sweeping French calvary charges led by Ney and General Kellermann were savagely battered by British fire, but nonetheless managed to inflict heavy losses on Wellington's troops, who were by now in urgent need of reinforcement from their Prussian allies.

Napoleon was waiting for reinforcements of 30 000 men from Maréchal de Grouchy, expected to arrive from Wavre to the east. Blücher, however, having regrouped his troops and evaded Grouchy, circumvented the French army's right flank to join the English army; in so doing, the Prussian front guard seized the village of **Plancenoit** and began to put pressure on Napoleon's southeast flank.

Surrounded, Napoleon finally sent his Imperial Guard to support Ney and engage with the British troops. The result was utter carnage in the valley, as Wellington had had time to reorganise his defence strategy to include the Prussian reinforcements, and the allied forces' fire shattered the closely packed ranks of Napoleon's Imperial Guard. As night fell over the battlefield, littered with the bodies of 49 000 men, the defeated French troops were running in disorderly retreat, completely routed despite Ney's efforts. Wellington joined Blücher at the **Belle Alliance inn** that evening shortly after the victory. Four days later Napoleon abdicated for the second and final time.

Every five years a historical re-enactment of the Battle of Waterloo takes place, with more than 2 000 soldiers participating.

THE BATTLEFIELD

Greatly changed since 1815 (a motorway now crosses it), the plain is nevertheless dotted with historical buildings and commemorative monuments.

Butte du Lion ⊙ – This 45m - 147ft high mound was constructed in 1826 by the kingdom of the Netherlands, on the spot where the Prince of Orange was wounded fighting the Imperial Guard. A cast-iron lion weighing 26 tons is at the top. An erroneous legend says that this was made with the metal of cannon gathered from the battlefield. There is a good view of the site from the top. At the foot of the mound, to the south, the famous battle valley ("chemin creux") has been largely levelled out, as the surrounding earth was taken to build the mound.

Visitor Centre – At the foot of the Butte du Lion this centre offers visitors two complementary presentations on the Battle of Waterloo. A film takes the spectator into the heart of events on 18 June 1815, and a model 10m^2 - 107ft^2 situates the strategic points of the battle and depicts its main stages.

Waxworks Museum (Musée de Cires) – This is a little museum near the mound in which a few waxwork figures represent Napoleon's last council with his staff at Caillou farmhouse.

Grand Panorama of the Battle of Waterloo – This enormous circular rotunda built in 1912 at the foot of the mound houses a grand panoramic painting 110m - 360ft in circumference, conceived by the French painter Dumoulin from 1913-1914. It represents the battle at the moment when Ney sent his calvary into the "chemin creux" valley.

Grand panorama paintings were one of the most popular forms of mass entertainment in the 19C, before the advent of photography and the motion picture. They were usually exhibited in purpose-built rotundas and were often on huge fully cylindrical canvases which entirely surrounded the viewer, who stood on a central viewing platform. The panorama painting technique is related to the exuberant mastery of baroque and the technique of trompe-l'oeil and was originally the idea of Robert Barker, an Irishman. By portraying vast panoramas in minute detail the painting enabled the public to glimpse foreign shores with an immediacy never before possible. Panorama paintings were generally executed by teams of artists, often drawing on specialised skills. Their most common subject matter tended to be military, more particularly the glorification of warfare. Preliminary sketches were rescaled onto the enormous canvas using a grid, but this did not entirely eliminate distortions of perspective caused by the curve of the cylindrical canvas. It took about a year to complete a painting, which was then exhibited in its rotunda with the area between it and the viewing platform converted into an elaborate extension of the painting's foreground by the dispersal of relevant objects all over it (known as a faux-terrain) to increase the effect of the illusion. Sadly, the popularity of the grand panorama diminished as that of the cinema grew, and many of the paintings were lost when the rotundas that housed them were demolished or put to other uses. There are now only nine left in western Europe (Austria: Salzburg, Innsbruck; Belgium: Waterloo, Brussels; Germany: Munich, Bad Frankenhausen; Switzerland: Einsiedelin, Thun, Lucerne).

Caillou Provincial Museum – This is located south of the battlefield. The Caillou farmhouse was Napoleon's headquarters on the eve of the combat. The room where he spent the night of 17-18 June 1815 has been re-constructed, and a few of his belongings are on display.

THE TOWN

Wellington Museum – The inn where Wellington set up his headquarters has been converted into a museum. In a series of little rooms, including Wellington's bedroom, there are engravings, arms, documents and mementoes evoking the history of Europe in 1815.
A large modern room is devoted to the Battle of Waterloo; the description of the battle can be read here in several languages.

St Joseph's Church (Église St-Joseph) – This church opposite the museum has a small royal chapel (1687) topped with a dome; inside, flagstones bear the names of the English and Dutch officers and soldiers who fell at Waterloo.

Museums of military history can be found at Arlon, Bastogne, Brussels, Mons, Tournai and Waterloo.
There are military cemeteries or memorials at Bastogne, Ieper, Mechelen (Fort Breendonk), Poperinge and Waterloo.

WAVRE Brabant

Pop 27 613

Michelin maps 409 G3 or 213 fold 19

Wavre (pronounced "whaavre") lies amidst the hills in the Dijle Valley and is an important communications node for several roads. The little statue of Maca, a laughing boy who symbolises the lighthearted spirit of the inhabitants, stands in an old church in front of the town hall.

Walibi – *2km - 1.25 miles southwest on the N 238 towards Ottignies.*
This huge 50ha - 123 acre recreation park, opened in 1975, is the most popular in the region. It offers a multitude of activities (dizzying Tornado, 50m-164ft high Ferris wheel, Ali Baba's palace) and entertainment shows (trained dolphins, etc.) In 1987 the vast tropical-atmosphere swimming pool complex called **Aqualibi** was inaugurated.

★ YPRES See IEPER

ZEEBRUGGE West-Vlaanderen

Michelin maps 409 C1 or 213 fold 3
Town plan in the current Michelin Red Guide Benelux

Zeebrugge (Bruges-sur-Mer to French-speakers) is the only Belgian deep-water coastal port. Inaugurated in 1907, it is linked to Bruges by the Baudouin Canal. It is also a pleasant seaside resort with a small marina.
Zeebrugge was a base for German submarines during the First World War. It was made famous by the English operation here during the night of 22-23 April 1918 which blocked the canal and made the port unusable.

A multi-purpose port – The outer harbour is accessible to very large vessels. As in Ostend, it has regular passenger services to England (car-ferries to Dover, Felixstowe and Hull). It is also a container and roll-on/roll-off port, in liaison with England, Norway, Australia, North America, New Zealand and West and South Africa, and functions as a stop-over port for cruise liners and as a marina. Last but not least, it is Belgium's foremost-ranking fishing port, both in terms of the quantity of fish caught and its value.
The outer harbour communicates via a lock with the **inner harbour** equipped with three docks between the Baudouin Canal and the Leopold and Schipdonk penstocks.

Port extension – New installations intended to enlarge the outer harbour by a further width of about 3km - 1.75 are under construction; in particular to the east, an arrivals terminal and a warehouse area for Algerian natural gas are being built. The construction of the new "West Pier" is being followed by the creation of two docks for container ships and roll-on/roll-off.
The new inner harbour, a part of which has been finished since 1984, covers an area of 1 300ha - 3 212 acres.
The industrial area of the port includes terminals to handle fruit, vegetables, cars, wood, coal, iron, etc.

SIGHT

Fishing port **(Vissershaven)** – In front of this there is a marina. It is fun to watch the fishing boats, a picturesque and colourful sight, and to go to the "vismijn" at the **fresh fish auction** ⏲.

EXCURSIONS

Lissewege – *4km - 2.5 miles on ② on the map.*
The charming village of Lissewege near the Baudouin Canal is overlooked by the brick **tower** of its church. Built in the 13C and rebuilt in the 16C to the 17C, the church has preserved its original charm (Tournai chancel, triforium).
All that remains of the **Ter Doest** *(1km - 0.5 miles south of Lissewege)*, a dependent of Coxyde's Dunes Abbey, are the chapel, a turreted farmhouse (part of which has been turned into a restaurant) and the vast and beautiful **abbey church barn★** (13C), decorated with Gothic brick mouldings and surmounted by wonderful oak timberwork.

★ ZOUTLEEUW Brabant

Pop 7 672

Michelin maps 409 I3 or 213 fold 21

This quiet and picturesque little Flemish village was once a stronghold protected by powerful walls (14C and 17C), in addition to being a clothmaking centre. It clusters around an interesting church.
Zoutleeuw was pillaged in 1678 by Louis XIV's troops; in the 18C its fortifications were demolished. The town has since lived very much on its past.

★★ ST LEONARD'S CHURCH (ST.-LEONARDUSKERK) ⏲ *time: 45min*

This is a beautiful building that was constructed over several centuries: the east end was built in the 13C, encircled by a colonnaded passageway, and so was the north arm of the transept; the nave and the south arm of the transept were built in the 14C.
In the 15C, Mathieu de Layens built the charming Late Gothic sacristy opposite the town hall. The 16C bell tower, rebuilt in 1926, has a 39-chime carillon.
The interior escaped the 16C iconoclasts and is a real **museum★★** of religious art. A "marianum" (1) a double-sided statue of the Virgin, dating from 1530 is suspended in the central nave.
The wooden altarpiece of St Anne (2) in the second chapel of the **south side aisle** has painted panels (1565); opposite, there is a 16C gilded wooden triptych, also with painted panels, depicting the Glorification of the Holy Cross (3). In the third chapel, there is a triptych painted by Pieter Aertsen in 1575; the medallions represent the Seven Sorrows of the Virgin (4). An interesting 11C Romanesque Christ (5) surmounts the Sacristy door.
The **south arm of the transept** has the most beautiful altarpiece (6) sculpted by the Brussels artist Arnould de Maeler in about 1478, a work recounting the life of St Leonard: an older statue of the saint (1300) has been placed in the centre. The old St Leonard's Chapel (7), at the far end of the transept arm, contains a beautiful collection of 16C and 17C statues as well as an interesting **treasury**: gold- and silver-work, coppersmith's work, liturgical ornaments.

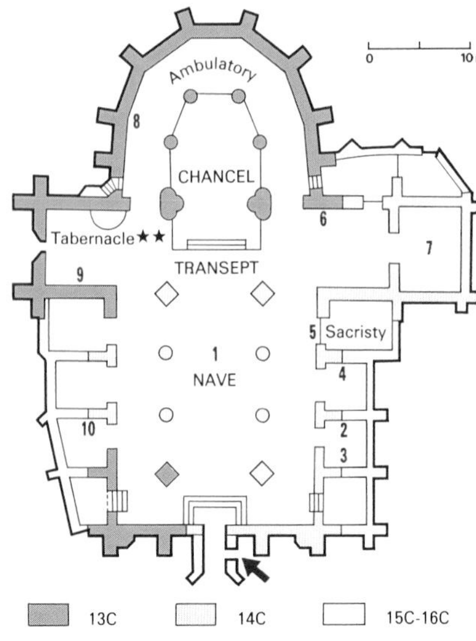

An exceptional series of 12C-16C statues runs along the **ambulatory**. There is also a superb six-armed brass paschal chandelier (**8**) on display, executed by Renier de Tirlemont in 1483; on top of this there is a calvary with figures of very moving plainness.
The magnificent Avesne stone **tabernacle★★** which is the pride of Zoutleeuw is in the **north arm of the transept**.
This masterpiece was completed in 1551 by the Antwerp native Cornelis Floris de Vriendt. Standing 18m - 59ft and 9 tiers high, it is decorated with groups consisting of 200 statues which are remarkably lifelike; both in their expressions and in the spontaneity of their poses. While their picturesque craftsmanship seems rather Gothic, the decoration and the composition are of Italian influence. There are scenes of the sacrifices from the Old Testament at the base; above that, scenes of earthly paradise; then, above the tabernacle alcove, the Last Supper and episodes from the Old Testament. The upper tiers, superposed in a pyramid, are decorated with a multitude of characters (the Virtues, Church Fathers); the Virgin is at the top.
Frans Floris, brother of Cornelis, is taken to be the creator of the triptych (**9**) of the Baptism of Christ, opposite the tabernacle.
Notice the statues in the **north side aisle** chapels and, in the Lady Chapel, painted medallions representing the Seven Joys of the Virgin (**10**) by Pieter Aertsen (1554).

ADDITIONAL SIGHT

Town Hall (Stadhuis) – This charming Renaissance building was constructed under Emperor Charles V (1530) following plans attributed to Mechelen-born Rombout Keldermans; there is an elaborate perron at the front, the façade is surmounted by a crowstepped gable and pierced by tall basket-handle windows. The town hall houses the tourist office.
The **drapers' hall** to the right, with a brick façade striped with bands of white stone, dates from the 14C.

Erasmus's Study at Anderlecht

Grand Duchy of Luxembourg

Vianden Castle

BERDORF

Pop 860

Michelin maps 409 M6 or 215 fold 3 – Local map see LUXEMBOURG'S "PETITE SUISSE"

This is a good departure point for excursions, situated at the heart of Luxembourg's so-called "Petite Suisse" (Mini-Switzerland) region, on a plateau with sides dropping steeply down to form crests or "escarpments" *(qv)* overlooking the Sûre Valley and the Mullerthal. A rock-climbing school comes here regularly to practise.

In the church, the high altar rests on a sculpted Romanesque block of stone on which four divinities are represented: Minerva, Juno, Apollo and Hercules.

RAMBLES

There are many footpaths which leave from Berdorf. They are marked on a noticeboard in the leisure centre next to the miniature golf course.

Promenade B – This path *(see also Luxembourg's "Petite Suisse")* which runs along the edge of the "escarpment" to the northwest of Berdorf before dropping down to Grundhof, is particularly spectacular along this stretch. It links several viewpoints that can also be reached by road from Berdorf:

★★ **Devil's Island** (l'Ile du Diable) – *Leave the Mullerthal road on the left and carry on towards the cemetery. Once past this, take the footpath on the left running along the right side of the campsite.*

Stroll through the pleasant pine forests to reach *(5min)* the end of the "escarpment": there are **magnificent views** of the Mullerthal and in the background the wooded, uncultivated countryside around Beaufort.

★ **The Seven Gorges** (Sieweschluff) – *Take the Hammhof (Hamm farmhouse) road north, then turn left.*

Follow the F 2 Promenade, then the footpath leading to the plateau *(10min)*; there is a marvellous **view** across the Sûre Valley and its wooded surroundings.

★ **Kasselt** – North of the Seven Gorges, this promontory 353m - 1 158ft in altitude affords an extensive **view** of the Sûre Valley, which forms a meander here at the point where its confluent the Ernz Noire flows into the Sûre, and of the village of Grundhof.

★ **Werschrumschluff** – *2km - 1.25 miles south on the Mullerthal road.*

A rock overhanging the road to the left is called the **pulpit rock** (Predigstuhl). From here it is possible to set off and explore the **Werschrumschluff**★, an immense gorge cut between two steep, rocky walls.

★ CLERVAUX

Pop 1 680

Michelin maps 409 L5 or 215 fold 10

Clervaux is an important tourist centre, built in a remarkable **setting**★★ at the heart of the thickly wooded Oesling region *(qv)*. The slate roofs cluster together on a promontory formed by the River Clerve, around a feudal castle and the parish church, which was built in 1910 in the Rhenish Romanesque style. St Maurice's Abbey, on the hill to the west, overlooks the valley, while its roofs disappear from view amidst the trees.

Clervaux is part of the Germano-Luxembourg nature reserve *(qv)*.

★★ **Viewpoints** – On the road coming from Luxembourg, there are two viewpoints giving good overall views of the town's setting.

SIGHTS

★ **Castle** ⊙ – This is a 12C fortress which was modified in the 17C with some adjoining towers added to it: to the south the Burgundy Tower surmounted by a small bell tower, and to the right the rather squat Brandenburg Tower.

In the restored Renaissance wing *(to the north)* there is an **exhibition of models**★ of the various manor-houses and fortresses in the Grand Duchy of Luxembourg.

On the second floor there is an exhibition of photography by Edward Steichen, the American photographer of Luxembourg origin: **The Family of Man**.

Mementoes of the Battle of the Bulge *(see Belgium: Bastogne)* are on display in the south wing.

Abbey of St Maurice and St Maur – This was founded in 1909 by Benedictines from Solesmes, a French abbey in the Sarthe Valley. It is a vast architectural unit in brown schist, rebuilt in 1945.

The **abbey church**, rebuilt in a style rather different from the original Rhenish church, has a beautiful hexagonal tower in the Burgundy Romanesque style in front of it, reminiscent of the "Holy Water" (Eau Bénite) bell tower of old Cluny Abbey.

The interior, with the austerity typical of Romanesque buildings, is lit by means of sparkling stained glass windows. Near the entrance, on the left, there is a 15C Pièta altarpiece with canopies in very delicate openwork. The high altar, by French sculptor Kaeppelin, is adorned with four winged subjects. There are two finely worked 16C Rhenish altarpieces, still essentially Gothic in style, in the arms of the transept, opposite one another.

An exhibition in the crypt explains 20C monastic life.

EXCURSIONS

Clerve Valley – *11km - 6.75 miles south as far as Wilwerwiltz.*
The river which gave Clervaux its name flows through this pleasant valley of meadows at the foot of wooded slopes.

From Clervaux to Troisvierges via Hachiville – *23km - 14.25 miles northwest on the N 18, the N 12 and then a road on the left.*

Hachiville – Near the Belgian-Luxembourg border, Hachiville is a village typical of the Oesling region *(qv).*
In the parish church there is an early 16C sculpted Brabant style **altarpiece**. This represents the joys and sorrows of the Virgin in a series of attractive compositions.
The **chapel-hermitage** built near a spring in the woods 2km - 1.25 miles northwest has been a site of pilgrimage to the Virgin for 500 years.

From Hachiville return to the N 12 and take this road to Troisvierges.

Troisvierges – Pop 1 920. This town is located on a plateau at an altitude of over 400m - 1 312ft. The River Woltz (which becomes the Clerve at Clervaux) flows right through the town. Troisvierges is overlooked by its onion-domed **church**, built by the Recollects in the 17C.
The interior is decorated with beautiful baroque furniture: pulpit, confessionals. The nave is separated from the chancel by two monumental altars. Niches in the left altarpiece contain statues of the three Virgins – Hope, Faith and Charity – which are venerated by pilgrims. *The Raising of the Cross* on the high altar is by the Rubens school.

DIEKIRCH

Pop 5 510

Michelin maps 409 L6 or 215 fold 3

Diekirch, a commercial and cultural centre, is spread along the lower Sûre Valley, on the borders of the Gutland and Oesling regions *(qv).* The Herrenberg (at a height of 394m - 1 292ft) overlooking the town marks the first foothills of the Oesling.
Diekirch is well-known for its brewery, which produces the famous Diekirch beer This is also a pleasant tourist centre with a pedestrian zone. The banks of the Sûre have been turned into a park. As far as the area around Diekirch is concerned, there are many signposted footpaths covering a total distance of 60km - 37 miles *(leaflet available from the tourist office – syndicat d'initiative).*

SIGHTS

Museum ⏲ – *In Place Guillaume, where the decanal church stands.*
This little museum is behind the kiosk. It houses in particular 3C **Roman mosaics** found during work on the Esplanade from 1926 to 1950.
The most remarkable of these ornate pavements (3.5m - 11ft by 4.75m - 15ft) depicts at its centre a Medusa's head with two faces.

St Laurence's Church (**Église St-Laurent**) ⏲ – *Access on foot from the decanal church; go via the Esplanade, then take the fourth street on the right.*
This little church is hidden behind a circlet of houses in the old district of the town. It has been a religious site since the 5C.
The Romanesque nave on the right was built over a Romanesque building. The nave on the left is Gothic, and contains frescoes dating from the 15C (above the altar) and the 16C (in the chancel).
About thirty sarcophagi were found beneath the church in 1961 during excavations; most of them are Merovingian.

EXCURSIONS

Devil's Altar (**Deiwelselter**) – *2km - 1.25 miles south on the Larochette road.*
After a hairpin bend and before the Gilsdorf road, take the Promenade D footpath on the right. It leads through the woods to this little monument of stones apparently from an ancient dolmen.
Outside the woods, there are beautiful views of the town.

Brandenbourg – *9km - 5.5 miles on the Reisdorf road to the east, and then the first left.*
This charming village is in the valley of the Blees, a tributary of the Sûre, and is overlooked by the ruins of a 12C castle on the top of a hill.
A small rural museum has been set up in the **Al Branebuurg House** ⏲; it contains literature on the region and a collection of everyday objects of olden days.

★ ECHTERNACH

Pop 4 360

Michelin maps 409 M6 or 215 fold 3 – Local map see LUXEMBOURG'S "PETITE SUISSE"

Located in the lower Sûre Valley, Echternach is a well-known tourist centre and the capital of the part of Luxembourg known as the "Petite Suisse" (Mini-Switzerland). Its overriding feature is the abbey founded in 698 by **St Willibrord**. This Anglo-Saxon, ordained Archbishop of Frisons by the Pope, lived in Utrecht in the Netherlands, before retiring to Echternach, where he died in 739. To the south, the town has preserved a few towers from the 13C ramparts (Rue des Remparts, near the hospice).

Echternach is renowned for its dancing procession which dates back to the late Middle Ages in honour of St Willibrord, healer of St Vitus' Dance (chorea). The dancers cross the town in leaps and bounds, linked to each other by white handkerchiefs, dancing to the tune of a polka march.

At the beginning of the summer, during the Echternach International Festival, musical events take place in the basilica or in the Church of St Peter and St Paul.

Market Square

★ **Market Square** (**Place du Marché**) – This is an attractive old square; it is ringed by traditional houses with flower-bedecked balconies. On one of the sides of the square stands the old law courts or **Denzelt**, a charming 15C building with arcades and corner turrets.

★ **Abbey** – This Benedictine monastery, a source of great cultural influence during the Middle Ages owing to its famous scriptorium, was abandoned in 1797. The abbey buildings (1727-1731), arranged in a quadrilateral and encircled by outbuildings, make a majestic and harmonious sight with the basilica next to them.

St Willibrord's Basilica was built in the 11C on the site of a Carolingian church, of which the crypt still exists, and then enlarged in the 13C. It was destroyed in December 1944, but its original charm has been restored to it during reconstruction. There is a neo-Gothic marble tomb in the crypt; the stone sarcophagus beneath it contains the relics of St Willibrord.

Abbey Museum ⏲ – This evokes Echternach's rich past since Roman days, in particular it illustrates the role of the abbey scriptorium, where the monks executed the most beautiful illuminated manuscripts from the 9C to the 11C. An exhibition shows the different phases in the elaboration of these manuscripts and displays some reproductions. The most famous was the "Code Aureus", a celebrated 11C Echternach gold gospel-book, now in the German National Museum in Nuremberg.

A pretty park north of the abbey extends as far as the Sûre, on the banks of which stands a graceful Louis XV style pavilion.

Roman villa – *1km - 0.5 mile on the E 29, towards Luxembourg. Upon leaving Echternach, turn left into a large car park.*

The vestiges of a large Roman villa dating from 1C can be seen here at the edge of the town. The villa was originally symmetrical, but was then enlarged and modified over the course of the following three centuries.

EXCURSION

★★ **Wolf Gorge** (**Wolfschlucht**) – *45min Rtn on foot. Take the car along Rue André Duscher from the Place du Marché and turn right towards Troosknepchen after the cemetery. The footpath leaves from Rue Emersinde near the bus station.*

The path follows Promenade B. It goes up to the pavilion of the **Troosknepchen viewpoint**: beautiful **views**★ of Echternach in the valley below. Continue along Promenade B, through a beech forest to Wolf Gorge. A great pointed rock is to the left of the entrance is known as Cleopatra's Needle. A staircase crosses from one side to the other of this dark, impressive gorge cutting between two jagged, sheer rock walls 50m - 164ft high. To leave the gorge, a staircase to the right leads to the **Bildscheslay viewpoint** from which there is a pretty view of the Sûre flowing through rich green countryside.

★ EISCH VALLEY

Michelin maps 409 K6-L6 or 215 folds 4 and 12

The River Eisch flows in sinuous meanders through meadows, forests and between high wooded walls of rock. The road runs along the river and enables visitors to discover the six remaining **castles** in this valley, also known as the Valley of the Seven Castles. A footpath runs through the valley as well, from Koerich to Mersch.

FROM KOERICH TO MERSCH

26km - 16 miles – allow 1 hour 30min

Koerich – Pop 1 560. The **church** is on a hill and has beautiful baroque furnishings, especially in the chancel. The ruins of a feudal **castle**, modified during the Renaissance (note the fireplace), stand near the river.

Septfontaines – Pop 570. This is a picturesque village clinging to the slopes which drop down towards the River Eisch. It is overlooked by the ruins of the **castle** (13C-15C).
The **church** contains an interesting Entombment. There are several elegantly carved baroque stelae forming a Stations of the Cross in the **cemetery** around the church *(illustration right)*. At the foot of the castle play the seven fountains, which gave their name to the village.

A Station of the Cross, Septfontaines

Ansembourg – This little town has two **castles**; on the hillside, a 12C castle modified in the 16C and 18C, and in the valley, a 17C palace, once the residence of a local forge owner, with a turreted doorway and beautiful 18C gardens.

Hollenfels Castle can be seen a little further on, on top of a ridge. It was enlarged in the 18C around a 13C keep. It now houses a Youth Hostel.

Hunnebour – *After the bridge over the Eisch, take the road on the right.*
At the foot of a high rocky bank, Hunnebour is a spring in a restful shady **setting★**.

Mersch – Pop 5 710. The feudal **castle**, extensively restored, is a tall square building in front of which there is a doorway with small turrets. Nearby is onion-domed **St Michael's Tower**, the only remnant of a church which has disappeared.

ESCH-SUR-ALZETTE

Pop 23 890

Michelin maps 409 K7 or 215 fold 14
Town plan in the current Michelin Red Guide Benelux

Esch-sur-Alzette, the Grand Duchy of Luxembourg's second city, is also the country's great iron and steel production centre. Its principal activity is steel manufacture, owing to the large ARBED factory. This cosmopolitan city – more than 30% of the inhabitants are foreigners – also plays an important role in the world of commerce.

City park – *Take the Dudelange road, then the first road on the right after the tunnel.* This vast flower-bedecked park of 57ha - 140 acres is laid out in tiers on a hill overlooking the town to the east of the station. There is a small game reserve at the top (402m - 1 318ft in altitude) at the **Galgenberg** open-air centre.

Resistance Museum ⌚ – *Place du Brill.* This little museum was built in 1956, at the heart of the city, to commemorate the heroism of the Luxembourg resistance to the occupying forces (1940-1944): the work in the mines and factories, the general strike of 1942, the battle of the underground forces and the deportations are evoked by bas-reliefs, frescoes, statues and documents.

EXCURSION

Rumelange – Pop 3 450. *6km - 3.75 miles. Take the Dudelange road, then turn right.* This mining community near the French border has an interesting **National Museum of Mining** ⌚. Part of the iron mines worked until 1958 in the hill crossed by the border is open to the public. The tour of 900m - 0.5 mile of galleries (temperature: 12°C - 53°F), part of which is by a small train, outlines the various extraction operations and the development of techniques and materials used since the opening of the mine.

★ LAROCHETTE

Pop 1 420

Michelin maps 409 L6 or 215 fold 4

Larochette is a pleasant holiday location in the Ernz Blanche Valley, which is dominated by Luxembourg's high rocky cliff walls of sandstone, on one of which there are two ruined castles.

Castles ⌚ – *Access via the Nommern road.*
The ruins of two buildings can be seen on the plateau; the 14C Gothic Créhange Castle, overlooking the town, and nearer at hand, the older Hombourg Castle, above the Mersch road.

EXCURSION

Round tour of 12km - 7.5 miles - *Allow 30min. Take the Nommern direction.*

Emerge from the pine forests and notice the nature reserve on the left. On the heathland amidst the broom there is the **Champignon** (Mushroom) rock, about 150m - 492ft from the road, a fine block of Luxembourg sandstone. There are good views of the locality from the road down to **Nommern** (Pop 770).

At Nommern, take the Larochette road.

The motoring-pedestrian tour route *(circuit auto-pédestre)* no 2 begins at a left-hand bend. It leads visitors to the magnificent crags called the **Nommerlayen★** in the forest; these are walls of sandstone in the most varied of forms scattered among the trees.

Return to Larochette on the N 8.

★★ LUXEMBOURG

Pop 74 400

Michelin maps 409 L7 or 215 fold 5

The initial impact of Luxembourg is striking, built as it is on a plateau crisscrossed by gullies, which are spanned by innumerable bridges. The city can come across as an urban, rural or military settlement, depending on the angle from which it is approached. Its squares, with their elegant façades painted in pastel colours, could be the backdrop for a theatre production. Its numerous viewpoints disclose vistas of lush green valleys. For all its apparent tranquillity, there is behind the scenes all the liveliness and activity to be expected of a capital city, money market and the headquarters for various European institutions. Luxembourg is also the headquarters for RTL, one of the largest broadcasting companies in Europe.

★★ **Magnificent setting** – The city and fortifications are perched on top of a sandstone outcrop with steeply sloping sides, skirted by two rivers, the Alzette and the Pétrusse. The old town is separated from the modern one to the south by the deep gash known as the Pétrusse gorge, which is spanned by bridges such as the well-known **Adolphe Bridge** (1899-1903) (**F**), built in a bold, impressive style. To the north, it is linked to the Kirchberg plateau by the red-painted **Grand Duchess Charlotte Bridge** (1964) (**DY**) spanning the Alzette. There are three districts situated in the valleys; Grund, Clausen and Pfaffenthal. Marvellous **views** of the city in all its varied guises can be enjoyed from around every bend along the cliff roads.
In high season the site is lit up at night, which shows it off to full advantage.

Festivals – The traditional folk festival of "l'Emais'chen", when young lovers exchange terracotta ware sold especially for the occasion, takes place every year where the fishmarket used to be (Place du Marché). From the end of August onwards there is the big Luxembourg fair and market (Schueberfouer/Schobermesse), which dates back to 1340.

HISTORICAL NOTES

The history of the city is closely connected with that of the country itself.
In Roman times, Luxembourg was situated at the intersection of two Roman roads, one going from Trier to Rheims via Arlon (now the Grand-Rue), and the other linking Metz to Aachen. The Bock outcrop had already been fortified. In the 10C, Count Sigefroi (from the Moselle), who gave himself the title Count of Luxembourg, built a castle near the upper town, on the Bock. A first defensive wall was erected around the upper town, then reinforced with a second the following century.
In the 12C the city, along with the Count of Luxembourg, came under the rule of Henry V the Blind ("l'Aveugle"), Count of Namur. His grandson **Henry VII** became **Emperor of Germany** in 1308. The House of Luxembourg held the imperial throne until 1437. In 1346 the son of Emperor Henry VII, **John the Blind**, King of Bohemia and Count of Luxembourg, was killed in the French ranks at the Battle of Crécy. In the 14C a third enclosure was built around the upper town, while the lower towns were also fortified.

Coveted territory – In the 15C, Luxembourg fell into the hands of the House of Burgundy. It next fell to Emperor Charles V (in 1555) who fortified the city, then to Philip II.
The city came under French rule in 1684, after being skilfully besieged by **Vauban**, who went on to strengthen its fortifications. Having fallen once more into the hands of the Spaniards in 1698, it was occupied by the French again in 1701, who were in turn replaced by the Austrians from 1715 to 1795. In spite of heavy reinforcement of its fortifications and the digging of casemates, the city yielded to Carnot in 1795 and was administered as part of the Département des Forêts until 1814. After the defeat of Napoleon, the Duchy was set up as a **Grand Duchy** by the Treaty of Vienna, administratively dependent on the German Confederation but belonging to the house of Orange-Nassau and governed by William I, King of the Netherlands. As a result, the city was occupied by a Prussian garrison which did not leave Luxembourg until 1867. Once the country's neutrality had been declared in the Treaty of London, the three rings of fortifications were dismantled.
Despite its neutrality, Luxembourg was invaded by the German army in 1914 and again in 1940. It was liberated by the American army under General Patton on 10 September 1944.

European Institutions – In 1952 Luxembourg became the headquarters of the ECSC, the European Coal and Steel Community, the organisation which was to pave the way for a federal Europe. **Robert Schuman** (1886-1963), the French statesman born in Luxembourg, developed the idea, and **Jean Monnet** (1888-1979) put it into action. There were six participating countries; Belgium, France, Italy, Luxembourg, the Netherlands and West Germany.
Since the signing of the Treaty of Rome in 1957, Luxembourg has been home to **The General Secretariat of the European Parliament**, which holds sessions in Strasbourg and Luxembourg. In 1966 the European Centre was inaugurated on Kirchberg. This building was intended to bring together the various departments of the General Secretariat of the European Parliament under one roof.
Since 1967, when the executives of the three committees – ECSC, EURATOM and EEC – combined to form one commission with its headquarters in Brussels, many institutions have been set up on the Kirchberg plateau. These include the European Investment Bank, departments of the Commission of European Communities (in particular the Statistics Department), the European School, the Court of Justice (founded in 1952) and the Revenue Court of the European Communities. As for the Official Publications Office for the European Communities, this is established in Luxembourg-Gare.
Since 1965 the Council of Ministers, the main source of decision-making for the European Communities, has held its sessions at Luxembourg three times a year (in April, June and October). There are currently about 7 000 European civil servants in Luxembourg.

View of the old town and St John's in Grund

★★ OLD TOWN *allow half a day*

Set off from the Place d'Armes.

Place d'Armes (F) – This shady square is the lively centre of the city. In high season the cafés spill decoratively onto the pavements. The main feature of the square is the **Municipal Palace** (palais municipal) (**F N**), built in 1907, which houses the tourist information office. In a building on the corner of the square, on the Rue du Curé, a **model** ⊙ of the Luxembourg fortress is on show.

Place Guillaume (F) – The equestrian statue of William II of the Netherlands (1792-1849), Grand Duke of Luxembourg, stands in the centre of the square. The **town hall** (**F H**) was begun in 1830 and built in the local architectural style.

Place de la Constitution (F) – This former Beck stronghold, which contains an obelisk (a memorial), affords marvellous **views★★** across the Pétrusse gorge, laid out as gardens, and the Adolphe Bridge. The entrance to the Pétrusse casemates *(see below)* is to be found here.

Take the Boulevard Roosevelt to get to St-Esprit Plateau.

The Boulevard Roosevelt is lined with the buildings of the **Old Jesuit School** (Ancien Collège des Jésuites) (**F S**), including the new section of the cathedral.

St-Esprit Plateau (G) – This impressive citadel designed by Vauban contains the monument to National Solidarity. There are **views★★** from the top of the citadel across the Pétrusse and Alzette Valleys, and of the Rham plateau and the lower town of Grund with St John's Church.

From the St-Esprit Plateau, go down to the car park.
From there take the stairs, or, in a modern building nearby, the lift up to the cliff path.

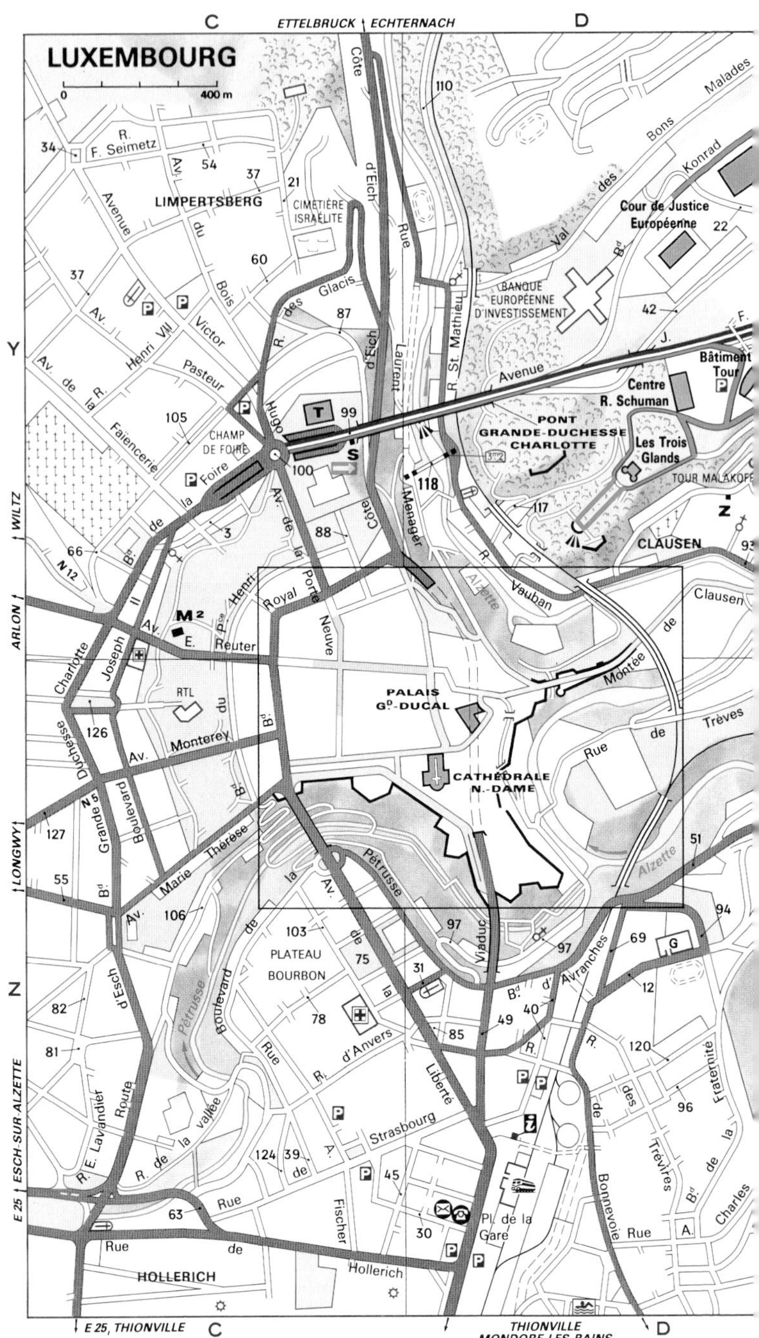

★★ **Cliff Path (Chemin de la corniche)** (G) – This has been called "the most beautiful balcony in Europe" because of its **views★★**. First, this walk goes past the old building in which the State Archives are kept, before joining the path that follows the old ramparts along the edge of the Alzette escarpment, and reaching the enormous **Grund Gate** (Porte de Grund) (1632) (**G E**). The elegant façades of houses belonging to the nobility line this path, overlooking the town of Grund and the church spire of St John's in the valley below.

The Bock (G) – This rocky spur used to be linked to the town by a drawbridge (now the Castle Bridge or Pont du Château). It has been smoothed off somewhat by the construction of the road up from Clausen (Montée de Clausen). The Bock forms the foundation of Luxembourg Castle (now ruined), which was built in the 10C, demolished in 1555 and converted into a small fort in the 17C. Destroyed in 1684 during the French siege, it was rebuilt by Vauban. In 1745 the Austrians took over the planning of the fortifications and dug the casemates. The Bock was razed in 1875; the only thing left standing is the tower called **"Hollow Tooth"** (Dent Creuse) (**G A**). From the top of the ruins there are **views★★** of the Rham plateau which was the site of a Gallo-Roman villa. To the left is the huge square gate called **Jacob Tower** (**G B**) or Dinselpuert. This was the gate to Trier and formed part of the 14C enclosure. The buildings on the right are the barracks built by Vauban (hospices). At the foot of the Bock, on the north side, is the old St-Esprit convent (17C).

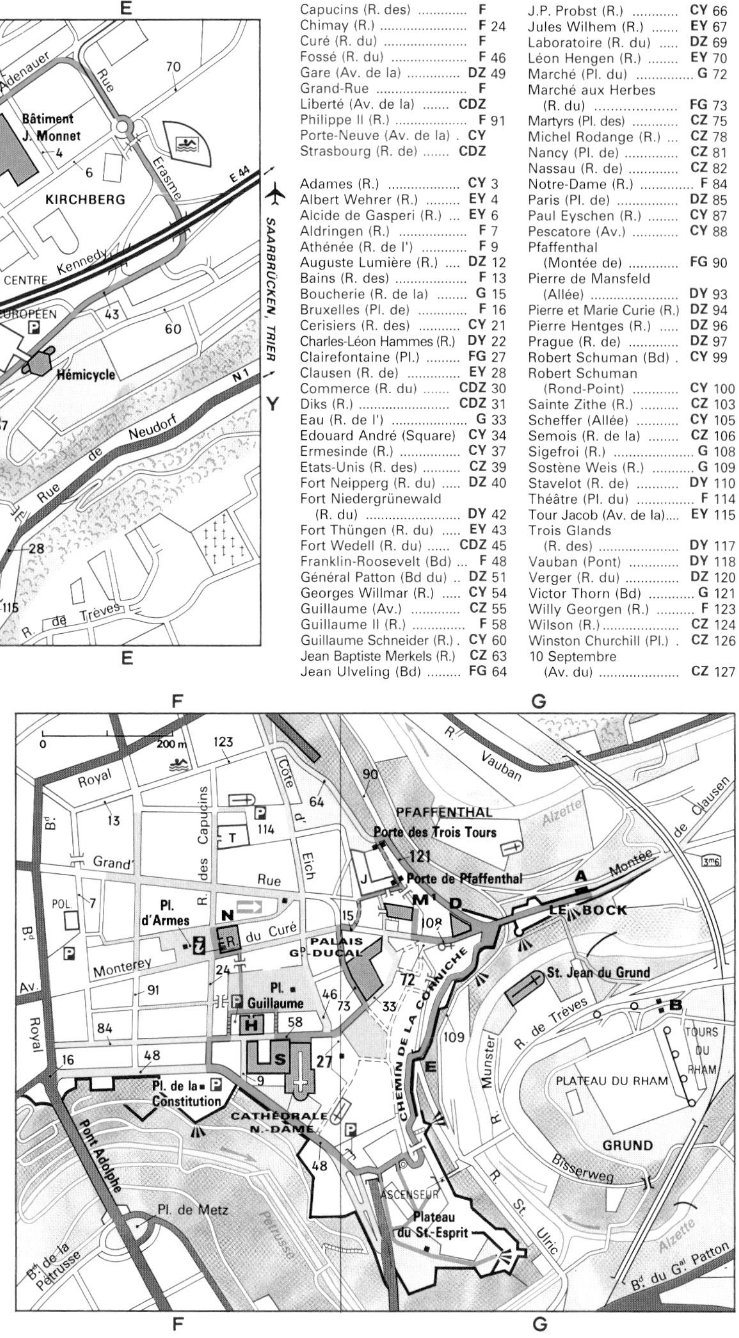

★★ **Bock Casemates** – In 1745, this defensive labyrinth was dug out of the sandstone outcrop which makes up the foundations of the city. There is a section open to the public – a minute part of a network of 23km - 14 miles of passages which acted as a shelter during the Second World War. Some of the openings have views of the gorge and Rham district.

On the right of the entrance to the upper town a **monument** has been built to commemorate visits to Luxembourg by famous people, most notably Goethe in 1792. Nearby is the porticoed building housing the **State Council** (**G D**).

Place du Marché (G 72) – Once the intersection of Roman roads and formerly also the fish market, this square is surrounded by old residential houses. The house known as "Underneath the Columns" (Sous les piliers) has Flamboyant Gothic style windows and a niche in the same style, containing a statue of St Anne and the Virgin and Child, above a Renaissance portico. Further along on the left there is an attractive house with a corbelled turret.

★ **National Museum of History and Art** (Musée national d'histoire et d'art) (**G M1**)

★ **Gallo-Roman collection** – This is to be found mainly on the ground floor and is very extensive. Excavations carried out in the south of the country (in Dalheim and Titelberg) have revealed that the area was densely inhabited during Roman times.

The exhibits are well-displayed and include bronzes, terracotta and fragile glassware. The numerous funeral monuments should be compared with those at Trier and Arlon. The little stelae in the shape of houses, which may have contained urns, and the stones carved to represent the four divinities were widespread in the south of Luxembourg. The particular legacy of the Merovingian period was weapons and beautiful jewellery. The **Medals Room** (salle des médailles), or treasury, displays rare items from all ages, including the remarkable **bronze mask of Hellange** dating from 1C.

Fine Art collection – A range of religious sculptures (from the 11C to the 18C) is distributed among various rooms in this section, as well as in those on the Gallo-Roman period and Luxembourg Life.

Medieval and Renaissance art *(third floor)* is represented principally by works from three collections: the Edmond Reiffers collection (Italian paintings from the 13C-16C); the Wilhelmy-Hoffmann collection (Northern European schools and Flemish works of the 16C and 17C; note a *Charity* by Cranach the Elder and a copy of the Hachiville altarpiece) and the Bentick-Thyssen collection (exhibited temporarily).

Modern art *(first and second floors)* includes, in addition to a few sculptures (by Rodin, Maillol, Lobo, Hadju), canvases and representational or abstract tapestries by the Paris school (Bertholle, Bissière, Borès, Chastel, Estève, Fautrier, Gilioli, Lurçat, Pignon, Soulages, Tápies, Veira da Silva) and works by the native Luxembourg Expressionist painter Joseph Kutter (1894-1941).

★★ **Luxembourg Life section (decorative arts, folk art and tradition)** – *Access via the first floor of the Museum of History and Art. Some of the rooms may be closed for staff reasons.* This outstanding section, set up in four old bourgeois houses, conjures up life in Luxembourg from the 17C to the 19C. The interiors are decorated with beautiful furniture, Boch faïence ware (Septfontaines), Nospelt pottery, pewterware, and a large collection of paintings under glass. Some firebacks are on display in the vaulted cellars. Part of the cellars is given over to Moselle viticulture.

A fireback (1586)

Boulevard Victor Thorn (**G 121**) – This affords **views**★ across the Alzette Valley, spanned by the Vauban bridge (**DY 118**), and the huddle of the Pfaffenthal suburbs. Above the valley, the Grand Duchess Charlotte Bridge connects the city with the Kirchberg plateau and the European Centre. The **Three Acorns Fortress** (Fort des Trois Glands) can be seen through a gap in the trees.

Three Towers Gate (Porte des Trois Tours) (**G**) – Built on the site of the second enclosure round the city, it actually consists of a gate flanked by two towers.

Now enter the city through the first **Pfaffenthal Gate** (17C).

★ **Grand Ducal Palace (Palais Grand-Ducal)** (**G**) ⊙ – The left wing, formerly the town hall, dates back to the 16C. Graceful turrets flank its façade, which is decorated with geometric patterns in bas relief.
The right wing, known as the "Pair of Scales" (La Balance), was added in 1741, and the wing at the back, which has a view of the garden, in 1891. The building (1859), on the right of the Pair of Scales houses the Chamber of Deputies.
Since 1895, most official functions have been held in this palace. A collection of well-preserved weapons is kept in the guardroom. The main staircase, with a charming balustrade decorated with the monogram of Adelaide-Marie, wife of the Grand Duke Adolphe, leads off to the suites. The former aristocrats' room, or **Kings' Chamber** (salon des rois), where portraits of all the past Grand Dukes are hung, is used for official audiences. In the dining room there are four tapestries, a gift from Napoleon after his stay at the palace in 1804, which illustrate the story of Telemachus.

Place Clairefontaine (FG 27) – A monument to Grand Duchess Charlotte has been put up in this attractive square.

★ **Cathedral of Our Lady (Cathédrale Notre-Dame)** (F) – This old Jesuit church with delicate 20C spires actually dates from the 17C; it opens to the north through an interesting **doorway** decorated with Renaissance and baroque motifs.
It is a good example of a hall-church, all three of its aisles being of a height. The style is on the whole Gothic, although the pillars are decorated with unusual arabesques in relief, and the gallery above the entrance is very delicately worked in a style half Renaissance and half baroque. On the left of the nave there is a gallery reserved for the Grand Ducal family. The neo-Gothic style choir was added in the 20C.
The wonderful statue of the Comforter of the Afflicted (national patron saint since 1678) is the object of particular worship; it is a shrine visited by many pilgrims during the third week after Easter. The exit by the door to the south of the chancel gives access to the Treasury Chapel and the **crypt**. The former contains the cenotaph of John the Blind (Jean l'Aveugle), who died at Crécy in 1346. This tomb was built in 1688 and depicts a burial scene. The crypt houses some interesting works by modern artists. It was at the cathedral that Josephine Charlotte of Belgium married Jean de Luxembourg in 1953. He went on to become Grand Duke in 1964 on the abdication of his mother, Grand Duchess Charlotte. The Jesuit School, adjacent to the cathedral is now the National Library (Bibliothèque Nationale).

Return to the Place d'Armes from the cathedral.

KIRCHBERG *allow 30min*

Several European institutions *(see above)* are on the Kirchberg plateau, which is crossed by a motorway; this has led to an increase in urbanisation (hotel, European school, etc.). The Parc des Expositions (exhibition centre) is beyond this at the far end of the motorway.
Before taking the bridge leading to the Kirchberg, notice the **municipal theatre** (**CY T**) on the left. It was built in 1964 and has a long façade with windows arranged in a geometric pattern.
To the right of the road leading onto the bridge, there is a monument to Robert Schuman, realised by architect Robert Lentz (**CY S**).

★ **Grand Duchess Charlotte Bridge** (DY) – This bridge of steel boldly painted in red, symbol of the ECSC, was inaugurated in 1966. It crosses the Alzette at a height of 300m - 984ft.

Take the second road on the right after the bridge, towards the European Centre.

Kirchberg European Centre (DEY) – The 23-storey **tower block**, inaugurated in 1966, is occupied by the General Secretariat of the European Parliament. The Council of Ministers holds sessions here for three months in every year. Additional space was created by a smaller building, the **Robert Schuman Centre**. A third construction, the **Hemicycle**, was finished in 1980 and serves as a conference centre.

Take the road which leads into the woods behind the European Centre to get to the Three Acorns (Trois Glands).

Three Acorns (Trois Glands) (DY) – This is the old Thungen stronghold in the forest. On top of its towers are stones shaped like acorns ("glands").

Turn left at the far end of the lawn.

A small viewpoint overlooks Clausen and its church; to the left is a house with turrets, in which Robert Schuman was born (**DY Z**). To the right, there is a **view★** of the city of Luxembourg, the Bock, and the Rham district with its towers.

Return to the European Centre and go under the motorway to reach the Court of Justice.

Court of Justice of the European Communities (DY) – The dark-brown painted steel elements of the four-storey CJEC building, built in 1973, stand on a vast terrace, on which there are also two sculptures by Henry Moore.
The **Jean Monnet building** nearby, with its walls of smoked glass, was constructed between 1976 and 1980 and houses the administration departments.

ADDITIONAL SIGHTS

Pétrusse Casemates – *Entrance in Place de la Constitution* (F).
This is a large underground network opening onto the Pétrusse Valley, created in 1746 by the Austrians to improve defences on the southern side of the plateau.

J P Pescatore Museum (CY M2) – This museum in the sophisticated 19C interior of the Vauban Villa houses three collectors' legacies of Belgian, Dutch and French painting from the 17C to the modern day.
After a few paintings attributed to Canaletto (Room 3), notice among the Flemish canvases works from the 17C by David Teniers the Younger *(Interior, The Smoker)*.
The rich 17C Dutch collection includes several genre paintings (Gérard Dou's *Empirical*, Jan Steen's *Festival of Kings*) and a Van de Capelle seascape.
19C French painting is represented notably by a Delacroix *(Young Turk Caressing his Horse)* and a Courbet *(Seascape)*.
The museum also organises temporary exhibitions.

Motor trip through the suburbs – A drive along the Alzette's right bank through the suburbs of lower Grund, Pfaffenthal and Clausen reveals a completely different side of the city: working class districts, maisonettes, breweries still making local beers. There are also very different views of the old town and its fortifications from these districts at the bottom of the gorges.

St John's Church in Grund (G) – This church belonged to the Benedictine abbey at Münster until the French Revolution. The present building dates from 1705. The interior is highlighted by three Flemish baroque altarpieces in the chancel. Note also: a Stations of the Cross in 16C Limoges enamel, signed by Leonard Limosin; the 18C organ; Gothic font; in a chapel to the left of the nave, a benevolent Black Virgin and Child of the Cologne school, sculpted in about 1360 and the object of great veneration.

EXCURSIONS

Military cemeteries – *5km - 3 miles east. Leave via the Boulevard du Général Patton* (**DZ 51**).
One of thirteen American Second World War cemeteries overseas, the Luxembourg American Cemetery at **Hamm**, just outside the capital, recalls the Grand Duchy of Luxembourg's gratitude to its liberators. This imposing 20ha - 50 acre cemetery is in the woods, overlooked by a memorial chapel built in 1960, and contains 5 076 tombs. Opposite the white crosses arranged in a curve stands that of General Patton, killed in December 1945, identical to the others.
Further to the east *(access via the Contern road)*, the **Sandweiler German cemetery**, inaugurated in 1955, can be visited by taking a detour from a forest road. Broad lawns, on which trees have been planted and short crosses made of dark Black Forest granite arranged in groups of five, cover an area of 4ha - 9.8 acres. A monumental cross surmounts the common grave in which 4 829 soldiers out of the 10 885 buried in this necropolis have been laid to rest.

From Luxembourg to Bettembourg – *15km - 9.3 miles south, towards Thionville.*

Hespérange – Pop 9 660. The most imposing feature of this picturesque town on the banks of the Alzette is the ruins of a 13C-14C castle, among which small homes with tiny front gardens have been built.

Bettembourg – Pop 7 950. This town has a large recreation park, the **Parc Merveilleux** ⊙. Animals and numerous attractions for children, in particular re-constructions of fairy tale scenes, abound in these vast 30ha - 74 acre grounds.

From Luxembourg to Junglinster – *13km - 8 miles north, towards Echternach.*

A beautiful road through the heart of a thick forest leads to Eisenborn, on the banks of the River Ernz Blanche. **Bourglinster**, a picturesque village at the foot of a restored castle, is to the right.

Junglinster – Pop 4 640. This small town has a charming 18C church in beige-grained stone, highlighted with pastel-toned paintings. It is surrounded by an old **cemetery** with 19C crosses that have a faintly archaic look.

★ LUXEMBOURG MOSELLE VALLEY

Michelin maps 409 M6-M7 and 215 folds 4, 5, 6

The Moselle (from the Roman name Mosella, or "little Meuse") separates the Grand Duchy of Luxembourg from Germany between the French frontier and Wasserbillig, at times reaching a width of about 100m - 109yds.
The navigability of the river has been substantially improved since the international agreement signed by France, Federal Germany and the Grand Duchy of Luxembourg; canalisation work finished in 1964 has made it accessible to 3 200-ton vessels between Thionville and Koblenz.
The two Grevenmarcher and Stadtbredimus dams, each equipped with a lock and a hydro-electric plant, interrupt the course of the river. So as not to disfigure the setting, they were built at water level.
The main attractions of the route along this valley are the bright landscape and, on the west bank, slopes of vines planted to grow up tall stakes (up to 2m - 6.5ft high).
Luxembourg Moselle vintage wines can be tasted in the principal wine cooperatives: white wines (Rivaner, Auxerrois, Pinot blanc, Pinot gris, Riesling, Traminer, Elbling) and sparkling wines.

Rambles – The Moselle footpath runs for about 40km - 25 miles along the river course from Stromberg, a hill south of Schengen, and Wasserbillig.

Boat trips ⊙ – A boat trip down the Moselle between Wasserbillig and Schengen is a marvellous way to enjoy the peaceful countryside of this region dotted with winegrowing villages.

Luxembourg Moselle Valley

FROM SCHENGEN TO WASSERBILLIG

46km - 28 miles - allow half a day

Schengen – It is in this border village, the prime winegrowing area of the Luxembourg Moselle region (wine cellars), that government representatives from Luxembourg, Germany, France, Belgium and the Netherlands met on the "Marie-Astrid" pleasure craft on 14 June 1985. They signed the **Schengen Convention**, in recognition of the gradual abolition of international borders between these countries. In 1990 Italy also signed this convention.

Remerschen – Pop 1 140. Set back slightly from the river, this town is at the foot of the Kapberg hills, covered with vines supported by stakes. A calvary is at the top of the slope and can be reached via a steep stairway.

Schwebsange – In a garden to the right of the road, a 15C winepress and a fruit-crushing machine can be seen.
Notice also some more winepresses opposite the church. In front of the church, the charming **Fountain of Children with Grapes** is the site of the annual wine festival *(see the Calendar of Events at the end of this guide)*.
Schwebsange also possesses the Grand Duchy's only marina.

Bech-Kleinmacher – The old winegrowers' houses, "A Possen" (1617) and "Muedelshaus", have been turned into a **Museum of Folklore and Viticulture** ⏲.
Small rooms with rustic furnishings (kitchen with an open fire) evoke the life of the past. Traditional activities are presented in workshops (spinning, coopering), and other attractions include a dairy, a wine museum and a wine cellar still with a grape-crushing tub.

Take the Wellenstein road which goes past the front of the museum.

Wellenstein – Pop 1 030. The **wine cellar cooperatives** ⏲ are at the entrance to the village, which is surrounded by 70ha - 172 acres of vineyards. The impressive installations make it possible to store as many as 10 million litres (2.2 million gallons) in enormous stainless steel vats, and to stock 1.5 million bottles.

The road climbs the **Scheuerberg** (views of the vineyards), then descends to Remich (views of the Moselle).

In Remich, return to the Moselle.

Remich – Pop 2 490. Remich has several wine cellars. The **St Martin cellars** ⏲ to the north of the town, hollowed out of the rock, are devoted to making sparkling wines. The bank of the Moselle at this point has been cleared to make a long footpath.

Stadtbredimus – Pop 860. Large wine cooperatives.

Shortly after Stadtbredimus, take the Greiveldange road on the left.

There are beautiful **views★** of the Moselle's meandering course, the steep Luxembourg slopes covered with vines supported by stakes and, on the German side towards Palzem, a more gently undulating countryside which is also planted with vineyards.

After **Greiveldange**, which has a large wine cooperative, return to the valley.

Ehnen – This winegrowing village is surrounded by vines on stakes and still has an old district with cobblestoned streets, in the middle of which stands a round church, built in 1826 and flanked with a Romanesque tower.
A winegrower's home has been turned into a **Wine Museum** ⏲. Tools used until the 1960s are on show here, and photographs give a pleasant illustration of the cultivation of vines and Moselle wine in days gone by. Related professions (coopering) are also mentioned, and the tour ends with some wine-tasting.

Wormeldange – Pop 2 100. This is the capital of the Luxembourg Riesling area. There are large **wine cooperatives** near the exit of the town, on the left.

St Donat's Chapel is at the top of the plateau, on the spot known as **Koeppchen**, where an old town once stood.

Machtum – This small village is in a bend in the river. A winepress and a fruit-crusher are on display on a lawn.

The great **dam-lock** of **Grevenmacher** is at the end of the meander; there is also an electrical power station here.

Grevenmacher – Pop 2 980. Surrounded by vineyards and orchards, this little town is an important viticultural centre with cooperative wine cellars and a private cellar. The **cooperative** (caves coopératives) is north of the town *(rue des Caves)*. South of the bridge are the **Bernard-Massard cellars** (caves), founded in 1921; they produce a sparkling wine by the champagne method. The tour of the lower cellars is completed by a documentary film on the Grand Duchy of Luxembourg, the Moselle, vine cultivation and the production of sparkling wine.

Mertert – Pop 3 030. This is an active river port linked to Wasserbillig by a footpath along the bank of the Moselle.

Wasserbillig – On the confluence of the Moselle and the Sûre *(qv)*, this international communications crossroads is also a tourist centre. Boat trips start from here.

★★★ LUXEMBOURG'S "PETITE SUISSE"

Michelin maps 409 L6-M6 and 215 folds 3, 4

The area known as Luxembourg's "Petite Suisse" (Mini-Switzerland) because of its rich green, undulating landscape has a wealth of natural beauty. Its rock formations and vegetation are among its most attractive features.

Parc Naturel Germano-Luxembourgeois

The Petite Suisse forms part of the Germano-Luxembourg nature park *(qv)*.

Romantic scenery – Forests thick with beech trees, hornbeams, pines, birches and oaks; forest floors covered with bilberry bushes, ferns, heather and moss; foaming waterfalls tumbling down onto rocky river beds; verdant pastures; all these make up the characteristic scenery of Luxembourg's Petite Suisse.

Variety of rock formations – Strangely-shaped rocks lying hidden in the heart of the forest further add to the charm of the landscape. Luxembourg sandstone, a mixture of sand and limestone and part of one of the main "escarpments" of Gutland *(see Introduction: Regions and Landscapes)*, has been sculpted by natural processes with amazing results.

Erosion has worn grooves into the rocks, which means they often look like tumble-down walls. Once water had eroded it, the sandstone plateau broke up, fissures appeared between the sedimentary layers, and huge blocks (diaclases) broke away and began to slide downhill towards the valley on their bed of argillaceous limestone.

The water table that collected in the lower section of the sandstone is the source of numerous springs. A kind of gully or crevice, known as a **"Schluff"**, can appear between the rock faces. If the rockfaces are sloping, then an actual gorge (schlucht) is formed.

Over a dozen signposted footpaths offer opportunities to roam all over the Petite Suisse and discover its most beautiful nooks and crannies.

Rock formations in Luxembourg's "Petite Suisse"

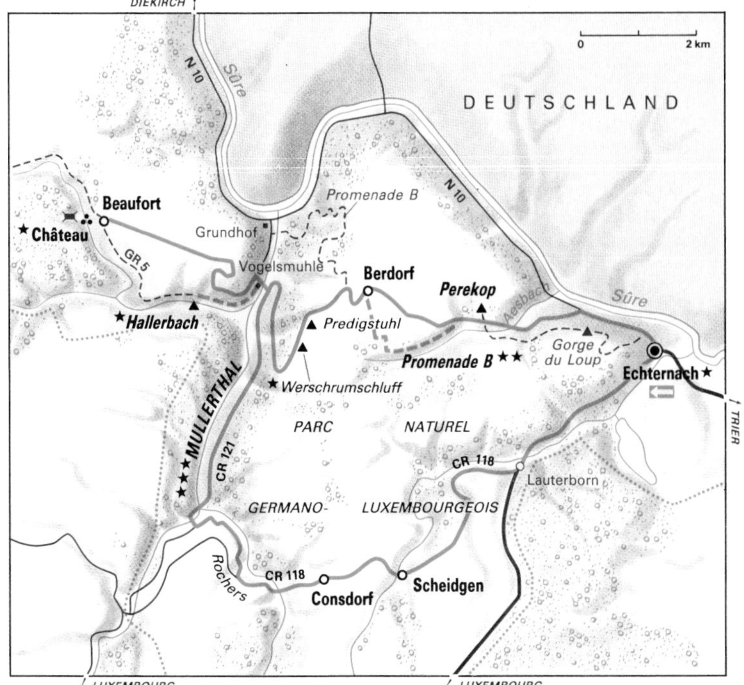

EXCURSION

Round tour of 34km - 21 miles from Echternach - allow 1 day.

★ **Echternach** – *See Echternach. Allow 45min.*

From Echternach take the road towards Diekirch.

The road follows the course of the river Sûre and passes close by Wolf Gorge (Wolfschlucht) *(qv)*.

Take the next turning on the left towards Berdorf.

About 1km - 0.5 mile on from the fork the road is joined by the **Promenade B** footpath *(see also Echternach: Excursion)* which goes down from Wolf Gorge into the Aesbach Valley.

The Perekop – This is a well-worn rock about 40m - 131ft high, which overhangs the road on the right. A set of stairs fitted into a crevice leads up to the top, where there is a view of the surrounding woods.

★★ **Walk** – At the Perekop the **Promenade B** footpath (from Echternach to Grundhof) joins the level of the road. The stretch towards the west along the river Aesbach until the point where the path diverges *(30min)* is among the most attractive in the area.
Notice the rocks misshapen by erosion: the Malakoff Tower and, further on, the Chipkapass.

On leaving the woods, the road reveals Berdorf ahead on the plateau.

Berdorf – *See Berdorf.*

From Berdorf take the road towards Mullerthal.

Not far along on the left is the **Predigstuhl** (pulpit) rock, which partially conceals among other things the **Werschrumschluff**★ gully *(qv)* behind it.

The road slopes steeply down into the Mullerthal valley.

At Vugelsmullen (or Vogelsmuhle) in the Mullerthal (see below), take a right turn immediately followed by a left towards Beaufort.

Beaufort – Pop 1 040. Set on a hill, this small district produces a blackcurrant liqueur called Cassero.

★ **Beaufort Castle** ⏲ – The romantic-looking ruins of this fortified castle (12C-16C) are in a wooded valley near a lake. In 1871, Victor Hugo wrote of the castle, "It comes into sight round a bend, at the foot of a gorge in a forest; it's a dream. It's magnificent." The old castle consists of a huge, towering keep attached to a fortress. Restorations in 1930 cleared the approach roads and reinforced the entrances.
The neighbouring castle was built by the lord of Beaufort in 1647.
The footpath which goes off to the west of the lake leads towards the Hallerbach waterfall *(see below)*.

Return towards Vogelsmuhle by car. Just before the hamlet, a small road branches off to the right along the Mullerthal. About 300m - 328yds along this, leave the car and take the Hallerbach footpath.

★ **Hallerbach** – This waterfall can be seen through the woods gushing down onto mossy piles of fallen rocks, off which charming mini-cascades splash down in their turn *(allow 30min there and back)*.

Return to Vogelsmuhle and turn right.

★★★ **Mullerthal** – This is the name given to the **Ernz Noire Valley**. Interrupted now and then by cascades, the river flows between two banks carpeted with meadows and backing onto wooded slopes. Spectacular outcrops of sandstone can be seen rising out of the trees.

About 200m - 218yds on from the Mullerthal, turn left towards Consdorf.

To get back to the top of the plateau the road goes along a little valley with attractive rock formations jutting out here and there along its sides.

Consdorf – Pop 1 380. This tourist village at the edge of the woods is very popular during the summer months.

Scheidgen – Holiday location.

Return to Echternach (qv) via Lauterborn.

★ MONDORF-LES-BAINS

Pop 2 830

Michelin maps 409 L7 and 215 fold 5

This popular spa town near the French border has two springs, the Kind and the Marie-Adélaïde bored respectively in 1846 and 1913, which bubble forth at a temperature of 24°C - 75°F. They are used for liver and intestinal problems as well as for treating rheumatism.
The spa establishment has modern facilities and is east of the old village.

★ **Park** – Near the spa, this 36ha - 88 acre park, with beautiful trees and shrubs and colourful flowerbeds *(rose garden in June)*, extends over a hillside, offering several pretty views of the local countryside. The new pavilion for the Kind spring is at its centre (1963).

St Michael's Church (Église St-Michel) ⏲ – This pink pebble-dashed church is on a hill overlooking the old town. It was built in 1764 and is surrounded by a cemetery. Inside it has sumptuous Louis XV **furniture**★. The organ on the balcony carved with musical emblems, the confessionals, the altars and the remarkable pulpit are all in perfect harmony with the stuccoes and *trompe-l'oeil* frescoes painted by Weiser (1766), a native of Bohemia.

★ RINDSCHLEIDEN

Michelin maps 214 fold 18 and 215 fold 11 - Local map see SÛRE VALLEY

This hamlet is tucked in the hollow of a valley around the parish church, which is much admired for the murals inside it.

★ PARISH CHURCH

This is Romanesque in origin. The chancel was modified in the Late Gothic period. The nave was enlarged in the 16C and given three equally high vaults.
Inside, all the vaulting and the walls of the chancel are covered with **frescoes**. Dating from the early 15C (chancel) and 16C (nave), they depict a multitude of figures, saints or royalty, and religious scenes in clear tints outlined in black. Note also the 17C and 18C wooden statues as well as some sculptures in stone: the 15C eucharistic cabinet surmounted by an oculus, keystones, capitals and 16C springer statues.
The miraculous well of St Willibrord, the object of an annual pilgrimage, is in a little garden near the church. An old 15C font is nearby.

RODANGE

Michelin maps 409 K7 and 215 fold 13 - 3km - 1.75 miles west of Pétange

This is a little industrial town near the Belgian and French borders.

Tourist train ⏲ – *From 2km - 1.25 miles south of the church on the Lasauvage road, as far as "Bois de Rodange".*
This train, pulled by turn-of-the-century steam engines, travels about 6km - 3.75 miles through the **Fond de Gras** valley overlooked by the Titelberg *(see the National Museum of History and Art, Luxembourg)*. A shuttle train operates between the road and the old Fond de Gras station. Once an iron mineral mine, this has become the starting point for a railway trip.

EXCURSION

Bascharage – Pop 4 920. *6km - 3.75 miles northeast on the Luxembourg road.*
The **National Brewery** (brasserie nationale) in this town makes light-coloured beer distributed mostly in the Grand Duchy of Luxembourg.
In the **Luxembourg Gem Stone-cutting Workshop** (Taillerie luxembourgeoise de pierres précieuses) ⏲ *(Rue de la Continentale, east of the station)* precious stones from all the continents are cut and polished. The stone-cutters may be seen at work, and there is a rich exhibition of minerals and jewels.

★★ SÛRE VALLEY

Michelin Maps 409 K6-L6-M6 and 215 folds 3, 4

The River Sûre, rising in Belgium between Neufchâteau and Bastogne, crosses the Grand Duchy of Luxembourg as far as the River Moselle and the German border, which it delimits from Wallendorf to Wasserbillig.
A large part of the valley can be explored by following signposted footpaths *(see the Practical Information section at the end of the guide).*

Esch-sur-Sûre

★★ 1 THE UPPER VALLEY

From Hochfels to Erpeldange

68km - 42 miles - allow half a day - local map overleaf

This is the most spectacular stretch, where the river cuts deeply into the ancient Oesling rocks. The valley through which the road runs is also followed by the Haute-Sûre footpath linking Martelange on the border to Ettelbruck 60km - 37 miles away.

★ **Hochfels** – From near the chalet on this crest 460m - 1 509ft high, there is a **bird's-eye view** of the winding valley and its wooded slopes.

Travel via Boulaide and cross the Sûre at **Pont-Misère**, surrounded by pretty countryside, to reach Insenborn. Going back up to the plateau reveals lovely **views** of part of the Haute-Sûre lake downstream of the bridge, as well as of the river upstream at the foot of the Hochfels, with Boulaide on the horizon.

Insenborn – This town on the **Haute-Sûre lake★** is a water sports centre *(sailing, windsurfing, boating, swimming, fishing, diving)*; these activities are authorised upstream of Lultzhausen.

From Insenborn to Esch-sur-Sûre the road runs along the shore of the Haute-Sûre lake; there are remarkable **viewpoints★** over the green, winding river banks covered with broom and bristling with firs.

Esch-sur-Sûre Dam – At the base of this 48m - 157ft high dam, which has a capacity of 62 million m^3 - 2 190 million ft^3, there is a hydro-electric plant. Two secondary dams for the purpose of absorbing river flood tides - Bavigne *(north-west)* and Pont-Misère *(upstream)* - make up the dam project.
There is a good **view★** of the lake from the Kaundorf road, in a bend 800m - 0.5 mile beyond the dam.

★ **Esch-sur-Sûre** – Pop 240. *Photograph above.*
This welcoming village, with its tiered, slate-roofed houses, has a pretty setting. It is tucked inside a meander of the river, which has twisted in almost a full circle at this point leaving only a narrow strip of land between the two stretches. The ruins of a castle stand on the neck of the meander, and a tunnel has been bored through beneath it.
From the round watch-tower at the top of the hill, there is an interesting **view★** of the setting with the castle keep and chapel in the foreground. The fortress dates back to the 10C and was demolished in 1795. The town still has some traces of its medieval fortified enclosure.

From Esch-sur-Sûre to Göbelsmuhle, the road rejoins the Sûre here and there, as it flows at the bottom of thickly wooded gorges.
Having entered the Germano-Luxembourg nature park *(qv)* and gone through Göbelsmuhle, the road comes within sight of Bourscheid Castle, perched on a hilltop.

After Lipperscheid take the road on the left.

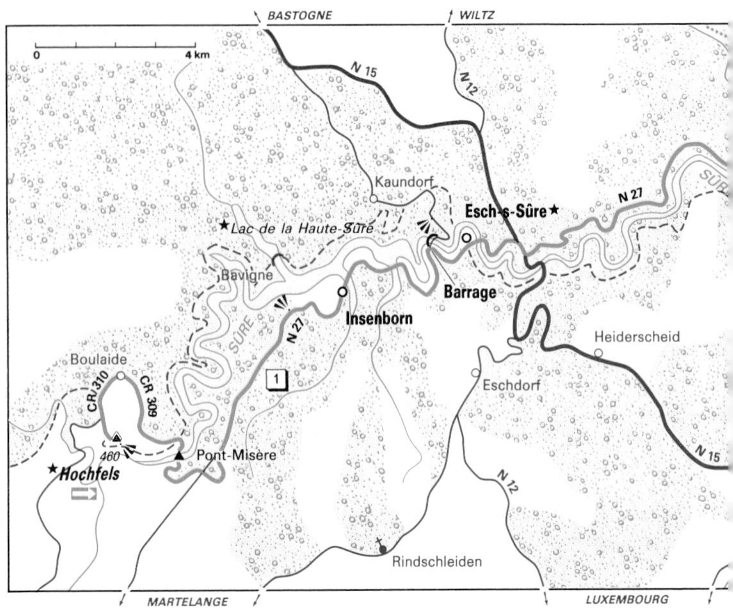

★★ **Grenglay Viewpoint** – *15min Rtn on foot, on a footpath through fields, signposted "Point de Vue".*
From the height of this impressive escarpment there is a beautiful **view** of the setting of Bourscheid Castle, set atop a promontory in a bend of the River Sûre.

Return to the N 27 and take a road on the right towards Bourscheid Castle.

★ **Bourscheid Castle** ⊙ – The **ruins**★ of this brown schist castle are 155m - 508ft above the Sûre. An 11C keep and a Gothic fireplace remain of the upper castle or fortress. The lower part of the castle, comprising the Stolzembourg mansion, was built in the 14C and modified many times up to the 18C. In the 19C it fell into ruins, but it has been restored since 1972 and is now a museum displaying objects excavated at the castle (earthenware, architectural fragments) as well as temporary exhibitions. Note the two reproductions of drawings of the castle by Victor Hugo (1871) on the ground floor; the originals are in the Bibliothèque Nationale in Paris.
There are beautiful and varied **views**★ of the valley and plateau from the towers of the fortress.

About 800m - 0.5 mile beyond the castle, on the right, there is the entrance to a campsite; a terrace here gives a pretty **glimpse**★★ of the ruins and the valley.

Return to the valley.

From here the river descends southwards to Erpeldange. The **setting**★ of groves and meadows is captivating.

★ 2 THE LOWER VALLEY

From Erpeldange to Wasserbillig

57km - 35 miles - allow half a day

The lower Sûre is less austere and is more pastural. After emerging from the Ardennes massif, the river flows between gentler slopes and wider fields. The road follows the course of the river almost continually until the confluence with the Moselle.

After Erpeldange, notice beyond the bridge over the Sûre ahead, towards Ettelbruck, the monument to General Patton.

Ettelbruck – Pop 6 740. This is a road and railway crossroads at the confluence of the Sûre and the Alzette, as well as a commercial and agricultural centre.

Diekirch – *See Diekirch.*

Reisdorf – Pop 550. This charming village was built at the opening of the pretty Ernz Blanche Valley.

Shortly after the village, the river Our flows into the Sûre, near Wallendorf.

★ **Echternach** – *See Echternach.*

Rosport Dam – Downstream from Rosport (Pop 1 430), the Sûre makes a gigantic loop. The river is contained by a large dam with a hydro-electric power station supplied by a pipe under pressure installed at the mouth of the meander. The river course is thus accelerated by an artificial variation in level.

At **Wasserbillig** *(qv)* the Sûre gushes into the Moselle.

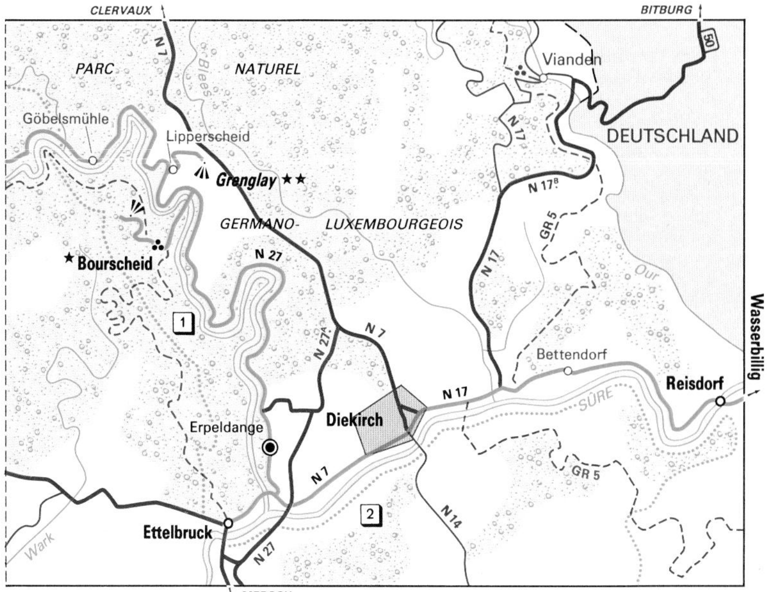

★★ VIANDEN

Pop 1 460

Michelin maps 409 L6 and 215 fold 3

The old houses of this charming little town cling to the slopes which fall away from the site of Our Castle. It is a splendid **setting**★.

★★ **Viewpoints** – The hills overlooking the town to the west offer beautiful views of Vianden's setting. The Mont St Nicolas *(see below)* road leads to a particularly interesting viewpoint. A **chairlift** ⊙ leads up to another viewpoint *(accessible also via a footpath leaving from the castle)*; there is an extensive **panorama**★★ over the town, the castle and the valley.

SIGHTS

★★ **Castle** ⊙ – *Photograph p 209.* The romantic outline of the castle dominates the town. It was built by the Counts of Vianden, and then belonged to the Orange-Nassau family from 1417 to 1977, except during a short period from 1820 to 1827, when it was bought by a speculator who demolished it.

In 1977 the Grand Duke Jean gave it up to the State of Luxembourg, and since then it has undergone a remarkable restoration which has returned it to its late-18C appearance.

Excavations have revealed the presence of a small fortress constructed during the early Empire (5C) and a first Carolingian medieval fortified enclosure from the 9C. The Counts of Vianden reached the height of their power from the 12C to the 13C, and it is from this period, a transition between Romanesque and Gothic, that most of the buildings date.

Tour – *1 hour 30min. A signposted route and numbered rooms lead the visitor through the maze of corridors, stairs and terraces.*

The castle consists of the 13C Petit Palais, a Romanesque building with Gothic ogive windows (Armoury and Byzantine Room) and the Grand Palais, with the gigantic **Knights' Hall** above the Counts' Hall.

The Romanesque **chapel** is at the far east end. It has a ten-sided base from the Carolingian period which is extended by the chancel and surmounted by a hexagonal upper storey with colonnettes.

An archaeological exhibition evokes the various stages of the castle's construction. From the watchpath and the garden, there are **views**★ of the Our Valley and the town.

Bridge over the Our – From this bridge, protected by a statue of St John of Nepomuk, patron saint of bridges, there is a pleasant **view** of the town and castle.

Victor Hugo's House ⊙ – After several trips through Vianden, Victor Hugo, in exile, stayed here in 1871 from 8 June to 22 August. The house has been turned into a museum and exhibits drawings and autographed letters by the great French writer. There is a bust of Victor Hugo by Rodin opposite the house.

Museum of Rustic Art (Musée d'Art rustique) ⊙ – *98 Grand-Rue.*
This museum in an old burgher's home consists of a delightful local interior decorated with rustic furniture. There is a beautiful collection of firebacks and another of dolls.

Trinitaires Church – *Grand-Rue.*
This old Gothic abbey church with two naves dates from the 13C; it has a pretty cloister, also from the 13C, which has been restored.

THE DAM AND POWER STATION *tour: 2 hours*

The Lohmühle Dam (Barrage) – *1km - 0.75 miles north.* This constitutes the lower basin of a large hydro-electric plant. The reservoir, with a capacity of 10 million m^3 - 107 million ft^3, is 8km - 5 miles long. The **Église Neuve** (church), built in 1770 in the old plague victims' district, is on the west bank at the foot of the dam.

Hydro-electric pumping station – *5km - 3 miles north of the dam, beyond Bivels.*
Hollowed out of the rock, the machine room is the underground link between the upper Mont St Nicolas basins and the lower Our reservoir. During hours of low consumption the reservoir water is pumped into the upper basins to be re-used in the periods of high consumption.
Annual energy production can reach 1 600 million kilowatts.
The visitors' gallery has models and illuminated explanatory displays.

Upper Mont St Nicolas Basins – *5km - 3 miles west on the Diekirch road, then right.*
After the crossroads, there is a beautiful **view**★★ of the castle and the town roofs. The **upper basins**, surrounded by 4.6km - 2.75 miles of dikes, form an artificial lake. This is between 14 and 35m - 45 and 114ft deep, and has a capacity of 6.6 million m^3 - 71 million ft^3. A set of stairs on a dike section lead to it; there is a **view** of the basin and the water tower, linked by a footbridge.
From the bottom of the basins there is a **view**★ of the Our Valley, scoured out of the cultivated Oesling plain and the hills of Germany.

EXCURSION

★★ **Our Valley** – *20km - 12.5 miles as far as Dasburg in Germany.*
In the area around Ouren in Belgium and Wallendorf, the River Our delineates the border between Germany and the Grand Duchy of Luxembourg. It cuts a deep and winding valley into the ancient rock, sometimes squeezing its way between sheer rock walls.

Leave Vianden by heading north.

The road runs initially along the crest of the **Lohmühle dam** *(see above).*

Bivels – This village is in a remarkable **setting**★ in the centre of an enormous Our meander.

Hydro-electric pumping station – *See above.*

Stolzembourg – The romantic ruins of a castle are perched over the village.

Dasburg – A charming town, in a pretty location on the German slopes.

WILTZ

Pop 3 880

Michelin maps 409 K6 and 215 folds 10, 11

Wiltz is at an altitude of 315m - 1 033ft on the Oesling plateau *(qv).* It is a commercial and industrial town (plastics, copper, brewing), a tourist centre and an international Scouting community: twelve chalets and about fifteen camps are dotted around the surrounding woods.
The lower town extends along the banks of the River Wiltz, while the upper town is a picturesque district squeezed onto a rocky spur between the church and the castle. Every year the castle gardens make a pretty setting for a European Festival of Open-air Theatre and Music *(see the Calendar of Events at the end of this guide).*

SIGHTS

Decanal church – This 16C church in the lower town was enlarged and restored in the 20C. Its two Gothic naves contain the tombstones of the Wiltz lords. A beautiful Louis XV grille closes off the counts' chapel.
On the climb up to the upper town, notice a **monument** on the left, recalling that it was at Wiltz that the first general strike against the German occupation began in September 1942.

Castle – The castle of the Counts of Wiltz still has a square 13C tower, modified in 1722. The main wing dates from 1631; it has now been turned into an old people's home. An amphitheatre was created in 1954 at the foot of the main staircase, which is where the festival events take place.

Cross of Justice – Dating from the 16C, it replaced a medieval cross and symbolises the rights the town had obtained (justice, freedom, trade).
Note also the statues of the Virgin and St John of Nepomuk, said to have saved the town from fire.

Monument Notre-Dame de Fatima – 1952. *Access via the Noertrange road CR 329, to the west.*
The road passes a brewery where copper cauldrons can be seen. There is an interesting **view** from the monument of the white-looking town with slate roofs arranged in tiers on the hillside.
The shrine is a pilgrimage site for Portuguese immigrants.

EXCURSION

Wiltz Valley – *11km - 6.75 miles east as far as Kautenbach.*
This pretty, winding valley runs between wooded hillsides.

Practical Information

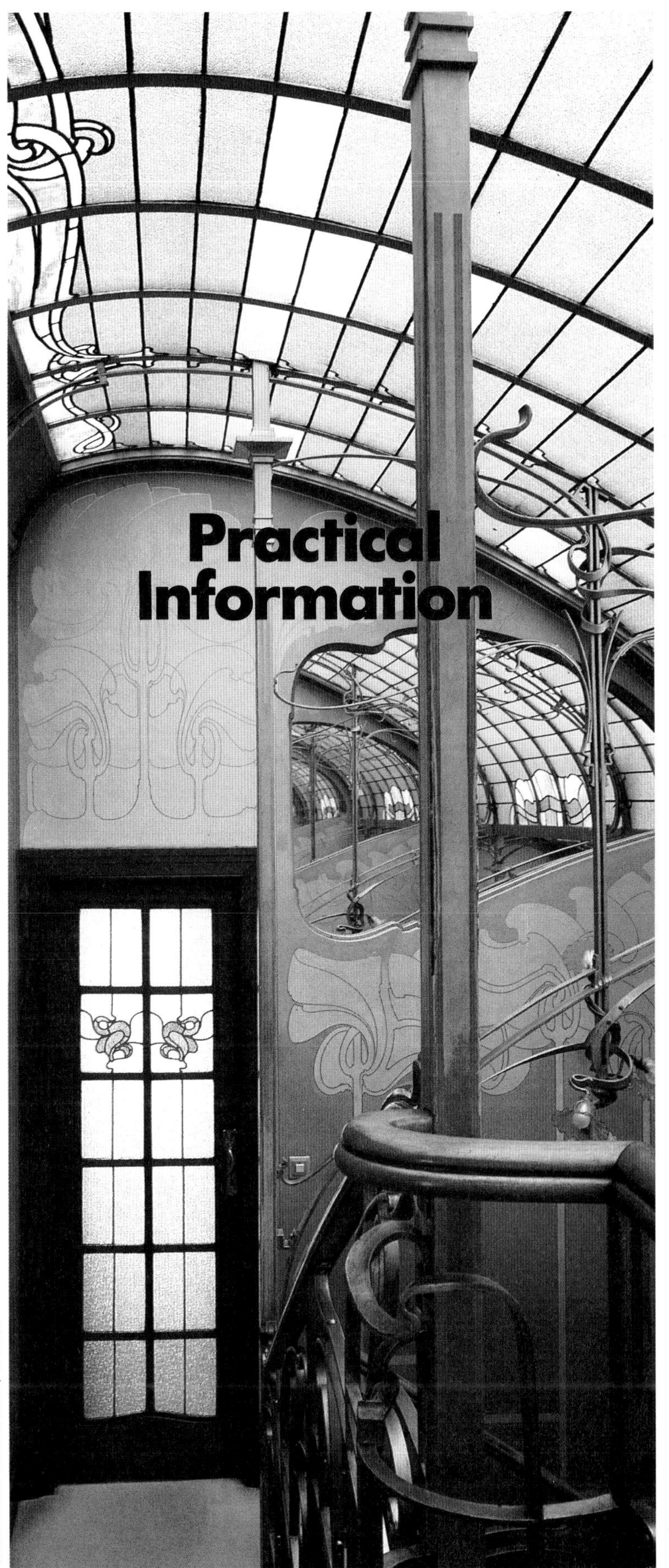

Stairwell in the Horta Museum, St-Gilles

TRAVELLING TO BELGIUM AND THE GRAND DUCHY OF LUXEMBOURG

Formalities - Despite the new law which came into force on 1 January 1993 authorising the free flow of goods and people within the EC, it is nonetheless advisable that travellers should be equipped with some valid piece of identification such as a **passport**. Holders of British, Irish and US passports require no visa to enter Belgium and the Grand Duchy of Luxembourg, although visas may be necessary for visitors from some Commonwealth countries, and for those planning to stay for longer than 3 months. US citizens should obtain the booklet *Your Trip Abroad* ($1) which provides useful information on visa requirements, customs regulations, medical care etc. for international travellers. Apply to the Superintendent of Documents, Government Printing Office, Washington DC 20402-9325.

Customs Regulations - There are no customs formalities between the countries of Benelux. Tax-free allowances for various commodities within the EC have increased with the birth of the EC Single Market. The HM Customs and Excise Notice 1 *A Guide for Travellers* explains how recent changes affect travellers within the EC. The US Treasury Department (☎ 202 566 8195) offers a publication *Know Before You Go* for US citizens.

By air - Various international airline companies operate regular services to the international airports in Belgium (Brussels, Antwerp) and the Grand Duchy of Luxembourg (Luxembourg). Contact airlines and travel agents for information and timetables.

By sea - There are numerous cross-Channel services (passenger and car ferries, hovercraft, SeaCat) from the United Kingdom and Eire. For details apply to travel agencies or to:

Hoverspeed, International Hoverport, Marine Parade, Dover, Kent CT17 9TG, ☎ 0304 240 241.
Maybrook House, Queen's Gardens, Dover, Kent CT17 9UQ, ☎ direct line from London 081 554 7061, Birmingham 021 236 2190, Manchester 061 228 1321.

P&O European Ferries, Channel House, Channel View Road, Dover, Kent CT17 9TJ, ☎ 0304 203 388; ticket collection: Russell Street, Dover, Kent CT16 1QB.

Sally Line, 81 Piccadilly, London W1V 9HF, ☎ 071 409 2240.
Argyle Centre, York St, Ramsgate, Kent CT11 9DS, ☎ 0843 595 522.

Sealink, Charter House, Park Street, Ashford, Kent TN24 8EX, ☎ 0233 647 047.

The Continental Ferry Port, Mile End, Portsmouth, Hampshire PO2 8QW, ☎ 0705 827 677.

By rail - The easiest travel route by rail and sea is from **London**, Victoria Station, via Dover and Ostend (sailing: 4 hours; jetfoil: 1 hour 40 min). Change at Brussels Midi station to travel on to Luxembourg.

By road - When driving to the continent the ideal ports of entry for Belgium are **Zeebrugge** (from Hull, Felixstowe and Dover), **Ostend** and **Calais** (both from Dover). There is a wide choice of routes using motorways or national roads into Belgium and the Grand Duchy of Luxembourg.
Ostend to Bruges: 28km - 17 miles, to Ghent: 64km - 40 miles, to Brussels: 115km - 72 miles;
Zeebrugge to Bruges: 14km - 9 miles, to Brussels: 111km - 69 miles;
Calais to Brussels: 213km - 132 miles (via Ostend) 231km - 144 miles (via Lille);
Brussels to Luxembourg: 219km - 136 miles.

The Channel Tunnel *- Due to open in 1994, this is the realisation of dreams of linking Britain to mainland Europe which date back over two hundred years. The Channel link consists of two single-track rail tunnels (7.60m - 24ft in diameter) for passenger and freight transport, and one service tunnel (4.80m - 15ft in diameter) for safety and ventilation. The tunnels are 50.5km - 31 miles long, 37km - 23 miles of which are under the Channel. Most of the tunnel is 40m - 131ft beneath the seabed, in a layer of blue chalk. The trains (800m - 2 624ft long) have two levels for passenger cars (capacity 118 cars per shuttle) and one level for coaches and caravans. Special services will operate for heavy goods vehicles. British, French and Belgian trains, including French TGVs, will also use the tunnel. Journey time will eventually be 35 minutes, 28 minutes of which are in the tunnel at a maximum speed of 130km - 80 miles per hour.*

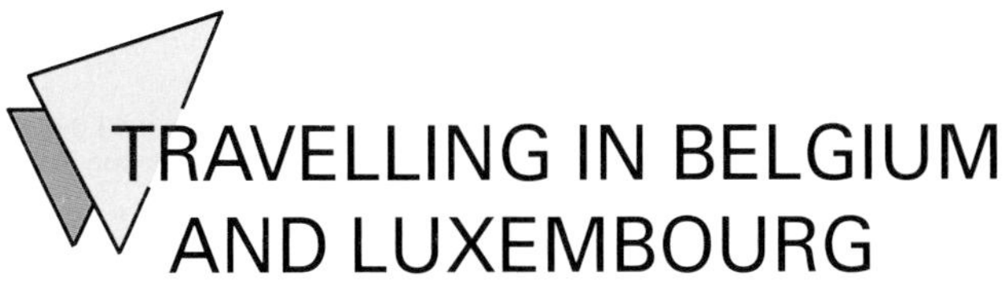

TRAVELLING IN BELGIUM AND LUXEMBOURG

By car

Documents - A valid **driving licence** is essential. Third party insurance is the minimum cover required by insurance legislation in Belgium, but it is advisable to take out additional insurance for fully comprehensive cover (the Green Card).

Driving regulations - Do not forget to **drive on the right**! The minimum age for driving is 18 for cars and motor-cycles and 16 for mopeds. Children under 12 are not allowed to travel in the front seat as long as there is room for them in the back. Seatbelts are compulsory in the back as well as the front of the car. Amber headlights are not necessary. Dipped headlights (not sidelights) are compulsory at night. Maximum **speed limits** for cars, caravans and small trailers are 50kph - 31mph in built-up areas, 90kph - 55mph on the open road, and 120kph - 75mph on motorways (minimum speed on motorways is 70kph - 45mph). Motorways are toll-free.
Priority must be given to cars coming from the right at junctions and on roundabouts, unless shown otherwise. Give way also to trams, pedestrians boarding or alighting from trams, and pedestrians crossing the road into which you are just turning.
The regulation **red warning triangle** must be carried, and displayed in the event of a breakdown. Dial 100 (in Belgium) for medical help for accidents involving injuries.

Breakdown service - The main organisations are:
- Touring Club de Belgique, rue Joseph II 25, Brussels, ☎ (02) 512 78 90 (for help anywhere in Belgium call ☎ (070) 34 47 77; this breakdown service operates 24h/24h; non-members have to pay three-months subscription for their first breakdown; on motorways, use the emergency telephones)
- Royal Automobile Club de Belgique, rue d'Arlon 53, 1040 Brussels, ☎ (02) 287 09 00
- Vlaamse Automobilistenbond, Sint-Jacobsmarkt 45, 2000 Antwerp, ☎ (03) 253 63 63.
- Automobile Club du Grand Duché de Luxembourg, route de Longwy 54, 8007 Bertrange, ☎ 45 00 45.

Petrol - Four-star ("super") petrol costs 34BF (25.5LF) per litre. Two-star ("normal") petrol, unleaded petrol and diesel are also available. Petrol is generally slightly more expensive in motorway service stations.
Access (Mastercard) and Barclaycard/Visa credit cards are not widely accepted at petrol stations; Eurocard, American Express and Diners Club are in wider use, but visitors are still strongly advised to have other means of payment with them.

Car Hire - Cars can be hired in most major towns and resorts. The minimum age limit is 21. A current driving licence is required.

Motorcyclists - Crash helmets are compulsory on motorcycles of 50cc and over. Dipped headlights must be used at all times of the day or night.

Signposting - In Flanders, French towns are often signposted in Dutch, so Parijs for Paris, Rijsel for Lille etc.

By train

Tickets and fares - The Belgian railway system is run by the Société Nationale de Chemin de Fer de Belgique/Belgische Spoorwegen, whose symbol is a "B" in an oval. For further information and reservations apply to

London - Belgian Railways, Premier House, 10 Greycoat Place, London SW1, ☎ 071 233 0360.

GENERAL INFORMATION

Currency - The unit of currency in Belgium is the Belgian franc, and in Luxembourg the Luxembourg franc. Belgian currency is used also in Luxembourg, but although the Luxembourg franc is theoretically valid currency in Belgium, it is generally only accepted in the province of Luxembourg.
Approximate exchange rate: £1 = 50BF.

To help with budgeting, here are some indications of **prices**:

	Belgian F
Two-star petrol (per litre)	29.6
Four-star petrol (per litre)	33.4
Diesel (per litre)	25.3
Bus ride	50
Underground ride (in Brussels)	50
Taxi ride (town centre rates)	95+38F/km
Local telephone call (3 min in town)	5
Posting a letter/postcard within the EC	15
Posting a letter/postcard outside the EC	28
Cinema (average price)	250
Theatre (average price)	600

For indications of prices of hotels and restaurants, consult the current Michelin Red Guide Benelux.

Opening hours and public holidays

In Belgium:

Banks open from 09.00 to 12.00 and from 14.30 to 15.30 (until 16.00 or even 19.00 on Fridays in branches near major commercial centres); in town centres they open from 08.30 to 15.30 (16.00 on Fridays); closed at weekends.

Post offices open from 09.00 to 12.00 and from 14.30 to 16.00; in city centres from 09.00 to 17.00; closed at weekends. Some post offices house telephone facilities, but check the town map or a telephone book for those which do not. Central telephone agency (bureau RTT) in Brussels at 19 boulevard l'Impératrice is open from 18.00 to 22.00 every day.

Shops open from 08.00 to about 19.00; closed on Sundays.

Public holidays are on 1 January, Easter Monday, 1 May, Ascension day, Whit Monday, 21 July (national holiday), 15 August, 1 November, 11 November, 25 December. Local festivals *(see the Calendar of Events)* can also mean that various public facilities will be closed.

In Luxembourg:

Banks open from 08.30 to 12.30 and from 13.30 to 16.30; closed at weekends.

Post and telephone facilities are not always in the same place; consult a town map or the telephone book.

Public holidays in Luxembourg are the same as those in Belgium (see above) except for the national holiday, which is on 23 June, and 11 November, which is not a public holiday.

Telephone - The international dialling code for Belgium is 32, and for Luxembourg 325. To telephone the UK from Belgium or Luxembourg, dial 00 + 44 + STD code (minus preceding 0) + number.

Some useful telephone numbers:

	Belgium	Luxembourg
Operator	1307	017
Police	101	113
Fire Brigade/Ambulance	100	112
Weather forecast	1703	18

ACCOMMODATION

Hotels and restaurants - For choosing a stopover for a few hours or a few days, the current Michelin Red Guide Benelux is an indispensable complement to this guide. It is updated every year and offers a range of hotels and restaurants with an indication of their standard of service and comfort, their location, their degree of pleasantness and their prices.
It is strongly advised to reserve hotel rooms in advance, especially for a weekend break, when visiting Bruges or any area where there is a local festival taking place.

Tips - An extra service charge of 15-16% is usually added to the bill in hotels and restaurants. It is customary to tip the waiter for particular service.
Tips are included in the prices of Belgian **taxis**.

Rented accommodation - Contact the local tourist office for details.

Farmhouse holidays - The following organisations provide information and make reservations:

- Fetourag, Fédération du Tourisme Agricole de l'Alliance Agricole Belge, rue de la Science 21, bte 2, 1040 Brussels, ☎ (02) 230 72 95.
- UTRA, Fédération du Tourisme des Unions Professionnelles Agricoles de Belgique, rue A Dansaert 94-96, 1000 Brussels, ☎ (02) 511 07 37.

  For Flanders, contact:
- Vlaamse Federatie voor Plattelandstoerisme, Minderbroederstraat 8, 3000 Leuven, ☎ (016) 24 21 58 - this organisation brings out a brochure with addresses.

  For West Flanders, contact:
- VZW, Hoevevakantie Kraaiehof, Proostdijk 28, 8480 Veurne, ☎ (058) 31 16 42.

In Tielt, contact the VVV, Stadhuis, 8800 Tielt, ☎ (051) 40 10 11.

For the Ardennes, contact the tourist offices of the provinces of Liège, Luxembourg and Namur *(see addresses below)*.

Back-to-Nature holidays - There are many opportunities for returning to nature, in the Ardennes in particular, in places with a minimum of facilities: setting, accommodation, sport, recreation. These are indicated by a special sign and known locally as *Stations vertes de vacances*.

Camping and Caravanning - Belgium has more than 350 campsites, divided into four categories. They are extremely crowded in July and August. The Grand Duchy of Luxembourg has over 100 campsites. Independent camping is permitted in Belgium and Luxembourg, but do not forget to ask the permission of the landowner first!

Youth Hostels - Belgian Youth Hostel associations:

- Centrale Wallonne des Auberges de la Jeunesse, rue Van Oost 52, 1030 Brussels, ☎ (02) 215 31 00.
- Vlaamse Jeugdherbergcentrale, Van Stralenstraat 40, 2060 Antwerpen, ☎ (03) 232 72 18.

For information on accommodation for young people, contact Inforjeunes, 2 Impasse des Capucins, Namur *(on weekdays from 12.00 to 17.40; no information given by telephone)*, or JIAC, Place Ste-Catherine 16, Brussels, ☎ (02) 218 11 80 *(on weekdays from 10.00 to 19.00; Saturdays from 12.00 to 17.00)*.

Luxembourg Youth Hostel association:

- Centrale des Auberges de Jeunesse Luxembourgeoises, 18 place des Armes, BP 374, 2013 Luxembourg, ☎ 22 55 88.

TOURIST INFORMATION

Belgian National Tourist Offices

London: Premier House, 2 Gayton Road, Harrow, Middx. HA1 2XU, ☎ 081 861 3300

New York: 745 Fifth Avenue, New York, NY 10151, ☎ 212 758 8130

Brussels: 61 rue du Marché-aux-Herbes, Brussels, ☎ (02) 504 03 90

There are also **Regional Belgian tourist offices** for each province:

- Antwerpen: Karel Oomstraat 11, 2018 Antwerpen, ☎ (03) 216 28 10
- Brabant: Rue du Marché-aux-Herbes 61, 1000 Brussels, ☎ (02) 504 04 55
- Hainaut: Rue des Clercs 31, 7000 Mons, ☎ (065) 36 04 64
- Liège: Boulevard de la Sauvenière 77, 4000 Liège, ☎ (041) 22 42 10
- Limburg: Thonissenlaan 27, 3500 Hasselt, ☎ (011) 22 29 58
- Luxembourg: Quai de l'Ourthe 9, 6980 La Roche-en-Ardenne, ☎ (084) 41 10 11
- Namur: Rue Notre-Dame 3, 5000 Namur, ☎ (081) 22 29 98
- Oost-Vlaanderen: Koningin Maria-Hendrikaplein 64, 9000 Gent, ☎ (09) 222 16 37
- West-Vlaanderen: Kasteel Tillegem, 8200 Brugge, ☎ (050) 38 02 96

Luxembourg National Tourist Offices

London: 36-7 Piccadilly, London, W1V 9PA, ☎ 071 434 2800

Luxembourg: Air Terminus, place de la Gare, Luxembourg, ☎ 48 11 99; Luxembourg-Findel Aérogare, ☎ 40 08 08

Brussels: 104 avenue Louise, Brussels, ☎ (02) 646 03 70

In Belgium and Luxembourg tourist offices are indicated with **i** (information). The tourist office is called Office de Tourisme/Syndicat d'Initiative in French, and Dienst voor Toerisme/VVV (Vereniging voor Vreemdelingen Verkeer, or Foreigners' Travel Association) in Dutch. Addresses and telephone numbers are in the current Michelin Red Guide Benelux, by the text entry.

DISCOVERING BELGIUM AND THE GRAND DUCHY OF LUXEMBOURG

Which is the best time of year to visit?

For those interested mainly in the cultural side of life, this can be enjoyed all year round. However, the countryside is at its best between April and October.

Spring - Burgeoning plant-life enhances avenues and squares, and delicate foliage along the borders of canals, in Bruges for example, makes a pretty scene. The forests of the Ardennes and Luxembourg are cloaked in myriad shades of green. In April, Watermael-Boitsfort, a suburb of Brussels, is a vision in pink amidst the blossom of its Japanese cherry trees.

Summer - The wide sandy beaches and sand dunes of the North Sea coast attract large crowds of holiday-makers. The rivers of the Ardennes cutting through their stunning backdrop of green hills are also extremely popular. In August the Lochristi region is resplendent with begonias in full bloom.

Autumn - This is the best time of year for visiting the Ardennes and Luxembourg, where richly stocked game forests take on magnificent seasonal hues. The city of Luxembourg is set jewel-like amidst the russet foliage of its trees.

Winter - Snow often covers the evergreen forests of the Ardennes, lending a magical quality to the beauty of the landscape. What better setting for a winter sports holiday?

Walking

An excellent network of clearly marked footpaths crisscrosses both Belgium, in particular the Ardennes, and the Grand Duchy of Luxembourg. Grande Randonnée or GR (long-distance) footpaths are marked on Michelin maps **212**, **213**, **214** and **215**.

Belgium - The network of marked footpaths covers 4 750km - 2 952 miles. The main footpaths are: GR 5 (Holland-Mediterranean), linking Rotterdam to Nice via the province of Liège (Spa, Liège) and the Grand Duchy of Luxembourg; GR AE (Ardennes-Eifel, part of European footpath 3) crossing the Ardennes from west to east through the Semois Valley; GR 12 (Brussels-Paris); GR 56 (Eastern Townships, Hautes-Fagnes, Helle Valley); GR 57 (Ourthe footpath linking Liège to the Grand Duchy); GR 129 (Scheldt-Meuse) linking Bruges with the Meuse Valley; GR 126 linking Brussels to the Semois Valley. There is also an interesting range of circular footpaths and footpaths in the Kempen region.
Two walking associations, "Sentiers de Grande Randonnée" (BP 10, 4000 Liège) and "Grote Routepaden" (Van Stralenstraat 40, 2060 Antwerpen, ☎ (03) 232 72 18), publish a quarterly periodical (GR Infos Sentiers and Wandelen GR) and have maps and literature on all the footpaths.
Elsewhere, public woods and recreation centres often have footpaths indicated by a special symbol depicting hikers. At the entrance to several nature reserves, routes for walks are suggested, with an indication of the length of the walk and posts painted in bright colours to act as markers.

Grand Duchy of Luxembourg - The national network of footpaths, marked in yellow, covers about 720km - 447 miles and is at its most dense around the main tourist centres: Diekirch, Echternach and Clervaux. The GR 5 crosses the country *(see above)*. Leaflets and small maps are available from tourist offices. Topographical maps (1:20 000) are on sale in bookshops or at the central office of the Youth Hostel association *(see previous page)*.
Similarly there are 171 **drive-and-walk** routes and 25 **train-and-walk** routes. These vary in length from 5-15km - 3-9 miles and enable tourists to leave their car and go for a walk in areas of particular interest or natural beauty, using footpaths designed to return to the point of departure. There is a guide of such walks on sale in bookshops; the guide of the train-and-walk routes is available from the central office of the Youth Hostel Association or from bookshops.

Sport

Canoeing - Certain stretches of several rivers can be navigated by canoe. On the Ourthe, the Semois, the Sûre and the Amblève there are organisations which hire canoes. Going down the river Lesse by canoe or punt is an unforgettable experience *(see Dinant: Excursion* 2*)*. The Royal Belgian Canoeing Association can be contacted at Geerdegemvaart 79, 2800 Mechelen, ☎ (015) 41 54 59.

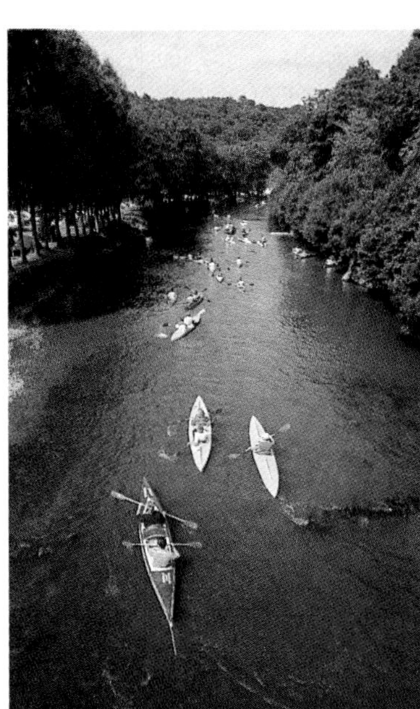
Canoeing on the River Lesse

Waterskiing - One of the best places for this activity is on the Upper Meuse (at Wépion, Profondeville, Yvoir and Waulsort), at Liège, Mons, Manage and Ronquières, on the Eau d'Heure lake and on the Albert Canal. Useful addresses for further information include the French-speaking Belgian waterskiing association (Fédération francophone du ski nautique belge, rue de Taervete 11, 1040 Brussels, ☎ (02) 734 93 73) and the Flemish watersports association (Vlaamse Vereniging voor Watersport, Sprenbonkstraat, 9000 Gent, ☎ (09) 345 0878).

Yachting - There are several marinas along the coast, at Zeebrugge, Blankenberge, Ostend and Nieuwpoort. Useful addresses include: Ligue régionale du yachting belge, avenue du Parc d'Armée 90, 5100 Jambes, ☎ (081) 30 49 79, Landelijke Bond voor Watersportverenigingen in België, IJzerweglaan 72, 9050 Gent/Ledeberg, ☎ (09) 231 26 35, Vlaamse Vereniging voor Watersport, Beatrijslaan 25, 2050 Antwerpen, ☎ (03) 219 69 67.

Hunting - Small game and water game can be found mainly to the north of the Sambre and Meuse trench, and large game (boar, various types of deer) in the Ardennes. It is compulsory to have either a shooting permit or game licence. For further information contact the Royal St-Hubert Club, place Jean-Jacobs 1, 1000 Brussels, ☎ (02) 511 89 75.

Fishing - Belgium offers opportunities for all sorts of angling. It is compulsory to have a fishing permit valid for a year, which can be obtained from a post office. Further details from the national angling association: Fédération sportive des pêcheurs francophones de Belgique, rue de Wynants 33, 1000 Brussels, ☎ (02) 511 68 48.

Horse-riding - This is possible throughout Belgium and Luxembourg. Some organisations set up horse-riding weekends. Horse racing takes place at Ostend, Groenendael, Watermael-Boitsfort, Kuurne and Sterrebeek (trotting), Waregem (steeplechase). Belgian horse-riding association: Fédération belge des sports équestres, Avenue Houba de Strooper 156, 1020 Brussels, ☎ (02) 478 50 56. Information on horse races can be obtained from the Jockey Club de Belgique, Avenue des Ombrages 16, 1200 Brussels, ☎ (02) 771 42 86.

Rock-climbing - A few of the rock faces overhanging the rivers of the Ardennes are sheer enough for rock-climbing *(see Meuse/Namur Region)*. Belgian rock-climbing club: Club alpin belge, rue de l'Aurore 19, 1050 Brussels, ☎ (02) 648 86 11.

Winter sports - The Ardennes climate is harsh enough for there to be substantial snowfall at quite low altitudes between December and March. In the provinces of Liège and Luxembourg, there are slopes for skiing and tobogganing. There are also outlets nearby which hire the necessary equipment. For further information contact the Liège or Luxembourg regional tourist offices *(see above)*.

Other sports - The reputation of Belgian cycling needs no further comment. Other popular sports in Belgium include swimming, tennis, bowling, clay-pigeon shooting and balle-pelote, a kind of bowls very popular in Wallonia.

A brochure published by the tourist office of the Grand Duchy of Luxembourg gives useful information about sports there.

Entertainment

See also the Calendar of Events.

Films are usually shown in their language of origin with subtitles in Flanders, or dubbed into French in Wallonia.

The Luxembourg tourist office publishes an Agenda Touristique six times a year which lists entertainments.

Belgians are great music-lovers; there are numerous **concerts** throughout the year, and during festivals in particular. From September to May, there is **opera** at Antwerp, Brussels, Ghent, Liège, Mons, Verviers and Charleroi, cities which have an opera house, as well as at Namur and Tournai.

In summer and autumn two major **festivals** take place: the Flanders Festival and the Wallonia Festival. These include performances from a variety of art forms (opera, concerts, recitals, ballet) in various towns of the region, usually set against the magnificent backdrop of an ecclesiastical building (church or cathedral) or a castle.

For further information on the Flanders Festival contact the Secretariat of the Flanders Festival, Place E. Flagey 18, 1050 Brussels, ☎ (02) 648 14 84.

For further information on the Wallonia Festival contact ☎ (041) 22 32 48.

The **Europalia** Festival takes place every two years with a large number of events all over the country, on the theme of a selected country (theatre, music, literature, exhibitions, cinema, ballet). For information on the programme contact the Europalia International Foundation, ☎ (02) 507 85 94 or the Belgian Tourist Office, Premier House, Gayton Road, Harrow, Middx HA1 2XU, ☎ 081 861 3300.

Last but not least, Belgium has no fewer than eight casinos open all year round: Blankenberge, Knokke, Ostend and Middelkerke on the coast, and Dinant, Chaudfontaine, Spa and Namur.

For entertainment in Luxembourg, consult the brochure available from the Luxembourg tourist office and the Calendar of Events in this guide.

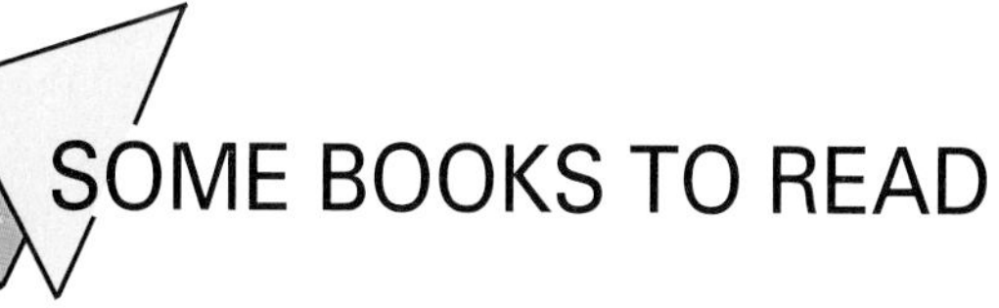

SOME BOOKS TO READ

Access to the Channel Ports (Guide for the Disabled), available from Access Project, Pauline Hephaistos Survey Projects, 39 Bradley Gardens, London W13 8HE

A New Guide to the Battlefields of Northern France and the Low Countries, M Glover (Michael Joseph)

Art Deco, A Duncan (Thames and Hudson)

Blue Guide Belgium and Luxembourg, J Tomes (A & C Black)

Civilisation (History/Flemish Primitives), K Clark (Penguin)

Dutch and Flemish Painting: Art in the Netherlands in the 17C, C Brown (Phaidon)

From Van Eyck to Brueghel, M Friedlander (Phaidon)

Medieval Flanders, D Nicholas (Longman)

Niccolò Rising (fiction), D Dunnett (Penguin)

Pieter Paul Rubens: Man and Artist, C White (Yale University Press)

The Sorrow of Belgium (fiction), H Claus (Penguin)

Through the Dutch and Belgian Canals, P Bristow (A & C Black)

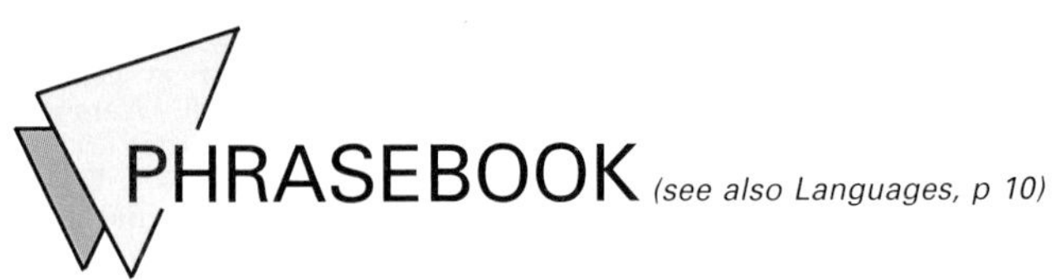

PHRASEBOOK

(see also Languages, p 10)

Some tips for pronunciation of Flemish:

h: is sounded *(het = the)*
j: yeh *(kindje = small child)*
s: is soft *(except in "mus(z)eum")*
g: between "gentle" and "guest" *(Gent)*
ng: more "n" than "ng" *(Tongeren)*
ch: guttural, as in Scottish "loch" *(Mechelen)*
sch: s + ch as above *(Aarschot)*
sch (at end of word): sh *(toeristisch)*

aa, ae: ah *(Laarne, Verhaeren)*
ee: eh *(meer, zee)*
ie: ee *(Tienen, Ieper)*
oo: oh *(Oostende)*
ij: ay *(Kortrijk, Rijssel)*
oe: oo *(Doest)*

ou: ow *(Oudenaarde, Turnhout)*
ui: oi *(Diksmuide, St.-Truiden)*

Common words

NB For restaurant terminology, consult the current Michelin Red Guide Benelux.

Dutch	French	English
U	vous	you
mijnheer	monsieur	Mr
mevrouw	madame	Mrs, Ms
juffrouw	mademoiselle	miss
toegang, ingang	entrée	entry
uitgang	sortie	exit
rechts; links	droite; gauche	right; left
koffiehuis	cafétéria	café
ja; nee	oui; non	yes; no
goedemorgen	bonjour	good morning
goedemiddag	bonjour	good afternoon
goedenavond	bonsoir	good evening
tot ziens	au revoir	goodbye
alstublieft	s'il vous plaît	please
hoeveel?	combien?	how much?
dank u (wel)	merci (bien)	thank you (very much)
postliggend	poste restante	poste restante
zegel	timbre	stamp

Tourist vocabulary

Dutch	French	English
abdij	abbaye	abbey
beeld	statue	statue
beiaard	carillon	chimes
begijnhof	béguinage	beguine convent
belfort	beffroi	belfry
beurs	bourse	stock exchange
burcht	forteresse	fortress
eeuw	siècle	century
gesloten	fermé	closed
gevel	façade	façade, front
gids	guide	guide
grote markt	grand-place	market square
haven	port	port
hof	cour	court(yard)
huis	maison	house
kaai	quai	quay
kapel	chapelle	chapel
kasteel	château	castle
kerk	église	church
kerkschat	trésor	treasury
koninklijk	royal	royal
koster	sacristain	sacristan
kunst	art	art
kursaal	casino	casino
lakenhalle	halle aux draps	cloth hall
meer; zee	lac; mer	lake; sea
molen	moulin	(wind)mill
museum	musée	museum
natuur-reservaat	réserve naturelle	nature reserve
O.L.Vrouw	Notre-Dame	Our Lady
oost; west	est; ouest	east; west
oud, oude	vieux	old, former
pastoor	curé	priest
paleis	palais	palace
plein	place	square
poort	porte	gate
schilderij	peinture	painting
sleutel	clé	key
stadhuis	hôtel de ville	town hall
stedelijk	municipal	town
straat	rue	road, street
toren	tour	tower
tuin	jardin	garden
uitzicht	vue, panorama	view
verdieping	étage	floor
vleeshuis	halle aux viandes	meat market
wandeling	promenade	walk

Road vocabulary

Dutch	French	English
doorgaand verkeer	voie de traversée	through traffic
fiets; fietsen	bicyclette(s)	cycle(s)
ijzel	verglas	ice
let op	attention	Look out!
moelijke doorgang	passage difficile	poor road
schijf verpflicht	disque obligatoire	(parking) disc compulsory
uitgezonderd plaatselijk verkeer	excepté circulation locale	local traffic only
uitrit	sortie	exit
weg	chemin	path
wegomlegging	déviation	detour
werken	travaux	roadworks

Incidentally, in Wallonia, "seventy" is "septante" (not "soixante-dix") and "ninety" is "nonante" (not "quatre-vingt-dix").

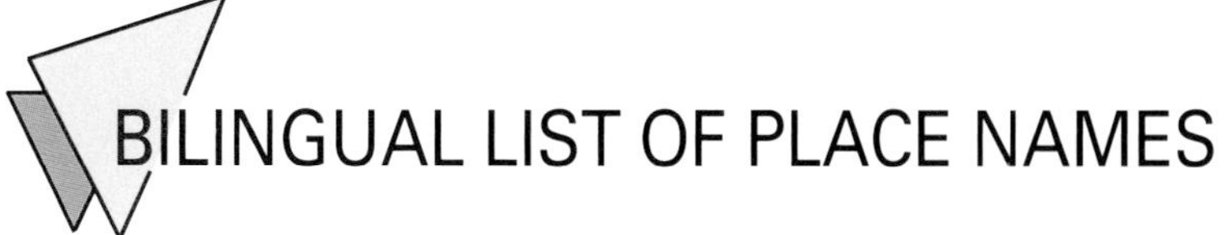

BILINGUAL LIST OF PLACE NAMES

Official names are given in **bold** *typeface:* **blue** *for French and* **black** *for Flemish. There is a more comprehensive list on Michelin map* **409**

Aalst	Alost
Aarlen	**Arlon**
Aat	**Ath**
Alost	**Aalst**
Antwerpen	Anvers
Arlon	Aarlen
Ath	Aat
Audenarde	**Oudenaarde**
Auderghem	**Oudergem**
Baarle-Duc	**Baarle-Hertog**
Bastenaken	**Bastogne**
Bergen	**Mons**
Braine-le-Château	Kasteelbrakel
Bruges	**Brugge**
Brussel	**Bruxelles**
Le Coq	De **Haan**
Courtrai	**Kortrijk**
Coxyde	**Koksijde**
Dendermonde	Termonde
Diksmuide	Dixmude
Doornik	**Tournai**
Edingen	**Enghien**
Ellezelles	Elzele
Elsene	**Ixelles**
Elzele	**Ellezelles**
Enghien	Edingen
Forest	**Vorst**
Furnes	**Veurne**
Gand	**Gent**
Geldenaken	**Jodoigne**
Gembloers	**Gembloux**
Gent	Gand
Geraardsbergen	Grammont
De **Haan**	Le Coq
Hal	**Halle**
Hoei	**Huy**
La **Hulpe**	Terhulpen
Huy	Hoei
Ieper	Ypres
Ixelles	**Elsene**
Jezus-Eik	N.-D.-au-Bois
Jodoigne	Geldenaken
Kasteelbrakel	**Braine-le-Château**
Koksijde	Coxyde
Kortrijk	Courtrai
Léau	**Zoutleeuw**
Lessen	**Lessines**
Leuven	Louvain
Liège	Luik
Lier	Lierre
Lombeek N.-D.	**O.-L.-V. Lombeek**
Louvain	**Leuven**
Luik	**Liège**
Malines	**Mechelen**
Mons	Bergen
Montaigu	**Scherpenheuvel**
Mont-St-Amand	**Sint-Amandsberg**
Namen	**Namur**
Nieuport	**Nieuwpoort**
Nijvel	**Nivelles**
N.-D.-au-Bois	**Jezus-Eik**
O.-L.-V. Lombeek	Lombeek N.-D.
Oostende	Ostende
Oudenaarde	Audenarde
Oudergem	**Auderghem**
De **Panne**	La Panne
Renaix	**Ronse**
Rhode St-Pierre	**Sint-Pieters-Rode**
Roeselare	Roulers
Ronse	Renaix
Roulers	**Roeselare**
St-Nicolas	**Sint-Niklaas**
St-Trond	**Sint-Truiden**
Scherpenheuvel	Montaigu
Sint-Amandsberg	Mont-St-Amand
Sint-Lambrechts-Woluwe	**Woluwe-St-Lambert**
Sint-Niklaas	St-Nicolas
Sint-Pieters-Rode	Rhode St-Pierre
Sint-Truiden	St-Trond
Soignies	Zinnik
Tamise	**Temse**
Terhulpen	La **Hulpe**
Termonde	**Dendermonde**
Tienen	Tirlemont
Tongeren	Tongres
Tournai	Doornik
Uccle	**Ukkel**
Veurne	Furnes
Vilvoorde	Vilvorde
Vorst	**Forest**
Watermaal-Bosvoorde	**Watermael-Boitsfort**
Wavre	Waver
Woluwe-St-Lambert	**Sint-Lambrechts-Woluwe**
Ypres	**Ieper**
Zinnik	**Soignies**
Zoutleeuw	Léau

Provinces: **Oost-Vlaanderen**, East Flanders; **West-Vlaanderen**, West Flanders.

French cities: **Paris**, Parijs; **Lille**, Rijsel.

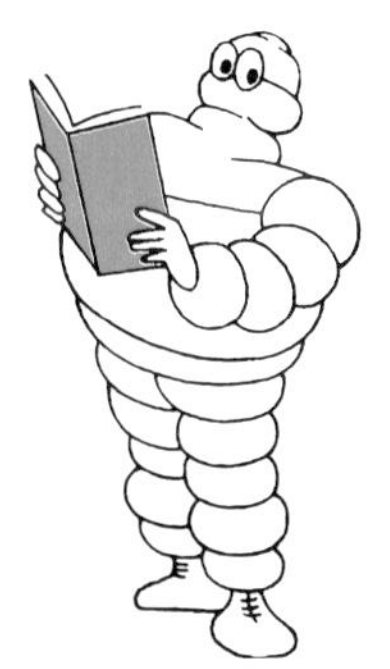

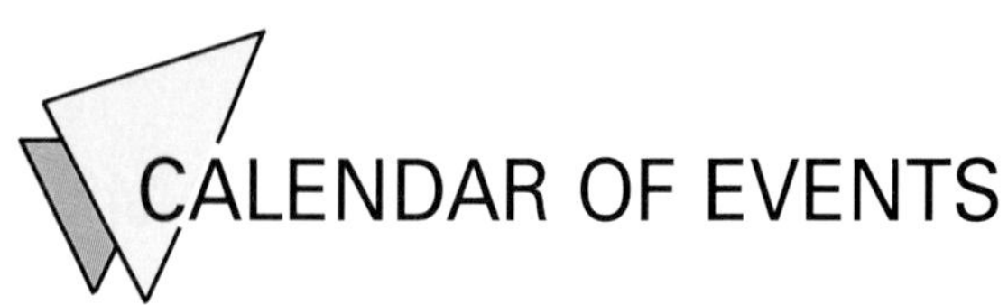

CALENDAR OF EVENTS

The following list includes the principal events among the very many that take place. Other events are described in the main body of the text. Detailed lists are distributed by the Belgian and Luxembourg tourist offices.

Belgium

Saturday, Sunday and Monday before Epiphany

Ronse . . . . Festival of Fools

Thursday, Friday, Saturday, Sunday, Monday and Shrove Tuesday

Eupen . . . . **Carnival★★** and Rosenmontag

Saturday, Sunday, Monday and Shrove Tuesday

Malmédy . . . . **Carnival★**
Blankenberge . . . . Carnival

Sunday, Monday, Shrove Tuesday

Aalst . . . . Carnival
Binche . . . . **Carnival★★★**

Every Sunday in Lent

Ligny *(see Waterloo)* . . . . Performance of the Passion at 15.30 (reservation advisable, contact the Syndicat d'Initiative ☎ (071) 88 80 57)

Refreshment Sunday (mid-Lent)

Halle . . . . Carnival
Fosses-la-Ville . . . . Carnival parade with "Chinels" *(see Namur: Excursions)*
Maaseik . . . . Carnival parade
Stavelot . . . . **Carnival parade★★** with Blancs Moussis

Last Sunday in February

Geraardsbergen . . . . Folklore parade and Krakelingen-throwing

First Saturday in March

Ostend . . . . Dead Rat Ball

Good Friday

Lessines . . . . Procession of the Penitents at 20.00

Easter Monday

Hakendover . . . . Procession of the Divine Redeemer at 10.00

Second Sunday in May

Ypres . . . . Cat Festival (every three years: 1994)

Sunday before Ascension Day

Mechelen . . . . Procession of Our Lady of Hanswijk

Ascension Day

Bruges . . . . **Holy Blood Procession★★★**

Weekend after Ascension

Blankenberge . . . . Harbour festivals

Third Sunday in May

Thuin . . . . St Roch military marches

Penultimate weekend in May

Arlon . . . . Maitrank festival

Saturday, Whit Sunday and Whit Monday

Écaussines-Lalaing . . . . Goûter matrimonial *(see Soignies: Excursions)*

Whit Sunday

Halle . . . . Procession at 15.00

Whit Monday

Gerpinnes . . . . Military marches *(see Charleroi)*
Soignies . . . . Grand Tour and Historical Pageant

Trinity Sunday (week after Whit Sunday)

Walcourt . . . . Grand Tour and military march
Mons. The "Lumeçon" and Chariot of Gold Procession
Ronse . . . . The Fiertel

First weekend in June

Ligny *(see Waterloo)*. . . . . Commemorative march for Napoleon's last victory

Second Saturday in June

Koksijde. . . . . Fishermen's Folklore Festival

Second weekend in June

Tournai . . . . Day of Four Parades

Penultimate weekend in June

Oostduinkerke. . . . . Shrimp Festival *(see Koksijde: Excursions)*

July

St-Hubert. . . . . "Juillet musical" and Summer Academy *(courses)*
Blankenberge . . . . Blessing of the Sea
Tongeren. . . . . Procession (every seven years: 1995)

July-August

Ostend . . . . Belgium Kites International
Stavelot. . . . . Vacances-Théâtre, then Festival of Chamber Music

First Thursday in July

Brussels. . . . . Ommegang Procession at 21.00; reservations: TIB (Town Hall), Grand-Place.

Sunday after 5 July

Gistel. St. Godelieve Procession *(see Ostend: Excursions)*

Friday after the first Sunday in July

Schoten **213** fold 7 *(1)* . . . . World Folklore Festival

Sunday nearest to 22 July

Jumet . . . . Military march *(see Charleroi)*

Last Sunday in July

Veurne . . . . **Procession of the Penitents★★** at 15.30

August

Spa . . . . Spa Festival of Theatre
Hasselt . . . . Virga Jesse Madonna Procession (every seven years: 1996)

First or second Sunday in August

Koksijde. . . . . Parade "In Homage to Flemish Painting"

14, 15, 16 August

Brussels. . . . . Carpet of Flowers on the Grand-Place (years ending in an even number)

15 August

Veurne . . . . " Anno 1900 " Festival

Sunday after 15 August

Ham-sur-Heure . . . . Military march *(see Charleroi)*

Fourth Sunday in August

Ath . . . . **"Ducasse"★★**

Thursday after the fourth Sunday in August

Dendermonde . . . . Giant's parade at 20.00

Last Sunday in August

Wingene **213** fold 3 *(1)*. . . . . . . **Brueghel Festival★★**: parade in costume, parts of which reproduce paintings by Pieter Brueghel, followed by a dinner (every two years: 1995)
Blankenberge . . . . Procession of floral floats

End of August

Overijse. . . . . Grape Festival *(see Leuven: Excursions)*

Tuesday following the last Sunday in August

Waregem. . . . . Flanders Obstacle Course *(see Oudenaarde: Excursions)*

First weekend in September

St-Hubert. . . . . International Days of Hunting and Nature

Third weekend in September

Namur	Wallonia Festival: people on stilts
Poperinge	Hops Festival (every three years: 1993)

29 September or the following Sunday

Nivelles	St Gertrude Procession

Sunday after 11 October

Lier	Procession

3 November

St-Hubert.	St-Hubert's Festival

Sunday after 1 November

Scherpenheuvel.	Candle Procession at 14.30 *(see Diest: Excursions)*

Sunday before 14 November

Tongerlo	Pilgrimage

December

Bastogne.	Walnut Fair

Luxembourg

Easter Monday

Luxembourg	"L'Emais'chen" Festival

Tuesday after Whitsun

Echternach	Dancing procession at 09.00

May-June

Echternach	International Festival of Classical Music

July (every Friday, Saturday and Sunday)

Wiltz	Festival of Theatre and Music

September

Moselle Valley	Wine Festival at **Grevenmacher** and **Schwebsange**

(1) Map references are given here for places not described in the main text of the guide.

Procession of Our Lady of Hanswijk at Mechelen

ADMISSION TIMES AND CHARGES

As admission times and charges are subject to modification due to increases in the cost of living, the information printed below is for guidance only.

The following list details the opening times and charges (if any) and other relevant information concerning all sights in the descriptive part of this Guide accompanied by the symbol ⊙. The entries given below are given in the same order as in the alphabetical section of the Guide.

Normally, especially in the case of large towns, the telephone number and/or address of the local Tourist Information Centre, indicated by the symbol 🅸, is given. Generally most efficient, these organisations are able the help passing tourists find accommodation (hotel, pension, camp site, youth hostel etc.) as well as providing information on exhibitions, performances, guided tours and other items of interest locally.

The prices quoted apply to individual adults but many places offer reduced rates for children, OAPs and some a family discount ticket.

The times are those of opening and closure but remember that some places do not admit visitors during the last hour or half hour.

BELGIUM

The prices are given in Belgian francs. The international dialling code for Belgium is 32.

A

AALST

🅸 Belfort, Grote Markt, ☎ (053) 73 22 62

St Martin's Collegiate Church – Open daily from 08.00 to 12.00 and from 13.30 to 19.00; further information from the tourist office; ☎ (053) 73 22 62.

Old Hospital – Open on weekdays from 10.00 to 12.00 and from 14.00 to 17.00 (19.00 on Wednesdays); at weekends from 14.00 to 17.00; closed Mondays, public holidays and between 1 and 15 January; ☎ (053) 70 26 60.

AARSCHOT

Collegiate Church of Our Lady – Open from 09.00 to 12.00; ☎ (016) 56 62 07.

AISNE VALLEY

Aisne Tourist Tramway (Part of the Musée vivant du Tram vicinal ardennais) – Service runs daily in July and August; on Sundays and public holidays only from mid-April to end of June and beginning of September to mid-October; Rtn: 140F; ☎ (041) 84 42 97 or (086) 47 72 69.

ANNEVOIE-ROUILLON DOMAIN

Gardens – Open between end of March and end of October daily from 09.00 to 19.00; guided tours (45 min) available from beginning of May to end of August; 170F (200F for palace and gardens).

Palace – Guided tour (20 min) in July and August daily from 09.30 to 13.00 and from 13.30 to 18.00; between mid-April and end of June and in September at weekends and on public holidays at same times; otherwise by appointment; 100F; ☎ (082) 61 15 55.

ANTWERPEN

🅸 Grote Markt 15, ☎ (03) 232 01 03

Antwerp offers a special combined ticket (combinatieticket) valid for a week for any three municipal museums of the visitor's choice at 150F.

Town Hall – Open on weekdays (except Thursdays) from 09.00 to 15.00; Saturdays from 12.00 to 16.00; closed Thursdays, Sundays, official public holidays and 2 January, 11 July, 2 November and 26 December; 30F; further information: ☎ (03) 232 01 03.

Cathedral – The pamphlet available at the entrance contains a diagram indicating the location of the works of art; open on weekdays from 10.00 to 17.00 (18.00 July to September); Saturdays from 10.00 to 15.00; Sundays and public holidays from 13.00 to 16.00; closed during services and 1 January; 60F.
Carillon concerts: Fridays at 11.30 and Mondays at 21.00.

Commodities Exchange – Open on weekdays from 09.00 to 12.00; closed at weekends, as well as on official public holidays and 2 January, 11 July and 26 December; ☎ (03) 232 01 03.

Butchers' Guild Hall – Open daily (except Mondays) from 10.00 to 17.00; closed Mondays, 1 and 2 January, 1 May, Ascension Day, 1 and 2 November, 25 and 26 December; 75F; ☎ (03) 233 64 04.

"Steen" Maritime Museum – Open daily (except Mondays) from 10.00 to 17.00; closed Mondays, 1 and 2 January, 1 May, Ascension Day, 1 and 2 November, 25 and 26 December; 75F; ☎ (03) 232 08 50.

Ethnography Museum – Open daily (except Mondays) from 10.00 to 17.00; closed Mondays, 1 and 2 January, 1 May, Ascension Day, 1 and 2 November, 25 and 26 December; 75F; ☎ (03) 232 08 82.

Folklore Museum – Open daily (except Mondays) from 10.00 to 17.00; closed Mondays, 1 and 2 January, 1 May, Ascension Day, 1 and 2 November, 25 and 26 December; 75 F; ☎ (03) 220 86 66.

Plantin-Moretus Museum – Open daily (except Mondays) from 10.00 to 17.00; closed Mondays, 1 and 2 January, 1 May, Ascension Day, 1 and 2 November, 25 and 26 December; 75F; ☎ (03) 233 02 94.

Mayer van den Bergh Museum – Open daily (except Mondays) from 10.00 to 17.00; closed Mondays, 1 and 2 January, 1 May, Ascension Day, 1 and 2 November, 25 and 26 December; 75F; ☎ (03) 232 42 37.

Maagdenhuis – Open on weekdays (except Tuesdays) from 10.00 to 17.00; at weekends from 13.00 to 17.00; closed Tuesdays, official and local public holidays; 75 F; ☎ (03) 223 56 10.

Rubens' House – Open daily (except Mondays) from 10.00 to 17.00; closed 1 and 2 January, Ascension Day, 1 May, 11 July, 21 July, 15 August, 1 and 2 November, 25 and 26 December; 75 F; ☎ (03) 232 47 47.

St James's Church – Open beginning of April to end of October from 14.00 to 17.00; closed Sundays and public holidays (except Whit Monday and 15 August: open from 14.00 to 18.00); 50F; ☎ (03) 827 50 43 or (03) 233 94 50.

Stock Exchange – Open on weekdays from 07.30 to 19.00; closed at weekends and on official and local public holidays; ☎ (03) 231 27 47.

Church of St Charles Borromeo – Open Mondays, Wednesdays and Fridays from 08.30 to 12.15, Tuesdays, Thursdays and Saturdays from 09.30 to 12.15, Sundays and public holidays from 09.30 to 12.45; also open Mondays, Wednesdays and Thursdays from 14.00 to 16.00, Tuesdays from 18.00 to 19.00, Fridays from 16.30 to 19.00 and Saturdays from 15.00 to 19.15; guided tour (1 hour) of the church, gallery, museum, sacristy and crypt on Wednesdays at 15.00; 40F; groups should contact Mr Philippé: ☎ (03) 233 02 29 or Mr Noppe: ☎ (03) 233 27 42.

Rockox House – Open daily (except Mondays and public holidays) from 10.00 to 17.00; closed Mondays, 1 and 2 January, Ascension Day, 1 November, 25 and 26 December; ☎ (03) 231 47 10.

St Paul's Church – Open beginning of May to end of September daily from 14.00 to 17.00; otherwise daily from 10.00 to 12.00; 50F; ☎ (03) 232 32 67.

St Elizabeth's Chapel – Open Wednesdays, Thursdays and Fridays from 13.00 to 16.00; 75F (ticket valid also for Maagdenhuis); ☎ (03) 223 56 20.

Royal Museum of Fine Art – Open daily (except Mondays) from 10.00 to 17.00; closed Mondays, 1 January, 1 May, Ascension Day and 25 December; ☎ (03) 238 78 09.

Photography Museum – Open daily (except Mondays) from 10.00 to 17.00; closed Mondays, 1 January, 25 and 26 December; ☎ (03) 216 22 11.

Antwerp Contemporary Art Museum – Open during exhibitions only from 10.00 to 17.00; closed Mondays, 1 January, 1 May, 15 August and 25 December; 200F; ☎ (03) 238 59 60.

Mini-Antwerpen – Open daily from 10.00 to 18.00; closed 1 January and 25 December; 160F (no charge for children less than 5 years old; 5-12 years old: 130F); ☎ (03) 237 03 29.

Zoological Garden – Open daily in July and August from 09.00 to 18.30; mid-March to end of June and in September from 09.00 to 18.00; first fortnight in March and first fortnight in October from 09.00 to 17.30; in February and mid-October to end of November from 09.00 to 17.00; in December and January from 09.00 to 16.45; 370F (children: 225F); ☎ (03) 231 16 40.

Open-Air Sculpture Museum Middelheim – Open in June and July from 10.00 to 21.00; in May and August from 10.00 to 20.00; in April and September from 10.00 to 19.00; beginning of October to end of March from 10.00 to 17.00; closed Mondays, 1 and 2 January, 1 May, Ascension Day, 1 and 2 November, 25 and 26 December; ☎ (03) 827 15 34.

Provincial Diamond Museum – Open daily from 10.00 to 17.00; closed 1 and 2 January, 25 and 26 December; ☎ (03) 231 00 87.
Demonstration by diamond cutters: Saturdays from 13.30 to 16.30.

Beguine Convent – Open daily from 09.00 to 17.00; ☎ (03) 232 01 03.

Brewers' Guild Hall – Open daily (except Mondays) from 10.00 to 17.00; closed Mondays, 1 and 2 January, 1 and 20 May, 1 and 2 November, 25 and 26 December; 75F; ☎ (03) 232 08 50.

Smidt van Gelder Museum – Open on Thursdays by prior appointment only; contact the tourist office: ☎ (03) 232 01 03.

Sterckshof Provincial Museum – Scheduled to reopen in 1994; further information: ☎ (03) 324 02 07.

Boat trip on the Scheldt – Time: 50 min. Between Easter and end of April at weekends only; beginning of May to end of September daily from 11.00 to 16.00; 230F (children: 160F); departure on the hour from Ponton Steen; further information: SA Flandria, Steenplein, Antwerpen, ☎ (03) 231 31 00.

Boat tour of the harbour – Time: 2 hours 30 min; beginning of May to end of August daily at 10.00 (except Saturday mornings) and 14.30; from Easter to end of April and in September on Saturdays at 14.30, Sundays and public holidays at 10.00 and 14.30; 375F (children: 250F); departure from quay (kaai) 13, Londenbrug; further information: SA Flandria, Steenplein, Antwerpen, ☎ (03) 231 31 00.

Excursions

Oelegem: Vrieselhof Provincial Estate Textile Museum – Open beginning of March to end of November from 10.00 to 17.00; closed Mondays; ☎ (03) 383 46 80.

Kalmthout Arboretum – Open mid-March to mid-November daily from 09.00 (10.00 at weekends and on public holidays) to 17.00; 100F; ☎ (03) 666 67 41.

ARLON

Pavillon, Parc Léopold, ☎ (063) 21 63 60

Viewpoint – 20F; ☎ (063) 91 63 60.

Luxembourg Museum – Open Mondays to Saturdays from 09.00 to 12.00 and from 14.00 to 17.00; mid-June to mid-September open also Sundays from 09.00 to 12.00 and from 14.00 to 17.00; otherwise closed Sundays, public holidays and between 15 and 31 December; 100F; ☎ (063) 22 61 92.

Roman Tower – Visitors should go to the Café d'Alby, Grand-Place 1; closed Mondays and Sunday mornings; 10F.

Roman baths and Basilica – Visitors should ring ☎ (063) 22 61 92 or (063) 22 12 36.

Excursion

Victory Memorial Museum – Open in July and August daily from 08.30 to 18.00, April to June from 09.00 to 17.00, beginning of October to end of March from 10.00 to 16.00; 295F; ☎ (063) 21 99 88.

ATH

Museum – Open beginning of April to end of October on Sundays only from 14.00 to 18.00; 70F; ☎ (068) 28 01 41.

Excursions

Moulbaix: Mill – Guided tour (30 min) beginning of April to end of October at weekends and on public holidays from 15.00 to 18.00 and during the week by appointment; contact Mr J. Dhaenens, ☎ (068) 28 27 91; 30F.

Chièvres: Church – Open beginning of April to end of September daily from 09.00 to 19.00; otherwise daily from 09.00 to 17.00; ☎ (068) 65 76 68.

Cambron-Casteau Abbey Estate – Open daily from sunrise to sunset; 45F; ☎ (068) 45 45 21.

ATTRE

Palace – Guided tour (45 min) in July and August daily (except Wednesdays) from 10.00 to 12.00 and from 14.00 to 18.00; final tour at 17.15; from beginning of April to end of June and in September and October at weekends and on public holidays only; 120F; ☎ (068) 45 44 60.

AULNE

Abbey – Open beginning of April to end of September Tuesdays to Fridays from 10.30 to 12.00 and from 13.30 to 18.00, Saturdays from 10.30 to 12.00 and from 13.00 to 19.00, Sundays and public holidays from 10.30 to 12.00 and from 13.00 to 19.00; 40F; ☎ (071) 51 52 98.

AVERBODE

Abbey: Conventual Buildings – Guided tours by written appointment only; contact: De Heer Prior, Abdijstraat 1, 3271 Averbode, ☎ (013) 77 29 01.

*The **Michelin Maps** for this region are shown in the diagram on the outside back cover of the guide.*

The text refers to the maps which, owing to their scale or coverage, are the clearest and most appropriate in each case.

B

BASTOGNE

i place McAuliffe 24, ☎ (061) 21 27 11

Bastogne Historical Center – Open daily in July and August from 09.00 to 18.00; in May, June and September from 09.30 to 17.00; in March, April and between October and mid-November from 10.00 to 16.00; open weekends only from mid-November to Christmas school holidays and from January to Carnival season; 225F (children: 165F); ☎ (061) 21 14 13.

BEAUMONT

Salamander Tower – Guided tour (1 hour) beginning of May to end of September daily from 09.00 to 12.00 and from 14.00 to 19.00; in October on Sundays only from 10.00 to 12.00 and from 14.00 to 17.00; 50F; ☎ (071) 58 81 91.

Excursions

Solre-sur-Sambre: Fortress – Closed for restoration work.

Rance: National Marble Museum – Open beginning of April to end of October Tuesdays to Saturdays from 09.30 to 18.00, Sundays from 14.00 to 18.00; otherwise Tuesdays to Saturdays from 08.30 to 17.00; closed Mondays (except public holidays), and on Sundays and public holidays between beginning of November and end of March; 100F; ☎ (060) 41 20 48.

BELŒIL

Castle and Gardens – Open beginning of April to end of October daily from 10.00 to 18.00; 390F (children: 200F) - ticket valid for gardens and Minibel also; ☎ (069) 68 94 26.

Excursion

Aubechies: Archaelogical Site – Open on weekdays from 09.00 to 17.00; mid-April to end of October also open at weekends and on public holidays from 14.00 to 18.00; 100F; ☎ (069) 66 29 38.

BINCHE

i Centre administratif, rue St-Paul 14, ☎ (064) 33 37 21

St Andrew's Chapel – Guided tour (15 min) by appointment on weekdays (excluding public holidays) only; contact tourist office; ☎ (064) 33 37 21.

St Ursmer's Collegiate Church – Open July and August; otherwise guided tours only; contact tourist office, Mme Antoine, ☎ (064) 33 37 21.

International Carnival and Mask Museum – Open beginning of April to mid-November Mondays to Thursdays from 09.00 to 12.00 and from 14.00 to 18.00, Saturdays from 14.00 to 18.00, Sundays and public holidays from 10.00 to 13.00 and from 14.00 to 18.00; mid-January to end of March Mondays to Thursdays from 09.00 to 12.00 and from 13.00 to 17.00, weekends and public holidays from 14.00 to 18.00; 120F; ☎ (064) 33 57 41.

Excursions

Mariemont Domain: Park – Open daily from 09.00 to 18.00 beginning of April to end of September, from 09.00 to 17.00 in February, March and October, from 09.00 to 16.00 beginning of November to end of January; open also on Sundays and public holidays from 09.00 to 19.00 between beginning of May and end of August; ☎ (064) 22 12 43.

Museum – Open daily (except Mondays) from 10.00 to 18.00; closed Mondays, 1 January and 25 December; ☎ (064) 21 21 93.

Library – Open Tuesdays to Saturdays from 10.00 to 12.30 and from 13.30 to 18.00 (except the first Saturday of the month and Saturdays during school holidays); closed Mondays and Sundays, public holidays and for fortnight last week of July/first week of August; ☎ (064) 21 21 93.

Bonne-Espérance Abbey – Tour by appointment all year; between Sunday after Easter and last Sunday in October tours on Saturdays at 15.00 and 17.00, Sundays at 10.00, 15.00 and 17.30; in July and August on weekdays at 15.00; ☎ (064) 33 20 21.

BLÉGNY-TREMBLEUR

Mine – Guided tour (2 hours) beginning of May to end of September daily from 10.00 to 16.30; in April and October weekends and public holidays only from 10.00 to 16.30; 250F (children: 165F); ☎ (041) 87 43 33.

Tourist train – Daily service in July and August at 14.30 and 16.30; Sundays and public holidays only in April, June, September and October; 160F (children: 90F).

Mortroux: Museum of Regional Life – Open daily beginning of May to end of September from 12.00 to 19.00; in April and October at weekends only from 12.00 to 19.00; 50F; ☎ (041) 87 43 33.

BOKRIJK PROVINCIAL DOMAIN

Open-Air Museum – Open beginning of April to end of September daily from 10.00 to 18.00; in October daily from 09.00 to 17.00; 180F (children: 60F); ☎ (011) 22 45 75.

BOUILLON

i Château fort, ☎ (061) 46 62 57

Castle – Open in July and August daily from 09.30 to 19.00; in April, May, June and September from 10.00 to 18.00; in March, October and November from 10.00 to 17.00; in December Wednesdays to Sundays from 10.00 to 17.00, in January at weekends only from 10.00 to 17.00; in February weekdays from 13.00 to 17.00, weekends from 10.00 to 17.00; closed 1 January and 25 December; 140F, joint ticket for Castle and Ducal Museum: 220F; ☎ (061) 46 62 57.

Ducal Museum – Open in July and August daily from 09.30 to 19.00; in April, May, June, September and October from 10.00 to 18.00; in November and December at weekends only from 10.00 to 17.00; 120F; recorded commentaries (in English also); ☎ (061) 46 69 56.

BRUGGE

i Burg 11, ☎ (050) 33 86 86

Canals Festival – Next festival in 1995.

Belfry – Open beginning of April to end of September daily from 10.00 to 17.15; otherwise from 10.00 to 11.45 and from 13.30 to 16.15; 80F.

Carillon concerts – Mid-June to end of September on Mondays, Wednesdays and Saturdays from 21.00 to 22.00, Sundays from 14.15 to 15.00; otherwise on Wednesdays and at weekends from 14.15 to 15.00.

Horse-drawn carriages – All year round daily from 10.00 to 18.00; 800F.

Holy Blood Basilica – Open beginning of April to end of September daily from 09.30 to 12.00 and from 14.00 to 18.00; otherwise from 10.00 to 12.00 and from 14.00 to 16.00 (closed Wednesday afternoons); Museum: 40F; closed Wednesday afternoons from beginning of October to end of March, 1 January, 1 November and 25 December; ☎ (050) 33 71 73.

Town Hall: Gothic Room – Open beginning of April to end of September daily from 09.30 to 17.00; otherwise daily (except Tuesdays) from 09.30 to 12.30 and from 14.00 to 17.00; 60F; ☎ (050) 33 99 11.

Freeman of Bruges Provincial Museum – Open daily (except Mondays) from 10.00 to 12.00 and from 13.30 to 17.00; closed Mondays and in January; 20F.

Groeninge Museum – Open beginning of April to end of September daily from 09.30 to 17.00; otherwise daily (except Tuesdays) from 09.30 to 12.30 and from 14.00 to 17.00; closed on Tuesdays between beginning of October and end of March, 1 January, afternoon of Ascension Day and 25 December; 130F; ☎ (050) 33 99 11.

Memling Museum – Open beginning of April to end of September daily from 09.30 to 17.00; otherwise daily (except Wednesdays) from 09.30 to 12.30 and from 14.00 to 17.00; closed on Wednesdays between beginning of October and end of March, 1 January, afternoon of Ascension Day and 25 December; 130F; ☎ (050) 33 99 11.

Beguine House – Open beginning of April to end of September on weekdays from 09.30 to 12.00 and from 13.45 to 17.30, Sundays and public holidays from 10.45 to 12.00 and from 13.45 to 18.00; otherwise on weekdays from 10.30 to 12.00 and from 13.45 to 17.00, Sundays and public holidays from 10.45 to 12.00 and from 13.45 to 18.00; 45F.

Boat trip – Beginning of March to end of November daily from 10.00 to 18.00; in December and February at weekends and on public holidays and during school holidays from 10.00 to 18.00; 150F (children less than 12 years old: 65F).

Gruuthuse Museum – Open beginning of April to end of September daily from 09.30 to 17.00; otherwise daily (except Tuesdays) from 09.30 to 12.30 and from 14.00 to 17.00; 130F; ☎ (050) 33 99 11.

Church of Our Lady – Open Mondays to Saturdays from 09.00 to 11.30 and from 14.30 to 17.00 (16.00 on Saturdays), Sundays and public holidays from 14.30 to 17.00; ☎ (050) 34 53 14; chancel open during the week from 10.00 onwards: 30F.

Brangwyn Museum – Open beginning of April to end of September daily from 09.30 to 17.00; otherwise daily (except Tuesdays) from 09.30 to 12.30 and from 14.00 to 17.00; closed 1 January, from 5 January to 5 February, afternoon of Ascension Day and 25 December; 80F; ☎ (050) 33 99 11.

Church of Jerusalem – Open Mondays to Saturdays from 08.30 to 12.00 and from 14.00 to 18.00 (17.00 Saturdays); closed Sundays and public holidays and from Christmas to the New Year.

Lace Centre – Open Mondays to Saturdays from 10.00 to 12.00 and from 14.00 to 18.00 (17.00 Saturdays); closed Sundays, public holidays and from Christmas to the New Year; 40F; ☎ (050) 33 00 72.

Folklore Museum – Open beginning of April to end of September daily from 09.30 to 17.00; otherwise daily (except Tuesdays) from 09.30 to 12.30 and from 14.00 to 17.00; closed on Tuesdays between beginning of October and end of March, and all January; 80F; ☎ (050) 33 99 11.

St.-Janshuismolen – Open beginning of May to end of September daily from 09.30 to 12.00 and from 12.45 to 17.00; 40F.

Guido Gezelle Museum – Open beginning of April to end of September daily from 09.30 to 12.00 and from 12.45 to 17.00; otherwise daily (except Tuesdays) from 09.30 to 12.30 and from 14.00 to 17.00; closed on Tuesdays between beginning of October and end of March, 1 January, afternoon of Ascension Day, 25 December, and from beginning of January to beginning of February; 40F; ☎ (050) 33 99 11.

St Sebastian's Archers' Guild Hall – Open Mondays, Wednesdays, Fridays and Saturdays from 10.00 to 12.00 and from 14.00 to 17.00; 20F; ☎ (050) 33 16 26.

English Convent Church – Open daily from 14.00 to 16.00 and from 16.30 to 17.30; closed every first Sunday of the month and some religious holidays.

St Saviour's Cathedral – Open Mondays to Saturdays from 08.00 to 12.00 and from 14.00 to 18.00 (17.00 Saturdays); Sundays and public holidays from 09.00 to 12.00 and from 15.00 to 18.00; ☎ (050) 33 61 88.

Treasury – Open in July and August Mondays to Saturdays from 10.00 to 12.00 and from 14.00 to 17.00 (15.00 Saturdays); Sundays and public holidays from 15.00 to 17.00; otherwise Mondays to Saturdays from 14.00 to 17.00 (15.00 Saturdays); Sundays and public holidays from 15.00 to 17.00; closed Wednesday afternoons and 1 January; 40F; ☎ (050) 33 61 88.

Museum Onze-Lieve-Vrouw ter Potterie – Open beginning of April to end of September daily from 09.30 to 12.00 and from 12.45 to 17.00; otherwise daily (except Wednesdays) from 09.30 to 12.30 and from 14.00 to 17.00; closed on Wednesdays between beginning of October and end of March, 1 January, afternoon of Ascension Day and 25 December; 60F; ☎ (050) 33 99 11.

Excursions

Access to Damme by boat – See Damme (below) for details.

Sint-Michiels: Boudewijnpark and Heirmanklok – Open beginning of May to end of August daily from 10.00 to 18.00; at Easter, and on Wednesdays and at weekends in September open from 12.00 to 18.00; joint ticket for Boudewijnpark, Heirmanklok and Dolfinarium: 380F (children younger than 12: 340F); ☎ (050) 38 38 38.

Dolfinarium – Displays all year at 11.00 and 16.00, also between third week of May and end of June at 10.00, and between third week of May and end of August at 14.00; 230F; ☎ (050) 38 38 38.

Loppem Palace – Open beginning of April to end of October from 10.00 to 12.00 and from 14.00 to 18.00; closed on those Mondays and Fridays which are not public holidays; 100F; ☎ (050) 82 22 45.

Maze – Open Easter to 1 November during holiday periods only from 13.30 to 18.00; 40F.

Male Castle – To visit, apply to Gastenzuster, Sint-Trudo Abdij, Male, 8310 Brugge, ☎ (050) 35 02 11.

BRUSSELS

ℹ Hôtel de Ville, Grand-Place, ☎ (02) 513 89 40

Brewery Museum – Open weekdays from 10.00 to 12.00 and from 14.00 to 17.00, Saturdays from 10.00 to 12.00; closed Sundays and public holidays; also closed Saturdays from beginning of November to end of March; 100F; ☎ (02) 511 49 87.

Town Hall – Open Tuesdays to Fridays from 09.30 to 12.15 and from 13.45 to 17.00 (16.00 beginning of October to end of March); Sundays and public holidays from 10.00 to 12.00 and from 14.00 to 16.00; closed 1 January, 1 May, 1 and 11 November and 25 December; 75F; ☎ (02) 512 75 54.

Museum of the City of Brussels – Open weekdays from 10.00 to 12.30 and from 13.30 to 17.00 (16.00 beginning of October to end of March); weekends and public holidays from 10.00 to 13.00; closed 1 January, 1 May, 1 and 11 November and 25 December; 80F; ☎ (02) 511 27 42.

Église Notre-Dame-de-la-Chapelle – Closed for restoration work; scheduled to reopen at the end of 1994.

Place du Grand-Sablon (Antique Dealers' District) – Antiques and book market on Saturday and Sunday mornings.

Palais Royal – Open from 21 July to end of September, usually from 10.00 to 16.00; closed Mondays.

Bellevue Museum – Open daily (except Fridays) from 10.00 to 16.45; closed 1 January, Easter Monday, 1 May, Whit Monday, 21 July, 1 and 11 November and 25 December; ☎ (02) 511 44 25.

Apartments of Charles of Lorraine – Guided tour (1 hour) on request, for groups only; ☎ (02) 519 53 71.

Albert I Royal Library – Guided tour (1 hour 15 min) on request: ☎ (02) 519 53 71.

Book Museum – Open Mondays, Wednesdays and Saturdays from 14.00 to 16.45; closed 1 January, Easter Monday, 1 May, Ascension Day, Whit Monday, 21 July, 15 August, last week of August, 1, 2, 11 and 15 November, 25 and 26 December; guided tour on request; ☎ (02) 519 53 71.

Printing Museum – Open Mondays to Saturdays from 09.00 to 17.00; guided tour on request; 500F per group; closed at same times as the Book Museum; ☎ (02) 519 53 56.

Toone Marionette Theatre – Performances all year on Fridays and Saturdays at 20.30; otherwise telephone for details; reservations ☎ (02) 511 71 37.

St Nicholas's Church – Open weekdays from 07.30 to 18.30; Saturdays from 09.00 to 18.30; Sundays and public holidays from 07.30 to 19.30; closed Easter Monday, 1 May, Whit Monday, 21 July and 26 December; ☎ (02) 513 80 22.

Historium – Open daily from 10.00 to 18.00; closed 1 January, 21 July and 25 December; 190F; ☎ (02) 217 60 23.

Belgian Centre for Comic Strip Art – Open daily (except Mondays) from 10.00 to 18.00, closed 1 January, 1 November and 25 December; 150F; ☎ (02) 219 19 80.

St Michael's Cathedral – Open weekdays from 07.00 to 19.00; Saturdays from 07.30 to 19.00; Sundays and public holidays from 08.00 to 19.00; closing time 18.00 from beginning of November to end of March; 30F; ☎ (02) 217 83 45.

Museum of Ancient (15C to 19C) Art – Open from 10.00 to 12.00 and from 13.00 to 17.00; closed Mondays and 1 January, 1 May, 1 and 11 November and 25 December; ☎ (02) 508 32 11.

Museum of Modern Art – Open from 10.00 to 13.00 and from 14.00 to 17.00; closed Mondays and 1 January, 1 May, 1 and 11 November and 25 December; ☎ (02) 508 32 11.

Museum of Musical Instruments – Open Tuesdays to Saturdays from 14.30 to 16.30; Sundays from 10.30 to 12.30; closed Mondays; ☎ (02) 512 08 48.

Palais de la Nation – Guided tour (1 hour 30 min) by prior appointment, for groups only; Mondays to Saturdays at 10.00, 11.00, 14.00 and 15.00; ☎ (02) 519 81 36.

Église St-Jean-Baptiste-au-Béguinage – Open Wednesdays to Fridays from 09.00 to 17.00; Tuesdays from 10.00 to 17.00; otherwise open the first, third and fifth Saturdays of the month from 10.00 to 17.00 and the second and fourth Sundays of the month from 10.00 to 17.00; for details of days when closed telephone ☎ (02) 217 87 42.

Costume and Lace Museum – Open weekdays from 10.00 to 12.30 and from 13.30 to 17.00 (16.00 beginning of October to end of March); weekends and public holidays from 14.00 to 16.30; closed 1 January, 1 May, 1 and 11 November and 25 December; 80F; ☎ (02) 512 77 09.

Law Courts – Open weekdays from 09.00 to 12.00 and from 14.00 to 16.00; closed at weekends and on public holidays.

Porte de Hal Folklore Museum – Open daily (except Mondays) from 10.00 to 17.00; closed Mondays, 1 January, 1 May, 1 and 11 November and 25 December; ☎ (02) 534 25 52.

Place du Jeu de Balle Flea Market – Every morning; main market on Sunday mornings.

Botanical Gardens – Open daily from 10.00 to 18.00; temporary exhibitions daily except Mondays from 11.00 to 18.00; ☎ (02) 217 63 86.

Royal Museums of Art and History – Open Tuesdays to Fridays from 09.30 to 17.00; weekends and public holidays from 10.00 to 17.00; closed Mondays, 1 January, 1 May, 1 and 11 November and 25 December; ☎ (02) 741 72 11.

Royal Museum of the Army and Military History – Open daily (except Mondays) from 09.00 to 12.00 and from 13.00 to 16.30; closed Mondays, 1 January, 1 May, 1 November and 25 December; ☎ (02) 733 44 93 (ext. 53).

Autoworld – Open daily from 10.00 to 18.00 (17.00 beginning of October to end of March); closed 1 January and 25 December; 150F; ☎ (02) 736 41 65.

Natural Science Museum – Open Tuesdays to Saturdays from 09.30 to 16.45; Sundays from 09.30 to 18.00; closed Mondays, 1 January and 25 December; 120F; ☎ (02) 627 42 38.

Brussels Communes

St-Gilles

Horta Museum – Open daily (except Mondays) from 14.00 to 17.30; closed Mondays, 1 January, Easter Day, 1 May, Ascension Day, Whit Sunday, 21 July, 15 August, 1 and 11 November and 25 December; 100F (200F at weekends); ☎ (02) 537 16 92.

Ixelles

Community Museum – Open Tuesdays to Fridays from 13.00 to 19.30, weekends from 10.00 to 17.00; closed Mondays and public holidays; ☎ (02) 511 90 84, ext. 1158; may close for restoration work end 1993/beginning 1994.

Abbey of Notre-Dame-de-la-Cambre Church – Open weekdays from 09.00 to 11.30 and from 15.00 to 17.00; Sundays from 15.00 to 18.00 on request only; closed during services and on public holidays; ☎ (02) 648 11 21.

Constantin Meunier Museum – Open from 10.00 to 12.00 and from 13.00 to 17.00; closed on Mondays, 1 January, 1 May, 1 and 11 November and 25 December; ☎ (02) 648 44 49.

Uccle

David and Alice van Buuren Museum – Guided tour (45 min; 20 min for gardens) Mondays (excluding public holidays) at 14.00 and 15.00; group visits by prior appointment Tuesdays to Saturdays; closed Easter Monday, 1 to 15 July, 1 November and 25 December; 150F; ☎ (02) 343 48 51.

Forest

St Denis's Church – By appointment only; contact Abbé Wayembergh, ☎ (02) 344 87 19.

Anderlecht

Erasmus's House – Open from 10.00 to 12.00 and from 14.00 to 17.00; closed Tuesdays and Fridays and 1 January; 20F; ☎ (02) 521 13 83.

Collegiate Church – Open Mondays to Saturdays from 09.00 to 12.00 and from 14.30 to 18.00 (17.00 during winter); closed Sundays and during services; ☎ (02) 521 84 15.

Gueuze Museum – Open weekdays from 08.30 to 16.30; Saturdays from 10.00 to 17.00 (13.00 beginning of June to mid-October); closed Sundays and public holidays; 70F; ☎ (02) 521 49 28.

Koekelberg

National Basilica of the Sacred Heart: Access to the Gallery-walkway – Open weekdays at 11.00 and 15.00; 50F; ☎ (02) 425 88 22.

Access to top of Dome – Guided tour (20 min) weekdays at 11.00 and 15.00; also open beginning May to mid-October on Sundays and public holidays from 14.00 to 17.45; visits on Saturdays by appointment only; 50F; ☎ (02) 425 88 22.

Jette

National Museum of Historical Figurines – Open Tuesdays to Fridays from 10.00 to 12.30 and from 14.00 to 16.00; also open on first weekend of every month; closed public holidays; ☎ (02) 479 00 52.

Laeken

Church of Our Lady of Laeken – Open beginning of April to end of October on first Sunday of the month only from 15.00 to 17.00.

Laeken Royal Palace: Royal Greenhouses – Open for a few days in the spring; for details telephone: ☎ (02) 513 89 40.

Japanese Tower – Open from 10.00 to 16.45; closed Mondays, 1 January, 1 May, 1 and 11 November and 25 December; ☎ (02) 268 16 08.

Chinese Pavilion – Due to reopen in 1994; open from 10.00 to 16.45; closed Mondays, 1 January, 1 May, 1 and 11 November and 25 December; ☎ (02) 268 16 08.

Heysel

Atomium – Open July and August daily from 09.30 to 18.00; beginning of September to end of June from 10.00 to 18.00; panorama open until 20.00; 160F; ☎ (02) 477 09 77.

Mini-Europe – The brochure given with the admission ticket explains the identity of the models; open daily end of March to beginning of January from 09.30 to 18.00 (20.00 in July and August); 360F; ☎ (02) 478 05 50.

Excursions

Soignes Forest

Tervuren: Royal Museum of Central Africa – Open mid-March to mid-October daily (except Mondays) from 09.00 to 17.30; otherwise daily (except Mondays) from 10.00 to 16.30; closed 1 January and 25 December; 50F; ☎ (02) 769 52 11.

Arboretum – Open sunrise to sunset.

La Hulpe: Solvay Estate Park – Open beginning of April to end of September daily from 08.00 to 21.00; otherwise daily from 09.00 to 18.00; ☎ (02) 653 64 04.

Rixensart Palace – Guided tour (35 min) from Passion Sunday to end of September on Sundays from 14.00 to 18.00; 150F; ☎ (02) 504 04 11.

Beersel and Huizingen

Beersel Fortress – *NB: upper floors and watch paths are dangerous*; open beginning of March to mid-November daily (except Mondays) from 10.00 to 12.00 and from 14.00 to 18.00; mid-November to end of February open weekends and public holidays from 10.00 to 12.00 from 14.00 to 18.00; 60F; ☎ (02) 331 00 24.

Huizingen Provincial Recreation Area – Admission: 40F (80F in high season); ☎ (02) 380 10 20.

Gaasbeek

Palace – Open in July and August daily (except Fridays) from 10.00 to 17.00; beginning of April to end of June and beginning of September to end of October open Tuesdays to Thursdays, at weekends and on public holidays from 10.00 to 17.00; closed beginning of November to end of March; 120F; ☎ (02) 532 43 72.

Grounds – Open in July and August daily (except Fridays) from 08.00 to 20.00; beginning of April to end of June and beginning of September to end of October open Tuesdays to Thursdays, at weekends and on public holidays from 08.00 to 20.00; closed beginning of November to end of March; ☎ (02) 532 43 72.

Meise

Bouchout Domain Park – Open Easter to end of October daily from 09.00 to 17.30 (18.00 on Sundays and public holidays); otherwise daily from 09.00 to 17.00; ☎ (02) 269 39 05.

National Botanical Garden: Plantenpaleis (greenhouses) – Open Easter to end of October Mondays to Thursdays from 13.00 to 16.00, Sundays from 14.00 to 17.30; otherwise Mondays to Thursdays from 13.00 to 15.30; 120F; ☎ (02) 269 39 05.

Vilvoorde

Church of Our Lady – Closed until further notice.

CANAL DU CENTRE

Strépy-Thieu Visitor Centre – Open daily from 10.00 to 18.00; 40F; ☎ (065) 36 04 64.

Boat trip – Daily in July and August; from beginning of May to end of June and in September on Saturdays only; Rtn: 370F (children: 300F); it is compulsory to book in advance; ☎ (065) 66 25 61.

Exhibition – Open in July and August daily from 10.00 to 18.00; in May, June and September at weekends and on public holidays only from 10.00 to 16.00.

CHARLEROI

🅸 Maison Communale Annexe Dampremy, av Mascaux 100, Marcinelle, ☎ (071) 43 49 55

Gerpinnes Museum of Entre-Sambre-et-Meuse Folklore Processions – Open beginning of May to end of September at weekends and on public holidays from 14.00 to 18.00; 50F; ☎ (071) 21 64 21.

Museum of Fine Art – Open Tuesdays to Saturdays from 09.00 to 17.00; also open Sundays during temporary exhibitions; closed Mondays, 1 and 2 January, during the Carnival, Easter, Ascension Day, Whitsun, 21 July, 15 August, 1, 2 and 11 November, 25 and 26 December, 50F; ☎ (071) 23 02 95.

Glass Museum – Open Tuesdays to Saturdays from 09.00 to 17.00; closed Sundays and public holidays; 50F; ☎ (071) 31 08 38.

Excursion

Mont-sur-Marchienne: Photography Museum – Open daily (except Mondays) from 10.00 to 18.00; closed 1 January, Easter, 1 May, Whitsun, Ascension Day, 21 July, 15 August, 1 and 11 November and at Christmas; 50F; ☎ (071) 43 58 10.

CHIMAY

Palace – Guided tour (45 min) beginning of March to 1 November daily from 10.00 to 12.00 and from 14.30 to 18.00; 150F; ☎ (060) 21 28 23.

Collegiate Church – Open weekdays from 09.00 to 12.00 and from 14.00 to 16.30 (18.30 beginning of October to end of April); Saturdays from 09.00 to 17.00; Sundays and public holidays from 11.00 to 17.00.

Excursion

Virelles Lake – Open beginning of May to end of September daily from 10.00 to 18.00; 80F; guided tours in June, July and August on Sundays at 10.00 and 15.00, otherwise on the first and third Sunday of the month at these times; tour: 100F; ☎ (071) 38 17 61 or (060) 21 13 63.

COUVIN

Cavernes de l'Abîme – Guided tour (45 min) mid-June to mid-September daily from 10.00 to 12.00 and from 13.30 to 18.00; beginning of April to end of September at weekends from 10.00 to 12.00 and from 13.30 to 18.00; in October on Sundays from 10.00 to 12.00 and from 13.30 to 18.00; 120F; ☎ (060) 31 19 54 (in season) and (02) 731 59 67.

Round tour (west)

Neptune Caves – Guided tour (45 min) beginning of April to end of September daily from 09.30 to 12.00 and from 13.30 to 18.00; in October at weekends from 09.30 to 12.00 and from 13.30 to 18.00; 200F (joint ticket with Cavernes de l'Abîme: 280F); ☎ (060) 31 19 54 (in season) of (02) 731 59 67.

Mariembourg Three Valleys Railway – Mariembourg-Treignes (time: 30 min) from beginning of April to beginning of October; 240F Rtn (children: 120F); Mariembourg-Chimay-Momignies (time: 1 hour) from beginning of April to beginning of October; 360F; further information from: ☎ (060) 31 24 40.

Excursion (French Border Region)

Brûly-de-Pesche: Hitler's Bunker – Open Easter to end of September daily from 09.30 to 12.00 and from 13.00 to 18.30; also at weekends in September and October; 100F; ☎ (060) 34 54 54.

Cul-des-Sarts: Regional Museum (des Rièzes et des Sarts) – Open Easter to end of September on Tuesdays and Thursdays from 09.00 to 16.00, weekends and public holidays from 15.00 to 18.00; 50F; ☎ (060) 37 70 03.

Join us in our constant task of keeping up-to-date.
Please send us your comments and suggestions.

Michelin Tyre PLC
Tourism Department
The Edward Hyde Building
38 Clarendon Road
WATFORD - Herts WD1 1SX
Tel : (0923) 415000

D

DAMME

Stadhuis, Markt, ☎ (050) 35 33 19

Access by boat (leaving from Bruges) – Time: 35 min; departures from Bruges: from beginning of April to end of September at 10.00, 12.00, 14.00, 16.20 and 18.00; departures from Damme (Damse Vaart Zuid 12): at 09.15, 11.00, 13.00, 15.00, 17.20; 130F, Rtn: 190F (children: 90F); ☎ (050) 35 33 19 (every day), or (052) 33 37 62 (except Sundays and Mondays).

Town Hall – Open beginning of May to end of September on weekdays from 09.00 to 12.00 and from 14.00 to 18.00; at weekends and on public holidays from 10.00 to 12.00 and from 14.00 to 18.00; otherwise open weekdays from 09.00 to 12.00 and from 14.00 to 17.00; weekends and public holidays from 14.00 to 17.00; closed 1 January and 25 December; 30F; ☎ (050) 35 33 19.

Church of Our Lady – Open beginning of April to end of September from 10.00 to 12.00 and from 14.30 to 17.30; access to top of tower: 20F; ☎ (050) 35 33 19.

St John's Hospital – Open beginning of April to end of September daily (except Mondays and Fridays) from 10.00 (11.00 Sundays and public holidays) to 12.00 and from 14.00 to 18.00; otherwise weekends only from 14.00 to 17.30; closed 1 January, first Sunday in September, and 25 December; 30F; ☎ (050) 35 88 10.

Till Eulenspiegel Museum – Closed for restoration work; scheduled to reopen at the end of 1994; further information from the tourist office: ☎ (050) 35 33 19.

Mill – Open in July and August daily from 10.00 to 12.30 and from 13.15 to 17.45; otherwise guided tours on request; ☎ (050) 35 33 19.

DENDERMONDE

Stadhuis, Markt, ☎ (052) 21 39 56

Municipal Museum – Open from beginning of April to end of September daily from 09.00 to 12.30 and from 13.30 to 17.30; otherwise guided visits on appointment; ☎ (052) 21 30 18 or (052) 21 39 56.

Church of Our Lady – Guided tour (30 min) Easter to beginning of October weekends and public holidays from 14.00 to 17.00; further information from tourist office; ☎ (052) 21 39 56.

Beguine Convent Museums – Open beginning of April to end of October daily from 09.00 to 12.30 and from 13.30 to 17.30; ☎ (052) 21 30 18.

DEURLE

Gust de Smet Museum – Guided tour (45 min) Wednesdays to Sundays from 14.00 to 18.00 (17.00 in February, March, April, October, November and December); also Sundays from 10.00 to 12.00 beginning of May to end of September; closed in January; 20F; ☎ (091) 82 77 42.

Léon de Smet Museum – Open mid-February to mid-December Wednesdays to Sundays from 14.00 to 18.00; closed Mondays, Tuesdays and from mid-December to mid-February; 30F; ☎ (091) 82 30 90.

Mevrouw Jules Dhondt-Dhaenens Museum – Open mid-February to mid-December Wednesdays to Fridays from 14.00 to 17.00 (18.00 during summer); also weekends and public holidays from 10.00 to 12.00 and from 14.00 to 17.00 (18.00 during summer); 40F; ☎ (09) 282 51 23.

DIEST

Stedelijk Museum, Stadhuis, Grote Markt 1, ☎ (013) 31 21 21 (ext. 271)

Church of St Sulpitius and St Dionysius – Open mid-May to end of September daily from 14.00 to 17.00; 30F; ☎ (013) 31 20 07.

Community Museum – Open beginning of January to end of October daily from 10.00 to 12.00 and from 13.00 to 17.00; otherwise Sundays only from 10.00 to 12.00 and from 13.00 to 17.00; closed 1 January and 25 December; ☎ (013) 31 21 21.

Beguine Convent Church – Guided tour by prior appointment, contact the tourist office; ☎ (013) 31 21 21.

Church (St.-Barbarakerk) – Open weekdays from 07.30 to 12.00 and from 18.45 to 19.30; Saturdays from 07.30 to 12.00 and from 19.00 to 20.00; Sundays and public holidays from 09.00 to 12.00; ☎ (013) 31 10 41.

DIKSMUIDE

Yser Tower – Open in July and August from 09.00 to 19.00, in June from 09.00 to 12.30 and from 13.30 to 18.00, Easter holidays to end of May and beginning of September to 11 November from 09.00 (10.00 weekends and public holidays) to 12.30 and from 13.30 to 17.00; 60F; ☎ (051) 50 02 86.

Trench of Death – Open beginning of June to end of August daily from 09.00 to 18.30, in May from 09.00 to 18.00, Easter to end of April and in September, on first two Sundays in October and 11 November from 09.00 to 17.00; last admissions 30 min before closing time; 60F; ☎ (051) 50 17 16.

DINANT

Rue Grande 37, ☎ (082) 22 28 70

Boat trips – Daily departures beginning of April to end of October from 10.00 to 19.00; 150F; further information: C. Marsigny, rue Daoust 64, 5500 Dinant, ☎ (082) 22 23 15.

Citadel – Guided tour (45 min) beginning of April to end of September daily from 09.30 to 18.00; otherwise daily from 10.00 to 12.00 and from 13.00 to 16.00; closed in January during the week, on Fridays from October to March, 1 January and 25 December; 160 F; ☎ (082) 22 21 19.

Cave (Grotte la Merveilleuse) – Guided tour (50 min) beginning of April to end of September daily on the hour from 10.00 to 18.00; otherwise weekends and public holidays from 11.00 to 16.00; also open during the Carnival and Christmas holidays; closed 1 January and 25 December; 160 F. ☎ (082) 22 22 10.

Mont-Fat Park – Open beginning of April to end of September; closed Mondays and Fridays in September; 150F (children: 100F) includes entrance to the tower, the cable car, the playing field and the Prehistoric Cave; ☎ (082) 22 27 83.

Prehistoric Cave – Same admission times and charges as for Mont-Fat Park (above).

Excursion 1

Bouvignes: Spanish House Museum of Local History – Open beginning of May to first weekend of October daily (except Mondays) from 13.00 to 18.00; 60F; ☎ (082) 22 49 10 or (082) 22 45 53.

St Lambert's Church – Visits by prior request to Révérend Raty, 1 rue des Potiers, 5500 Dinant, ☎ (082) 22 30 25 or 22 32 59.

Excursion 2

Down the River Lesse – Anseremme-Houyet can be reached by train or SNCV bus; there are several departures every morning. Reservations can be made with Lesse kayaks, place de l'Église 2, 5500 Dinant, ☎ (082) 22 43 97 or Meuse et Lesse, Libert Frères, rue Cousin 13, 5500 Dinant, ☎ (082) 22 61 86, or Kayaks Ansiaux, rue du Vélodrome 15, 5500 Dinant, ☎ (082) 22 23 25.

Excursion 3

Furfooz Park – Open beginning of February to end of November daily from 10.00 to sunset; otherwise from 10.00 to 16.00; closed 1 to 15 December and 15 to 31 January; 70F; ☎ (082) 22 34 77.

Vêves Castle – Open Easter to 1 November Mondays to Saturdays from 10.00 to 12.00 and from 14.00 to 18.00, Sundays from 10.00 to 18.00; 150F; ☎ (082) 66 63 95.

E

ENGHIEN

Castle Gardens – Open Easter to end of September daily from 13.00 to 20.00; otherwise weekends and public holidays only from 13.00 to 18.00; 80F; ☎ (02) 395 84 48.

Capuchin Church – Guided tour (1 hour) by written request to: Archives of Arenberg, Kapucijnenstraat 5, 7850 Edingen; 20 F.

St Nicholas's Church – Open mid-March to end of April daily (including public holidays) from 08.00 to 12.00 and from 14.00 to 17.00 (19.30 Saturdays); otherwise from 09.00 (08.00 on Sundays and public holidays) to 17.00 (19.30 on Saturdays); ☎ (02) 395 54 61.

Tapestry Museum – Open Tuesdays to Fridays from 14.00 to 17.00; Saturdays from 14.00 to 19.00; Sundays and public holidays from 10.00 to 12.00 and from 14.00 to 19.00; ☎ (02) 395 83 60.

EUPEN

i Marktplatz 7, ☎ (087) 55 34 50

Eupen Town Museum – Open weekdays from 09.30 to 12.00 and from 13.00 to 16.00, Wednesdays from 18.00 to 20.00, Saturdays from 14.00 to 17.00, Sundays and public holidays from 10.00 to 12.00 and from 14.00 to 17.00; closed 1 January, during the Carnival and the *Kermesse* in June, and 25 December; 30F; ☎ (087) 74 00 05.

Excursions

Vesdre Dam Viewpoint – Admission: 25F;

Henri-Chapelle: Memorial Museum – Open daily from 09.00 to 18.00 (17.00 beginning of November to end of March); ☎ (087) 68 71 73.

Triple Milestone: Baldwin Tower – Open beginning of April to end of October daily from 10.00 to 18.00; otherwise at weekends and on public holidays only from 10.00 to 16.00; 40F.

F

FOURNEAU-ST-MICHEL

Museum of Walloon Country Life – Open in July and August daily from 09.00 to 18.00; beginning of April to end of June and first fortnight in September from 09.00 to 17.00 (18.00 at weekends and on public holidays); mid-September to mid-November weekends and public holidays only from 09.00 to 18.00; closed beginning of December to end of March; 100F; ☎ (084) 21 06 13.

Iron and Ancient Metallurgy Museum – Open in July and August daily from 09.00 to 18.00; beginning of March to end of June and beginning of September to end of December open weekdays from 09.00 to 17.00, weekends from 09.00 to 18.00; closed in January and February; 100F; ☎ (084) 21 06 13.

P J Redouté Museum – Same admission times as for the Museum of Walloon Country Life; 20F.

FREŸR

Château and Gardens – Guided tour (75 min) in July and August at weekends and on public holidays from 14.00 to 18.00; 200F; ☎ (082) 22 22 00.

G

GEMBLOUX

Bailli House – Museum on Local Life on first floor: open daily from 10.00 to 12.00 and from 14.00 to 16.00; closed on public holidays; ☎ (081) 61 51 71.

Excursion

Corroy-le-Château: Feudal Castle – Guided tour (1 hour) beginning of May to end of September at weekends and on public holidays from 10.00 to 12.00 and from 14.00 to 18.00; 100F; ☎ (081) 63 32 32.

GENK

🅸 Gemeentehuis, Dieplaan 2, ☎ (089) 35 39 11

Excursions

De Maten Nature Reserve – Open beginning of July to end of February from sunrise to sunset; ☎ (089) 35 41 25.

Zwartberg: Limburgse Zoo – Open beginning of April to mid-November daily from 09.00 to 19.00; 290F (children: 145F); ☎ (089) 38 18 44.

GENT

🅸 Stadhuis-krypte, Botermarkt, ☎ (09) 24 15 55

Boat trips – On the canals: departures from Graslei and Korenlei; further information from Benelux-Gent-Watertoerist, Baarledorpstraat 87, ☎ (09) 282 92 48 or from De Bootjes van Gent, Rederij Dewaele, Halvemaanstraat 41, 9040 St.-Amandsberg, ☎ (09) 223 88 53. See also under Leie River Trip (Excursions below).

Old Town: illuminations – Every evening from beginning of April to end of October and during second fortnight of December; otherwise on Fridays and Saturdays only.

St Bavo's Cathedral – Open beginning of April to end of September Mondays to Saturdays from 09.30 to 12.00 and from 14.00 to 18.00, Sundays and public holidays from 13.00 to 18.00; otherwise Mondays to Saturdays from 10.30 to 12.00 and from 14.30 to 16.00, Sundays and public holidays from 14.00 to 17.00; closed 1 January and 25 December; access to the tower between the Saturday before 21 July and the Monday after this date from 11.00 to 18.00: 10F; to view the polyptych and crypt: 50F (joint ticket).

Belfry – Open beginning of April to end of October daily from 10.00 to 12.30 and from 14.00 to 17.30; 80F; ☎ (09) 233 39 54.

Town Hall – Guided tour (40 min) beginning of April to end of October Mondays to Thursdays at 16.00 (in English); closed Easter Monday, 1 and 28 May and 8 June; 60F; ☎ (09) 224 15 55 or (09) 233 07 72 (mornings only).

Folklore Museum – Open daily beginning of April to beginning of November from 09.00 to 12.30 and from 13.30 to 17.30; otherwise daily (except Mondays) from 10.00 to 12.00 and from 13.30 to 17.00; closed 1 January and 25 December; 50 F; ☎ (09) 223 13 36.

Marionette Theatre – Performances from beginning of September to end of July on Wednesdays at 14.30 and Saturdays at 15.00; closed 1 January and 25 December; 50F; ☎ (09) 223 13 36.

Gravensteen – Open daily from 09.00 to 17.15 (16.15 beginning of October to end of March); closed 1 and 2 January, 25 and 26 December; 80 F; ☎ (09) 223 99 22.

Fine Art Museum – Open daily (except Mondays) from 09.30 to 17.30; closed 1 and 2 January, 25 and 26 December; 80F; ☎ (09) 222 17 03.

Bijloke Museum – Open daily (except Mondays) from 09.30 to 17.00; closed 1 and 2 January, 25 and 26 December; 80F; ☎ (09) 225 11 06.

Museum of Decorative Arts – Open daily (except Mondays) from 09.30 to 17.00; closed 1 and 2 January, 25 and 26 December; 80F; ☎ (09) 225 66 76.

St.-Bavo's Abbey Ruins – Open beginning of April to beginning of November daily (except Mondays) from 09.30 to 17.00; closed 1 and 2 January, 25 and 26 December; 80F; ☎ (09) 225 11 06.

Excursions

St.-Amandsberg Large Beguine Convent Museum – Open beginning of April to end of October on Wednesdays, Thursdays, at weekends and on public holidays from 09.00 to 11.00 and from 14.00 to 17.30; 25F; ☎ (09) 228 19 13.

Leie River Trip – May to September; further information from Rederij Benelux, Recollettenlei 10, 9000 Gent, ☎ (09) 224 32 33. During the same period Rederij Benelux organises day trips by boat every Thursday, stopping at St.-Martens-Latem, Deinze and Deurle and allowing time to visit various museums, for reservations (compulsory) and further details call: ☎ (09) 224 32 33.

Ooidonk Palace – Guided tour (50 min) Easter to end of October on Sundays and public holidays from 14.00 to 17.30; in July and August also on Saturdays from 14.00 to 17.30; otherwise visit by prior appointment only; 120F; ☎ (09) 282 61 23.

Museum of Deinze and the Leie region – Open weekdays (except Tuesdays) from 14.00 to 17.30; weekends and public holidays from 10.00 to 12.00 and from 14.00 to 17.00; closed 1 January, 25 and 26 December; 40F; ☎ (09) 386 00 11.

GERAARDSBERGEN

i Stadhuis, ☎ (054) 41 41 21

St Adrian's Abbey Museum – Open Easter to first weekend of October weekdays from 09.30 to 11.30 and from 13.00 to 16.30, Sundays and public holidays from 14.00 to 18.00; 30F; ☎ (054) 41 13 94.

GRAND HORNU

Tour – Open beginning of March to end of September Tuesdays to Sundays from 10.00 to 12.00 and from 14.00 to 18.00; beginning of October to end of February from 10.00 to 12.00 and from 14.00 to 16.00 (17.00 at weekends); closed Mondays, 1 January and 25 December; 100F; ☎ (065) 77 07 12.

H

HAKENDOVER

Church (Kerk van de Goddelijke Zaligmaker) – To visit, contact the presbytery, Schoolpad 43, ☎ (016) 78 80 98.

HALLE

Basilica – Open daily from 08.00 to 18.00; guided tour (1 hour) of the tower; on 31 May from 14.30 to 16.00, 20 June from 14.45 to 15.45, 5 September from 14.30 to 16.00; 40F; ☎ (02) 356 42 59.

Crypt (Treasury) – Open 20 and 29 May from 14.00 to 17.00, 30 May from 15.00 to 18.00, 31 May from 14.00 to 17.00 and 5 September from 14.00 to 17.00; otherwise by appointment only; 20F; ☎ (02) 356 42 59.

Southwest Brabant Museum – Open beginning of April to end of October on Sundays from 14.00 to 18.00; also beginning of May to end of August on Saturdays from 14.00 to 18.00; 40F; ☎ (02) 356 42 59.

Excursion

Rebecq Tourist Train – Departures between beginning of May and end of September on Sundays and public holidays at 14.30, 16.00 and 17.30; time: 1 hour; 100F (children: 80F).

HAN-SUR-LESSE

Han Cave – Guided tour (1 hour 45 min) May to August every 30 min from 09.30 to 11.30 and from 13.00 to 18.00 (17.00 in May and June); in April, September and October every hour from 10.00 to 12.00 and from 13.30 to 16.30; in March and November and during Christmas school holidays every two hours from 10.00 to 12.00 and from 14.00 to 16.00; 275F (children: 195F): ☎ (084) 37 72 13.

Museum – Open in July and August daily from 10.00 to 20.00; also in April, May, June and beginning of September to mid-November from 10.00 to 18.00; 70F; ☎ (084) 37 70 07.

Safari – Guided tour (1 hour 15 min) same opening times as Han Cave; 185F (children: 130F); ☎ (084) 37 72 13.

Excursion

Lavaux-Ste-Anne: Museum of Hunting, Game, Falconry and Nature – Open beginning of March to end of October from 09.00 to 18.00; otherwise from 09.00 to 17.00; closed 1 January; 150F; ☎ (084) 38 83 62.

HASSELT

ℹ Lombaardstraat 3 ☎ (011) 22 22 35

Gin Museum – Open Tuesdays to Fridays from 10.00 to 17.00, at weekends and on public holidays from 14.00 to 18.00; closed in January, at Easter, 1, 2 and 11 November and 24 to 31 December; 60F; ☎ (011) 24 11 44.

Beguine Convent Provincial Museum of Modern Art – Open Tuesdays to Saturdays from 10.00 to 12.00 and from 13.00 to 17.00, on Sundays from 14.00 to 17.00; closed Mondays and public holidays.

Stellingwerff-Waerdenhof Museum – Same admission times and charges as the Gin Museum; ☎ (011) 24 10 70.

Excursions

't Fonteintje Recreation Area – Open in July and August daily from 10.00 to 19.00; Easter to end of September on Wednesdays and at weekends from 13.00 to 18.00, public holidays from 10.00 to 19.00; 60F (children: 40F); ☎ (011) 42 20 03.

Molenheide Game Park – Open all year round from 10.00 to 19.00; 180F; ☎ (011) 52 10 44.

HAUTES FAGNES

Nature Reserve – Accompanied walks are organised leaving from Botrange Nature Centre; ☎ (080) 44 57 81.

Botrange Nature Centre – Open daily from 10.00 to 18.00; closed mid-November to mid-December; 70F; ☎ (080) 44 57 81.

Signal de Botrange: Tower – Closed due to work in progress.

HERENTALS

Fraikin Museum – To visit, contact VVV Herentals, ☎ (014) 21 90 88.

St Waudru's Church – Guided tour (1 hour) on request; contact VVV Herentals, ☎ (014) 21 90 88.

Beguine Convent – Guided tour on request, further information from VVV Herentals; ☎ (014) 21 90 88.

Excursions

Geel: St Dympna's Church – Guided tour (50 min) weekdays from 09.00 to 16.00; at weekends on request; closed public holidays; 10F; ☎ (014) 59 14 43.

Sluis: Jakob Smits Museum – Open Wednesdays to Sundays from 14.00 to 18.00; closed Mondays, Tuesdays, 1 January and 25 December; 40F; ☎ (014) 31 74 35.

Papekelders Viewpoint – Open beginning of May to end of September and during school holidays daily from 10.00 to 18.00; otherwise at weekends from 10.00 to 18.00; 25F; ☎ (014) 21 90 88.

HUY

ℹ Quai de Namur 4, ☎ (085) 21 29 15/23 45 69

Boat trip on the Meuse – Departure from below the Collegiate Church from April to September; time: 1 hour; 120F; ☎ (085) 21 29 15.

Collegiate Church of Our Lady – Open Mondays to Saturdays from 09.00 to 12.00 and from 14.00 to 17.00, Sundays and public holidays from 09.00 to 12.30 and from 14.00 to 17.00.

Treasury – Open daily from 09.00 to 12.00 and from 14.00 to 17.00; 50F; ☎ (085) 21 20 05.

Fortress – Open in July and August daily from 10.00 to 18.00 (20.00 weekends and public holidays); beginning of April to end of June and in September daily from 10.00 to 18.00; 120F; ☎ (085) 21 29 15.

Town Museum – Open beginning of April to the third week of October daily from 14.00 to 18.00; 60F; ☎ (085) 23 24 35.

La Sarte Playing Fields – Open beginning of April to end of October daily from 10.00 to 20.00; 100F; ☎ (085) 23 29 96.

Excursions

Amay Town Museum of Archaeological and Religious Art – Restoration work in progress; visit by prior appointment only; contact Mr J Willems: ☎ (085) 31 37 62 or Mr E Davin: ☎ (085) 31 11 44.

Château de Jehay – Open in July and August weekends and public holidays from 14.00 to 18.00; 150F (château and museum); ☎ (085) 31 17 16.

Museum of Archaeology and Speleology – Same opening times as the Château above.

The star ratings are allocated for various categories:

- ***regions of scenic beauty with dramatic natural features***
- ***cities with a cultural heritage***
- ***elegant resorts and charming villages***
- ***ancient monuments and fine architecture***
- ***museums and picture galleries.***

I

IEPER

ℹ Stadhuis, Grote Markt 1 ☎ (057) 20 07 24

Cloth Halls: Ascent of the Belfry and Memorial Museum – Open beginning of April to mid-November daily from 09.30 to 12.00 and from 13.30 to 17.30; 30F (joint ticket); ☎ (057) 20 07 24.

Hotel Museum Merghelynck – Guided tour (1 hour) Mondays to Saturdays from 10.00 to 12.00 and from 14.00 to 17.00; closed 15 to 31 July and on Sundays and official public holidays; 50F; ☎ (057) 20 30 42.

OCMW Museum – Open beginning of April to end of October daily from 09.30 to 12.00 and from 13.30 to 17.30; 30F; ☎ (057) 20 48 31.

St George's Memorial Church – Open daily from 09.00 to 18.00 (19.30 in summer); closed during services, on the first and third Sunday of the month between 10.30 and 11.30 and on the second, fourth and fifth Sunday of the month between 18.00 and 19.00; ☎ (057) 20 18 79.

Excursions

Bellewaerde Park – Open daily in July and August from 09.30 to 19.00; beginning of April to end of June and beginning of September to 12 September from 10.00 to 18.00; otherwise the two last weekends in September; 530F (children: 480F); ☎ (057) 46 86 86.

Kemmelberg Tower – Open daily (except Thursdays) from 10.00 to 20.00; closed Thursdays, also Fridays between beginning of November and beginning of May; 20F; ☎ (057) 44 69 50.

KNOKKE-HEIST

ℹ Zeedijk 660, ☎ (050) 60 16 16

Walks – Contact the tourist office for suggested routes.

Het Zwin Nature Reserve – Open beginning of April to end of September daily from 09.00 to 19.00; otherwise daily from 09.00 to 17.00; closed Wednesdays between beginning of November and end of March; 140F; ☎ (050) 60 70 81; the section of the reserve normally closed to the public can be visited as part of the guided tour (on Thursdays at 10.00 in spring and summer and on Sundays at 10.00 all year round; boots are indispensable and field glasses are recommended).

KOKSIJDE

Flower Market – Holy Saturday from 10.30 to 18.00.

Dunes Abbey – Open mid-June to mid-September daily from 10.00 to 18.00 (in July and August on Wednesdays from 10.00 to 22.00); otherwise weekdays from 09.00 to 12.30 and from 13.30 to 17.00, weekends and public holidays from 10.00 to 17.00; during Easter holidays daily from 10.00 to 18.00 and Christmas holidays daily from 10.00 to 17.00; closed in January and 25 December; 80F; ☎ (058) 51 19 33.

Church (Onze-Lieve-Vrouw ter Duinenkerk) – Open daily from 09.00 to 12.00 and from 14.30 to 18.00; ☎ (058) 52 15 15.

Paul Delvaux Museum (Sint-Idesbald) – Open in July and August daily from 10.30 to 18.30; in April, May, June and September daily (except Mondays) from 10.30 to 18.30; in October, November and December open Fridays, weekends and public holidays from 10.30 to 17.30; 150F; ☎ (058) 52 12 29.

Excursions

Oostduinkerke St Nicholas's Church – Guided tour (30 min) by prior appointment only; contact: Pastorie, Witte Burg 90, 8670 Oostduinkerke-Koksijde, ☎ (058) 51 23 33.

National Museum of Fishing – Open daily from 10.00 to 12.00 and from 14.00 to 18.00; closed 1 January, 1 November and 25 December; 80F; ☎ (058) 51 24 68.

Florishof Folklore Museum – Open Easter to mid-September daily (except Tuesdays) from 10.00 to 12.00 and from 13.00 to 18.00; otherwise open at weekends and during holiday periods from 10.00 to 12.00 and from 13.00 to 18.00; 45F; ☎ (058) 51 12 57.

KORTRIJK

ℹ Schouwburgplein, ☎ (056) 23 93 71

Town Hall – Open weekdays from 09.00 to 12.00 and from 14.00 to 17.00; closed weekends and public holidays; ☎ (056) 23 93 71.

Beguine Convent Museum – Open Mondays, Wednesdays, Thursdays and weekends from 14.00 to 17.00; 30 F; ☎ (056) 22 83 74.

Church of Our Lady – Open weekdays from 08.30 to 12.00 and from 14.00 to 18.30, Saturdays from 08.30 to 12.00, 14.00 to 16.00 and from 17.15 to 18.15, Sundays and public holidays from 09.00 to 12.00 and from 18.00 to 18.30; ☎ (056) 21 38 09.

Town Museum – Open Tuesdays to Sundays from 10.00 to 12.00 and from 14.00 to 17.00; closed 1 January and 25 December and the afternoons of 24 and 31 December; ☎ (056) 25 78 92.

KORTRIJK

National Linen Museum – Open beginning of March to end of November Tuesdays to Fridays from 09.30 to 12.30 and from 13.30 to 18.00, on Mondays from 13.30 to 18.00, weekends from 14.00 to 18.00; closed official public holidays and 11 July; 60F; ☎ (056) 21 01 38.

Excursion

Rumbeke Palace – Guided tour (1 hour 30 min) by appointment; contact N V Domein Sterrebos, Kerkplein 30, 8800 Rumbeke; 300F.

L

LAARNE

Castle – Open Easter to beginning of November from 14.00 to 17.30; closed Mondays and Fridays (except during July and August); 150F; ☎ (09) 230 91 55.

LESSINES

Hospital Notre-Dame à la Rose – Guided tour (1 hour 30 min) in July and August daily (except Saturdays) at 15.00; beginning of April to end of June and beginning of September to first Sunday in October on Sundays at 15.00; 120F; ☎ (068) 33 21 13.

Excursions

Ellezelles Wild Cat Mill – Guided tour (30 min) beginning May to end of September on Sundays from 14.00 to 18.00; 30F; ☎ (068) 54 22 12.

LEUVEN — **i** Stadhuis, Naamsestraat 1a, ☎ (016) 21 15 39

Brewery – Groups visits can be arranged in advance, ☎ (016) 24 74 61.

Town Hall – Guided tour (30 min) weekdays at 11.00 and 15.00, weekends at 15.00; closed 1 January and 25 December; 20F; ☎ (016) 21 15 39.

St Peter's Church: Museum of Religious Art – Open Tuesdays to Saturdays from 10.00 to 12.00 and from 14.00 to 17.00, Sundays and public holidays from 14.00 to 17.00; closed Mondays; 50F; ☎ (016) 22 69 06.

Vander Kelen-Mertens Town Museum – Open Tuesdays to Saturdays from 10.00 to 17.00, Sundays and public holidays from 14.00 to 17.00; closed Mondays; 50F; ☎ (016) 22 69 06.

St Gertrude's Church – Open beginning of June to end of September on Thursdays from 10.00 to 12.00 and from 14.00 to 17.00; closed on public holidays; ☎ (016) 23 68 74.

Park Abbey – Guided tour (1 hour 30 min) on Sundays and public holidays at 16.00; 80 F; ☎ (016) 40 63 29.

Excursions

Korbeek-Dijle St Bartholomew's Church – Visit by prior appointment only; contact ☎ (016) 47 77 42.

LIÈGE — **i** En Féronstrée 92, ☎ (041) 21 24 56

Fort Loncin – Grounds open (interior can only be visited as part of a guided tour) Wednesdays to Sundays from 09.00 to 18.00 (10.00 to 16.00 between beginning of October and end of March); guided tours (2 hours 30 min) beginning of April to beginning of October on Saturdays at 14.30; 60F; ☎ (041) 63 42 35.

Museum of Walloon Life – Open Tuesdays to Saturdays from 10.00 to 17.00, Sundays and public holidays from 10.00 to 16.00; closed Mondays, 1 January, 1 May, 1 November and 25 December; 80F; ☎ (041) 23 60 94.

Marionette Theatre – Performances beginning of November to end of April on Wednesdays at 14.30 and Sundays at 10.30; 80F; ☎ (041) 23 60 94.

Museum of Religious and Mosan Art – Open Tuesdays to Saturdays from 13.00 to 18.00, Sundays from 11.00 to 16.00; closed 1 January, 1 and 8 May, 1, 2, 11 and 15 November, and 24, 25, 26 and 31 December; 50F; ☎ (041) 23 18 93.

St Bartholomew's Church (font) – Open from 10.00 to 12.00 and from 14.00 to 17.00; closed mornings on Sundays and religious holidays, also Mondays between beginning of October and end of April; 80F; ☎ (041) 21 92 21.

Curtius Museum and Glass Museum – Open Mondays, Thursdays and Saturdays from 14.00 to 17.00, Wednesdays and Fridays from 10.00 to 13.00, second and fourth Sunday of the month from 10.00 to 13.00; closed Tuesdays, 1 January, 1 and 8 May, 1, 2, 11 and 15 November, 24, 25, 26 and 31 December; 50F; ☎ (041) 21 94 04.

Arms Museum – Open Mondays, Thursdays and weekends from 10.00 to 13.00, Wednesdays and Fridays from 14.00 to 17.00; closed Tuesdays, 1 January, 1 and 8 May, 1, 2, 11 and 15 November, 24, 25, 26 and 31 December; 50F; ☎ (041) 21 94 16.

Ansembourg Museum – Open daily (except Mondays) from 13.00 to 18.00; guided tour daily (except Mondays) at 13.00, 14.00, 15.00, 16.00 and 17.00; closed Mondays, 1 January, 1 and 8 May, 1, 2, 11 and 15 November, 24, 25, 26 and 31 December; 50F; ☎ (041) 21 94 02.

Museum of Walloon Art – Open Tuesdays to Saturdays from 13.00 to 18.00, Sundays and public holidays from 11.00 to 16.30; closed Mondays, 1 January, 1 and 8 May, 1, 2, 11 and 15 November, 24, 25, 26 and 31 December; 50F; ☎ (041) 21 92 31.

St Paul's Cathedral: Treasury – Guided tour (30 min) daily from 10.00 to 12.00 and from 14.00 to 17.00; 50F; 50 F. ☎ (041) 22 04 26.

St James's Church – Open beginning of May to end of September Mondays to Saturdays from 08.00 to 12.00 and from 17.00 to 19.00 (also from 14.00 to 18.00 during Easter school holidays and from beginning of July to mid-September), and on Sundays from 08.00 to 12.00 (also from 14.00 to 18.00 during Easter school holidays and from beginning of July to mid-September); otherwise from 08.00 to 12.00; closed 1 January, Easter Monday, 1 May, Whit Monday, 11 November, and 25 December; ☎ (041) 22 14 41.

St John's Church – Open during Easter fortnight and from mid-June to mid-September daily from 10.00 to 12.00 and from 14.00 to 17.00; otherwise daily (except Sundays) from 16.00 to 17.45; closed Sundays and public holidays; ☎ (041) 23 70 42.

Church of the Holy Cross: Treasury – Apply to the Sacristan, no 9 in the cloisters.

Metallurgy Centre – Open weekdays from 09.00 to 17.00, Saturdays from 09.00 to 12.00; closed Sundays and public holidays; 100F; ☎ (041) 42 65 63.

Aquarium – Open weekdays from 10.30 to 12.30 and from 13.30 to 17.30, weekends and public holidays from 10.30 to 12.30 and from 14.00 to 18.00; closed 1 January, 24, 25 and 31 December; 120F; ☎ (041) 66 50 00.

Tchantchès Museum – Open Tuesdays and Thursdays from 14.00 to 16.00; closed in July and on official public holidays; 20F; ☎ (041) 42 75 75.

Puppet Show – From mid-September to Easter holidays on Sundays at 10.30 and Wednesdays at 14.30.

Liège Public Transport Museum – Open beginning of April to end of October weekends and public holidays from 14.00 to 18.00; 40F; ☎ (041) 67 00 64.

Excursions

Boat trips – From Liège to Maastricht (3 hours 30 min) in July and August on Wednesdays and Fridays: leave from Liège at 08.30, from Coronmeuse at 09.00; 420F Rtn (children: 260F); in July and August a cruise is organised every Sunday from Liège to Visé, including a visit to the old Blégny coalmine, for further information contact ☎ (041) 87 43 33.

Chaudfontaine Maison Sauveur – Open weekdays from 09.00 to 12.00 and from 13.15 to 17.00; closed weekends and public holidays; ☎ (041) 65 18 34.

Aigremont Castle – Open daily (except Mondays) July and August from 10.00 to 12.00 and from 14.00 to 18.00; at weekends only from beginning of April to end of June and during September and October from 10.00 to 12.00 and from 14.00 to 18.00; 120F; ☎ (041) 36 16 87.

LIER

i Stadhuis, Grote Markt ☎ (03) 489 11 11 (ext. 212)

Zimmer Tower – Open Easter to end of October daily from 09.00 to 12.00 and from 13.00 to 19.00; otherwise daily from 09.00 to 12.00 and from 14.00 to 16.00; 50F; ☎ (03) 489 11 11.

Wuyts-Van Campen en Baron Caroly Museum – Open beginning of April to end of October from 10.00 to 12.00 and from 13.30 to 17.30; closed Mondays and Fridays; 40F; ☎ (03) 489 11 11 (ext. 278).

Timmermans-Opsomer House – Same admission times and charges as for Wuyts-Van Campen en Baron Caroly Museum, except on Sundays from beginning of November to end of March: open from 10.00 to 12.00 and from 13.30 to 16.30.

LOUVAIN-LA-NEUVE

Louvain-la-Neuve Museum – Open weekdays from 10.00 to 18.00, Sundays and public holidays (except in July and August) from 14.00 to 18.00; closed 1 January, Easter, 1 May, and from 24 to 31 December; ☎ (010) 47 48 41.

M

MAASEIK

i Markt 45, ☎ (089) 56 63 72

Boat trips – Mid-April to mid-October; further information from Maaseik tourist office, Markt 45, 3680 Maaseik, ☎ (089) 56 63 72.

Museactron – Open in July and August daily from 10.00 to 18.00; otherwise daily (except Mondays) from 10.00 to 12.00 and from 14.00 to 17.00; closed 1 January and 25 December; 50F; ☎ (089) 56 68 90.

St Catherine's Church: Treasury – Can be visited only by prior appointment; apply to Maaseik tourist office, Markt 45, 3680 Maaseik, ☎ (089) 56 63 72 or the Secretariaat Dekenij Maaseik, Mgr. Koningsstraat 5, 3680 Maaseik, ☎ (089) 56 41 08.

Aldeneik Church – Visit by prior appointment only: ☎ (089) 56 46 02 or tourist office ☎ (089) 56 78 25; closed Wednesday afternoons.

MALMÉDY

Ancienne Abbaye, place du Châtelet 10, ☎ (080) 33 02 50

Cathedral of SS Peter, Paul and Quirinus – Open daily from 09.00 to 18.00; closed during the carnival; ☎ (080) 33 00 26.

Excursion

Reinhardstein Castle – Guided tour (75 min) in July and August on Tuesdays, Thursdays and Saturdays at 15.30, Sundays and public holidays at 14.15, 15.15, 16.15 and 17.15; during the second fortnight of June and the first fortnight of September on Sundays and public holidays, also Easter Day, Ascension Day and Whit Sunday at 14.15, 15.15, 16.15 and 17.15; 150F; ☎ (080) 44 68 68.

MECHELEN

Stadhuis, Grote Markt, ☎ (015) 29 76 55

Carillon concerts – On Saturdays from 11.30 to 12.30 and Sundays from 15.00 to 16.00; also on Mondays (between beginning of June and end of September) from 20.30 to 21.30.

St Rumbald's Cathedral – Open beginning of April to end of September Mondays to Saturdays from 10.00 to 12.00 and from 13.00 to 18.00, Sundays from 13.00 to 18.00; otherwise Mondays to Saturdays from 10.00 to 12.00 and from 13.00 to 16.00, Sundays from 13.00 to 16.00; ☎ (015) 29 10 68.

Gaspard De Wit Royal Tapestry Works – Guided tour (1 hour 30) on Saturdays at 10.30; closed on public holidays, the period between Christmas and the New Year and in July; 150F; ☎ (015) 20 29 05.

St John's Church – Can be visited by prior appointment; ☎ (015) 20 50 27.

Church (Kerk van O.-L.-Vrouw over de Dijle) – Open beginning of May to end of September on Wednesdays and Saturdays from 14.00 to 17.00.

Excursions

Fort Breendonk – Open beginning of April to end of September daily from 09.00 to 17.00; otherwise daily from 10.00 to 16.00; closed 1 January and 25 December; 75F; ☎ (03) 886 62 09.

Muizen Plankendael zoological garden – Open June to August daily from 09.00 to 18.30; in March, April, May, September and October from 09.00 to 18.00; in January, February, November and December from 09.00 to 17.00; 320F (children: 195F); ☎ (015) 41 49 21 or (015) 41 43 49.

Elewijt Het Steen Castle – Only open to visitors on officially designated national visiting days; further information from the town hall (gemeentehuis) at Zemst (Elewijt).

Tremelo Father Damien Museum – Open on Sundays and public holidays from 14.00 to 17.00; April to end of June open also on Saturdays at these times; in July and August open daily (except Mondays) at these times; closed Mondays, 1 November and 25 December; ☎ (016) 53 05 19.

MEUSE/NAMUR REGION

Hastière-Lavaux Pont d'Arcole Caves – Guided tour (45 min) in July and August daily from 09.30 to 18.00; Easter to end of June and in September daily from 10.30 to 16.00; beginning of October to end of November at weekends from 13.00 to 16.00; 150F; ☎ (082) 64 44 01 or ☎ (081) 56 88 07.

Poilvache Castle – Open in July and August daily from 10.30 to 18.00; beginning of April to end of June and in September open weekends and public holidays from 10.30 to 18.00; 40F; ☎ (082) 61 35 14.

Yvoir Recreation Centre – Open in June, July and August daily from 10.30 to 20.00 (21.00 at weekends); in April and May on Saturdays from 11.00 to 18.30 and Sundays from 10.30 to 18.30; in September and October at weekends from 11.00 to 18.00; 35F; ☎ (082) 61 12 43.

Nature Oasis – Open in July and August daily from 10.00 to 19.00; in May, June and September at weekends from 10.00 to 18.00; 230F; ☎ (082) 61 10 84.

Frênes Rocks – Open daily (except Wednesdays) from 10.30 to 18.30; closed Wednesdays and during the Carnival; 50F; ☎ (081) 41 11 23.

Goyet caves and caverns – Guided tour (1 hour 30 min) beginning of March to end of November daily from 09.00 to 17.00; 220F; ☎ (081) 58 85 45.

Andenne: St Begga's Collegiate Church Museum and Treasury – Open Sundays from mid-July to mid-August from 14.30 to 18.00; also on first Sunday of May, June, September and October; closed from end of October to end of April; 75F; ☎ (085) 84 13 44.

MODAVE CASTLE

Castle – Open beginning of April to mid-November daily from 09.00 to 18.00; otherwise by appointment only; 150F; ☎ (085) 41 13 69.

Excursions

Bois-et-Borsu Church – Open at weekends and on public holidays beginning of April to end of October from 11.00 to 17.00, or on request; ☎ (086) 34 41 02.

MOLIGNÉE VALLEY

Falaën fortified farm – Open in July and August daily from 13.00 to 20.00; beginning of April to end of June and in September open weekends and public holidays from 13.00 to 20.00; 75F; ☎ (082) 69 96 26.

Maredsous Abbey – Open Mondays to Saturdays from 09.00 to 18.00, Sundays from 09.00 to 20.00; closed 1 January; ☎ (082) 69 91 55.

MONS

Grand'Place 22, ☎ (065) 33 55 80

St Waudru's Collegiate Church – Open Mondays to Saturdays from 09.00 to 18.30; closed Sundays from 13.00 to 16.00.

Treasury – Open end of June to end of September daily (except Mondays) from 14.00 to 17.00; 30F; ☎ (065) 33 55 80.

Town Hall – Guided tour (1 hour) by written request (a fortnight in advance) to: Office de Tourisme de Mons, Grand-Place 22, 7000 Mons; ☎ (065) 33 55 80.

Centenaire Museums – Open daily (except Mondays) from 10.00 to 12.00 and from 14.00 to 18.00 (between beginning of May and end of September closed at 17.00 on Fridays, beginning of October and end of April closed at 17.00 on Sundays); closed 1 November and during Christmas school holidays; 30F; ☎ (065) 33 52 13.

Museum of Life in Mons – Open beginning of May to end of September daily from 10.00 to 12.30 and from 14.00 to 18.00 (17.00 on Fridays); otherwise from 10.00 to 12.30 and from 14.00 to 18.00 (17.00 on Sundays); closed 1 November and during the Christmas school holidays; 30F; ☎ (065) 34 95 55.

Fine Art Museum – Same admission times and charges as Museum of Life in Mons; ☎ (065) 34 77 63.

Le Vieux Logis: Chanoine Puissant Museum – Same admission times and charges as Centenaire Museums; ☎ (065) 33 66 70.

Excursions

Cuesmes Van Gogh's House – Open daily (except Mondays) from 10.00 to 18.00; closed Mondays, 1 January and 25 December; 50F; ☎ (065) 33 55 80.

Roisin Verhaeren Museum – Guided tour (30 min) by prior appointment daily (except Fridays) from 10.00 to 12.00 and from 14.00 to 17.00; 50F; ☎ (065) 75 93 52.

N

NAMUR

Square de l'Europe Unie, ☎ (081) 22 28 59

Boat trips on the Meuse – Rtn trip Namur-Dinant in July and August on Sundays at 10.00 (Rtn at 19.00): 550F; Rtn trip Namur-Wépion in July and August daily at 15.00: 270F; Cruise along the Sambre and Meuse between beginning of April and end of August daily leaving at 10.00, 11.15, 13.30 and 17.00 (April and May at 13.30, 15.00 and 17.00 only); 150F; departure from the confluence of the Sambre and the Meuse; ☎ (081) 24 64 33 or (082) 22 23 15.

Citadel – Access by cablecar (time: 15 min) or road from beginning of April to first weekend in October daily from 11.00 to 19.00 (last admission at 17.30); 195F.

Fortified Estate – Open beginning of April to beginning of October daily from 11.00 to 19.00 (last admission at 17.30); 195F; ☎ (081) 22 68 29.

Provincial Forest Museum – Open beginning of April to end of October daily (except Fridays) from 09.00 to 12.00 and from 14.00 to 17.00 (open also on Fridays from mid-June to mid-September); 50F; ☎ (081) 74 38 94.

Archaelogical Museum – Open daily (except Tuesdays) from 10.00 to 17.00; 40F.

Oignies Treasury – Guided tour (40 min) on Mondays and on Wednesdays to Saturdays from 10.00 to 12.00 and from 14.00 to 17.00, Sundays from 14.00 to 17.00; closed Tuesdays and public holidays, and from 11 to 26 December; 50F; ☎ (081) 23 03 42.

Museum of Ancient Arts of the Namur Region – Open from 10.00 to 12.30 and from 13.30 to 17.00 (18.00 Easter to 1 November); closed Tuesdays and between Christmas and the New Year; 50F; ☎ (081) 22 00 65.

St Loup's Church – Currently under restoration.

Diocesan Museum and Cathedral Treasury – Open Easter to end of October from 10.00 to 12.00 and from 14.30 to 18.00; otherwise from 14.30 to 16.30; closed Mondays and Sunday mornings; 50F; ☎ (081) 22 21 64.

Musée de Croix – Guided tour (1 hour) daily at 10.00, 11.00, 14.00, 15.00 and 16.00; closed Tuesdays and between 23 December and 3 January; 50F; ☎ (081) 22 21 39.

Félicien Rops Museum – Open daily from 10.00 to 18.00 (17.00 from 1 November to Easter); closed Tuesdays (except in July and August) and during Christmas holidays; 100F; ☎ (081) 22 01 10.

Excursions

Franc-Waret Castle – Guided tour (1 hour) beginning of June to end of September weekends and public holidays from 14.00 to 17.30; 120F; ☎ (081) 83 34 04.

Floreffe Abbey – Guided tour (1 hour) in July and August daily at 10.30, 11.30, 13.30, 14.30, 16.00, 17.00 and 18.00; mid-March to end of June and beginning of September to end of October daily at 13.30, 14.30, 16.00 and 17.00; otherwise by appointment only; closed first week of January; 70F; ☎ (081) 44 53 03.

Fosses-la-Ville Petit Chapitre collection of traditional dolls – Open in July and August daily from 14.00 to 18.00; otherwise open weekends, public holidays and during school holidays from 14.00 to 18.00; 60F; ☎ (071) 71 12 02.

NIEUWPOORT

i Marktplein 7, ☎ (058) 23 55 94

Church (O.-L.-Vrouwekerk): carillon concerts – Mid-June to mid-September on Wednesdays and Saturdays at 20.30.

King Albert I Monument – Open daily from 09.00 to 12.00 and from 13.30 to 17.00 (19.00 during summer); closed in January and February; 30 F; ☎ (058) 23 55 87.

K R Berquin Museum – Closed until further notice.

Ornithological Museum – Open during Easter holidays and in July and August daily from 09.30 to 12.00 and from 14.00 to 17.30 (mornings only on Fridays in June and September); 20F; ☎ (058) 22 55 94.

De IJzermonding – Guided tour in July and August on Wednesdays at 10.30; otherwise by prior appointment, contact: Natuurreservaten VZW, Iepersesteenweg 56, 8600 Woumen, ☎ (051) 54 52 44.

NINOVE

Abbey Church – Open Mondays to Saturdays from 09.00 to 12.00 and from 14.00 to 17.00; closed mornings on Sundays and public holidays; ☎ (054) 33 78 58.

NIVELLES

i Waux-Hall, Grand'Place ☎ (067) 21 54 13

St Gertrude's Collegiate Church – Open beginning of April to end of September Mondays to Saturdays from 08.00 to 18.00; otherwise from 09.00 to 17.00; closed Sunday mornings; guided tour between beginning of April and end of September Mondays to Saturdays at 10.00, 11.00, 14.00 and 15.00, Sundays at 15.00; 70F; ☎ (067) 21 54 13.

Museum of Archaeology, History and Folklore – Open daily (except Tuesdays) from 09.30 to 12.00 and from 14.00 to 17.00 (open on Wednesdays from 09.30 to 17.00); 40F; ☎ (067) 21 21 61.

Excursions

Ronquières Inclined Plane – Open beginning of May to end of August daily from 10.00 to 18.00; access to tower: 70F; joint ticket with the Tourist Boat Ride: 130F.

Tourist Boat Ride (Parcours en bateau mouche) – Time: 1 hour; departures daily except on those Wednesdays and Saturdays which are not public holidays; weekdays at 12.00, 15.00 and 17.00, Sundays and public holidays at 12.00, 14.00, 15.30 and 17.00; 80F.

Bois-Seigneur-Isaac Manor-house – Open last two Sundays of June and first Sunday of July from 14.00 to 18.00; 100F; ☎ (067) 21 38 80.

O

OOSTENDE

i Monacoplein 2, ☎ (059) 70 34 77

North Sea Aquarium – Open weekends from 10.00 to 12.00 and from 14.00 to 18.00; between beginning of April and end of September open daily from 10.00 to 12.00 and from 14.00 to 18.00; 50F; ☎ (059) 32 16 69.

Fine Art Museum – Open daily (except Tuesdays) from 10.00 to 12.00 and from 14.00 to 17.00; closed Tuesdays, 1 January, 25 December; 50 F. ☎ (059) 80 53 35.

De Plate Museum of Local History – Open beginning of July to end of September and during Easter holidays daily (except Tuesdays and Sundays) from 10.00 to 12.00 and from 15.00 to 17.00; otherwise open only Saturdays and Whit weekend from 10.00 to 12.00 and from 15.00 to 17.00; 50F; ☎ (059) 80 53 35.

James Ensor's House – Open beginning of June to end of September and during Easter holidays daily (except Tuesdays) from 10.00 to 12.00 and from 14.00 to 17.00; during Christmas holidays open weekends (not public holidays) from 14.00 to 17.00; closed 1 January and 25 December; 50F; ☎ (059) 80 53 35.

Mercator Sailing Ship – Open in July and August daily from 09.00 to 19.00; in May, June, September and during the Easter holidays open daily from 09.00 to 12.00 and from 13.00 to 18.00; in March open at weekends from 10.00 to 12.00 and from 13.00 to 17.00; in April open weekends and public holidays from 09.00 to 12.00 and from 13.00 to 18.00; in October weekends from 10.00 to 12.00 and from 13.00 to 16.00; beginning of November to end of February open on Sunday and public holidays from 10.00 to 12.00 and from 13.00 to 16.00; 75F; ☎ (059) 70 56 54.

Modern Art Museum – Open daily (except Tuesdays) from 10.00 to 18.00; closed 1 January and 25 December; 100F; ☎ (059) 50 81 18.

Excursion

Jabbeke Provinciaal Museum Constant Permeke – Open daily (except Mondays) from 10.00 to 12.30 and from 13.30 to 18.00 (17.00 beginning of October to end of March); closed 1 January and 25 December; 50F; ☎ (059) 50 81 18.

ORVAL

Abbey Ruins – Open beginning of March to end of October daily from 09.30 to 12.30 and from 13.30 to 18.00 (18.30 between beginning of May and end of September); otherwise from 10.30 to 12.30 and from 13.30 to 17.30; 80F; ☎ (061) 31 10 60.

OUDENAARDE

i Stadhuis, Markt, ☎ (055) 31 72 51

Town Hall – Guided tour (1 hour) for groups of at least 20 by prior appointment between beginning of April and end of October daily at 10.00, 11.00, 14.00, 15.00 and 16.00; open also for visits without a tour at weekends from 14.00 to 17.00; closed Friday afternoons, last weekend in June and between beginning of November and end of March; 80 F. ☎ (055) 31 72 51.

Church (O.-L.-Vrouwekerk van Pamele) – Guided tour (30 min) from beginning of April to end of October by prior appointment only; 40F; contact the tourist office; ☎ (055) 31 72 51.

Tapestry Museum and Restoration Workshop – Open weekdays from 09.00 to 17.00; closed public holidays and weekends; ☎ (055) 31 48 63.

Excursion

Kruishoutem Veranneman Foundation – Open daily (except Mondays and Sundays) from 14.00 to 18.00; closed official public holidays; 50F; ☎ (09) 383 52 87.

OURTHE VALLEY

Hotton Caves – Guided tour (50 min) beginning of April to end of October daily from 10.00 to 17.00 (18.00 in July and August); 180F; ☎ (084) 46 60 46.

Logne Castle – Guided tour (1 hour) in July and August daily from 10.30 to 19.00; in May, June, September and October weekends and public holidays from 13.00 to 18.00; during Easter school holidays daily from 13.00 to 18.00; 90F; ☎ (086) 21 20 33.

Bouverie farm (Vieuxville) – Open in July and August daily from 13.00 to 18.00 or by appointment: ☎ (086) 21 20 33.

Comblain-au-Pont Caves – Closed until further notice.

Tilff Bee Museum – Open in July and August daily from 10.00 to 12.00 and from 14.00 to 18.00; April to June and in September at weekends and on public holidays from 14.00 to 18.00; 50F; ☎ (041) 88 22 63.

P

DE PANNE

i Gemeentehuis, Zeelaan 21, ☎ (058) 41 13 02

Excursions

Westhoek Nature Reserve guided walks – Contact the tourist office: Dienst voor Toerisme, Gemeentehuis, Zeelaan 21, 8660 De Panne, ☎ (058) 41 13 02.

Adinkerke: Meli Recreation Park – Open daily from beginning of April to mid-September, at weekends only during last two weeks of September, on Sundays only during October from 09.30 to 17.30 (in good weather the park may stay open until 19.00); 490F (no charge for children less than 1m - 3.28ft tall); ☎ (058) 42 02 02.

PHILIPPEVILLE

Underground installations – Guided tour (45 min) by appointment in July and August daily from 14.00 to 18.00; 100F; ☎ (071) 66 62 13.

POPERINGE

i Stadhuis, Grote Markt 1, ☎ (057) 33 40 81

National Hops Museum – Open daily in July and August and on Sundays and public holidays in May, June and September from 14.30 to 17.30; 50 F; ☎ (057) 33 40 81.

R

REDU-TRANSINNE

Euro Space Center – Open daily from 10.00 to 17.00; closed for a few weeks in January; 395 F; ☎ (061) 65 64 65.

LA ROCHE-EN-ARDENNE

i Place du Marché, ☎ (084) 41 13 42

Castle – Open in July and August daily from 10.00 to 19.00; in April, May, June, September and October daily from 10.00 to 12.00 and from 14.00 to 17.00; otherwise weekdays from 14.00 to 16.00 and weekends from 10.00 to 12.00 and from 14.00 to 16.00; 70F; ☎ (084) 41 13 42.

LA ROCHE-EN-ARDENNE

Blue Sandstone Ware Pottery – Guided tour (30 min) in July and August weekdays from 10.00 to 12.00 and from 14.00 to 17.30, weekends and public holidays from 14.00 to 17.30; during Easter holidays, and on 1 May, Ascension Day and at Whitsun open from 14.00 to 17.00; 75F; ☎ (084) 41 18 78.

Excursion

Six Ourthes Viewpoint tower – Open all year; 30F; ☎ (084) 44 41 93.

ROCHEFORT — i Rue Behogne 5, ☎ (084) 21 25 37

Cave – Guided tour (1 hour) May to August daily from 09.45 to 17.15 (every 45 min, except at 12.00); in April, September, October and during the first fortnight of November daily at 10.00, 11.30, 13.30, 15.00 and 16.30; 150F; ☎ (084) 21 20 80.

Excursions

Chevetogne Valery Cousin Provincial Estate – Open beginning of April to end of September from 10.00 to 20.00; 200F per motor vehicle plus a supplement in July and August of 50F per person; ☎ (083) 68 88 21.

Lessive Belgian Earth Station of Satellite Telecommunications – Guided tour (1 hour 30 min) mid-April to end of October daily from 09.30 to 17.00 (17.30 in July and August); 150F; ☎ (078) 11 88 22.

Jannée Castle – Guided tour (35 min) Easter to end of September daily from 10.00 to 18.00; 140F; ☎ (084) 68 82 07.

RONSE — i Stadhuis, Grote Markt, ☎ (055) 21 25 01 (ext. 24)

St Hermes Collegiate Church: crypt – Open Easter to mid-November Tuesdays to Saturdays from 10.00 to 12.00 and from 14.00 to 17.00; Sundays and public holidays from 10.00 to 12.00 and from 15.00 to 18.00; otherwise by appointment only; 40F; ☎ (055) 21 17 30.

Excursion

Hotond Mill – Open all year; 5F; ☎ (055) 21 33 05.

S

ST-HUBERT — i Palais Abbatial, Place de l'Abbaye, ☎ (061) 61 30 10

Basilica – Guided tour (1 hour 30 min) beginning of April to end of October; contact the warden at the basilica; otherwise make an appointment with Abbé G Leemans, rue Saint-Gilles 56, ☎ (061) 61 15 85.

Excursion

Game park – Open from 09.00 to 17.00 (18.00 beginning of April to end of September); 60F; ☎ (061) 61 17 15.

SEMOIS VALLEY

Chiny: Boat trip from Chiny to Lacuisine – Contact the Société des Passeurs Réunis, 6810 Chiny; ☎ (061) 31 19 03, from beginning of April to end of September daily; 200F.

Florenville Viewpoint – Open in July and August daily from 10.00 (11.00 Sundays) to 12.00 and from 14.00 to 18.00; closed during religious services; 30F; ☎ (061) 31 12 29.

2

Vresse-sur-Semois Museum of Tobacco and Folklore – Open in July and August daily from 11.00 to 13.00 and from 15.00 to 19.00; otherwise (except in January and February) on weekdays from 10.00 to 12.00 and from 13.00 to 17.00, at weekends and on public holidays from 11.00 to 13.00 and from 15.00 to 17.00; 100F; ☎ (061) 50 08 27.

SINT-NIKLAAS — i Grote Markt 45, ☎ (03) 777 26 81

St Nicholas's Church – Guided tour (30 min) by prior appointment; contact the tourist office: ☎ (03) 777 26 81.

Waas Region Historical Museum – Open beginning of April to end of September Tuesdays to Saturdays from 14.00 to 17.00, Sundays from 10.00 to 17.00; otherwise by appointment; closed 1 and 3 January and 25 December; 30F; ☎ (03) 777 29 42.

Music Box and Gramophone section – Same admission times and charges as Waas Region Historical Museum.

Historical Collections – Same admission times and charges as Waas Region Historical Museum.

International Ex-Libris Centre – Same admission times and charges as Waas Region Historical Museum.

Fine Art Salons – Open Tuesdays to Saturdays from 14.00 to 17.00 and Sundays from 10.00 to 17.00; closed 1 and 3 January and 25 December; 30 F; ☎ (03) 777 29 42.

Excursion

Bornem Castle – Guided tour (2 hours) for groups from mid-April to end of October by appointment only; telephone at 09.00: ☎ (03) 889 21 05 or (03) 889 01 79.

SINT-TRUIDEN

ℹ Stadhuis, Grote Markt, ☎ (011) 68 68 72

Beguine Convent Church – Open beginning of April to end of October weekdays from 10.00 to 12.30 and from 13.30 to 17.00, weekends and public holidays from 13.30 to 17.00; closed Mondays, Easter Monday and Whit Monday; 100F; ☎ (011) 68 85 79.

Studio Festraets – Tours from beginning of April to end of September Tuesdays to Fridays at 09.45, 10.45, 11.45, 13.45, 14.45, 15.45 and 16.45; weekends and public holidays afternoons only; 60F; ☎ (011) 68 87 52.

Brustem Gate – Guided tour (45 min) beginning of April to end of September by appointment only; contact the tourist office: ☎ (011) 68 68 72.

Lace Exhibition – Guided tour (20 min) Sundays and public holidays from 10.00 to 12.00 and from 14.00 to 18.00; 30F; ☎ (011) 68 23 56.

Excursion

Colen Abbey – Open Mondays to Saturdays from 10.00 to 11.30 and from 14.00 to 17.00; Sundays from 10.00 to 11.30 and from 15.30 to 17.45; closed at Easter, Whitsun, on 24 May, 15 August, 20 August, 1 November and 25 December; 30F; ☎ (012) 74 14 67.

SOIGNIES

St Vincent's Collegiate Church Treasury – Temporarily closed to visitors.

Excursions

Ecaussines-Lalaing fortress – Open in July and August daily (except Tuesdays and Wednesdays which are not public holidays) from 10.00 to 12.00 and from 14.00 to 18.00; in April, May, June, September and October open weekends and public holidays from 10.00 and 12.00 and from 14.00 to 18.00; 120F; ☎ (067) 44 24 90 or ☎ (02) 673 01 21.

Le Rœulx Palace – Closed for restoration work; scheduled to reopen in spring 1994.

SOUGNÉ-REMOUCHAMPS

Cave – Guided tour (1 hour 20 min) June to August daily from 09.00 to 19.00 (last admission 18.00); March to May, September and October daily from 09.30 to 17.30 (last admission 16.30); beginning of November to end of February daily from 10.00 to 17.00 (last admission 16.00); 225F; ☎ (041) 84 46 82.

Excursion

Deigne-Aywaille Monde Sauvage safari park – Open daily mid-March to mid-November from 10.00 to 19.00; otherwise weekends and public holidays only from 10.00 to 17.00; 225F; closed from 15 December to 5 January; ☎ (041) 60 90 70.

SPA

ℹ Pavillon des Petits Jeux, Place Royale 41, ☎ (087) 77 17 00

Pouhon Pierre-le-Grand – Open beginning of April to end of October daily from 10.00 to 12.00 and from 14.00 to 17.30; otherwise weekdays from 14.00 to 17.00, weekends and public holidays from 10.00 to 12.00 and from 14.00 to 17.00; tasting: 7F; ☎ (087) 77 17 00.

Guided tours – Walks are organised in July and August, and during the Christmas and Easter holidays; contact Office du Tourisme, Place Royale 41, 4900 Spa; ☎ (087) 77 25 10.

Spa Town Museum – Open mid-June to mid-September daily from 14.30 to 17.30; otherwise at weekends and on public holidays and during school holidays from 14.30 and 17.30; 60F.

Horse Museum – Same admission times as Spa Town Museum; 40F.

Excursions

Berinzenne Forest Museum – Open daily (except Mondays) in July and August from 14.00 to 17.00; on Wednesdays, at weekends and on public holidays beginning of March to end of June and beginning of September to mid-November from 14.00 to 17.00; closed on Mondays which are not public holidays; 60F; ☎ (087) 77 33 20.

Franchimont Castle – Open beginning of April to end of September daily from 10.00 to 19.00; otherwise weekends only from 10.00 to 19.00; 60F; ☎ (087) 54 10 27.

Theux Church of SS Hermes and Alexander – Open beginning of June to end of September from 10.00 to 18.00 (17.00 on Saturdays); beginning of October to end of May from 10.00 to 17.00; closed Sundays between 10.00 and 11.00; ☎ (087) 54 12 37.

La Reid Game Park – Open daily from 09.00 to 18.00 (17.00 beginning of October to end of March); 120F (children: 50F); ☎ (087) 54 10 75.

SPONTIN

Castle – Open beginning of April to end of September daily from 10.00 to 17.00; otherwise weekends only from 10.00 to 17.00; 125F; ☎ (083) 69 90 55.

STAVELOT

Regional Religious Museum – Open beginning of April to beginning of November daily from 10.00 to 12.30 and from 14.30 to 17.30; 120F (ticket also valid for Spa-Francorchamps Speed Track Museum); ☎ (080) 86 23 39 or 86 23 43.

Guillaume Apollinaire Museum – Open in July and August daily from 10.30 to 12.30 and from 14.30 to 17.30; otherwise on Tuesdays from 13.00 to 16.00, Wednesdays from 13.00 to 17.00, Thursdays from 09.00 to 11.00 and from 14.00 to 18.00, Fridays from 16.00 to 18.00 and Saturdays from 09.00 to 12.00; 50F; ☎ (080) 86 21 24.

Spa-Francorchamps Speed Track Museum – Open daily from 10.00 to 12.30 and from 14.30 to 17.30 (from 10.00 to 12.30 and from 14.00 to 16.30 between 1 November and Easter); closed 1 January, Refreshment Sunday and 25 December; 125F; ☎ (080) 86 27 06.

St Sebastian's Church Treasury – Guided tour (20 min) all year by appointment, contact: Mr Kinet, 109 rue Neuve, 4970 Stavelot, ☎ (080) 86 44 37.

T

TIENEN

Grote Markt 4, ☎ (016) 81 97 85

Church (O.-L.-Vrouw-ten-Poelkerk) – Open Mondays to Saturdays from. 09.00 to 19.00.

Het Toreke Town Museum – Open weekdays from 09.00 to 12.00 and from 14.00 to 16.30, weekend and public holidays from 14.00 to 18.00; closed at weekends and on public holidays between Christmas and Easter; ☎ (016) 81 73 19.

St Germanus's Church: summer carillon concerts – In July and August on Wednesdays at 21.00 and from September to June on Sundays at 11.30; ☎ (016) 81 99 97 or (015) 41 47 28.

Excursions

Hoegaarden 't Nieuwhuys Folklore Museum – Open daily (except Sundays) from 10.00 to 19.00; 30F; ☎ (016) 76 62 94.

TONGEREN

Stadhuisplein 9, ☎ (012) 23 29 61

Basilica of Our Lady – Open beginning of April to end of September daily from 09.00 to 11.45 and from 13.30 to 16.45; 100F; ☎ (012) 23 90 66.

Concerts: for dates, contact: Basilica Concerten, Vlasmarkt 4, 3700 Tongeren ☎ (012) 23 57 19.

Provincial Gallo-Roman Museum – Scheduled to reopen in mid-1994.

Museum of the Town's Military History – Open beginning of May to end of September weekends and public holidays from 10.00 to 17.00; 30F; ☎ (012) 23 29 61.

Town Museum – Open weekdays from 10.00 to 12.00 and from 14.00 to 16.30; beginning of May to end of September open also weekends and public holidays from 10.00 to 12.00 and from 14.00 to 17.00; 30 F; ☎ (012) 23 29 61.

TONGERLO

Leonardo da Vinci Museum – Open beginning of March to end of October daily (except Fridays) from 13.30 to 16.30; closed Easter Day; 40 F; ☎ (014) 54 10 01.

TORHOUT

Kasteel Ravenhof, ☎ (050) 22 07 70

St Peter's Church – Open weekdays from 07.00 to 12.00 and from 15.30 to 18.30, Saturdays from 07.00 to 12.00 and from 14.30 to 18.30, Sundays from 08.00 to 12.30 and from 17.30 to 19.00.

TOURNAI

Vieux Marché-aux-Poteries 14, ☎ (069) 22 20 45

Cathedral of Our Lady: treasury – Open beginning of April to end of October Mondays to Saturdays from 10.15 to 13.00 (12.00 on Saturdays) and from 14.00 to 18.00, on Sundays from 14.00 to 17.30; beginning of November to end of March Mondays to Saturdays from 10.15 to 12.00 and from 14.00 to 16.00, on Sundays from 14.00 to 15.30; closed 1 January, Easter, Whitsun, 15 August, second weekend of September, 1 November and 25 December; 25F.

Fine Art Museum – Open daily (except Tuesdays) from 10.00 to 12.00 and from 14.00 to 17.30; closed Tuesdays, 1 January, the Monday of the annual jumble sale (*braderie* in September), 11 November and 25 December; 50F; ☎ (069) 22 20 45.

Tapestry Museum – Open from 10.00 to 12.00 and from 14.00 to 17.30; closed Tuesdays, the Monday of the annual jumble sale (*braderie* in September), 11 November, 25 and 31 December; ☎ (069) 84 20 74.

Folklore Museum – Same admission times and charges as the Fine Art Museum ☎ (069) 22 40 69.

Museum of Decorative Arts – New address from end of 1992: 50, rue St-Martin; same admission times and charges as the Fine Art Museum.

Museum of History and Archaeology – Same admission times and charges as the Fine Art Museum.

Henry VIII Tower: Arms Museum – Open from 10.00 to 12.00 and from 14.00 to 17.30; closed 1 January and on Tuesdays; ☎ (069) 22 38 78.

Excursion

Antoing Castle – Guided tour (1 hour 30 min) Sundays and public holidays from mid-May to end of September at 15.00, 16.00 and 17.00; 100F; ☎ (069) 44 17 29.

TROIS PONTS

ℹ Place Communale 10, ☎ (080) 68 40 45

Excursion

Grand-Halleux Monti Estate – Open daily from 09.00 to 17.00 (18.00 in July and August); 100F; ☎ (080) 21 49 45.

TURNHOUT

St Peter's Church – Open daily from 09.00 to 19.00; ☎ (014) 44 89 41 (ext. 192).

Taxandria Museum – Scheduled to reopen in 1994; ☎ (014) 41 13 77.

Beguine Convent Museum – Open Wednesdays and Fridays from 14.00 to 17.00 and Sundays from 15.00 to 17.00; in July and August open also on Tuesdays from 14.00 to 17.00; 30F; ☎ (014) 42 21 96.

Playing Cards Museum – Open on Wednesdays, Fridays and Saturdays from 14.00 to 17.00 and Sundays from 10.00 to 12.00 and from 14.00 to 17.00; in June, July and August open also on Tuesdays and Thursdays from 14.00 to 17.00; closed 1 and 2 January, 25 and 26 December; 30F; ☎ (014) 41 56 21.

Excursion

Hoogstraten St Catherine's Church – Open Easter to end of September daily from 09.00 to 18.00; ☎ (03) 314 50 07.

V

VERVIERS

ℹ Rue Xhavée 61, ☎ (087) 33 02 13

Museum of Fine Art and Ceramics – Open Mondays, Wednesdays and Saturdays from 14.00 to 17.00 and Sundays from 15.00 to 18.00; ☎ (087) 33 16 95.

Museum of Archaeology and Folklore – Open Tuesdays and Thursdays from 14.00 to 17.00, Saturdays from 09.00 to 12.00 and Sundays from 10.00 to 13.00; ☎ (087) 33 16 95.

Wool Museum – Open Mondays to Saturdays from 14.00 to 17.00 (18.00 on Wednesdays); closed Sundays and public holidays; ☎ (087) 33 16 95.

VEURNE

ℹ Landshuis, Grote Markt 29, ☎ (058) 31 21 54

Town Hall – Guided tour (45 min) beginning of April to end of September daily at 11.00, 14.00, 15.00 and 16.30; otherwise weekdays only at 11.00 and 15.00; 40F; ☎ (058) 31 21 54.

St Walburga's Church – Open beginning of April to end of September daily from 10.00 to 12.00 and from 14.00 to 18.00; ☎ (058) 31 21 54.

St Nicholas's Church Tower – Open mid-June to mid-September from 10.00 to 11.45 and from 14.00 to 17.00; 30F.

Excursions

Wulveringem Beauvoorde Manor-house – Guided tour (1 hour) beginning of June to end of September daily (except Mondays) at 14.00, 15.00, 16.00 and 17.00; closed Mondays and the third Tuesday and Wednesday of July; 50F; ☎ (058) 29 92 29.

Izenberge Bachen de Kupe Open-Air Museum "Village of the Past" – Open weekdays from 13.00 to 17.00; also between beginning of April and mid-November at weekends and on public holidays from 14.00 to 18.00; 80F; ☎ (058) 29 80 90.

VILLERS-LA-VILLE

Abbey Ruins – Open beginning of July to end of September daily from 10.00 to 18.00; between beginning of April and end of June on Wednesdays to Sundays from 10.00 to 18.00; otherwise Wednesdays to Sundays from 13.00 to 17.00; closed 1 January and 25 December; 60F; ☎ (071) 87 95 55.

Church of the Visitation – To arrange a visit contact the Sacristan, rue de Sart 28, or telephone ☎ (071) 87 73 27.

VIRTON

ℹ Pavillon, Rue Croix-le-Mairie 2, ☎ (063) 57 89 04

Gaume Museum – Open beginning of April to end of November daily from 09.30 to 12.00 and from 14.00 to 18.00; closed Tuesdays (except in July and August); 100F; ☎ (063) 57 03 15.

Excursion

Montquintin Museum of Peasant Life – Open in July and August daily from 14.00 to 18.00; otherwise by appointment only; 50F; ☎ (063) 57 03 15.

WALCOURT

St Materne's Basilica Treasury – Guided tour by appointment; contact Abbé Pivetta, 12 rue de la Basilique, 5650 Walcourt, ☎ (071) 61 13 66.

WATERLOO

Chaussée de Bruxelles 149, ☎ (02) 354 99 10

Butte du Lion – Open between beginning of April and end of October daily from 09.30 to 18.30; otherwise from 10.30 to 16.00; closed 1 January and 25 December; 40F; ☎ (02) 385 19 12.

Visitor Centre – Same admission times as the Butte du Lion; 180F; ☎ (02) 385 19 12.

Waxworks Museum – Open between beginning of April and end of October daily from 09.00 to 18.30; otherwise on Sundays and public holidays from 10.00 to 16.45; 60F; ☎ (02) 384 67 40.

Grand Panorama of the Battle of Waterloo – Same opening times as the Butte du Lion; 70F; ☎ (02) 384 31 39.

Caillou Provincial Museum – Open between beginning of April and end of October daily (except Mondays) from 10.00 to 18.30; otherwise daily (except Mondays) from 13.30 to 17.00; closed in January; 40F; ☎ (02) 348 24 24.

Wellington Museum – Open between beginning of April and mid-November daily from 09.30 to 18.00; otherwise daily from 10.30 to 17.00; closed 1 January and 25 December; 70F; ☎ (02) 354 78 06.

WAVRE

Hôtel de Ville, ☎ (010) 23 03 52

Walibi – Open in July and August daily from 10.00 to 19.00; between first Sunday in April and end of June and in September on weekdays from 10.00 to 18.00, Sundays and public holidays from 10.00 to 19.00; 590F (no charge for children less than 1m - 3.3ft tall), ticket for Walibi is valid also for Aqualibi; ☎ (010) 41 44 66.

Aqualibi – Open between beginning of April and end of September daily from 14.00 to 22.00; between beginning of October and end of March open Tuesdays to Fridays from 14.00 to 22.00, Saturdays from 10.00 to 23.00 and Sundays from 10.00 to 22.00; 400F; ☎ (010) 41 44 66.

Z

ZEEBRUGGE

Fishing port Fresh fish auction – On weekdays fish is sold at 07.00 and shrimps are sold at 09.30; no auction at weekends or on public holidays.

ZOUTLEEUW

St Leonard's Church – Open Easter to end of October daily (except Mondays and public holidays) from 14.00 to 17.00; 30F; ☎ (011) 78 11 07.

A Flemish Proverb, by Brueghel the Elder, Mayer van den Bergh Museum, Antwerp

GRAND DUCHY OF LUXEMBOURG

The prices are given in Luxembourg francs. The international dialling code for the Grand Duchy of Luxembourg is 325.

CLERVAUX

Castle – Open in June daily from 13.00 to 17.00; between 1 July and mid-September daily from 10.00 to 17.00; 40F for the model exhibition; 40F for the Battle of the Bulge exhibition; ☎ 91048.

DIEKIRCH

ℹ Place Guillaume, ☎ 80 30 23

Museum – Open beginning of May to end of October and for one week before and after Easter daily from 10.00 to 12.00 and from 14.00 to 18.00; 120F; ☎ 80 89 08.

St Laurence's Church – Open Easter to end of October daily (except Mondays) from 10.00 to 12.00 and from 14.00 to 18.00; ☎ 80 30 23.

Excursion

Brandenbourg: Al Branebuurg House – Open in July and August on Sundays and public holidays from 14.00 to 18.00; otherwise on the first Sunday of the month and public holidays only from 14.00 to 18.00; 30F; ☎ 90475.

ECHTERNACH

ℹ Porte St-Willibrord, ☎ 72230

Abbey Museum – Open Easter to end of October daily from 10.00 to 12.00 and from 14.00 to 18.00; in November, December and between the second week of February and the end of March open weekends and public holidays only from 14.00 to 17.00; 40F; ☎ 72 74 72.

ESCH-SUR-ALZETTE

ℹ Hôtel de Ville, ☎ 54 73 83 (ext. 246)

Resistance Museum – Open Thursdays and weekends 15.00 to 18.00; ☎ 54 73 83.

Excursion

Rumelange: National Museum of Mining – Guided tour (1 hour 45 min) Easter to end of October daily from 14.00 to 17.00; otherwise on the second Saturday and Sunday of the month from 14.00 to 17.00; 100F; ☎ 56 31 21.

LAROCHETTE

ℹ Hôtel de Ville, ☎ 87676

Castles – Open mid-April to end of October daily from 10.00 to 18.00; 50F; ☎ 87676.

LUXEMBOURG

ℹ Place d'Armes, ☎ 22 28 09

Old Town Model – Open during the tourist season from 10.00 to 12.20 and from 14.00 to 18.00; 40F; ☎ 22 67 53.

Bock Casemates – Open beginning of March to end of October daily from 10.00 to 17.00; 50F; ☎ 22 67 53.

National Museum of History and Art – Open Tuesdays to Fridays from 10.00 to 16.45, Saturdays from 14.00 to 17.45, Sundays from 10.00 to 11.45 and from 14.00 to 17.45; closed Mondays, 1 January, Easter, Ascension, Whitsun, 23 June, 15 August and 25 December; ☎ 47 93 30.

Grand-Ducal Palace – Closed for restoration work.

Cathedral of Our Lady –Open Easter to end of October weekdays from 10.00 to 17.00, Saturdays from 08.00 to 18.00 and Sundays from 10.00 to 18.00; otherwise weekdays from 10.00 to 11.30 and from 14.00 to 17.00, Saturdays from 08.00 to 11.30 and from 14.00 to 17.00 and Sundays from 10.00 to 17.00; ☎ 22 29 70-1.

Pétrusse Casemates – Guided tour (30 min) in season; see admission times posted on site; 50F.

J-P Pescatore Museum – Scheduled to reopen in 1995.

Excursion

Bettembourg: Parc Merveilleux – Open beginning of April to end of September daily from 09.30 to 19.00; 120F (children: 100F); ☎ 51 10 48.

LUXEMBOURG MOSELLE VALLEY

Boat trips – Wasserbillig-Schengen from Easter to September, contact the Navigation Touristique de l'Entente de la Moselle Luxembourgeoise-Grevenmacher, ☎ 75 82 75, for details; selected railway stations sell joint tickets for trips by train and boat, or by bus and boat.

Bech-Kleinmacher: Museum of Folklore and Viticulture – Open between beginning of April and end of October daily (except Mondays) from 14.00 to 19.00; otherwise on Fridays, at weekends and on public holidays from 14.00 to 19.00; closed in January; 100F; ☎ 69 82 33.

Wellenstein: Wine Cellar Cooperatives – Guided tour (1 hour) beginning of May to end of August daily from 09.00 to 17.00; 70F; ☎ 69 83 14.

Remich: St-Martin Cellars – Guided tour (45 min) beginning of April to end of October daily from 09.00 to 11.30 and from 13.30 to 17.30; 80F; ☎ 69 90 91.

Ehnen: Wine Museum – Open between beginning of April and end of October daily (except Mondays) from 09.30 to 11.30 and from 14.00 to 17.00; on Mondays and during the rest of the year by appointment only; 60F; ☎ 76026.

LUXEMBOURG MOSELLE VALLEY

Wormeldange: Wine Cooperatives – Guided tour (1 hour) beginning of May to end of August from 09.00 to 17.00; closed Sundays and public holidays; 80F; ☎ 69 83 14.

Grevenmacher: Cooperative Wine Cellars – Open beginning of May to end of August daily from 09.00 to 17.00; 70F; ☎ 69 83 14.

Bernard-Massard Cellars – Guided tour (1 hour) beginning of April to end of October daily from 09.00 to 12.00 and from 14.00 to 18.00; 80F; ☎ 75545-228.

LUXEMBOURG'S "PETITE SUISSE"

Beaufort Castle – Open between end of March and beginning of November daily from 09.00 to 18.00; 60F; ☎ 86002.

MONDORF-LES-BAINS — Av. Fr. Clement, ☎ 67575

St Michael's Church – Open daily (except Wednesdays) from 14.00 to 18.00 (16.00 beginning of October to end of February); ☎ 68020.

RODANGE

Tourist train – Departures between beginning of May and end of September on Sundays and public holidays (except 23 June) at 15.00 and 16.40; first class Rtn: 220F, second class Rtn: 150F (children's second class Rtn: 70F); ☎ 31 90 69; there is a rail-car shuttle link between Rodange and Fond-de-Gras at 15.15.

Excursions

Bascharage: Luxembourg Gemstone-cutting Workshop – Guided tour all year round by appointment; contact (at least a fortnight in advance) the Taillerie Luxembourgeoise de Pierres Précieuses, Mr Klein, rue de la Continentale, Bascharage/Gare, ☎ 50 90 32.

SÛRE VALLEY 1

Bourscheid Castle – Open beginning of April to beginning of November daily from 10.00 to 19.00; 80F; ☎ 90570 or 90564.

VIANDEN — Maison Victor-Hugo, Rue Gare 37, ☎ 84257

Chairlift – This runs from beginning of April to end of September; 140F; ☎ 84323.

Castle – Open beginning of April to end of September daily from 10.00 to 18.00; in March and October from 10.00 to 17.00; in November and December daily from 10.00 to 16.00; in January and February weekends and public holidays from 10.00 to 16.00; guided tours by appointment, contact Madame G Frantzen-Heger, Cité Scheuerhof, L-9440 Vianden; closed 1 January, 2 November and 25 December; 110F; ☎ 84108.

Victor Hugo's House – Open beginning of April to mid-October daily (except Thursdays between beginning of April and end of May) from 09.30 to 12.00 and from 14.00 to 18.00; 25F; ☎ 84257.

Museum of Rustic Art – Open between Easter and the third week of October and between Christmas and the New Year daily from 10.00 to 12.00 and from 14.00 to 18.00; closed Mondays (except public holidays); 80F; ☎ 84821.

House in the old town of Luxembourg displaying the national motto

INDEX

Brussels Brabant ..... Towns, sights and tourist regions followed by name of the province.

Egmont, Count of ... People, historical events, artistic styles and local terms explained in the text.

Cloth Halls .... Sights in important towns.

NB A bilingual list of place names is given on pp 4 and 237.

BELGIUM

A

B

C

D

E

F

G

H

I

J

L

M

N

T - U

V

W

X - Y

Z

Landsailing

GRAND DUCHY OF LUXEMBOURG

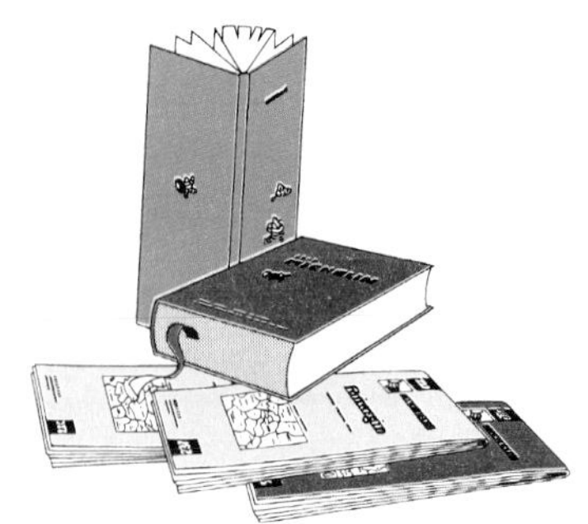

ILLUSTRATION ACKNOWLEDGEMENTS

p. 11 K Straiton/EXPLORER, Paris
p. 14 B Brillion/MICHELIN, Paris
p. 15 After photo by Ed. Thill
p. 19 A2M/VLOO, Paris
p. 20 After photo by CGT, Robijns
p. 21 After photo by CGT, Esterhazy
p. 23 MICHELIN, Paris
p. 24 Museum of Ancient (15C to 19C) Art, Brussels/ARTEPHOT-COLORTHEQUE, Paris
p. 26 Royal Museums of Art and History, Brussels/LAUROS GIRAUDON, Paris
p. 30 © Hergé/Casterman - Extract from the album "Prisoners of the Sun" by Hergé
p. 31 Kouprianoff/EUREKA SLIDE, Paris
p. 37 GIRAUDON, Paris
p. 38 MICHELIN, Paris
p. 43 J L Barde/SCOPE, Paris
p. 48 Mayer van den Bergh Museum, Antwerp
p. 51 Ph Gajic/MICHELIN, Paris
p. 53 After photo by L Lefebre
p. 58 Ph Gajic/MICHELIN, Paris
p. 59 Recchia/EUREKA SLIDE, Brussels
p. 61 J Evrard, Brussels
p. 63 MICHELIN, Paris
p. 64 Ph Gajic/MICHELIN, Paris
p. 69 C Bowman/SCOPE, Paris
p. 71 B Brillion/MICHELIN, Paris *(above)*
p. 71 Gruuthuse Museum, Bruges *(below)*
p. 73 Ph Gajic/MICHELIN, Paris
p. 74 Ph Maille/EXPLORER, Paris
p. 77 J Evrard, Brussels
p. 81 Museum of Ancient (15C to 19C) Art, Brussels/ARTEPHOT-COLORTHEQUE, Paris
p. 86 Autoworld, Brussels - Ph Gajic/ MICHELIN, Paris
p. 92 After photo by ARDH of Belgium
p. 93 After photo by CGT, L Philippe
p. 94 J Evrard, Brussels
p. 97 J D Sudrès/SCOPE, Paris
p. 100 After photo by F Loosen, Diest
p. 103 J Evrard, Brussels
p. 107 B Brillion/MICHELIN, Paris
p. 108 J Evrard, Brussels
p. 109 B Brillion/MICHELIN, Paris
p. 111 GIRAUDON, Paris
p. 115 Ph Gajic/MICHELIN, Paris *(above)*
p. 115 After photo by ACL *(below)*
p. 118 Grand-Hornu Images, Grand-Hornu
p. 122 Ph Gajic/MICHELIN, Paris
p. 125 Ph Gajic/MICHELIN, Paris
p. 126 L Y Loirat/EXPLORER, Paris
p. 127 Ph Roy/EXPLORER, Paris
p. 131 A Saucez/EXPLORER, Paris
p. 133 Eka/EUREKA SLIDE, Brussels
p. 135 Print Room, Albert I Royal Library, Brussels
p. 138 After photo by ACL
p. 142 Ph Gajic/MICHELIN, Paris
p. 145 Ph Gajic/MICHELIN, Paris
p. 148 Ph Gajic/MICHELIN, Paris
p. 150 After photo by CGT, Sutter
p. 157 J Evrard, Brussels
p. 159 Print Room, Albert I Royal Library, Brussels
p. 164 J Evrard, Brussels
p. 165 Royal Museum of Fine Art, Antwerp/GIRAUDON, Paris
p. 173 J Vernin/TRAVEL PICTURES, Brussels
p. 180 J Evrard, Brussels
p. 187 Ph Gajic/MICHELIN, Paris
p. 188 Ph Gajic/MICHELIN, Paris
p. 190 Ph Gajic/MICHELIN, Paris
p. 193 Ph Gajic/MICHELIN, Paris
p. 201 J Evrard, Brussels
p. 202 Roland/EUREKA SLIDE, Brussels
p. 204 J Evrard, Brussels
p. 208 Ph Gajic/MICHELIN, Paris
p. 209 F Wilkin/TRAVEL PICTURES, Brussels
p. 212 B Brillion/MICHELIN, Paris
p. 213 MICHELIN, Paris
p. 215 B Brillion/MICHELIN, Paris
p. 218 National Museum of Art and History, Luxembourg
p. 221 Eka/EUREKA SLIDE, Brussels
p. 222 Ph Gajic/MICHELIN, Paris
p. 225 Ph Gajic/MICHELIN, Paris
p. 229 J Evrard, Brussels
p. 234 J Evrard, Brussels
p. 240 J Evrard, Brussels
p. 266 Mayer van den Bergh Museum, Antwerp
p. 268 Luxembourg Tourist Office, Paris
p. 277 Belgian Tourist Office, Paris

MANUFACTURE FRANÇAISE DES PNEUMATIQUES MICHELIN
Société en commandite par actions au capital de 2 000 000 000 de francs
Place des Carmes-Déchaux - 63 Clermont-Ferrand (France)
R.C.S. Clermont-Fd B 855 200 507

Dépôt légal Mars 94 - ISBN 2-06-151401-4 - ISSN 0763-1383

Printed in the EC 02-94-30
Photocomposition: TALLON TYPE à Bruxelles
Impression et Brochage: AUBIN Imprimeur à Ligugé, Poitiers